MOTIVATING STUDENTS TO LEARN

Written specifically for teachers, this book offers a wealth of research-based principles for motivating students to learn. Its focus on motivational principles rather than motivation theorists or theories leads naturally into discussion of specific classroom strategies. Throughout the book these principles and strategies are tied to the realities of contemporary schools (e.g., curriculum goals) and classrooms (e.g., student differences, classroom dynamics). The author employs an eclectic approach to motivation that shows how to effectively integrate the use of extrinsic and intrinsic strategies. Guidelines are provided for adapting motivational principles to group and individual differences and for doing "repair work" with students who have become discouraged or disaffected learners.

- Changes—In addition to updating, this edition features new material on the role of parents in their children's school motivation, on goal theory and self-determination theory, on the value aspects of motivation, on the self and identity aspects of motivation, and on the teacher's role in scaffolding students' motivation.
- Teacher Oriented—The coverage focuses on those aspects of the motivational literature that are directly applicable to classroom teaching, that is, it focuses on the teacher as the motivator more than it does on the student as the motivatee.
- Organizing Perspectives—The author uses three general perspectives to organize the field: 1) social milieu/learning community, 2) expectancy/confidence/efficacy aspects of motivation, and 3) value aspects of motivation. This helps readers see the connections among related theories as well as teachers' strategies for motivating students.
- Value Aspects of Motivation—More than other texts, this one emphasizes the value aspects of motivation. This is what most teachers have in mind when they talk about school-based motivation, that is, "how can I get my students to see value in the curriculum and lessons I am teaching."

Jere Brophy is University Distinguished Professor of Teacher Education and of Counseling, Educational Psychology, and Special Education at Michigan State University.

MOTIVATING STUDENTS TO LEARN

Third Edition

Jere Brophy

Michigan State University

Routledge
Taylor & Francis Group

NEW YORK AND LONDON

First edition published 1997
by The McGraw-Hill Companies, Inc.

Second edition published 2004
by Lawrence Erlbaum Associates, Inc.

This edition published 2010
by Routledge
270 Madison Avenue, New York, NY 10016

Simultaneously published in the UK
by Routledge
2 Park Square, Milton Park, Abingdon, Oxon OX14 4RN

Routledge is an imprint of the Taylor & Francis Group, an informa business

© 1997 The McGraw-Hill Companies, Inc.
© 2004 Lawrence Erlbaum Associates, Inc.
© 2010 Taylor & Francis

Typeset in Minion and Gill Sans by EvS Communication Networx, Inc.
Printed and bound in the United States of America on acid-free paper by Edwards Brothers, Inc.

Library of Congress Cataloging in Publication Data
Brophy, Jere E.
Motivating students to learn / Jere Brophy. — 3rd ed.
p. cm.
Includes bibliographical references and index.
1. Motivation in education. I. Title.
LB1065.B776 2010
370.15'4—dc22
2009033156

ISBN 10: 0-415-80069-2 (hbk)
ISBN 10: 0-415-80070-6 (pbk)
ISBN 10: 0-203-85831-x (ebk)

ISBN 13: 978-0-415-80069-3 (hbk)
ISBN 13: 978-0-415-80070-9 (pbk)
ISBN 13: 978-0-203-85831-8 (ebk)

For my grandchildren,

Mark Speier, Chris Speier, Jered Brophy, and Carmen Brophy.

Contents

    Needs for Autonomy, Competence, and Relatedness   152

        Connecting with Students' Existing Intrinsic Motivation   *152*
        Conceptions of Intrinsic Motivation   *153*
        Deci and Ryan's Self-Determination Theory   *154*
        Autonomy, Competence, and Relatedness as Bases for Autonomous
            Motivation   *158*
        Responding to Students' Autonomy Needs   *160*
        Responding to Students' Competence Needs   *165*
        Responding to Students' Relatedness Needs   *169*
        Self-Determination Theory: Looking Ahead   *173*
        Summary   *177*
        Reflection Questions   *177*
        References   *178*

8   Other Ways to Support Students' Intrinsic Motivation   184

        Theory and Research on Interest   *184*
        Adapting Activities to Students' Interests   *189*
        Adapting Traditional Learning Activities to Enhance their Intrinsic
            Motivation Potential   *190*
        Instructional Approaches That Reflect Multiple Principles
            Working in Combination   *196*
        Teachers' Experience-Based Motivational Strategies   *198*
        Conclusion   *201*
        Summary   *202*
        Reflection Questions   *203*
        References   *203*

9   Stimulating Students' Motivation to Learn   208

        Motivation to Learn   *208*
        Related Motivational Concepts   *209*
        Bringing Students to the Lesson   *212*
        Paving the Way for Motivation to Learn: Socializing   *214*
        Teachers Often Need to Scaffold Students' Appreciation of their Learning,
            by Helping Them to Build Motivated Learning Schemas   *219*
        Socializing Motivation to Learn as a General Disposition   *227*
        Stimulating Students' Motivation to Learn in Specific Learning Situations   *230*
        Strategies for Shaping Students' Expectations about the Learning   *231*
        Strategies for Inducing Motivation to Learn   *232*
        Strategies for Scaffolding Students' Learning Efforts   *240*
        Self-Regulated Learning   *248*
        Conclusion   *249*
        Summary   *249*
        Reflection Questions   *250*
        References   *251*

Preface

This book offers principles and strategies to use in motivating students to learn. It is not a "bag of tricks" developed from my own personal philosophy or culled randomly from everywhere. Instead, it is the product of a systematic review of the motivational literature followed by synthesizing that involved: identifying those portions of this vast literature that are most relevant to teachers, summarizing this relevant material using a basic vocabulary to counteract the proliferation of multiple terms for the same basic concept, and organizing the material within a few categories that are rooted in motivational theory and research but also supportive of teachers' efforts to incorporate motivational principles into their instructional planning.

My treatment of relatively obvious principles (e.g., warm, caring teachers are more likely to be successful motivators than indifferent or rejecting teachers) emphasizes their fundamental importance but does not go on to include unnecessarily detailed explanation or documentation. More detail is provided for less obvious and familiar principles, although even here I have focused on key ideas and application guidelines rather than providing broad coverage of the history and development of related theory and research. Similar concepts are treated together with emphasis on their common implications, avoiding "distinctions without difference."

Much of the scholarly literature on motivation has limited relevance to teachers because it does not apply in classrooms or uses differences in individuals' motivational systems to predict differences in their behavior (e.g., students who value success and do not fear failure are more likely to prefer challenging tasks than students with the opposite motivational pattern). Concepts such as success seeking or failure avoidance are useful to the extent that they help teachers to understand their students' current motivational orientations. However, teachers mostly need to learn strategies for socializing their students' motivational orientations toward optimal patterns (in this example, strategies for helping students to reduce their fear of failure and become more persistent in their efforts to achieve success). Consequently, although the book explains concepts needed to understand students' motivational orientations, it focuses on teachers' strategies for optimizing those orientations.

Furthermore, it does so with an eye toward the realities of classroom teaching. First, it recognizes that schools are not day camps or recreational centers: They feature an instructional agenda that teachers and students are expected to accomplish. Consequently, teachers' motivational strategies need to focus on motivating their students to learn—to achieve the intended curricular outcomes—not merely to enjoy their time in school. Learning should be experienced as meaningful and worthwhile, but it requires sustained goal-oriented efforts to construct understandings.

Second, the classroom setting complicates the motivational challenges facing teachers. Instruction can be individualized only to an extent, so some students may often be bored and others may often be confused or frustrated. Also, students' concentration on learning may be impaired by worries about getting bad grades or by embarrassing themselves in front of their classmates.

These and other features of classrooms underscore the need for an emphasis on motivational goals and strategies that are feasible for use in that setting. Consequently, although I describe forms of motivation that may be observed when people are engaged in activities of their own choosing without pressure to respond to external constraints, I emphasize that such conditions of self-determination can only be achieved partially and occasionally in classrooms. Thus, the motivational challenge facing teachers is to find ways to encourage their students to seek to develop the knowledge and skills that learning activities were designed to develop, whether or not they enjoy the activities or would choose to engage in them if other alternatives were available. This is what I mean by motivating students to learn, and the book emphasizes strategies for doing so.

The book also presents strategies for capitalizing on students' existing intrinsic motivation and for reinforcing their learning efforts using rewards and other extrinsic incentives. In the process, I review the often-contentious literature on these topics and develop principles for using intrinsic and extrinsic motivational strategies compatibly. An eclectic approach to motivation that incorporates both sets of strategies (as well as strategies for motivating students to learn) is likely to be much more powerful than a more limited approach.

Finally, the book offers guidelines for adapting motivational principles to group and individual differences in students and for doing "repair work" with students who have become discouraged or disaffected learners. These adaptation and problem-solving suggestions are embedded within the overall approach developed throughout the book. They are extensions of it, compatible with its basic principles.

Along with a general updating of relevant theory and research, this third edition offers several noteworthy new features. Chapter 4 updates the controversy surrounding performance approach goals and outlines a potential consensus that distinguishes outcome goals that are focused on achieving some standard of excellence from performance goals that are focused on self-validation or competition with peers. Chapter 6 explains the emerging consensus that extrinsic rewards can be used in ways that are complementary to strategies for nurturing intrinsic motivation, and provides guidelines for doing so. Chapter 7 traces the evolution and expansion of self-determination theory, including its recent emphasis on extrinsic forms of autonomous motivation, calling attention to instructional goals and the value of learning as forms of autonomy support, connections between self-determination and general well-being, and the universality of the basic needs for autonomy, competence, and relatedness, even in collectivist cultures.

Chapters 8–10 provide unique coverage of the value aspects of motivation in education, synthesizing the flowering of theory and research on value-related topics that have finally begun to appear after decades of relative neglect. This includes recent European work on interest, the four-phase model of movement from initial situational interest to developed individual interest, new implications of self and identity concepts, new work on aesthetic and transformative experiences, and supplementing of the traditional emphasis on affective and hedonic pleasures with a growing emphasis on cognitive and eudaimonic pleasures. After laying the groundwork in chapter 1, I provide in chapter 9 a newly elaborated version of my theorizing about why and how teachers need to socialize their students' appreciation of the value of school content, supported with several new graphics. Finally, chapter 11 contains expanded coverage of the concept of stereotype threat and of contrasts between independent/Western and interdependent/East Asian self-construals and related motivation.

To reduce the verbiage and passive-voice sentence constructions that accompany third-person language, I have written much of the book in second-person language addressed directly to the reader, who is construed as a teacher. Readers who are inservice teachers or student teachers can respond to this directly; preservice teacher education majors or other readers who are not currently teaching can respond by projecting themselves into the teacher role. Non-teachers should find the book almost as useful as teachers will, although they will need to substitute their own application context (e.g., parent–child, coach–player, supervisor–subordinate) for the teacher-student context used here. The research-based, generic principles emphasized in the book should be useful to anyone who holds a leadership position that calls for motivating people to accomplish an agenda.

I have eliminated most gender-specific language by pluralizing. Where this was not feasible (e.g., in examples involving individual students), I have standardized the format by routinely referring to the teacher as female and the student as male. Finally, in sections on gender differences, I have referred to teachers as male or female teachers and to students as boys or girls.

Acknowledgments

The first edition of this book was completed in part while I was on sabbatical from Michigan State University and in residence as a Fellow at the Center for Advanced Study in the Behavioral Sciences. I wish to thank both of these institutions for their financial support during that sabbatical year. In addition I wish to thank the Spencer Foundation, which provided part of the funds for the support I received through the Center for Advanced Study in the Behavioral Sciences (Spencer Foundation Grant No. B-1074).

I thank Lane Akers for helping me to develop my ideas into book form, as well as Phyllis Blumenfeld, Lyn Corno, and Allan Wigfield, who provided detailed feedback on an earlier draft.

I thank the many colleagues and students who contributed to my thinking through discussions about motivation over the years, particularly Carole Ames, Cheng Chen, Michael Deschryver, Lori Gano-Overway, J. David Gallagher, Tom Good, Amanda Hawkins, Neelam Kher, Denice Blair Leach, Ohkee Lee, Mary McCaslin, James Middleton, Jane Pizzolato, Lisa Raphael, Karen Shellberg, Eva Sivan, Emily Sportsman, Tat Ming Sze, and Andrea Weber.

Finally, I wish to thank Amy Peebles for her outstanding assistance with the manuscript preparation work involved in developing this edition.

1

Student Motivation:
The Teacher's Perspective

Learning is fun and exciting, at least when the curriculum is well matched to students' interests and abilities and the teacher emphasizes hands-on activities. When you teach the right things the right way, motivation takes care of itself. If students aren't enjoying learning, something is wrong with your curriculum and instruction—you have somehow turned an inherently enjoyable activity into drudgery.

School is inherently boring and frustrating. We require students to come, then try to teach them stuff that they don't see a need for and don't find meaningful. There is little support for academic achievement in the peer culture, and frequently in the home as well. A few students may be enthusiastic about learning, but most of them require the grading system and the carrots and sticks that we connect to it to pressure them to at least do enough to get by.

These italicized paragraphs express the core ideas behind much of the advice traditionally offered to teachers about motivating students. The two views are contradictory, even though both are frequently expressed. Neither is valid, but each contains elements of truth.

The first view incorporates overly romantic views of human nature and unrealistic expectations about school learning. We can expect students to find learning activities to be meaningful and worthwhile, but not to experience them as "fun" in the same sense that they experience recreational games and pastimes. Even when they find the content interesting and the activity enjoyable, learning requires sustained concentration and effort.

The second view incorporates overly cynical views of human nature and negative expectations about teachers' potential for inducing motivation to learn. Besides seeking to maximize pleasure and minimize pain, children can learn to experience satisfaction in acquiring knowledge, developing skills, satisfying curiosity—in a word, learning. Teachers can shape students' behavior by manipulating reinforcement contingencies, but they also can help students to appreciate their learning opportunities—to find them meaningful and worthwhile for reasons that include intrinsic motivation and self-actualization.

If the two extreme views are not valid, what might be a more balanced and fruitful way to think about student motivation? I will develop my answer throughout the book, based on the notion of socializing students' motivation to learn. Before you read my views, however, take stock of your own. Motivation reflects the reasons behind our choices and actions. Our beliefs about these reasons anchor our understandings about our own motivation, which we tend to project to other people when we try to understand their motivation. So, to sharpen your awareness of your own current motivational thinking, take time to reflect on the following questions and write down your answers.

1. What activities do you engage in frequently because you enjoy them? Why? (What makes these activities so enjoyable? What do you get out of them?)
2. What activities do you engage in frequently even though you don't enjoy them (because they are responsibilities that you can't evade or necessary steps toward some important goal)? How do you motivate yourself to perform these unenjoyed activities well (or at least, well enough)?
3. Most people prefer certain kinds of books, movies, television programs, and hobbies over others. For example, they may prefer realistic fiction over fantasy, comedy over drama, golf over tennis, or collecting historical memorabilia over collecting stamps. What might account for these contrasting preferences? Why do you prefer certain types of books, movies, sports, or hobbies over others, especially others that appear similar but don't quite "do it" for you?
4. As a student, which subjects or learning activities have you found most enjoyable or rewarding? Which are boring or merely "OK" rather than stimulating or worthwhile? Are some anxiety-provoking, irritating, or in some other way aversive for you, so that you try to avoid them? What explains your contrasting motivational responses?
5. What self-motivational and coping strategies do you call on to help you do what you need to do when you find a school activity boring or aversive? When you find the activity frustrating or overly difficult?
6. In what ways have your teachers and professors affected your motivation positively or negatively (not just your liking for their subject matter and learning activities, but also your motivation to learn with understanding and to do your best work on assignments)?
7. Have your answers to these questions evolved as you progressed from childhood through adolescence into adulthood? If so, how and why?
8. Do you think that people who differ from you in gender, race, or cultural background would generate similar or different answers to these questions? Why?
9. What do your answers suggest about strategies to emphasize or avoid in your attempts to motivate students to learn (given the ages of your students)?

Save your responses to these questions. As you read through the book, revisit them to compare your own experience-based ideas about motivation with ideas from the scholarly literature. If you note any contradictions, try to identify the reasons for them and any implications for your practice as a teacher.

The remainder of this chapter provides a general introduction to motivation and to my perspective on it. First, it offers definitions of some basic concepts and a summary of ways in which theorizing about motivation has evolved, culminating in notions of intrinsic motivation or flow as the ideal state. Next, it argues that it is unrealistic to expect to routinely produce intrinsic motivation in the classroom and proposes producing motivation to learn as a more feasible alternative. A preview of what is involved in stimulating and socializing students' motivation to learn follows. Finally, the chapter concludes with an overview of the rest of the book.

DEFINITION AND OVERVIEW OF MOTIVATION

Motivation is a theoretical construct used to explain the initiation, direction, intensity, persistence, and quality of behavior, especially goal-directed behavior (Maehr & Meyer, 1997). *Motives* are hypothetical constructs used to explain why people do what they do. Motives are distinguished from related *goals* (the immediate objectives of action sequences) and *strategies* (the methods used to achieve goals and thus to satisfy motives). For example, a person responds to hunger (motive) by going to a restaurant (strategy) to get food (goal).

Motives are relatively general needs or desires that energize people to initiate purposeful action sequences. In contrast, goals (and related strategies) are more specific and used to explain the direction and quality of action sequences in particular situations (Thrash & Elliot, 2001).

In the classroom context, the concept of *student motivation* is used to explain the degree to which students invest attention and effort in various pursuits, which may or may not be the ones desired by their teachers. Student motivation is rooted in students' subjective experiences, especially those connected to their willingness to engage in learning activities and their reasons for doing so. This book develops the argument that teachers should focus on encouraging students to engage in activities with *motivation to learn*: the intention of acquiring the knowledge or skills that learning activities are designed to develop.

EVOLVING VIEWS OF MOTIVATION

Behavior Reinforcement Theories

Most contemporary views on motivation emphasize its cognitive and goal-oriented features. Earlier views were influenced heavily by behavioral theory and research (much of it done on animals rather than humans). *Early behavioral views depicted humans as responsive to basic drives or needs*, but otherwise relatively passive: "… a creature quietly metabolizing in the shade, occasionally goaded into action by the hot sun or the lure of a cold glass of beer" (Murray, 1964, p. 119).

Behaviorists later shifted from drives or needs to focus on *reinforcement* as the primary mechanism for establishing and maintaining behavior patterns. A *reinforcer* is anything that increases or maintains the frequency of a behavior when access to it is made contingent on performance of that behavior. For example, careful work on assignments might be reinforced by giving verbal or written praise, awarding high grades, affixing stars, allowing access to some privilege, awarding points that can be exchanged for prizes, or in some other way compensating students for their efforts or recognizing their accomplishments by providing rewards that they value.

In explaining how to establish and maintain desired behavior patterns, behaviorists usually talk about control rather than motivation. They speak of *using reinforcement to bring behavior under stimulus control.* The stimulus is a situational cue that reminds learners that performing a certain behavior pattern in this situation will gain them access to reinforcement. If the learners are not able to perform this pattern immediately, *gradual improvement toward the target level is shaped through successive approximations.* Once the desired pattern is established, it is maintained by reinforcing it often enough to ensure its continuation. Any behaviors that are incompatible with the desired pattern are extinguished through nonreinforcement or (if necessary) suppressed through punishment.

Much of the culture of schooling reflects the behavioral view, especially report card systems, conduct codes, and honor rolls and awards ceremonies. In the classroom, behavioral views lead to carrot-and-stick approaches: teachers are advised to reinforce students when they display desired learning efforts and withhold reinforcement when they do not (Alberto & Troutman, 1999; Schloss & Smith, 1994).

Behavioral reinforcement models are still emphasized in applied behavior analysis treatments, especially in school psychology and special education (Landrum & Kauffman, 2006). However, most behavioral models have evolved into more complicated forms that consider learners' thoughts and intentions. Meanwhile, *cognitive models of motivation have developed that emphasize learners' subjective experiences such as their needs, goals, or motivation-related thinking.* These cognitive models include the concept of reinforcement but portray its effects as mediated through learners' cognitions. That is, the degree to which task engagement can be motivated by reinforcer availability depends on the degree to which learners value the reinforcer, expect its delivery upon completion of the task, believe that they can complete the task successfully, and believe that doing so will be worth the costs in time, effort, and foregone opportunities to pursue alternative agendas.

Need Theories

Need theories were among the first motivational theories to emerge as alternatives to behavior reinforcement theories. *Need theories explain behaviors as responses to felt needs.* The needs may be either inborn and universal (self-preservation, hunger, thirst) or learned through experience and developed to different degrees in different cultures and individuals (achievement, affiliation, power).

Need theories have been criticized for relying on circular logic that fails to separate the hypothesized motive (need) from the behavior that it supposedly explains (e.g., students who work hard in school are said to do so because they are high in need for achievement, and the evidence that they are high in need for achievement is that they work hard in school). Such circular "explanations" identify and label clusters of behaviors without really explaining them. Scientific psychologists have rejected need theories because of these circular logic problems and a lack of convincing support for the lists of supposed needs that have been compiled (e.g., Murray, 1938). Nevertheless, one need theory has remained popular and influential:

Abraham Maslow's Hierarchy of Human Needs

Maslow (1962) suggested that needs function within a hierarchy arranged in the following order of priority:

1. Physiological needs (sleep, thirst)
2. Safety needs (freedom from danger, anxiety, or psychological threat)
3. Love needs (acceptance from parents, teachers, peers)
4. Esteem needs (mastery experiences, confidence in one's ability)
5. Needs for self-actualization (creative self-expression, satisfaction of curiosity)

The hierarchy implies that needs must be satisfied in the order given. Unless lower needs are satisfied, higher needs may not even be recognized, let alone motivate behavior. Physiological needs are basic to survival, but once they are met, attention can be directed to higher needs. If both physiological and safety needs are satisfied, people can appreciate warm, interpersonal relationships, and love needs may begin to motivate their behavior. If love needs are reasonably satisfied, people may seek to satisfy esteem needs or even self-actualization needs.

In the classroom, Maslow's hierarchy implies that students who come to school tired or hungry are unlikely to become engrossed in lessons. Similarly, students who feel anxious or rejected are unlikely to take the intellectual risks involved in seeking to overcome confusion, and even less likely to try to be creative when working on assignments. This is especially the case when need frustration is chronic. Rational people want arrangements in place that will enable them to meet their basic needs routinely, not just for the moment (Frame, 1996).

Students do not always act in accord with Maslow's hierarchy. They may deprive themselves of sleep in order to study for a test, or become so engrossed in an activity that they forget about their fatigue, hunger, or personal problems (Neher, 1991; Wahba & Bridwell, 1976). Even so, the hierarchy is a useful reminder that, in order to motivate students successfully, we may need to address their lower needs along with higher needs associated with school learning.

Goal Theories

Behavior reinforcement theories and need theories both depicted motivated actions as *reactive* to pressures, either from extrinsic incentives or from internally felt needs. Gradually, motivation theories began to acknowledge that in addition to being pushed and pulled in this manner, we are sometimes more *proactive* in deciding what we want to do and why. As biological organisms, we are naturally active (except when sleeping), so motivational concepts usually are not needed to explain the energization of behavior (why we are doing something instead of nothing). They are needed, however, to explain the direction, intensity, persistence, and quality of behavior. That is, given all the possibilities that a situation affords, why does the person choose a subset of them, to the exclusion of the rest, and pursue those possibilities in a particular way?

Reflecting this evolution in theorizing, most motivational researchers have shifted from talking about needs to talking about *goals*: the objectives or intended outcomes of planned sequences of behavior. Most human activity is purposeful, although not necessarily from its inception (when free from pressing needs, we may seek "down time," although even then we usually make action decisions that imply goals, such as taking a nap or a bath to refresh ourselves or reading or watching television to inform ourselves or enjoy entertainment). *Implied goals are built into activity settings*, such as workplaces, gymnasiums, or classrooms. In classrooms, students are expected to engage in activities with the goal of achieving their intended learning outcomes. However, they may pursue other goals in addition or instead.

Goals vary in scope, from primitive or concrete goals (grasping an object) through somewhat more abstract goals (seek out activities that you enjoy) to highly abstract goals (try to be the kind of person you want to be). Whatever its scope, *the existence of a goal indicates that the person has made a commitment to achieve some state or outcome, that progress in doing so can be monitored and assessed, and that the person can use the resulting feedback to make any needed adjustments* in the strategies used to pursue the goal. Many goals subsume complex activities played out across extended periods of time. For example, the goal of climbing a mountain implies not just wanting to experience standing on top, but experiencing all of the things involved in doing the climbing. In this case, the "going" is the main goal of the activity, not the "arriving" (Carver & Scheier, 1999).

Martin Ford (1992) developed a theory of human motivation that included a taxonomy of 24 goals arranged within six categories:

1. *Affective goals*: entertainment, tranquility, happiness, pleasurable bodily sensations, and physical well being
2. *Cognitive goals*: exploration to satisfy one's curiosity, attaining understanding, engaging in intellectual creativity, and maintaining positive self-evaluations
3. *Subjective organization goals*: unity (experiencing a spiritual sense of harmony or oneness with people, nature, or a greater power) and transcendence (experiencing optimal or extraordinary states of functioning that go beyond ordinary experience)
4. *Self-assertive social relationship goals*: experiencing a sense of individuality, self-determination, superiority (in comparisons with others), and resource acquisition (obtaining material and social support from others)
5. *Integrative social relationship goals*: belongingness, social responsibility (meeting one's ethical and social obligations), equity (promoting fairness and justice), and resource provision (giving material and social support to others)
6. *Task goals*: mastery, task creativity, management (handling everyday tasks with organization and efficiency), material gain, and safety.

Ford's list is unusually lengthy. Goal theorists usually work with simpler taxonomies that contain just a few categories of goals that are more convenient and flexible to apply. However, longer lists are useful as reminders of the many competing agendas facing teachers who seek to motivate their students to focus on learning goals. To do so successfully, teachers need to make it possible for students to coordinate their goals so that many different goals are being satisfied, and few if any are being frustrated, as they engage in classroom activities with motivation to learn.

Many of the concepts and motivational strategies discussed in chapters 3–5 were developed within *goal theory* frameworks that have shifted focus from quantitative aspects (strength) of motivation to qualitative aspects of the goals that people adopt in achievement situations and the strategies they use to pursue those goals. When students adopt *learning goals* (also called mastery goals or task-involvement goals), they focus on trying to learn whatever the activity is designed to teach them. In contrast, when students adopt *performance goals* (also called ego-involvement goals), they focus on preserving their self-perceptions and public reputations as capable individuals more than on learning what the activity is designed to teach. Finally, when students adopt *work-*

avoidant goals, they refuse to accept the achievement challenges inherent in the activity and instead seek to minimize the time and effort they devote to it.

Goal theorists have developed information about situational characteristics that predict people's tendencies to adopt these different goals. Other motivational researchers have explored related cognitive and affective experiences (success or failure expectations, self-efficacy perceptions, attributions of performance outcomes to causes), and the ways in which these motivational factors influence the quality of people's engagement in activities and the ultimate levels of success they achieve. Classroom applications of goal theories emphasize (a) establishing supportive relationships and collaborative learning arrangements that encourage students to adopt learning goals and (b) minimizing the sorts of pressures that dispose students toward performance goals or work-avoidant goals.

Intrinsic Motivation Theories

The shift in emphasis from motivation as response to felt pressures to motivation as self-determination of goals and self-regulation of actions is most obvious in theories of intrinsic motivation. Even if they include need concepts, theories of intrinsic motivation depict people as pursuing their own agendas—doing what they do because they want to, rather than because they need to.

Self-Determination Theory. A prominent example is the self- determination theory of Edward Deci and Richard Ryan (1985, 2002). When people are motivated, they intend to accomplish something and undertake goal-oriented action to do so. Motivated action may be either self-determined or controlled. To the extent that it is self-determined, it is experienced as freely chosen and emanating from one's self, not done under pressure from some internal need or external force.

The prototype of self-determined behavior is intrinsically motivated action that we engage in because we want to. Intrinsically motivated actions require no separate motivating consequences; the only necessary "reward" for them is the interest and enjoyment that we experience as we do them.

Self-determination theory specifies that social settings promote intrinsic motivation when they satisfy three innate psychological needs: autonomy (self-determination in deciding what to do and how to do it), competence (developing and exercising skills for manipulating and controlling the environment), and relatedness (affiliation with others through prosocial relationships). In other words, people are inherently motivated to feel connected to others within a social milieu, to function effectively in that milieu, and to feel a sense of personal initiative while doing so. Students are likely to experience intrinsic motivation in classrooms that support satisfaction of these autonomy, competence, and relatedness needs. Where such support is lacking, students will feel controlled rather than self-determined, so their motivation will be primarily extrinsic rather than intrinsic.

Flow. Mihaly Csikszentmihalyi (1993) captured what peak experiences of intrinsic motivation feel like in his concept of *flow*. He interviewed people about their subjective experiences during times when they were absorbed in activities they enjoyed. He expected to find that most flow experiences occur during relaxing moments of leisure and entertainment. Instead, he found that they usually occur when we are actively involved in challenging tasks that stretch our physical or mental abilities. He listed *eight characteristic dimensions of the flow experience*:

1. The activity has clear goals and provides immediate feedback about the effectiveness of our responses to it.
2. There are frequent opportunities for acting decisively, and these are matched by our perceived ability to do so effectively. In other words, our personal skills are well suited to the activity's challenges.
3. Action and awareness merge; we experience one-pointedness of mind.
4. Concentration on the task at hand; irrelevant stimuli disappear from consciousness and worries and concerns are temporarily suspended.
5. A sense of potential control.
6. Loss of self-consciousness, transcendence of ego boundaries, a sense of growth and of being part of some greater entity.
7. Altered sense of time, which usually seems to pass faster.
8. Experience becomes autotelic: the activity becomes worth doing for its own sake.

In summary, we tend to experience flow when we become absorbed in doing something challenging. We remain aware of the goals of the activity and of the feedback generated by our responses to it, but we concentrate on the activity itself without thinking about success or failure, reward or punishment, or other personal or social agendas. At least for awhile, we focus completely on meeting the challenges that the activity offers, refining our response strategies, developing our skills, and enjoying a sense of control and accomplishment. We are most likely to experience flow when engaged in hobbies or recreational activities (e.g., artistic endeavors, sports, arcade or computer games), but we may also experience it on the job, in the classroom, or in any other activity setting.

Flow potential differs across both persons and situations. Some people develop a "flow personality." They seek out challenges and relish stretching their limits. When required to engage in a routine activity (e.g., mowing a lawn or working on a practice assignment), they tend to "complexify" it by trying to do it artistically, seeking to increase their efficiency, or in other ways setting goals that will make the activity more challenging and interesting for them. Other people rarely experience flow because they fear failure and therefore try to avoid challenging situations, or because they lack the general action orientation and ability to sustain concentration that are needed to maintain oneself in a state of flow (Keller & Bless, 2008; Shernoff, Csikszentmihalyi, Schneider, & Shernoff, 2003).

In the original flow research, people reported flow experiences most frequently during activities that offered high degrees of challenge in areas in which they possessed high degrees of skill. Other situations produced different experiences. When skill was high but the activity was not challenging, they experienced boredom; when both challenge and skill levels were low, they experienced apathy, and when they faced a challenge for which they possessed low levels of skill, they experienced anxiety.

The original flow findings seemed to imply that people would always prefer situations that offered challenges well matched to their current skill levels. However, subsequent work has shown that this is true primarily for situations in which we are engaging in activities voluntarily and with the understanding that no high-stakes consequences are attached to the quality of our performance. If our participation is mandatory, and espe-

TABLE 1.1
Subjective Experiences during Goal-Oriented Activity as Related to
Perceived Levels of Challenge and Skill.

		Perceived Level of Skill	
		Low	*High*
Perceived Level of Challenge	Low	Apathy	Boredom or Relaxation
	High	Anxiety	Flow

Note: Based on Csikszentmihalyi (1993, 1997a).

cially if we need to meet challenges successfully for reasons that are important to us, we are likely to prefer situations in which our skills exceed the challenges. Although we appreciate opportunities for flow-like experiences as we engage in an activity, we also want to experience the satisfaction of successful closure upon completing it. Because it is so important to succeed in these situations, we are more likely to experience flow and related forms of intrinsic motivation when we can succeed with relative ease (whereas having to sustain effort at the limits of our capacities is exhausting and anxiety-producing). Findings like these, including many in school situations, led to recognition that flow can also be experienced when skills exceed task challenges, and these situations are often better characterized as relaxing than as boring (Ainley, Enger, & Kennedy, 2008; Csikszentmihalyi, 1997a; Engeser & Rheinberg, 2008; Schweinle, Turner, & Meyer, 2009; see Table 1.1).

In school, anxiety is the chief threat to flow potential. If students are routinely faced with performance demands that they cannot handle, they may come to prefer the boredom of "safe" routines to the flow opportunities embodied in challenges. Eventually, their potential for experiencing flow in the classroom will erode away. Insufficient challenge also can be a problem, however: Students report low involvement in classes where activity demands are well below their current knowledge and skill levels (Turner et al., 1998).

Csikszentmihalyi, Rathunde, & Whalen (1993) suggested that teachers can encourage flow experiences in three ways:

1. being knowledgeable about their subjects, teaching them enthusiastically, and acting as models pursuing the intrinsic rewards of learning;
2. maintaining an optimal match between what is demanded and what students are prepared to accomplish (urging but also helping students to achieve challenging but reasonable goals); and
3. providing a combination of instructional and emotional support that enables students to approach learning tasks confidently and without anxiety.

Subsequently, Csikszentmihalyi (1997b) singled out *modeling* as the key to stimulating students' intrinsic motivation to learn. Ideal teachers are intrinsically motivated to both learn and teach their subjects. They display this enthusiasm in ways that encourage students to view the content as relevant and to enjoy and look forward to learning about it themselves.

Key ideas relating to the four general types of motivational theories featured in this historical overview are given in Table 1.2.

TABLE 1.2
Views of the Human Condition and Implications for Motivating Students Embedded in Four Types of Motivational Theories

Theories	Views of the Human Condition	Implications for Motivating Students to Learn
Behavior Reinforcement	Reactive to external reinforcement and associated situational cues	Cue and reinforce desired learning behavior (attention to lessons, careful work on assignments, etc.)
Needs	Reactive to felt pressures from internal needs	Make sure that competing needs are satisfied or at least muted so that students can focus on mastery- and achievement-related needs; design curriculum and instruction to help them meet the latter needs without undue difficulties
Goals	Both reactive and proactive in formulating and coordinating goals so as to satisfy needs and desires	Coordinate classroom climate, curriculum, instruction, and assessment practices so as to encourage students to adopt learning goals
Intrinsic Motivation	Autonomously determining goals and regulating actions to pursue interests, gain satisfactions	Emphasize curriculum content and learning activities that connect with students' interests; provide opportunities for them to make choices in deciding what to do and to exercise autonomy in doing it

MOTIVATION IN THE CLASSROOM

The concepts of intrinsic motivation and flow are very appealing, but I do not believe that they can serve as the primary concepts underlying models of motivation in education. These concepts apply best when people are freely engaging in self-chosen activities, usually play or recreational activities rather than work or learning activities. Even when people are intrinsically motivated to learn, their learning usually features leisurely exploration to satisfy personal curiosity rather than sustained efforts to accomplish explicit curricular goals. Finally, even when intrinsically motivated learning is more goal oriented, it tends to occur under autonomous and self-determined conditions. These conditions are difficult to establish in classrooms, for several reasons.

First, school attendance is compulsory and curriculum content and learning activities reflect what society believes students need to learn, not what students would choose if given the opportunity. Schools are established for students' own benefit, but from their point of view, time in the classroom is devoted to enforced attempts to meet externally imposed demands. Second, teachers usually must work with classes of 20 or more students and therefore cannot always meet each individual's needs. As a result, some students sometimes are bored and others sometimes are confused or frustrated. Third, classrooms are social settings, so failures often produce not only personal disappointment but public embarrassment. Finally, students' work on assignments and performance on tests are graded, and periodic reports are sent home to their parents. In combination, *these factors focus students' attention on concerns about meeting demands rather than on any personal benefits they might derive from learning experiences.* It's hard to just enjoy an activity and "go with the flow" when the activity is compulsory and your performance will be evaluated, especially if you fear that your efforts will not be successful.

Even in classrooms where fear of failure is minimized, both teachers and students tend to settle into familiar routines as the school year progresses. To the extent that these routines become the "daily grind," classroom activities that were designed as means toward curricular ends tend to become ends in themselves. That is, *attention becomes focused on what must be done to complete the activities rather than on the knowledge or skills that the activities were designed to develop.*

You can make curricular and instructional adjustments that will increase your students' opportunities to experience intrinsic motivation and flow in your classroom. Strategies for doing so are discussed in chapters 7 and 8. For now, however, I ask you to face up to some important constraints on your options for motivating students: As a teacher, you are not a recreational worker who provides experiences that are enjoyable but not necessarily educational. Nor are you a private tutor who can individualize the curriculum to a single learner's needs and interests. Instead, you must work with classes of 20 or more students and concentrate on helping them to accomplish curricular goals.

These constraints make it unrealistic to adopt intrinsic motivation or flow as the model of student motivation that you will seek to maintain on an all-day, everyday basis. You can provide frequent opportunities for choice and autonomy, and you can phrase instructions and feedback in ways that downplay your control over students, but it will remain true that the students are required to come to your class to try to master an externally-imposed curriculum, and that their efforts will be graded. Under these conditions, intrinsic motivation will be the exception rather than the rule.

The same will be true of flow experiences, especially for students who are underchallenged and thus bored much of the time or overchallenged and thus anxious much of the time. Even students who enjoy a consistently good match between your demands and their current readiness to meet them will vary in their desire for flow experiences. Some will prefer the boredom of safety over the risk of challenge. Even those who are more disposed toward flow experiences cannot be in flow continuously because this would be exhausting (Csikszentmihalyi, 2003).

It is worth noting that *teachers are not the only people who experience constraints on their options as motivators.* Most leadership roles (parent, coach, boss, political or corporate executive) are played out in contexts in which supervisees do not necessarily share their supervisors' goals, yet must be motivated to adopt those goals or at least commit to accomplishing the agenda that goes with them. Furthermore, they often must be willing to do so even though they will not be rewarded as generously as their supervisors and possibly some of their peers. Therefore, the aspects of motivational theory and research that are most relevant to potential appliers involve motivating people to commit to goals that they ordinarily would not adopt on their own initiative.

STUDENT MOTIVATION TO LEARN AS YOUR GOAL

If intrinsic motivation is ideal but unattainable as an all-day, everyday motivational state to seek to develop in your students, what is a more feasible goal? I believe that it is realistic for you to seek to develop and sustain your students' motivation to learn: their tendencies to find learning activities meaningful and worthwhile and to try to get the intended benefits from them.

Motivation to learn differs both from extrinsic, reinforcement-driven motivation and from intrinsic, enjoyment-driven motivation, although it may coexist with either of them. The difference between motivation to learn and extrinsic motivation is closely related to the difference between learning and performance. *Learning* refers to the information processing, sensemaking, and advances in comprehension or mastery that occur when one is acquiring knowledge or skill; *performance* refers to the demonstration of that knowledge or skill after it has been acquired. Strategies for stimulating students' motivation to learn apply not only to performance (work on assignments or tests) but also to the information processing that is involved in learning content or skills in the first place (attending to lessons, reading for understanding, comprehending instructions, putting things into one's own words). Thus, *stimulating students' motivation to learn includes encouraging them to use thoughtful information-processing and skill-building strategies when they are learning. This is quite different from merely offering them incentives for good performance later.*

The difference between intrinsic motivation and motivation to learn is closely related to the difference between affective and cognitive engagement experiences. Intrinsic motivation refers primarily to *affective* experience—enjoyment of the processes involved in engaging in an activity. In contrast, motivation to learn is primarily a *cognitive* experience involving attempts to make sense of the information that an activity conveys, to relate this information to prior knowledge, and to master the skills that the activity develops. *Students may be motivated to learn from a lesson or activity whether or not they find its content interesting or its processes enjoyable.*

Student motivation to learn can be viewed as either a general disposition or a situation-specific state. As a *disposition*, it is an enduring tendency to value learning--to approach the process of learning with effort and thought and to seek to acquire knowledge and skill. In specific situations, a *state* of motivation to learn exists when a student engages purposefully in an activity by adopting its goal and trying to learn the concepts and master the skills it develops. Students who are high in motivation to learn (as a disposition) tend to do these things routinely, as if they possess a "motivated learning schema" that is triggered whenever they enter a learning situation. Even students who do not have much motivation to learn as a general disposition may display it in specific situations because the teacher has sparked their interest or made them see the importance of the content or skill (Deci, Vallerand, Pelletier, & Ryan, 1991). Students who are motivated to learn do not necessarily find classroom activities intensely pleasurable or exciting, but they do find them meaningful and worthwhile, and therefore take them seriously by trying to get the intended enrichment and empowerment benefits from them.

Focus on the Nature and Quality of Motivation, Not its Quantity

Motivation to learn refers primarily to the quality of students' cognitive engagement in a learning activity, not the intensity of the effort they devote to it or the time they spend on it. For most tasks, there is a curvilinear relationship between motivational intensity and degree of success achieved. That is, *performance is highest when motivation is at an optimal level rather than either below or above this optimal level.* Furthermore, the optimal level varies with the nature of the task: High levels of arousal facilitate performance on tasks that call for extraordinary effort, but lower levels facilitate performance on tasks that call for controlled application of refined technique. Thus, it helps to be "psyched up" if your task is to smash open a door or win a 50-meter dash, but such high arousal is counterproductive if your task is to sink a putt or make a free throw.

High arousal is likely to interfere with performance on activities that call for sustained mental concentration and thought, such as the learning activities facing students in classrooms. Students are likely to handle these activities most successfully when their motivation is positive (they are engaged and free from distractions, anxieties, and fear of failure) but not overly high in an absolute sense. They are alert and oriented toward learning, but not "psyched up" or focused on winning a competition or obtaining a reward.

In other words, we always want to maximize students' motivation to learn, but not necessarily to maximize their total motivation. Similarly, we want to maximize successful achievement outcomes, but only insofar as this can be done by maximizing motivation to learn and supplying supportive incentives and rewards. Attempts to increase motivation still further are likely to be counterproductive, especially if they involve inappropriately pressuring students or making them unnecessarily anxious or dependent. We want to develop life-enhancing dispositions in students, not neurotic needs.

MOTIVATION AS A COMPONENT OF SITUATED ACTION SCHEMAS

Most motivated human activity occurs because people recognize the affordances (opportunities to engage in goal-oriented behavior) that an activity arena presents and exploit these affordances by activating previously developed schemas for operating in the arena. If the arena has been designed for people to carry out particular activities by playing particular roles, they are likely to act accordingly. However, if the arena affords opportunities for activities and roles other than the intended or expected ones, they might enact one of these alternatives instead. For example, tennis court complexes are designed to facilitate tennis-related activities and roles, but some people might use them for skating or hopscotch activities (see Table 1.3).

Table 1.4 applies this model to students' motivation at school. It shows how optimally motivated students (Example A) may construe the classroom as an arena for learning

TABLE 1.3

Tennis Courts as Arenas for Situated Activity: Examples of Conventional and Alternative Activities and Roles

	Situation: Tennis Court Complex			
	Conventional Activities: Tennis			
Activity:	Practice Alone	Practice with Partner	Play Singles	Play Doubles
Role:	Practice Targeted Skills	Cooperate to Practice Targeted Skills	Compete to Defeat Opponent	Cooperate with Partner to Defeat Opponents
	Alternative Activities: Skating and Hopscotch			
Activity:	Roller Skating	In-Line Skating	Solo Hopscotch	Competitive Hopscotch
Role:	Skate for Fun, Exercise	Skate for Fun, Exercise	Practice, Challenge Self	Compete to Defeat Opponent

TABLE 1.4
General Model of Situated Activity, Elaborated to Show Motivational Aspects of School Learning.

| General Model (Applies to Any Action Arena) | | Application to School Context | |
General Components of Motivation	General Components of Situated Activity	Example A: Optimal Conditions for Learning	Example B: Suboptimal Conditions for Learning
Motives	*Situation*	*Situation*	*Situation*
Reasons for being in this situation, engaged in this activity	Physical and social context in which the activity takes place	Classroom or other school learning context, viewed primarily as an arena for enrichment, empowerment	Classroom or other school learning context, viewed primarily as an arena for potential failure or embarrassment
Goals	*Activity*	*Activity*	*Activity*
Intended outcomes of engagement in the activity	Goal-oriented action sequence intended to attain the goal(s)	Autonomously motivated acquisition and use of school content	Meeting imposed demands without suffering failure or embarrassment
Strategies	*Role*	*Role*	*Role*
Means used to attain the goals	Network of schemas activated (if necessary, generated) and organized to carry out the activity successfully	Seek to understand the content, integrate it with prior knowledge, and retain it for access in future application situations	Focus on determining what demands will have to be met and how to meet them with minimal risk of failure or embarrassment

(leading to enrichment or empowerment) and thus activate learning-related schemas. However, students with histories of failure and frustration (Example B) might construe the same classroom primarily as an arena for struggling to cope with imposed demands (often leading to failure and embarrassment), so they activate schemas that focus more on ego protection than on learning.

Motivational thinking and decision making are simplest in optional, pressure-free action arenas. People need only to decide whether to enter the arena (go to the tennis courts), what activities/roles to enact there (skate for fun), and when to move on (when they get tired, satiated, etc.). The situation becomes more complicated if the action arena's expected role involves achievement striving. Instead of doing only what they want, when and how they want to do it, and only for as long as they want to continue, people who choose to enter achievement arenas incur responsibilities to respond to performance pressures and deal with whatever consequences might be attached to performance outcomes. The situation is most threatening and pressuring when participation in the achievement arena is required, high-stakes consequences are attached to performance levels, and people lack confidence in their ability to meet the imposed demands successfully.

STIMULATING AND SOCIALIZING MOTIVATION TO LEARN

Much of the motivational advice typically offered to teachers boils down to the following principle: Find out what topics your students want to learn about and what activities they enjoy doing, then build these into your curriculum as much as possible. This principle is useful as far as it goes, but building on students' existing motivation is only part of what teachers need to do. *If you confine yourself to responding to the motivational orientations that your students bring into your classroom, you will limit your options and fail to capitalize on opportunities to guide their motivational development in desirable directions.*

People are born with the potential to develop a great range of motivational dispositions. A few appear to be inborn as part of the human condition and can be observed in everyone. Most, however, especially higher level dispositions such as motivation to learn, are developed gradually through exposure to learning opportunities and socialization influences. The degree to which a particular motivational disposition develops, as well as the qualitative nuances it takes on in the individual person, are influenced by the modeling and socialization (communication of expectations, direct instruction, corrective feedback, reward and punishment) provided by "significant others" in the person's social environment. Along with family members and close friends, teachers are "significant others" in the lives of their students, and thus in a position to influence the students' motivational development.

It is helpful to view motivation to learn as a schema—a network of connected insights, skills, values, and dispositions that enable students to understand what it means to engage in learning activities with the intention of accomplishing their goals and with awareness of the strategies they use in attempting to do so. The total schema cannot be taught directly, although some of its conceptual and skill components can. In addition, its value and dispositional components can be stimulated and supported by teachers through modeling, communication of expectations, and socialization of students into a cohesive learning community.

Development of motivation to learn and related self-actualization motives is especially dependent on modeling and socialization by adults, at home and at school. Students who have not had much exposure to these cognitive aspects of motivation may view school activities as imposed demands rather than as learning opportunities, and thus engage in them with work-avoidant goals and perhaps performance goals, but not learning goals. They will have to be helped to appreciate what motivation to learn means before such motivation can begin to influence their decisions and actions (see chapter 10).

Therefore, besides capitalizing on students' existing motivation, make the best of your opportunities to stimulate and socialize their motivation to learn. In each teaching situation, stimulate motivation to learn the knowledge or skills that the activity is designed to develop. These everyday motivational efforts should have cumulative effects encouraging your students to develop motivation to learn as an enduring disposition. In addition, you can socialize this disposition more directly, using the strategies described in chapter 9.

MOTIVATION AS EXPECTANCY × VALUE REASONING, OFTEN WITHIN A SOCIAL CONTEXT

Much of what researchers have learned about motivation can be organized within an expectancy × value model (Feather, 1982; Pekrun, 1993; Wigfield & Eccles, 2000). The expectancy × value model of motivation holds that the effort that people are willing to invest in an activity is the product of (a) the degree to which they *expect* to be able to perform the activity successfully if they apply themselves (and thus expect to get whatever rewards that successful performance will bring), and (b) the degree to which they *value* those rewards as well as the opportunity to engage in the processes involved in carrying out the activity itself. [Note: The word "value," used here as a verb meaning to appreciate or see worth in, should not be confused with the noun "values," meaning ethical principles or ideals.]

Effort investment is viewed as the product rather than the sum of the expectancy and value factors because it is assumed that no effort at all will be invested if either factor is missing entirely. People do not willingly invest effort in activities that they do not enjoy and that do not lead to valued outcomes, even if they know that they can perform successfully. Nor do they willingly invest effort in even highly valued activities if they believe that they cannot succeed no matter how hard they try. If required to engage in such activities unwillingly, they are likely to experience negative reactions (see Tables 1.5 and 1.6). Thus, *the expectancy × value model of motivation implies that teachers need to (a) help students appreciate the value of school activities and (b) make sure that students can achieve success if they apply reasonable effort.*

Unique expectancy × value reasoning concerning potential engagement occurs within each individual, but it is influenced by the social context in which the activity is embedded. Classrooms are highly charged social contexts that complicate individual students' expectancy × value reasoning, for good or ill (see chapter 2).

Hansen (1989) suggested that students tend to adopt one of four general approaches to classroom activities, depending on their expectations and values (see Table 1.7). *Engaging* is likely when students see value in the activity and are confident of their ability to meet its demands. When engaged, they seek to make sense of the activity by discovering meanings, grasping new insights, and generating integrative interpretations. Unfamil-

TABLE 1.5
Students' Subjective Experiences Relating to the Expectancy Aspects of Task Engagement.

	Anticipated Implications Prior to Task Engagement	Reaction to Task Processes During Task Engagement
When Fearing or Expecting Failure	*Affect:* Apathy, resignation, resentment of forced participation.	*Affect:* Anxiety, embarrassment, fear of failure.
	Cognition: Perception that one cannot "win," that one has no realistic chance to earn desired rewards, satisfactory grades, etc.	*Cognition:* Task focus is "invaded" by perception of confusion, failure, helplessness. Attribution of (poor) performance to insufficient ability.
When Expecting to Succeed	*Affect:* Excitement, happy anticipation of success, reward.	*Affect:* Satisfaction (perhaps occasional excitement) as skills or insights develop. Pride in craftsmanship, successful performance.
	Cognition: Recognition that one can attain desired rewards with reasonable effort. Focus on meeting stated performance criteria.	*Cognition:* Perception of progress toward goals, attribution of (successful) performance to (sufficient) ability plus (reasonable) effort. Focus on one's developing knowledge and skills.

TABLE 1.6
Students' Subjective Experiences Relating to the Value Aspects of Task Engagement.

	Anticipated Implications Prior to Task Engagement	Reaction to Task Processes during Task Engagement
When Engaged in a Negatively Valued Task	*Affect:* Alienation, resistance. Student doesn't want to acquire this knowledge or skill	*Affect:* Anger or dread. Student dislikes the task, which is in effect a punishment.
	Cognition: Perceptions of conflict between what this task represents and one's self-concept, gender role identification, etc. Anticipation of undesirable consequences to involvement in such tasks.	*Cognition:* Task focus is "invaded" by resentment, awareness of being coerced into unpleasant, pointless, or negatively-valued activity.
When Engaged in a Positively Valued Task	*Affect:* Energized, eager to learn this knowledge or skill (for its instrumental value).	*Affect:* Enjoyment, pleasure. Engagement in this task is a reward in its own right.
	Cognition: Recognition that the task is a sub-goal related to attainment of important future goals (often as a "ticket" to social advancement). Focus on the "relevant" aspects of the learning.	*Cognition:* Relaxed concentration on the processes involved in doing this task. Flow. Metacognitive awareness of what the task requires and how one is responding to it. Focus on the academic content when learning, and on the quality of the product when performing.

iar aspects are viewed as challenging but valued because they provide a basis for extending one's understandings.

Dissembling is likely when students recognize value in the activity but do not feel capable of meeting its demands. They are uncertain of what to do, how to do it, or whether they can do it. These uncertainties threaten their identity and self-esteem, so they pretend to understand, make excuses, deny their difficulties, or otherwise focus more on protecting their ego than on developing knowledge and skill.

Evading is likely when success expectancies are high but value perceptions are low. The students feel confident of their ability to meet the activity's demands but don't see a reason to do so. They may go through the motions by focusing sufficiently to avoid teacher interventions and perhaps even accomplish the goal. However, their attention frequently drifts to competing interests such as daydreaming, interacting with classmates, or thinking about their personal lives.

TABLE 1.7
Students' Strategies for Responding to Classroom Activities as Related to Their Expectancy and Value Perceptions.[1]

	Has Low Success Expectations	Has High Success Expectations
Does Not Value the Activity	*Rejection:* Refuses to Participate	*Evading:* Does the Minimum
Values the Activity	*Dissembling:* Protects image of competence	*Engagement:* Seeks to learn

1. Based on Hansen (1989).

Finally, *rejecting* is likely when both success expectations and value perceptions are low. Lacking both reasons to care about succeeding and confidence that they could do so if they tried, students withdraw. Some become passive and psychologically numbed. Others smolder with anger or alienation. Rejecting the activity completely, they not only don't engage in it but don't even feel the need to dissemble by pretending to meet its demands.

ORGANIZATION OF THE BOOK

This first chapter has introduced the concept of motivation, described how motivational theories have evolved, argued for student motivation to learn as the primary focus of your motivational efforts, and introduced the expectancy × value (within a social context) model. Chapter 2 focuses on the social context, emphasizing the importance of establishing your classroom as a learning community in which the participants collaborate in pursuing worthwhile learning goals. It describes classroom management and student socialization strategies that produce a positive classroom climate and set the stage for use of the motivational strategies presented in chapters 3–10. It also summarizes key curricular and instructional features that complement the motivational features of powerful learning programs.

Chapters 3–10 are organized within the expectancy × value model.[1] Chapters 3–5 focus on expectancy issues: protecting students' confidence as learners and providing extra support to those who have become discouraged. Chapters 6–10 focus on strategies for helping students to appreciate the value of engaging in learning activities (because

---

1. As introduced in this chapter and as used to organize chapters 3–10, the notion of motivation as expectancy × value (within a social context) is used as a relatively informal general model. It is *not* meant to refer to the more formal and specific expectancy × value theory of achievement motivation, or to convey the precise definitions, assumptions, or connotations associated with particular versions of that theory (which stretch from Atkinson's 1957 original version through more recent and elaborated versions such as that of Wigfield and Eccles, 2000). For example, applications of the more specific theory are usually limited to achievement situations that call for meeting clear standards of excellence, but I also apply the more general model to informal learning situations that do not involve striving to accomplish well-articulated goals. As another example, the meaning of the value term is usually restricted to the value that the person places on the rewards that may be earned by completing an activity successfully. In contrast, I also include within the value term any intrinsic enjoyment or satisfaction that the person may anticipate or derive from engaging in the processes involved in carrying out the activity.

I have used the expectancy × value model as an organizer for the book because I find it most useful for synthesizing the motivational literature to focus on strategies that teachers might use with their students. It complements organizing and synthesizing schemes that focus on other motivational characteristics of students, and facilitates a shift in primary attention from descriptive concepts to intervention principles. Consequently, it better meets teachers' needs for information about ways to establish and maintain desired motivational patterns in their students.

There have been too many attempts to establish fine distinctions between too many overlapping motivational concepts (Boekaerts, 2001; Bong, 1996; Murphy & Alexander, 2000; Stipek, 1996), so my treatment of related theoretical concepts emphasizes their commonalities and complementary implications for teachers, not their differences. Thus, for the most part I have omitted arguments about issues such as whether adaptive achievement goals are best construed as learning goals, task goals, or mastery goals, or whether adaptive expectancy-related perceptions are best construed as success expectations, confidence, efficacy perceptions, attributions of success to internal and controllable causes, internal locus of control, etc. Instead, I have focused on the common implications of theory and research relating to all these concepts, namely that teachers should seek to foster learning goals and success expectations.

successful engagement will earn extrinsic rewards, bring intrinsic satisfactions, or allow them to develop worthwhile knowledge).

For the most part, the material in chapters 1–10 reflects principles that apply to all students, regardless of age, gender, social class, race, culture, or other personal characteristics. Certain principles might be more applicable with certain students (e.g., younger ones rather than older ones) or in certain situations (e.g., a whole-class lesson versus a follow-up assignment). Wherever the principle is applicable, however, it should have the same implications for practice (i.e., that motivational strategies consistent with the principle are advisable but contradictory strategies are not).

The focus on universally applicable principles in chapters 1–10 reflects my belief that, at least with respect to motivation, people are much more similar than different. I acknowledge the need to adapt motivational strategies to students' individual needs and experiences. However, I believe that this individualization mostly involves adaptations of a single set of basic principles. I do not see a scientific basis for assuming that separate sets of motivational principles (and separate psychologies generally) are needed in order to understand and work effectively with students who differ in age, gender, or cultural background. However, researchers have identified some group and individual differences that seem worth bringing to your attention, and these are discussed in chapter 11. Most of what I have to say about adapting motivational strategies to different students or situations is found in that chapter.

Chapter 12 concludes the book. First it offers suggestions about ways to incorporate the ideas developed in chapters 1–11 into your instructional planning. Then it shifts attention from the motivation of students to the motivation of teachers. It points out that the same principles used to understand the motivation of students facing learning challenges can be used to understand the motivation of teachers facing professional challenges, including difficulties in motivating students. It also calls attention to some of the pitfalls you may encounter in your efforts to become a successful classroom motivator and suggests ways to avoid or overcome them.

SUMMARY

Theories of human motivation have evolved from an emphasis on reactive responses to pressures (external reinforcement contingencies or internally felt needs) to an emphasis on intrinsically motivated, self-determined actions. Flow experiences and other manifestations of intrinsic motivation are usually considered ideal and thus held up to teachers as goals to achieve with their students. I agree that these motivational states should be developed in the classroom when it is feasible to do so. However, the goal of achieving sustained intrinsic motivation is not realistic as a basis for planning your all-day, everyday motivational strategies, because classroom learning requires students to try to master an externally imposed curriculum while often being observed by peers and evaluated by teachers.

It is realistic to expect (and help) your students to experience learning activities as meaningful and worthwhile, and to try to get the intended benefits from them. You can encourage this by stimulating students to engage in the activities with motivation to learn, which they can do whether or not they find the activities intrinsically enjoyable.

The conception of motivation as expectancy × value (within a social context) is useful as a general model for thinking not only about students' existing motivation but also about potential intervention strategies. This model has been used to organize the book. Chapter 2 focuses on the social context, chapters 3–5 address expectancy aspects of motivation, and chapters 6–10 address value aspects. Individual and group differences that may provide a basis for adapting motivational strategies to students' personal characteristics are addressed in chapter 11. Finally, chapter 12 concludes the book by offering suggestions about ways to address motivational issues in your instructional planning and to apply the ideas presented here to your attempts to optimize your own motivation as a teacher.

REFLECTION QUESTIONS

1. Did one of the two italicized paragraphs that began the chapter seem right to you, at least at first? Why?
2. What insights or questions arose from your answers to the self-quiz?
3. What implications stem from the distinction between motivation and control (concerning the appropriate content scope for a book on motivation, distinctions between student motivation and classroom management, and what principles of motivation to suggest to teachers)? See also Box 6.1, pp. 130.
4. Does Czikszentmihalyi's description of "flow" fit your experiences?
5. Do you see any problems with my argument/assumptions about schooling?
6. Why do I claim that we always want to maximize students' motivation to learn, but not necessarily their total motivation?
7. What are some similarities and differences between the approaches to motivation typically taken by psychologists vs. educators? (See Preface)
8. Most motivation attempts take place within relationships that involve power differentials. Does this raise ethical issues? What are the similarities and differences between motivational techniques and brainwashing or propaganda techniques?

REFERENCES

Ainley, M., Enger, L., & Kennedy, G. (2008). The elusive experience of 'flow': Qualitative and quantitative indicators. *International Journal of Educational Research, 47*, 109–121.

Alberto, P., & Troutman, A. (1999). *Applied behavior analysis for teachers* (5th ed.). Columbus, OH: Merrill.

Atkinson, J. (1957). Motivational determinants of risk taking behavior. *Psychological Review, 64*, 359–372.

Boekaerts, M. (2001). Motivation, learning, and instruction. In N. Smelser & P. Baltes (Eds.), *International encyclopedia of the social and behavioral sciences* (pp. 10112–10117). New York: Elsevier Science.

Bong, M. (1996). Problems in academic motivation research and advantages and disadvantages of their solutions. *Contemporary Educational Psychology, 21*, 149–165.

Carver, C., & Scheier, M. (1999). A few more themes, a lot more issues: Commentary on the commentaries. In R. Wyer, Jr. (Ed.), *Perspectives on behavioral self-regulation* (Advances in social cognition series, Vol. 12, pp. 261–302). Mahwah, NJ: Erlbaum.

Csikszentmihalyi, M. (1993). *The evolving self: A psychology for the third millennium.* New York: HarperCollins.

Csikszentmihalyi, M. (1997a). *Finding flow: The psychology of engagement with everyday life.* New York: Basic Books.

Csikszentmihalyi, M. (1997b). Intrinsic motivation and effective teaching: A flow analysis. In J. Bess (Ed.), *Teaching well and liking it: Motivating faculty to teach effectively* (pp. 72–89). Baltimore: The Johns Hopkins Press.

Csikszentmihalyi, M. (2003). *Good business: Leadership, flow, and the making of meaning.* New York: Viking.

Csikszentmihalyi, M., Rathunde, K., & Whalen, S. (1993). *Talented teenagers: The roots of success and failure.* Cambridge, UK: Cambridge University Press.

Deci, E., & Ryan, R. (1985). *Intrinsic motivation and self-determination in human behavior.* New York: Plenum.

Deci, E., & Ryan, R. (Eds.). (2002). *Handbook of self-determination research.* Rochester, NY: University of Rochester Press.

Deci, E., Vallerand, R., Pelletier, L., & Ryan, R. (1991). Motivation and education: The self-determination perspective. *Educational Psychologist, 26,* 325–346.

Engeser, S., & Rheinberg, F. (2008). Flow, performance and moderators of challenge-skill balance. *Motivation and Emotion, 32,* 158–172.

Feather, N. (Ed.). (1982). *Expectations and actions.* Hillsdale, NJ: Erlbaum.

Ford, M. (1992). *Motivating humans: Goals, emotions, and personal agency beliefs.* Newbury Park, CA: Sage.

Frame, D. (1996). Maslow's hierarchy of needs revisited. *Interchange, 27,* 13–22.

Hansen, D. (1989). Lesson evading and lesson dissembling: Ego strategies in the classroom. *American Journal of Education, 97,* 184–208.

Keller, J., & Bless, H. (2008). Flow and regulatory compatibility: An experimental approach to the flow model of intrinsic motivation. *Personality and Social Psychology Bulletin, 34,* 196–209.

Landrum, T., & Kauffman, J. (2006). Behavioral approaches to classroom management. In C. Evertson & C. Weinstein (Eds.), *Handbook of Classroom Management* (pp. 47–71). Mahwah, NJ: Erlbaum.

Maehr, M., & Meyer, H. (1997). Understanding motivation and schooling: Where we've been, where we are, and where we need to go. *Educational Psychology Review, 9,* 371–409.

Maslow, A. (1962). *Toward a psychology of being.* Princeton, NJ: VanNostrand.

Murphy, P., & Alexander, P. (2000). A motivated exploration of motivation terminology. *Contemporary Educational Psychology, 25,* 3–53.

Murray, E. (1964). *Motivation and emotion.* New York: Prentice-Hall.

Murray, H. (1938). *Explorations in personality.* New York: Oxford University Press.

Neher, A. (1991). Maslow's theory of motivation: A critique. *Journal of Humanistic Psychology, 31,* 89–112.

Pekrun, R. (1993). Facets of adolescents' academic motivation: A longitudinal expectancy-value approach. In P. Pintrich & M. Maehr (Eds.), *Advances in motivation and achievement* (Vol. 8, pp. 139–189). Greenwich, CT: JAI.

Schloss, P., & Smith, M. (1994). *Applied behavior analysis in the classroom.* Boston: Allyn & Bacon.

Schweinle, A., Turner, J., & Meyer, D. (2009). Understanding young adolescents' optimal experiences in academic settings. *Journal of Experimental Education, 77,* 125–143.

Shernoff, D., Csikszentmihalyi, M., Schneider, B., & Shernoff, E. (2003). Student engagement in high school classrooms from the perspective of flow theory. *School Psychology Quarterly, 18,* 158–176.

Stipek, D. (1996). Motivation and instruction. In D. Berliner & R. Calfee (Eds.), *Handbook of educational psychology* (pp. 85–113). New York: Macmillan.

Thrash, T., & Elliot, A. (2001). Delimiting and integrating achievement motive and goal constructs. In A. Efklides, J. Kuhl, & R. Sorrentino (Eds.), *Trends and prospects in motivation research* (pp. 3–21). Boston: Kluwer.

Turner, J., Meyer, D., Cox, K., Logan, C., DiCintio, M., & Thomas, C. (1998). Creating contexts for involvement in mathematics. *Journal of Educational Psychology, 90,* 730–745.

Wahba, M., & Bridwell, L. (1976). Maslow reconsidered: A review of research on the need hierarchy theory. *Organizational Behavior and Human Performance, 15,* 212–240.

Wigfield, A., & Eccles, J. (2000). Expectancy-value theory of achievement motivation. *Contemporary Educational Psychology, 25,* 68–81.

2

Establishing a Learning Community in Your Classroom

This chapter describes key features of classroom management, curriculum, instruction, and teacher–student relationships that create a social context that prepares the way for successful use of the motivational strategies discussed in the rest of the book. Those strategies are meant to be subsumed within an overall pattern of effective teaching that includes compatible approaches to managing the classroom and teaching the curriculum. Students will not respond well to motivational attempts if they are fearful, resentful, or otherwise focused on negative emotions. To create conditions that favor your motivational efforts, you will need to establish and maintain your classroom as a learning community—a place where students come primarily to learn, and succeed in doing so through collaboration with you and their classmates. You also will need to focus your curriculum on things that are worth learning and to develop this content in ways that help students to appreciate its significance and application potential.

BUILD A LEARNING COMMUNITY

Certain preconditions must be in place before motivational strategies can be effective. Maslow's hierarchy of needs, for example, implies that lower level needs must be satisfied before higher level needs can become operative. Studies of workers' satisfaction and productivity indicate that workers' motivation is affected not only by the nature of their work and the rewards they expect to earn, but also by their job environment, their social relationships with co-workers, and especially, their feelings about their boss. Even workers who do not derive much intrinsic satisfaction from their work will put forth reasonable effort if they like their boss. However, they may develop apathy or resistance if they view their boss as oppressive.

William Glasser (1990) urged teachers to act as lead managers rather than boss managers. Lead managers motivate by reinforcing rather than punishing, showing rather than telling, empowering rather than overpowering, and emphasizing cooperative work toward shared goals rather than rule enforcement. Lead managers are more likely than boss managers to elicit students' cooperation and empower them to assume responsibility for controlling their lives at school.

Ideas about establishing caring and collaborative relationships with students and their families have been advanced by James Comer (1980) in *School Power*, by Nel Noddings (2005) in *The Challenge to Care in Schools*, by Robert Pianta (1999) in *Enhancing Relationships Between Children and Teachers*, by William Purkey and John Novak (1996) in *Inviting School Success*, and by Carl Rogers and H. Jerome Freiberg (1994) in *Freedom to Learn*. These books advocate creating a school environment in which students feel comfortable, valued, and secure. This encourages them to form positive emotional bonds with teachers and peers and a positive attitude toward school, which in turn facilitates their academic motivation and learning.

Many emerging ideas about optimal social contexts in classrooms center around the concept of a *learning community* (Baker, Terry, Bridger, & Winsor, 1997; Watson & Battistich, 2006), which points directly to two key features of optimal classroom environments. First, it emphasizes learning, which implies something more than merely completing tasks or even passing tests. It serves as a reminder that students come to school to acquire important knowledge, skills, values, and dispositions, and that their learning is supposed to be enriching and empowering.

Second, the term emphasizes that this learning will occur within a community—a group of people with social connections and responsibilities toward one another and the group as a whole. The learning will be collaborative as community members encourage and support one another's efforts. This social context enables students to feel comfortable asking questions, seeking help, and responding to questions when unsure of the answer. Members share the belief that "We're all learning together," so confusion and mistakes are understood as natural parts of the learning process. The teacher is a learner too, and models this role frequently (Matsumura, Slater, & Crosson, 2008).

Three important agendas for you to accomplish in establishing a learning community will set the stage for motivating your students: (a) make yourself and your classroom attractive to students, (b) focus their attention on individual and collaborative learning goals and help them to achieve these goals, and (c) teach things that are worth learning, in ways that help students to appreciate their value. The first two of these agendas address the communal aspects of a learning community; the third addresses the learning aspects.

MAKE YOURSELF AND YOUR CLASSROOM ATTRACTIVE TO STUDENTS

You—your own personality and everyday behavior in the classroom—can become your most powerful motivational tool, if you *cultivate and display the attributes of effective models and socializers*. These begin with characteristics that make people well liked: a cheerful disposition, friendliness, emotional maturity, sincerity, and other qualities that indicate good mental health and personal adjustment. Your attempts to socialize students will have positive effects to the extent that the students admire you, value your opinions, and believe that you are sincere in what you say and have their best interests in mind when saying it. Students' motivation to learn and sense of belonging in the classroom tend to be high when students perceive their teachers as involved with them (liking them, sympathetic and responsive to their needs), but students become disaffected when they do not perceive such involvement (Davis, 2001; Elias & Haynes, 2008; Martin & Dowson, 2009; McMahon, Wernsman, & Rose, 2009; McCombs, Daniels, & Perry, 2008; Murdock, 1999; Nichols, 2008; Osterman, 2000; Wentzel, 1999).

Therefore, *get to know and enjoy your students.* Learn their preferred names quickly and use these names frequently as you interact with them. Greet them warmly each day and spend some time getting to know them as individuals. In the process, you will learn a lot about their backgrounds and interests that you can incorporate into your teaching in ways that are compatible with curricular goals. *Also, help your students get to know and appreciate you as a person* by sharing some of your background, experiences, interests, and opinions. This will help your students to become more open and genuine in their interactions with you, even while retaining their respect for your authority as the teacher. *Finally, help them get to know one another* by interviewing them publicly in ways that allow them to share information about their families, interests, hobbies, and noteworthy experiences (Morganett, 1995).

Create an inviting physical environment in your classroom. To the extent possible, see that it is furnished comfortably and arranged in a way that is both aesthetically pleasing and compatible with your instructional methods. Include attractive displays and decorations that relate to the curriculum. As photos of your students and products from their completed assignments become available, incorporate these into your displays in ways that encourage the students to take pride in their accomplishments and appreciate those of their classmates.

Be an Authoritative Manager and Socializer of Students

In managing your classroom and socializing students, emphasize the strategies that have emerged repeatedly in studies of effective teachers: Approach management as a process of establishing a productive learning environment. That is, *focus on helping students learn what is expected and how to meet those expectations, not on threatening or punishing them for failing to do so.* Successful managers are clear and consistent in articulating their expectations. If necessary, they model and instruct students in desired procedures and remind students when these procedures are needed. They keep students engaged in worthwhile lessons and activities, monitor their classrooms continually and respond to emerging problems before they become disruptive, and when possible, intervene in ways that do not disrupt lesson momentum or distract students who are working on assignments (Brophy, 1988, 2006; Evertson & Weinstein, 2006; Freiberg, 1999).

Why am I discussing management strategies in a section on making yourself and your classroom attractive to students? Because students want and expect teachers to create predictable structures in their classrooms (Askell-Williams & Lawson, 2001; Cothran, Kulinna, & Garrahy, 2003). Unsurprisingly, students describe their favorite teachers as caring about them, helping them to succeed as learners, teaching interesting things, explaining content clearly, being pleasant and friendly, and being fair, as well as not playing favorites, humiliating them, appearing to look down on them when they make mistakes or ask for help, yelling at them, or overreacting to their minor misbehavior. However, students also say that they want teachers to articulate and enforce clear standards of behavior. They view this not just as part of the teacher's job but as evidence that the teacher cares about them (Cabello & Terrell, 1994; Hayes, Ryan, & Zseller, 1994; Hoy & Weinstein, 2006).

A dependable classroom structure provides students with the information and assistance they need to enable them to learn successfully. You can provide structure by communicating your expectations clearly; by responding consistently, predictably, and contingently to students' behavior; by offering help and support to those who are struggling; and by adjusting your teaching strategies to individual differences. Students who experience optimal levels of this kind of structure are likely to be the most effortful, persistent, and highly engaged in classroom activities (Skinner & Belmont, 1993).

Parents who are the most successful in getting their children to adopt their ideals and internalize their standards for behavior use authoritative rather than authoritarian strategies (Baumrind, 1991). *Authoritarian* parents make little attempt to explain their demands, which they expect to be obeyed without questioning or discussion. In contrast, *authoritative* parents explain the rationales for their demands and help their children to understand that the demands are made for the children's own good. The authoritative pattern includes:

- Accepting the child as an individual
- Communicating this acceptance through warm, affectionate interactions
- Socializing by teaching the child prosocial values and behavioral guidelines, not just imposing "discipline"
- Clarifying rules and limits, but with input from the child and flexibility in adapting to developmental advances (e.g., allowing more opportunities for autonomy and choice as children develop greater ability to handle these opportunities responsibly)
- Presenting expectations in ways that communicate respect for and concern about the child, as opposed to "laying down the law"
- Explaining the rationales underlying demands and expectations
- Justifying prohibitions by citing the effects of children's actions on themselves and others rather than by appealing to fear of punishment or essentially empty logic such as "good children don't do that"
- Teaching desired values and modeling their applications
- Continually projecting positive expectations and attitudes: treating children as if they already are, or at least are becoming, prosocial and responsible people.

Authoritative socialization practices are optimal in the classroom as well as the home. Besides supporting your management system, they set the stage for successful motivation efforts by creating a positive classroom atmosphere and encouraging students to view you as a caring teacher whom they trust and want to please (vanWerkhoven, vanLonden, & Stevens, 2001; Wentzel, 1999).

In summary, seek to maintain a classroom structure that is optimal not only in the degree of direction you provide but also in the manner in which you exercise leadership. *Use authoritative strategies that help students to become active, self-regulated learners*; avoid both (a) authoritarian strategies that produce passive obedience rather than thoughtful self-regulation and (b) laissez-faire strategies that offer students autonomy but fail to provide them with needed guidance (McCaslin & Good, 1992).

USE APPEALING COMMUNICATION PRACTICES

The linkage between authoritative classroom management and successful student motivation was demonstrated in college classrooms in studies done by communication theorists. Some of these studies focused on instructors' *compliance-gaining strategies*. They indicated that coercive, authoritarian approaches to gaining compliance had very negative effects on students' liking of instructors and achievement of the classes' learning goals. In contrast, authoritative techniques paved the way for motivational efforts by developing positive relationships between the instructors and their students.

Other studies showed the importance of teacher *immediacy*: actions that enhance physical and psychological closeness with students. Nonverbal immediacy includes eye contact, smiling, positive gestures, vocal variety, movement around the classroom, forward body lean, and a relaxed body position. Verbal immediacy includes use of humor, personal examples, and other self-disclosure, "we" and "our" language, and students' first names. Immediacy behaviors increase students' liking for the instructor, their interest in the course, and their desire to study thoughtfully and do good work on assignments. Working together, the compliance-gaining and immediacy aspects of teachers' communication styles produce positive effects on motivation and learning, especially in students who are not highly motivated at the beginning of the term (Allen, Witt, & Wheeless, 2006; Richmond, 2002). In contrast, students avoid interactions with instructors they perceive as uncaring or uninterested in them, and they stop coming to ask for help if repeated attempts do not elicit effective responses (Martin, Meyers, & Mottet, 2002).

This book is about motivating students rather than managing classrooms, so I will not pursue the latter topic further. For more research-based information about classroom management and detailed suggestions about applications, see Emmer and Evertson (2008), Evertson and Emmer (2008), Good and Brophy (2008), Jones and Jones (2007), or Weinstein and Mignano (2006). For now, bear in mind that an important part of making your students feel comfortable in your classroom is providing them with a reliably safe and humane learning environment. If you interact with them in an authoritative manner, you will be viewed as meeting their needs and helping them to accomplish shared goals rather than as "bossing them around."

FOCUS STUDENTS' ATTENTION ON INDIVIDUAL AND COLLABORATIVE LEARNING GOALS

At any given time, you will want your students to focus on certain goals but may find that some of them pursue other goals in addition or instead. Many of these will be social goals. Social goals sometimes complement learning goals (as when students seek to achieve at a high level in order to please you, their parents, or peers who value such achievement). However, social goals also can undermine learning goals (as when students minimize their work output to please peers who have rejected the school's agenda, or more typically, when their attention is distracted from lessons and assignments to social interactions with classmates). You can increase the power of your motivational efforts by attending to your students' social goals (Urdan & Maehr, 1995; Wentzel, 1992). In particular, *create a social environment in which everyone feels welcome and learning is accomplished through the collaborative efforts of yourself and your students.*

During lessons and times when students are working on assignments individually, however, you will need to *keep attention focused on learning goals rather than on social goals or other competing agendas.* You are likely to get the best results if you *help students to frame their learning goals* in terms of acquiring knowledge or skills (e.g., learning to find the lowest common denominator), not just in terms of completing tasks or obtaining particular grades. This will encourage them to take responsibility for managing their own learning by actively setting goals, seeking to construct understandings, persisting in their efforts to overcome confusions, and assessing and reflecting on what they have learned.

Teach Things That Are Worth Learning, in Ways That Help Students to Appreciate their Value

Even if you have set the stage by making yourself and your classroom attractive to students and by focusing their attention on individual and collaborative learning goals, you cannot expect them to sustain much motivation to learn unless they view the learning as meaningful and worthwhile. *Students are not likely to be motivated to learn when engaged in pointless or meaningless activities such as the following*: continued practice on skills that already have been mastered thoroughly; memorizing lists for no good reason; looking up and copying definitions of terms that are never used in activities or assignments; reading material that is written in such sketchy, technical, or abstract language as to make it essentially meaningless; or working on tasks assigned merely to fill time rather than to support worthwhile learning.

Plan with Major Goals in Mind

The key to making learning experiences worthwhile is to *focus your planning on major instructional goals, phrased in terms of desired student outcomes*—the knowledge, skills, attitudes, values, and dispositions that you want to develop in your students. Goals, not content coverage or learning processes, provide the rationale for curriculum and instruction. All of the elements of your instructional program—content sources, discussion questions, activities, assignments, and assessment methods—should be included because you consider them useful as means to accomplish important instructional goals.

It may seem obvious that curriculum planning should be guided by major instructional goals, but research on instructional materials and on teachers' planning and teaching suggest that this principle is not often realized in classrooms. Teachers typically plan by concentrating on the content they will teach and the activities their students will do, without giving much thought to the goals that provide the rationale for including the content and activities (Clark & Peterson, 1986).

In effect, most teachers leave crucially important decisions about goals to the publishing companies who supply their instructional materials. This would work out well if sustained focus on important goals guided the development of these materials. However, the textbook series typically treat content coverage as an end in itself. As a result, too many topics are covered in not enough depth; content exposition often lacks coherence and is cluttered with insertions and illustrations that have little to do with the key ideas that should be developed; skills are taught separately from knowledge content rather than integrated with it; and in general, neither the students' texts nor the questions and activities suggested in the teachers' manuals are structured around powerful ideas connected to important goals (Beck & McKeown, 1988; Brophy, 1992b; Dreher & Singer, 1989; Elliott & Woodward, 1990; Tyson-Bernstein, 1988).

Adapt Instructional Materials to Your Goals

You will not be able to achieve a coherent program of curriculum and instruction simply by following the teaching suggestions that come with your textbooks. Instead, you will need to elaborate on or even substitute for much of the content in the texts and many of the activities suggested in the accompanying manuals.

To do so, examine your instructional materials and unit plans in light of your major instructional goals. Identify what content to ignore or downplay and what content to emphasize. You may need to augment the latter content if major ideas or themes are not well developed in the texts. Skip pointless questions and activities, and develop alternatives that will support progress toward major goals. Treat the textbook as just one among many potential resources to draw upon in planning and implementing curricula. There is no need to view the textbook as "the" curriculum and thus limit yourself and your students to its contents.

Develop Powerful Ideas in Depth

You won't have time to teach everything worth learning. Only so many topics can be included in the curriculum, and not all of these can be developed in sufficient depth to promote deep understanding of key ideas, appreciation of their significance, and exploration of their applications to life outside of school. This tension between breadth of coverage and depth of topic development is an enduring dilemma that teachers have to manage as best they can; it is not a problem that you can solve in any permanent or completely satisfactory manner.

In recent years, curricula have drifted into an overemphasis on breadth at the expense of depth. Critics routinely complain that textbooks offer "mile-wide but inch-deep" curricula featuring parades of disconnected facts instead of coherent networks of connected content structured around powerful ideas. Reports of teaching in classrooms suggest a similar picture. Although there are exceptions, most of these descriptions portray teachers as hurriedly attempting to cover too much content and students as frequently memorizing but not often reflecting and discussing. *Students spend too much time reading, reciting, filling out worksheets, and taking memory tests, and not enough time engaging in sustained discourse about powerful ideas or applying these ideas in authentic activities* (Goodlad, 1984; Stodolsky, 1988). These unfortunate curricular trends have been exacerbated by increasing emphasis on high-stakes testing.

Disconnected factual information is not very meaningful or memorable. When students lack contexts within which to situate such information and richly connected networks of ideas to enhance its meaningfulness, they are forced to rely on rote memorizing instead of using more sophisticated learning and application strategies. They remember as much as they can until the test, but then forget most of it afterwards. Furthermore, most of what they do remember is inert knowledge that they are not able to use in relevant application situations (Bransford, Brown, & Cocking, 1999; Palincsar, 1998; Prawat, 1989).

There is general agreement about what needs to be done to enable students to construct meaningful knowledge that they can access and use in their lives outside of school. First, there needs to be a retreat from breadth of coverage in order to allow time to develop the most important content in greater depth. Second, this important content needs to be represented as networks of connected information structured around powerful ideas. Third, the content needs to be developed with a focus on explaining these important ideas and the connections among them (see Box 2.1).

Box 2.1   Teaching with Emphasis on Powerful Ideas

As an example of the value of structuring content around powerful ideas, consider the topic of shelter. Elementary social studies textbook series typically emphasize that shelter is a basic human need and then go on to identify and illustrate a great variety of shelter forms (tipis, igloos, stilt homes, etc.). However, the texts typically say very little about why people live in these different kinds of homes and nothing at all about advances in construction materials and techniques that have made possible the features of modern housing that most children in the United States take for granted. Students often emerge from these units thinking that people from the past or from other societies have inexplicably chosen to live in strange or exotic forms of housing, without appreciating that local responses to shelter needs usually are quite inventive given the available construction knowledge, technology, and materials.

Units on shelter and other cultural universals (food, clothing, transportation, communication, occupations, government, etc.) will be much more powerful if taught with emphasis on how practices relating to the cultural universal have evolved over time, how and why they vary across societies today, and what all of this might mean for personal, social, and civic decision making. This will expand students' purviews on the human condition and help them to put the familiar into historical, geographical, and cultural perspective.

For example, instruction on shelter might help students to understand and appreciate the reasons for its different forms. Students could learn that shelter needs are determined by local climate and geographical features, and that most housing is constructed using materials adapted from natural resources that are plentiful in the local area. Certain forms of housing reflect cultural, economic, or geographic conditions (tipis and tents as easily portable shelters used by nomadic societies, stilt homes as adaptation to periodic flooding, highrises as adaptation to land scarcity in urban areas). Inventions, discoveries, and improvements in construction knowledge and materials have enabled many modern people to live in housing that offers better durability, weatherproofing, insulation, and temperature control, with fewer requirements for maintenance and labor (e.g., cutting wood for a fireplace or shoveling coal for a furnace) than what was available to even the richest of our ancestors.

These and related ideas would be taught with appeal to students' sense of imagination and wonder, and with emphasis on values and dispositions (e.g., consciousness-raising through age-suitable activities relating to the energy efficiency of homes or the plight of the homeless). Development and application might include a tour of the neighborhood (in which different types of housing are identified and discussed) or taking home an energy-efficiency inventory to fill out and discuss with their parents. There might also be reading and discussion of children's literature selections on life in the past (e.g., in log cabins on the frontier) or in other societies or about the homeless in our society today, as well as activities calling for students to plan their ideal homes or simulate the thinking involved in making decisions about where to live given certain location and budgetary constrictions. For a complete shelter unit developed according to these principles, see Alleman and Brophy (2001).

(continued)

Box 2.1   Continued

Similarly, units on history need not be seemingly random parades of facts. If planned with focus on instructional goals, they can be structured around powerful ideas that students can appreciate and apply. For example, units on the American Revolution might be planned to develop understanding and appreciation of the origins of American political values and policies. Treatment of the Revolution and its aftermath would emphasize the historical events and political philosophies that shaped the thinking of the writers of the Declaration of Independence and the Constitution. Content coverage would focus on the issues that developed between England and the colonies and the ways that these impacted various types of people, as well as on the ideals, principles, and compromises that went into the construction of the Constitution (especially the Bill of Rights). Assignments calling for research, critical thinking, or decision making would focus on topics such as the various forms of oppression that different colonial groups had experienced (and the influence of this on their thinking about government), as well as the ideas of Jefferson and other key framers of the Constitution. There would be less emphasis on Paul Revere or other revolutionary figures who were not known primarily for their contributions to American political values and policies, and no emphasis at all on the details of particular battles. Students might role play journalists or pamphleteers writing about the Boston Massacre or the Boston Tea Party, simulate a town meeting or Continental Congress session discussing possible responses to the Intolerable Acts, hold a debate on whether the Revolution was justified, or pretend to be citizens of Boston writing to friends elsewhere about their experiences.

These suggested approaches are not the only or even necessarily the best ones to take in addressing these two topics. However, they illustrate how clarity of primary goals encourages development of units and lessons likely to cohere and function as tools for accomplishing those goals, and in the process, to produce instruction that students find meaningful, relevant, and applicable to their lives outside of school. The particular goals to emphasize will vary with one's educational philosophy, the ages and needs of the students, and the purposes of the course. Teachers of military history in a service academy, for example, would have very different goals and would approach the unit on the American Revolution with very different content emphases than those in the example.

Structure Activities and Assignments Around Powerful Ideas

The best learning activities and assignments are built around powerful ideas. Students will not necessarily learn anything important from merely spending "time on task." The key to the effectiveness of good activities is their *cognitive engagement potential*—the degree to which they get students actively thinking about and applying key ideas, preferably with conscious awareness of their learning goals and control of their learning strategies. The most valuable activities are not merely hands-on, but minds-on.

The success of an activity in producing thoughtful student engagement with key ideas depends not only on the activity itself but on the teacher structuring and the teacher-student discourse that occur before, during, and after the activity. *Activities are likely to have maximum impact when* you (a) introduce them in ways that clarify their purposes and engage students in seeking to accomplish those purposes; (b) scaffold students' work, monitor their progress, and provide appropriate feedback; and (c) lead the students through post-activity sharing of and reflection on the insights that have been developed. [Instructional *scaffolding* is a general term for the task assistance or simplification strategies that teachers use to bridge the gap between what students are capable of doing on their own and what they are capable of doing with help. Scaffolds help students progress from their current abilities toward the intended goal. As with the scaffolds used by house painters, the support provided by instructional scaffolds is temporary, adjustable, and removed when it is no longer needed. Examples of scaffolds include cognitive modeling (in which the teacher demonstrates what to do, thinking aloud while doing so), prompts or cues that help students move on to the next step when they are temporarily stuck, and questions that help them to diagnose the reasons for errors and develop repair strategies.]

In planning activities and assignments, begin with a focus on the unit's major goals and consider what kinds of activities would promote progress toward those goals. This will help you to make good decisions about whether to use activities suggested in the manual and about what other activities might need to be included. A synthesis of principles for designing and implementing learning activities (Brophy & Alleman, 1991) concluded that all of the activities in a unit of instruction should meet four *primary criteria*:

1. *Goal relevance.* Each activity is essential, or at least directly relevant and useful, for enabling students to achieve the unit's learning goals.
2. *Difficulty level.* Each activity is pitched within the optimal range of difficulty--challenging enough to extend learning, but not so difficult as to leave many students confused or frustrated.
3. *Feasibility.* Each activity is feasible for implementation within the constraints under which you must work (space and equipment, time, types of students, etc.).
4. *Cost effectiveness.* The learning benefits derived from each activity justify its anticipated costs in time and trouble (both for you and for your students).

In selecting from among activities that meet all four of these primary criteria, you might consider applying several *secondary criteria*:

1. Students are likely to find the activity interesting or enjoyable.
2. The activity provides opportunities for interaction and reflective discourse, not just solitary seatwork.
3. If the activity involves writing, students will compose prose, not just fill in blanks.
4. If the activity involves discourse, students will engage in critical or creative thinking, inquiry, problem solving, or decision making, not just regurgitate facts and definitions.
5. The activity focuses on application of important ideas, not incidental details or interesting but ultimately trivial information.
6. As a set, the activities offer variety and in other ways appeal to student motivation to the extent that this is consistent with curriculum goals.
7. As a set, the activities include many ties to current events or local and family examples or applications.

Emphasize Authentic Activities

When selecting and implementing learning activities, be conscious of potential applications of powerful ideas. As much as possible, allow your students to learn through engagement in authentic activities. *Authentic activities* require using what is being learned for accomplishing the very sorts of life applications that justify inclusion of this learning in the curriculum in the first place. If it is not possible to engage students in the actual life applications that the learning experiences are designed to prepare them for, then at least engage them in discussions or simulations of these applications.

Where skills must be practiced until they become smooth and automatic, most practice should occur within whole-task applications rather than be confined to isolated practice of subskills. Elementary students should have opportunities to read for pleasure in addition to practicing word attack skills, to solve problems and apply mathematics in addition to practicing number facts and computations, and to write prose or poetry compositions or actual correspondence in addition to practicing spelling and penmanship. All students should learn how and why knowledge was developed in addition to acquiring the knowledge itself, and should have opportunities to apply what they are learning to their own lives or to current social, civic, or scientific issues.

Educators who do not distinguish between school subjects and the academic disciplines that inform them sometimes define authentic activities narrowly, as activities that engage students in doing things that disciplinary practitioners do (e.g., conduct inquiry using the forms of discourse and the investigatory tools that characterize the discipline). However, most educators (myself included) view schooling more broadly—as development of students' full human potential and preparation for life in general, not just as induction into the disciplines. This broader view leads to definitions of authentic activities that emphasize life applications (Brophy, 2001; King, Newmann, & Carmichael, 2009; Shaffer & Resnick, 1999; Wells, 1999).

Newmann and colleagues (1996), for example, specified that authentic activities should provide opportunities to construct knowledge through disciplined inquiry that has value beyond the classroom. Perkins (1993) suggested that mathematics curricula might place more emphasis on probability and statistics relative to quadratic equations, and that social studies curricula might place more emphasis on the roots of ethnic hatreds than on the details of the French Revolution. The authenticity of literacy education has been augmented by establishing authentic audiences for students' reading and writing activities, such as by creating pen pal programs (Austin, 2000) or student-run newspapers (Cazden, 2002).

These examples illustrate that authentic activities involve both curricular elements (focusing on content that has potential applications in life outside of school) and instructional elements (developing this content through activities that allow students to use what they are learning for authentic purposes). Research on authentic activities indicates that they occur infrequently in classrooms, but when they do, they are associated with a variety of positive outcomes (Avery, 1999; Hickey, Moore, & Pellegrino, 2001; Newmann and colleagues, 1996; Purcell-Gates, Degener, Jacobsen, & Soler, 2002).

TEACH FOR UNDERSTANDING

In recent years, both the findings of research on effective teaching and the instructional guidelines issued by organizations serving subject-matter specialists have emphasized the importance of teaching school subjects for understanding. *Students who learn content with understanding not only learn the content itself but appreciate the reasons for learning it and retain it in a form that makes it usable when needed.* When the new learning is complex, the construction of meaning required to develop clear understanding of it takes time and is facilitated by the interactive discourse that occurs during lessons and activities. Clear explanations and modeling from the teacher are important, but so are opportunities to answer questions about the content, discuss or debate its meanings and implications, and apply it in problem-solving or decision-making contexts.

These activities allow students to process the content actively and make it their own by paraphrasing it into their own words, exploring its relationships to other knowledge and to past experience, appreciating the insights it provides, and identifying its implications for personal decision making or action. The teacher provides whatever structuring and scaffolding that students need in order to accomplish the goals, but gradually fades this assistance as students develop expertise. Ultimately, the students engage in independent and self-regulated learning.

Analysis of programs that have been developed to teach school subjects for understanding have identified a set of principles that are common to most if not all of them (Brophy, 1992a). These common elements are shown in Table 2.1. Although these principles emerged from research on learning, note how well they complement the principles emerging from research on motivation. They fit especially well with the principles for establishing a learning community and encouraging students to adopt learning goals rather than performance or work-avoidant goals when engaging in activities. The case examples in Box 2.2 further illustrate this complementarity. For more information about teaching for understanding, see Good and Brophy (2008).

TABLE 2.1
Teaching for Understanding: 10 Key Features

1. The curriculum is designed to equip students with knowledge, skills, values, and dispositions that they will find useful both inside and outside of school
2. Instructional goals emphasize developing student expertise within an application context and with emphasis on conceptual understanding of knowledge and self-regulated application of skills
3. The curriculum balances breadth with depth by addressing limited content but developing this content sufficiently to foster conceptual understanding
4. The content is organized around a limited set of powerful ideas (basic understandings and principles)
5. The teacher's role is not just to present information but also to scaffold and respond to students' learning efforts
6. The students' role is not just to absorb or copy input but also to actively make sense and construct meaning
7. Students' prior knowledge about the topic is elicited and used as a starting place for instruction, which builds on accurate prior knowledge and stimulates conceptual change if necessary
8. Activities and assignments feature tasks that call for critical thinking or problem solving, not just memory or reproduction
9. Higher order thinking skills are not taught as a separate skills curriculum. Instead, they are developed in the process of teaching subject-matter knowledge within application contexts that call for students to relate what they are learning to their lives outside of school by thinking critically or creatively about it or by using it to solve problems or make decisions
10. The teacher creates a social environment in the classroom that could be described as a learning community featuring discourse or dialogue designed to promote understanding

Box 2.2   Contrasting Mastery Orientations

Meece (1994) reported case studies of fifth- and sixth-grade science teachers whose students showed contrasting degrees of orientation toward learning (mastery) goals. Analyses indicated that differences in students' goal orientations and related achievement behaviors were associated with differences in their teachers' approaches to motivation and instruction.

In the low mastery classes, learning activities emphasized memorization and recall of isolated bits of information. Students had limited opportunities to actively construct meaning, view themselves as sources of knowledge, or apply what they were learning to new situations. Their teachers made little effort to adapt lessons to the students' ability levels and interests, and provided few opportunities for peer collaboration or self-directed learning. Motivational attempts were focused on the grading system (via reminders to students that their work would be evaluated or that they needed to prepare for an upcoming test). These instructional practices that emphasized simple transmission and recall of facts did not encourage the development of mastery goals and self-regulated learning.

In contrast, the high mastery teachers expected their students to understand, apply, and make sense of what they were learning. To encourage active involvement in lessons, they modified material to increase its personal relevance to their students, emphasized its intrinsic value, and provided opportunities for peer collaboration. They did not place much emphasis on grades or other extrinsic incentives for learning.

Students in one of the two high mastery classes reported more active engagement than those in the other high mastery class. The teacher in the first class presented coherent lessons that proceeded in small steps and allowed students to see the connections between ideas. She also regularly monitored her students' comprehension and held them individually accountable for what they were learning. The other high mastery teacher summarized and connected ideas for his students but did not follow up by monitoring their understanding closely and helping them to construct understandings. When his students were confused, he was more likely to simply provide the correct answer than to help the students figure it out for themselves.

Although both high mastery teachers used motivational strategies that helped generate interest in the content, one was less successful because he did not provide adequate instructional support or consistently hold his students accountable for learning with understanding. He was good at conveying the inherent value of learning the content, but less skilled at involving all of his students in learning activities and supporting their independent problem-solving efforts.

SOCIOCULTURAL VIEWS OF TEACHING

Sociocultural views of teaching and learning also fit well with ideas about teaching for understanding within a learning community. Sociocultural theorists view learning in classrooms as part of the more general socialization that takes place as societies equip their new members with the knowledge and skills that they believe to be important. Based on the metaphor of on-the-job training, sociocultural theorists speak of learners as novices undergoing a *cognitive apprenticeship* under the supervision of one or more mentors. In addition to society in general, such enculturation occurs within smaller *communities of practice* when mentors impart to novices the knowledge and skills involved in functioning as a mathematician, historian, or chemist (or out of school, as a carpenter, baker, etc.).

At first, novices learn through legitimate peripheral participation in communities of practice. They are legitimate members of the community, but their participation is peripheral because they mostly watch, listen, and carry out beginner-level activities under the supervision of mentors. *As they gain expertise, they move from peripheral toward more central forms of participation.* They begin to function more fully as equals with their mentors and to assume increasing responsibilities for regulating their own learning and for acting as mentors themselves in socializing new members into the community.

As novices acquire expertise, they learn to use the community's specialized discourse and tools. Communities of practice develop specialized vocabulary and forms of discourse that help them to carry out their activities (e.g., analyze a story using concepts such as plot or characterization, or analyze a historical account using concepts such as bias or primary vs. secondary sources). Communities of practice use not only physical tools but cognitive tools such as mathematical formulas, musical notation, or any of the processes and skills commonly taught as part of the academic disciplines (Roelofs & Terwell, 1999; Salomon & Perkins, 1998; Wells, 2001). Novices ordinarily acquire the community's specialized discourse and learn to use its specialized tools in the context of carrying out the very kinds of activities that led the community to invent the specialized discourse and tools in the first place.

Sociocultural theorists emphasize that learning activities and situations are characterized by affordances and constraints (Gresalfi, Martin, Hand, & Greeno, 2009). *Affordances* are exploitable opportunities—the potential for thought and action that the activity offers. For example, a discussion affords opportunities to students to engage in verbal interaction about a topic, whereas an essay assignment affords opportunities to organize their thinking and communicate their ideas in writing. *Constraints* are limitations on the range of thinking and action that an activity imposes. A teacher might constrain a discussion by requiring that students' contributions be polite and on topic, or constrain an essay assignment by limiting it to 300 words and requiring that each paragraph begin with a clear topic sentence. Some school activities and assignments are severely constrained, such as worksheets that limit students' responses to filling in a blank, circling an alternative, or supplying the answer to a calculation problem.

Sociocultural theorists emphasize the importance of learning activities that embody affordances and constraints that are well matched to the major instructional goals. In particular, they emphasize allowing students to learn primarily through engagement in authentic activities. Book-length presentations of sociocultural models of learning communities can be found in Rogoff, Turkanis, and Bartlett (2001), Tharp, Estrada, Dalton, and Yamauchi (2000), and Wells (1999).

TWO TEACHERS WITH CONTRASTING MOTIVATIONAL ORIENTATIONS

As an opportunity to apply learning community principles, let us consider two teachers who are good at relating to their students and committed to supporting their progress as learners, but who approach motivation quite differently. Despite their similar student orientations, the teachers' ideas about motivation create contrasting learning contexts for their students.

Laura Hirsch and Rachel Dewey both teach language arts and social studies at a large middle school. Their classes are similar in size and student composition. Both teachers are authoritative in managing their classes and interacting with students, so their classes generally run smoothly, with high rates of student engagement in activities and low rates of disruption. Both Laura and Rachel are warm, friendly, and optimistic people who are devoted to their profession and well liked by their students. Each devotes considerable attention to student motivation in planning her classroom routines, lessons, and learning activities. However, the motivational principles that they emphasize are quite different. As you read about these two teachers, think about the motivational strategies they use and consider their probable effects on students' motivation and learning.

Laura Hirsch

Laura makes sure that her students can achieve success if they invest reasonable effort. In her class, grades are determined by performance on daily assignments (one-third) and on weekly quizzes and unit tests (two-thirds). Laura prepares her students well for these assignments and tests.

First, she leads the class through a reading of the story in the reader or the chapter section in the social studies textbook. She works her way methodically through the rows, allowing each student an opportunity to read a paragraph or two, then moving on to the next student. She suspends the reading periodically to provide explanations or ask questions to underscore key ideas that were developed in the section just read or will be developed in the upcoming section. Laura's students know that they should take notes on these explanations and questions, because they are likely to appear on the assignments, quizzes, and tests. As the reading progresses, Laura also invites and responds to students' questions and comments about the material, but she makes sure that the discourse doesn't stray too far from the key ideas she wants to emphasize.

Following these text-based lessons, students work individually on assignments. Laura insists on quiet during these work times, so everyone can concentrate. The worksheets feature comprehension questions, mostly calling for matching, true/false, or fill-in-the-blank responses. Most questions have been supplied by the textbook publishers, although Laura has eliminated a few ambiguous or controversial items and added some items of her own on points that had been neglected in the publisher-supplied exercises and tests. As students work, she circulates to help those who need it. A few students may finish these assignments during class, but most will have some items left to complete as homework.

Prior to major quizzes and tests, Laura leads the class through reviews to prepare them for the assessment. She usually structures these reviews as elimination bees or games, especially the popular Jeopardy format. Occasionally she announces that prizes (small treats such as candy bars) will be awarded to winning individuals or team members. She reminds everyone, though, that the main purpose of these contests and games is to review the material for the upcoming test.

The major quizzes and tests include some short-answer essay questions in addition to the more familiar matching, true/false, and fill-in-the-blank questions. Unit tests also include questions that call for integrating across chapter sections or relating material from the chapter to big ideas being developed across the school year. However, none of these questions strays too far from the text or contains elements that students who have studied carefully would find surprising or unfair. As Laura frequently reminds her students, if they pay attention to lessons and work conscientiously on assignments, they should be successful on her tests.

Even so, Laura includes "safety nets" for students who struggle. First, everyone is allowed to have one bad day: When Laura calculates total scores to use for grading, she disregards each student's worst daily assignment score. Second, students can partially regain lost credit on quizzes (although not on unit tests): If they return the quizzes to her with correction of each mistake accompanied by a statement about why the original answer was incorrect, they will receive half credit for these items. Third, students can earn a few points during each unit by selecting from a menu of extra credit assignments and completing a maximum of three of these successfully.

During English classes, Laura's questions focus on the details of the stories and how these exemplify the genre (e.g., mystery stories) and techniques (e.g., foreshadowing) under study. Daily assignment and weekly quiz questions focus on defining and recognizing examples of these genres and techniques. Unit tests call for more integrated responses through series of questions such as the following: define foreshadowing; give three examples of foreshadowing in stories read during the unit; and give two reasons why an author might use foreshadowing (for extra credit, give additional valid reasons).

In social studies, Laura's daily assignments and weekly quizzes focus on basic facts about the South American nations under study: the nation's geographical location, climate, major cities and places of interest, historical highlights, primary imports and exports, etc. Unit tests also include short-answer essay questions calling for students to demonstrate understanding of connections among these facts, such as by showing awareness that much of the economy and cultures of Chile reflect the fact that it is a mountainous country in which internal travel is difficult and access to the sea is limited.

Rachel Dewey

Rachel's motivational strategies emphasize personalizing the curriculum and collaborative learning rather than preparing students for tests. She does give a short test early in each unit as a way to make sure that all of her students can define and give examples of key terms, and sometimes she includes a major unit test as a way to assess students' accomplishment of unit goals. For the most part, however, her students' grades are determined by their work on a variety of learning activities and assignments, and her feedback to them emphasizes qualitative critiques and suggestions for improvement rather than letter grades or numerical scores.

In English, Rachel covers fewer stories than Laura does but spends more time on the stories that she does cover. Instead of beginning by leading her students through a reading of the story in class, she has the students read each new story and discuss it with a partner. She prepares them for this by introducing the genre and some of its key techniques and providing questions to guide their analyses. First, the students read the story individually to enjoy the aesthetic experience. Next, they discuss the story with their partner, focusing on what they liked and didn't like about it and why, and noting questions or comments to bring up in class. Then the partners work through

Rachel's questions to analyze the story with respect to genre techniques. They record their answers and again make notes about questions and comments to raise in class.

During the whole-class discussion that follows, Rachel first focuses on the students' aesthetic reactions and related questions and comments. She tosses in a few of her own as food for thought (e.g., Would the story have been better if it had been set in the present instead of the past, or if it had a happier ending? What might have happened if the hero had kept his secret instead of telling it to his friend?). When discussion of the aesthetic appreciation aspects of the story has run its course (or if necessary, when time constraints loom), Rachel shifts to the topic of genre techniques, starting by eliciting students' answers to her questions and listing these on the board. She then leads a discussion of these issues, making sure to highlight ways that the author used key techniques and how they enhanced the story. Her goal is not just to help students to understand key features of the genre, but also to enable them to appreciate what the genre has to offer them as readers and the ways that good applications of genre techniques enhance the power and enjoyment of the stories they read.

Following these class discussions are quiet times during which students work individually to write in their journals about their reactions to the story and its "moral" and what they learned about the genre and its characteristic techniques. Rachel supplies a list of questions that the students can use to guide their journal writing if they wish. However, she encourages them to write in depth about aspects that they found especially interesting or meaningful, rather than to answer each question or confine themselves to the issues raised on the list. At minimum, she wants them to address two main areas of response to the story (their personal aesthetic response and what they have learned about the genre from reading it).

As a culmination activity for genre-based units, students compose an original example of the genre (e.g., a mystery story). These are published in a class anthology and some of the best ones are read (or acted out in drama form) in class or at performances staged in other classrooms or at school assemblies.

In social studies, rather than give equal time to each South American nation, Rachel introduces the continent as a whole and its major regions and characteristics but then focuses on a few nations in more depth. These countries are selected because they exemplify key ideas or social studies themes that she wants to emphasize in her teaching (e.g., Brazil for its rain forest and the cultural and ecological preservation issues it raises, Venezuela for studying the effects of a modern oil industry on a traditional agrarian economy, and Chile as an example of life in a mountain region).

For most of the countries studied, and in particular for those addressed in depth, Rachel supplements the text with nonfiction tradebooks, children's literature, videos, and classroom visits by people who come from or have visited the country. She wants to personalize what her students learn about the country, and especially about the everyday lives and activities of families that include children their age.

Rachel assigns her students to work in four- or five-member teams to develop illustrated booklets about these key countries. One member of each team focuses on the country's geography and climate; another on its history, language, and culture; another on its economy and natural resources; and so on. Rachel meets with these "specialists" as groups to suggest encyclopedias, books, websites, and other data sources for them to consult, and to encourage them to help one another to develop expertise in their specialization area. In addition to acquiring this specialized knowledge and collaborating with group mates in producing the illustrated booklets, each student writes an individual report summarizing what he or she has learned about the country. These reports call for information about all aspects studied, not just the area in which the student has specialized, so the student will be required to learn from the textbook and from the supplementary information accumulated by group mates.

The students also write in their journals about what they are learning in social studies. They are asked to record their thinking on two questions: What I would and would not like about living in the country, and What I have learned about why things in that country are as they are and why they are similar to or different from the way they are in our country. In addition, students are encouraged to elaborate about whatever aspects of the country they have found particularly interesting or meaningful to learn about.

In grading, Rachel emphasizes students' performance on individual and group assignments as much as their performance on tests. For tests she assigns credit points for each item and notes the total score, provides qualitative feedback, and invites students to revise their responses to earn partial credit for items on which they failed to receive credit. She responds similarly to group and individual reports. Finally, she holds biweekly meetings with each student, during which she reads and comments on the students' journal entries and reviews and makes suggestions about the students' general progress in the subject.

The Two Teachers Compared

Laura Hirsch and Rachel Dewey are similar in their emphasis on authoritative classroom management strategies but different in their orientation toward learning goals. The activity and reward structures emphasized by Laura are primarily individual but also somewhat competitive and not at all collaborative. In contrast, those emphasized by Rachel are primarily collaborative and secondarily individual, with very little emphasis on competition. Rachel's class is more of a learning community.

Despite the competitive elements in her approach to motivation, Laura tries to emphasize learning goals over performance goals. She minimizes ambiguity and risk, practically guaranteeing good grades in exchange for paying attention to class, working conscientiously on assignments, and studying for tests. Rachel offers no such guarantees, but her emphasis on collaborating with peers and exploring the personal implications of learning tends to focus her students on learning goals without causing them to worry much about performance goals. Also, she allows her students more choice and autonomy in working on assignments, so they are more likely to experience intrinsic motivation. Even so, students who fear ambiguity and risk may be anxious in her class unless she is sufficiently specific in answering their questions about what she expects from them and sufficiently reassuring in giving them feedback about how well they are doing.

Along with these differences in motivational strategies, there are associated differences in the two teachers' general approaches to curriculum and instruction--differences likely to affect their students' motivation and learning. By sticking so closely to the text in her curriculum, instruction, and assessment practices, Laura is restricting her curriculum to broad but shallow coverage of mostly disconnected content. This encourages students to focus on memorizing material for tests rather than constructing more elaborate and better connected representations of learning that are likely to be more permanent and more available for application.

In contrast, Rachel covers more limited content but focuses on developing key ideas in depth, seeks to personalize to her students' backgrounds and experiences, and provides them with opportunities to elaborate and connect their learning both through communication with peers and through individual report and journal writing. Rachel's teaching exemplifies many of the principles involved in teaching school subjects for understanding, appreciation, and application to life outside of school, whereas Laura's approach is more confined to content coverage via transmission of information.

SUMMARY

Certain preconditions must be in place before motivational strategies can be effective. Establish and maintain your classroom as an attractive and psychologically supportive learning community by accomplishing three important agendas: Make yourself and your classroom attractive to students; focus their attention on individual and collaborative learning goals and help them to achieve these goals; and teach things that are worth learning, in ways that help students to appreciate their value.

Optimal instruction implies classroom management and motivational strategies and curriculum and instructional features that all function as mutually supportive components of a coherent program of effective teaching. The remainder of this book will focus on the motivational components, but bear in mind that successful use of motivational strategies requires that the prerequisites discussed in this chapter are already in place. To the extent that this assumption does not hold true in your classroom, your efforts to improve your students' motivation to learn will require adjustments in your approach to classroom management, your curriculum, or your instructional practices in addition to appropriate motivational strategies.

REFLECTION QUESTIONS

1. What are some things you can do to ensure that you function as a lead manager rather than a boss manager in your classroom?
2. What personal things about yourself might you share with your students to help them get to know and appreciate you as an individual?
3. What seating arrangements best support the teaching/learning formats that you intend to use? How will you manage transitions from one to another?
4. Is authoritative management simply a midway point between laissez-faire management and authoritarian management, or does it have distinctive qualitative features that will be important for you to implement?
5. How might you help students frame learning goals so as to make the learning more meaningful to them?
6. If goals are so important, why is so much instruction planned and carried out without apparent reference to them?
7. Are you surprised to learn that the textbook series leave much to be desired as instructional materials? How can you prepare yourself to adapt or substitute for these materials in order to teach things that are worth learning, in ways that help students to appreciate their value?
8. What should teachers do when they find that they lack good answers to students' questions about why they are learning particular content or why particular tasks are required of them?

9. Given the grade levels and subjects that you teach or intend to teach, what are examples of the kinds of authentic activities to emphasize?
10. What affordances and constraints of learning activities are important to take into account when assessing their suitability for use in the classroom?
11. Would you rather be a student in Laura Hirsch's class or Rachel Dewey's class? Why?
12. Why do you think that the author has given Laura and Rachel the surnames Hirsch and Dewey?
13. Why will failure to follow the advice in this chapter negate the effectiveness of the motivational strategies discussed in the rest of the book?

REFERENCES

Alleman, J., & Brophy, J. (2001). *Social studies excursions, K-3. Book One: Powerful units on food, clothing, and shelter.* Portsmouth, NH: Heinemann.

Allen, M., Witt, P., & Wheeless, L. (2006). The role of teacher immediacy as a motivational factor in student learning: Using meta-analysis to test a causal model. *Communication Education, 55*, 21–31.

Askell-Williams, H., & Lawson, M. (2001). Mapping students' perceptions of interesting class lessons. *Social Psychology of Education, 5*, 127–147.

Austin, P. (2000). Literary pen pals: Correspondence about books between university students and elementary students. *Reading Horizons, 40*, 273–294.

Avery, P. (1999). Authentic assessment and instruction. *Social Education, 63*, 368–373.

Baker, J., Terry, T., Bridger, R., & Winsor, A. (1997). Schools as caring communities: A relational approach to school reform. *School Psychology Review, 26*, 586–602.

Baumrind, D. (1991). The influence of parenting style on adolescent competence and substance abuse. *Journal of Early Adolescence, 11*, 56–94.

Beck, I., & McKeown, M. (1988). Toward meaningful accounts in history texts for young learners. *Educational Researcher, 17*(6), 31–39.

Bransford, J., Brown, A., & Cocking, R. (Eds.). (1999). *How people learn: Brain, mind, experience, and school.* Washington, DC: National Academy Press.

Brophy, J. (1988). Educating teachers about managing classrooms and students. *Teaching and Teacher Education, 4*, 1–18.

Brophy, J. (1992a). Probing the subtleties of subject-matter teaching. *Educational Leadership, 49*(7), 4–8.

Brophy, J. (1992b). The de facto national curriculum in U.S. elementary social studies: Critique of a representative example. *Journal of Curriculum Studies, 24*, 401–447.

Brophy, J. (Ed.). (2001). *Subject-specific instructional methods and activities.* New York: Elsevier Science.

Brophy, J. (2006). History of research on classroom management. In C. Evertson & C. Weinstein (Eds.), *Handbook of classroom management: Research, practice, and contemporary issues* (pp. 17–43). Mahwah, NJ: Erlbaum.

Brophy, J., & Alleman, J. (1991). Activities as instructional tools: A framework for analysis and evaluation. *Educational Researcher, 20*(4), 9–23.

Cabello, B., & Terrell, R. (1994). Making students feel like family: How teachers create warm and caring classroom climates. *Journal of Classroom Interaction, 29*, 17–23.

Cazden, C. (2002). A descriptive study of six high school Puente classrooms. *Educational Policy, 16*, 496–521.

Clark, C., & Peterson, P. (1986). Teachers' thought processes. In M. C. Wittrock (Ed.), *Handbook of research on teaching* (3rd ed., pp. 255–296). New York: Macmillan.

Comer, J. (1980). *School power: Implications of an intervention project.* New York: The Free Press.

Cothran, D., Kulinna, P., & Garrahy, D. (2003). "This is kind of giving a secret away…": Students' perspectives on effective classroom management. *Teaching and Teacher Education, 19*, 435–444.

Davis, H. (2001). The quality and impact of relationships between elementary school children and teachers. *Contemporary Educational Psychology, 26*, 431–453.

Dreher, M., & Singer, H. (1989). Friendly texts and text-friendly teachers. *Theory Into Practice, 28*, 98–104.

Elias, M., & Haynes, N. (2008). Social competence, social support, and academic achievement in minority, low-income, urban elementary school children. *School Psychology Quarterly, 23*, 474–495.

Elliott, D., & Woodward, A. (Eds.). (1990). Textbooks and schooling in the United States. *89th yearbook of the National Society for the Study of Education, part* I. Chicago: University of Chicago Press.

Emmer, E., & Evertson, C. (2008). *Classroom management for middle and high school teachers* (8th ed.). Boston: Pearson/Addison-Wesley.

Evertson, C., & Emmer, E. (2008). *Classroom management for elementary teachers* (8th ed.). Boston: Allyn & Bacon.

Evertson, C., & Weinstein, C. (2006). *Handbook of classroom management: Research, practice, and contemporary issues.* Mahwah, NJ: Erlbaum.

Freiberg, H. J. (Ed.). (1999). *Beyond behaviorism: Changing the classroom management paradigm.* Boston: Allyn and Bacon.

Glasser, W. (1990). *The quality school: Managing students without coercion.* New York: Harper & Row.

Good, T., & Brophy, J. (2008). *Looking in classrooms* (10th ed.). Boston: Allyn & Bacon.

Goodlad, J. (1984). *A place called school*. New York: McGraw-Hill.

Gresalfi, M., Martin, T., Hand, V., & Greeno, J. (2009). Constructing competence: An analysis of student participation in the activity systems of mathematics classrooms. *Educational Studies in Mathematics, 70,* 49–70.

Hayes, C., Ryan, A., & Zseller, E. (1994). The middle-school child's perceptions of caring teachers. *American Journal of Education, 103,* 1–19.

Hickey, D., Moore, A., & Pellegrino, J. (2001). The motivational and academic consequences of two innovative mathematics environments: Do curricular innovations and reforms make a difference? *American Educational Research Journal, 38,* 611–652.

Hoy, A., & Weinstein, C. (2006). Student and teacher perspectives on classroom management. In C. Evertson & C. Weinstein (Eds.), *Handbook of Classroom Management: Research, practice, and contemporary issues* (pp. 181–219). Mahwah, NJ: Erlbaum.

Jones, V., & Jones, L. (2007). *Comprehensive classroom management* (8th ed.). Boston: Pearson/Merrill.

King, M. B., Newmann, F., & Carmichael, D. (2009). Authentic intellectual work: Common standards for teaching social studies. *Social Education, 73*(1), 43–49.

Martin, A., & Dowson, M. (2009). Interpersonal relationships, motivation, engagement, and achievement: Yields for theory, current issues, and educational practice. *Review of Educational Research, 79,* 327–365.

Martin, M., Meyers, S., & Mottet, T. (2002). Students' motives for communicating with their instructors. In J. Chesebro & J. McCroskey (Eds.), *Communication for teachers* (pp. 35–46). Boston: Allyn & Bacon.

Matsumura, L., Slater, S., & Crosson, A. (2008). Classroom climate, rigorous instruction and curriculum, and students' interactions in urban middle schools. *Elementary School Journal, 108,* 293–312.

McCaslin, M., & Good, T. (1992). Compliant cognition: The misalliance of management and instructional goals in current school reform. *Educational Researcher, 21*(3), 4–17.

McCombs, B., Daniels, D., & Perry, K. (2008). Children's and teachers' perceptions of learner-centered practices, and student motivation: Implications for early schooling. *Elementary School Journal, 109,* 16–35.

McMahon, S., Wernsman, J., & Rose, D. (2009). The relation of classroom environment and school belonging to academic self-efficacy among urban fourth-and fifth-grade students. *Elementary School Journal, 109,* 267–281.

Meece, J. (1994). The role of motivation in self-regulated learning. In D. Schunk & B. Zimmerman (Eds.), *Self-regulation of learning and performance: Issues and educational applications* (pp. 25–44). Hillsdale, NJ: Erlbaum.

Morganett, L. (1995). Ten tips for improving teacher-student relationships. *Social Education, 59,* 27–28.

Murdock, T. (1999). The social context of risk: Status and motivational predictors of alienation in middle school. *Journal of Educational Psychology, 91,* 62–75.

Newmann, F., & associates. (1996). *Authentic achievement: Restructuring schools for intellectual quality.* San Francisco: Jossey-Bass.

Nichols, S. (2008). An exploration of students' belongingness beliefs in one middle school. *Journal of Experimental Education, 76,* 145–169.

Noddings, N. (2005). *The challenge to care in schools: An alternative approach to education* (2nd ed.). New York: Teachers College Press.

Osterman, K. (2000). Students' need for belonging in the school community. *Review of Educational Research, 70,* 323–367.

Palincsar, A. (1998). Social constructivist perspectives on teaching and learning. *Annual Review of Psychology, 49,* 345–375.

Perkins, D. (1993). Teaching for understanding. *American Educator, 17*(3), 8, 28–35.

Pianta, R. (1999). *Enhancing relationships between children and teachers.* Washington, DC: American Psychological Association.

Prawat, R. (1989). Promoting access to knowledge, strategy, and disposition in students: A research synthesis. *Review of Educational Research, 59,* 1–41.

Purcell-Gates, V., Degener, S., Jacobson, E., & Soler, M. (2002). Impact of authentic literacy instruction on adult literacy practices. *Reading Research Quarterly, 37,* 70–92.

Purkey, W., & Novak, J. (1996). *Inviting school success: A self-concept approach to teaching, learning, and democratic practice* (3rd ed.). Belmont, CA: Wadsworth.

Richmond, V. (2002). Teacher nonverbal immediacy: Uses and outcomes. In J. Chesebro & J. McCroskey (Eds.), *Communication for teachers* (pp. 65–82). Boston: Allyn & Bacon.

Roelofs, E., & Terwell, J. (1999). Constructivism and authentic pedagogy: State of the art and recent development in the Dutch national curriculum in secondary education. *Journal of Curriculum Studies, 31,* 201–227.

Rogers, C., & Freiberg, H. J. (1994). *Freedom to learn* (3rd ed.). New York: Merrill.

Rogoff, B., Turkanis, C., & Bartlett, L. (2001). *Learning together: Children and adults in a school community.* New York: Oxford University Press.

Salomon, G., & Perkins, D. (1998). Individual and social aspects of learning. In P. D. Pearson & A. Iran-Nejad (Eds.), *Review of research in education* (Vol. 23, pp. 1–24). Washington, DC: American Educational Research Association.

Shaffer, D., & Resnick, M. (1999). "Thick" authenticity: New media and authentic learning. *Journal of Interactive Learning Research, 10,* 195–215.

Skinner, E., & Belmont, M. (1993). Motivation in the classroom: Reciprocal effects of teacher behavior and student engagement across the school year. *Journal of Educational Psychology, 85,* 571–581.

Stodolsky, S. (1988). *The subject matters.* Chicago: University of Chicago Press.

Tharp, R., Estrada, P., Dalton, S., & Yamauchi, L. (2000). *Teaching transformed: Achieving excellence, fairness, inclusion, and harmony.* Boulder, CO: Westview Press.

Tyson-Bernstein, H. (1988). *A conspiracy of good intentions: America's textbook fiasco.* Washington, DC: Council for Basic Education.

Urdan, T., & Maehr, M. (1995). Beyond a two-goal theory of motivation and achievement: A case for social goals. *Review of Educational Research, 65,* 213–243.

VanWerkhoven, W., vanLonden, A., & Stevens, L. (2001). Teaching and parenting styles related to children's achievement motivation and learning outcomes. In A. Efklides, J. Kuhl, & R. Sorrentino (Eds.), *Trends and prospects in motivation research* (pp. 85–99). Boston: Kluwer.

Watson, M., & Battistich, V. (2006). Building and sustaining caring communities. In C. Evertson & C. Weinstein (Eds.), *Handbook of classroom management: Research, practice, and contemporary issues* (pp. 253–279). Mahwah, NJ: Erlbaum.

Weinstein, C., & Mignano, A., Jr. (2006). Elementary classroom management: Lessons from research and practice (4th ed.). New York: McGraw-Hill.

Wells, G. (1999). *Dialogic inquiry: Towards a sociocultural practice and theory of education.* New York: Cambridge University Press.

Wells, G. (2001). The case for dialogic inquiry. In G. Wells (Ed.), *Action, talk, and text: Learning and teaching through inquiry* (pp. 171–194). New York: Teachers College Press.

Wentzel, K. (1992). Motivation and achievement in adolescence: A multiple goals perspective. In D. Schunk & J. Meece (Eds.), *Student perceptions in the classroom* (pp. 287–306). Hillsdale, NJ: Erlbaum.

Wentzel, K. (1999). Social-motivational processes and interpersonal relationships at school: Implications for understanding motivation at school. *Journal of Educational Psychology, 91,* 76–97.

3

Supporting Students' Confidence as Learners

Self-efficacy beliefs touch virtually every aspect of people's lives—whether they think productively or self-debilitatingly; how well they motivate themselves and persevere in the face of adversities; their vulnerability to stress and depression; and the life choices they make. People with a strong sense of efficacy approach difficult tasks as challenges to be mastered rather than as threats to be avoided. They have greater intrinsic interest and deep engrossment in activities, and they set themselves challenging goals and maintain a strong commitment to them. High self-efficacy also helps create feelings of serenity in approaching difficult tasks and activities. As a consequence, self-efficacy beliefs powerfully influence the level of accomplishment that one ultimately achieves. (Pajares, 2008, p. 113)

Chapter 1 focused on helping you to think about motivation and identify realistic motivational goals for your students. Chapter 2 focused on establishing your classroom as a learning community that both reflects and supports your efforts to motivate students to learn. Beginning here in chapter 3, I address these motivational efforts directly, working within the expectancy × value model. Chapters 3–5 focus on expectancy issues: protecting students' confidence as learners and providing extra support to those who have become discouraged.

ACHIEVEMENT SITUATIONS

Information about the expectancy aspects of motivation has been developed by studying reactions to *achievement situations* that require people to perform a goal-oriented task knowing that their performance will be evaluated. Some achievement situations pit people in direct competition and produce winners and losers. Others do not involve such personal competition but evaluate performance with reference to standards of excellence. If there is a single clear-cut goal, people either succeed or fail to meet it. If the task allows for more graduated or varied assessment, the quality of performance may be characterized more comprehensively.

Performance can be evaluated with reference either to absolute standards or to norms that allow comparisons to some reference group (e.g., one's classmates). *Subjective expe-*

riences of relative success or failure flow from these evaluations, viewed in the light of one's prior expectations (e.g., among students who earn a B, any who expected a lower grade will feel successful, but any who expected an A will feel that they failed to accomplish what they should have).

EARLY WORK ON TASK CHOICE AND GOAL SETTING IN ACHIEVEMENT SITUATIONS

People approach achievement situations differently depending on the makeup of their achievement motivation. Atkinson (1964) noted that two key components of *achievement motivation* are motivation to succeed and motivation to avoid failure. *Motivation to succeed* is determined by the strength of one's overall need for achievement, one's estimate of the probability of succeeding on the task at hand, and the degree to which one values the rewards that such success would bring. There also are parallel components of *motivation to avoid failure*: the strength of one's overall need to avoid failure, one's estimate of the probability of failing the task, and the degree to which one fears the negative outcomes that such failure would bring (e.g., private disappointment, public embarrassment).

Individual differences in approach to achievement situations are predictable from the relative strengths of people's motivation to succeed and to avoid failure. When our motivation to succeed is stronger, we engage in the task willingly. When our motivation to avoid failure is stronger, we seek to avoid the task. If we cannot avoid it, we seek to minimize the likelihood of failure. Atkinson and Litwin (1960) showed this in an experiment in which people played a ring-toss game. They were free to stand anywhere from 1 to 15 feet from the target peg. Success seekers tended to toss their rings from 9 to 11 feet away. This was a moderate-difficulty, optimal-challenge distance: far enough away to challenge them (they would be successful only about half the time), but not so far away that success depended more on luck than skill.

In contrast, people concerned about avoiding failure tended to respond in either of two contrasting ways. Some stood very close to the peg, so most if not all of their tosses would be successful. This ensured a high probability of success, but these frequent "successes" were not significant accomplishments. Other people who sought to avoid failure were less obvious about it. In fact, they tossed the rings from the maximum distances of 12 to 15 feet away. This enabled them to give the appearance of taking risks and accepting challenges without really doing so. By standing so far away, they converted a skill task into a luck task. Any successes they achieved were causes for celebration, but their frequent misses were not considered embarrassing failures because most long tosses were expected to be misses.

Other work confirmed these early findings. *People who focus on achieving success* tend to approach achievement situations willingly, to prefer activities that are moderately difficult for them, and to engage in those activities with emphasis on developing their skills. In contrast, *people who focus on avoiding failure* tend to fear achievement situations and try to avoid them if possible. When required to engage in them, they do so in ways that minimize their risk of failure. One way is to stick with easy tasks and avoid risks. Another is to set goals so high that failure is virtually certain but does not carry the stigma attached to failure to accomplish more realistic goals.

Attempts to draw teaching implications from early achievement motivation studies are hampered by contrasts between the situations facing the people in those studies and the situations facing students in classrooms. The experiments often involved informal or play settings and engagement in physical activities such as ring toss games. Under these conditions, success seekers' achievement motivation was maximized when their success probability was 50% (rather than either lower or higher). This does not mean that students' motivation will be maximized when classroom activities produce a 50% success rate, however, for several reasons.

First, most classroom tasks involve cognitive rather than physical activity, so a higher success rate is necessary. Learning proceeds most smoothly when it involves continuous progress through small, easy steps with consistent success all along the way. Novelty and challenge are important, but overly difficult tasks produce confusion and discouragement. The degree of cognitive strain produced by learning activities that allowed only a 50% success rate would discourage most students and make learning unduly difficult for the rest.

Also, the 50% figure refers to the person's estimate of the probability of attaining his or her own goal, not a score of 50% on some absolute scale. In theory, teachers could maximize students' achievement motivation by inducing them to set goals that they believed they had 50% chances to attain. The corresponding performance levels would vary with individual students.

However, even this idea only takes into account success seeking; it does not consider fear of failure. Individuals who fear failure try to avoid achievement situations in which their chances of success hover around 50%. In the classroom, where activities are compulsory, performance is often public, and failure has consequences, few students are likely to be optimally motivated when they believe they have only a 50% chance of succeeding. Most will prefer a much higher probability.

SUBSEQUENT WORK ON EXPECTATION ASPECTS OF ACHIEVEMENT SITUATIONS

Research on thinking and behavior in achievement situations has continued, but its emphasis has shifted from achievement needs to achievement goals. Also, it has broadened from recreational settings to include learning in classrooms, and broadened from a focus on goal difficulty to consider qualitative aspects of goals and related strategies.

Achievement motivation research initially established that effort and persistence are greater in people who set goals of moderate difficulty, commit to pursuing these goals rather than treat them as mere "pie-in-the sky" hopes, and concentrate on trying to achieve success rather than avoid failure (Dweck & Elliott, 1983). As this work extended to include more cognitive factors, information was developed about the role of other perceptions and concepts:

Effort-outcome covariation. Effort and persistence are greater when people perceive a continuing connection between the level of effort they invest and the level of mastery they achieve (Cooper, 1979).

Internal locus of control. Effort and persistence are greater when people believe that the potential to control outcomes (e.g., achieve success) lies within themselves rather than external factors they cannot control (Stipek & Weisz, 1981; Thomas, 1980).

Concept of self as origin rather than pawn. Effort and persistence are greater when people believe that they can bring about desired outcomes through their own actions (act as origins) rather than feeling that they are pawns whose fate is determined by factors beyond their control (deCharms, 1976).

Recent work on the expectancy aspects of motivation includes these and many other cognitive features. Three lines of work have been especially productive: research on implicit theories of ability, causal attributions, and self-efficacy perceptions.

Implicit Theories of Ability

Carol Dweck and her colleagues have explored the connections between people's implicit theories of ability and their goal setting and behavior in achievement situations. Their work began with description of the contrasting ways in which two groups of children responded to a concept-formation experiment that allowed them to succeed on the first eight problems but then presented four problems that were too difficult for them. The children were asked to think aloud as they worked. Soon after the onset of the difficult problems, *helpless* children began to define themselves as having failed and to attribute this failure to limited ability. They also began to express negative affect toward the task, to make pessimistic predictions about their future performance, and to show declines in the sophistication of their strategies. In summary, helpless children quickly perceived themselves to be failing, construed these failures as indicators of limited ability, and "became mired in them as past and future successes seemed to recede from their grasp" (Dweck, 1991, p. 203).

Mastery-oriented children responded much more productively. When they encountered the difficult problems, they did not become upset or talk about how they were failing. Instead, they redoubled their concentration and began issuing more self-instructions—verbalizing plans and problem solving strategies. Instead of losing confidence and predicting continued failure, they maintained positive affect and spoke of mastering the more difficult problems. In summary, "the mastery-oriented children appeared to see failure as an interlude between past and future successes and as an opportunity for new learning and mastery" (Dweck, 1991, p. 203).

The next stage in the research was aimed at understanding why helpless children react to failure as though their ability is being assessed and discredited, whereas mastery-oriented children react to it as an opportunity for learning. Elliott and Dweck (1988) showed that these contrasting response patterns were linked to contrasting goals. Children who established *learning goals* focused on learning something new or mastering the task. They processed information for its relevance for problem solving and responded to errors as indications that they needed to adjust their strategies. In contrast, children who set *performance goals* were more concerned about gaining favorable judgments of their competence than about learning something new. Consequently, they processed information primarily for its relevance for assessing their ability. This made them vulnerable to the helpless pattern because when they encountered failure, they called their ability into question. Once this occurred, they were prone to lose confidence, become upset, and begin to use less sophisticated strategies.

In summary, children with comparable ability levels may respond to achievement situations very differently. Those who set learning goals tend to adopt a mastery orientation and focus on improving their ability, whereas those who set performance goals tend to focus on displaying their ability and are prone to adopt a helpless orientation if they fail to do so. To explain these contrasting patterns, Dweck (1991) suggested that children with different goals have different conceptions of ability—different implicit theories about its nature.

Those who subscribe to the *entity theory* think of ability as a fixed entity over which they have no control. In contrast, those who hold an *incremental theory* believe that ability can be increased incrementally through effort. Entity theorists are more likely to set performance goals and develop helplessness in achievement situations, whereas incremental theorists are more likely to set learning goals and persist in their efforts to attain them. Following failure experiences, entity theorists tend to withdraw and seek to repair their damaged self-esteem (such as by comparing themselves with others who did even worse than they did), but incremental theorists tend to focus on remediating their deficiencies (Niiya, Crocker, & Bartmess, 2004; Nussbaum & Dweck, 2008).

Subsequent work by Dweck and her colleagues focused on entity versus incremental theories, extending their application from theories about ability to theories about personality traits, moral dispositions, and other human characteristics (Dweck, 1999; Dweck & Grant, 2008; Dweck & Master, 2008). This work indicated that among both children and adults, about 40% favor entity theories, another 40% favor incremental theories, and the remaining 20% are undecided. These implicit theories are relatively stable, and their effects can cumulate over time. When studied across years, entity theorists tend to show drops in self esteem, grade-point average, and related measures, whereas incremental theorists tend to maintain or gain (Blackwell, Trzesniewski, & Dweck, 2007; Robins & Pals, 2002). Studies of self-theories in domains other than academic achievement show similar patterns. For example, among people who currently feel shy or limited in sports ability, those who hold incremental theories are likely to be oriented toward and ultimately successful at improving in these areas, but those who hold entity theories (e.g., my shyness is something that I can't change very much) are likely to feel helpless and unwilling to even try to improve (Molden & Dweck, 2006).

Entity theorists are likely to retain their theories if left to their own devices, but intervention studies have shown that temporary shifts to incremental theories can be primed when orienting people to particular situations, and that more significant shifts from entity to incremental thinking can be stimulated through more extensive interventions (Dweck, 2008). For example, Aronson, Fried, and Good (2002) showed college students a film about how the brain is capable of making new connections throughout life and grows in response to intellectual challenges. Then they asked these college students to write letters to struggling younger students, explaining that the brain is malleable and that intelligence expands with hard work. At the end of the semester, the treatment students showed greater valuing of academics, more enjoyment of assignments, and higher grade-point averages than other college students.

Blackwell and colleagues (2007) intervened with students making the transition from elementary to junior high school. All students received an eight-session workshop on study skills, but the malleable-intelligence group also learned that the brain is like a muscle that gets stronger with use and that it forms new connections every time learning occurs. Compared to control students, these students became more motivated to learn (putting more effort into classroom activities and being more conscientious about homework and studying). Dweck and her colleagues have developed a computer-based version of this malleable-intelligence intervention (called "Brainology").

The classroom implications of Dweck's work are straightforward. As a teacher, encourage your students to adopt incremental rather than entity theories of ability, to set learning rather than performance goals, and to adopt a mastery rather than a helpless orientation to achievement situations.

Encouraging learning goals is accomplished primarily by establishing your class as the kind of learning community described in chapter 2. This will focus your students' attention on self-improvement rather than comparisons with classmates. It also will lend credibility to your efforts to counter any ego-protective behavior that does occur by reminding students that mistakes are part of learning, that ordinarily we move toward mastery through successive approximations rather than attain it quickly in giant steps, and that we are in the classroom to learn, not to compete or show off.

You can *encourage the incremental theory of ability and a mastery orientation toward learning activities* by portraying these activities as opportunities to acquire (not just to display) knowledge or skill and by giving feedback that reinforces this idea. Where relevant, help students to see how an activity fits into a larger strand ("We've been learning how to compose well-structured paragraphs. Starting today, we're going to learn how to combine a sequence of paragraphs into a well-structured composition that starts with a clear statement of purpose and then builds toward a conclusion.").

When giving feedback, *stimulate appreciation of accomplishments to date and imply confidence that ultimate goals will be attained* ("You've done a good job of establishing your purpose in the first paragraph and structuring each paragraph around a main idea. However, the idea flow across paragraphs is a little choppy. As you revise (or, in your next composition), take time to outline the flow of ideas so your argument builds step-by-step from start to finish, and use this outline to sequence your paragraphs. Then you'll have a nicely constructed argument!"). Notice that nothing in this example says anything directly about the students' abilities or the teacher's confidence that they will be successful. Yet, both by what it does and what it does not say, the statement implies that the teacher is pleased (or at least satisfied) with the students' progress, unbothered by the need for improvements in some aspects of performance, and fully expecting those improvements to emerge as students continue to develop their expertise.

Dweck recommended avoiding generic evaluative comments and instead providing more specific feedback when reacting to students' work. In particular, she cautioned against praising their ability or intelligence, because this orients them toward global self-assessment and eventual entity theorizing. She suggested focusing feedback on the care, concentration, or effort that students put into the work or on their development of effective strategies for accomplishing it. Useful alternatives to direct feedback include asking questions that show appreciation for the work and initiating discussion of what was learned (Dweck, 1999; Mueller & Dweck, 1998).

Causal Attributions

Bernard Weiner (1992, 2001) and other attribution theorists have focused on the *causal attributions* that people make in achievement situations—*the explanations we generate to explain our behavior*. Some causal attributions address value aspects of motivation (What benefits do I expect to derive from engaging in this activity?). However, attribution theorists have focused on causal attributions for the level of performance achieved (Why did I fail that math test?), and their implications concerning future performance (I must not be very smart in math, so I'm never going to do well on math tests). People are most likely to engage in attributional thinking when what occurs is different from what they expected, and especially when their performance falls below their expectations (Whitley & Frieze, 1985).

Causal attributions generated during or after a performance are likely to affect subsequent motivation in that situation and others like it. The effects will depend on the causes to which the performance is attributed. Causal attributions have been distinguished according to whether they are used to explain success or failure, as well as whether the attributed causes are internal or external to the person, controllable or uncontrollable by the person, and stable or unstable across situations (Forsyth, Story, Kelley, & McMillan, 2009).

Effort and persistence are greater when we attribute our performance to internal and controllable causes rather than to external or uncontrollable causes. Concerning explanations for successful performance, optimal patterns of motivation are associated with attributions of successes to the combination of sufficient ability and reasonable effort. "Sufficient" ability implies that we entered the achievement situation already possessing whatever abilities were needed or that we were able to develop those abilities in the process of responding to its demands. "Reasonable" effort implies that we had to maintain focus in order to succeed, but we did not have to extend ourselves to the limits of our capacities. That is, we were able to succeed through relatively normal levels of effort, rather than only through heroic efforts that we would not be able to sustain on a daily basis.

Attributing successful performance to internal and mostly stable and controllable causes gives us reason to believe that we will continue to succeed on similar tasks in the future. We would have less reason for confidence if we attributed our success to more external, less stable and controllable causes (e.g., we were successful because this task happened to be an easy one; we lucked into the solution; we got unexpected help that we probably would not get the next time).

Concerning explanations for unsuccessful performance, effort and persistence are greater when we attribute our failures to internal but controllable causes such as insufficient knowledge (of task-relevant information or response strategies) *or insufficient effort* (we did not prepare or concentrate as much as we should have). These failure attributions provide a basis for believing that we can improve and ultimately achieve success (by acquiring the needed knowledge or increasing our level of effort). We would have less basis for confidence if we attributed our failure to external causes (e.g., poor textbook or teacher). Worse yet, we would establish a basis for continued failure expectations if we attributed our failure to the internal cause of low ability, especially if we viewed this cause as stable and uncontrollable (i.e., if we held an entity theory of ability).

Attributions also affect our emotional responses to successes and failures. Successes attributed to internal causes result in enhanced self-esteem and feelings of pride in accomplishment, whereas failures attributed to internal causes result in feelings of guilt (if attributed to lack of effort) or shame (if attributed to lack of ability). In contrast, successes attributed to external causes (such as extra help from a teacher) result in feelings of gratitude, whereas failures attributed to external causes (such as a teacher not caring enough to explain clearly or respond to a request for help) result in feelings of anger and blame (Hareli & Hess, 2008).

Again, implications for the classroom seem straightforward. As a teacher, *help your students learn to attribute their successes to the combination of sufficient ability and reasonable effort, and to attribute their failures to (temporary) lack of information or response strategies (or to lack of effort, where this has been the case).* At the same time, avoid leading students to infer that their failures are due to fixed ability limitations. This requires subtlety, because your communications to students ordinarily should focus on building understanding and providing informative feedback, not making performance attributions.

Success attributions ordinarily should be implied rather than stated directly, so as to avoid calling students' attention to self-worth issues. Give feedback that expresses appreciation for effort and subtly reinforces confidence in abilities ("I appreciate the careful work that you put into your writing. It's really paid off—that's a set of compositions you can be proud of! They are very clear and interesting to read."). *Failure attributions* to individuals ordinarily should be expressed privately. If the class as a whole has performed poorly, but not for lack of effort, you might tell them that: their poor performance was surprising given your experience with previous classes; apparently you didn't teach key ideas or skills effectively this time, and therefore you'll reteach and make sure that they attain the learning goals.

Individual students may verbalize attributions to low ability (e.g., "I can't do math.") if you ask why they "blew" an assignment or test. When this occurs, gently but firmly refuse to accept this explanation. Instead, suggest that the student has the ability to succeed but failed to do so because he lacked key knowledge or used an ineffective strategy (or if relevant, because he failed to put forth sufficient effort). If possible, cite evidence that the student possesses the needed ability (e.g., successful performance on similar tasks; McCabe, 2006). Otherwise, construct a success scenario (e.g., based on your teaching experience and your personal observations of this student, you know that he will soon be successful if he trusts you and makes an honest effort to do what you ask him to do). If you are unable to "turn around" such a student immediately, at least make it clear that you have confidence in his abilities.

Self-Efficacy Perceptions

Albert Bandura has conducted and inspired a great deal of research on *self-efficacy perceptions*, which he defines as "beliefs in one's capabilities to organize and execute the courses of action required to produce given attainments" (Bandura, 1997, p. 3). People who enter achievement situations with self-efficacy perceptions believe that they can accomplish what the situation calls for, whereas people who lack these perceptions are unsure that they can succeed or even convinced that they cannot.

Perceptions of self-efficacy are most commonly acquired through *mastery experiences* in which success is attributed to internal and controllable causes (we had what it took to do it this time, so we have good reason to believe that we can do it again in the future). However, they also can be acquired through *vicarious learning* (by watching the successes and failures of others, especially people similar to ourselves), *persuasion* (a trustworthy source convinces us that we can accomplish the task if we apply reasonable effort), or *emotional arousal* (we are likely to feel efficacious if we are relaxed and at ease in the situation, but not if we are tense or anxious).

Interviews with middle school students indicated that they drew on all four of these sources in forming their mathematics self-efficacy. Students with high self-efficacy perceptions pointed to high math grades and test scores and noted that math was easy for them; reported parental modeling of math abilities and noted that they did as well or better than high performing classmates; frequently received feedback from parents, teachers, and peers praising their mathematics abilities; and typically felt relaxed and happy to be in math classes. In contrast, their low-efficacy classmates reported histories of struggles in mathematics, featuring low grades and test scores attributed to limited ability; parental modeling of difficulties with mathematics and perceptions of less math ability than most classmates; direct or indirect communications from parents, teachers, and peers that they had limited math abilities or that little was expected of them; and histories of feeling depressed, anxious, pressured, or angry in mathematics classes (Usher, 2009).

Bandura and those who follow his lead define and assess self-efficacy perceptions with reference to particular achievement situations, so they intend self-efficacy perceptions to have a more specific meaning than terms such as confidence or academic self-concept (Bong & Skaalvik, 2003). However, researchers have studied the role of self-efficacy perceptions in contexts ranging from a single elementary lesson to college students' choices of majors and careers (Pajares, 1996). Scholz, Gutiérrez Doña, Sud, and Schwarzer (2002) developed a scale for measuring general self-efficacy, which they described as an optimistic sense of global confidence in one's coping ability across a wide range of domains or activity arenas. Judge (2009) proposed an even broader integrative trait called core self-evaluation. It subsumes measures of self-esteem, locus of control, generalized self-efficacy, and neuroticism. People high in core self-evaluation report high self-esteem, an internal locus of control, high generalized self-efficacy, and low neuroticism (high emotional stability).

Pajares (2008) noted that self-efficacy theorists distinguish between self-efficacy beliefs (judgments of capability) and self-concept (a broader evaluation of oneself, often accompanied by judgments of worth or esteem). They also distinguish between *self-efficacy beliefs* about personal capabilities and more general *outcome expectations* about the consequences that behaviors will produce. For example, people familiar with bowling understand that bowling 12 consecutive strikes in a game would produce a perfect 300 score (outcome expectation), but few of them believe that they are personally capable of doing so (self-efficacy perception). Like other self-efficacy theorists, Pajares typically treated the concept as domain-specific rather than generalized. Yet, he also produced the quotation that begins the chapter.

Most research on the topic leaves the impression that the higher the learner's self-efficacy perceptions, the better. However, recent findings indicate the need to qualify this conclusion. In a study of college students learning technology skills, Koh (2006) obtained the usual findings that high technology self-efficacy students were more at ease and successful, as well as more resilient in the face of frustrations, than low self-efficacy students. However, the high self-efficacy students sometimes overestimated their knowledge, displaying overconfidence to the point of persistently defending misconceptions. Also, several investigators have noted that extremely high levels of self-efficacy can create a sense of complacency, leading people to slack off from the sustained efforts that led them to high levels of achievement. Debates are currently in progress about the validity and generalizability of these findings and their implications, especially regarding the issue of whether self-efficacy perceptions should be viewed as causes of subsequent performance, outcomes of prior performance, or both (Bandura & Locke, 2003; Feltz, Short, & Sullivan, 2008; Vancouver & Kendel, 2006).

Implications for practice depend on whether the context calls for learning or performance. For example, on game days (performance contexts) coaches want their players' self-efficacy perceptions to be sky high (ready to play with confidence, expecting to win or at least acquit themselves well). However, during the practices that take place between that game and the next (learning contexts), the coaches want their players to recognize and focus on remediating their weaknesses. Teaching presents similar challenges: you want your students to feel relaxed and confident when taking tests, and you always want them to feel that they have sufficient ability to enable them to succeed with reasonable effort. However, you also want them to perceive both their strengths and their weaknesses accurately, and to do what is needed to remediate weaknesses and make good progress through expected learning trajectories (Schunk & Pajares, 2005).

Self-efficacy perceptions can influence activity choices and engagement quality. When their self-efficacy perceptions are high, people are likely to approach achievement situations with confidence and engage in them willingly and persistently. However, if they doubt their capabilities for succeeding, they are likely to try to avoid the situation, or if this is not possible, to give up easily when they encounter frustration or failure. In these and other respects, the implications of high versus low self-efficacy perceptions are similar to those for mastery versus helpless orientations and for attributing performance outcomes to internal and controllable causes versus external or uncontrollable causes.

Self-efficacy theorists have been especially active in identifying ways that teachers can support their students' self-efficacy perceptions, and in the process optimize their motivation and engagement patterns. *Increases in self-efficacy perceptions, effort, persistence, and ultimate performance levels can be achieved by (a) encouraging students to set specific and challenging but attainable goals; (b) modeling and cueing effective strategies; (c) providing feedback that helps students to achieve success; and (d) making attributional statements that help them to appreciate that they are developing their abilities by accepting challenges and applying consistent effort* (Bandura, 1997; Schunk & Zimmerman, 2006). These findings provide the basis for many of the suggestions about protecting your students' success expectations that are given in the remainder of this chapter and in chapter 5.

Integration of Expectancy-Related Concepts and Principles

The motivational concepts and principles introduced in this chapter were derived from different theoretical traditions. Some refer to general dispositions, others to specific situations. Some refer to perceptions, some to cognitive inferences, some to affective experiences, and some to strategies for accomplishing goals. All of them, however, refer to the expectancy (rather than the value) aspects of motivation in situations that call for striving to accomplish goals. Taken together, they compose a rich portrait of adaptive versus maladaptive response to these achievement situations.

Elements drawn from different theoretical traditions have been combined into more complete packages that simultaneously address several expectancy-related aspects of motivation. Shawaker and Dembo (1996) incorporated a motivational component into reading comprehension instruction for middle school students. Its five elements were:

1. *Task analysis.* Students were taught a four-step procedure: read each paragraph reflectively, identify its main idea, decide what type of paragraph it was (concept, generalization, sequence, process, or comparison), and mark evidence that supported these decisions.
2. *Proximal goal-setting.* Students were taught to work through the task analysis sequence one step at a time, using the steps as proximal goals to guide their information processing.

3. *Reciprocal teaching.* Students took turns with the teacher or with other students in modeling task processes (thinking aloud while doing so).
4. *Attribution training.* Attributional statements were incorporated into the feedback given to students, reinforcing the notion that they had the ability to succeed if they applied themselves.
5. *Self-talk reminders.* Students occasionally were reminded to use their own self-talk to guide their behavior. ("Talk yourself through the steps and be sure to compliment yourself when you work hard.")

Martin (2008) developed an intervention designed to help students increase six adaptive aspects of their school-related motivation (self-efficacy perceptions, mastery orientations, valuing of school, planning their work on assignments, managing this work effectively, and persisting through difficulties) as well as reduce five maladaptive aspects (anxiety, failure avoidance, uncertainty about outcome control, self-handicapping, and disengagement from learning activities). The intervention involved classroom discussions of each topic, followed by individualized reflection on problems they had had in the past and generation of ideas about how to function more effectively in the future. Use of the program with high school students performing below their potential produced improvements on all 11 aspects of motivation, often significantly in comparison to changes in the control group.

SUPPORTING STUDENTS' CONFIDENCE AS LEARNERS

As a teacher, you will want to help your students to maintain their confidence as learners and approach learning activities with productive goals and strategies. The next three sections of the chapter suggest ways for you to take these motivational concerns into account when planning the three major features of your teaching: curriculum, instruction, and assessment.

CURRICULUM: PROGRAM FOR SUCCESS

The simplest way to ensure that students expect success is to make sure they achieve it consistently so they can adjust to each new step without much confusion or frustration. However, two points need to be made to clarify that this strategy does not mean assigning underchallenging busy work.

First, "success" means gradual mastery of appropriately challenging objectives, not application of overlearned skills to overly familiar tasks. You should pace your students through the curriculum as briskly as they can progress without undue frustration. Programming for success is not an end in itself but a means toward maximizing your students' ultimate achievement.

Second, keep in mind your role as the teacher. *Potential levels of success depend not only on the difficulty of the task itself, but also on the degree to which you prepare students through advance structuring and scaffold their learning efforts through instruction, guidance, and feedback.* A task that would be too difficult for students left to their own devices might be just right when learned with your help. In fact, *instruction should focus on the zone of proximal development*: the range of knowledge and skills that students are not yet ready to learn on their own but can learn with help from their teachers (Tharp & Gallimore, 1988).

Programming for success involves continually challenging students within their zones of proximal development, yet making it possible for them to meet these challenges by providing sufficient scaffolding. You may need to provide extra instruction to slower students, to monitor their progress more closely, and to give them briefer or easier assignments if they cannot handle the regular ones even with extra help. Even so, continue to expect these students to put forth reasonable effort and progress as far as their abilities will allow. Don't give up on them or allow them to give up on themselves. Continue to encourage them and convey positive expectations concerning their ability to achieve success with your help (more on this in chapter 5).

One paradoxical feature of the success expectancy aspects of motivation is that *self-efficacy perceptions are optimized when they are not at issue at all. That is, learning proceeds most smoothly when students are concentrating on the task rather than on evaluating their performance, even successful performance.* In effect, student motivation is optimized not only by teaching techniques traditionally recognized as motivational, but also by techniques traditionally considered instructional: clarity and specificity of explanations and demonstrations, modeling of strategies, and provision of informative feedback (Koh, 2006; Pajares, 2008). Modeling of strategies is especially important, because so many learning activities are primarily cognitive rather than physical (so the processes used to accomplish their goals cannot be observed directly).

By thinking out loud while modeling use of a strategy, a teacher makes overt the otherwise covert thought processes that guide its implementation. Such modeling provides learners with first-person language ("self-talk") that they can adapt directly when using the strategy themselves. This eliminates the need for translation of instruction presented in the impersonal third-person language of explanation or even the second-person language of coaching. Learners can focus directly on the processes to be learned, with minimal cognitive strain.

INSTRUCTION: HELP STUDENTS TO SET GOALS, EVALUATE THEIR PROGRESS, AND RECOGNIZE EFFORT-OUTCOME LINKAGES

Teach Goal Setting, Performance Appraisal, and Self-Reinforcement

Students' reactions to their own performance depend on both the absolute level of success they achieve and their perceptions of what this level means. Some may not fully appreciate their accomplishments unless you help them to use appropriate evaluation standards. You can provide such help in your everyday teaching, especially when introducing assignments or providing feedback.

Goal setting. The process begins with goal setting. *Setting goals and committing to trying to reach these goals increase performance levels* (Bandura, 1997; Locke & Latham, 2002). Goal setting is especially effective when goals are (a) *proximal* rather than distal (they refer to a task to be attempted here and now rather than to some ultimate goal for the distant future), (b) *specific* (e.g., complete a page of math problems with no more than one mistake) rather than global (e.g., do a good job), and (c) *challenging* (difficult but reachable) rather than too easy or too hard.

For example, suppose that you have assigned 20 problems of varying difficulty. If it is not realistic to expect struggling students to solve all 20 on their own, you might ask them to adopt the goals of making a serious attempt to solve each problem and persisting until confident that at least 15 have been solved correctly. This is likely to lead to more persistent and higher quality efforts than asking them to "do the best you can" or "do as many as you can." These suggestions are too vague to function as specific challenges toward which students can work as goals.

For a brief assignment, meeting the instructional objective is the appropriate goal. On more comprehensive assignments or tests, however, perfect performance is not realistic for many students, and they may need help in formulating challenging but reachable goals. For a long series that ultimately leads to some distal goal, establish proximal goals for each successive activity (Houser-Marko & Sheldon, 2008). Then, as students accomplish these goals, remind them of the linkages between successive advances and their eventual achievement of the ultimate goal. *Proximal goals usually seem attainable with reasonable effort even to students who doubt their capacities for attaining ultimate goals*, and "keeping your eye on the prize" (bearing in mind that what you are doing now is another step toward an important ultimate goal) can help people persist through frustrations (Morgan, 1985; Tabachnick, Miller, & Relyea, 2008; Turner & Schallert, 2001).

Along with establishing expectations about reasonable levels of challenge, *goal setting can include specifications of the characteristics of desired outcomes. This helps learners develop subgoals and assess their work*. For example, Page-Voth and Graham (1999) used a goal-setting treatment with junior high students learning to write argumentative essays. All of the students received instruction describing the features of good essays and strategies for planning them. In addition, the experimental students were asked to adopt goals of increasing the number of reasons given to support the premise, the number of counterarguments refuted, or both, and to talk about how they would realize these goals. These students wrote longer and better essays. The authors concluded that setting specific goals helps learners because: (a) the goals focus attention on important aspects of the task, (b) they help motivate and sustain mastery efforts, and (c) they provide learners with criteria they can use to assess and if necessary adjust their strategies as they work. For additional information about goal setting, see Box 3.1.

Goal setting is not enough by itself; students must show *goal commitment* by taking goals seriously and committing themselves to trying to reach them. You may need to negotiate goal setting with some students, or at least encourage them to commit to reasonable challenges. One way is to list potential goals and ask students to commit to a particular subset. Another is *contracting*, in which students formally contract for a certain level of performance in exchange for specified grades or rewards (Tollefson, Tracy, Johnsen, Farmer, & Buenning, 1984). Contracting is time consuming and may call more attention to rewards than is desirable, but it does ensure active negotiation about goal setting and formal commitments to goals. Students are more likely to follow through on goal commitments when they have had a voice in establishing them.

Performance appraisal and feedback.   Students also are more likely to follow through when their performance will be monitored and evaluated. Unless students are held accountable for following through on commitments and making progress toward curricular goals, goal setting may not have performance enhancement effects (Harkins, White, & Utman, 2000). Furthermore, unless the monitoring leads to needed feedback, some learners may fail to accomplish key goals even if highly motivated to do so.

Box 3.1   Things to Keep in Mind When Helping Students Set Goals

Goal setting can be a powerful motivational technique, but it also can be used counterproductively. Keep in mind the following qualifications on its use (Bandura & Wood, 1989; Deci, 1992; Pomerantz, Saxon, & Oishi, 2000).

First, make sure that your suggested goals are realistic for the student. Difficult goals are likely to yield better performance than easier goals, but beyond some optimal level, goals become too difficult. If you consistently urge students to perform beyond their capacities, you will lose your credibility. Students will begin to find your urgings irritating or depressing rather than encouraging and energizing. Especially for tasks that must be confronted day after day, establish goals that call for reasonable rather than extraordinary effort. Most students find it exhilarating to push themselves to their limits on occasion, but few want to be required to do so on a daily basis.

Second, setting highly specific goals is most appropriate when the activity is relatively uninteresting, repetitive, or amenable to quantitative assessment (e.g., arithmetic computation, spelling, typing, free-throw shooting). For complex tasks that require creativity or cognitive flexibility, overly specific goals may undermine intrinsic motivation and lead to a lower quality of performance. In giving instructions for a composition or research assignment, for example, it is better to focus on qualitative goals (build a coherent argument that leads to and supports your conclusions; identify relevant information and then synthesize it so as to address your question), rather than to be overly specific about the formal aspects of the product to be developed (the composition will consist of at least 300 words and be comprised of at least five paragraphs, each beginning with a topic sentence; the research report will include reference to at least 10 sources). Students should see the goals as helpful guides to their learning efforts, not hoops that they must jump through.

Finally, attempts to influence students' notions of reasonable effort are most likely to be successful if goals are established before the students have gained experience with the task and begun to set their own goals informally. A difficult but reasonable teacher-suggested goal might be viewed as an appropriate challenge initially, but students might reject the same goal if it were imposed later after they had established expectations for themselves. Goal-setting programs that rely on externally imposed goals tend to lose their effectiveness over time, so help your students learn to evaluate their own work and reset goals in response to their growing expertise.

Some forms of feedback are ineffectual or even counterproductive. Kluger and DeNisi (1998) found that feedback actually reduced performance more than a third of the time. *Unhelpful feedback merely informs learners about how well they did, whereas informative feedback identifies which aspects of their performance were unacceptable and how they will need to improve.* With complex learning that takes time to develop, focus goal setting and feedback on the processes needed to accomplish the task rather than the ultimate end product, especially during earlier stages in the learning (McNeil & Alibali, 2000; Schunk & Ertmer, 2000; Zimmerman & Kitsantas, 1997).

In addition to being informative, feedback should be delivered in ways that convey respect for learners and sensitivity to their self-esteem (Brinko, 1993; Hareli & Hess, 2008). Avoid accusatory statements, attributions likely to lead to anger or hurt feelings, or other counterproductive responses, but make sure that your students get the feedback they need in order to recognize and remediate their deficiencies.

Teachers sometimes fail to provide needed feedback (or provide misleading feedback) because of misguided concerns about protecting students' self-esteem. Pajares and Graham (1998) presented teachers with the following vignette:

> An eighth grade language arts teacher is interested in students learning to be poetically expressive. She assigns them the task of composing a free verse poem. A 13-year-old boy submits the following:
>
> *When the wild west winds are blowing*
> *the tall trees will tremble.*
> *When heavy rains fall from the skies*
> *and a torrential downpour hits the earth,*
> *when the tall trees are struck with lightning*
> *and whole forests catch on fire,*
> *that is when we feel nature at its greatest.*
>
> After the teacher reads it, the student asks, "Do you like it? Is it good?" How ought the teacher to respond? (p. 856)

Most teachers would not provide a direct and honest answer to the student's question, because they endorsed one or more of the following beliefs: You should always find something good to say about a student's work and generally offer positive feedback; regardless of a poem's merits, you should praise the poet for effort and creativity; criticism will crush students' creative propensities and turn them off to writing; you should not answer such questions but redirect them to the student; and the value of poetry is relative and thus cannot be judged in any case. Ironically, these teachers' views were endorsed, respectively, by only 7%, 3%, 2%, 3%, and 5% of their students. Instead, most of their students believed that teachers should answer such questions by identifying what is good and why, as well as what needs to be improved and how. Many did say that teachers should be respectful of their feelings and keep criticism constructive, but they wanted informative feedback, not gratuitous praise. Teachers interpreted caring as helping students feel good about their work independent of its merits, whereas students interpreted caring as providing whatever assistance they needed to enable them to meet learning goals.

Straub (1997) reported similar findings in a study of students' reactions to teacher comments on written compositions. The students expressed strong preferences for specific and detailed comments over vague generalizations. Although they resented gratuitous attacks on themselves or their ideas, they welcomed constructive criticism that called for better support of their conclusions, clearer arguments, and so on.

In giving feedback, help students to use appropriate standards for judging levels of success. In particular, teach them to compare their work with absolute standards or with their own previous performance rather than with the performance of classmates (Shih & Alexander, 2000). Provide accurate feedback about specific responses (errors must be labeled as such if they are to be recognized and corrected), but also provide encouragement in your more general evaluative comments (e.g., "You've shown good understanding of the events that led up to the Revolutionary War, but not the reasons why the colonies were able to win it. Go over those reasons again and discuss them with your study partner until you're sure that you know them."). You might note levels of progress made toward established goals or describe accomplishments with reference to what is reasonable to expect, rather than absolute perfection (e.g., "You know the basic steps in multiplying and reducing fractions. The errors you're still making are mostly computation errors. You can eliminate most of them if you check your answers before you turn in your assignment.").

Some students need specific, detailed feedback concerning both the strengths and weaknesses of their performance (Butler, 1987; Elawar & Corno, 1985; Krampen, 1987). Those who have only a vague appreciation of when and why they have done well or poorly will need *feedback that includes concepts and language they can use to describe their performance with precision.* This is especially true for compositions, research projects, laboratory experiments, and other complex activities that are evaluated qualitatively.

Concerning compositions, for example, you might comment on the relevance, accuracy, and completeness of the content; its organization and sequencing into a coherent beginning, middle, and end; the structuring of paragraphs to feature main ideas; the appropriateness of the style and vocabulary; and the mechanics of grammar, spelling, and punctuation. If performance is unsatisfactory, provide additional instruction and opportunities for improvement, along with continued encouragement that realistic goals will be achieved if the student continues to put forth reasonable effort.

Self-reinforcement. Students who have been working toward specific proximal goals and who have the concepts and language needed to evaluate their performance accurately are in a position to *reinforce themselves* for their successes. Many do this habitually, but others will need encouragement to check their work and take credit for their successes. If necessary, compare current accomplishments with samples from earlier in the year or have students keep portfolios, graphs, or other records to document their progress. *Arranging for students to periodically assess their progressively improving performance has positive effects on their motivation and learning* (Schunk, 1996).

In monitoring performance and giving feedback, focus on mastery. Stress the quality of your students' engagement and the degree to which they are making continuous progress rather than comparisons with how their classmates are doing. Treat failures as indicators of a need for additional instruction and learning opportunities, not as evidence of lack of ability in the domain. For additional information about giving feedback to students, see Box 3.2.

Help Students to Recognize Effort-Outcome Linkages

In your everyday teaching, help your students to appreciate the connections between learning efforts and learning outcomes. The following strategies are useful for developing an internal locus of control and a sense of efficacy in students and helping them to recognize that they can achieve success if they put forth reasonable effort.

First, *model beliefs about effort-outcome linkages* when talking about your own

Box 3.2   Attributional Aspects of Feedback

Research done or influenced by attribution theorists offers relatively clear guide-lines for feedback following student failures: Unless the failures are clearly due to lack of effort, attribute them to lack of information or strategy knowledge but not to lack of ability. Wrong-strategy attributions are preferable to low-ability attribu-tions because they preserve learners' self-efficacy beliefs much longer (Anderson & Jennings, 1980; Clifford, 1986; Zimmerman & Kitsantis, 1999).

Implications are less clear concerning feedback following success. Opinions vary on the degree to which feedback should emphasize attributions of success to ability or effort. Schunk (1983) found that attributing students' success to (high) ability was more effective than attributing it to effort or even to ability plus effort. Apparently, even mentioning effort can cause some students to doubt their abili-ties. Also, effort attributions tend to remind students that their performance is being evaluated by an authority figure, whereas ability attributions tend to be experienced simply as praise. Findings by Burnett (2003), by Hau and Salili (1996) and by Koestner, Zuckerman, and Koestner (1987) suggest similar conclusions.

Nicholls (1989) questioned the wisdom of attributions that stress ability, noting that you can't make all of your students feel smart. As alternatives, he suggested allowing students to evaluate their own work as much as possible so that they are less likely to see it as teacher imposed, and also giving feedback that stresses intrinsic or "motivation to learn" reasons for successful engagement.

Covington (1992) cautioned against telling individual students that they achieved success because they worked very hard. To the extent that those students are aware that others achieved similar success without working so hard, they may appreciate your praise of their hard work but also infer that you believe that their ability is limited. Effort praise is encouraging to students who believe that effort and ability are related positively (incremental theorists), but demotivating to entity theorists who believe that effort and ability are related negatively (Lam, Yim, & Ng, 2008).

These cautions are well taken. Ordinarily, the notions that students have the ability to succeed, are making good progress, and are putting forth sufficient effort should be implied rather than stated directly in your feedback. Students who are clearly achieving well below their capabilities need to be informed of this and motivated to commit to higher goals. However, effort probably should not be men-tioned at all if it is satisfactory. If you want to express appreciation to students whose efforts are more than satisfactory, do so in ways that do not imply limited ability (e.g., note their careful work or their willingness to stick with a problem until they solve it, but don't tell them that they succeeded because they worked hard).

With struggling students, feedback usually should not emphasize praise of hard work so much as encouragement of persistence and patience to allow time for skills to develop. Focus attention on their accomplishments ("Yes, it's hard, but look at what you can do now!"). Portray difficult work not so much as hard and therefore requiring strenuous effort, but as challenging them to stay goal oriented and per-sist in using adaptive learning strategies ("Don't work hard, work smart!").

> When giving help, emphasize instrumental help (probing and prompting) rather than gratuitous help (giving answers). Gratuitous help is likely to be perceived as evidence that you believe that the student lacks the ability needed to succeed on the task. So are gratuitous praise of minor accomplishments or gratuitous expressions of sympathy to struggling students, especially if these affective supports are not accompanied by assistance designed to help the student master the task (Graham, 1984; Graham & Barker, 1990; Horn, 1985; Meyer, 1982).

learning and when thinking out loud as you demonstrate tasks. When you encounter temporary failure in performing everyday classroom activities, model confidence that you will succeed if you persist by searching for a better strategy or for some error in your application of strategies already tried.

Also, *stress effort-outcome linkages when socializing your students or giving them feedback.* Explain that your curricular goals and instructional practices have been established to make it possible for them to succeed if they apply themselves. If necessary, reassure them that persistence (perhaps augmented by extra help) eventually pays off. Some students may need repeated statements of your confidence in their abilities to do the work or your willingness to accept slow progress so long as they keep at it.

Extra socialization will be needed with low achievers when grades must be assigned according to fixed standards or comparisons with peers rather than effort expended or success achieved in meeting individually negotiated goals. *You may need to socialize low achievers to take satisfaction in receiving Bs or Cs when such grades represent, for them, significant accomplishments.* Express to these students (and their parents) recognition of their accomplishments and appreciation of the progress they are making.

Acknowledge that learning takes effort, but *portray effort as investment rather than risk.* Learning may take time and involve confusion or mistakes, but persistence and careful work eventually yield knowledge or skill mastery. Furthermore, such mastery empowers them with knowledge or skills that make them more prepared to handle higher-level tasks in the future. If they give up because of frustration or fear of failure, they cheat themselves out of this growth potential.

In characterizing achievement progress, *portray skill development as incremental and domain-specific.* Help your students to appreciate that their intellectual abilities are open to improvement rather than fixed and that they possess a great many such abilities rather than just a few. Difficulties in learning usually occur not because they lack ability but because they lack experience with the type of task involved. With patience, persistence, and help from you, they can acquire domain-specific knowledge and skills that will enable them to succeed on this task and others like it. Difficulty in learning mathematics need not imply difficulty in learning other subjects, and within mathematics, difficulty in learning to graph coordinates need not mean difficulty in learning to solve differential equations or to understand geometric relationships. Even within a domain that is difficult for them, students can expect to build up knowledge and skills gradually if they persistently apply themselves, accept your help, and do not lose patience or give up whenever success is not achieved easily.

ASSESSMENT: EMPHASIZE INFORMATIVE FEEDBACK, NOT GRADING OR COMPARING STUDENTS

Even if it were not required for report card purposes, assessment of students' progress would be needed to generate feedback, to both you as the teacher and your students as learners. Therefore, *help your students to understand that getting and following up productively on informative feedback is integral to the learning process.*

If assessment methods are goal-oriented and aligned with the larger program of curriculum and instruction, they will provide valuable information. When students are clear about what they are expected to learn and how this learning will be evaluated, they can guide their learning efforts accordingly. After they engage in an evaluation activity and get the feedback it generates, both you and they will have a clearer picture of strength areas in which they have progressed nicely as well as weakness areas in which they need follow-up instruction and learning activities. Certain mistakes (minor factual or computational errors) may require only brief correction, but others (misunderstandings of basic concepts) may require more sustained follow up.

Unfortunately, classroom evaluation and grading systems also have the potential to undermine students' motivation and learning strategies. If they are perceived as controlling students by placing extrinsic pressures on them to study or do homework, they are likely to erode the students' intrinsic motivation. If test content is confined to matching or fill-in-the-blank items, students are likely to emphasize surface-level memorizing rather than deeper-level information processing strategies as they study the material. If you have been overly specific about the nature and content of test items, students may narrow their focus to preparing to answer the kinds of questions they expect on the test, rather than engaging in more integrative learning.

Finally, if testing and grading are not well matched to the knowledge and skill levels of some of your students, the desired covariation between effort and outcome will be missing. Some students can get high grades without exerting much effort, and others cannot get high grades no matter how hard they try. These undesirable effects of assessment and grading systems are always lurking as potential problems to teachers, for reasons explained in chapter 1. However, researchers have developed suggestions to help you get the most out of your evaluation and grading strategies (Ames, 1992; Andrade, 2009; Baron & Wolf, 1996; Butler, 1987; Butler & Nisan, 1986; Covington & Omelich, 1984; Crooks, 1988; Natriello, 1987; Wlodkowski & Jaynes, 1990).

Uses and Forms of Assessment

Think of assessment as part of your larger program of curriculum and instruction—a set of tools to help your students reach your instructional goals. Assessment is required to keep track of the progress of the class as a whole and alert you to the need for adjustments in your instructional plans, not just to provide a basis for grading.

Closed-ended, "one right answer" questions may be needed to test mastery of certain basic knowledge and skills (e.g., spelling, multiplication tables). Also, some use of matching or fill-in-the-blank items may be appropriate for testing basic vocabulary knowledge. Unfortunately, however, studies of teacher-made tests and the tests supplied with instructional materials indicate widespread overreliance on these low-level recognition or memory reproduction items. *Assessment information will be most useful to you and your students if it reflects progress made toward major instructional goals.* Ordinarily, this will mean emphasizing authentic tasks that require students to integrate and apply what they are learning, not just to recognize or retrieve miscellaneous items of information.

Tests ought to sample from the full range of content taught and include enough items to allow reliable measurement. Sampling from all content taught alerts you to areas of weakness and holds your students accountable for learning all of the material. It also helps ensure that your students will view the test as fair. They may not view it as fair if it emphasizes only a small portion of what was taught in a unit, especially if they concentrated their study efforts on other material.

Grant Wiggins (1993) detailed ways for teachers to make assessments both more fair and more authentic: (a) use assessments that feature worthwhile tasks that are educative and engaging; (b) instead of being secretive about grading standards, clarify to students what constitutes exemplary performance and provide models; (c) use methods that allow students the time to produce thoughtful and complete work; and (d) follow up with opportunities to improve on areas of weakness and ultimately produce products in which the students can take pride.

"Assessment" and "evaluation" are much broader terms than "testing," and should not be equated with it. *Ordinarily, daily lesson participation and work on assignments, especially work on significant projects, should be used at least as much as tests to provide a basis for assessing progress and grading students.* In the elementary grades, students' cognitive developmental levels and skill repertoires limit the kinds of tests that can be used productively. Even in the secondary grades, overreliance on tests is likely to lead to memorizing and forgetting instead of connected understandings.

Portfolio assessment is often recommended as better suited than testing as a way to meet students' informational and motivational needs. Portfolios are organized sets of student work that illustrate their progress over time. Students have opportunities to exercise a degree of choice in deciding what to include in their portfolios, and to revise and improve the items in response to feedback from the teacher or their peers. The portfolio approach reflects several motivational principles by focusing attention on quality standards rather than just grades or scores, incorporating assessment data as informative feedback, encouraging students to become reflective about their work and oriented toward improvement over time, and allowing them to assemble a collection of their best work that they can share with family members.

Helping Students Prepare for Assessment

In talking about assessment generally, and in preparing students for any particular experience, *emphasize the role of assessment in providing informative feedback about progress, not its role in providing a basis for grading or a means to pressure students to keep up with study assignments.* Portray tests as opportunities to find out how "we" are doing and projects as opportunities to apply what "we" are learning. Express confidence that students will succeed if they apply themselves to lessons and learning activities.

Also, *portray yourself as a helper and resource person who assists your students in learning and preparing for assessment, not as a remote evaluator.* Encourage students to see you as allied with them in preparing for tests, not as allied with the tests in pressuring or threatening them.

Clarify your goals and assessment criteria to help students understand what they need to learn and what strategies will enable them to do so. Let them know how their learning will be assessed, but avoid overspecificity that might tempt some of them to focus only on what is needed to pass the test and thus fail to develop more integrated learning.

Follow-Up Feedback and Grading

Some of your best opportunities for encouraging incremental theories of ability and desirable performance attributions and efficacy perceptions occur when you are giving feedback following assessment experiences. In addition to (or instead of) letter, number, or percentage grades, provide students with informative feedback designed to help them appreciate their accomplishments but also recognize areas of weakness and commit themselves to making needed improvements. Deliver such feedback privately and emphasize students' progress relative to their own prior accomplishments rather than comparisons with classmates. The feedback should imply continuous progress in learning with your assistance (e.g., "Here is where you are progressing nicely and here is where we need to improve"), not a closing of the book on that domain of learning (e.g., "You got a B.").

Include "safety nets" for struggling students as part of your assessment follow-up and grading system. That is, allow students who have failed to earn satisfactory grades the opportunity to do so by taking an alternative test following a period of review and relearning. Or, allow them to earn extra credit by engaging in learning activities and producing some product to indicate that they have overcome the deficiencies identified in their test performance. Such safety nets encourage struggling students to make the extra effort needed to accomplish your instructional goals.

If the cumulative level of performance that would earn a report card grade of A is not a realistic goal, help students to identify and commit themselves to realistic goals that, if reached, would yield grades of B or C (Forsterling & Morgenstern, 2002). In doing so, you might use a strategy emphasized in Mastery Learning programs: Provide a list of potential goals (graduated in terms of the effort required to meet them and the grades earned if success is achieved) and ask the students to commit themselves to particular goals and associated levels of effort. Be sure to arrange conditions so that every student who consistently puts forth reasonable effort can earn report card grades of C or better. Otherwise, your struggling low achievers will have little incentive to keep trying and your efforts to motivate them will not have much chance to succeed.

Wlodkowski and Jaynes (1990) suggested that a well-designed report card informs students about their progress in learning and encourages their continuing motivation to learn. This is accomplished more through qualitative comments than letter or number grades. Separate sets of comments can be made for the students' achievement progress, effort and persistence in learning, noteworthy academic strengths and talents, areas needing improvement, and social development (cooperation, maturity, classroom participation). Where weaknesses are identified, the comments should emphasize the kinds of improvements needed.

Reducing Test Anxiety

Certain students show symptoms of text anxiety: they may learn effectively in informal, pressure-free situations but become anxious and perform below their potential on tests or during testlike situations in which they are monitored and evaluated. Several strategies have been developed for minimizing test anxiety problems (Hembree, 1988; Hill & Wigfield, 1984; Neveh-Benjamin, 1991; Wigfield & Eccles, 1989; Zeidner, 1998):

1. rather than "spring" a test on students, let them know well in advance the date of an upcoming test, its general scope and nature, and how they can best prepare for it;
2. be friendly and encouraging when administering the test, so as not to make the testing situation any more threatening than it needs to be;
3. avoid time pressures unless they are truly central to the skill being tested;
4. stress the feedback functions rather than the grading functions of tests when discussing them with your students;
5. portray tests as opportunities to assess progress rather than as measures of ability;
6. where appropriate, tell your students that some problems are beyond their present achievement level (so they will not become upset if they fail to solve these problems);
7. give pretests to accustom students to "failure" and provide base rates for comparison when you administer posttests later;
8. teach your students stress management skills and effective test-taking skills and attitudes; and
9. help your students to understand that the best way for them to prepare for tests is to concentrate on learning what they need to know, without worrying about what will be on the test or how they will cope with anxiety in the test situation.

SUMMARY

Much of this book is organized according to the expectancy × value model of motivation, which holds that the effort that people are willing to expend on an activity is the product of (a) the degree to which they expect to be able to perform successfully and garner whatever rewards this will bring, and (b) the degree to which they value those rewards. Chapters 3–5 focus on expectancy aspects of motivation.

Expectancy concepts are especially relevant to achievement situations that require people to perform some goal-oriented task knowing that they will be evaluated. Early work indicated that people focused on motivation to succeed approach achievement situations willingly, prefer tasks that are moderately difficult for them, and engage in these tasks with emphasis on developing their skills. In contrast, people focused on avoiding failure tend to fear and avoid achievement situations. When required to engage in them, they seek to minimize risk of failure by setting goals either very low or impossibly high.

More recent work on achievement situations has shown that effort and persistence are greater when people perceive effort-outcome covariation, believe that the potential to control outcomes lies within themselves rather than in external factors that they cannot control, view themselves as origins rather than pawns, possess an incremental rather than an entity theory of intelligence, attribute their performance to internal and controllable causes, and possess a sense of efficacy or competence. People who possess these desirable dispositions are likely to engage in achievement situations with an emphasis on learning goals and to process information using deeper-level strategies rather than surface-level memorizing (more on this in chapter 4).

Research findings on the expectancy aspects of motivation underscore the importance of supporting your students' confidence as learners and helping them to focus on learning rather than worry about potential failure. You can do this through your curriculum (teaching students in their zones of proximal development and helping them to achieve success), your instruction (including instruction in goal setting, performance appraisal, and self-reinforcement along with instruction in the formal curriculum), and your assessment (using assessment methods that are aligned with your instructional goals, emphasizing informative feedback over comparing students, and taking steps to minimize test anxiety).

As theory and research on achievement motivation shifted focus from needs to goals and from quantitative to qualitative aspects of goal setting and task engagement, much of it eventually became synthesized as part of the emergence of achievement goal theory. These developments and their implications for teachers are addressed in chapter 4.

REFLECTION QUESTIONS

1. Are all learning situations achievement situations? Are all achievement situations learning situations? Or what?
2. What are classroom equivalents of standing either too close to or too far away from the ring toss peg? How might you deal with students who show these dispositions?
3. How might you try to shift students' entity theories of ability to incremental theories?
4. Why is attributional thinking more likely when something unexpected happens, especially an unpleasant surprise?
5. Why do I keep referring to "sufficient" ability and "reasonable" effort?
6. Why should success attributions ordinarily be implied rather than stated? (See Box 3.2)
7. Why do you think that mastery experiences are usually more powerful than vicarious learning experiences, persuasion, or emotional arousal as means of building self-efficacy perceptions?
8. What is involved in programming for success in achieving curricular goals?
9. Why is cognitive modeling so valuable as an instructional and motivational tool?
10. How might you induce resistant students to commit to challenging proximal goals?
11. What are some differences between highly helpful and less helpful feedback?
12. Why might some students resist taking credit for their successes?
13. Would it be a good idea if teachers could give As to all of their students? Why or why not?
14. More than likely, you will be assigning a range of grades. How will you help your students interpret and respond to the grades they receive?
15. Why might some students consider effort a risk rather than an investment?
16. Given your intended grading system, what safety nets might you include to allow students to boost unsatisfactory grades?
17. A teacher could distribute several hundred potential test items at the beginning of a term and then randomly select 50 of these items to be on the final exam. What trade-offs are embodied in this practice?

REFERENCES

Ames, C. (1992). Classrooms: Goals, structures, and student motivation. *Journal of Educational Psychology, 84,* 261–271.

Anderson, C., & Jennings, D. (1980). When experiences of failure promote expectations of success: The impact of attributing failure to ineffective strategies. *Journal of Personality, 48,* 393–405.

Andrade, H. (Guest Ed.). (2009). Special issue on classroom assessment. *Theory into Practice, 48,* 1–93.

Aronson, J., Fried, C., & Good, C. (2002). Reducing the effects of stereotype threat on African American college students by shaping theories of intelligence. *Journal of Experimental Social Psychology, 38,* 113–125.

Atkinson, J. (1964). *An introduction to motivation.* Princeton, NJ: VanNostrand.

Atkinson, J., & Litwin, G. (1960). Achievement motive and test anxiety as motives to approach success and avoid failure. *Journal of Abnormal and Social Psychology, 60,* 52–63.

Bandura, A. (1997). *Self-efficacy: The exercise of control.* New York: Freeman.

Bandura, A., & Locke, E. (2003). Negative self-efficacy and goal effects revisited. *Journal of Applied Psychology, 88,* 87–99.

Bandura, A., & Wood, R. (1989). Effect of perceived controllability and performance standards on self-regulation of complex decision making. *Journal of Personality and Social Psychology, 56,* 805–814.

Baron, J., & Wolf, D. (Eds.). (1996). *Performance-based student assessment: Challenges and possibilities. Ninety-fifth yearbook of the National Society for the Study of Education, Part I.* Chicago: University of Chicago Press.

Blackwell, L., Trzesniewski, K., & Dweck, C. (2007). Implicit theories of intelligence predict achievement across an adolescent transition: A longitudinal study and an intervention. *Child Development, 78,* 246–263.

Bong, M., & Skaalvik, E. (2003). Academic self-concept and self-efficacy: How different are they really? *Educational Psychology Review, 15,* 1–40.

Brinko, K. (1993). The practice of giving feedback to improve teaching: What is effective? *Journal of Higher Education, 64,* 574–594.

Butler, R. (1987). Task-involving and ego-involving properties of evaluation: Effects of different feedback conditions on motivational perceptions, interest, and performance. *Journal of Educational Psychology, 79,* 474–482.

Butler, R., & Nisan, M. (1986). Effects of no feedback, task-related comments, and grades on intrinsic motivation and performance. *Journal of Educational Psychology, 78,* 210–216.

Clifford, M. (1986). Comparative effects of strategy and effort attributions. *British Journal of Educational Psychology, 56,* 75–83.

Cooper, H. (1979). Pygmalion grows up: A model for teacher expectation communication and performance influence. *Review of Educational Research, 49,* 389–410.

Covington, M. (1992). *Making the grade: A self-worth perspective on motivation and school reform.* Cambridge, UK: Cambridge University Press.

Covington, M., & Omelich, C. (1984). Task-oriented versus competitive learning structures: Motivational and performance consequences. *Journal of Educational Psychology, 76,* 1038–1050.

Crooks, T. (1988). The impact of classroom evaluation practices on students. *Review of Educational Research, 58,* 438–481.

deCharms, R. (1976). *Enhancing motivation: Change in the classroom.* New York: Irvington.

Deci, E. (1992). On the nature and functions of motivation theories. *Psychological Science, 3,* 167–171.

Dweck, C. (1991). Self-theories and goals: Their role in motivation, personality, and development. In R. Dienstbier (Ed.), *Perspectives on motivation: Nebraska Symposium on Motivation 1990* (Vol. 38, pp. 199–235). Lincoln: University of Nebraska Press.

Dweck, C. (1999). *Self-theories: Their role in motivation, personality, and development.* Philadelphia: Taylor & Francis.

Dweck, C. (2008). Can personality be changed? The role of beliefs in personality and change. *Current Directions in Psychological Science, 17,* 391–394.

Dweck, C., & Elliott, E. (1983). Achievement motivation. In P. Mussen (Ed.), *Handbook of child psychology Vol. IV: Socialization, personality, and social development* (4th ed., pp. 643–691). New York: Wiley.

Dweck, C., & Grant, H. (2008). Self-theories, goals, and meaning. In J. Shah & W. Gardner (Eds.), *Handbook of motivation science* (pp. 405–416). New York: Guilford.

Dweck, C., & Master, A. (2008). Self-theories motivate self-regulated learning. In D. Schunk & B. Zimmerman (Eds.), *Motivated and self-regulated learning: Theory, research, and applications* (pp. 31–51). Mahwah, NJ: Erlbaum.

Elawar, M. C., & Corno, L. (1985). A factorial experiment in teachers' written feedback on student homework: Changing teacher behavior a little rather than a lot. *Journal of Educational Psychology, 77,* 162–173.

Elliott, E., & Dweck, C. (1988). Goals: An approach to motivation and achievement. *Journal of Personality and Social Psychology, 79*, 474–482.

Feltz, D., Short, S., & Sullivan, P. (2008). *Self-efficacy and sport.* Champaign, IL: Human Kinetics.

Forsterling, F., & Morgenstern, M. (2002). Accuracy of self-assessment and task performance: Does it pay to know the truth? *Journal of Educational Psychology, 94*, 576–585.

Forsyth, D., Story, P., Kelley, K., & McMillan, J. (2009). What causes failure and success? Students' perceptions of their academic outcomes. *Social Psychology of Education, 12*, 157–174.

Graham, S. (1984). Teacher feelings and student thoughts: An attributional approach to affect in the classroom. *Elementary School Journal, 85*, 91–104.

Graham, S., & Barker, G. (1990). The down side of help: An attributional-developmental analysis of helping behavior as a low-ability cue. *Journal of Educational Psychology, 82*, 7–14.

Hareli, S., & Hess, U. (2008). When does feedback about sucess at school hurt? The role of causal attributions. *Social Psychology of Education, 11*, 259–272.

Harkins, S., White, P., & Utman, C. (2000). The role of internal and external sources of evaluation in motivating task performance. *Personality and Social Psychology Bulletin, 26*, 100–117.

Hau, K., & Salili, F. (1996). Motivational effects of teachers' ability versus effort feedback on Chinese students' learning. *Social Psychology of Education, 1*, 69–85.

Hembree, R. (1988). Correlates, causes, effects, and treatment of test anxiety. *Review of Educational Research, 58*, 47–77.

Hill, K., & Wigfield, A. (1984). Test anxiety: A major educational problem and what can be done about it. *Elementary School Journal, 85*, 105–126.

Horn, T. (1985). Coaches' feedback and changes in children's perceptions of their physical competence. *Journal of Educational Psychology, 77*, 174–186.

Houser-Marko, L., & Sheldon, K. (2008). Eyes on the prize or nose to the grindstone? The effects of level of goal evaluation on mood and motivation. *Personality and Social Psychology Bulletin, 34*, 1556–1569.

Judge, T. (2009). Core self-evaluations and work success. *Current Directions in Psychological Science, 18*, 58–62.

Kluger, A., & DeNisi, A. (1998). Feedback interventions: Toward the understanding of a double-edged sword. *Current Directions in Psychological Science, 7*, 67–72.

Koestner, R., Zuckerman, M., & Koestner, J. (1987). Praise, involvement, and intrinsic motivation. *Journal of Personality and Social Psychology, 53*, 383–390.

Koh, J. (2006). Motivating students of mixed efficacy profiles in technology skills classes: A case study. *Instructional Science, 34*, 423–449.

Krampen, G. (1987). Differential effects of teacher comments. *Journal of Educational Psychology, 79*, 137–146.

Lam, S., Yim, P., & Ng, Y. (2008). Is effort praise motivational? The role of beliefs in the effort-ability relationship. *Contemporary Educational Psychology, 33*, 694–710.

Locke, E., & Latham, G. (2002). Building a practically useful theory of goal setting and task motivation: A 35-year odyssey. *American Psychologist, 57*, 705–717.

Martin, A. (2008). Enhancing student motivation and engagement: The effects of a multidimensional intervention. *Contemporary Educational Psychology, 33*, 239–269.

McCabe, P. (2006). Convincing students they can learn to read: Creating self-efficacy props. *Clearing House, 79*, 252–257.

McNeil, N., & Alibali, M. (2000). Learning mathematics from procedural instruction: Externally imposed goals influence what is learned. *Journal of Educational Psychology, 92*, 734–744.

Meyer, W. (1982). Indirect communications about perceived ability estimates. *Journal of Educational Psychology, 74*, 888–897.

Molden, D., & Dweck, C. (2006). Finding "meaning" in psychology: A lay theories approach to self-regulation, social perception, and social development. *American Psychologist, 61*, 192–203.

Morgan, M. (1985). Self-monitoring and attained subgoals in private study. *Journal of Educational Psychology, 77*, 623–630.

Mueller, C., & Dweck, C. (1998). Praise for intelligence can undermine children's motivation and performance. *Journal of Personality and Social Psychology, 75*, 33–52.

Natriello, G. (1987). The impact of evaluation processes on students. *Educational Psychologist, 22*, 155–175.

Neveh-Benjamin, M. (1991). A comparison of training programs intended for different types of test-anxious students: Further support for an information-processing model. *Journal of Educational Psychology, 83*, 134–139.

Nicholls, J. (1989). *The competitive ethos and democratic education.* Cambridge, MA: Harvard University Press.

Niiya, Y., Crocker, J., & Bartmess, E. (2004). From vulnerability to resilience: Learning orientations buffer contingent self-esteem from failure. *Psychological Science, 15*, 801–805.

Nussbaum, A. D., & Dweck, C. (2008). Defensiveness versus remediation: Self-theories and modes of self-esteem maintenance. *Personality and Social Psychology Bulletin, 34*, 599–612.

Page-Voth, V., & Graham, S. (1999). Effects of goal setting and strategy use on the writing performance and self-efficacy of students with writing and learning problems. *Journal of Educational Psychology, 91*, 230–240.

Pajares, F. (1996). Self-efficacy beliefs in academic settings. *Review of Educational Research, 66*, 543–578.

Pajares, F. (2008). Motivational role of self-efficacy beliefs in self-regulated learning. In D. Schunk & B. Zimmerman (Eds.), *Motivation and self-regulated learning: Theory, research, and applications* (pp. 111–139). Mahwah, NJ: Erlbaum.

Pajares, F., & Graham, L. (1998). Formalist thinking and language arts instruction: Teachers' and students' beliefs about truth and caring in the teaching conversation. *Teaching and Teacher Education, 14*, 855–870.

Pomerantz, E., Saxon, J., & Oishi, S. (2000). The psychological trade-offs of goal investment. *Journal of Personality and Social Psychology, 79*, 617–630.

Robins, R., & Pals, J. (2002). Implicit self-theories in the academic domain: Implications for goal orientation, attributions, affect, and self-esteem change. *Self and Identity, 1*, 313–336.

Scholz, U., Gutiérrez-Doña, B., Sud, S., & Schwarzer, R. (2002). Is perceived self-efficacy a universal construct? Psychometric findings from 25 countries. *European Journal of Psychological Assessment, 18*, 242–251.

Schunk, D. (1983). Ability versus effort attributional feedback: Differential effects on self-efficacy and achievement. *Journal of Educational Psychology, 75*, 848–856.

Schunk, D. (1996). Goal and self-evaluative influences during children's cognitive skill learning. *American Educational Research Journal, 33*, 359–382.

Schunk, D., & Ertmer, P. (2000). Self-regulation and academic learning: Self-efficacy enhancing intervetions. In M. Boekaerts, P. Pintrich, & M. Zeidner (Eds.), *Handbook of self-regulaton* (pp. 631–649). San Diego, CA: Academic Press.

Schunk, D., & Pajares, F. (2005). Competence perceptions and academic functioning. In A. Elliot & C. Dweck (Eds.), *Handbook of competence and motivation* (pp. 85–104). New York: Guilford.

Schunk, D., & Zimmerman, B. (2006). Competence and control beliefs: Distinguishing the means and ends. In P. Alexander & P. Winne (Eds.), *Handbook of educational psychology* (2nd ed., pp. 349–367). Mahwah, NJ: Erlbaum.

Shawaker, T., & Dembo, M. (1996). *The effects of efficacy-building instruction on the use of learning strategies.* (ERIC Document No. ED 395301)

Shih, S., & Alexander, J. (2000). Interacting effects of goal setting and self- or other-referenced feedback on children's development of self-efficacy and cognitive skill within the Taiwanese classroom. *Journal of Educational Psychology, 92*, 536–543.

Stipek, D., & Weisz, J. (1981). Perceived personal control and academic achievement. *Review of Educational Research, 51*, 101–137.

Straub, R. (1997). Students' reactions to teacher comments: An exploratory study. *Research in the Teaching of English, 31*, 91–116.

Tabachnick, S., Miller, R., & Relyea, G. (2008). The relationships among students' future-oriented goals and subgoals, perceived task instrumentality, and task-oriented self-regulation strategies in an academic environment. *Journal of Educational Psychology, 100*, 629–642.

Tharp, R., & Gallimore, R. (1988). *Rousing minds to life: Teaching, learning, and schooling in social context.* Cambridge, UK: Cambridge University Press.

Thomas, J. (1980). Agency and achievement: Self-management and self-reward. *Review of Educational Research, 30*, 213–240.

Tollefson, N., Tracy, D., Johnsen, E., Farmer, W., & Buenning, M. (1984). Goal setting and personal responsibility for LD adolescents. *Psychology in the Schools, 21*, 224–233.

Turner, J., & Schallert, D. (2001). Expectancy-value relationships of shame reactions and shame resiliency. *Journal of Educational Psychology, 93*, 320–329.

Usher, E. (2009). Sources of middle school students' self-efficacy in mathematics: A qualitative investigation. *American Educational Research Journal, 46*, 275–314.

Vancouver, J., & Kendel, L. (2006). When self-efficacy negatively relates to motivation and performance in a learning context. *Journal of Applied Psychology, 91*, 1146–1153.

Weiner, B. (1992). *Human motivation: Metaphors, theories and research.* Newbury Park, CA: Sage.

Weiner, B. (2001). Intrapersonal and interpersonal theories of motivation from an attribution perspective. In F. Salili, C. Chiu, & Y. Hong (Eds.), *Student motivation: The culture and context of learning* (pp. 17–30). New York: Kluwer Academic/Plenum.

Whitley, B., & Frieze, I. (1985). Children's causal attributions for success and failure in achievement settings: A meta-analysis. *Journal of Educational Psychology, 77*, 608–616.

Wigfield, A., & Eccles, J. (1989). Test anxiety in elementary and secondary school students. *Educational Psychologist, 24*, 159–183.

Wiggins, G. (1993). Assessment: Authenticity, context, and validity. *Phi Delta Kappan, 75*, 200–214.

Wlodkowski, R., & Jaynes, J. (1990). *Eager to learn: Helping children become motivated and love learning.* San Francisco: Jossey-Bass.

Zeidner, M. (1998). *Test anxiety: The state of the art.* New York: Plenum.

Zimmerman, B., & Kitsantas, A. (1997). Developmental phases in self-regulation: Shifting from process goals to outcome goals. *Journal of Educational Psychology, 89,* 29–36.

Zimmerman, B., & Kitsantas, A. (1999). Acquiring writing revision skill: Shifting from process to outcome self-regulatory goals. *Journal of Educational Psychology, 91,* 241–250.

4

Goal Theory

"I can't afford to get interested in this course because I've got to get a good grade." (College student cited in Lin, McKeachie, & Kim, 2003, p. 252)

"I recently tried a little experiment with my undergraduate developmental psychology class. During the first half hour of the class the students took a quiz. The remainder of the class was to be spent discussing moral development, a topic that the students knew would not be covered on the quiz. To begin our discussion of moral development, I asked my students to write down their responses to [questions about whether and why they did the readings]… Among the students who had done the assigned readings, their reasons for doing the readings included a range of purposes including personal gain, fear of punishment, not wanting to sound stupid in front of the class if called upon, fulfilling a social obligation to participate in class discussions, and wanting to show respect for oneself, the teacher and one's classmates. Among the students who did not read for class, all said that they should have read but chose not to because they had to study for the quiz and knew that the quiz would not include questions about moral development." (Urdan, 1997, pp. 99–100)

ANTECEDENTS OF GOAL THEORY

As work on achievement motivation broadened from experimental situations to naturally occurring achievement situations, investigators began addressing the motivational implications of school as an institution and classrooms as learning communities featuring ongoing interpersonal relationships. Much of this was fueled by findings indicating that although most students begin school eager to learn, their motivation tends to drop as they progress through the grades. John Nicholls (1984, 1989) noted that most children initially assume that ability flows from effort (so you can increase your ability by engaging in learning activities), but many later shift to the idea that ability and effort are related inversely (so if you can handle tasks with relative ease, you have high ability, but if you have to expend noteworthy effort, you lack ability in the domain).

Martin Covington (1992) emphasized that classrooms create situations in which students are publicly revealed to be ignorant or confused, leading to embarrassment and other social costs. He developed a *self-worth perspective* on achievement motivation, suggesting that in classrooms where ability comparisons are often made or easily inferred, students may become more concerned with preserving their sense of self-worth than with learning. This can lead them to face-saving but ultimately counterproductive reactions such as:

Defense mechanisms. Instead of increasing effort or activating other coping resources to improve performance following failure, employing defense mechanisms such as devaluing the domain ("I don't care about math anyway") or the importance of appearing competent to others ("Who cares what they think?") (Kurman, 2006; Park, Crocker, & Kiefer, 2007).

Sandbagging. Lowering others' expectations by pretending to have less ability than one has (Gibson & Sachau, 2000).

Defensive pessimism. Keeping one's own expectations low, to avoid disappointment if one does not do well (Martin, Marsh, Williamson, & Debus, 2003).

Self-handicapping. Providing oneself with an excuse for potential poor performance, such as by not studying much or partying the night before the test (Leondari & Gonida, 2007; McCrea, 2008; Ommundsen, Haugen, & Lund, 2005; Thomas & Gadbois, 2007).

Procrastination. Putting off studying or working on an assignment until the last minute. Used in this way, procrastination is a form of self-handicapping (Howell & Buro, 2009; Wolters, 2003), although some students use it more as a coping mechanism than a defense mechanism. That is, they delay starting the work until the time is right for doing it efficiently (Schraw, Wadkins, & Olafson, 2007; Wolters, 2003).

Cheating. Copying test answers, plagiarizing research reports, etc. (Anderman & Murdoch, 2007).

Carole Ames (1984) examined the *reward structures* and related *goal structures* operating in classrooms. She identified three structures likely to have contrasting effects on motivation. In an *individualistic structure*, students work on their own and are rewarded (e.g., with grades) according to how much they achieve relative to absolute standards, regardless of what classmates might achieve. An individualistic structure orients students toward personal achievement goals (i.e., they try to learn as much as they can). In a *competitive structure*, students are required to compete with classmates for available rewards (because they will be graded on a curve). This structure orients students toward interpersonal competitive goals. They may even focus more on competition than on learning, and refuse to collaborate with peers. Finally, in a *cooperative structure*, students work together in groups and are rewarded at least in part according to the quality of the products their groups create. Cooperative reward structures orient students toward fulfilling their moral responsibilities to do their parts for their groups, perhaps even more than meeting individual learning goals.

In contrast to Dweck, who treated goal orientations primarily as predictable from stable personal traits (entity vs. incremental theories of ability), Ames treated goal orientations primarily as responses to the reward structures operating in the situation. Most other goal theorists lie somewhere between these positions (Kaplan & Maehr, 2007).

DEVELOPMENT OF GOAL THEORY

As work by Ames, Covington, Nicholls, and others became established and work by Bandura, Dweck, Weiner, and others continued, a sizeable research literature accumulated on motivation in achievement situations, especially classrooms. Most of it focused on expectancy aspects and supported the conclusion that *it is desirable for people to focus on mastering the tasks involved in achievement situations rather than on competing with peers or worrying about how their performance will be judged by others*. The implication is that teachers should employ instructional and motivational practices that will focus attention on the learning activity and avoid practices that encourage peer comparisons and competition concerns.

Commenting on this knowledge base, reviewers celebrated its rapid development but expressed concern about the proliferation of terms that mean essentially the same thing (Boekaerts, 2001; Bong, 1996; Murphy & Alexander, 2000; Pintrich, 2003). Theorists associated with particular concepts (e.g., attributions, efficacy perceptions, theories of ability) sometimes argued for a synthesis built around these concepts, but the field never coalesced around any single theorist's work. Instead, syntheses developed around the goal orientations emphasized in achievement goal theory or simply *goal theory* (Ames, 1992; Blumenfeld, 1992; Meece, 1994). These *goal orientations refer to beliefs about the purposes of engaging in achievement-related behavior*. Students who approach the same activity with different goal orientations may engage in it quite differently and emerge with different outcomes.

Early Goal Theory Studies

Early studies focused on two contrasting goal orientations, variously called learning vs. performance goals (Dweck & Leggett, 1988), mastery vs. performance goals (Ames & Archer, 1988) or task vs. ego goals (Nicholls, 1984). They found that *students who approach activities with learning goals* (also called mastery or task goals) *focus on acquiring knowledge or skills.* They seek to construct accurate understandings by paraphrasing the material into their own words and connecting it to prior knowledge. When they encounter difficulties, they seek help or if necessary persist with their own self-regulated learning efforts, expecting these efforts to pay off eventually.

In contrast, students who approach activities with performance goals (also called ego goals) *treat these activities as tests of their ability to perform rather than as opportunities to learn.* Their primary concern is preserving their self-perceptions and public reputations as capable individuals who possess the ability needed to succeed. In striving to meet task demands, they may rely on rereading, rote memorizing, and other surface-level learning strategies instead of deeper-level knowledge construction strategies, and their learning efforts may be impaired by fear of failure or other negative emotions. If they are focused on avoiding failure, they may give up easily when frustrated because they lack confidence that persistent efforts will pay off. Rather than ask for help, they prefer to conceal their difficulties by leaving items blank, taking wild guesses, or perhaps copying from neighbors.

Note that goal theorists assign a special definition to the term performance goals. In everyday language, performance goals usually refer to criterion-referenced standards, such as batting .300 or getting at least a B in a course. For goal theorists, however, *operating from performance goals means seeking to display high ability for the task at hand, or at least to avoid appearing low in ability.* Whereas learning goals are about *developing* ability, performance goals are about *displaying* ability. Given this meaning, it would have been better if performance goals had been called ego-protective goals, ability display goals, image preservation goals, or some other term that clearly communicated a preoccupation with displaying ability rather than developing it. However, the term "performance goals" is now firmly established, so it is used consistently in this book.

If people engage in achievement situations with performance goals but not mastery goals, they have little interest in learning anything and may want to disengage if they run into difficulties. In several of Dweck's studies, for example, students with performance goals (especially if they also were entity theorists) showed marked losses in interest and enjoyment in courses or experimental situations as soon as they received feedback that they were not doing well. In an especially revealing experiment, college students wore caps outfitted with electrodes as they sought to answer difficult questions about history, geography, or popular culture. The electrodes were attached to machines used to track the students' attention during the activity. Each time they typed in an answer, they were first told whether or not the answer was correct (ability-relevant feedback), and then given information about the correct answer (learning-relevant feedback). Analyses indicated that incremental theorists who were focused on learning goals paid attention to both kinds of feedback, but entity theorists who were focused on performance goals only paid close attention to the initial ability-relevant feedback. That is, "...once they found out whether they were right or wrong, that was it. They showed little sign of interest in learning the right answer." Unlike the students focused on learning, these performance-focused students did not tend to improve their scores on a retest by answering previously missed questions (Dweck & Grant, 2008, p. 410).

GOAL THEORY AS SYNTHESIS

Goal theory provided a base for synthesizing emerging research on the expectancy aspects of motivation in education. It fit well with shifts in emphasis from behavior to cognition, from quantitative to qualitative aspects of motivation, from traits to situations, and from individual to social purviews. It complemented theorizing based on needs or other motives by accommodating cultural and situational factors that influence goal striving, as well as the subjective experiences that mediate or accompany it (Boekaerts, 2001; Thrash & Elliot, 2001). It also appealed to educators because it appeared to support straightforward guidelines for application.

As goal theory developed, new studies continued to indicate that learning goals were associated with desirable correlates such as greater effort and persistence, deeper processing strategies, and more positive attitudes toward school and oneself as a learner. Most also continued to indicate that performance goals were associated with undesirable correlates (Bereby-Meyer & Kaplan, 2005; El-Alayli, 2006; Elliot, 2005; Gehlbach, 2006; Kaplan & Maehr, 2007; Linnenbrink & Pintrich, 2002; Roney & O'Connor, 2008; Tuominen-Soini, Salmela-Avo, & Niemivirta, 2008; Veermans & Järvelä, 2004; Vrugt & Oort, 2008; Wolters, 2004).

Thus, *early goal theory research supported the simple conclusion that learning goals are desirable and performance goals are counterproductive. However, the picture soon became more complicated. Newly developed findings indicated that performance goals sometimes were associated with desirable outcomes.* For example, Valle et al. (2003) identified groups who showed either a predominance of performance goals, a predominance of learning goals, or a multiple goals pattern that included both of these plus social reinforcement goals. They found that the multiple goals students were the most successful, because they were mindful of both task characteristics and evaluation criteria. Learning-oriented students attended closely to task characteristics but not the evaluation criteria, and performance-oriented students did the opposite.

Emergence of the 2×2 Goal Theory Model

Several studies done by Judith Harackiewicz, Andrew Elliot, and their colleagues suggested that performance goals could complement mastery goals in some circumstances, if the performance goals focused on achieving success rather than avoiding failure. These studies, conducted in large introductory college courses, indicated that learning goals were associated with interest in the content, long-term retention, and plans to take related courses in the future, but success-oriented performance goals were associated with higher course grades and scores on short-term retention tests (Barron & Harackiewicz, 2001; Harackiewicz, Barron, Tauer, Carter, & Elliot, 2000; Hulleman, Durik, Schweigert, & Harackiewicz, 2008).

These findings led to a distinction between *performance-approach goals* that focus on achieving success and *performance-avoidance goals* that focus on avoiding failure. Performance-avoidance goals are associated with negative correlates such as low self-efficacy perceptions, high test anxiety, avoidance of help seeking, disorganized study strategies, and low test scores and grades, but performance-approach goals are associated with a mixed pattern that includes high need for achievement but also high fear of failure, strong needs to please parents, high effort and persistence in studying but with an emphasis on surface-level processing, high competitiveness, and high grades and test scores (Elliot & McGregor, 2001; Harackiewicz, Barron, Tauer, & Elliot, 2002; Lopez, 1999; Okun, Fairholme, Karoly, Ruehlman, & Newton, 2006).

For example, McGregor and Elliot (2002) found that college students' mastery goals predicted early preparation (studying well in advance of the exam), absorption during this preparation, a sense of challenge with respect to the exam, and a sense of calm preparedness at exam time. Performance-approach goals predicted high grade aspirations, perceiving the exam as both a challenge and a threat, and concentrating study in the days immediately prior to the exam. Finally, performance-avoidance goals predicted low ability self-concepts, high test anxiety, desire to escape the exam, procrastination and disorganization in preparing for it, and feeling anxious and unprepared during it.

Such findings have led to expansion of goal theory into a 2×2 framework that considers goals with respect to both the learning-performance distinction and the approach-avoidance distinction (Elliot & McGregor, 2001; Linnenbrink & Pintrich, 2002). That is, goal theorists now distinguish between mastery-approach, mastery-avoidance, performance-approach, and performance-avoidance goals.

Little is known about mastery goals that are framed within an avoidance orientation (e.g., striving not to make mistakes or fail to learn in the short run, and striving not to lose one's accumulated skills in the longer run). Early work on *mastery-avoidance goals* suggests that they are common in struggling students who seek to master the material but fear failure. Their pattern of correlates is less positive than for students who emphasize mastery-approach goals, but not as negative as for students who emphasize performance-avoidance goals (Cury, Elliot, Da Fonseca, & Moller, 2006; Elliot & McGregor, 2001; Elliot & Murayama, 2008; Howell & Watson, 2007; Kaplan & Maehr, 2007; Witkow & Fuligni, 2007). As this literature develops, it will be interesting to find out more about mastery-avoidance goals (for example, whether they are common in students who are overly perfectionistic). For now, however, because research on mastery goals has focused almost exclusively on mastery-approach goals, approach motivation is implied whenever the terms "learning goals" or "mastery goals" are used in this text.

Relationships Between Achievement Goals and Other Responses to Achievement Situations

The motivational concepts introduced in chapters 3 and 4 were derived from different theoretical traditions. Some refer to general dispositions, while others refer to thinking or behavior in specific situations. Some refer to perceptions, some to cognitive inferences, some to affective experiences, and some to strategies for accomplishing goals or solving problems. All of them, however, refer primarily to the expectancy (vs. value) aspects of motivation in situations that call for striving to accomplish goals, so they can be synthesized around the goal orientations emphasized in goal theory. Taken together, they compose a rich portrait of adaptive vs. maladaptive patterns of response to achievement situations (see Table 4.1).

Conflicting Views on Performance-Approach Goals

Recent research has clarified that the negative correlates previously associated with performance goals in general are associated primarily with performance-avoidance goals. At least in the short run, performance-approach goals usually do not have these negative correlates and may even have positive correlates that complement those associated with mastery goals. Such findings have led some goal theorists to adopt a *multiple goals perspective*, implying that optimal motivation includes both mastery-approach and performance-approach goals, but not avoidance goals.

Other goal theorists are not as accepting of performance-approach goals. Midgley, Kaplan, and Middleton (2001) warned that any emphasis on performance-approach goals needs to be coupled with an emphasis on learning goals. Performance-approach goals alone might help students get high test scores in the short run, but also encourage them to avoid challenging tasks, compete rather than cooperate with peers, and cheat if they fear failure. In the longer run, these students would be vulnerable to developing learned helplessness and shifting to performance-avoidance goals if they encountered failure.

Performance-approach goals have more positive correlation patterns for students high in perceived competence, for boys, and for older students in competitive learning contexts. If these relationships are causal, they imply that performance-approach goals lead to desirable outcomes for some students in some learning contexts. However, at least some of the relationships may be merely correlational. High achievers are likely to adopt performance-approach goals because they can do so with reasonable expectation of success. In contrast, low achievers have more reason to fear failure and thus are more likely to adopt performance-avoidance goals. So, the contrasting patterns of correlates

TABLE 4.1

General Dispositions, Situational Goals, Subjective Experiences, and Response Strategies Relating to the
Expectancy Aspects of Motivation in Achievement Situations

Productive/Adaptive Alternatives	Unproductive/Maladaptive Alternatives
GENERAL DISPOSITIONS	
• Perceived effort-outcome covariation	• Perceived lack of covariation
• Internal locus of control	• External locus of control
• Concept of self as origin	• Concept of self as pawn
• Incremental theory of ability	• Entity theory of ability
• Outcomes attributed to internal and controllable causes	• Outcomes attributed to external or uncontrollable causes
• Perceived self-efficacy	• Perceived lack of efficacy
SITUATIONAL GOALS/FOCUS	
• Learning goals and outcome goals (approach versions)	• Performance-avoidance goals , work-avoidant goals
• Focus on task, learning progress	• Focus on ego, self-worth protection
• Seek to acquire knowledge, skill that task can develop	• Seek to meet evaluation criteria at a sufficiently high level
• Seek optimal challenges, flow experiences	• Minimize risk of failure
SUBJECTIVE EXPERIENCES AND COPING RESPONSES	
If success is achieved easily:	
• Complete task, integrate learning	• Complete task, feel relieved/reinforced
• Attribute success to sufficient ability plus reasonable effort	• Attribute failure to fixed limitations in ability
If difficulties are encountered:	
• Continued focus on task	• Task focus invaded by ego concerns
• Continued emphasis on deep-processing strategies	• Increased reliance on surface-level strategies
• Calm, analytic problem solving	• Increasingly anxious, frustrated
• Sustained confidence	• Fear of failure, plunging confidence, eventual learned helplessness
If success is not achieved:	
• Attribute failure to remediable deficits in knowledge, strategy selection, or effort	• Attribute success to ability alone or to ability plus external, uncontrollable causes
• Seek to acquire needed knowledge and skill, eventually reach mastery	• Seek to avoid such tasks if possible; otherwise, defend against perception of incompetence or at least hide one's incompetence from others

for performance-approach and performance-avoidance goals may occur merely because
they are part of a larger set of contrasts between high- and low-achieving students, and
not because the students' stated goals have causal effects on their subsequent learning
strategies or outcomes (Roney & O'Connor, 2008).

Controversy over the multiple goals perspective has broadened the focus of debate
from individuals' goals to the goal structures of learning situations. Goal theory has

roots stretching back to the philosophy of John Dewey (Urdan, 1997) and several prominent goal theorists have advocated wholesale school reforms that would replace competition for limited rewards with a system that makes it possible for all students who invest reasonable effort to earn comparable rewards by achieving individualized criterion-referenced attainment levels (Ames, 1990; Covington, 1992, 2000; Maehr & Midgley, 1996; Nicholls, 1989).

Confronted with data suggesting that performance-approach goals can complement learning goals, goal theorists of this persuasion do not admit a need to shift to a multiple goals perspective. Instead, they question the advisability of learning contexts that make such findings possible. As Kaplan and Middleton (2002) put it, "…instead of interpreting the finding that performance-approach goals contribute to achievement whereas mastery goals contribute to interest as indicating that the most desirable motivational orientation is high performance approach-high mastery, one might question the educational characteristics of a context in which a focus on mastering and understanding the material does not contribute to a higher grade" (pp. 647–648). This quote illustrates that disputes about desirable motivational practices often embody conflicting value-based positions on the purposes and nature of education, and thus are only partially resolvable through scientific evidence.

Goals, Strategies, and Achievement Outcomes

The above quote also alludes to *a troubling enigma in goal theory research: disappointing correlations between motivation measures and achievement measures*. Overall, this body of research has produced widely replicated and theoretically pleasing findings showing relationships of motivational measures to one another and to measures of information processing and learning strategies (see Table 4.1). Furthermore, individual studies, such as that of Miller, Greene, Montalvo, Ravindran, and Nichols (1996), occasionally show reassuringly robust correlations between goal measures, strategy measures, and achievement measures, and a meta-analysis indicated an overall positive relationship between mastery goals and achievement measures (Payne, Satoris, & Beaubien, 2007). Even so, correlations with achievement often are disappointingly low. Most findings show strong relationships between goal measures and strategy measures, but much weaker relationships with achievement measures. Sometimes they even show unexpected relationships, such as positive correlations between mastery goals and surface information processing strategies, or positive relationships between surface strategies and achievement test scores.

As findings accumulated, new distinctions were introduced and new insights were developed that began to clear up some of the confusion. Instead of looking just at the relative emphasis on mastery vs. performance goals, researchers began to take into account students' absolute scores on both measures. This led to recognition that, although mastery goals may be ideal, performance goals are better than no achievement goals at all. Furthermore, they can be productive in some situations, especially if they accompany a strong mastery orientation (mastery goals and performance goals often occur together; Senko, Durik, & Harackiewicz, 2008).

It also became clear that relationships between goals and strategies, and between strategies and outcomes, were not as simple as initially assumed. Deep processing strategies are preferable in the long run, especially if the material is meaningful to learners and will need to be accessible to them in the future. However, these strategies take time to apply and integrate. Sometimes the advantages of using them do not appear on short-term retention tests, but do appear if the assessment includes long-term retention or ability to access the information in application situations (Yeo, Sorbello, Koy, & Smillie, 2008).

However, if time is limited, and especially if the material is not particularly meaningful to the learner or not well structured around organizing concepts, surface memorization may be more productive than deeper processing. To the extent that students accurately perceive the nature of the material to be learned and the kinds of learning strategies likely to be most successful (given the timing and nature of the assessment), exceptions to the usual correlational patterns may occur. Mastery-oriented students may rely on surface strategies when it makes sense for them to do so, and performance-oriented students may include deep processing strategies if they must do so in order to meet their performance goals (Rozendaal, Minnaert, & Boekaerts, 2003; Senko & Miles, 2008).

One last reason why mastery goal measures do not correlate highly with learning outcome measures is social desirability influences on students' questionnaire responses. To the extent that students are aware that mastery goals are considered desirable, they may be tempted to claim greater degrees of mastery orientation than they actually possess (Dompnier, Darnon, & Butera, 2009).

CLARIFYING THE MEANINGS AND IMPLICATIONS OF STUDENTS' PERSONAL ACHIEVEMENT GOALS

After several years of debate, a new consensus is emerging about the meanings and implications of students' mastery and performance goals. Grant and Dweck (2003) identified three types of performance goals: *outcome goals* that are simply focused on obtaining positive outcomes (do well in my courses, get good grades), *ability goals* that are linked to validating one's ability (confirm my intelligence through my schoolwork, demonstrate my intellectual ability), and *normative goals* that include social comparisons (do better in my classes than other students, confirm that I am more intelligent than they are). These three types of performance goals have unique patterns of correlation with other motivational variables and with learning strategies.

The experimental procedures or goal orientation questionnaires used by goal theorists to induce or measure performance goal orientations have differed in their relative emphasis on these three types. Consequently, what were called performance goals in one study were not always the same as what were called performance goals in another study. This contributed to some of the confusion about the meanings and implications of performance goals.

Grant and Dweck's analysis led me to suggest that goal theorists phase out the term performance goals altogether, or at least treat outcome goals as a separate category. We might distinguish between learning/mastery goals and validation goals. Subtypes of validation goals would include ability goals (validating one's ability by doing well on assessments) and normative goals (validating one's ability by outperforming peers). Outcome goals would be a separate type, differing from learning/mastery goals in that they focus more on successfully meeting assessment criteria than on learning, but also differing from validation goals because the learner does not view the assessment as a test of or opportunity to display ability (Brophy, 2005).

I emphasize this point because there is reason to believe that whatever benefits performance goals may add to mastery goals resides in their focus on outcomes rather than self-validation. Adopting a specific outcome goal (getting an A in a course or at least 90% on a test) helps you to mobilize all of your resources to do what is needed to attain that goal. In contrast, adopting a self-validation goal will divert some of your resources from doing what is needed to maximize your achievement to worrying about impressing others or besting your peers (Crocker & Park, 2004).

In an important contribution, Senko and Miles (2008) offered convincing arguments and new findings to help explain why mastery goals do not consistently predict achievement and why performance-approach goals do. First, they reaffirmed that mastery goals predict interest in the content and use of deep (and sometimes also, surface) learning strategies, but not necessarily in ways that translate into higher course grades. This is because students who adopt mastery goals tend to pick and choose what they want to learn, and often spend most of their study time on topics that are of most interest to them. In short, they pursue their own agenda, which may or may not correspond well with the teacher's agenda. They are likely to emerge with deeper rooted and better integrated learning than students who lack much mastery orientation, but they may not perform any better on the test (they may even perform worse, if their priorities have little overlap with the teacher's).

In contrast, although performance-approach goals orient students toward using surface learning strategies, they help the students attain high grades in at least two ways. First, adopting performance-approach goals means committing oneself to striving for high levels of achievement. This requires putting pressure on oneself to sustain high efforts to do very well (Senko & Harackiewicz, 2005). Second, instead of following their own self-generated agenda, students who adopt performance-approach goals align their study efforts with the teacher's agenda. They adopt a strategic preparation approach that includes cue-seeking, careful planning, and using whatever learning strategies will produce the best grades (Entwistle & Tait, 1990; Senko & Miles, 2008).

In summary, when attention is shifted from *how* students are studying (deep or surface processing) to *what* they are studying (their own or the teacher's agenda), it becomes clear why performance-approach goals typically correlate more strongly with grades and test scores than mastery goals do. These findings support the multiple goals perspective. They imply that whenever students have little or no mastery orientation, as well as whenever they are mastery oriented but their mastery goals do not closely overlap the teacher's agenda, performance-approach goals should support productive achievement striving. *Performance-approach goals should be especially helpful in the following situations*:

- When the material to be learned is a parade of disconnected information rather than a network of content structured around big ideas (learners are unlikely to have much mastery motivation for mile-wide but inch-deep content, and even if they do, deep learning strategies will not be very helpful in learning it. Such content virtually forces reliance on rote memorization).
- When the learning situation is highly competitive and achievement outcomes are tied to high-stakes rewards (as when attaining a high grade in an introductory survey course is a precondition to being accepted as a major in the subject).
- When the culture as a whole or the particular learning circumstances call for inclusion of performance goals and surface learning strategies. Liem, Lau, and Nie (2008) illustrated this in a study of students learning English in Singapore. They noted that Asian, and especially Chinese, students rely on an approach to learning

called *memorization with understanding*, in which deep and surface learning strategies are used simultaneously. Furthermore, surface learning strategies took on special importance in the students' English classes. To insure access to advanced educational opportunities and the best jobs, they needed to gain facility in English. However, English was not their first language, so they needed not only to understand but also to memorize their English-related lessons.

Although the potential benefits of performance-approach goals are mostly limited to these special circumstances, mastery goals are likely to be associated with a broad pattern of desirable motivational and strategic variables (shown in Table 4.1) in all learning situations. Furthermore, they are likely to promote higher achievement when meeting the learning objectives requires deep processing of complex content, lengthy persistence, or overcoming obstacles (Grant & Dweck, 2003), when the assessment focuses on long-term retention rather than short-term memory (Yeo et al., 2008); when the learner is highly motivated to master the content, as in specialized vocational training (Simons, Dewitte, & Lens, 2004); or when the learner's agenda closely overlaps the teacher's (Senko & Miles, 2008).

Implications for Teaching

All goal theorists recommend that teachers encourage mastery goals and avoid actions that may lead some students to adopt performance-avoidance goals. Opinions still differ about performance-approach goals. However, even the multiple-goals theorists usually do not recommend that teachers encourage students to adopt performance goals.

This is true despite the fact that most students do not generate performance-approach goals spontaneously. Frequent use of achievement goal questionnaires has given the impression that performance goals are common, but this is not the case. It is true that, when given questionnaires containing performance-goal items, many students endorse these items. However, it also is true that, when asked to describe their achievement-related goals in their own words, students often mention mastery goals and outcome goals, but not ability goals or normative goals. That is, they often speak of learning or getting a high grade, but rarely speak of validating their abilities or outperforming their peers (Brophy, 2005; Dolan & McCaslin, 2008; Kember, Hong, & Ho, 2008; Urdan, 2001).

Open-ended interviews with students about the goals they pursue in classrooms have elicited responses that line up only partially with the goals emphasized by goal theorists. Lemos (1996) interviewed Portuguese sixth graders and found that seven types of goals were mentioned frequently:

Work completion goals (29%): Engaging in academic work in order to "get it done" or "finish it and go on to the next one."

Evaluation goals (21%): Working in order to garner positive evaluations or avoid negative ones. This is similar to outcome goals.

Learning goals (19%): Seeking to learn, to know more about, to find out how, etc.

Complying goals (17%): Seeking to meet student role requirements by adapting to the pace of the class, following the rules, paying attention, etc.

Interpersonal relationship goals (6%): Seeking to develop positive relationships with teachers or peers.

Enjoyment goals (5%): Engaging in activities for pleasure, enjoyment, or fun.
Discipline goals (3%): Wanting to engage in ethical behavior and avoid getting into
    disciplinary trouble.

Note that although learning goals were represented, performance goals were not (students talked about getting good grades but not about displaying ability or looking good in comparisons with classmates). Also, the most commonly mentioned goal, simply completing the work, has not been studied by goal theorists.

Even college students, either when asked to generate their own goals or when allowed to select from a goals menu, seldom adopt ability or normative versions of performance goals. They often adopt outcome goals (get a good grade), but without speaking of validating their abilities or besting peers (Okun et al., 2006; VanYperen, 2006).

This low incidence of performance goals is desirable from several perspectives, including not only much of goal theory but theory and research on collaborative learning communities (which emphasize cooperation over competition as the desired classroom ethos). Also, if students are not displaying much mastery orientation toward the teacher's agenda, improving curriculum and instruction so that they do value the teacher's agenda (and seek to master it because they see good reasons for doing so) seems more advisable than urging the adoption of performance goals to provide extra achievement pressure. Students' levels of mastery orientation can increase, even if they currently are very low (Shim, Ryan, & Anderson, 2008).

Several other characteristics of performance-approach goals also caution against recommending them. First, although they do support achievement striving, *performance-approach goals carry affective costs.* Compared to classmates operating primarily from learning goals, students operating primarily from performance-approach goals derive less enjoyment but experience more anxiety and tension as they engage in learning activities (Daniels et al., 2008; Witkow & Fuligni, 2007). They also experience more distraction by intrusive thoughts (Button, Mathieu, & Zajac, 1996, Vansteenkiste et al., 2004).

Another concern is that performance-approach goals (particularly the normative versions) imply a selfish and competitive focus that conflicts with learning community norms (Darnon, Muller, Schrager, Pannuzzo, & Butera, 2006; Harris, Yuill, & Luckin, 2008; Levy-Tossman, Kaplan, & Assor, 2007; Poortvliet, Janssen, VanYperen, & Van de Vliert, 2007; Stornes & Ommundsen, 2004). Performance-oriented students have been found to be more elitist and self-centered than mastery-oriented students, as well as more concerned about social status (wanting to work on their own or collaborate only with an in-group, instead of the full range of their peers; Levy, Kaplan, & Patrick, 2004; Liem et al., 2008).

Finally, saying or doing anything that might orient students toward self-validation or social comparisons can open the door to performance-avoidance goals and ultimately learned helplessness. Encouraging performance-approach goals establishes or reinforces students' dispositions toward including social comparison components in their goal orientations. This might be beneficial (or at least, not harmful) in the short run, or for as long as the students continue to be successful in achieving their goals of displaying high ability. However, if their success rates begin to drop as they move into higher grades and encounter more challenging tasks, they will be at risk for shifting from performance-approach goals to performance-avoidance goals.

Goal theory researchers have shown that sixth graders who expressed performance-approach goals were prone to shifting to performance-avoidance goals in seventh grade (Middleton, Kaplan, & Midgley, 2004), and college students who expressed performance-approach goals early in the semester were prone to shifting to performance-avoidance goals later in the semester (Senko & Harackiewicz, 2004; Shim & Ryan, 2005). *Apparently, the approach aspects of performance-approach goals are fragile, so these goals can quickly shift to become performance-avoidance goals if doubts about prospects for success set in* (Darnon, Harackiewicz, Butera, Mugny, & Quiamzade, 2007).

EXPANDING BEYOND ACHIEVEMENT GOALS

Learning and performance goals are similar in *content* (they both focus on achievement) but imply contrasts in the ways that achievement is defined and the *processes* used to pursue it. Recently, goal theorists have been studying other kinds of goals (Kaplan & Maehr, 2007).

Work-Avoidant Goals

Alienated or discouraged students may not show much evidence of either type of achievement goal and instead adopt *work-avoidant goals*: Rather than becoming cognitively engaged in learning activities, they seek to minimize effort investment by tuning out lessons, copying the work of peers, frequently seeking teacher or peer help, or negotiating less demanding assignments (Dowson & McInerny, 2001; Meece & Holt, 1993). Work-avoidant goals correlate negatively with indicators of motivation and achievement, such as use of deep processing, reading voluntarily for fun, positive attitudes toward the class or the subject, and test scores (Baker & Wigfield, 1999; Newstead, Franklyn-Stokes, & Armstead, 1996; Somuncuoglu & Yildirim, 1999). Students operating from work-avoidant goal orientations are not striving to achieve anything in particular. Instead, they are trying to get away with putting in as little work as possible (Nolen, 1988; Tapola & Niemvirta, 2008; Urdan, 1997).

Social Goals

Students pursue *social goals* that include building friendships, maintaining their reputation as a good and likeable person, assisting others, pleasing the teacher or peers, and enjoying social interactions (Anderman & Kaplan, 2008). They are likely to be achievement oriented if their social goals include pleasing their teachers or parents or take the form of *social responsibility goals* that emphasize keeping interpersonal commitments, meeting social role obligations, and conforming to social expectations. However, some students may focus less on social responsibility goals than on other social goals such as *intimacy goals* (maintaining close friendships with peers) or *status goals* (being admired by peers). For these students, the effects of social goals on achievement orientations will depend on the values of peers with whom they share intimate friendships (Juvonen & Wentzel, 1996; Miller et al., 1996; Wentzel, 1999; Wentzel & Wigfield, 1998). Students sometimes might perform less than their best to maintain popularity or avoid hurting the feelings of friends (White, Sanbonmatsu, Croyle, & Smittipatana, 2002).

Extrinsic Goals

Students' achievement orientations may focus on garnering extrinsic rewards. In the short run, extrinsic goal orientations focus on earning good grades and related contingencies (eligibility for extracurricular activities, money from parents, prizes from the teacher, etc.). In the longer run, they include such things as opportunities to win scholarships, gain admittance to good colleges, or qualify for good jobs. Unlike learning goals, which focus on developing understandings, *extrinsic goals* focus on rewards associated with displays of successful performance. However, extrinsic goals are not the same as performance goals because they do not involve desires to display high ability.

Extrinsic goals help mobilize learners to put forth the effort and persistence needed to earn good grades, but they also correlate with cheating or relying on surface processing strategies (Anderman, Griesinger, & Westerfield, 1998; Miller et al., 1996; Newstead, Franklyn-Stokes, & Armstead, 1996; Urdan, 1997). Lin et al. (2003) found that college students who combined high levels of intrinsic motivation with medium levels of extrinsic motivation were the most successful achievers.

Purpose versus Target Goals

Harackiewicz and Elliot (1998) distinguished between higher level *purpose goals* that represent the reason for task engagement and task-specific *target goals* that guide the person's task behavior. Purpose goals explain the "why" for performing an activity and target goals provide the "how." People are more likely to enjoy an activity (i.e., to have intrinsic motivation to engage in it) when their target goals are well matched to their purpose goals. As they accomplish their target goals, they not only feel more competent at the task but value that competence and seek to continue building it, because it serves their longer run purposes. One implication is that, in performance purpose goal contexts, performance target goals are more optimal than mastery target goals. This explains the quotation that begins the chapter. Other findings also support the conclusion that people enjoy performing actions that help them meet their larger purpose goals (Carver & Scheier, 1999; Freitas & Higgins, 2002).

Promotion Focus versus Prevention Focus

E. Tory Higgins (2006) developed similar notions of regulatory fit by contrasting promotion focus and prevention focus, both as stable personal traits and as situational strategies for goal pursuit. When *promotion focused*, people are seeking to realize their hopes or aspirations. Their goal striving features approach-motivated strategies include eager goal pursuit, creative thinking, and risk taking. When people are *prevention focused*, they are careful to make sure that they meet their duties or obligations. They rely more on avoidance-motivated strategies such as being vigilant against making mistakes and carefully following prescribed steps or procedures. Promotion-focused people tend to be happier and more productive in open and unstructured achievement situations, whereas prevention-focused people tend to be less anxious and more productive in situations that call for careful application of specified procedures (Brodscholl, Kober, & Higgins, 2006; Sideridis, 2006; Vaughn, Baumann, & Klemann, 2008). Although approach motivation is generally preferable to avoidance motivation, the latter can be beneficial when striving to meet prevention-focused goals such as staying away from cigarettes after resolving to quit smoking (Worth, Sullivan, Hertel, Jeffery, & Rothman, 2005).

Goal Coordination

Students in classrooms, like people in any social situation, typically seek to optimize multiple goals and agendas simultaneously. They want to please teachers and parents by earning good grades, but also to maintain their self-esteem and their social reputations and friendships. This requires them to coordinate their goal striving by taking advantage of opportunities to pursue more than one goal simultaneously and by trying to avoid getting caught in situations where what they must do to satisfy one goal will interfere with their attempts to satisfy another (Urdan, 1999).

Goal coordination can get complicated quickly. For one thing, investment in any goal implies commitments to whatever efforts are required to accomplish it, often accompanied by worry about the consequences of failure (Pomerantz, Saxon, & Oishi, 2000). Also, some goals are much closer than others to individuals' core values and developing interests, so they will be assigned higher priorities (Sheldon & Elliot, 1999).

Goal coordination is especially difficult for struggling students, because maintaining commitment to learning goals will require them to work harder than their peers (Hong, 2001). Even then, their work may still result in lower grades if teachers grade on a curve or hold all students to identical high standards (Church, Elliot, & Gable, 2001).

APPLYING GOAL THEORY

Most goal theorists emphasize managing classrooms in ways that encourage students to adopt learning goals (and if relevant, performance-approach goals) rather than performance-avoidance goals, work-avoidant goals, extrinsic goals, or other goals that would distract from a focus on learning. Much of what they suggest involves establishing the classroom as a learning community, as described in chapter 2. They condemn *two particularly counterproductive practices: harsh grading standards* that make it unduly difficult for students to be successful (and create anxiety about grades) *and grading on a curve*, which guarantees that some students will not be successful. They also caution against public evaluations and other practices that focus attention on social comparisons rather than one's own trajectory of progress. These practices make it difficult for learners to establish and maintain focus on learning goals, and more likely that any performance goals they adopt will be performance-avoidance goals.

Even theorists who emphasize that performance-approach goals can complement learning goals tend to qualify their recommendations about performance-approach goals when talking about implications for practice. Pintrich (2000) suggested that performance-approach goals can be helpful but primarily as complements rather than alternatives to learning goals. He added that habitual adoption of performance-approach goals is likely to be effective only so long as the students are successful. If they begin to encounter failure consistently, they will become vulnerable to shifting to performance-avoidance goals and eventual learned helplessness.

Harackiewicz, Barron, and Elliot (1998) noted that performance-approach goals can complement learning goals in highly competitive classes that are graded on a curve, especially for highly competitive students. However, they also pointed out that these goals can be counterproductive in neutral and especially learning-oriented contexts. For them, the key is an optimal match of goal to context: "Successful negotiation of academic life at the college level may require a performance orientation in some contexts, but a mastery orientation in others, and the wisdom to know which one to adopt when" (p. 17). Others would argue that a more fundamental principle is to avoid creating such highly competitive contexts in the first place and instead create learning communities that support continued focus on learning goals.

Classroom Goal Structures: Focus on Learning

Most of the findings discussed in previous sections of the chapter came from studies of the *personal goal orientations that students brought with them into their classes*, measured using items such as "I want to show my teacher that I am smarter than the other students" (performance goal) or "The main reason I do my work is that I like to learn" (learning goal). However, other investigators began to measure perceptions of the *goal orientations that students found when they entered their classes*, using items such as "In this school, we are encouraged to compete against each other for grades" (perceived performance orientation) or "Our teachers want us to really understand our work, not just memorize it" (perceived learning orientation). Their studies indicated that a perceived learning orientation in a classroom or school was associated with student tendencies to adopt personal learning goals, use deep processing study strategies, and have higher self-efficacy perceptions and more positive attitudes toward school. Meanwhile, perceptions of a performance orientation were associated with adoption of performance goals, use of surface processing strategies, lower self-efficacy perceptions, more cheating, more self-handicapping, less willingness to seek help, and negative attitudes toward school (Anderman & Wolters, 2006; Church, Elliot, & Gable, 2001; Patrick, Anderman, Ryan, Edelin, & Midgley, 2001; Ryan & Patrick, 2001; Turner et al., 2002; Wolters, 2004).

These studies suggested that, although students enter classes with already developed dispositions toward particular goal orientations, their personal goal orientations can be modified in response to the goal orientations emphasized by their teachers or their school as a whole. This was confirmed in several experimental studies in which participants were induced to adopt either learning or performance goals (Button, Mathieu, & Zajac, 1996; Hole & Crozier, 2007; Jagacinski, Madden, & Reider, 2001; Thompson & Musket, 2005). Learning goals led to more positive outcomes, although the effects were greater for challenging and complex tasks than for easy or rote tasks, and greater for college students than for elementary students (Utman, 1997). Among college students, learning goals had especially positive effects on those who were low in achievement motivation (Barron & Harackiewicz, 2001; Harackiewicz et al., 1998).

Although the research findings and implications concerning students' personal achievement goals are complicated, the story is much simpler for classroom level goal orientations. *If students perceive a mastery-oriented goal orientation in their classroom, they are likely to adopt mastery goals, but if they perceive a performance-oriented goal orientation, they are likely to adopt performance goals* (Lau & Nie, 2008; Midgley, 2002; Patrick & Ryan, 2009; Wolters, 2004). Thus, teaching practices can orient the class as a whole toward adopting mastery goals, which, in turn, leads to a variety of desirable outcomes (Anderman & Wolters, 2006; Bong, 2005; Corpus, McClintic-Gilbert, & Hayenga, 2009; Greene et al., 2004; Kaplan, Gheen, & Midgley, 2002; Ommundsen & Kvalo, 2007; Turner et al., 2002; VanYperen, 2006).

Meece, Herman, and McCombs (2003) found that teachers who promoted mastery goal orientations emphasized the importance of attempting challenging assignments, pursuing ideas and interests, and taking responsibility for learning. In contrast, teachers who promoted performance goal orientations frequently provided public recognition to the best students, gave special privileges to them, or emphasized high test scores in lieu of more specific learning goals.

Patrick and Ryan (2009) asked students to rate their teachers on five items associated with mastery goal orientations and then explain their ratings. The students' explanations indicated that teachers establish mastery goal orientations in their classrooms through a combination of instructional and affective/social aspects of their teaching.

Teachers rated high on wanting their students to understand the work, not just memorize it, were described as: using a variety of explanations and examples to relate content to students' prior knowledge, encouraging students' participation and questions, and showing concern that their students understand, get help when needed, and are prepared for successful futures. Teachers rated highly on thinking that mistakes are okay so long as the students are learning were described as: encouraging or allowing students to redo homework, quizzes, or tests; giving grades for homework completion rather than correctness of answers; using different approaches to explain the content; and displaying support and positive affect when interacting with students. Teachers rated highly on really wanting us to enjoy learning new things were described as: being friendly, making lessons pleasurable, showing concern that students learn and do well, using interesting and enjoyable tasks, and teaching in ways that helped students to pay attention and learn. Teachers rated highly on providing time to really explore and understand new ideas were described as: being friendly and approachable, using a variety of interesting tasks, and taking time to provide examples and explanations and respond to students' questions. Finally, teachers rated highly on recognizing students for trying hard were described as: telling students when they had done well, noticing improvement, attending to effort, and encouraging and assisting progress.

Dresel, Martschinke, and Kopp (2009) found that teachers' feedback was a key predictor of students' perceptions of the goal structures in their classrooms. Teachers who promoted mastery goal structures gave most of their feedback privately, whereas teachers who promoted performance goal structures frequently gave feedback publicly. Public negative feedback appeared particularly counterproductive, because it was associated not only with performance goal structures at the classroom level but also with performance-avoidance goals at the individual level. Teachers who frequently criticized their students publicly conditioned them to anticipate and fear public humiliation and embarrassment.

The TARGET Program

The most comprehensive classroom intervention rooted in goal theory is the TARGET Program, developed by Carole Ames (1990). Ames began with Joyce Epstein's (1989) synthesis of research on family structures that influence children's developing motivational systems at home (see chapter 11). Epstein organized her findings within six categories that are represented in the TARGET acronym: Task, Authority, Recognition, Grouping, Evaluation, and Time. Noting that these home structures have parallels at school, Ames blended in additional principles from goal theory to develop TARGET into a program for managing these six facets of classrooms in ways that encourage students to focus on learning.

Tasks are selected to provide an optimal level of challenge and to emphasize activities that students find interesting and engaging. *Authority* is shared with students and exercised with consideration of their needs and feelings. *Recognition* is provided to all students who make noteworthy progress, not just the highest achievers. *Grouping* is managed in ways that promote cooperative learning and minimize interpersonal competition and social comparison. *Evaluation* is accomplished using multiple criteria and methods, focusing on individualized assessment of progress rather than comparisons of individuals or groups. Finally, *Time* is used in creative ways that ease the constraints of rigid scheduling and allow for more use of valuable learning activities that are hard to fit into 30-60 minute class periods.

TARGET is adaptable to different teaching situations and useful for building motivational considerations into your instructional plans. Table 4.2 summarizes ways in which the TARGET recommendations contrast with traditional classroom structures.

Ames (1990) compared data from at-risk students in TARGET and comparison classrooms. The TARGET students perceived their classrooms as more learning oriented.

TABLE 4.2
TARGET Recommendations Contrasted with Traditional Classroom Structures

TARGET	Traditional Practices	TARGET Recommendations
Task	Textbook-based curriculum emphasizing textbook reading, recitation lessons, workbook tasks, and tests. All students are exposed to the same input and engaged in the same activities, with emphasis on content coverage and memorization. Motivation is addressed primarily through the grading system, perhaps augmented by various forms of extrinsic rewards.	There is a greater variety of learning activities, selected to emphasize tasks that students find interesting and intrinsically engaging and to connect with students' backgrounds and experiences. Activities are introduced with emphasis on their purposes and are developed in ways designed to maximize their intrinsic appeal and help students to appreciate the value of what they are learning (rather than with emphasis on tests, grades, or extrinsic rewards). To help ensure that activities are optimally challenging for all students, students are taught goal-setting and self-regulation skills, and if necessary, are assigned to information sources and learning tasks of varying difficulty
Authority	The teacher dictates classroom rules and makes unilateral decisions regarding curriculum and instruction. Students' general behavior is tightly regimented within school and classroom rules and their exposure to learning opportunities is heavily determined by the teacher and their textbooks.	Authority is shared with students and exercised with consideration of their needs and feelings. Their content-related interests and questions are solicited and addressed. They frequently have opportunities to make choices in deciding what to do, to exercise autonomy in deciding how to do it, and to participate in decision making about classroom rules, procedures, or learning opportunities.

TARGET	Traditional Practices	TARGET Recommendations
Recognition	At least implicitly, students are always in competition for recognition and rewards. Certain students consistently receive high grades, have their work praised and publicly displayed, and win whatever competitions, prizes, or awards are made available. Other students rarely if ever enjoy these recognitions and rewards, which are based primarily if not solely on absolute levels of accomplishment, without regard to individual differences in the levels of effort that went into the accomplishments.	Recognition is provided to all students who make noteworthy progress, not just to the highest achievers. Students are recognized for a broad range of achievements (not just high scores on tests); recognition is based on levels of progress made toward individually established goals; and most recognition takes the form of privately communicated appreciations of effort and progress rather than public celebration of the accomplishments of the highest achievers.
Grouping	The class is an aggregate of individuals rather than a coherent learning community. Students interact frequently with the teacher but rarely with one another, and they work mostly alone on assignments. If used at all, grouping is used to set up competitions or to differentiate students by ability or achievement level.	The class functions as a learning community that features collaborative norms and expectations. Students frequently work in pairs or small groups to engage in the social construction of knowledge. Group assignments are varied and based on friendships, common interests, or other considerations in addition to or instead of achievement level, and students are encouraged to cooperate rather than compete as learners.
Evaluation	All students are evaluated using the same assessment instruments (typically conventional tests). Feedback is often public and emphasizes absolute levels of performance (number or percentage of items answered correctly) or normative comparisons (a students' relative standing within the class or some larger sample). It often is delivered in ways that encourage students to view it as assessment of fixed levels of performance capacity rather than of increments in ability development.	Evaluation features a variety of assessment instruments and an emphasis on helping students to recognize and appreciate the progress they have made toward individually suitable goals. The system for converting assessment results into report card grades includes provision for allowing students to take alternate tests, revise their work on assignments, and in other ways improve on initially disappointing performance levels.
Time	Teacher and students are locked into a rigid schedule in which each day is divided into 30-60 minute periods. Activities that require more time than this schedule allows are not included in the curriculum, and even scheduled activities frequently must be cut short or interrupted and resumed on another day because a time period is ending.	Time is scheduled more flexibly so that a greater range of activities can be included. In addition, instead of always being told what to do and when to do it, students frequently work on major projects that allow them to exercise autonomy in managing time and other learning resources (e.g., interactions with information sources or collaborating classmates). Students who need it are given extra time to complete their assignments.

Furthermore, they maintained their perceptions of competence, positive attitudes toward their classes, intrinsic motivation, and use of productive learning strategies, whereas the comparison students showed deterioration on all of these measures as the semester progressed.

Fuchs et al. (1997) incorporated the task, authority, recognition, and evaluation components of TARGET into interventions in elementary mathematics teaching. They found that, compared to control students, low achieving students in the treatment classrooms reported enjoying and benefiting from the intervention, chose more challenging and varied learning topics to address, and increased their levels of effort.

Experiments in physical education classes have shown that students taught in task-involving climates tended to become more task-involved, and students taught in ego-involving climates tended to become more ego-involved. The former students reported positive changes in their views of the motivational climate of the class, willingness to attempt more challenging tasks and persist longer at them, and in some cases, improvement of skills at a faster rate (Solmon, 1996; Theeboom, DeKnop, & Weiss, 1995; Todorovich & Curtner-Smith, 2003).

Studies of teacher characteristics associated with students' perceptions of classroom goal structures have shown that, in addition to the categories included within the TARGET system, students typically talk about the presence or absence of close, supportive teacher-student relationships. This has led to suggestions that the system be expanded to include a category of social relationships, so TARGET would become TARGETS (Kaplan & Maehr, 1999; Patrick & Ryan, 2009).

Maehr and Midgley extended Ames's TARGET model from the classroom level to the school level. The schoolwide TARGET model calls for adjustments such as reinforcing the intrinsic value of learning by extending it through field experiences and other extracurricular participation, arranging for public recognition of students' accomplishments, creating opportunities for students to learn study skills and strategies for managing their own learning, and revising time schedules to allow for more flexible curricular planning. At the end of a three-year intervention, TARGET school students were more learning oriented, whereas comparison school students were more performance oriented (Maehr & Midgley, 1996).

GOAL THEORY: LOOKING AHEAD

An optimistic summary of goal theory to date would go something like the following. Goal theory was the natural result of the realization that the aspects of human activity most in need of motivational explanation were not its energization or initiation aspects but its directional and quality aspects. This dictated a shift from needs or other general motives to the goals and associated strategies operating in particular situations. Goals and related cognitions are key concepts in any cognitive theory of motivation in achievement situations, so goal theory provided a venue for synthesis of the contributions of the theorists cited in chapters 3 and 4. Early work supported the idea that learning goals are productive and performance goals are counterproductive, but this generalization broke down as it became clear that goal theory would have to include the approach-avoidance distinction as well as other kinds of goals such as work-avoidant goals, social goals, and extrinsic goals.

These developments led to the *multiple goals perspective, which depicts learners as matching their goals to the contingencies of situations and coordinating their goal striving so as to pursue multiple goals efficiently and minimize the likelihood that they will find themselves working at cross purposes*. They will pursue learning goals to the extent that they value the content and are taught in ways that encourage or at least allow deep-processing strategies and a focus on mastery; they will pursue performance-approach goals where an emphasis on competition and test preparation make this necessary to earn good grades; and they will coordinate these achievement agendas with social and other agendas so that they support or at least do not conflict with one another (Harackiewicz, Barron, Pintrich, Elliot, & Thrash, 2002).

The multiple goals perspective resolves some of the problems inherent in the earlier perspective, but it introduces some new problems of its own. *The notion of coordinating efforts so as to address multiple goals simultaneously is appealing in theory but difficult to accomplish in reality*, as the two quotations that began this chapter illustrate. In a study of people engaged in volunteer efforts, Kiviniemi, Snyder, and Omoto (2002) found that those who volunteered in response to a single motivation reported more positive experiences and fulfillment than those who volunteered in the service of multiple motivations. Emmons and King (1988) showed that mobilizing to accomplish particular goals involves focusing attention on what is relevant and shutting out what is not. Attempting to accomplish multiple goals simultaneously tends to reduce our capacities to focus on any one of them (Carver & Scheier, 2008; Louro, Pieters, & Zeelenberg, 2007).

This point was demonstrated with respect to approach vs. avoidance goals by Coats, Janoff-Bulman, and Alpert (1996), who showed that phrasing goals positively (e.g., try to be creative) tended to focus attention on progress and produce more favorable self-evaluations and greater psychological well-being than phrasing goals negatively (e.g., try not to be uncreative), which tended to focus attention on indications of failure. Performance-avoidance goals reduce students' capacities for mobilizing to meet task demands, because they lead to "invasion" of concentration by concerns about possible failure (Forster, Grant, Idson, & Higgins, 2001; Snyder et al., 2002).

There are other complications as well. Some goal theorists have treated goal orientations as highly stable dispositions that learners take with them into any learning situation. Others have treated them as highly malleable, responsive to the reward contingencies and related social atmospheres operating in the learning situation. The success of experiments that involved inducing goal orientations suggests that they are easy to manipulate in the laboratory, but the relatively modest findings of school intervention studies suggest that students' goal orientations toward their everyday classroom work may be much more difficult to change significantly (Urdan, 1997). For example, some students, including high achievers, persistently report performance-avoidance goal orientations even in learning communities that de-emphasize competition and support learning goals (Dai, 2000; Miserandino, 1996; Turner & Meyer, 1999).

Also, students in the same class vary in their perceptions of their teacher's relative emphasis on learning vs. performance (Tapola & Niemivirta, 2008; Urdan, 2004). Furthermore, some students are learning oriented in some school subjects, but performance orientated in others (Bong, 2001; Marsh, Kong, & Hau, 2001). Finally, although goal theory research consistently produces coherent results when contrasting goal orientations are induced or when goal orientations are measured using self-report questionnaires, students ordinarily do not mention performance goals spontaneously when interviewed about what goals they are pursuing.

CONCLUSION

Much of the theory and research on the expectancy and learning community aspects of motivation in classrooms (summarized in Table 4.1) can be synthesized around a goal theory perspective. *The philosophy that led to the original goal theory stands as a vision of what schooling might become, and the emergent multiple goals perspective offers a sensible compromise for making the best of schooling as it has been and continues to be in most places.* Both versions imply that teachers should minimize elements of competition and social comparison in the learning community norms and evaluation and reward structures operating in their classrooms, while at the same time encouraging students to adopt learning goals and providing the instructional scaffolding and personal support needed to enable them to attain these goals successfully. The multiple goals perspective adds that, in situations where competition cannot be eliminated in favor of criterion-referenced grading, teachers can at least follow the same principles just outlined so as to make it more likely that their students' performance goals will be performance-approach goals rather than performance-avoidance goals.

My own advice is similar, except that in talking about upcoming examinations, *I would emphasize learning goals and outcome goals* (striving to master the material and thus position oneself to earn a high grade) *rather than learning goals and performance goals* (striving to outperform one's classmates or validate one's ability). This is because *I see no reason to believe that performance-approach goals would support students' achievement striving more effectively than outcome goals* (on the contrary, they inject concerns about competition and peer comparisons that are likely to distract the students from an exclusive focus on preparing for the test). *Furthermore, anything done to encourage performance goals would work against efforts to create a learning community* as described in chapter 2.

Kaplan (2004) elaborated on this point by noting that performance goals are related to attempts to protect or enhance social self-worth. In turn, these self-worth concerns are associated with tendencies to perceive social environments as composed of an in-group and one or more out-groups, and to discriminate accordingly. Compared to students who emphasize mastery goals, students who emphasize performance goals are more concerned about social status and less willing to cooperate with peers from different social groups.

Interviews typically reveal that students are focused primarily on just getting their work completed rather than on acquiring the intended learning benefits. Consequently, Urdan (2001) advised teachers not only to regularly explain the intended outcomes of lessons and learning activities, but to regularly assess students' appreciation of these goals. This is good advice.

Focusing students' attention on individual and collaborative learning goals means much more than merely keeping them on task. It means creating a supportive, collaborative learning environment that enables students to feel comfortable in accepting the challenges implied in learning goals, persisting with self-regulated learning efforts when they encounter failure or frustration, and asking for help when they need it. It also means seeing that they get the help they need, building confidence that persistent efforts will eventually pay off, and treating mistakes as expected parts of an ongoing learning process rather than as evidence of limited ability. Finally, it means avoiding practices that tend to make students feel psychologically isolated or threatened in their efforts to meet your academic expectations.

In combination with the principles outlined in chapters 2 and 3, consistent application of the principles outlined in this chapter will enable you to support your students' confidence as learners and thus encourage them to adopt learning rather than performance goals, to focus on processing information and developing skills rather than worrying about failing or being embarrassed, and to persist and stay focused on the task when they encounter difficulties. This combination of preventive and supportive strategies will be sufficient for many if not most of your students. However, some will require more intensive attention to the expectancy aspects of their motivation. Strategies for assisting these students are discussed in chapter 5.

SUMMARY

Theory and research on human motivation gradually shifted focus from questions about the energization and initiation of action sequences to questions about their direction and quality. A large literature developed concerning motivation in achievement situations, as work by Bandura, Dweck, and Weiner was joined by work by Ames, Covington, Nicholls, and others who studied qualitative aspects of achievement goal orientations. Much of the early work appeared to support the generalization that learning goals are productive but performance goals are not.

However, further studies indicated that the negative motivational and strategic correlates previously ascribed to performance goals in general were linked primarily with performance-avoidance goals. Performance-approach goals showed a more mixed pattern. This led to the multiple goals perspective that depicted performance-approach goals as complementary to learning goals, at least for some people in some achievement situations. Performance-approach goals appeared to be more closely related to short-run retention and grades, whereas learning goals appeared more closely related to long-run retention and interest in the subject.

Goal theorists began looking at the content of goals other than achievement goals. Research on work-avoidant goals, social goals, and extrinsic goals revealed predictable relationships with achievement goals and led to an appreciation of students as coordinating multiple goals to address multiple agendas simultaneously. The implication is that optimizing motivation means adopting goals that are well matched to the situation's embedded achievement tasks and assessment criteria.

At this point, some theorists view the 2×2 goal model and the associated multiple goals perspective as a pleasing synthesis of much of the literature on the expectancy aspects of motivation and their cognitive, affective, and strategic correlates (summarized in Table 4.1). Others, however, argue that something is wrong with an educational system that appears to reward performance goals but not mastery goals. In addition, goal theorists face persistent empirical anomalies (goal coordination sounds good in theory but is difficult to accomplish in practice; when asked to talk about their goals in their own words, students usually do not mention performance goals but often mention work completion goals; goal measures usually do not correlate very well with achievement measures; and patterns of stability and change in students' goal orientations are not yet well understood).

As you think about how to apply goal theory in your own practice, you will need to consider not only research findings but your own educational philosophy. If you share the philosophy common among the original goal theorists and believe that its vision of schooling is feasible, you might consider attempting to implement the TARGET program or a comparably broad package of motivational interventions. If you are less hopeful about fundamentally reforming schooling as we know it, you might adopt the multiple goals perspective. This would involve routinely teaching in ways that encourage your students to formulate and follow through on learning goals, but also supporting their adoption of performance-approach goals when this might help them to accomplish certain tasks and meet associated grading criteria. If you do the latter, be sure to limit yourself to outcome goal versions of performance-approach goals. That is, emphasize mobilizing to do well on the test but not focusing on validating ability or competing with classmates. At the very least, take the advice offered by all goal theorists and avoid harsh grading standards, grading on a curve, and public comparisons of students' accomplishments.

REFLECTION QUESTIONS

1. Have you had experiences similar to those featured in the two quotes that began the chapter? If so, what do they imply about goal theory applications in your teaching practice?

2. Self-handicapping and other variables associated with self-worth theory have been especially popular among investigators working at the college level. Why do you think this is so?

3. What might you say to a student whom you observed engaging in self-handicapping behavior?

4. What do you view as an optimal combination of individualistic, competitive, and cooperative reward structures in classrooms? Would you answer be the same across all grade levels?

5. How does adopting a performance goal (as defined by goal theorists) differ from mobilizing to do your very best on a test?

6. Why do you think that approach goals have mixed or even generally positive relationships with other variables, but avoidance goals have strongly negative relationships?

7. It is not surprising that learning goals are associated with deep-level processing strategies, but why should performance goals be associated with surface-level strategies?

8. Why might current performance-approach goals predict a shift to performance-avoidance goals in the future?

9. Should teachers ever encourage performance goals? If so, when, why, and how?

10. How do you view the TARGET model: Strengths? Weaknesses? Significant omissions? Classroom feasibility?

11. Should we socialize students to <u>achieve</u> or instead to <u>compete</u>? Why?

12. Why is it important to look at the quality of motivation, not just the amount?

13. Why is criterion-referenced grading preferable to grading on a curve?

14. Given that learning goals routinely correlate with quite a range of motivational and strategy measures (Table 4.1), why don't they show consistent relationships with achievement?

15. Why does the author recommend a combination of learning goals and outcome goals over a combination of learning goals and performance-approach goals?

REFERENCES

Ames, C. (1984). Competitive, cooperative and individualistic goal structures: A cognitive-motivational analysis. In R. Ames & C. Ames (Eds.), *Research on motivation in education: Volume 1. Student motivation* (pp. 177–207). New York: Academic Press.

Ames, C. (1990). Motivation: What teachers need to know. *Teachers College Record, 91*, 409–421.

Ames, C. (1992). Classrooms: Goals, structures, and student motivation. *Journal of Educational Psychology, 84*, 261–271.

Ames, C., & Archer, J. (1988). Achievement goals in the classroom: Students' learning strategies and motivational processes. *Journal of Educational Psychology, 80*, 260–267.

Anderman, E., Griesinger, T., & Westerfield, G. (1998). Motivation and cheating during adolescence. *Journal of Educational Psychology, 90*, 84–93.

Anderman, L., & Kaplan, A. (Guest Eds.). (2008). Special issue on the role of interpersonal relationships in student motivation. *Journal of Experimental Education, 76*, 115–240.

Anderman, E., & Murdoch, T. (2007). *Psychology of academic cheating.* Boston: Elsevier.

Anderman, E., & Wolters, C. (2006). Goals, values, and affects: Influences on student motivation. In P. Alexander & P. Winne (Eds.), *Handbook of educational psychology* (2nd ed., pp. 369–390). Mahwah, NJ: Erlbaum.

Baker, L., & Wigfield, A. (1999). Dimensions of children's motivation for reading and their relations to reading activity and reading achievement. *Reading Research Quarterly, 34*, 452–477.

Barron, K., & Harackiewicz, J. (2001). Achievement goals and optimal motivation: Testing multiple goal models. *Journal of Personality and Social Psychology, 80*, 706–722.

Bereby-Meyer, Y., & Kaplan, A. (2005). Motivational influences on transfer of problem-solving strategies. *Contemporary Educational Psychology, 30*, 1–22.

Blumenfeld, P. (1992). Classroom learning and motivation: Clarifying and expanding goal theory. *Journal of Educational Psychology, 84*, 272–281.

Boekaerts, M. (2001). Motivation, learning, and instruction. In N. Smelser & P. Baltes (Eds.), *International encyclopedia of the social and behavioral sciences* (pp. 10112–10117). New York: Elsevier Science.

Bong, M. (1996). Problems in academic motivation research and advantages and disadvantages of their solutions. *Contemporary Educational Psychology, 21*, 149–165.

Bong, M. (2001). Between- and within-domain relations of academic motivation among middle and high school students: Self-efficacy, task-value, and achievement goals. *Journal of Educational Psychology, 93*, 23–34.

Bong, M. (2005). Within-grade changes in Korean girls' motivation and perceptions of the learning environment across domains and achievement levels. *Journal of Educational Psychology, 97*, 656–672.

Brodscholl, J., Kober, H., & Higgins, E. T. (2006). Strategies of self-regulation in goal attainment versus goal maintenance. *European Journal of Social Psychology, 37*, 628–648.

Brophy, J. (2005). Goal theorists should move on from performance goals. *Educational Psychologist, 40*, 167–176.

Button, S., Mathieu, J., & Zajac, D. (1996). Goal orientation in organizational research: A conceptual and empirical foundation. *Organizational Behavior and Human Decision Processes, 67*, 26–48.

Carver, C., & Scheier, M. (1999). A few more themes, a lot more issues: Commentary on the commentaries. In. R. Wyer (Ed.), *Perspectives on behavioral self-regulation* (pp. 261–302). Mahwah, NJ: Erlbaum.

Carver, C., & Scheier, M. (2008). Feedback processes in the simultaneous regulation of action and affect. In J. Shah & W. Gardner (Eds.), *Handbook of motivation science* (pp. 308–324). New York: Guilford.

Church, M., Elliot, A., & Gable, S. (2001). Perceptions of classroom environment, achievement goals, and achievement outcomes. *Journal of Educational Psychology, 93*, 43–54.

Coats, E., Janoff-Bulman, R., & Alpert, N. (1996). Approach versus avoidance goals: Differences in self-evaluation and well-being. *Personality and Social Psychology Bulletin, 22*, 1057–1067.

Corpus, J., McClintic-Gilbert, M., & Hayenga, A. (2009). Within-year changes in children's intrinsic and extrinsic motivational orientations: Contextual predictors and academic outcomes. *Contemporary Educational Psychology, 34*, 154–166.

Covington, M. (1992). *Making the grade: A self-worth perspective on motivation and school reform.* New York: Cambridge University Press.

Covington, M. (2000). Goal theory, motivation, and school achievement: An integrative review. *Annual Review of Psychology, 51*, 171–200.

Crocker, J., & Park, L. (2004). The costly pursuit of self-esteem. *Psychological Bulletin, 130*, 392–414.

Cury, F., Elliot, A., Da Fonseca, D., & Moller, A. (2006). The social-cognitive model of achievement motivation and the 2 × 2 achievement goal framework. *Journal of Personality and Social Psychology, 90*, 666–679.

Dai, D. (2000). To be or not to be (challenged), that is the question: Task and ego orientations among high-ability, high-achieving adolescents. *Journal of Experimental Education, 68*, 311–330.

Daniels, L., Haynes, T., Stupnisky, R., Perry, R., Newall, N., & Pekrun, R. (2008). Individual differences in achievement goals: A longitudinal study of cognitive, emotional, and achievement outcomes. *Contemporary Educational Psychology, 33,* 584–608.

Darnon, C., Harackiewicz, J., Butera, F., Mugny, G., & Quiamzade, A. (2007). Performance-approach and performance-avoidance goals: When uncertainty makes a difference. *Personality and Social Psychology Bulletin, 33,* 813–827.

Darnon, C., Muller, D., Schrager, S., Pannuzzo, N., & Butera, F. (2006). Mastery and performance goals predict epistemic and relational conflict regulation. *Journal of Educational Psychology, 98,* 766–776.

Dolan, A., & McCaslin, M. (2008). Student perceptions of teacher support. *Teachers College Record, 110,* 2423–2437.

Dompnier, B., Darnon, C., & Butera, F. (2009). Faking the desire to learn: A clarification of the link between mastery goals and academic achievement. *Psychological Science, 20,* 939–943.

Dowson, M., & McInerny, D. (2001). Psychological parameters of students' social and work avoidance goals: A qualitative investigation. *Journal of Educational Psychology, 93,* 35–42.

Dresel, M., Martschinke, S., & Kopp, B. (2009, April). *Elementary school teachers' feedback practices, perceived classroom goal structures, and students' personal achievement goals.* Paper presented at the annual meeting of the American Educational Research Association, San Diego, California.

Dweck, C., & Grant, H. (2008). Self-theories, goals, and meaning. In J. Shah & W. Gardner (Eds.), *Handbook of motivation science* (pp. 405–416). New York: Guilford.

Dweck, C., & Leggett, E. (1988). A social-cognitive approach to motivation and personality. *Psychological Review, 95,* 256–273.

El-Alayli, A. (2006). Matching achievement contexts with implicit theories to maximize motivation after failure: A congruence model. *Personality and Social Psychology Bulletin, 32,* 1690–1702.

Elliot, A. (2005). A conceptual history of the achievement goal construct. In A. Elliot & C. Dweck (Eds.), *Handbook of competence and motivation* (pp. 52–72). New York: Guilford.

Elliot, A., & McGregor, H. (2001). A 2×2 achievement goal framework. *Journal of Personality and Social Psychology, 80,* 501–519.

Elliot, A. J., & Murayama, K., (2008). On the measurement of achievement goals: Critique, illustration, and application. *Journal of Educational Psychology, 100,* 613–628.

Emmons, R., & King, L. (1988). Conflict among personal strivings: Immediate and long-term implications for psychological and physical well-being. *Journal of Personality and Social Psychology, 54,* 1040–1048.

Entwistle, N., & Tait, H. (1990). Approaches to learning, evaluations of teaching, and preferences for contrasting academic environments. *Higher Education, 19,* 169–194.

Epstein, J. (1989). Family structures and student motivation: A developmental perspective. In C. Ames & R. Ames (Eds.), *Research on motivation in education. Volume 3. Goals and cognitions* (pp. 259–295). San Diego, CA: Academic Press.

Forster, J., Grant, H., Idson, L., & Higgins, E. T. (2001). Success/failure feedback, expectancies, and approach/avoidance motivation: How regulatory focus moderates classic relations. *Journal of Experimental Social Psychology, 37,* 253–260.

Freitas, A., & Higgins, E. T. (2002). Enjoying goal-directed action: The role of regulatory fit. *Psychological Science, 13,* 1–6.

Fuchs, L., Fuchs, D., Karns, K., Hamlett, C., Katzaroff, M., & Dutka, S. (1997). Effects of task-focused goals on low-achieving students with and without learning disabilities. *American Educational Research Journal, 34,* 513–543.

Gehlbach, H. (2006). How changes in students' goal orientations relate to outcomes in social studies. *Journal of Educational Research, 99,* 358–370.

Gibson, B., & Sachau, D. (2000). Sandbagging as a self-presentational strategy: Claiming to be less than you are. *Personality and Social Psychology Bulletin, 26,* 56–70.

Grant, H., & Dweck, C. (2003). Clarifying achievement goals and their impact. *Journal of Personality and Social Psychology, 85,* 541–553.

Greene, B., Miller, R., Crowson, H., Duke, B., & Akey, K. (2004). Predicting high school students' cognitive engagement and achievement: Contributions of classroom perceptions and motivation. *Contemporary Educational Psychology, 29,* 462–482.

Harackiewicz, J., Barron, K., & Elliot, A. (1998). Rethinking achievement goals: When are they adaptive for college students and why? *Educational Psychologist, 33,* 1–21.

Harackiewicz, J., Barron, K, Pintrich, P., Elliot, A., & Thrash, T. (2002). Revision of achievement goal theory: Necessary and illuminating. *Journal of Educational Psychology, 94,* 638–645.

Harackiewicz, J., Barron, K., Tauer, J., Carter, S., & Elliot, A. (2000). Short-term and long-term consequences of achievement goals: Predicting interest and performance over time. *Journal of Educational Psychology, 92,* 316–330.

Harackiewicz, J., Barron, K., Tauer, J., & Elliot, A. (2002). Predicting success in college: A longitudinal study of achievement goals and ability measures as predictors of interest and performance from freshman year through graduation. *Journal of Educational Psychology, 94,* 562–575.

Harackiewicz, J., & Elliot, A. (1998). The joint effects of target and purpose goals on intrinsic motivation: A mediational analysis. *Personality and Social Psychology, 24,* 675–689.

Harris, A., Yuill, N., & Luckin, R. (2008). The influence of context-specific and dispositional achievement goals on children's paired collaborative interaction. *British Journal of Educational Psychology, 78,* 355–374.

Higgins, E. D. (2006). Value from hedonic experience and engagement. *Psychological Review, 113,* 439–460.

Hole, J., & Crozier, W.R. (2007). Dispositional and situational learning goals and children's self-regulation. *British Journal of Educational Psychology, 77,* 773–786.

Hong, Y. (2001). Chinese students' and teachers' inferences of effort and ability. In F. Salili, C. Chiu, & Y. Hong (Eds.), *Student motivation: The culture and context of learning* (pp. 105–120). New York: Kluwer Academic/ Plenum.

Howell, A., & Buro, K. (2009). Implicit beliefs, achievement goals, and procrastination: A mediational analysis. *Learning and Individual Differences, 19,* 151–154.

Howell, A., & Watson, D. (2007). Procrastination: Associations with achievement goal orientation and learning strategies. *Personality and Individual Differences, 43,* 167–178.

Hulleman, C., Durik, A., Schweigert, S., & Harackiewicz, J. (2008). Task values, achievement goals, and interest: An integrative analysis. *Journal of Educational Psychology, 100,* 398–416.

Jagacinski, C., Madden, J., & Reider, M. (2001). The impact of situational and dispositional achievement goals on performance. *Human Performance, 14,* 321–337.

Juvonen, J., & Wentzel, K. (Eds.). (1996). *Social motivation: Understanding children's school adjustment.* New York: Cambridge University Press.

Kaplan, A. (2004). Achievement goals and intergroup relations. In P. Pintrich & M. Maehr (Eds.), *Motivating students, improving schools: The legacy of Carol Midgley* (pp. 97–136). New York: Elsevier.

Kaplan, A., Gheen, M., & Midgley, C. (2002). Classroom goal structure and student disruptive behavior. *British Journal of Educational Psychology, 72,* 191–211.

Kaplan, A., & Maehr, M. (1999). Enhancing the motivation of African American students: An achievement goal theory perspective. *Journal of Negro Education, 68,* 23–41.

Kaplan, A., & Maehr, M. (2007). The contributions and prospects of goal orientation theory. *Educational Psychology Review, 19,* 141–184.

Kaplan, A., & Middleton, M. (2002). Should childhood be a journey or a race? Response to Harackiewicz et al. (2002). *Journal of Educational Psychology, 94,* 646–648.

Kember, D., Hong, C., & Ho, A. (2008). Characterizing the motivational orientation of students in higher education: A naturalistic study in three Hong Kong universities. *British Journal of Educational Psychology, 78,* 313–329.

Kiviniemi, M., Snyder, M., & Omoto, A. (2002). Too many of a good thing? The effects of multiple motivations on stress, cost, fulfillment, and satisfaction. *Personality and Social Psychology Bulletin, 28,* 732–743.

Kurman, J. (2006). Self-enhancement, self-regulation and self-improvement following failures. *British Journal of Social Psychology, 45,* 339–356.

Lau, S., & Nie, Y. (2008). Interplay between personal goals and classroom goal structures in predicting student outcomes: A multilevel analysis of person-context interactions. *Journal of Educational Psychology, 100,* 15–29.

Lemos, M. (1996). Students' and teachers' goals in the classroom. *Learning and Instruction, 6,* 151–171.

Leondari, A., & Gonida, E. (2007). Predicting academic self-handicapping in different age groups: The role of personal achievement goals and social goals. *British Journal of Educational Psychology, 77,* 595–611.

Levy, I., Kaplan, A., & Patrick, H. (2004). Early adolescents' achievement goals, social status, and attitudes toward cooperation with peers. *Social Psychology of Education, 7,* 127–159.

Levy-Tossman, I., Kaplan, A., & Assor, A. (2007). Academic goal orientations, multiple goal profiles, and friendship intimacy among early adolescents. *Contemporary Educational Psychology, 32,* 231–252.

Liem, A., Lau, S., & Nie, Y. (2008). The role of self-efficacy, task value, and achievement goals in predicting learning strategies, task disengagement, peer relationship, and achievement outcome. *Contemporary Educational Psychology, 33,* 486–512.

Lin, Y., McKeachie, W., & Kim, Y. (2003). College student intrinsic and/or extrinsic motivation and learning. *Learning and Individual Differences, 13,* 251–258.

Linnenbrink, E., & Pintrich, P. (2002). Achievement goal theory and affect: An asymmetrical bidirectional model. *Educational Psychologist, 37,* 69–78.

Lopez, D. F. (1999). Social cognitive influences on self-regulated learning: The impact of action-control beliefs and academic goals on achievement-related outcomes. *Learning and Individual Differences, 11,* 301–319.

Louro, M., Pieters, R., & Zeelenberg, M. (2007). Dynamics of multiple-goal pursuit. *Journal of Personality and Social Psychology, 93,* 174–193.

Maehr, M., & Midgley, C. (1996). *Transforming school cultures.* Boulder, CO: Westview Press.

Marsh, H., Kong, C., & Hau, K. (2001). Extension of the internal/external frame of reference model of self-concept formation: Importance of native and nonnative languages for Chinese students. *Journal of Educational Psychology, 93,* 543–553.

Martin, A., Marsh, H., Williamson, A., & Debus, R. (2003). Self-handicapping, defensive pessimism, and goal orientation: A qualitative study of university students. *Journal of Educational Psychology, 95,* 617–628.

McCrea, S. (2008). Self-handicapping, excuse making, and counterfactual thinking: Consequences for self-esteem and future motivation. *Journal of Personality and Social Psychology, 95,* 274–292.

McGregor, H., & Elliot, A. (2002). Achievement goals as predictors of achievement-relevant processes prior to task engagement. *Journal of Educational Psychology, 94,* 381–395.

Meece, J. (1994). The role of motivation in self-regulated learning. In D. Schunk & B. Zimmerman (Eds.), *Self-regulation of learning and performance: Issues and educational applications* (pp. 25–44). Hillsdale, NJ: Erlbaum.

Meece, J., Herman, P., & McCombs, B. (2003). Relations of learner-centered teaching practices to adolescents' achievement goals. *International Journal of Educational Research, 39,* 457–475.

Meece, J., & Holt, K. (1993). A pattern analysis of students' achievement goals. *Journal of Educational Psychology, 85,* 582–590.

Middleton, M., Kaplan, A., & Midgley, C. (2004). The change in middle school students' achievement goals in mathematics over time. *Social Psychology of Education, 7,* 289–311.

Midgley, C. (Ed.). (2002). *Goals, goal structures, and patterns of adaptive learning.* Mahwah, NJ: Erlbaum.

Midgley, C., Kaplan, A., & Middleton, M. (2001). Performance-approach goals: Good for what, for whom, under what circumstances, and at what cost? *Journal of Educational Psychology, 93,* 77–86.

Miller, R., Greene, B., Montalvo, G., Ravindran, B., & Nichols, J. (1996). Engagement in academic work: The role of learning goals, future consequences, pleasing others, and perceived ability. *Contemporary Educational Psychology, 21,* 388–422.

Miserandino, M., (1996). Children who do well in school: Individual differences in perceived competence and autonomy in above-average children. *Journal of Educational Psychology, 88,* 203–214.

Murphy, P. K., & Alexander, P. (2000). A motivated exploration of motivation terminology. *Contemporary Educational Psychology, 25,* 3–53.

Newstead, S., Franklyn-Stokes, & Armstead, P. (1996). Individual differences in student cheating. *Journal of Educational Psychology, 88,* 229–241.

Nicholls, J. (1984). Achievement motivation: Conceptions of ability, subjective experience, task choice, and performance. *Psychological Review, 91,* 328–346.

Nicholls, J. (1989). *The competitive ethos and democratic education.* Cambridge, MA: Harvard University Press.

Nolen, S. (1988). Reasons for studying: Motivational orientations and study strategies. *Cognition and Instruction, 5,* 269–287.

Okun, M., Fairholme, C., Karoly, P., Ruehlman, L., & Newton, C. (2006). Academic goals, goal process cognition, and exam performance among college students. *Learning and Individual Differences, 16,* 255–265.

Ommundsen, Y., Haugen, R., & Lund, T. (2005). Academic self-concept, implicit theories of ability, and self-regulation strategies. *Scandanavian Journal of Education Research, 49,* 461–474.

Ommundsen, Y., & Kvalo, S. (2007). Autonomy-mastery, supportive or performance focused? Different teacher behaviours and pupils' outcomes in physical education. *Scandinavian Journal of Educational Research, 51,* 385–413.

Park, L., Crocker, J., & Kiefer, A. (2007). Contingencies of self-worth, academic failure, and goal pursuit. *Personality and Social Psychology Bulletin, 33,* 1503–1517.

Patrick, H., Anderman, L., Ryan, A., Edelin, K., & Midgley, C. (2001). Teachers' communication of goal orientations in four fifth-grade classrooms. *Elementary School Journal, 102,* 35–58.

Patrick, H., & Ryan, A. (2009). What do students think about when evaluating their classrooms' mastery goal structure? An examination of young adolescents' explanations. *Journal of Experimental Education, 77,* 99–124.

Payne, S., Satoris, S., & Beaubien, J. (2007). A meta-analytic examination of the goal orientation nomological net. *Journal of Applied Psychology, 92,* 128–150.

Pintrich, P. (2000). Multiple goals, multiple pathways: The role of goal orientation in learning and achievement. *Journal of Educational Psychology, 92,* 544–555.

Pintrich, P. (2003). A motivational science perspective on the role of student motivation in learning and teaching contexts. *Journal of Educational Psychology, 95,* 667–686.

Pomerantz, E., Saxon, J., & Oishi, S. (2000). The psychological trade-offs of goal investment. *Journal of Personality and Social Psychology, 79,* 617–630.

Poortvliet, P. M., Janssen, O., VanYperen, N., & Van de Vliert, E. (2007). Achievement goals and interpersonal behavior: How mastery and performance goals shape information exchange. *Personality and Social Psychology Bulletin, 33,* 1435–1447.

Roney, C., & O'Connor, M. (2008). The interplay between achievement goals and specific goals in determining performance. *Journal of Research in Personality, 42,* 482–489.

Rozendaal, J. S., Minnaert, A., & Boekaerts, M. (2003). Motivation and self-regulated learning in secondary vocational education: information-processing type and gender differences. *Learning and Individual Differences, 13,* 273–289.

Ryan, A., & Patrick, H. (2001). The classroom social environment and changes in adolescents' motivation and engagement during middle school. *American Educational Research Journal, 38,* 437–460.

Schraw, G., Wadkins, T., & Olafson, L. (2007). Doing the things we do: A grounded theory of academic procrastination. *Journal of Educational Psychology, 99,* 12–25.

Senko, C., Durik, A., & Harackiewicz, J. (2008). Historical perspectives and new directions in achievement and goal theory: Understanding the effects of mastery and performance-approach goals. In J. Shah & W. Gardner (Eds.), *Handbook of motivation science* (pp. 100–113). New York: Guilford.

Senko, C., & Harackiewicz, J. (2005). Regulation of achievement goals: The role of competence feedback. *Journal of Educational Psychology, 97,* 320–326.

Senko, C., & Miles, K. (2008). Pursuing their own learning agenda: How mastery-oriented students jeopardize their class performance. *Contemporary Educational Psychology, 33,* 561–583.

Sheldon, K., & Elliot, A. (1999). Goal striving, need satisfaction, and longitudinal well-being: The self-concordance model. *Journal of Personality and Social Psychology, 76,* 482–497.

Shim, S., & Ryan, A. (2005). Changes in self-efficacy, challenge avoidance, and intrinsic value in response to grades: The role of achievement goals. *Journal of Experimental Education, 73,* 333–349.

Shim, S., Ryan, A., & Anderson, C. (2008). Achievement goals and achievement during early adolescence: Examining time-varying predictor and outcome variables in growth-curve analysis. *Journal of Educational Psychology, 100,* 655–671.

Sideridis, G. (2006). Goal orientations and strong oughts: Adaptive or maladaptive forms of motivation for students with and without suspected learning disabilities? *Learning and Individual Differences, 16,* 61–77.

Simons, J., Dewitte, S., & Lens, W. (2004). The role of different types of instrumentality in motivation, study strategies, and performance: Know why you learn, so you'll know what you learn! *British Journal of Educational Psychology, 74,* 343–360.

Snyder, C., Shorey, H., Cheavens, J., Pulvers, K., Adams, V., & Wiklund, C. (2002). Hope and academic success in college. *Journal of Educational Psychology, 94,* 820–826.

Solmon, M. (1996). Impact of motivational climate on students' behaviors and perceptions in a physical education setting. *Journal of Educational Psychology, 88,* 731–738.

Somuncuoglu, Y., & Yildirim, A. (1999). Relationship between achievement goal orientations and use of learning strategies. *Journal of Educational Research, 92,* 267–277.

Stornes, T., & Ommundsen, Y. (2004). Achievement goals, motivational climate and sportspersonship: A study of young handball players. *Scandinavian Journal of Educational Research, 48,* 205–221.

Tapola, A., & Niemvirta, M. (2008). The role of achievement goal orientations in students' perceptions of and preferences for classroom environment. *British Journal of Educational Psychology, 78,* 291–312.

Theeboom, M., DeKnop, P., & Weiss, M. (1995). Motivational climate, psychological responses, and motor skill development in children's sport: A field-based intervention study. *Journal of Sport and Exercise Psychology, 17,* 294–311.

Thomas, C., & Gadbois, S. (2007). Academic self-handicapping: The role of self-concept clarity and students' learning strategies. *British Journal of Educational Psychology, 77,* 101–119.

Thompson, T., & Musket, S. (2005). Does priming for mastery goals improve the performance of students with an entity view of ability? *British Journal of Educational Psychology, 75,* 391–409.

Thrash, T., & Elliot, A. (2001). Delimiting and integrating achievement motive and goal constructs. In A. Efklides, J. Kuhl, & R. Sorrentino (Eds.), *Trends and prospects in motivation research* (pp. 3–21). Boston: Kluwer.

Todorovich, J., & Curtner-Smith, M. (2003). Influence of the motivational climate in physical education on third grade students' task and ego orientations. *Journal of Classroom Interaction, 38,* 36–46.

Tuominen-Soini, H., Salmela-Avo, K., & Niemivirta, M. (2008). Achievement goal orientations and subjective well-being: A person-centred analysis. *Learning and Instruction, 18,* 251–266.

Turner, J., & Meyer, D. (1999). Integrating classroom context into motivation theory and research: Rationales, methods, and implications. In T. Urdan (Ed.), *The role of context* (Vol. 11 in the *Advances in motivation and achievement* series, pp. 87–121). Stamford, CT: JAI.

Turner, J., Midgley, C., Meyer, D., Gheen, M., Anderman, E., Kang, Y., & Patrick, H. (2002). The classroom environment and students' reports of avoidance strategies in mathematics: A multi method study. *Journal of Educational Psychology, 94,* 88–106.

Urdan, T. (1997). Achievement goal theory: Past results, future directions. In P. Pintrich & M. Maehr (Eds.), *Advances in motivation and achievement* (Vol. 10, pp. 99–141). Greenwich, CT: JAI.

Urdan, T. (Ed.). (1999). *The role of context* (Volume 11 in the *Advances in motivation and achievement* series). Stamford, CT: JAI.

Urdan, T. (2001). Contextual influences on motivation and performance: An examination of achievement goal structures. In F. Salili, C. Chiu, & Y. Hong (Eds.), *Student motivation: The culture and context of learning* (pp. 171–201). New York: Kluwer/Plenum.

Urdan, T. (2004). Using multiple methods to assess students' perceptions of classroom goal structures. *European Psychologist, 9,* 222–231.

Utman, C. (1997). Performance effects of motivational state: A meta-analysis. *Personality and Social Psychology Review, 1,* 170–182.

Valle, A., Cabanach, R., Nunez, J., Gonzalez-Pienda, J., Rodriguez, S., & Pineiro, I. (2003). Multiple goals, motivation and academic learning. *British Journal of Educational Psychology, 73,* 71–87.

Vansteenkiste, M., Simons, J., Lens, W., Soenens, B., Matos, L., & Lacante, M. (2004). Less is sometimes more: Goal content matters. *Journal of Educational Psychology, 96,* 755–764.

VanYperen, N. (2006). A novel approach to assessing achievement goals in the context of the 2 x 2 framework: Identifying distinct profiles of individuals with different dominant achievement goals. *Personality and Social Psychology Bulletin, 32,* 1432–1445.

Vaughn, L., Baumann, J., & Klemann, C. (2008). Openness to experience and regulatory focus: Evidence of motivation from fit. *Journal of Research in Personality, 42,* 886–894.

Veermans, M., & Järvelä, S. (2004). Generalized achievement goals and situational coping in inquiry learning. *Instructional Science, 32,* 269–291.

Vrugt, A., & Oort, F. (2008). Metacognition, achievement goals, study strategies and academic achievement: Pathways to achievement. *Metacognition and Learning, 3,* 123–146.

Wentzel, K. (1999). Social-motivational processes and interpersonal relationships: Implications for understanding motivation at school. *Journal of Educational Psychology, 91,* 76–97.

Wentzel, K., & Wigfield, A. (1998). Academic and social motivational influences on students' academic performance. *Educational Psychology Review, 10,* 155–175.

White, P., Sanbonmatsu, D., Croyle, R., & Smittipatana, S. (2002). Test of socially motivated underachievement: "Letting up" for others. *Journal of Experimental Social Psychology, 38,* 162–169.

Witkow, M., & Fuligni, A. (2007). Achievement goals and daily school experiences among adolescents with Asian, Latino, and European-American backgrounds. *Journal of Educational Psychology, 99,* 584–596.

Wolters, C. (2003). Understanding procrastination from a self-regulated learning perspective. *Journal of Educational Psychology, 95,* 179–187.

Wolters, C. (2004). Advancing achievement goal theory: Using goal structures and goal orientations to predict students' motivation, cognition, and achievement. *Journal of Educational Psychology, 96,* 236–250.

Worth, K., Sullivan, H., Hertel, A., Jeffery, R., & Rothman, A. (2005). Avoidance goals can be beneficial: A look at smoking cessation. *Basic and Applied Social Psychology, 27,* 107–116.

Yeo, G., Sorbello, T., Koy, A., & Smillie, L. (2008). Goal orientation profiles and task performance growth trajectories. *Motivation and Emotion, 32,* 296–309.

5

Rebuilding Discouraged Students' Confidence and Willingness to Learn

Certainly, it is unfair to force tortoises to race against hares. Hares will become lazy and fall asleep while tortoises will become discouraged at the impossibility of winning. Both, however, can benefit from a system that helps all participants become better runners.

If the goal is maximum performance from all *students, the schools must provide hope to all students that increased effort can result in success.* (Raffini, 1988, pp. 13–14; emphasis in original)

Some of your students will achieve less than most of their classmates, even if you meet their individual needs effectively and they progress as rapidly as they can. You can help protect their confidence as learners by establishing the kind of learning community described in chapter 2 and consistently implementing the curriculum, instruction, and assessment principles put forth in chapters 3 and 4. Even so, these students may need additional motivational support. Also, many will bring into your classroom motivational problems developed through prior experiences with failure and its consequences. These problems may continue unless you address them effectively.

This chapter considers four types of expectancy-related motivational problems:

1. students with limited ability who have difficulty keeping up, develop chronically low expectations, and become resigned to failure;
2. students whose failure attributions or ability beliefs make them susceptible to learned helplessness in failure situations;
3. students who are obsessed with self-worth protection and thus focus on performance goals but not learning goals; and
4. students who underachieve due to a desire to avoid responsibilities.

Students who do not put forth much effort because they do not find school very meaningful or worthwhile also require special motivational attention. However, their problems lie in the value aspects rather than the expectancy aspects of motivation (see chapter 10).

SUPPORTING THE MOTIVATION OF LOW ACHIEVERS

Some students continuously struggle to keep up, due to limitations in ability or to learning disabilities that impede their progress. For example, they may be able to decode text, yet not understand and remember enough of what they read to learn efficiently through independent study. Or, they may know basic number facts but have difficulty generating solutions to application problems. As these students fall behind, it becomes more difficult to teach them using instructional materials and methods developed for the grade level. Some may be able to keep up if provided with tutoring or other special help, but others may begin to require individualized materials and instruction.

If you are able to provide them with sufficient instructional support, slow learners can make steady progress and achieve enough to satisfy both you and themselves, even though they may remain at or near the bottom of the class in overall achievement. However, if they often become frustrated because they cannot handle tasks or get help when they need it, or if they frequently feel humiliated because they are not keeping up, they may begin to show *failure syndrome symptoms*. That is, they may lose their motivation to persist with learning efforts and instead begin to give up quickly at the first sign of failure. Or, they may become more concerned with covering up their confusion than with learning what the activity is intended to teach. Some may begin to withdraw into passivity rather than participate in lessons, to leave items blank or simply guess at answers instead of seeking help, or to develop behavior problems. At this point, *low achievement* due to limited ability becomes compounded by *underachievement* due to motivational problems.

Strategies for Helping Low Achievers

Theorists and researchers who discuss strategies for teaching low achievers tend to disagree about what can be expected from these students and how much effort should be devoted to their needs relative to the needs of the rest of the class. However, reviews of this literature do converge on certain strategies, especially providing tutorial help to low achievers and individualizing their assignments.

McIntyre (1989) culled four sets of suggestions from a variety of sources. First, *individualize activities and assignments*: reduce the length and difficulty levels of the tasks that you assign to struggling students; use multisensory input sources to reduce their need to learn from texts; build assignments around their interests; make sure that assignments are well structured and within their ability level; and make sure that the first part of the assignment is easy or familiar enough to provide initial success experiences.

Second, *provide directions to structure tasks* for low achievers: have them repeat the instructions to make sure they know what to do; model the task for them by thinking out loud as you perform demonstrations; train them in methods of self-instructional guidance; outline what must be done to achieve the objectives; and set time limits within which the work should be done, preferably generous limits that allow these students to "beat the clock."

Third, *provide for assistance or tutoring* from yourself or an aide, adult volunteer, older student, or classmate. Rephrase questions or provide hints when these students are unable to respond; praise them when they do well; have them revise work that is unacceptable; reassure them that help is available if needed; sit them among average (not superior) classmates with whom they enjoy friendly relationships, and ask these classmates to help keep the low achievers "on track" by providing help and reminders of assignments and due dates; and set up a "study buddy" system to encourage low achievers to collaborate with a neighborhood friend during study sessions at their homes.

Fourth, *maintain motivation*. Provide encouragement and positive comments on papers; help low achievers to establish realistic goals and evaluate their accomplishments; call attention to their successes and send home positive notes; encourage them to focus on trying to surpass their previous day's or week's performance rather than to compete with classmates; use performance contracting methods; and give marks and report card grades on the basis of effort and production rather than in relation to the rest of the class.

Along with many of the strategies mentioned by McIntyre, Abbott (1978) included: keep directions simple, if necessary by dividing the task into parts; seat the student toward the front of the class and maintain frequent eye contact; provide extra assignments that address learning needs and allow the student to earn extra credit; and keep in close communication with tutors, to make sure that the tutoring focuses on primary needs and that you keep abreast of progress and problems.

Margolis and McCabe (2006) developed a set of principles for motivating struggling readers that included using materials and assignments that promote successful performance, increasing expectations of success by ensuring adequate background and vocabulary, and teaching these students to make facilitative attributions. They suggested that reading materials might be too difficult for struggling readers if they cannot recognize at least 95% of the words and answer at least 75% of questions about the content. To help get them ready for reading, you might read critical portions of the material to them and then have them retell it in their own words, pair them with more advanced readers to read to one another prior to group lessons, have them preview materials and generate a list of words with which they want help, give them brief summaries of material written at lower reading levels and review the summaries with them, or send home materials that parents can use to help them learn key words or develop background knowledge related to upcoming reading.

When they are successful, help them attribute this success to their own effort and persistence (You stuck to it and didn't give up), correct selection and application of a strategy (You examined the pages for clues to figure out the hard words), and growth in modifiable abilities (You're getting better everyday at reading and understanding what you read). When they struggle, help them to attribute their failures to inadequate effort and persistence (if relevant), incorrect selection or application of a strategy, and the need to learn modifiable abilities. Other recommendations included: identify what struggling readers are doing right and complement them with specific feedback; supplement difficult text materials with graphic organizers; make it easy for them to request and get help when they need it; and scaffold their reading by teaching them specific coping strategies and providing outlines, study guides, or other resources.

Low achievers may benefit from strategies used in *mastery learning* approaches: make success likely by giving them tasks that they should be able to handle, provide them with individualized tutoring as needed, and allow them to contract for a particular level of performance and then continue to study, practice, and take tests until that level is achieved. By virtually guaranteeing success, this approach builds confidence and increases willingness to take the risks involved in adopting challenging goals (Grabe, 1985). For more information about mastery learning, see Box 5.1.

Good and Brophy (2008) reviewed research indicating that low achievers need frequent

---

Box 5.1   Mastery Learning

Mastery learning adjusts whole-class pacing by allowing slower students more time, and usually providing them with tutoring or other special assistance, to enable them to learn material that classmates have mastered more quickly. Originally mastery learning emphasized individualized tutoring, but the approach has since been adapted for use in tandem with whole-class or group-based instruction (Anderson, 1985; Bloom, 1980; Levine, 1985).

Mastery learning principles are often used with curricula that feature clearly specified learning objectives, preset mastery performance standards, and frequent assessment using criterion- referenced tests. The heart of mastery learning is the cycle of teaching, testing, reteaching, and retesting. Students are informed of the unit's objectives and then receive instruction designed to enable them to master those objectives. Upon completion of instruction and related practice activities, the students take mastery tests. Those who achieve preset performance standards (usually, passing at least 80% of the items) are certified as having mastered the unit and then move on to the next unit, or more typically, work on enrichment activities or activities of their own choosing until the entire class is ready to move on. Meanwhile, students who do not meet mastery criteria receive corrective instruction and additional practice before their mastery levels are assessed again. Theoretically, cycles of assessment and reteaching would go on until all students reached mastery, but in practice, attempts to bring students to mastery usually cease after the second test, and the class then moves on to the next unit.

Mastery Learning methods increase, often dramatically, the percentage of students who master basic objectives. They benefit low achievers by providing extra time and instruction to enable them to master more content than they would otherwise, and this additional mastery is likely to bring motivational benefits as well (Guskey & Pigott, 1988; Kulik, Kulik, & Bangert-Drowns, 1990). However, the approach is time consuming and often viewed as impractical by teachers (Kurita & Zarbatany, 1991).

Also, its potential benefits for slower learners may be counterbalanced by deficits to faster learners, unless the needs of all students in the classroom are taken into account in designing the system (Livingston & Gentile, 1996). Activities planned for faster learners should be selected for sound pedagogical reasons and not as mere time fillers to give them something to do while they wait for slower students to catch up. A feasible adaptation of the mastery learning approach may be to identify those learning objectives that seem most essential and see that all of your students master them, while tolerating more variable performance on objectives that are less essential. You then can supplement the basic curriculum with enrichment opportunities that classmates work on individually or in groups during times when you are busy teaching a remedial or enrichment lesson to a small group of students.

---

monitoring and supplementary tutoring from their teacher (or an adequate substitute), not just exposure to so-called individualized instructional materials. Too many of these materials are restricted to low-level repetitive tasks that amount to busy work rather than truly remedial instruction. Also, low achievers often need to be retaught using varied and enriched forms of instruction, not just to be recycled through the original instruction followed by additional drill and practice.

Other strategies included: collect books and instructional materials that address content taught at your grade but are written at easier reading levels; tutor slow learners in independent reading and study skills, not just in subject-matter content; provide them with study guides and related learning supports; and combine empathy for these students with determination to see that they meet established learning goals.

Findings from the Classroom Strategy Study

I collected advice on teaching low achievers as part of the Classroom Strategy Study. For this study, 98 K–6 teachers were interviewed concerning their strategies for working with 12 categories of students who present chronic achievement, motivation, or behavior problems (Brophy, 1996). Half of these teachers had been rated as outstanding in their ability to teach such students effectively, whereas the other half had been rated as average. Analyses focused on common themes in the teachers' responses, especially those of the higher rated teachers.

Concerning low achievers, these teachers' responses centered around the following principles: focus on providing academic help; supplement this with counseling or motivational support if needed; provide extra monitoring, feedback, and tutoring; enlist help from peers, parents, or other students or adults; and view low achievers as challenges to your professionalism as a teacher rather than as candidates for retention in grade or transfer into special education.

At first, I was surprised that the higher rated teachers emphasized providing low achievers with academic help, not motivational support. However, follow-up analyses indicated that much of the intended motivational support reported by lower rated teachers amounted to ineffectual attempts at encouragement. The difference is illustrated in the following examples of two teachers' handling of a situation in which a student is "stuck" on a math problem.

Here is how the situation might be handled effectively:

Stuent: I can't do Number 4.
Teacher: What part don't you understand?
Student: I just can't do it, it's too hard!
Teacher: I know you can do part of it because you've done the first three problems correctly. The fourth one is similar, but just a little more complicated. You start out the same way, but there's one extra step. Review the first three; then see if you can figure out Number 4. I'll come back in a few minutes to see how you are doing.

Compare this with the following less effective scenario:

Student: I can't do Number 4.
Teacher: You can't! Why not?
Student: I just can't do it, it's too hard!
Teacher: Don't say you can't do it—we never say we can't do it. Did you try hard?
Student: Yes, but I can't do it.
Teacher: You did the first three; maybe if you worked a little longer you could do the fourth. Why don't you do that and see what happens?

The first teacher communicated positive expectations and provided a specific suggestion about how to proceed, yet did not give the answer or do the work. In giving feedback about performance on the first three problems, she was more specific in noting that the answers were correct and attributing this success to the student's knowledge and abilities, thus supporting the student's self-efficacy beliefs. She also provided some instructional assistance, and in the process, embedded some socialization of the student's expectancy-related beliefs. The second teacher provided neither useful instructional guidance nor a credible basis for encouragement. Instead, she communicated half-hearted and somewhat contradictory expectations, leaving the student with no reason to believe that further effort would succeed.

Concluding Comments About Low Achievers

In elaborating on principles culled from the research literature and from interviewing experienced teachers, I would stress the following suggestions for teaching low achievers. First, accept the situation and make the best of it. *Identify the most essential (although not necessarily low-level or easily attained) objectives of each curriculum unit and make sure that low achievers master these, even if this means skipping other things. Also, help them to view their situation realistically, yet still try to progress as best they can* (Fosterling & Morgenstern, 2002). Let them know that their work is acceptable to you so long as they apply themselves, even if they are unable to keep up with most of their classmates. *Elicit their commitment to establishing and working on feasible goals.* Explain that extra practice may be necessary for them, even if it is not enjoyable (you empathize, but you want to see them learn, too).

Low achievers need extra help, especially individualized tutoring. However, their tutors will need to be patient and caring. If you use peer or cross-age tutors, make sure that they understand this. Also, arrange for low achievers to tutor peers or younger students. This will help them to master material more thoroughly and also avoid making them always the receivers but never the givers of help (Bar-Eli & Raviv, 1982; Shanahan, 1998; Topping & Ehly, 1998).

As soon as your class settles into assignments, give personal attention to low achievers to make sure that they understand what to do and get off to a good start. Don't let them "practice errors" or end up turning in completed papers that are "all wrong." If they are not ready for extended independent work, build toward it through successive approximations. If they don't read well, help them learn to do so. At other times, engage them in worthwhile learning activities that do not require significant reading skills or that can be explained to them orally. In mathematics, use concrete manipulables to help them grasp basic concepts. In language arts and the content subjects, ask them questions that focus on key ideas and require them to compose thoughtful oral or written responses. Then provide feedback focused on their grasp of the key ideas rather than on the formal correctness of their language or writing.

In effect, "cut a deal" with low achievers: It's OK if they can't keep up with the rest of the class, because you have special goals and activities for them. You will be pleased if they accomplish these goals and are prepared to help them do so, but they will have to work persistently and hold up their end, too. You are demanding effort and progress, but not necessarily the attainment of grade-level norms or the performance of the class as a whole.

RESOCIALIZING STUDENTS WITH "FAILURE SYNDROME" PROBLEMS

Failure syndrome is one of several terms that teachers use to describe students who approach assignments with very low expectations and tend to give up at the first sign of difficulty. Other such terms include "low self-concept," "defeated," and "frustrated." Unlike low achievers, who often fail despite their best efforts, failure syndrome students often fail needlessly because they do not invest their best efforts. Instead, they begin half-heartedly and give up easily. Motivation theorists use other terms to describe these students, such as "low self-efficacy," "entity theorist," or "attributes failure to internal, stable, and uncontrollable causes" (i.e., low ability).

Motivation theorists also refer to *learned helplessness*. Compared to students who develop a more generalized failure syndrome, students who develop learned helplessness can be found at all levels of academic ability, and their helplessness may appear only in particular achievement situations. For example, students may show learned helplessness symptoms in mathematics but not in English, or vice versa (Galloway, Leo, Rogers, & Armstrong, 1996).

Students who are prone to learned helplessness may not always develop anxiety in response to evaluation cues or begin all tasks with failure expectations. As long as they do not question their ability to succeed, they may be able to handle even challenging activities. However, when they encounter frustration, they are prone to develop "catastrophic" reactions, followed by deterioration in the quality of their coping (Dweck & Elliott, 1983).

Butkowsky and Willows (1980) noted the following tendencies in learned helplessness students confronted with challenging tasks:

1. they had low initial expectancies for success,
2. they gave up quickly when they encountered difficulty,
3. they attributed their failures to lack of ability rather than to controllable causes such as insufficient effort or inappropriate strategies,
4. they attributed their successes to external and uncontrollable causes (luck, easy task) rather than to their own abilities and efforts, and
5. following failure, they made unusually severe reductions in their estimates of future success probabilities.

Some students, especially in the early grades, show failure syndrome tendencies as part of a larger pattern of emotional immaturity that includes low frustration tolerance and avoidance, inhibition, or overdependency on adults as reactions to stress. Other students acquire failure expectations from their parents or teachers. Parents sometimes lead their children to believe that school will be difficult for them or that they have only limited academic potential, especially if the children's first few report cards contain low grades (Entwisle & Hayduk, 1982).

Teachers communicate low expectations through a variety of direct and indirect means, especially to students who have been assigned labels such as "learning impaired" (Brophy, 1998; Weinstein, 2002) or who come from minority or low socioeconomic status families (McKown & Weinstein, 2008; Mertzman, 2008; see Box 5.2).

However, most failure syndrome problems develop through social learning mechanisms centered around experiences with failure. Children usually begin school with enthusiasm, but many begin to find it psychologically threatening. They are accountable

Box 5.2   How Some Teachers Communicate Low Expectations to Their Low Achievers

Like some students who have become discouraged by repeated academic failures, some teachers become discouraged by repeated instructional failures and begin to show the same kinds of symptoms: lowered self-efficacy perceptions, reduced expectations for future success, attribution of failure to external and uncontrollable causes, and a shift from persistent and adaptive problem-solving strategies to half-hearted and maladaptive ones. In extreme cases, teachers "burn out" and display such behavior most of the time with most of their students. More typically, however, teachers develop learned helplessness in teaching certain students, particularly low achievers who continue to struggle to keep up with the rest of the class. Some teachers redouble their efforts and make the best of the situation, but others gradually give up and begin just going through the motions with these students, communicating their low expectations in the process.

For example, most teachers know that low achievers need patience and encouragement. However, Brophy and Good (1970) observed teachers who were not practicing these seemingly obvious strategies, at least not toward the end of the school year, when the observations were made. Consider these teachers' behavior when they called on a student to answer a question and the student made no response, said "I don't know," or answered incorrectly. At these times, the teachers could either stay with the student by repeating the question, giving a clue, or asking a new question, or else give up on the student by giving the answer or calling on someone else. Observations indicated that these teachers were twice as likely to stay with high-achieving students than with low-achieving students.

There also were differences in the teachers' rates of praise and criticism of students' responses. Good answers from high achievers were praised 12% of the time, but good answers from low achievers were praised only 6% of the time. Meanwhile, 6% of the high achievers' response failures yielded teacher criticism, whereas this occurred 18% of the time with low achievers. Thus, the students who most needed patience and encouragement often were treated with impatience when they struggled to respond. They also were less likely to be praised when they responded correctly (even though this happened less often), and more likely to be criticized when they were unable to respond correctly (even though this happened more often). Clearly, these teachers had drifted into counterproductive patterns of interacting with their low achievers.

Subsequent research has shown that some teachers do provide their low achievers with patience, encouragement, and support. Other teachers, however, drift into maladaptive patterns. Examples that have been documented in various studies (reviewed by Good and Brophy, 2008) include the following:

1. waiting less time for low achievers to answer a question (before giving the answer or calling on someone else)
2. giving answers to low achievers or calling on someone else rather than trying to improve their responses by giving clues or repeating or rephrasing questions

3. inappropriate reinforcement: rewarding inappropriate behavior or incorrect answers by low achievers
4. criticizing low achievers more often for failure
5. praising low achievers less often for success
6. failing to give feedback following the public responses of low achievers
7. generally paying less attention to low achievers or interacting with them less frequently
8. calling on them less often to respond to questions, or asking them only easier, nonanalytic questions
9. seating them farther away from the teacher
10. generally demanding less from them (attempting to teach them less than they are capable of learning, accepting low-quality or even incorrect responses from them and treating them as if they were correct responses, substituting misplaced sympathy or gratuitous praise for sustained teaching that ultimately leads to mastery)
11. interacting with low achievers more privately than publicly, and monitoring and structuring their activities more closely
12. giving high achievers but not low achievers the benefit of the doubt in grading tests or assignments
13. being less friendly in interactions with low achievers, including less smiling and fewer other nonverbal indicators of support
14. providing briefer and less informative answers to their questions
15. interacting with them in ways that involve less eye contact and other nonverbal communication of attention and responsiveness (e.g., forward lean, positive head nodding)
16. less use of effective but time-consuming instructional methods with low achievers when time is limited
17. less acceptance and use of low achievers' ideas
18. limiting low achievers to an impoverished curriculum (low-level and repetitive content, factual recitation rather than lesson-extending discussion, drill and practice rather than application and higher-level thinking)

Some of these differences are due at least in part to the behavior of the students. For example, if low achievers seldom raise their hands, it is difficult for the teacher to ensure that they get as many response opportunities as high achievers, and if their contributions to lessons are of lower quality, the teacher cannot accept and use their ideas as frequently. Also, some forms of differential treatment may represent appropriate individualizing of instruction. Low achievers may require more structuring of their activities and closer monitoring of their work, for example, and under some circumstances it may make sense to interact with them more privately than publicly or to ask them easier questions. However, these differential patterns are danger signals, especially if the differences are large and occur on many dimensions rather than just one or two. Such differences suggest that a teacher is merely going through the motions of instructing low achievers, without seriously working to help them achieve their potential.

for responding to questions, completing assignments, and taking tests. Their performances are monitored, graded, and reported to their parents. Failure carries the danger of public humiliation.

Given these conditions, it is not surprising that students who have experienced a continuing history of failure, or a recent progressive cycle of failure, begin to believe that they lack the ability to succeed. Once this belief takes root, failure expectations and other self-conscious thoughts begin to disrupt their concentration and limit their coping abilities. Eventually they abandon serious attempts to master tasks and begin to concentrate on preserving their self-esteem in their own eyes and their reputations in the eyes of others.

Failure syndrome problems that took a long time to develop are not going to disappear overnight. For example, it is important to avoid communicating low expectations, but simply communicating high expectations or even giving more demanding assignments is not likely to accomplish much unless the higher expectations are accompanied by scaffolding to help the students meet them (Miller, Heafner, & Massey, 2009; Warrican, 2006). These students are likely to need initial successes and other confidence-building experiences, assistance in setting goals and planning strategies, modeling of productive responses to frustration, and so on (Koh, 2006). Successful teachers develop "academic momentum" with these students, starting by establishing supportive relationships and creating trust, then encouraging them to increasingly adopt challenging goals and develop strategic plans, persist through difficulties, and ask for help when they need it, until they eventually become more willing and self-regulated learners (Strahan, 2008).

Strategies for Helping Students with Failure Syndrome Problems

Failure syndrome problems become especially deeply rooted in entity theorists who attribute their failures to limited ability. They can get so accustomed to this idea that they become anxious or at best only cautiously hopeful in response to feedback indicating that they might have more ability than they thought (Plaks & Stecher, 2007). Teachers need to keep chipping away at these entrenched entity beliefs, using practices that promote an incremental theory of ability. These include portraying ability as achieved through effort and growing with learning, portraying effort as necessary for everyone (not just less able students), portraying challenge as a way to learn and thus something to be valued, and praising for process, strategy, or effort rather than talent or intelligence (Dweck & Master, 2008).

Students with failure syndrome problems need assistance in regaining self-confidence and developing strategies for coping with failure and persisting when they experience difficulty. Reviewers have identified many strategies for accomplishing these goals. Wlodkowski (1978) suggested that teachers

- guarantee that failure syndrome students experience success regularly (by seeing that they know what to do before asking them to do it independently, providing immediate feedback to their responses, and making sure that they know the evaluation criteria);
- give them recognition for real effort, show appreciation for their progress, and project positive expectations;
- emphasize personal causation by allowing them to set goals, make choices, and use self-evaluation procedures to check their progress; and

- use group process methods to enhance positive self-concepts (activities that orient these students toward appreciating their positive qualities and getting recognition for them from their peers).

Swift and Spivack (1975) suggested most of these same strategies. In addition, they recommended exploring with these students which classroom situations they find comfortable and which anxiety-provoking, and why; helping them to gain better insight into and sense of control over their anxieties; and reassuring them of your willingness to help. Forms of help might include minimizing evaluation and competition, marking and grading with emphasis on noting successes rather than failures, using individualized instructional materials, and calling on these students only when they volunteer or are likely to be able to respond successfully (or alternatively, when you have prepared them through advance warnings or study suggestions).

McIntyre (1989) suggested reading and discussing with these students *The Little Engine That Could*; praising them for attempting difficult tasks as well as for whatever successes they achieve; requiring them to complete (or at least to make a serious attempt to complete) a certain portion of an assignment before asking you for help; pointing out the similarities between the present task and work completed successfully earlier; and allowing them extra time if necessary but insisting that their work be completed.

More specific and elaborated suggestions have emerged from research on particular theoretical concepts or treatment approaches. Many of these involve what Ames (1987) called "cognition retraining." Three prominent approaches to cognition retraining are attribution retraining, efficacy training, and strategy training (see Table 5.1).

TABLE 5.1
Cognition Retraining Methods

Cognition retraining methods use combinations of direct instruction, modeling with verbalized self-instruction (thinking aloud), coaching, and scaffolded practice under controlled task conditions to teach students productive strategies for responding to achievement situations and help them learn to self-regulate their application of these strategies. Different cognitive retraining methods have been developed to pursue different goals by focusing on different aspects of students' coping strategies.

Training Method	Primary Focus	Major Goals
Attribution retraining	Performance attributions (especially explanations for and strategies for recovering from failures	Teach students to attribute failures to remediable causes (insufficient knowledge or effort, reliance on an inappropriate strategy) and thus to persist with problem-solving efforts instead of giving up
Efficacy training	Self-efficacy perceptions	Teach students to set and strive to attain reasonable proximal goals and approach ultimate goals through successive approximations, and in the process, to appreciate their developing expertise in the domain
Strategy training	Domain- and task-specific skills and strategies	Help students to acquire and self-regulate their use of effective learning and problem-solving strategies, through comprehensive instruction that includes attention to propositional knowledge (what to do), procedural knowledge (how to do it) and conditional knowledge (when and why to do it)

Attribution retraining.   Attribution retraining involves inducing changes in students' tendencies to attribute their failures to lack of ability rather than to remediable causes such as insufficient effort or inappropriate strategies. Typical treatments use modeling, socialization, practice, and feedback to teach students to (a) concentrate on the task rather than worry about failing, (b) cope with failures by retracing their steps to find their mistake or analyzing the problem to find another approach, and (c) attribute their failures to insufficient effort, lack of information, or ineffective strategies rather than to lack of ability (Craske, 1998; Dweck & Elliott, 1983; Hall et al., 2007; Haynes, Daniels, Stupinsky, Perry, & Hladkyj, 2008). Failure syndrome students are especially likely to benefit from programs that combine attribution retraining with training in strategies for accomplishing tasks (Borkowski, Weyhing, & Carr, 1988; Carr & Borkowski, 1989; Dresel & Haugwitz, 2008; Margolis & McCabe, 2006; Robertson, 2000; VanOverwalle, Segebarth, & Goldschstein, 1989).

Research on attribution retraining has led to significant advances over the common-sense idea of programming students for success. This work has shown that *success alone is not enough*—even a steady diet of success will not change an established pattern of learned helplessness. In fact, *a key to successful attribution retraining is controlled exposure to failure*. Rather than being exposed only to "success models" who handle tasks with ease, students are exposed to "coping models" who struggle to overcome mistakes before finally succeeding. In the process, they *model constructive responses to mistakes* as they occur (e.g., by verbalizing continued confidence, attributing failures to remediable causes, and coping by first diagnosing the source of the problem and then correcting the mistake or approaching the problem in a different way). Following exposure to such modeling, students begin to work on the tasks themselves. Conditions are arranged so that they sometimes experience difficulty or failure, but accompanied by coaching that encourages them to respond constructively rather than becoming frustrated and giving up (Borkowski, Weyhing, & Carr, 1988; Schunk, 1999).

Successful socialization of motivational attitudes and beliefs includes attention to frustration tolerance, persistence, and other constructive responses to failure. This is quite different from programming for success, especially attempts to enable students to avoid experiencing failure altogether (Clifford, 1984; Rohrkemper & Corno, 1988).

Early attribution retraining programs stressed attribution of failures to insufficient effort (I didn't try hard enough or concentrate carefully enough). More recent programs stress attributing failures to using ineffective strategies (I went about the problem in the wrong way; I misunderstood the directions; I made a mistake at a certain point that negated my efforts thereafter). This shift recognizes the fact that most students at least subjectively put forth their best efforts, so that failure results not from lack of effort but from a limited repertoire of relevant knowledge and coping strategies. That is, they do everything they know how to do but still don't succeed, and they don't know how to diagnose and overcome the problem on their own. For these students, attributing their failures to lack of effort is both inaccurate and insulting, but attributing them to ineffective strategies is reassuring and re-energizing. By consistently modeling strategy attributions and helping your students to determine when and why they are succeeding and failing, you can promote the core idea that effort + strategy = success (Kozminsky & Kozminsky, 2003).

Efficacy training.   Efficacy training also involves exposing students to a planned set of challenges and providing them with modeling, instruction, and feedback. However, whereas attribution retraining programs were developed specifically for learned helplessness students and thus focus on teaching constructive response to failure, efficacy training programs were developed primarily for low achievers who have become accustomed to failure and developed generalized low self-concepts of ability. Consequently, efficacy training helps students to set realistic goals and pursue them with the recognition that they have the ability (efficacy) needed to reach these goals if they apply reasonable effort (Gerhardt & Brown, 2006; Koestner et al., 2006).

Schunk (1985) identified the following practices as effective for *increasing students' self-efficacy perceptions*:

- cognitive modeling that includes verbalization of task strategies, the intention to persist despite problems, and confidence in achieving eventual success;
- explicit training in strategies for accomplishing the task;
- performance feedback that points out correct operations, remedies errors, and reassures students that they are developing mastery;
- attributional feedback that emphasizes successes and attributes them to the combination of sufficient ability and reasonable effort;
- encouraging students to set goals prior to working on tasks (goals that are challenging but attainable, phrased in terms of specific performance standards and oriented toward immediate short-term outcomes);
- focusing feedback on how students' current performance surpasses their prior attainments rather than on how they compare with other students; and
- supplying rewards contingent on actual accomplishment (not just task participation).

Strategy training.   In strategy training, modeling and instruction are used to teach problem-solving strategies that students will need to handle tasks successfully. *Strategy training is a component of good cognitive skills instruction to all students; it is not primarily a remedial technique. However, it is especially important to use with discouraged students* who have not developed effective learning and problem-solving strategies on their own but who can learn them through modeling and explicit instruction.

Poor readers, for example, can be taught reading comprehension strategies such as identifying the purpose of the assignment and keeping it in mind when reading, activating relevant background knowledge, identifying major points and attending to the outline and flow of content, monitoring their understanding by generating and trying to answer questions about the content, and drawing and testing inferences by making interpretations, predictions, and conclusions (Duffy & Roehler, 1989; Meichenbaum & Biemiller, 1998; Palincsar & Brown, 1984; Paris & Paris, 2001; Pressley, 1998; Raphael, 1984). Poor writers can be taught strategies for planning, drafting, and revising text (De La Paz & Graham, 2002; Graham, Harris, Fink-Chorzempa, & MacArthur, 2003) Two keys to effective strategy instruction are that (a) it includes attention not just to propositional knowledge (what to do) but also to procedural knowledge (how to do it) and conditional knowledge (when and why to do it) and (b) it includes cognitive modeling (thinking out loud that makes visible the covert thought processes that guide problem solving).

Programs also have been developed for training students in general study skills (Devine, 1987) and learning strategies (Weinstein & Mayer, 1986). Cognitive elements of these programs include instruction in strategies such as rehearsal (repeating material to remember it more effectively), elaboration (putting material into one's own words and relating it to prior knowledge), organization (outlining material to highlight its structure and remember it), comprehension monitoring (keeping track of the strategies used and the degree of success achieved with them, and adjusting strategies accordingly), and affect monitoring (maintaining concentration and task focus, minimizing performance anxiety and fear of failure). The programs also contain affective management components similar to those used in attribution retraining and efficacy training programs (McCombs & Pope, 1994; Rohrkemper & Corno, 1988; Toland & Boyle, 2008), and they also are likely to be more successful when learners observe a coping model improve gradually than when they observe a success model perform flawlessly (Zimmerman & Kitsantas, 2002). A comprehensive cognition retraining program for failure syndrome students will include attention to both the cognitive and the affective aspects of task engagement and persistence.

Dweck and Elliott (1983) recommended that strategy training programs encourage incremental rather than entity views of ability. This involves: acting more as a resource person than a judge, focusing students more on learning processes than on outcomes, reacting to errors as natural and useful parts of the learning process rather than as evidence of failure, stressing effort over ability and individualized standards over normative standards when giving feedback, and using intrinsic rather than extrinsic motivational strategies.

Findings from the Classroom Strategy Study

Teachers interviewed for the Classroom Strategy Study (Brophy, 1996) also were asked about strategies for teaching failure syndrome students. The higher rated teachers suggested a combination of support, encouragement, and task assistance to shape gradual improvement in work habits. They would make it clear that these students were expected to work conscientiously and persistently so as to turn in assignments done completely and correctly. However, they also would reassure the students that they would be given work that they could do, monitor their progress and provide any needed help, and reinforce them by praising their successes, calling attention to their progress, and providing them with opportunities to display their accomplishments publicly. Such special treatment would be faded gradually as the students gained confidence and began to work more persistently and independently.

None of these teachers were familiar with the term "efficacy training," but most of them intuitively favored strategies stressed in efficacy training programs (negotiating agreement to strive to meet specific proximal goals, giving feedback indicating that the student has the ability to succeed). However, their responses appeared less satisfactory from the standpoints of attribution retraining and remediation of learned helplessness. Most mentioned support, encouragement, and instructional assistance but did not say much about learned helplessness symptoms (e.g., catastrophic reactions to frustration, giving up quickly, attributing failure to lack of ability). Nor was there much mention of modeling to teach better coping strategies or of teaching the student how to persist in the face of difficulty. Thus, it bears repeating that *failure syndrome students, especially those with learned helplessness symptoms, do not so much need a steady diet of success as they need to learn how to cope with frustration and failure productively.*

Concluding Comments About Failure Syndrome Students

Failure syndrome students require patience and persistence, especially if their problems have been developing for years. You cannot quickly "cure" those who have become convinced that they lack ability by providing a few success experiences and words of encouragement. However, you can begin to undermine their certainty of failure and get them moving toward confidence by making sure that they are prepared to handle the challenges you present, teaching them needed task skills and more general learning and study strategies, and applying the principles involved in attribution retraining, efficacy training, and related treatment approaches.

Whether or not you undertake such treatments formally, you can include relevant messages in your everyday interactions with failure syndrome students. Much of this socialization can be subtle and informal, as in the earlier example of effective handling of a student who was "stuck" on a math problem (see p. 105). Students treated in this manner every day should slowly but surely begin to gain confidence and become less prone to catastrophic reactions to failure.

Additionally, help these students to recognize when they need help and become willing to get help when they need it. Give them procedures to follow when they encounter difficulties, starting with strategies for diagnosing possible causes of their problem and perhaps solving it on their own. If they cannot solve the problem on their own, they then should seek help. You may need to encourage them to do so, because most are not willing to seek help overtly (Good, Slavings, Harel, & Emerson, 1987; Newman & Goldin, 1990; van der Meij, 1988).

Therefore, give them methods to use to signal their need for help unobtrusively. Then, get to them as quickly as you can to provide the help they need. Also, teach them to distinguish when they do and do not need help. If they have not used the strategies you taught them and thus have not yet determined whether they can handle the problem on their own, require them to engage these strategies before seeking help. If they really do need help, provide it, but emphasize "instrumental" help (explanations, questions, or hints that will stimulate them to think about the problem and encourage them to work out the rest of it on their own) rather than "executive" help (giving them answers). Instrumental help scaffolds students' problem solving just enough to enable them to make needed connections and construct the knowledge or skill that the task was intended to teach, whereas executive help eliminates the need for further thinking and leaves them possessing correct answers but lacking key understandings (Butler & Neuman, 1995; Nelson-LeGall, 1987).

WEANING STUDENTS AWAY FROM PERFORMANCE GOALS AND OVEREMPHASIS ON SELF-WORTH PROTECTION

Struggling low achievers or students beset with failure syndrome problems are especially likely to focus on performance goals instead of learning goals. However, certain capable or even confident students also may emphasize performance goals, especially as they approach adolescence and become more concerned about social comparison and their reputation. Some may become predisposed toward learned helplessness in a steadily growing range of achievement situations. In other cases, the problem may be less extreme but still worrisome because self-worth preoccupations distract attention from learning goals and cause students to engage in activities using less-than-ideal strategies (Covington, 1992; Crocker & Niiya, 2008; Hansen, 1989; Nicholls, 1989).

Such students may attempt to escape being called on by scrunching down in their seats and avoiding eye contact with you (or by conspicuously waving their hands and looking confident, if they have discovered that this will make you less likely to call on them). If you do call on them and they are not sure how to answer, they may hesitate in the hope that you will help them. Or, they may offer a vague and rambling response in the hope that you will accept it and move on. During work times they may appear to be working thoughtfully when they are actually just guessing at answers or copying from a neighbor. They may procrastinate in getting started and then hurry to finish as time runs out. They may skip items, do the minimum required, or in other ways perform marginally rather than accept the challenge of working up to their capabilities. Or, they may display unrealistic perfectionism by constantly rejecting their partially completed efforts and starting over (thus giving the appearance of commitment to high goals while actually not accomplishing much). These and related stratagems allow students who are obsessed with self-worth protection to go through the motions of achievement striving while actually avoiding acceptance of genuine challenges and arming themselves with excuses for potential failures.

Lehtinen, Vauras, Salonen, Olkinuora, and Kinnunen (1995) described several of these mechanisms in a student named Heli whom they studied between third and sixth grade. Heli was a fluent decoder and viewed herself as one of the top students. However, she had great difficulties with text comprehension, restlessness, and lack of concentration, so her teacher rated her much lower. Fear of failure and symptoms of learned helplessness emerged whenever Heli encountered difficulty in her work or even picked up a cue that the task was going to be difficult. She often complained that a new task was too long, too hard, or that she didn't like it. She would attempt to wheedle help through social dependence strategies (e.g., appealing for help, babyish chatting, or smooth-tongued questioning aimed at eliciting teacher guidance). If this did not succeed, she would escalate to passive avoidance strategies (e.g., absent-minded staring, averting her gaze from the task, or "silent treatment" of the teacher). At other times, she proceeded to more active or manipulative forms of avoidance (e.g., attempting to leave the classroom, engaging in stereotyped rituals or mannerisms, signaling tiredness, or resorting to intensive whining or tantrums).

Heli's symptomatic behaviors typically escalated as long as the stress continued, and sometimes carried over to the next activity. However, they typically disappeared and were replaced by a smiling, cooperative demeanor if the teacher gave up attempts to get more out of her. Over time, Heli perfected her techniques to the point that they were quite successful in limiting her teachers' (and her parents') persistence in seeking to get her to work up to her abilities.

Some students do not usually fear failure and thus are not obsessed with protecting their self-worth, but they are frequently distracted from learning goals by social goals such as trying to please you as the teacher or trying to impress their peers (sometimes by displaying intelligence or task skills, but often by showing off or acting "cool"). To the extent that students are distracted from learning goals by these social concerns, they are less likely to use optimal learning strategies (Lehtinen et al., 1995; Meece & Holt, 1993).

Strategies for Reducing Preoccupation with Self-Worth Protection

The most powerful strategies focus on prevention rather than cure. You can minimize your students' needs for self-worth protection by establishing your classroom as a learning community (chapter 2) and consistently modeling, socializing, and instructing students in ways that orient them toward learning goals rather than performance goals (chapters 3 and 4).

Martin Covington (1992) has experimented with methods for minimizing self-worth protection problems. He recommended the following strategies:

1. *Provide engaging assignments* that appeal to curiosity and personal interests and offer challenging yet manageable goals. To the extent feasible, allow students some choice of tasks and control over the levels of challenge they face (but encourage them to increase levels of challenge in response to increases in their levels of expertise).

2. *Provide sufficient rewards.* Make sure that all students (not just the brighter ones) can earn desired rewards. Also, dispense rewards in ways that reinforce students for setting meaningful goals, posing challenging questions, and working to satisfy their curiosity. Seek to make learning itself a sought-after goal.

3. *Enhance effort-outcome covariation beliefs.* Help students learn to set realistic goals and develop confidence that they can be successful and earn rewards through reasonable effort.

4. *Strengthen the linkage between achievement efforts and self-worth.* Help students learn to take pride in their accomplishments and their developing expertise, and to minimize attention to social comparison.

5. *Promote positive beliefs about ability.* Help students to adopt multidimensional definitions of their abilities and take an incremental rather than an entity view towards them.

6. *Improve teacher-student relations.* Emphasize your role as a resource person who assists these students' learning efforts, not your role as an authority figure who controls their behavior.

Other sources offer similar advice, suggesting the following strategies: Attempt to socialize the students' values and learning goals by helping them see the need for what they are learning in their present and future lives outside of school; teach them cognitive and metacognitive strategies for regulating their learning more effectively, so they will have less need for self-worth protection; encourage them to ask for help when they need it and make it possible for them to get such help without suffering public embarrassment; emphasize cooperative learning and avoid competition; and use individual criterion-referenced grading standards rather than absolute standards or grading on a curve (Adelman & Taylor, 1983; Lehtinen et al., 1995; Nicholls, 1989; Raffini, 1988).

Concluding Comments about Students Obsessed with Self-Worth Protection

I would add the following suggestions about socializing the attitudes and beliefs of students who are obsessed with self-worth protection. First, help these students to understand how this focus ironically limits their current performance and future development (in effect, explain Table 4.1 to them). Help them to appreciate that they develop their abilities only by accepting new challenges: sticking to what is easy and familiar minimizes risk but keeps them standing still while their classmates are moving forward.

Similarly, help them to understand that a focus on competing with peers is ultimately a losing game, even if they win most of the time. It distracts attention from learning efforts and is likely to create problems with peers. It also diverts energies that should be devoted to synthesizing their learning, appreciating its value, and remembering it with an eye toward using it in their lives outside of school. Portfolio assessment and related approaches for focusing on progress over time can be helpful here.

Finally, take seriously these students' needs to look good in public situations. Don't dismiss their fears or suggest that they are groundless. Instead, ask if there are things that you can do to help them feel more comfortable and become more willing to accept genuine challenges. Follow through on any feasible requests. Make sure that your everyday interactions with these students are consistent with the notions that you care about them personally, do not want to embarrass them, and will try to provide any help they may need.

RESOCIALIZING "COMMITTED UNDERACHIEVERS"

Most students with expectancy-related issues would like to achieve more than they do but are hampered by problems described earlier in this chapter. However, you may encounter a few "committed underachievers" who set low goals and resist accepting responsibility for their successes because they do not want to be expected to maintain higher levels of performance. These students need reassurance that they can attain consistent success with reasonable (i.e., not superhuman) effort. Also, help them see that their deliberate underachievement is contrary to their own long-run best interests.

McCall, Evahn, and Kratzer (1992) completed a large study of underachievers, following them into adulthood. As students, they displayed low self-concept, low perception of abilities, unrealistic goal setting, lack of persistence, impulsive rather than thoughtful responses to assignments, social immaturity and poor peer relationships, oppositional and aggressive response to authority, and a tendency to make excuses rather than accept responsibility and make a serious commitment to change.

These school problems were part of a larger syndrome characterized by failure to persist in the face of challenge: Underachievers were less likely to complete college and to display job and marital stability than comparison groups, including a group that earned similar grades but had lower aptitude. Thus, there is no reason to believe that underachievement problems will take care of themselves once underachievers "find what interests them" or "leave school and enter the work world." This type of underachievement syndrome tends to persist if left untreated.

Strategies for Helping Committed Underachievers

McCall and his colleagues also reviewed the treatment literature and concluded that many programs failed to improve achievement because they targeted peripheral symptoms such as self-esteem or social relationships but not the core symptoms of low achievement motivation and the desire to minimize expectations and responsibilities. The best results are obtained with comprehensive programs that address the full range of symptoms and include elements aimed at parents and teachers as well as students. The most common approach is teacher-parent collaboration: the teacher sends home a daily or weekly report of the student's efforts and accomplishments, and the parents withhold or dispense privileges or other rewards contingent on their child's achievement of previously negotiated academic and behavioral goals.

A confrontational strategy.   Mandel and Marcus (1988) described a strategy designed to pressure committed underachievers to stop making excuses and instead begin to take responsibility for applying themselves. These authors argued that less confrontive strategies, such as providing a lot of encouragement or making the work easier or more interesting, will not lead to fundamental change because these students are motivated to minimize expectations and responsibilities. Their approach calls for patiently working through the student's excuses and resistance strategies.

The first step is to ask underachievers whether they want to get better grades (as opposed to announcing that you are going to help them do so). For the overwhelming majority who respond positively, the relationship has now been structured such that it is the responsibility of the student to set goals, whereas your role is to help the student achieve them. Step 2 involves taking stock of progress and problems in each subject, along with any plans the student may have for addressing the problems. At this point, your role is to elicit information nonjudgmentally, without making interpretations or recommendations.

Step 3 involves focusing on specific problems and isolating the student's excuses for them. You ask what problems are getting in the way of better grades, probe for specifics when the student offers only vague generalizations, and if necessary, challenge questionable claims. For example, the student might claim to spend an hour per day studying, but questions about the last few days might establish that the real average is more like 20 minutes. Step 4 involves linking each excuse to its natural consequence by describing (or better yet, eliciting) what will happen if the student does not address this problem effectively. Step 5 involves asking the student to suggest solutions for each identified hindrance to success, then discussing these suggestions to clarify their practicality, anticipate snags, and refine plans. Here, you need to be careful to elicit plans from the student rather than tell the student what to do. Once the student "owns" the goal of better grades, has recognized the connection between current study habits and future consequences, and has identified a specific and workable solution, there is no way to "unrecognize" these connections again. The student must accept personal responsibility for improving the grades.

The sixth step is a call for action ("OK, now what do you propose to do?" followed by questions about specifics). The seventh step is follow-up to assess whether the student has implemented the plan. Given the student's motivation to continue to underachieve, it is likely that the assessment will indicate either that the student continued to underachieve but simply dropped one excuse and substituted another, or else began to achieve in just one area but not in others. This leads to a possibly lengthy Step 8, which involves repeating Steps 3–7 with a different excuse each time. Eventually, the student will run out of excuses and be forced to accept personal responsibility for underachievement.

When this occurs, there may be accompanying reactions such as panic, depression, anxiety, anger, regret, energy toward achievement, confusion, changes in social relationships, or intense introspection. At this point, your role shifts from taking away excuses and pressing for acceptance of responsibility to becoming a supportive, nonjudgmental listener and resource person who helps the student begin to express and struggle with questions such as "Why did I allow myself to get such poor grades?" and "What do I want my future to be?"

Other strategies.   Other sources of advice about coping with underachievers describe strategies that range between the confrontive and the supportive. For example, Blanco and Bogacki (1988) culled the following recommendations from school psychologists: peer and cross-age tutoring; contracts that feature collaboration with the student in setting goals and with the parents in withholding or providing performance-contingent rewards; counseling sessions designed to allow underachievers to vent their concerns but also to pressure them to accept responsibility for their performance and commit themselves to realistic goals; and requiring the students to make up missed homework assignments during recess or after school.

McIntyre (1989) emphasized many of the same strategies, especially contracts and reward systems, collaborative learning with peers, improving performance gradually through successive approximations, and requiring the student to redo shoddy work and complete unfinished work. Other suggestions included:

- small-group cooperative learning methods in which each individual has a unique function to perform (thus creating peer pressure on underachievers to do their part);
- monitoring these students closely and checking back with them frequently to make sure that they stay on task during work times;
- teaching them study habits and self-regulation skills;
- making their work as interesting as possible and helping them to see its current or future application potential, but at the same time making it clear that they are responsible for applying themselves to accomplishing all curricular goals (boredom is not a valid excuse);
- letting them do extra credit work in areas of interest;
- discussing their occupational plans and then helping them to see how academic skills are required in those occupations; and
- soliciting their suggestions about how you might be helpful to them and following through on those that are feasible.

Thompson and Rudolph (1992) developed a similar list and also included:

- increase work production gradually through escalating contracts;
- avoid lecturing, nagging, or threatening;
- where feasible, have underachievers study or at least talk about study habits with a friend who models motivation to learn and conscientious work on assignments;
- reinforce and build on current accomplishments rather than emphasizing past faults and failures; and
- structure the students' work by providing clear instructions and identifying specific goals.

Findings from the Classroom Strategy Study

The higher rated teachers in the Classroom Strategy Study (Brophy, 1996) would be more demanding and less willing to make allowances with students who underachieved because they were unmotivated, compared to students who believed that the work was too difficult for them. Most of these teachers recommended performance contracting and related approaches that call for rewarding unmotivated students if they meet imposed or negotiated performance expectations but punishing them if they do not. However, the higher rated teachers also spoke of *building positive relationships with these students and resocializing their attitudes* by helping them to appreciate the connections between school work and their current or future needs or by stressing the work's potential for enriching their lives. Teachers who believed that devaluing of school work reflects attitudes modeled at home tended to speak of working with the parents, whereas teachers who thought the problem was lack of interest tended to speak of making changes in the curriculum.

Several teachers noted that underachievement problems do not so much indicate alienation from school work as lack of a positive value on it, which leads to a "do as little as you can get away with" attitude. Reward and punishment systems can control work output but socialization is needed to change students' attitudes. The goal is not just to get underachievers to perform more acceptably, but to *teach them to see benefit in school work and take pride in their efforts and successes*. A variation on this idea, expressed by teachers in the early grades, was that underachievers aren't so much alienated as lacking in direction. They need imposition of responsibilities and expectations, at home as well as at school.

Concluding Comments about Underachievers

Themes noted both in the scholarly literature and in the teacher interviews suggest that, until they reach age 10 or so, most underachievers do not systematically avoid responsibility. They may be adult dependent, attention seeking, unprepared to assume responsibilities, or otherwise immature, but not yet systematically working below their potential because they are consciously or unconsciously motivated to do so.

This implies that encouraging and instructional strategies might be more effective with younger underachievers, but confrontive and persuasive strategies might be more effective with older ones. This implication has not been tested directly, but research findings that favor supportive strategies tend to come from the elementary grades, whereas findings that favor confrontive strategies tend to come from junior high and high schools. Thus, it may be best to avoid treating young underachievers as "hardened" cases unless there is clear evidence that they have become so. Instead, give them the benefit of the doubt and treat them as well meaning but in need of socialization and instruction concerning what they will need to do in order to get the most out of lessons and assignments. In short, teach these students about motivation to learn (see chapter 9).

CONCLUSION

The expectancy aspects of student motivation depend less on the degree of objective success that students achieve than on how they view their performance: what they see as possible for them to achieve with reasonable effort, whether or not they define this achievement as success, and whether they attribute their performance to controllable or uncontrollable causes. *The motivation of all students, even the most extreme cases of learned helplessness, is open to reshaping.* Empty reassurances or a few words of encouragement will not do the job, but a combination of appropriately challenging demands, socialization designed to make the students see that success can be achieved with reasonable effort, and coaching them in strategies for self-regulating their learning should be effective.

Students need to learn to view academic frustrations and failures realistically and respond to them adaptively. As Rohrkemper and Corno (1988) pointed out, not only is some failure inevitable, but a manageable degree of failure is desirable. When students are challenged at optimal levels of difficulty, they make mistakes. The important thing about these mistakes is that they trigger informative feedback and students use this feedback to respond to the mistakes with renewed motivation rather than discouragement.

SUMMARY

This chapter suggested strategies for working with four types of expectancy-related motivational problems that require additional attention beyond the preventive strategies discussed in chapters 2–4. *Low achievers* who have difficulty keeping up and have developed chronically low expectations and resignation to failure will require continuous reassurance that they can meet your demands, that you will provide whatever help they may need, and that you appreciate their efforts and accept their progress so long as they continue to put forth reasonable effort. These students will need instructional assistance along with motivational encouragement, and perhaps individualized instructional materials or activities as well. If they are not able to keep up despite their best efforts, at least make sure that they master the most important learning objectives.

Students with failure syndrome problems need attribution retraining, efficacy training, and strategy training to help them learn to cope productively rather than give up when faced with frustration or failure. Bear in mind that even a steady diet of success experiences will not eliminate their potential for catastrophic reactions to failure; they need to realize that they can remain focused on the task and employ strategies for working through such problems, and in the process, increase their levels of knowledge and skill in the domain.

Students obsessed with self-worth protection need help in realizing that this preoccupation is contrary to their own best interests. At the same time, however, communicate empathy with their concerns and willingness to take steps to help them feel more comfortable in the classroom. With less serious cases of students who focus on social goals rather than learning goals, help them to realize that their preoccupation with short-term social goals is keeping them from developing integrated understandings that will provide a basis for applying what they are learning in their lives outside of school.

Finally, *"committed" underachievers* also need help in realizing that their behavior is contrary to their long-run best interests. They need reassurance and perhaps a degree of task assistance in coming to understand that they can expect to enjoy continuous success if they continuously put forth reasonable effort—that you do not expect them to extend themselves to their limits every day. In "hardened" cases that feature work avoidance and excuses, you may need to supplement encouragement and motivational resocialization attempts with pressuring strategies such as home-school collaboration on behavior contracts or the confrontational approach recommended by Mandel and Marcus (1988).

Like people in any setting, students in classrooms pursue multiple goals and experience shifting priorities. Your goal as the teacher is to focus them on learning goals, while minimizing their attention to other goals. Regarding the expectancy aspects of motivation, this means minimizing threats to students' egos or self-worth perceptions. Systematic implementation of the principles outlined in chapters 2–4 will minimize the need for students to worry about embarrassment or self-worth protection. Those who do so anyway will need additional treatment using strategies described in chapter 5.

Chapters 3–5 have addressed the expectancy aspects of motivation. Chapters 6–10 now turn to the value aspects.

REFLECTION QUESTIONS

1. How can teachers keep expectations in the "realistic optimism" zone between counterproductive pessimism on one side and unrealistic optimism on the other? Is this the same as teaching in the zone of proximal development?
2. Why is "let them experience success" an incorrect or at least incomplete remedy for struggling students?
3. What should teachers do about individual differences among learners? (Ignore them? Try to eliminate them? Cater to preferences and build on strengths? Try to remediate weaknesses? Or...?)
4. Would you use mastery learning? If so, when and how? If not, why not?
5. You will need to monitor struggling students closely and be available to provide them with needed assistance. How will you make time to do this?
6. The author recommends making sure that low achievers master the most essential objectives of each unit, even if this means skipping other things. Is this caving in to negative expectations, committing to challenging but realistic goals rather than verbalizing pie-in-the-sky hopes, or what?
7. Supposedly, we are eager to think well of ourselves, even to the point of self-delusion. If so, why do negative self-efficacy perceptions sometimes become firmly rooted and resistant to change?
8. When and how might you set goals for students as a motivational technique? When and why might you avoid this technique?
9. Why can even high achievers develop learned helplessness problems?
10. Why are "coping" models generally more successful than "success" models in attribution retraining?
11. Write out a plan for supporting the mathematics self-efficacy perceptions of students who are struggling in this subject.
12. Why does efficacy training emphasize good modeling, instruction, and feedback about accomplishments instead of "motivational" pep talks?
13. What are the trade-offs embodied in using "safety nets" for struggling students?
14. Write out a plan for coping with resistant students like Heli.
15. What might you say to the parents of committed underachievers in an attempt to enlist their help in changing the students' attitudes and behavior?

REFERENCES

Abbott, J. (1978). *Classroom strategies to aid the disabled learner.* Cambridge, MA: Educators Publishing Service.

Adelman, H., & Taylor, L. (1983). Enhancing motivation for overcoming learning and behavior problems. *Journal of Learning Disabilities, 16,* 384–392.

Ames, C. (1987). The enhancement of student motivation. In M. Maehr & D. Kleiber (Eds.), *Advances in motivation and achievement, Vol. 5: Enhancing motivation* (pp. 123–148). Greenwich, CT: JAI Press.

Anderson, L. (1985). A retrospective and prospective view of Bloom's "learning for mastery." In M. Wang & H. Walberg (Eds.), *Adapting instruction to individual differences* (pp. 254–268). Berkeley, CA: McCutchan.

Bar-Eli, N., & Raviv, A. (1982). Underachievers as tutors. *Journal of Educational Research, 75,* 139–143.

Blanco, R., & Bogacki, D. (1988). *Prescriptions for children with learning and adjustment problems: A consultant's desk reference* (3rd ed.). Springfield, IL: Charles C. Thomas.

Bloom, B. (1980). *All our children learning.* Hightstown, NJ: McGraw-Hill.

Borkowski, J., Weyhing, R., & Carr, M. (1988). Effects of attributional retraining on strategy-based reading comprehension in learning disabled students. *Journal of Educational Psychology, 80,* 46–53.

Brophy, J. (1996). *Teaching problem students.* New York: Guilford.

Brophy, J. (Ed.). (1998). *Advances in research on teaching. Volume 7: Expectations in the classroom.* Greenwich, CT: JAI.

Brophy, J., & Good, T. (1970). Teachers' communication of differential expectations for children's classroom performance: Some behavioral data. *Journal of Educational Psychology, 61,* 365–374.

Butler, R., & Neuman, O. (1995). Effects of task and ego achievement goals on help-seeking behaviors and attitudes. *Journal of Educational Psychology, 87,* 261–271.

Butkowsky, I., & Willows, D. (1980). Cognitive motivational characteristics of children varying in reading ability: Evidence for learned helplessness in poor readers. *Journal of Educational Psychology, 72,* 408–422.

Carr, M., & Borkowski, J. (1989). Attributional training and the generalization of reading strategies with underachieving children. *Learning and Individual Differences, 1,* 327–341.

Clifford, M. (1984). Thoughts on a theory of constructive failure. *Educational Psychologist, 19,* 108–120.

Covington, M. (1992). *Making the grade: A self-worth perspective on motivation and school reform.* Cambridge, UK: Cambridge University Press.

Craske, M. (1998). Learned helplessness, self-worth, motivation and attribution retraining for primary school children. *British Journal of Educational Psychology, 58,* 152–164.

Crocker, J., & Niiya, Y. (2008). Contingencies of self-worth: Implications for motivation and achievement. In M. Maehr, S. Karabenick, & T. Urdan (Eds.), *Social psychological perspectives* (*Advances in motivation and achievement* series, Vol. 15, pp. 49–79). Bingley, UK: Emerald.

De La Paz, S., & Graham, S. (2002). Explicitly teaching strategies, skills, and knowledge: Writing instruction in middle school classrooms. *Journal of Educational Psychology, 94,* 687–698.

Devine, T. (1987). *Teaching study skills: A guide for teachers* (2nd ed.) Boston: Allyn & Bacon.

Dresel, M., & Haugwitz, M. (2008). A computer-based approach to fostering motivation and self-regulated learning. *Journal of Experimental Education, 77,* 3–18.

Duffy, G., & Roehler, L. (1989). The tension between information-giving and mediation: Perspectives on instructional explanation and teacher change. In J. Brophy (Ed.) *Advances in research on teaching: Vol. 1. Teaching for meaningful understanding and self-regulated learning* (pp. 1–33). Greenwich, CT: JAI Press.

Dweck, C., & Elliott, E. (1983). Achievement motivation. In P. Mussen (Ed.), *Handbook of child psychology: Vol. 4. Socialization, personality, and social development* (pp. 643–691). New York: Wiley.

Dweck, C., & Master, A. (2008). Self-theories motivate self-regulated learning. In D. Schunk & B. Zimmerman (Eds.), *Motivation and self-regulated learning: Theory, research, and applications* (pp. 31–51). Mahwah, NJ: Erlbaum.

Entwisle, D., & Hayduk, L. (1982). *Early schooling: Cognitive and affective outcomes.* Baltimore: Johns Hopkins University Press.

Forsterling, F., & Morgenstern, M. (2002). Accuracy of self-assessment and task performance: does it pay to know the truth? *Journal of Educational Psychology, 94,* 576–585.

Galloway, D., Leo, E., Rogers, C., & Armstrong, D. (1996). Maladaptive motivational style: The role of domain specific task demand in English and mathematics. *British Journal of Educational Psychology, 66,* 197–207.

Gerhardt, M., & Brown, K. (2006). Individual differences in self-efficacy development: The effects of goal orientation and affectivity. *Learning and Individual Differences, 16,* 43–59.

Good, T., & Brophy, J. (2008). *Looking in classrooms* (10th ed.). Boston: Allyn & Bacon.

Good, T., Slavings, R., Harel, K., & Emerson, H. (1987). Student passivity: A study of question-asking in K-12 classrooms. *Sociology of Education, 60,* 181–199.

Grabe, M. (1985). Attributions in a mastery instructional system: Is an emphasis on effort harmful? *Contemporary Educational Psychology, 10,* 113–126.

Graham, S., Harris, K., Fink-Chorzempa, B., & MacArthur, C. (2003). Primary grade teachers' instructional adaptations for struggling writers: A national survey. *Journal of Educational Psychology, 95,* 279–292.

Guskey, T., & Piggott, T. (1988). Research on group-based mastery learning programs: A meta-analysis. *Journal of Educational Research, 81,* 197–216.

Hall, N., Perry, R., Goetz, T., Ruthig, J., Stupnisky, R., & Newall, N. (2007). Attributional retraining and elaborative learning: Improving academic development through writing-based interventions. *Learning and Individual Differences, 17,* 280–290.

Hansen, D. (1989). Lesson evading and lesson dissembling: Ego strategies in the classroom. *American Journal of Education, 97,* 184–208.

Haynes, T., Daniels, L., Stupnisky, R., Perry, R., & Hladkyj, S. (2008). The effect of attributional retraining on mastery and performance motivation among first-year college students. *Basic and Applied Social Psychology, 30,* 198–207.

Koestner, R., Horberg, E., Gaudreau, P., Powers, T., DiDio, P., Bryan, C., et al. (2006). Bolstering implementation plans for the long haul: The benefits of simultaneously boosting self-concordance or self-efficacy. *Personality and Social Psychology Bulletin, 32,* 1–12.

Koh, J. (2006). Motivating students of mixed efficacy profiles in technology skills classes: A case study. *Instructional Science, 34,* 423–449.

Kozminsky, E., & Kozminsky, L. (2003). Improving motivation through dialogue. *Educational Leadership, 61,* 50–54.

Kulik, C., Kulik, J., & Bangert-Drowns, R. (1990). Effectiveness of mastery learning programs: A meta-analysis. *Review of Educational Research, 60,* 265–299.

Kurita, J., & Zarbatany, L. (1991). Teachers' acceptance of strategies for increasing students' achievement motivation. *Contemporary Educational Psychology, 16,* 241–253.

Lehtinen, E., Vauras, M., Salonen, P., Olkinuora, E., & Kinnunen, R. (1995). Long-term development of learning activity: Motivational, cognitive, and social interaction. *Educational Psychologist, 30,* 21–35.

Levine, D. (1985). *Improving student achievement through mastery learning programs.* San Francisco: Jossey-Bass.

Mandel, H., & Marcus, S. (1988). *The psychology of underachievement: Differential diagnosis and differential treatment.* New York: Wiley.

Margolis, H., & McCabe, P. (2006). Motivating struggling readers in an era of mandated instructional practices. *Reading Psychology, 27,* 435–455.

McCall, R., Evahn, C., & Kratzer, L. (1992). *High school underachievers.* Newbury Park, CA: Sage.

McCombs, B., & Pope, J. (1994). *Motivating hard to reach students.* Washington, DC: American Psychological Association.

McIntyre, T. (1989). *A resource book for remediating common behavior and learning problems.* Boston: Allyn & Bacon.

McKown, C., & Weinstein, R. (2008). Teacher expectations, classroom context, and the achievement gap. *Journal of School Psychology, 46,* 235–261.

Meece, J., & Holt, K. (1993). A pattern analysis of students' achievement goals. *Journal of Educational Psychology, 85,* 582–590.

Meichenbaum, D., & Biemiller, A. (1998). *Nurturing independent learners: Helping students take charge of their learning.* Cambridge, MA: Brookline.

Mertzman, T. (2008). Individualizing scaffolding: teachers' literacy interruptions of ethnic minority students and students from low socioeconomic backgrounds. *Journal of Research in Reading, 31,* 183–202.

Miller, S., Heafner, T., & Massey, D. (2009). High-school teachers' attempts to promote self-regulated learning: "I may learn from you, yet how do I do it?" *Urban Review, 41,* 121–140.

Nelson-LeGall, S. (1987). Necessary and unnecessary help seeking in children. *Journal of Genetic Psychology, 148,* 53–62.

Newman, R., & Goldin, L. (1990). Children's reluctance to seek help with homework. *Journal of Educational Psychology, 82,* 92–100.

Nicholls, J. (1989). *The competitive ethos and democratic education.* Cambridge, MA: Harvard University Press.

Palincsar, A., & Brown, A. (1984). Reciprocal teaching of comprehension-fostering and comprehension-monitoring activities. *Cognition and Instruction, 1,* 117–175.

Paris, S., & Paris, A. (2001). Classroom applications of research on self-regulated learning. *Educational Psychologist, 36,* 89–101.

Plaks, J., & Stecher, K. (2007). Unexpected improvement, decline, and stasis: A prediction confidence perspective on achievement success and failure. *Journal of Personality and Social Psychology, 93,* 667–684.

Pressley, M. (1998). *Reading instruction that works: The case for balanced teaching.* New York: Guilford.

Raffini, J. (1988). *Student apathy: The protection of self-worth.* Washington, DC: National Education Association.

Raphael, T. (1984). Teaching learners about sources of information for answering comprehension questions. *Journal of Reading, 27,* 303–311.

Robertson, J. (2000). Is attribution training a worthwhile classroom intervention for K-12 students with learning difficulties? *Educational Psychology Review, 12,* 111–134.

Rohrkemper, M., & Corno, L. (1988). Success and failure on classroom tasks: Adaptive learning and classroom teaching. *Elementary School Journal, 88,* 299–312.

Schunk, D. (1985). Self-efficacy and classroom learning. *Psychology in the Schools, 22,* 208–223.

Schunk, D. (1999). Social-self interaction and achievement behavior. *Educational Psychologist, 34,* 219–227.

Shanahan, T. (1998). On the effectiveness and limitations of tutoring in reading. *Review of Research in Education, 23,* 217–234.

Strahan, D. (2008). Successful teachers develop academic momentum with reluctant students. *Middle School Journal, 39,* 4–12.

Swift, M., & Spivack, G. (1975). *Alternative teaching strategies: Helping behaviorally troubled children achieve.* Champaign, IL: Research Press.

Thompson, C., & Rudolph, L. (1992). *Counseling children* (3rd ed.). Pacific Grove, CA: Brooks/Cole.

Toland, J., & Boyle, C. (2008). Applying cognitive behavioural methods to retrain children's attributions for success and failure in learning. *School Psychology International, 29,* 286–302.

Topping, S., & Ehly, S. (1998). *Peer-assisted learning.* Mahwah, NJ: Erlbaum.

van der Meij, H. (1988). Constraints on question-asking in classrooms. *Journal of Educational Psychology, 80,* 401–405.

VanOverwalle, F., Segebarth, K., & Goldschstein, M. (1989). Improving performance of freshmen through attributional testimonies from fellow students. *British Journal of Educational Psychology, 59,* 79–85.

Warrican, S. J. (2006). Promoting reading amidst repeated failure: Meeting the challenges. *High School Journal, 90,* 33–43.

Weinstein, C., & Mayer, R. (1986). The teaching of learning strategies. In M. Wittrock (Ed.), *Handbook of research on teaching* (3rd ed., pp. 315–327). New York: Macmillan.

Weinstein, R. (2002). *Reaching higher: The power of expectations in schooling.* Cambridge, MA: Harvard University Press.

Wlodkowski, R. (1978). *Motivation and teaching: A practical guide.* Washington, DC: National Education Association.

Zimmerman, B., & Kitsantas, A. (2002). Acquiring writing revision and self-regulatory skill through observation and emulation. *Journal of Educational Psychology, 94,* 660–668.

6

Providing Extrinsic Incentives

THE VALUE ASPECTS OF STUDENTS' MOTIVATION

The expectancy × value model implies the need to attend to the value aspects of students' motivation, not just the expectancy aspects. Otherwise, your students may be asking themselves, "I know I can do this, but where is my motivation?" To be motivated to do something, we need good reasons for doing it, not just confidence that we can do it if we try.

Subjective task value has three major components: *attainment value* (the importance of attaining success on the task in order to affirm our self-concept or our core needs, values, or identities); *intrinsic or interest value* (the enjoyment that we get from engaging in the task); and *utility value* (the role that engaging in the task may play in helping us to reach larger goals such as advancing our career; Eccles, 2009; Wigfield & Eccles, 2000). This is a useful classification scheme, but for applications to the classroom I would expand it to place more emphasis on the cognitive aspects of motivation to learn school content. A broadened version would include *experiencing the satisfaction of achieving understanding or skill mastery* under attainment value, *aesthetic appreciation of the content or skill* under intrinsic value, and *awareness of the role of the learning in improving the quality of one's life or making one a better person* under utility value.

Attention to the value aspects of motivation is needed to broaden from focus on achievement situations that feature relatively specific goals to consideration of the complete range of learning situations. Attribution theory, self-efficacy theory, and even goal theory apply most clearly to achievement situations that call for some particular performance that will be evaluated with reference to success criteria. In contrast, theories dealing with the value aspects of motivation apply not only to these achievement situations but also to self-guided exploration and discovery learning, curricular enrichment activities, interest-driven reading, and other activities that offer opportunities for learning but do not involve striving to accomplish a particular goal.

The expectancy aspects of motivation feature beliefs about performance attainment (Can I succeed on this task? Why did I achieve the level of success that I did?). In contrast, the value aspects feature beliefs about the reasons for engaging in the first place

(Why should I care about this activity? What benefits will I obtain from engaging in it?). Traditionally, teachers have been advised to address value questions either by offering incentives for good performance (extrinsic motivation approach) or by teaching content and designing activities that students find enjoyable (intrinsic motivation approach).

Strategies reflecting these two general approaches are described here in chapter 6 (extrinsic strategies) and in chapters 7 and 8 (intrinsic strategies). Chapter 9 presents strategies for implementing a third approach: stimulating students' motivation to learn. Coverage of the value aspects of motivation then concludes in chapter 10 with discussion of strategies for working with alienated or unmotivated students who do not value schooling.

The ordering of these five chapters (and of the book as a whole) has been established to facilitate the coherent flow of ideas, and has nothing to do with the relative importance of their content. Each chapter contributes to a network of ideas that, taken as a whole, constitutes a comprehensive approach to motivating students. A complete system that incorporates the whole network will be more powerful than a partial system that omits parts of it.

COMMON BELIEFS ABOUT REWARDS

To begin thinking about the effects of extrinsic incentives, consider Students A and B: A and B are both fourth graders who enjoy and do well in school, although they approach school and relate to their teachers in different ways. For example, B did all this week's reading on the solar system knowing that completing assignments pleases the teacher. B made a couple of points during class discussion so the teacher would know B had done the reading. A also finished the reading because A got really interested in knowing all about the solar system. A continued to ask questions during the discussion, even after some of the other kids seemed tired of the topic. Since A knows grades don't always reflect work quality, A isn't that interested in grades and doesn't pay much attention to them, but B pays close attention to grades and uses them as a gauge by which to judge how B has been doing on recent work... (Flink, Boggiano, Main, Barrett, & Katz, 1992, p. 208)

Given this information, how would you rate Students A and B in basic ability, degree of responsibility as students, or overall effort in school work? Which student would exert greater effort following failure? Which would show enhanced performance following success?

Barrett and Boggiano (1988) put these questions to groups of parents and college students. They found that the majority of both groups believed that extrinsically motivated Student B would exert more effort after failure, show enhanced performance following success, exert more overall effort in school work, and take more responsibility for completing work than intrinsically motivated Student A. However, they believed that B would have lower self-esteem than A. Only the last belief is supported by research comparing extrinsically and intrinsically motivated students.

Other studies presented descriptions of students displaying either high or low intrinsic interest in various learning activities, then asked parents or college students to rate the effectiveness of four social control techniques (rewards, reasoning, punishment, or noninterference) for maximizing the student's enjoyment or interest. Both groups rated rewards as more effective than the other three strategies. Most adults believe that rewards are effective, not only as incentives for motivating students to put forth effort, but also for stimulating their intrinsic interest in the activities (Boggiano, Barrett, Weiher, McClelland, & Lusk, 1987; Flink et al., 1992).

You probably share these beliefs in the effectiveness of rewards as motivators, at least in part. Do you? Before reading on, pause to take stock. Is using rewards an effective way to motivate students? A desirable way? Are rewards helpful for certain students or situations but not for others? If so, why?

CONTROVERSY OVER EXTRINSIC REWARDS IN EDUCATION

In some respects, extrinsic motivation strategies are the simplest, most direct, and most adaptable of the methods for addressing the value aspects of motivation. These strategies do not attempt to increase the value that students place on the activity itself. Instead, they link successful completion of the activity to delivery of consequences that students already do value. By reminding students that successful completion is instrumental to accomplishment of some valued goal (where this contingency exists naturally) or by establishing an incentive system that offers extrinsic rewards contingent on successful completion, you can spur students to invest more effort than they might invest otherwise. *Rewards are one proven way to spur students to put forth effort.*

However, from the standpoint of most motivational theorists, this is control of behavior, not motivation of learning (see Box 6.1). Some educators oppose extrinsic rewards on principle, viewing them as bribing students for doing what they should be doing anyway because it is in the best interests of themselves or of society. Kohn (1993) claimed that the effectiveness of rewards has been exaggerated and that rewarding students for learning undermines their intrinsic interest in the content. The subtitle of his book refers to "gold stars, incentive plans, A's, praise, and other bribes." More recently, educators have become concerned about the extrinsic pressures on teachers and students exerted by high-stakes testing programs (Nichols & Berliner, 2008), which have led to policies calling for offering monetary rewards for students who do well on the tests (Farley & Rosario, 2008).

Early Findings

Research findings from the 1970s and 1980s provided what appeared to be strong support for opponents of extrinsic rewards. These findings indicated that if you begin to reward people for doing what they already were doing for their own reasons, you may decrease their intrinsic motivation to continue that activity in the future (Deci & Ryan, 1985; Heckhausen, 1991; Lepper & Greene, 1978). Furthermore, to the extent that you focus their attention on the reward rather than the activity, their performance tends to deteriorate (Condry & Chambers, 1978). They do whatever will garner them the most rewards with the least effort, rather than trying to do the job as well as they can to create a high quality product. If allowed to choose, they select tasks that will maximize their access to rewards over tasks that offer more challenge or opportunities for them to develop their knowledge or skills (e.g., choose "easy A" courses over more demanding courses so as to preserve high grade point averages).

For a time, it was thought that these undesirable outcomes were inherent in the use of

Box 6.1   A Note on Reinforcement and Behavior Modification

Chapter 6 includes a section on using rewards as incentives but does not include sections on contingency contracting, behavior modification, token economy programs, or related applications of applied behavior analysis used to bring selected behaviors under stimulus control. This is because these methods are conceived and implemented as behavioral control strategies rather than as motivation strategies. They work by making desired behavior (e.g., careful and persistent work on assignments) instrumental to attainment of contingent extrinsic rewards, usually by making this contingency explicit to students in advance. Heavy emphasis on these behavioral control techniques, and in particular, use of a token economy or some other earned-credits incentive system as one's basic approach to classroom management, is in many respects incompatible with the strategies that have emerged from research on motivation in education.

You will need to choose between a behavioral control system or a student motivational system as your basic approach to classroom management and motivational issues. The two are not completely incompatible, so if you choose one as your basic approach, you can still supplement it with selected strategies drawn from the other. You cannot implement each approach fully, however, because there are too many contradictions. This book is for teachers who opt for the motivational approach, which I recommend for two primary reasons. First, although it is more difficult to learn to implement consistently, the motivational approach is nevertheless more feasible for most teachers. In order to use reinforcement to shape students' behavior in ways that reflect consistent application of behavior modification principles, teachers have to be in position to supply reinforcement when and where it is needed. This is not possible in regular classrooms where teachers work with 20 or more students. It may be possible in special classrooms with very low student-to-teacher ratios, but even there it will require heavy reliance on programmed instructional materials, rather than tutoring or small-group instruction from the teacher, as the primary approach to curriculum and instruction (thus leaving the teacher free to circulate, monitor progress, and dispense rewards). A great deal of classroom research suggests that students need active instruction from their teachers, not solitary work with instructional materials, in order to make good achievement progress (Good & Brophy, 2008).

Second, the motivational approach seems clearly preferable to the behavioral control approach when students' long-run best interests are taken into account. Even when behavioral control methods work effectively, they accomplish only temporary, situational, and external control over students' behavior (Stipek, 1996, 2002). This behavior can and often does change drastically when the incentive system is terminated or when the students are in situations in which the system is not operative. In contrast, motivational approaches are designed not just to induce situational compliance but to develop attitudes, values, beliefs, and self-regulated learning strategies that students will use in and out of school throughout their lives.

> Although this book clearly focuses on motivational strategies, it discusses the use of contracts in chapter 5 and the use of rewards in chapter 6. Note, however, that it advocates using these strategies in ways that deemphasize their behavioral control aspects to make them compatible with more purely motivational strategies. In particular, it calls for encouraging students to commit themselves to challenging yet realistic goals and helping them to appreciate their progress and accomplishments, while avoiding placing too much emphasis on reinforcement contingencies or salient rewards.

rewards (or other extrinsic pressures—see Box 6.2). Later work clarified that *the effects of rewards depend on what rewards are used and how they are presented*. Decreases in performance quality and intrinsic motivation are most likely when rewards have the following characteristics:

High salience (the rewards are very attractive or are presented in ways that call attention to them)

Noncontingency (the rewards are given for mere participation in the activity, rather than being contingent on achieving specific goals)

Unnatural/unusual (the rewards are artificially tied to behaviors as control devices, rather than being natural outcomes of the behaviors)   book-it

Attempts to use rewards to motivate students often have these characteristics. For example, a well-known program that awards coupons for free pizzas to students who read books incorporates all three of them. Pizzas are very attractive rewards to most children, the program artificially makes reading a certain number of books instrumental to receiving the pizzas, and the pizzas are awarded merely for certifying that the books have been read (not for reading them carefully, responding to them thoughtfully, or taking something meaningful away from the experience). This contingency could undermine students' intrinsic motivation to read because it implies that their reading is controlled externally—that they read the books only because they must do so to earn pizzas. It might encourage them to select short, simple books, zip through them quickly, and move on to the next one. As John Nicholls (quoted by Kohn, 1993, p. 73) once noted, this approach could produce "a lot of fat kids who don't like to read" rather than a nation of thoughtful and intrinsically motivated readers.   elementary kids...

Later Findings

Debate over the claim that rewards might bring short-term increases in motivation or performance but undermine intrinsic interest produced a great deal of research, including a book devoted to the topic (Sansone & Harackiewicz, 2000) and a series of literature reviews and meta-analyses that yielded divergent results.

It became clear that *addressing questions about the appropriate use of rewards requires attention to the nature of the rewards, the ways in which they are introduced and delivered, and the student outcomes under consideration*. Rewards can be verbal or tangible, large or small, and salient or non-salient. They can be given for simply engaging in an

Box 6.2   Undermining Intrinsic Motivation

Research on ways in which extrinsic considerations can undermine intrinsic motivation initially focused on use of rewards offered as incentives, and explanations for the undermining effect focused on people's attributional inferences. In fact, an early term for this undermining was the *overjustification effect*: To the extent that people become aware that they are being "bribed" to engage in a particular behavior, they are likely to infer that bribing is considered necessary because they are not expected to engage in the behavior voluntarily. That is, the opportunity to engage in the behavior is not sufficient justification for doing so, and therefore extra incentives must be added. This line of reasoning leads to the inference that the overjustified behavior is aversive, or at least not worth performing in the absence of an extrinsic incentive to do so. This inference would undermine any intrinsic motivation for performing the behavior that might have been present originally.

As research findings accumulated, it became clear that undermining can occur not only when people are offered rewards, but when any extrinsic factor leads them to attribute their engagement to external pressures rather than their own intrinsic motivation. Other examples include awareness that the behavior is required, that one's performance will be evaluated or compared to that of others, or that one is under pressure to meet a time deadline (Kohn, 1993; Lepper, 1983). Therefore, what undermines intrinsic motivation is not the use of rewards as such but offering rewards in advance as incentives and following through in ways that lead students to believe that they engaged in the rewarded behaviors only because they had to do so to earn the rewards (not because these behaviors have value in their own right or produce other outcomes that are in the students' best interests).

Pintrich, Marx, and Boyle (1993) noted that students often are in situations where multiple incentives or goals are operating. For example, they may have intrinsic interest in a topic or activity, may also value learning about it because it is important to their future career plans, and furthermore may be aware of the need to display their learning by meeting performance standards that will enable them to get acceptable grades. The important thing is to see that these and any other motivational influences that might be operating work in such a way as to encourage students to "think it through" rather than just to "get it done."

activity (engagement-dependent), for completing the activity (completion-dependent), or for not only completing it but doing so in a way that fulfills some criterion (performance-dependent). Effects of rewards might be considered with respect to immediate effort or performance, changes in attitudes toward the activity (e.g., finding it interesting), or changes in intrinsic motivation to engage in it voluntarily when future opportunities arise.

Using such distinctions, Eisenberger and Cameron (1996) performed a meta-analysis of existing research and concluded that verbal rewards have positive effects on motivation but tangible rewards sometimes have negative effects (when they are given merely for participation in the activity without attention to quality of engagement or level of performance, and even then, only when the students expected the rewards because they had been announced in advance). These authors claimed that the supposedly harmful effects of rewards had been overstated, and advised use of verbal rewards and performance-dependent tangible rewards.

Subsequently, they published another meta-analysis (Eisenberger, Pierce, & Cameron, 1999) and interpreted the results as showing that:

- rewards will increase people's perceived self-determination, because the reward is a signal that the offerer does not control the person, who is voluntarily accepting an invitation to perform the task;
- the effects of reward on other aspects of intrinsic motivation are mostly positive or neutral; these effects depend mostly on the nature of the performance requirement. Vague or minimal standards indicate that the reward offerer doesn't care much about the task, but specific and high standards indicate that the offerer cares about the task or considers it important; and
- there is no reason for concern about using rewards with low-interest tasks, but with high-interest tasks it is important to link delivery of rewards to accomplishment of specific (preferably challenging) performance criteria.

Eisenberger, Cameron, and their behaviorist colleagues represent one side of the argument, claiming that the concern about rewards undermining intrinsic motivation has been mostly a false alarm. The other side has been represented by Deci, Ryan, Lepper, and other investigators whose work has focused on intrinsic motivation. They claimed that the meta-analyses just described produced misleading conclusions because the authors were inappropriately selective in deciding which studies to include, combined types of studies that should have been treated separately, and failed to distinguish between dull tasks and more interesting tasks (Deci, Koestner, & Ryan, 1999b; Lepper, Henderlong, & Gingras, 1999).

In support of their position, Deci, Koestner, and Ryan (1999a) reported findings from the largest meta-analysis done to date, which indicated that expected tangible rewards undermine intrinsic motivation, whether those rewards are engagement-contingent, completion-contingent, or even performance-contingent. In fact, the most detrimental effects were observed when the size of the reward was a direct function of the level of performance. This is the reward system most commonly used in applied settings, including school grading practices.

Rewards had strong negative effects on subsequent intrinsic motivation to engage in interesting tasks, but no effects on subsequent intrinsic motivation to engage in uninteresting tasks. Verbal rewards (positive feedback or praise) enhanced intrinsic motivation when they were primarily informational but decreased it when they were primarily controlling. The positive effects of verbal rewards were found primarily among college students, whereas the detrimental effects of tangible rewards were noticed primarily with children.

These authors concluded that although rewards can control behavior, they undermine people's taking responsibility for motivating and regulating themselves. Verbal rewards can be used effectively if they are delivered in an informational rather than a controlling manner, and tangible rewards might not be harmful if given occasionally and unexpectedly (rather than being announced in advance as reinforcers contingent on attaining specified performance levels). Making rewards more informational requires minimizing authoritarian or pressuring language when delivering the rewards, acknowledging good performance but not using the rewards as reinforcers to control behavior, providing opportunities for choice about how to do the tasks, and emphasizing the interesting or challenging aspects of the tasks rather than treating them as work that must be completed.

Subsequently, Cameron, Banko, and Pierce (2001) published yet another meta-analysis, and Deci, Koestner, and Ryan (2001) published yet another retrospective on the controversy. They actually agreed more than they disagreed, although they continued to talk past each other on the few points of disagreement, especially regarding material rewards. However, in a review of the controversy written from a behavioral point of view, Akin-Little, Eckert, Lovett, and Little (2004) added an interesting qualification. They noted that in performance-contingent reward situations, in which the size of the reward depends on the level of performance, receiving anything less than maximal reward signals failure (or at least, something less than success), so it may be experienced more as punishing than rewarding. Therefore, they concluded, the problem lies not with rewarding successful performance but with poor calibration of goals to individual students' current performance capabilities (i.e., failure to individualize criteria for full reward eligibility).

Cameron, Pierce, Banko, and Gear (2005) and Pierce, Cameron, Banko, and So (2003) conducted laboratory experiments indicating that extrinsic (monetary) rewards for achievement on a puzzle task increased college students' intrinsic motivation to continue working on the puzzles during subsequent free time. However, these results were produced in artificial, individualized, low-stakes situations and do not appear applicable to classrooms. Meanwhile, a more realistic study done with fourth and fifth graders found that both completion-dependent and performance-dependent rewards increased performance on mathematics problems during the reward condition, but decreased both performance and intrinsic motivation during a no-rewards follow-up (Oliver & Williams, 2006). These investigators were behaviorists who had expected the rewards to have positive effects, but they admitted that their findings show an overjustification effect.

Houlfort, Koestner, Joussenet, Nantel-Vivier, and Lekes (2002) introduced a further distinction that clarifies seemingly conflicting findings. They noted that Deci and Ryan measured autonomy by asking people if they felt pressured in the situation, whereas Eisenberger and his colleagues measured autonomy by asking them if they felt free to choose to do something other than what the experimenter was asking them to do in exchange for a reward. In two new studies of the effects of performance-contingent rewards ($5 if performance met criteria), Houlfort et al. measured both aspects of autonomy. They found that performance-contingent rewards increased peoples' perception of competence (because earning the reward indicated that they had done well on the task), had negative effects on the affective aspects of autonomy (feeling pressured), and had no effect on the decisional aspect of autonomy (feeling free to decline the offer). Thus, the results supported Eisenberger and Cameron's claims that performance-contingent rewards enhance competence perceptions, as well as encourage (or at least, do not undermine) autonomy perceptions, because they leave it up to the person whether or not to accept the invitation to pursue the reward. However, they also supported Deci and Ryan's claim that such rewards undermine autonomy perceptions in that they make the person feel pressured to perform. Later research showed that people felt depleted and suffered reduction in their coping resources after performing tasks they felt compelled to perform in order to earn rewards, but did not experience such depletion if they performed the same tasks while autonomously motivated (Muraven, Rosman, & Gagné, 2007).

Ryan et al. (1999) extended this controversy from specific situations to general dispositions. They reported that people express greater overall satisfaction with their lives if their most prominent goals and aspirations are primarily intrinsic (relatedness, helpfulness to others, physical health, self-acceptance) rather than extrinsic (money, fame, social attractiveness to others). Ryan and Deci (2000) claimed that our culture has become strongly reward-oriented, leading us away from our interests and desires for challenge, and toward a narrow instrumental focus. They added that over time, neglecting important needs to focus on pursuing rewards will be perceived as coercive and alienating, at cost to our well-being.

Conclusions About the Use of Rewards

This debate has been lively and the research connected with it has been informative. *We now realize that the issues are much more complicated than they seemed at first. I believe that intrinsic motivation theorists are correct in raising concerns about overuse or inappropriate use of rewards.* In classrooms, it is difficult to reward students in ways that (a) take into account their individual learning efforts and progress and (b) avoid communicating that they engage in activities to obtain the rewards rather than to learn. *However, I also believe that behaviorists are correct in claiming that rewards can be used effectively in classrooms.* The motivational problems facing teachers primarily involve getting students to put forth consistent learning efforts whether or not they find activities interesting or enjoyable, not just maintaining intrinsic motivation to engage in interesting tasks. That is, *motivating students is mostly about fostering identified regulation, not preserving existing intrinsic motivation.*

What about those corporate-sponsored programs that offer pizzas or other rewards for reading a specified number of books? These programs have been criticized as violating important principles of motivation theory and literacy engagement (Fawson & Moore, 1999; Kohn, 1993). However, a study of college students who had or had not participated in the "Book It!" program as children indicated that participation was not correlated with the college students' interest in reading (nor was having been paid to read by their parents when they were children; Flora & Flora, 1999). Thus, fears that this program would undermine intrinsic motivation for reading were unfounded. On the other hand, the millions of dollars spent implementing (and publicizing) this program did not yield positive results, either.

Such findings apparently are to be expected: McQuillan (1997) reviewed 10 studies of reading encouragement programs that included incentives for reading, and found that five had at least some positive results and five did not. However, none of the positive effects could be attributed clearly to the incentives. McQuillan concluded that no clear causal relationship had yet been established between reading incentives and reading attitudes, achievement, or habits.

Gambrell and Marinak (1997) reported positive effects for the "Running Start" program that offers first graders the opportunity to select a book of their choice as a reward for reading 21 books in 10 weeks. Classrooms are given 60–80 high-quality children's literature books (selected by the teacher), the students choose 21 books to read or listen to, and family members and older students participate by listening to the first graders read or by reading to them. Participating first graders showed increased reading

[handwritten marginal notes: "Family support" / "not simple" / "not" / "declare/shame"]

motivation relative to a control group, presumably because they were presented with a challenging goal but given choices about how to meet it, they got a lot of support and encouragement from significant others, and the reward (a book to keep) was linked to the desired behavior rather than tied to it artificially (as with candy or pizza).

In a later study, Marinak and Gambrell (2008) asked third graders to select one of six books to read, then give their opinion about whether the book should be purchased for the school library. For this, the students received either no reward, a book, or a token reward (Nerf ball, Pez dispenser, bracelet, or key chain). Then the students were given the opportunity to read another book, play a math game, or work on a jigsaw puzzle. During the latter activity, the token reward group showed less intrinsic motivation to read than either of the other groups.

The key to rewarding effectively is to do so in ways that support students' motivation to learn and do not encourage them to conclude that they engage in activities only to earn rewards. For example, if students are offered rewards simply for participating in a reading incentive program or are offered significant prizes for reading 100 books, they might well begin to view reading as drudgery and expect to be rewarded if they agree to do it. More positive effects might result if students were invited to: identify a rationale or set of themes for selecting books to read; after reading the books, write a report that illustrates how these themes have played out; and make a brief presentation to classmates (followed by questions and answers). Looking back on their own and others' contributions to the "rewards for reading" controversy, Marinak and Gambrell (2009) concluded that engaging students in authentic literacy activities was more fundamental than rewards as a way to develop interest in reading. This approach is similar to other methods (e.g., science fairs where students demonstrate projects to an interested audience) that allow students to enjoy public recognition for significant accomplishments.

In conclusion, extrinsic rewards do not necessarily undermine intrinsic motivation and even can be used in ways that support its development (Covington, 2000; Gehlbach & Roeser, 2002; Lepper & Henderlong, 2000). One way is to provide unannounced rewards *following* task completion, so that the rewards are seen as expressions of appreciation of effort or recognitions of accomplishment rather than as delivery of promised incentives. Other ways involve using rewards as informative feedback rather than as control mechanisms. It also helps to emphasize social rewards over material rewards and to deliver rewards in ways that encourage students to value their accomplishments. These principles are illustrated in the following section.

STRATEGIES FOR REWARDING STUDENTS

Most teachers want to reward their students' praiseworthy efforts and accomplishments. They find it natural to do so in the process of building good relationships with students and encouraging and supporting their learning efforts. Hoffmann, Huff, Patterson, and Nietfeld (2009) found that all 86 of the elementary teachers they surveyed used rewards, although with large individual differences in reward types and in the frequencies and purposes of reward usage. Verbal rewards (praise) and tangible rewards (prizes) were the most common types, with praise used more for rewarding achievement and prizes more for rewarding good behavior. Most of the teachers used rewards informally, without systematically tying them to specific behaviors as part of a formal reinforcement or token economy system.

Types of rewards commonly used by teachers include material rewards (money, prizes, trinkets, consumables), activity rewards and special privileges (opportunities to play games, use special equipment, or engage in self-selected activities); grades, awards, and recognitions (honor rolls, displaying good papers); praise and social rewards; and teacher rewards (special attention, personalized interaction, opportunities to go places or do things with the teacher).

If you enjoy rewarding your students in one or more of these ways, you do not need to stop doing so for fear of undermining their intrinsic motivation. Intrinsic motivation and extrinsic motivation are relatively independent, so in a given situation students can be high in both or low in both, not just high in one and low in the other (Lepper & Henderlong, 2000). *Rewards can be used in ways that support or at least do not undermine intrinsic motivation. However, it is important to learn when and how to dispense rewards effectively.*

When to Reward

Rewards are more effective for increasing the intensity or duration of effort than for improving the quality of performance. They support learning more effectively when there is a clear goal and a clear strategy to follow than when goals are more ambiguous or when students must discover or invent new strategies rather than merely activate familiar ones. Therefore, *rewards are better used with routine tasks than with novel ones, better with specific intentional learning tasks than with incidental learning or discovery tasks, and better with tasks where steady performance or quantity of output is of more concern than creativity, artistry, or craftsmanship.*

It is better to offer rewards as incentives for meeting performance improvement standards on skills that require a great deal of drill and practice (arithmetic computation, musical scales, typing, spelling, free-throw shooting) than for work on a research or demonstration project. With low-level tasks that demand rote learning, no other source of motivation may be operating, so rewards may be needed to motivate sustained effort (although a more basic strategy is to minimize students' encounters with such boring or aversive activities).

It is not wise to offer rewards as primary incentives to motivate students to do things that you want them to continue to do on their own, such as watch educational television programs, read quality books, or participate in civic affairs or community improvement efforts. However, rewards may be helpful when initial levels of interest in the activity are low or its value becomes apparent only after engaging in it long enough to reach a critical level of mastery.

Rewards can act as motivators only for students who believe that they have a chance to get the rewards if they put forth reasonable effort. Traditional grading systems and other common school practices (e.g., multiple levels of honors) violate this principle routinely. Remember, if you wish to create incentives for the whole class and not just your high achievers, you will need to ensure that all students have equal (or at least reasonable) access to the rewards. This may require performance contracting or some less formal method of individualizing criteria for success.

For example, MacIver and Reuman (1993/94) described an incentives program in which students were rewarded either for maintaining high performance or for improving less satisfactory performance. Each week, students attempted to beat their current "base score" on an important test, project, or assignment. They were rewarded according to the "improvement points" they earned. Those who turned in perfect tests or papers or beat their current base score by more than nine points were awarded 30 improvement points in that subject for that week; those who scored within five points of a perfect paper or beat their current base score by five to nine points were awarded 20 improvement points; those who scored within four points of their current base score were awarded 10 improvement points; and those who scored more than four points below their current base score were not awarded any improvement points.

Midgley and Urdan (1992) offered useful suggestions about the kinds of accomplishments that you might emphasize in rewarding students. First, recognize the quality of accomplishments rather than the quantity, and in particular, recognize students for taking on challenging work or stretching their abilities (even if they make mistakes). Also, recognize them for coming up with different or unusual ways to solve problems. These priorities give powerful messages about what is valued in your classroom.

Use multiple criteria that allow you to adapt recognitions to individual differences, rather than always applying the same criteria to all students and thus comparing them directly. However, make sure that your recognitions are for genuine accomplishments (given what is reasonable to expect from the student). Finally, although you may want to provide recognition to students in a variety of domains (athletics, good citizenship, etc.), make sure that every student has the opportunity to earn recognition in the academic domain.

How to Reward

Deliver rewards in ways that provide students with informative feedback and encourage them to appreciate their developing knowledge and skills, not just to think about the rewards. If you offer rewards in advance as incentives, emphasize your major instructional goals in setting criteria for determining credits. Reward students for mastering key ideas and skills (or showing improvement in their mastery levels), not merely for participating in activities or turning in assignments. Include provisions for redoing work that does not meet standards.

In explaining and following through on incentive systems, emphasize the importance of the learning and help students to appreciate and take pride in their accomplishments. *Portray the rewards as verifications of significant and worthwhile achievements, not as the whole point of their efforts.* This is less crucial when rewards are not announced in advance as incentives, but even when delivering surprise rewards it is wise to cast them as expressions of appreciation for your students' efforts and accomplishments, without making too much of the "big surprise."

Additional guidelines about rewarding students are implied in the following section on praising in ways that emphasize providing students with informative feedback rather than exercising control over their behavior. Most of what is said about praise also applies to other forms of rewards, and in particular, to what you might say to students as you deliver the rewards.

PRAISING YOUR STUDENTS EFFECTIVELY

Most teachers enjoy delivering praise and most students enjoy receiving it, at least when it is delivered as a spontaneous, genuine reaction to an accomplishment rather than as part of a calculated manipulation attempt (Burnett, 2001). Praise is widely recommended as a way to reward students, although it does not always have this effect (Brophy, 1981; Delin & Baumeister, 1994). Some teacher praise is not even intended as a reward for a specific accomplishment, as when the praise is used in an attempt to build a social relationship with an alienated student ("I like your new shirt, John.").

Even when praise is intended as a reward, students may not perceive it that way (Larrivee, 2002). Some students do not attach much value to teacher praise and thus do not feel particularly rewarded when they receive it (Ware, 1978). Also, many appreciate praise communicated in private but are less enthused about being praised in front of their classmates (Caffyn, 1989) or given public recognition for their achievements (Dresel, Martschinke, & Kopp, 2009; Exline, Single, Lobel, & Geyer, 2004).

Students may find it embarrassing to be singled out, humiliating to be praised for some minor accomplishment, or irritating to have classmates' attention called to their neatness, punctuality, or conformity rather than to more clearly noteworthy achievements. For example, a teacher's statement that "I like the way Susie is sitting up straight and ready to listen" is likely to embarrass Susie. It may even alienate her if she is sophisticated enough to realize that the statement is not really praise of her but an attempt to cue some of her classmates.

As related examples, consider the following: "John, I really enjoyed your story, especially the machine that converts peanut butter into energy. I'd like you to read it to the class later. Also, how about drawing what that machine might look like?...Mary, you did a fine job. I especially liked the way you wrote your story so neatly—centered headings, no smudges, writing carefully on the lines—keep up the good work!"

The teacher's praise of John's work focuses on its substance and is likely to be appreciated because it identifies noteworthy accomplishments. By drawing attention to a particular detail of John's story, the teacher shows that she has paid attention to its content and appreciates its creativity. In contrast, her praise of Mary's work focuses on form and neatness rather than its substantive content or the creativity of her writing. She does not mention any particulars of Mary's story or even indicate that she remembers any of it. Although apparently sincere, such praise may cause Mary to suspect that the teacher does not like her story or does not think highly of her writing abilities.

Public praise can be problematic even when it is recognized as praise and appreciated as such both by the recipient and by classmates. Students who are eager for teacher attention may begin clamoring for it, and students who believe that they are just as deserving as praised classmates may begin to feel slighted (Ollendick & Shapiro, 1984).

Praise should be informative and appreciative rather than controlling (Kast & Connor, 1988). Sometimes this is easier said than done. As Kohn (1993, p. 102, italics in original) observed, "...the most notable aspect of a positive judgment is not that it is positive but that it is a *judgment*." Therefore, it is important to phrase praise statements as communication of informative feedback rather than as evaluation. Effective praise expresses appreciation for students' efforts or admiration for their accomplishments, in ways that call attention to the efforts or accomplishments themselves rather than to their role in pleasing the teacher. This helps students learn to attribute their *efforts* to their own motivation rather than to external incentives, and to attribute their *successes* to their own abilities and efforts rather than to external supports. You might express such praise as part of a "celebration" of what has been learned as you bring a unit or series of activities to closure.

Effective praise is genuine.   Brophy and Evertson (1981) found that teachers were credible and spontaneous when praising students whom they liked, often smiling as they spoke and praising genuine accomplishments. These teachers praised students whom they disliked just as frequently, but usually without accompanying spontaneity and warmth and often with reference to appearance or conduct rather than accomplishments.

Some teachers praise poor responses as part of a well-intentioned attempt to encourage low achievers (Nafpaktitis, Mayer, & Butterworth, 1985; Natriello & Dornbusch, 1985; Pajares & Graham, 1998). This tactic often backfires, however, because it undermines the teacher's credibility and confuses or depresses the students (if they realize that they are being treated differently from their classmates). For example, students who notice that they are frequently praised for minor accomplishments (e.g., answering a relatively routine question or completing an easy task) may infer that the teacher does not have much confidence in their abilities or potential (Miller & Hom, 1997; Thompson, 1997). Students generally prefer private, quietly delivered praise to public, loudly delivered praise, and praise for their academic accomplishments as well as praise for their good conduct (Burnett, 2001; Elwell & Tiberio, 1994; Sharp, 1985).

Even when praising significant achievements, it is better to focus on the effort and care that the student put into the work, on the gains in knowledge or skills that the achievement represents, or on its more noteworthy features, than to portray the achievement as evidence of the student's intelligence or aptitude. The problem with the latter kind of praise (e.g., "Wow—you're really good at this!") is that it creates vulnerabilities for the future. Students who become accustomed to interpreting successes as evidence of high aptitude in a domain (e.g., mathematics) will also tend to interpret failures as evidence of low aptitude. This makes them vulnerable to developing learned helplessness beliefs (Kamins & Dweck, 1999; Mueller & Dweck, 1998).

Students need informative feedback to support their learning efforts, but they do not need more intensive expressions of praise.   Correlations between teachers' rates of praise and their students' achievement gains are low in magnitude and mixed in direction, suggesting that the most effective teachers are sparing rather than effusive in their praise (Brophy & Good, 1986). Keep this in mind when deciding when and how to praise students. Other guidelines for praising effectively are given below and in Table 6.1.

1.   Praise simply and directly, in a natural voice, without gushing or dramatizing.
2.   Praise in straightforward, declarative sentences ("I never thought of that before.") instead of exclamations ("Wow!") or rhetorical questions ("Isn't that terrific!"). The latter are condescending and more likely to embarrass than reward.
3.   Specify the particular accomplishment being praised and recognize any noteworthy effort, care, or perseverance ("Good! You figured it out all by yourself. I like the way you stuck with it without giving up" instead of "Good work"). Call attention to new skills or evidence of progress ("I notice you've learned to use different kinds of metaphors in your compositions. They're more interesting to read now.").

4. Use a variety of phrases for praising students. Overused stock phrases soon begin to sound insincere and give the impression that you have not paid much attention to the accomplishments you are praising.

5. Combine verbal praise with nonverbal communication of approval. "Good job!" is much more rewarding when delivered with a smile and a tone that communicates appreciation or warmth.

6. Avoid ambiguous statements that students may take as praise for compliance rather than for learning (e.g., "You were really good today."). Instead, be specific ("I'm very pleased with the way you read with so much expression. You made the conversation between Billy and Mr. Taylor sound very real.").

TABLE 6.1
Guidelines for Effective Praise

Effective Praise	Ineffective Praise
1. Is delivered contingently	1. Is delivered randomly or unsystematically
2. Specifies the particulars of the accomplishment	2. Is restricted to global positive reactions
3. Shows spontaneity, variety and other signs of credibility; suggests clear attention to the student's accomplishment	3. Shows a bland uniformity that suggests a conditioned response made with minimal attention
4. Rewards attainment of specified performance criteria (which can include effort criteria, however)	4. Rewards mere participation, without consideration of performance processes or outcomes
5. Provides information to students about their competence or the value of their accomplishments	5. Provides no information at all or gives students information about their status relative to peers
6. Orients students toward better appreciation of their own task-related behavior and thinking about problem solving	6. Orients students toward comparing themselves with others and thinking about competing
7. Uses student's own prior accomplishments as the context for describing present accomplishments	7. Uses the accomplishments of peers as the context for describing student's present accomplishments
8. Is given in recognition of noteworthy effort or success at difficult (for this student) tasks	8. Is given without regard to the effort expended or the meaning of the accomplishment
9. Attributes success to effort and ability, implying that similar success can be expected in the future	9. Attributes success to ability alone or to external factors such as luck or (easy) task difficulty
10. Fosters endogenous attributions (students believe that they expend effort on the task because they enjoy the task and/or want to develop task-relevant skills)	10. Fosters exogenous attributions (students believe that they expend effort on the task for external reasons—to please the teacher, win a competition or reward, etc.
11. Focuses students' attention on their own task-relevant behavior	11. Focuses students' attention on the teacher as an external authority figure who is manipulating them
12. Fosters appreciation of, and desirable attributions about, task-relevant behavior after the process is completed	12. Intrudes into the ongoing process, distracting attention from task-relevant behavior

Source: Brophy, J. (1981). Teacher praise: A functional analysis. *Review of Educational Research, 51*, 5–32.

7. *Ordinarily, students should be praised privately.* This underscores that the praise is genuine and avoids the problem of sounding as though you are holding the student up as an example to the rest of the class.

Wlodkowski (1985) summarized many of these same principles in his "3S-3P" guidelines: Praise (or other rewards) should be Sincere, Specific, Sufficient (adapted to the accomplishment), and Properly attributed for genuinely Praiseworthy accomplishments, in a manner Preferred by the learner.

Henderlong and Lepper (2002) completed a meta-analysis of the research on praise. They concluded that praise enhances intrinsic motivation and increases perseverance when it is perceived as sincere, encourages adaptive performance attributions, promotes perceived autonomy, provides information about competence without relying heavily on social comparisons, and conveys standards and expectations that are realistic for the student.

CAPITALIZING ON EXISTING EXTRINSIC REWARDS: CALL STUDENTS' ATTENTION TO THE INSTRUMENTAL VALUE OF LEARNING

Often it is possible to make students aware of naturally existing extrinsic incentives for mastering school content or skills. A good curriculum moves students toward outcomes that will enrich their lives and empower them to function successfully in our society. At least in theory, it is in a student's best interest to engage in any learning activity seriously and complete it successfully, so as to obtain the benefits it was designed to yield.

However, *school activities differ in the degree to which their life application potential is immediate and obvious to students.* Some knowledge and skills can be applied in the students' current lives or obviously will be needed as "life skills" later. These natural consequences of mastery can be powerful incentives for motivating learning efforts. Therefore, whenever you see the opportunity to do so, help your students to appreciate that the knowledge or skills developed by an activity will help them to meet their own current needs, provide them with a "ticket" to social advancement, or prepare them for occupational or other success in life. Cite examples by relating your own personal experiences or anecdotes about individuals with whom your students can identify (such as famous people that they look up to or former students from your school).

The strategy of calling students' attention to life applications of what they are learning is not used as often or effectively as it could be. Rather than stress life applications in positive terms, many teachers only mention negative outcomes that may result from failure to learn. These include personal embarrassment ("You don't want people to think you are ignorant") or future educational or occupational disasters ("You'll never get through the sixth grade"; "How are you going to get a job if you can't do basic math?"). Other teachers use variations that cast the student in a more positive light but portray society as a hostile environment (learn to count so merchants don't shortchange you; learn to read so you don't get cheated when signing contracts).

Be more positive as you *help students appreciate the potential applications of what they are learning.* Basic literacy and mathematics skills are used daily when shopping, banking, driving, reading instructions for using products, paying bills, carrying on business correspondence, and planning home maintenance projects or family vacations. Scientific knowledge is useful for everything from coping effectively with minor everyday challenges to making good decisions in emergency situations. History and social studies provide a basis for making good personal, social, and civic decisions. In general, a good working knowledge of the information, principles, and skills taught in school prepares people to make well-informed decisions that can save time, trouble, expense, or even lives. It also empowers people to appreciate and take advantage of the life-enriching opportunities that society offers.

Help your students to recognize such connections to life outside of school, so that they *come to see learning activities as enabling opportunities.* More generally, help them to appreciate that schools are established by society for their benefit. In this regard, you might note that the educational opportunities we take for granted in our country are available only to the privileged few in many countries. Do not preach or make your students feel guilty, but do heighten their awareness of education as an opportunity and underscore the idea that conscientious learning efforts are in their own best interests, not just duties to perform to please you or their parents.

COMPETITION: A POWERFUL BUT PROBLEMATIC EXTRINSIC INCENTIVE

Competition can add excitement to classroom activities, whether for prizes or merely the satisfaction of winning. Competitions may be either individual (students compete in pairs or as individuals working against everyone else) or group (students are divided into teams that compete with one another, or the class competes with other classes). Despite its popularity among many teachers and students, *most motivational theorists oppose the use of competition or place heavy qualifications on its applicability as a motivational strategy. There are several good reasons for this.*

First, classroom activities already involve risking public failure, and a great deal of competition is already built into the grading system. Why introduce additional competitive elements?

Second, competition is even more salient and distracting than rewards. Ames and Ames (1981) found that students working on their own evaluated their progress with reference to their prior performance, noting and appreciating developments in knowledge and skill. In contrast, students working in competitive structures were so focused on winning that they paid little attention to what they were supposed to be learning.

Third, competitions are more coercive than motivational when participation is mandatory; the games and rules are imposed by authority figures, and high stakes are attached to the outcomes.

Fourth, the qualifications that apply to the use of rewards also apply to competition. Competition is more appropriate for use with routine practice tasks than with tasks calling for discovery or creativity, and it can be effective only if everyone has a good (or at least an equal) chance of winning. To ensure this, it may be necessary to use team competition in which the teams are balanced by ability profiles or to use individual competition in which a handicapping system enables each student to compete with his or her own previous performance rather than with classmates.

Finally, competition creates losers as well as winners (usually many more losers). Even when there is no rational reason for it, a loser's psychology tends to develop whenever individuals or teams lose competitions. Individuals may suffer at least temporary embarrassment, and those who lose consistently may suffer more permanent losses in confidence, self-esteem, and enjoyment of school (Chan & Lam, 2008; Epstein & Harack- iewicz, 1992; Moriarty, Douglas, Punch, & Hattie, 1995; Reeve & Deci, 1996). Members of losing teams may devalue one another and scapegoat those they hold responsible for the team's loss (Ames, 1984; Johnson & Johnson, 1985).

In combination, these considerations should give you pause about introducing com- petition as a motivational strategy. If you are thinking about doing so, plan to minimize its risks by making sure that all students have an equal chance to win, that winning is determined primarily by degree of effort (and perhaps a degree of luck) rather than by level of ability, that attention is focused more on learning than on who wins or loses, and that reactions to the outcome emphasize the positive (winners are congratulated but losers are not criticized or ridiculed; the accomplishments of the class as a whole, not just of the winners, are acknowledged).

Traditionally, competitions have been structured around test scores, but competitive elements can be infused into ordinary instruction through activities such as argumenta- tive essays, debates, or simulation games (Keller, 1983). In fact, debates or other activities that encourage students to develop conflicting positions rather than seek concurrence can have both motivation and learning benefits, if the discourse remains constructive (Johnson, & Johnson, 2009).

There are ways to depersonalize competition (Johnson & Johnson, 1999). For example, you might divide the class into several teams and ask each team to develop a campaign speech based on specified criteria. Next, the class would use these criteria to critique the speeches. Then, each team would take the best features from all of the initial versions and produce speech that represents the class's best thinking.

Student Team Learning Methods

One way to exploit the motivational potential of competition while avoiding most of its undesirable effects is to use student team learning methods in which students cooperate in addition to compete. These methods feature both a handicapping system to supply individual criteria for scoring each student's work and an incentive system that offers group rewards to teams whose combined individual scores enable them to win competi- tions against other teams (Slavin, 1995).

TGT. The original student team learning method was called Teams-Games- Tournament (TGT). In TGT, students work together in four- or five-member heterogeneously composed teams to help one another master content and prepare for competitions against other teams. The teacher first presents the material to be learned, then team members work together filling out worksheets. They discuss the material, tutor one another, and quiz one another to assess mastery. These forms of cooperative learning continue throughout the week in preparation for tournaments held on Fridays.

For the tournaments, students are assigned to three-person tables composed of stu- dents from different teams who are similar in achievement level. The three students compete at games covering the content taught that week and practiced during team meetings. Most of these games are simply numbered questions on a handout. A student draws a number card and attempts to answer the corresponding question. Students can earn points by responding to questions correctly or by successfully challenging and correcting the answers of the other two students at the table. These points are later summed to determine each team's score, and the teacher prepares a newsletter that recognizes successful teams and unusually high scores attained by individuals. Prior to the next tournament, the teacher may assign certain students to different tables to keep the competition as even as possible. This ensures that even though team membership remains the same, all students begin each tournament with an equal chance to earn points for their teams because they are competing against similar peers.

STAD.   Student Teams-Achievement Divisions (STAD) is a simplification of TGT. STAD follows the same heterogeneous grouping and cooperative learning procedures as TGT but replaces the games and tournaments with a quiz. Quiz scores are translated into team competition points based on how much students have improved their performance over past averages.

Both TGT and STAD combine cooperative learning with team competition and use group rewards for cumulative individual performance. However, STAD depersonalizes the competition. Rather than compete face-to-face at tournament tables, STAD students try to do their best on quizzes taken individually. STAD is an improvement on TGT because it is easier to implement and it reduces the salience of the competition.

Jigsaw II.   Jigsaw II is an adaptation of the original Jigsaw (described in chapter 7), a cooperative learning method that ensures that students interact with and learn from one another because each team member possesses unique information that must be communicated to the others. Jigsaw II combines competitive elements with these cooperative elements. Students begin by reading a narrative (such as a chapter in a history text or a biography of an accomplished person) to acquire a common base of information. Then, to develop the material, each member of a team is given a separate topic on which to become an expert. Students from different teams who have been assigned to the same topic meet in "expert groups" to discuss their topics. Then, they return to their teams to teach what they have learned to their teammates.

Except for the topic on which they have become expert, students must depend on their classmates for information that is not included in the base narrative. Team members have responsibilities not only to master the material themselves but to teach it effectively to teammates. At the end of the week, students take a quiz, individual scores are summed to compute team scores, and accomplishments are recognized through the class newsletter. Despite their potential motivational benefits, many educators are skeptical of Jigsaw methods because they fear that students will learn an incomplete or distorted version of the content because their peers will not teach it as effectively as the teacher would and because they will not have texts to support their efforts to learn on their own (Battista, 2001; Stein, 2001).

TAI.   Team-Assisted Individualization (TAI) is an adaptation of individualized mathematics instruction that introduces cooperative learning methods and team competition with group reward, as in STAD. TAI combines direct instruction by the teacher (to small, homogeneously formed groups), follow-up practice using programmed instructional materials, and a student team learning approach to seatwork management.

Student team learning methods consistently show positive effects on achievement, related to the use of group rewards based on team scores. Methods that ensure the accountability of individual members to their groupmates produce higher achievement than methods that allow one or two students to do the work while the others take more passive roles. The highest achievement outcomes result from methods that combine group goals with individual accountability (Shepperd & Taylor, 1999; Slavin, 1995).

Note that the achievement advantages of student team learning methods reside in their group reward and individual accountability features, not their competitive features. There is no evidence that group competition offers advantages over other cooperative learning methods so long as arrangements are made to provide group rewards based on the cumulative performance of individual group members. Besides using direct competitions (as in TGT and STAD), good results have been obtained by giving teams certificates for meeting preset standards (independently of the performance of other teams) and by using task specialization to motivate students to encourage their teammates. Thus, although the effects of student team learning on achievement appear to be primarily motivational, the key is not motivation to win competitions against other teams but motivation to assist one's teammates to meet their individual goals and thus ensure that the team will do well.

Like other forms of cooperative learning, student team learning methods have produced positive effects on outcomes other than achievement. These methods promote friendships and prosocial interaction among groupmates as well as positive outcomes on affective variables such as self-esteem, academic self-confidence, and liking for the class and for classmates.

CONCLUSION

Extrinsic motivational strategies can be effective in certain circumstances, but you should not rely on them too heavily. If your students become preoccupied with rewards or competition, they may not pay enough attention to what they are supposed to be learning or develop much appreciation for its value. Quality of engagement and ultimate achievement tend to be higher when students perceive themselves to be engaged for their own reasons rather than in order to please an authority figure, obtain a reward, or escape punishment (Deci & Ryan, 1985; Flink et al., 1992; Lepper, 1983; Sweet, Guthrie, & Ng, 1998). Therefore, confine your extrinsic motivational strategies to noting the instrumental value of what is being learned or offering after-the-fact praise or rewards to show appreciation for students' learning efforts and achievements.

If you use rewards and other extrinsic incentives, use them in ways that encourage students to commit themselves to your instructional goals, so they engage in activities with the intention of acquiring the knowledge and skills that these activities are meant to develop (and in doing so, obtaining extrinsic rewards as well). This may produce a form of motivation to learn that is comparable to that produced by intrinsic motivation, or at least close enough to serve your purposes. To the extent that students focus primarily on obtaining rewards rather than on accomplishing learning goals, less satisfactory results can be expected.

If students perceive themselves as performing a task solely to obtain a reward, they tend to concentrate on meeting minimum standards for performance rather than on doing a high-quality job. They may write 300-word essays containing exactly 300 words or read only those parts of the text that they need to read to answer the questions on an assignment. You can minimize these dangers by using extrinsic motivation approaches sparingly, keeping in mind the qualifications on when they might be used, and implementing the methods and delivering the rewards in ways that reflect the guidelines for praising given in Table 6.1.

SUMMARY

This has been the first of five chapters on the value aspects of motivation, which focus on people's reasons for engaging in activities and the benefits that they expect to derive from doing so. The chapter described strategies for supplying extrinsic incentives to motivate engagement. These strategies do not attempt to increase the value that students place on an activity, but instead link successful completion of the activity to delivery of consequences that they do value.

Three general strategies for supplying extrinsic motivation were discussed: (a) rewarding students for good performance, (b) calling attention to the instrumental value of the learning, and (c) occasionally structuring appropriate forms of competition. The discussion emphasized using these extrinsic incentives in ways that are compatible with other motivational principles, rather than incorporating them within a behavioral control approach to classroom management.

Extrinsic motivational methods are more suited to increasing the intensity of effort than improving the quality or creativity of performance, and more suited to motivating steady performance on tasks requiring following a clear strategy to reach a clear goal than on more open, divergent, or complex tasks. If you announce rewards in advance to create an incentive system, make sure that the system motivates students to focus on accomplishing your instructional goals (not just on obtaining the rewards) and that each student has an equal (or at least reasonable) opportunity to earn the rewards. When delivering praise or rewards, help students to appreciate and take pride in their accomplishments, both as a class and as individuals. Praise of individuals ordinarily should be done in private, be appreciative and informative rather than controlling, and display the characteristics summarized in Table 6.1.

Where appropriate, call students' attention to naturally existing extrinsic incentives for mastering content or skills. More generally, infuse your everyday teaching with modeling and socialization designed to build students' appreciation of the fact that schools are established to prepare them for life in the present and future, and that the curriculum was designed with this in mind.

Competition provides another potential source for extrinsic motivation. However, it is even more salient and distracting than rewards and it adds higher stakes to classroom activities that already involve risk of public failure and competition for grades. Consequently, if you use competition at all, do so in ways that depersonalize it and focus students primarily on learning goals. This may be accomplished through methods that combine competition with cooperative learning, including the student team learning methods that have produced positive effects on achievement, affect, and social and motivational outcomes.

Extrinsic motivational strategies can be used in ways that complement the strategies described in other chapters in this book, provided that they are not overemphasized; they are implemented in ways that focus students' attention primarily on what they are learning rather than on the rewards; and they preserve and support intrinsic motivation by avoiding incentive systems or explanations that lead students to infer that they engage only to please you or to obtain rewards.

REFLECTION QUESTIONS

1. Before reading this chapter, did you share the beliefs of the people interviewed about the efficacy of rewards? What do you think now?
2. In your own words, when and how do extrinsic rewards decrease intrinsic motivation? Complement or support intrinsic motivation?
3. Will you seek to motivate using praise or extrinsic rewards? If so, when and how? If not, why not?
4. Would you require or encourage your students to participate in science fairs, writing contests, or similar competitions? Why or why not?
5. Would you encourage them to participate in programs that offer pizza for reading books? Why or why not?
6. Your most outstanding student once again does an excellent job. What would be appropriate things to say to him? What might be inappropriate?
7. A struggling student gets 68% of the items correct on a test, which for him, is part of a pattern of slow but steady improvement over much worse performance. However, the class averaged 84%. What would be appropriate things to say to him in this situation? What might be inappropriate?
8. Why is motivating students mostly about fostering identified regulation, not preserving existing intrinsic motivation?
9. Why is the way in which rewards are presented more important than the rewards themselves?
10. If you plan to use rewards, how do you plan to ensure that all students have equal (or at least reasonable) access to them?
11. Think of situations in which you would likely praise students. For each of them, write down some highly appropriate and some less appropriate praise statements.
12. Review a series of lessons that you teach or are likely to teach. For each lesson, identify at least one way in which what is taught will be used in life outside of school, and write out how you would convey this life application potential to students.
13. Some theorists believe that competition is bad for everyone, even winners. Is this a valid conclusion? Why or why not?
14. Would you use competition? If so, when and how? What steps would you take to depersonalize it and make sure that all students have equal opportunities to win?

REFERENCES

Akin-Little, K. A., Eckert, T., Lovett, B., & Little, S. (2004). Extrinsic reinforcement in the classroom: Bribery or best practice. *School Psychology Review, 33*, 344–362.

Ames, C. (1984). Competitive, cooperative, and individualistic goal structures: A cognitive-motivational analysis. In R. Ames & C. Ames (Eds.), *Research on motivation in education. Volume 1: Student motivation* (pp. 177–208). New York: Academic Press.

Ames, C., & Ames, R. (1981). Competitive versus individualistic goal structures: The salience of past performance information for causal attributions and affect. *Journal of Educational Psychology, 73*, 411–418.

Barrett, M., & Boggiano, A. (1988). Fostering extrinsic orientations: Use of reward strategies to motivate children. *Journal of Social and Clinical Psychology, 6*, 293–309.

Battista, M. (2001). A research-based perspective on teaching school geometry. In J. Brophy (Ed.), *Subject-specific instructional methods and activities* (pp.145–185). New York: Elsevier Science.

Boggiano, A., Barrett, M., Weiher, A., McClelland, G., & Lusk, C. (1987). Use of the maximal operant procedure to motivate children's intrinsic interest. *Journal of Personality and Social Psychology, 53,* 866–879.

Brophy, J. (1981). Teacher praise: A functional analysis. *Review of Educational Research, 51,* 5–32.

Brophy, J., & Evertson, C. (1981). *Student characteristics and teaching.* New York: Longman.

Brophy, J., & Good, T. (1986). Teacher behavior and student achievement. In M. Wittrock (Ed.), *Handbook of research on teaching* (3rd ed., pp. 328–375). New York: Macmillan.

Burnett, P. (2001). Elementary students' preferences for teacher praise. *Journal of Classroom Interaction, 36,* 16–23.

Caffyn, R. (1989). Attitudes of British secondary school teachers and pupils to rewards and punishments. *Educational Research, 31,* 210–220.

Cameron, J., Banko, K., & Pierce, W. (2001). Pervasive negative effects of rewards on intrinsic motivation: The myth continues. *Behavior Analyst, 24,* 1–44.

Cameron, J., Pierce, W. D., Banko, K., & Gear, A. (2005). Achievement-based rewards and intrinsic motivation: A test of cognitive mediators. *Journal of Educational Psychology, 97,* 641–655.

Chan, J., & Lam, S. (2008). Effects of competition on students' self-efficacy in vicarious learning. *British Journal of Educational Psychology, 78,* 95–108.

Condry, J., & Chambers, J. (1978). Intrinsic motivation and the process of learning. In M. Lepper & D. Greene (Eds.), *The hidden costs of reward: New perspectives on the psychology of human motivation* (pp. 61–84). Hillsdale, NJ: Erlbaum.

Covington, M. (2000). Intrinsic versus extrinsic motivation in schools: A reconciliation. *Current Directions in Psychological Science, 9,* 22–25.

Deci, E., Koestner, R., & Ryan, R. (1999a). A meta-analytic review of experiments examining the effects of extrinsic rewards on intrinsic motivation. *Psychological Bulletin, 125,* 627–668.

Deci, E., Koestner, R., & Ryan, R. (1999b). The undermining effect is a reality after all—extrinsic rewards, task interest, and self-determination. *Psychological Bulletin, 125,* 692–700.

Deci, E., Koestner, R., & Ryan, R. (2001). Extrinsic rewards and intrinsic motivation in education: Reconsidered once again. *Review of Educational Research, 71,* 1–27.

Deci, E., & Ryan, R. (1985). *Intrinsic motivation and self-determination in human behavior.* New York: Plenum.

Delin, C., & Baumeister, R. (1994). Praise: More than just social reinforcement. *Journal for the Theory of Social Behaviour, 24,* 219–241.

Dresel, M., Martschinke, S., & Kopp, B. (2009, April). *Elementary school teachers' feedback practices, perceived classroom goal structures, and students' personal achievement goals.* Paper presented at the annual meeting of the American Educational Research Association, San Diego.

Eccles, J. (2009). Who am I and what am I going to do with my life? Personal and collective identities as motivators of action. *Educational Psychologist, 44,* 78–89.

Eisenberger, R., & Cameron, J. (1996). The detrimental effects of reward: Myth or reality? *American Psychologist, 51,* 1153–1166.

Eisenberger, R., Pierce, W. D., & Cameron, J. (1999). Effects of reward on intrinsic motivation: Negative, neutral, and positive. *Psychological Bulletin, 125,* 677–691.

Elwell, W., & Tiberio, J. (1994). Teacher praise. *Journal of Instructional Psychology, 21,* 322–328.

Epstein, J., & Harackiewicz, J. (1992). Winning is not enough: The effects of competition and achievement orientation on intrinsic interest. *Personality and Social Psychology Bulletin, 18,* 128–138.

Exline, J., Single, P., Lobel, M., & Geyer, A. (2004). Glowing praise and the envious gaze: Social dilemmas surrounding the public recognition of achievement. *Basic and Applied Social Psychology, 26,* 119–130.

Farley, D., & Rosario, H. (2008). A critique of monetary educational incentives for elementary and middle school students in New York City public schools. Retrieved July 9, 2008, from http://www.tcrecord.org, ID #15257

Fawson, P., & Moore, S. (1999). Reading incentive programs: Beliefs and practices. *Reading Psychology, 20,* 325–340.

Flink, C., Boggiano, A., Main, D., Barrett, M., & Katz, P. (1992). Children's achievement-related behaviors: The role of extrinsic and intrinsic motivational orientations. In A. Boggiano & T. Pittman (Eds.), *Achievement and motivation: A social-developmental perspective* (pp. 189–214). Cambridge, UK: Cambridge University Press.

Flora, S., & Flora, D. (1999). Effects of extrinsic reinforcement for reading during childhood on reported reading habits of college students. *Psychological Record, 49,* 3–14.

Gambrell, L., & Marinak, B. (1997). Incentives and intrinsic motivation to read. In J. Guthrie & A. Wigfield (Eds.), *Reading engagement: Motivating readers through integrated instruction* (pp. 205–217). Newark, DE: International Reading Association.

Gehlbach, H., & Roeser, R. (2002). The middle way to motivating middle school students: Avoiding false dichotomies. *Middle School Journal, 33,* 39–46.

Good, T., & Brophy, J. (2008). *Looking in classrooms* (10th ed.). Boston: Allyn & Bacon.

Heckhausen, H. (1991). *Motivation and action* (2nd ed.). New York: Springer-Verlag.

Henderlong, J., & Lepper, M. (2002). The effects of praise on children's intrinsic motivation: A review and synthesis. *Psychological Bulletin, 128,* 774–795.

Hoffmann, K., Huff, J., Patterson, A., & Nietfeld, J. (2009). Elementary teachers' use and perceptions of rewards in the classroom. *Teaching and Teacher Education, 25,* 843–849.

Houlfort, N., Koestner, R., Joussenet, M., Nantel-Vivier, A., & Lekes, N. (2002). The impact of performance-contingent rewards on perceived autonomy and competence. *Motivation and Emotion, 26,* 279–295.

Johnson, D., & Johnson, R. (1999). *Learning together and alone: Cooperative, competitive, and individualistic learning* (5th ed.). Boston: Allyn & Bacon.

Johnson, D., & Johnson, R. (1985). Motivational processes in cooperative, competitive, and individualistic learning situations. In C. Ames & R. Ames (Eds.), *Research on motivation in education. Volume 2: The classroom milieu* (pp. 249–286). Orlando, FL: Academic Press.

Johnson, D., & Johnson, R. (2009). Energizing learning: The instructional power of conflict. *Educational Researcher, 38,* 37–51.

Kamins, M., & Dweck, C. (1999). Person versus process praise and criticism: Implications for contingent self-worth and coping. *Developmental Psychology, 35,* 835–847.

Kast, A., & Connor, K. (1988). Sex and age differences in response to informational and controlling feedback. *Personality and Social Psychology Bulletin, 14,* 514–523.

Keller, J. (1983). Motivational design of instruction. In C. Reigeluth (Ed.), *Instructional-design theories and models: An overview of their current status* (pp. 383–434). Hillsdale, NJ: Erlbaum.

Kohn, A. (1993). *Punished by rewards: The trouble with gold stars, incentive plans, A's, praise, and other bribes.* Boston: Houghton Mifflin.

Larrivee, B. (2002). The potential perils of praise in a democratic interactive classroom. *Action in Teacher Education, 23*(4), 77–88.

Lepper, M. (1983). Extrinsic reward and intrinsic motivation: Implications for the classroom. In J. Levine & M. Wang (Eds.), *Teacher and student perceptions: Implications for learning* (pp. 281–317). Hillsdale, NJ: Erlbaum.

Lepper, M., & Greene, D. (Eds.). (1978). *The hidden costs of reward: New perspectives on the psychology of human motivation.* Hillsdale, NJ: Erlbaum.

Lepper, M., & Henderlong, J. (2000). Turning "play" into "work" and "work" into "play." In C. Sansone & J. Harackiewicz (Eds.), *Intrinsic and extrinsic motivation: the search for optimal motivation and performance* (pp. 257–307). San Diego: Academic Press.

Lepper, M., Henderlong, J., & Gingras, I. (1999). Understanding the effects of extrinsic rewards on intrinsic motivation—uses and abuses of meta-analysis. *Psychological Bulletin, 125,* 669–676.

MacIver, D., & Reuman, D. (1993/94). Giving their best: Grading and recognition practices that motivate students to work hard. *American Educator, 17*(4), 24–31.

Marinak, B., & Gambrell, L. (2008). Intrinsic motivation and rewards: What sustains young children's engagement with text? *Literacy research and instruction, 47,* 9–26.

Marinak, B., & Gambrell, L. (2009, April 7). Rewarding reading?: Perhaps authenticity is the answer. *Teachers College Record.* Retrieved from http://www.tcrecord.org. ID Number: 15608.

McQuillan, J. (1997). The effects of incentives on reading. *Reading Research and Instruction, 36,* 111–125.

Midgley, C., & Urdan, T. (1992). The transition to middle level schools: Making it a good experience for all students. *Middle School Journal, 24,* 5–14.

Miller, A., & Hom, H. (1997). Conceptions of ability and the interpretation of praise, blame, and material rewards. *Journal of Experimental Education, 65,* 163–177.

Moriarty, B., Douglas, G., Punch, K., & Hattie, J. (1995). The importance of self-efficacy as a mediating variable between learning environments and achievement. *British Journal of Educational Psychology, 65,* 73–84.

Mueller, C., & Dweck, C. (1998). Praise for intelligence can undermine children's motivation and performance. *Journal of Personality and Social Psychology, 75,* 33–52.

Muraven, M., Rosman, H., & Gagné, M. (2007). Lack of autonomy and self-control: Performance contingent rewards lead to greater depletion. *Motivation and Emotion, 31,* 322–330.

Nafpaktitis, M., Mayer, G., & Butterworth, T. (1985). Natural rates of teacher approval and disapproval and their relation to student behavior in intermediate school classrooms. *Journal of Educational Psychology, 77,* 362–367.

Natriello, G., & Dornbusch, S. (1985). *Teacher evaluative standards and student effort.* New York: Longman.

Nichols, S., & Berliner, D. (2008). Why has high-stakes testing so easily slipped into contemporary American life? *Phi Delta Kappan, 89,* 672–676.

Oliver, R., & Williams, R. (2006). Performance patterns of high, medium, and low performers during and following a reward versus non-reward contingency phase. *School Psychology Quarterly, 21,* 119–147.

Ollendick, T., & Shapiro, E. (1984). An examination of vicarious reinforcement processes in children. *Journal of Experimental Child Psychology, 37,* 78–91.

Pajares, F., & Graham, L. (1998). Formalist thinking and language arts instruction: Teachers' and students' beliefs about truth and caring in the teaching conversation. *Teaching and Teacher Education, 14,* 855–870.

Pierce, W. D., Cameron, J., Banko, K., & So, S. (2003). Positive effects of rewards and performance standards on intrinsic motivation. *Psychological Record, 53,* 561–579.

Pintrich, P., Marx, R., & Boyle, R. (1993). Beyond cold conceptual change: The role of motivational beliefs and classroom contextual factors in the process of conceptual change. *Review of Educational Research, 63,* 167–199.

Reeve, J., & Deci, E. (1996). Elements of the competitive situation that affect intrinsic motivation. *Personality and Social Psychology Bulletin, 22,* 24–33.

Ryan, R., Chirkov, V., Little, T., Sheldon, K., Timoshina, E., & Deci, E. (1999). The American dream in Russia: Extrinsic aspirations and well-being in two cultures. *Personality and Social Psychology Bulletin, 25,* 1509–1524.

Ryan, R., & Deci, E. (2000). When rewards compete with nature: The undermining of intrinsic motivation and self-regulation. In C. Sansone & J. Harackiewicz (Eds.), *Intrinsic and extrinsic motivation: The search for optimal motivation and performance* (pp. 13–54). San Diego, CA: Academic Press.

Sansone, C., & Harackiewicz, J. (2000). *Intrinsic and extrinsic motivation: The search for optimal motivation and performance.* San Diego, CA: Academic Press.

Sharp, P. (1985). Behaviour modification in the secondary school: A survey of students' attitudes to rewards and praise. *Behavioral Approaches with Children, 9,* 109–112.

Shepperd, J., & Taylor, K. (1999). Social loafing and expectancy-value theory. *Personality and Social Psychology Bulletin, 25,* 1147–1158.

Slavin, R. (1995). *Cooperative learning: Theory, research, and practice* (2nd ed.) Boston: Allyn & Bacon.

Stein, M. (2001). Teaching and learning mathematics: How instruction can foster the knowing and understanding of number. In. J. Brophy (Ed.), *Subject-specific instructional methods and activities* (Vol. 8, pp. 111–143). New York: Elsevier Science.

Stipek, D. (1996). Motivation and instruction. In D. Berliner & R. Calfee (Eds.), *Handbook of educational psychology* (pp. 85-113). New York: Macmillan.

Stipek, D. (2002). *Motivation to learn: Integrating theory and practice* (4th ed.). Boston: Allyn & Bacon.

Sweet, A., Guthrie, J., & Ng, M. (1998). Teacher perceptions and student reading motivation. *Journal of Educational Psychology, 90,* 210–223.

Thompson, T. (1997). Do we need to train teachers how to administer praise? Self-worth theory says we do. *Learning and Instruction, 7,* 49–63.

Ware, B. (1978). What rewards do students want? *Phi Delta Kappan, 59,* 355–356.

Wigfield, A., & Eccles, J. (2000). Expectancy-value theory and achievement motivation. *Contemporary Educational Psychology, 25,* 68–81.

Wlodkowski, R. (1985). *Enhancing adult motivation to learn.* San Francisco: Jossey-Bass.

7

Self-Determination Theory of Intrinsic Motivation: Meeting Students' Needs for Autonomy, Competence, and Relatedness

That children can be regulated by external constraints and controls is without dispute. The question is whether this describes the atmosphere and goals of education to which we as educators, and as a culture, aspire.

    An alternative perspective, more complex and subtle than the one just described, considers the motivation to learn to be a developmental issue. While learning can be wholly controlled and prompted from the outside (i.e., externally regulated), the goal of education is, from the alternative view, the development of self-regulation *for learning. This is conceptualized as a movement away from heteronomy and toward autonomy in the acquisition of knowledge, away from reliance on others for the incentives to learn and toward internal satisfaction with accomplishment and the learning process itself.* (Ryan, Connell & Grolnick, 1992, p. 168, emphasis in original)

CONNECTING WITH STUDENTS' EXISTING INTRINSIC MOTIVATION

The extrinsic motivation strategies described in chapter 6 are designed to stimulate students to engage in classroom activities effortfully because completing these activities successfully will bring them valued rewards. When motivation is purely extrinsic, the activity itself is not valued except as an instrument that students can use to obtain rewards that they do value. In contrast, *intrinsic motivational strategies apply when students value (or can learn to value) the activity itself.* These strategies are based on the idea that teachers should emphasize activities that students find interesting or enjoyable, so that they engage in these activities willingly without any need for extrinsic incentives.

    For reasons described in chapter 1, it is not feasible to base your all-day, everyday motivational strategies on the principle of connecting with students' existing intrinsic motivation. However, you can use three general sets of strategies to increase the role of intrinsic motivation in your students' classroom experiences: (a) use classroom management and teaching styles that address students' needs for autonomy, competence, and relatedness; (b) plan learning activities that students are likely to find enjoyable or intrinsically rewarding; and (c) modify the design of other learning activities to include features that will enhance the activities' appeal. The first approach is discussed in this chapter. The other two approaches are discussed in chapter 8, along with teachers' views concerning their applications.

CONCEPTIONS OF INTRINSIC MOTIVATION

Some treatments of intrinsic motivation emphasize the *affective* quality of students' engagement in an activity—the degree to which they enjoy or derive pleasure from the experience. This kind of intrinsic motivation is more typical of play or recreational activities than learning activities. Other treatments of intrinsic motivation place more emphasis on its *cognitive* aspects—the degree to which students find participation in the activity to be self-actualizing, enriching, empowering, or otherwise meaningful and worthwhile. To the extent that these cognitive aspects predominate, intrinsic motivation begins to resemble motivation to learn as defined in chapter 9.

Most intrinsic motivation theorists do not directly address distinctions between its affective/fun aspects and its cognitive/learning aspects. Instead, they focus on the issue of control, emphasizing that actions must be experienced as self-determined if intrinsic motivation is to develop. This emphasis is seen in the quotation that begins the chapter.

Until recently, intrinsic motivation theorists tended to depict intrinsic motivation and extrinsic motivation as incompatible opposites, and to caution teachers against using extrinsic incentives lest they erode their students' intrinsic motivation. This tendency to portray a simple dichotomy has receded in favor of the idea that *relative autonomy* increases by degrees as one moves from purely extrinsic motivation (externally controlled) through mixed forms to purely intrinsic motivation (autonomous). Most intrinsic motivation theorists now concede that extrinsic incentives can be used in ways that complement other motivational strategies and do not undermine students' intrinsic motivation. Even so, they still argue that intrinsic motivational approaches to teaching are preferable to extrinsic approaches. Guay, Ratelle, and Chanal (2008) reviewed several studies indicating that self-determined learning tends to be of higher quality than extrinsically motivated learning. Teachers tend to agree (Sweet, Guthrie, & Ng, 1998).

The concept of intrinsic motivation began as part of the attempt to balance the notion that people are driven by felt needs with the notion that we often engage in activities because we want to, not because we feel a need to (Collier, 1994). Abraham Maslow (1962) spoke of self-actualization needs that we begin to express when our lower needs are satisfied. These include needs for creative self-expression, satisfaction of curiosity, and other exploratory or skill- enhancing activities that appear to be intrinsically motivated.

Robert White (1959) suggested that we often act out of competence motivation: We want to deal effectively with the environment and master and control the things around us. This energizes activities such as attention, exploration, thought, and play. It also causes us to seek new challenges rather than wait for events to happen, and to experience such challenges as intrinsically motivating.

Contemporary intrinsic motivation theorists define intrinsic motivation in terms of the presence of subjective perceptions of self-determination rather than the absence of extrinsic incentives or pressures (Condry & Stokker, 1992). That is, if we feel self-determined, then, for practical purposes, we are self-determined, even if extrinsic incentives are in effect or if our behavior is constrained in various ways. As an extreme example, consider a murderer sentenced to life in prison without possibility of parole. Although incarcerated, this man can exercise autonomy in managing those aspects of his life over which he still has control. Rather than descend into chronic rage or depression, he can make the best of the situation by keeping fit, cultivating friendships, and engaging in educational and recreational activities (and feel self-determined in doing so).

Other conceptions of intrinsic motivation also emphasize our subjective experiences. In discussing flow, for example, Csikszentmihalyi (1993) emphasized the experience of becoming absorbed in an activity that offers challenges that are well matched to our current skills (see chapter 1). Eckblad (1981) defined extrinsically motivated activity as involving a clear differentiation in awareness between means and ends. In contrast, intrinsically motivated activity is not experienced as a means undertaken to achieve some goal. There is no awareness of means-end separation, of the self, or of striving to achieve some goal separate from the ongoing activity.

DECI AND RYAN'S SELF-DETERMINATION THEORY

Most of these themes are included in the self-determination theory put forth by Edward Deci and Richard Ryan, which has inspired a great deal of research on the value aspects of motivation in education. Deci and Ryan believe that a full understanding of goal-directed behavior, and of psychological development and well-being generally, requires addressing the needs that give goals their psychological potency and influence people's self-regulated activities. They have identified *three psychological needs—for autonomy, competence, and relatedness—as universal, fundamental, and broad ranging in their influences on goal-oriented pursuits.* If those needs are fulfilled, people's motivation will be autonomous: Their pursuits will be well aligned with their sense of self and reflect what they view as interesting or important. If not, their motivation will be more controlled and their pursuits less self-determined (Deci & Ryan, 2008; Heppner et al., 2008; Vansteenkiste, Lens, & Deci, 2006).

Satisfaction of the three basic needs provides the necessary conditions for people to engage in self-determined activity. Free from concern about satisfying these needs, they can do whatever they find interesting or important, such as read a book or play music. When their fundamental needs are being thwarted, however, their behavior is less likely to be self-determined. Instead of intrinsically motivated pursuits, they are likely to focus on getting their needs met, or if that cannot be done easily, on developing defenses or pursuing need gratification substitutes (such as wealth, fame, or popularity). If sustained over time, this will have negative consequences for their integrity, vitality, and health (Ryan, Huta, & Deci, 2008).

Intrinsically motivated actions are performed out of interest and require no external prods, promises, or threats. They are experienced as wholly self-determined, emanating from our sense of self. *Extrinsically motivated actions* are performed instrumentally to attain some separate consequence. They usually would not occur spontaneously and therefore must be prompted by incentives or other external pressures.

Levels of Extrinsic Regulation That Increasingly Resemble Intrinsic Motivation

Deci and Ryan have elaborated self-determination theory to include a developmental analysis of extrinsic motivation. This analysis differentiates subtypes of extrinsic motivation and explains how *extrinsically motivated actions can become self-determined through the developmental processes of internalization and integration*. Internalization refers to the transformation of an externally prescribed regulation or value into an internally adopted one. *Integration* is the process through which internalized regulations and values become integrated into the self.

By enabling us to assimilate external values and reconstitute them into personally endorsed values, internalization allows us to feel self-determined when we enact these values. When the process functions optimally, we identify with the values, assimilate them into our integrated sense of self, and thus fully accept them as our own. However, internalization can become forestalled, so that some values remain external or only partially internalized. *Deci and Ryan identified four types of extrinsic regulation that can be ordered along a continuum from external control to autonomous self-regulation.*

External regulation occurs when our actions are regulated by external rewards, pressures, or constraints. Students are externally regulated when they attend to lessons or work on assignments solely because they will be rewarded if they do or punished if they do not.

Introjected regulation occurs when we act as we do because we think we should or would feel guilty if we did not. These dispositions to action are internalized to the extent that we have learned to produce the expected behavior and no longer require external prodding to do so. However, we are responding to felt pressure that is still external to our sense of self. Introjected regulation is seen in students who attend to lessons or work on assignments primarily because they do not want to get bad grades and disappoint their parents.

Identified regulation occurs when the regulation or value is adopted by the self as personally important and valuable. Identified regulation is seen in students who attend to lessons and work on assignments because they view these activities as important for their self-selected goal of attending college or entering a particular occupation.

Integrated regulation is the most self-determined form of extrinsic motivation. It results from the integration of identified values and regulations into one's coherent sense of self. Any conflicts between different values and associated action tendencies (e.g., the desire to be both a good student and a rock musician) are eliminated by making whatever adjustments might be needed to achieve harmonious coexistence.

In a given situation, people may be either amotivated, extrinsically motivated, or intrinsically motivated. When amotivated, we do not seek to enact any particular behavior or to pursue any particular goal. If certain goal-oriented behavior is expected in the situation, we may seek to avoid it because we do not value the behavior or believe that we can enact it successfully. To the extent that we are motivated to do something in particular, we may be extrinsically motivated (at varying levels of self-determination) or intrinsically motivated (fully self-determined).

Among extrinsically motivated activities, those that are lower on the continuum (external regulation, introjected regulation) are enacted in response to external pressures and thus considered forms of *controlled motivation*. In contrast, those that are higher on the continuum (identified and integrated regulation) are enacted voluntarily for our own reasons (because we view them as important). Because identified and integrated regulations are experienced as self-determined, they are classified along with intrinsic regulation as forms of *autonomous motivation*. Nevertheless, identified and integrated regulation are still considered forms of extrinsic motivation because they are performed as means to attain separate goals. In contrast, intrinsically motivated actions are done "for their own sake." We do them because we view them as interesting or enjoyable.

These distinctions are illustrated in representative items from a scale developed by Pelletier et al. (1995) to measure sport motivation. The scale incorporates three of the four levels of extrinsic regulation (it does not attempt to distinguish between identified and integrated regulation, which also is true of most other measures of extrinsic regulation). In addition, the scale distinguishes among three subtypes of intrinsic motivation. As adapted by Standage, Duda, and Ntoumamis (2003), it asks for students to rate the degree to which the items correspond to their reasons for participating in physical education (PE):

- Intrinsic motivation to know ("For the fun of discovering new skills/techniques")
- Intrinsic motivation toward accomplishments ("For the satisfaction I experience while I am perfecting my abilities")
- Intrinsic motivation to experience stimulation ("For the excitement I feel when I am really involved in the activity")
- Identified regulation ("Because it is one of the best ways I have chosen to develop other aspects of myself")
- Introjected regulation ("Because I must do PE to feel good about myself")
- External regulation ("To show others that I am good at PE")
- Amotivation ("I used to have good reasons for doing PE, but now I am asking myself why I have to")

Expansion from an exclusive focus on intrinsic motivation to include attention to several forms of extrinsic regulation has greatly increased the applicability of self-determination theory to the classroom. Given the nature of schooling as described in chapter 1, the primary motivational issues facing teachers are not about intrinsic motivation but about helping students come to appreciate the value of school learning activities, and thus shift from external or introjected (controlled) regulation to identified or integrated (autonomous) regulation. This is illustrated in the findings of the following studies.

Losier and Koestner (1999) found that college students who talked about following political campaigns and voting in an upcoming election out of identified motivation ("It's for my own good") rather than intrinsic motivation ("For the pleasure of doing it") were more likely to appreciate the relevance and importance of the election, to actively seek information, and to vote on election day. They concluded that identification (rather than intrinsic motivation) is key to the successful regulation of behaviors that are socially valued but not necessarily fun, such as voting in an election (and I would add, engaging in most school activities).

Norwich (1999) collected data on students' reported reasons for putting forth effort on schoolwork. The students' identified reasons were closely related to their intrinsic reasons, whereas both of those were contrasted with their introjected reasons. This suggests that identified regulation has more in common with intrinsic motivation than it does with introjected regulation (at least in students' thinking), even though identified regulation is classified as a form of extrinsic motivation.

Other studies indicate that relationships among the different forms of motivation identified by self-determination theory tend to follow a pattern in which each form is correlated most highly with the forms that are adjacent to it on the continuum from amotivation through extrinsic motivation to intrinsic motivation. External regulation tends to correlate most highly with amotivation and with introjected regulation, for example, and integrated regulation tends to correlate most highly with identified regulation and intrinsic motivation. These findings support self-determination theory's postulate that the different forms of motivation are organized along a continuum of self-determination (Guay, Ratelle, & Chanal, 2008; Otis, Grouzet, & Pelletier, 2005).

Although motivation for engaging in a particular activity is likely to be more specific, all forms of motivation apply to activity arenas as extensive as schooling. Otis et al. (2005) demonstrated this in a study of French Canadian students followed from eighth through tenth grades. Each year, the students were asked to reply to the question, "Why do you go to school?" by indicating the degree to which each of several response alternatives corresponded to their own reasons. The response alternatives were constructed to represent intrinsic motivation to know (e.g., because I experience pleasure and satisfaction while learning new things), identified regulation (e.g., because I think that education will help me better prepare for the career I have chosen), introjected regulation (e.g., to show myself that I am an intelligent person), external regulation (e.g., to have a better salary later), or amotivation (e.g., I cannot see why I go to school and frankly I could not care less).

The eighth graders most frequently endorsed items reflecting identified regulation (mean = 4.42 of a possible 5), followed by external regulation (4.21), intrinsic motivation (3.72), and introjected regulation (3.52). Few students endorsed items reflecting amotivation (1.48). By tenth grade, they still were unlikely to endorse amotivation items (1.50), but their responses to the other items indicated a general drop in motivation for schooling. They still were most likely to endorse items reflecting identified regulation, followed by external regulation, intrinsic motivation, and introjected regulation, but the means had fallen to 4.02, 3.98, 3.15, and 2.82, respectively. Across all three years, they were much more likely to say that they went to school for career preparation and access to well paid jobs than for the pleasure or satisfaction of learning new things or pursuing their interests.

These findings further illustrate that the forms of value afforded by K–12 schooling derive mostly from activities that are important (and thus amenable to identified regulation) but not necessarily interesting or fun (and thus amenable to intrinsic motivation). This was underscored in a subsequent study, also done with French Canadian high school students (Ratelle, Guay, Vallerand, Larose, & Senècal, 2007). In this study, the authors used the same data collection methods but then classified students into three groups. The first group (6%) had low levels of autonomous motivation and moderate to high levels of both controlled motivation and amotivation. The second group (46%) had moderate levels of both autonomous and controlled motivation but low levels of amotivation. The third group (48%) had high levels of both autonomous and controlled motivation and low levels of amotivation. Notice that among these high school students, all but 6% reported moderate to high levels of autonomous motivation, but always accompanied by moderate to high levels of controlled motivation. No identifiable group was characterized primarily by autonomous motivation, let alone specifically intrinsic motivation.

A follow-up study in another city produced similar but even less encouraging results. The same three groups were identified, but their relative percentages were 7%, 59%, and

33%. Thus, statements reflecting autonomous motivation were endorsed even less frequently in this second sample of high school students than in the first sample.

However, a third study done with college students produced quite different results. This time, 39% of the sample was high in both autonomous and controlled motivation, 25% was low to moderate in both autonomous and controlled motivation, and 36% was high in autonomous motivation but low in controlled motivation. Furthermore, across the college sample as a whole, students were more likely to endorse items reflecting autonomous (intrinsic, identified) forms of motivation than controlled (introjected, external) forms. Thus, autonomous motivation is more prominent in college, where students attend voluntarily and have much more autonomy in deciding what and how to study, than it is in high school, where attendance is compulsory for most students and opportunities to make choices are limited (Ratelle et al., 2007).

Similar studies done in East Asia revealed patterns in both seventh graders in Singapore (Liu, Wang, Tan, Koh, & Ee, 2008) and college students in South Korea (Lee, 2005) that were closer to those for the college students than the high school students in Canada. Apparently, high school is a particularly controlling learning environment relative to other educational levels.

AUTONOMY, COMPETENCE, AND RELATEDNESS AS BASES FOR AUTONOMOUS MOTIVATION

The degree to which people are able to synthesize cultural values and regulations and incorporate them into the self depends on the degree to which fulfillment of their basic psychological needs is supported as they engage in relevant activities. People tend naturally to internalize the values and regulations of their social groups, but the process is facilitated by feelings of relatedness to the socializers and perceptions of competence to perform the expected behaviors. This includes understanding the meaning or rationale behind a regulation as well as the ability to enact it. Support for relatedness and competence needs may promote partial internalization of a regulation or value, but support for autonomy needs is also needed to enable internalization to progress to the level of integration. Excessive external pressures, controls, or evaluations are likely to forestall this process (Ryan & Deci, 2006).

Social settings promote autonomous motivation when they satisfy people's needs for autonomy, competence, and relatedness their needs to feel connected to others within the setting, to function effectively in it, and to feel a sense of personal initiative while doing so. When teachers and classroom climates support satisfaction of these needs, students will feel self-determined and autonomously motivated; when they do not, students will feel controlled and pressured.

At first glance, there appears to be a contradiction between the need for autonomy and the need for relatedness. For example, to the extent that a teacher requires students to do things they would not do otherwise, the students' desire to please the teacher (part of their need for relatedness) would motivate them to adopt the teacher's agenda rather than pursue their own (Buunk & Nauta, 2000; Carver & Scheier, 2000). However, the defining feature of the sense of autonomy is the students' subjective sense of self-determination, not the presence of external incentives or pressures. Hodgins, Koestner, and Duncan (1996) have shown that when the need for autonomy is expressed as a tendency to experience self-determination of one's behavior (rather than as a tendency to prefer acting independently without any influence from others), it actually promotes connectedness with others and positive perceptions of social experiences. In this regard, self-determination theorists distinguish autonomy from independence, noting that one can be autonomously dependent or be forced into undesired independence (Ryan & Deci, 2006).

Learners' reports from settings ranging from academic learning in classrooms to exercise or physical education activities in gyms to game play in laboratories all indicate that satisfaction of the three basic needs is associated with positive outcomes such as higher intrinsic motivation, higher feelings of satisfaction or well-being, better performance, and desire to repeat the experience (Edmunds, Ntoumanis, & Duda, 2007; Filak & Sheldon, 2008; Krapp, 2005; Legault, Green-Demers, & Pelletier, 2006; Ntoumanis, 2005; Reinboth, Duda, & Ntoumanis, 2004; Ryan, Rigby, & Przybylski, 2006; Shih, 2008; Skinner, Furrer, Marchand, & Kindermann, 2008; Standage, Duda, & Ntoumanis, 2005; Vansteenkiste et al., 2006). An experimental study in which need satisfaction was manipulated yielded similar findings (Sheldon & Filak, 2008).

Even though self-determination theorists have broadened from their original focus on intrinsic motivation to include attention to several forms of extrinsic regulation, their emphasis on intrinsic motivation has continued. As a complement to conceptualizing learners' quality of motivation as autonomous versus controlled, they have begun addressing the content of the goals that students value. Much of this work contrasts intrinsic goals, which focus on growth, relationships, community, or health, with extrinsic goals, which focus on wealth, fame, image, or power. Compared to people who focus on extrinsic goals, people who focus on intrinsic goals tend to behave more prosocially and show higher and more stable levels of psychological well-being (Ryan et al., 2008; Vansteenkiste et al., 2006).

Classroom applications of this work have employed a technique called *goal framing*. In several experiments, self-determination theorists have presented learners with the same learning activity, but framed it within an intrinsic goal rationale for one group but an extrinsic goal rationale for the other. Examples include:

- Learn about the Father Damien Foundation to learn more about how you can help people with tuberculosis (intrinsic goal frame), or because doing so might help you to collect a lot of money for the Foundation and hence be admired by others (extrinsic goal frame; Vansteenkiste, Timmermans, Lens, Soenens, & Van den Broeck, 2008).
- Learn about recycling so you can teach your future children to contribute to a clean and healthy environment (intrinsic), or so you can save money on your future job by recycling materials (extrinsic; Vansteenkiste, Simons, J., Lens, W., Sheldon, K., & Deci, 2004a).
- Learn about business communication styles to contribute to your personal development (intrinsic), or because this could help your chances of getting a well-paid job in the future (extrinsic; Vansteenkiste, et al, 2004b).
- Read about how to perform a card trick because you could use it to entertain your friends and because you can help us (the experimenters) by taking a test on the material to enable us to evaluate the clarity of our instructions (intrinsic), or because you want to do well on the subsequent test which is a good measure of people's learning skills (extrinsic; Schaffner & Schiefele, 2007).

These studies indicated that, compared to students exposed to extrinsic goal framing, students exposed to intrinsic goal framing showed more interest and autonomous motivation, less anxiety, more persistence, and sometimes better performance. Note, however, that the goals emphasized within the intrinsic goal framing treatments were largely cognitive and appealed to the students' identities as prosocial people who wanted to be helpful to others and to the world generally. These were quite different from the affective goals of pleasure or enjoyment that have been emphasized in most studies of intrinsic motivation.

Deci and Ryan's (1994) suggestions to teachers emphasized socializing and instructing students in ways that encourage self-determined learning initiatives and thus result in intrinsically motivated learning. They identified three factors that promote self-determination in classrooms:

1. providing meaningful rationales that will enable students to understand the purpose and personal importance of each learning activity;
2. acknowledging students' feelings when it is necessary to require them to do something they don't want to do (by letting them know that you are aware of their feelings and taking time to explain why the requirement is needed); and
3. managing the classroom and instructing students using a style that emphasizes choice rather than control.

To the extent that the goal of intrinsic motivation is not fully attainable and extrinsic motivation enters the picture, they favor teaching in ways that produce autonomous rather than controlled forms of extrinsic regulation. Their ideas, presented in the following sections, overlap considerably with principles for orienting students toward learning goals rather than performance goals (see chapter 4).

RESPONDING TO STUDENTS' AUTONOMY NEEDS

As its very name indicates, self-determination theory places special emphasis on the importance of feeling self-determined (versus controlled) in carrying out human activities. Studies indicate that autonomous motivation enables people to exert more effort and feel less conflict when pursuing goals, perform more successfully (especially when the activity requires creativity, flexibility, or dealing with complexities), and experience a sense of well-being (Koestner, 2008; Ryan & Deci, 2006). When addressing teachers, self-determination theorists strongly emphasize the importance of meeting students' autonomy needs, citing research indicating that most teachers tend to be controlling when they could get better results by being autonomy supportive (Assor, Kaplan, & Roth, 2002; Bozack, Vega, McCaslin, & Good, 2008; Reeve, 2009; Wiley, Good, & McCaslin, 2008). You can support your students' sense of self-determination by offering them opportunities for autonomy and choice and by minimizing overtly controlling behaviors.

Encourage Students to Function as Autonomous Learners

Autonomous forms of student motivation are associated with desirable correlates, whereas controlled forms are associated with undesirable correlates. For example, Ryan and Connell (1989) found that externally regulated students showed little interest, value, and effort at school and tended to disown responsibility for failures by blaming the teacher or the school. Introjected students reported more effort, but also more anxiety and self-blame. They reacted to failure by amplifying anxiety and self-criticism. Identified students showed higher levels of effort, interest, enjoyment of school, and positive coping than the introjected or externally regulated students. Finally, students who were intrinsically motivated showed the highest levels of interest, enjoyment, confidence, and effort.

Subsequent research done at several grade levels and in several countries has yielded similar findings (Conroy & Coatsworth, 2007; Hayamizu, 1997; Ryan & LaGuardia, 1999; Sheldon & Elliot, 1998; Sheldon & Kasser, 1998; Shih, 2008; Standage, Duda, & Ntoumanis, 2003; Taylor & Ntoumanis, 2007; Tsai, Kunter, Lüdtke, Trautwein, & Ryan, 2008; Wong, 2000; Yamauchi & Tanaka, 1998). Some studies have extended these findings to other measures such as grades or test scores (Conti, 2001; Grolnick & Ryan, 1989; Miserandino, 1996) or staying in vs. dropping out of school (Hardré & Reeve, 2003; Vallerand, Fortier, & Guay, 1997). However, some also have suggested that the benefits of intrinsic motivation or perceptions of autonomy are limited to the affective aspects of task engagement and do not result in better achievement (Garcia & Pintrich, 1996).

Deci, Ryan, and their colleagues have investigated what is involved in autonomy-supportive teaching. Deci, Schwartz, Sheinman, and Ryan (1981) asked teachers to rate the appropriateness of various responses to problems that students might display (e.g., not turning in homework, misbehaving). Autonomy-supportive teachers endorsed investigating and working from the child's perspective, whereas controlling teachers endorsed rewards and punishments, social comparisons, or application of external praise, pressure, or contingencies. Later in the school year, the researchers assessed these teachers' students' motivation. They found that students of autonomy-supportive teachers showed more curiosity, desire for challenge, and other evidence of mastery motivation, whereas students of controlling teachers showed less mastery motivation, lower confidence in their abilities, and lower self-worth perceptions. Other investigators also have reported more positive patterns of motivation among students of autonomy-supportive teachers (Adie, Duda, & Ntoumanis, 2008; Assor, Kaplan, Kanat-Maymon, & Roth, 2005; Black & Deci, 2000; Conroy & Coatsworth, 2007; Guay, Boggiano, & Vallerand, 2001; Noels, Clement, & Pelletier, 1999; Ommundsen & Kvalo, 2007; Pelletier, Fortier, Vallerand, & Briere, 2002; Reeve & Jang, 2006; Ryan & Grolnick, 1986; Taylor & Ntoumanis, 2007; Tsai et al., 2008; Valas & Sovik, 1994), and some have reported higher grades or test scores as well (Black & Deci, 2000; Jang, 2008; Soenens & Vansteenkiste, 2005; Vansteenkiste et al., 2004a,b; Vansteenkiste et al., 2005).

Reeve and Jang (2006) reviewed indicators of autonomy-supportive versus controlling teacher behavior identified by previous researchers and verified that most of them were correlated with students' perceptions of being autonomous or controlled in their classrooms. *Autonomy-supportive teacher behaviors included*: time spent listening to students (vs. speaking to them), asking students what they want, time spent allowing students to work in their own way, time devoted to student talk (vs. teacher talk), inviting students to sit close to learning materials, providing rationales for suggestions or directives, delivering praise as informational feedback rather than contingent reward, encouraging students, offering cues or hints when they were stuck, being responsive to their questions, and communicating perspective taking statements (especially expressions of empathy when students were struggling with difficult challenges). *Teacher behaviors identified as controlling included*: time spent holding or monopolizing learning materials, stating or showing answers or solutions (rather than allowing students time to discover these for themselves), uttering directives or commands, making "should" or "must" statements, and asking controlling questions (issuing directives but phrasing them in question form). Essentially, autonomy-supportive teachers provide opportunities for their students to think and solve problems, while scaffolding their efforts relatively indirectly, whereas control-oriented teachers overmanage their students by using highly detailed directives to guide them through fixed programs of steps in learning and problem solving.

In addition to many correlational studies, self-determination theorists have completed several experiments testing the effects of presenting instruction in an autonomy-supportive manner (and in particular, providing rationales explaining why the learning was worth pursuing). These studies indicated that autonomy-supportive instruction had positive effects on students' motivation and engagement, and sometimes on their learning as well (Jang, 2008; Koestner et al., 2006; Reeve, Jang, Carrell, Jeon, & Barch, 2004).

Some investigators have expressed concern that autonomy support has been defined too narrowly, such as by equating it with provision of choice without considering the meaningfulness of the choices to students (Assor et al., 2002). Others warn against treating autonomy support as if it were an end in itself, instead of viewing it within the context of the teacher's responsibility to scaffold student learning. Stefanou, Perencevich, Di Cintio, and Turner, (2004) classified autonomy-support strategies as organizational (opportunities for students to select groupmates or seating arrangements, participate in creating and implementing classroom rules and work evaluation procedures, or take responsibility for due dates for assignments), procedural (opportunities to choose materials to use in class projects, choose the way competence will be demonstrated, display work in an individual manner, discuss their wants, and handle materials), or cognitive (opportunities to discuss strategies for addressing problems or finding multiple solutions to them, justify solutions for the purpose of sharing expertise, have ample time for decision making, be independent problem solvers (with sufficient scaffolding), reevaluate their mistakes and seek to correct them, receive informational feedback, formulate personal goals or realign tasks to correspond with their interests, debate ideas freely, and ask questions and articulate their ideas). They viewed these forms of autonomy support as increasing in personal and instructional relevance: organizational autonomy support provides the least opportunity for making meaningful choices, and cognitive autonomy support provides the most.

In summary, autonomy-supportive teachers promote self-determination by understanding students' perspectives, supporting their initiatives, creating opportunities for choice, being encouraging rather than demanding or directive, and allowing students to work in their own way. They also promote internalization by encouraging questions and allowing expression of negative feelings, providing rationales that help students understand the purpose and value of activities, stimulating interest, and supporting confidence. Fundamentally, autonomy support is more about how expectations are communicated than about the number or extent of these expectations.

Allow Students to Make Choices

Offer your students choices of activities and opportunities to exercise autonomy in pursuing alternative ways to meet requirements. For example, allow them to select topics for book reports, composition assignments, and research projects, and perhaps also to select from alternative ways of reporting to you or the class as a whole (e.g., work with a partner to present a biography as an interview of the person, present a book review using a conversational format). If they are likely to make undesirable choices if left completely on their own, provide a menu of choices or help them make choices that are well-suited to their interests and reading levels (Starnes & Paris, 2000; Worthy, Patterson, Salas, Prater, and Turner, 2002). Take students' interests into account when considering choice options (see Box 7.1).

Many instructional goals involve developing skills and strategies rather than learning information. In these situations, many different information sources and instructional materials or media may be useful as means for accomplishing the learning goals. You might ask your students to suggest means that you had not considered but would be willing to approve as equivalent alternatives. By offering such choices, you provide students with opportunities to assume responsibility for regulating their own learning and to experience a sense of self-determination as they do so.

Offer autonomy and choice opportunities to all students, not just higher achievers. Some teachers provide frequent autonomy and choice opportunities for their higher achievers but micromanage the learning efforts of their lower achievers. Low achievers often do need more explicit structuring and scaffolding of their learning efforts, but they also need opportunities to experience self-determination and self-regulation of their learning (Weinstein, 2002).

Box 7.1   Connecting with Students' Interests

Students develop abiding interests in certain domains of knowledge (pioneer life, dinosaurs). They also discover that they enjoy certain activities that provide bases for learning (reading certain literary genres, writing poetry, acting in plays or simulations, conducting experiments, doing research). The reasons for unique patterns of interest development are not clear. Most theorists assume that interests begin when children are exposed to a knowledge domain or type of activity and discover that they value it because they identify with it in some fashion or because it meets some salient need. As interests take hold and develop, they begin to motivate action sequences that incorporate the experience of flow as described by Csikszentmihalyi (1993). That is, as people pursue their interests they develop domain-specific knowledge and skills, leading them to seek out interest-related activities that feature optimal matches between their current knowledge and skill levels and the levels of challenge embedded in the activities.

To the extent that doing so is feasible given your instructional goals, you may find it worthwhile to incorporate your students' interests into your curriculum (or at least to point out connections between the curriculum and those interests), as well as to offer students choice options that allow them to pursue their interests as they work on reading, research, and writing assignments. Researchers who have studied the role of interest in learning have found that students sustain their attention more continuously and process information at deeper levels when they have a personal interest or investment in the knowledge domain (Alexander, Kulikowich, & Jetton, 1994; Renninger, Hidi, & Krapp, 1992; Schiefele, 1991).

One way to build in choice opportunities for all students is to set up *learning centers* where students can work individually or in collaboration with peers on a variety of projects. Some of the projects may be required because they are essential to accomplishment of your unit goals, but others might be optional—viewed as enrichment activities and included at least in part because most students find them interesting or enjoyable.

For example, a language arts or social studies center might feature children's literature selections relating to your current social studies unit. The collection would include a variety of genres of children's literature written at a range of reading levels, although it would be limited to books considered suitable as content sources for enriching knowledge about the unit topic (e.g., pioneer life or the Civil War). Students might be required to read and write their reactions to one or more of these books, but they could decide which books to read. They also might be allowed at least some autonomy (along with any needed guidance) concerning the content and organization of their reports.

Reynolds and Symons (2001) engaged third graders in an activity calling for them to locate information in books. Some were allowed to choose which of three books they would use, but others were assigned to the books randomly. Students allowed to choose their books used more efficient search strategies and were faster at locating information than students not given this choice.

Morrow (1992, 1993) developed a writing and reading appreciation program that included significant provisions for student autonomy and choice in working on projects. Several times each week, students worked in a literacy center that contained 5–8 books per child, including picture story books, poetry, informational books, magazines, biographies, and other fictional and nonfictional sources. The selections were related to topics being taught in science or social studies. The center also included six types of manipulative materials that students might use with their projects:

- felt board stories (characters from a book made of oaktag or construction paper that could be used when retelling the story by displaying them on a felt board);
- taped stories that children could listen to through headsets as they followed along in the accompanying book;
- roll movies (illustrated stories that could be advanced scene by scene by scrolling them through a viewing apparatus);
- prop stories (collections of materials for use in retelling a story, such as three stuffed bears, three bowls, and a yellow-haired doll for telling the story of *Goldilocks*);
- puppet stories (various types of puppets to use in retelling stories); and
- chalk talks (materials for drawing a story on a chalkboard or sheet of paper while the story is being read or told).

Students could use these or other materials to: read a book, magazine, or newspaper; read to a friend; listen to someone read to them; listen to a taped story and follow the words in the book; use the felt board with a storybook and felt characters; use the roll movie with its storybook; write a story; draw a picture about a story they had read; write a story and then make it into a book; make a felt story or a tape for a book they had read or a story they had written; write and perform a puppet show; record activities in the log; check out books to take home and read; or follow directions on a task card for some other selected activity.

Students could choose to work alone or with peers. They operated mostly independently of the teacher in deciding what tasks to work on and how to complete them. However, they were encouraged to select activities that included both reading and writing, to try activities they had not tried before and classmates they had not worked with before, and to take on significant projects and follow them through to completion rather than flit from one thing to another.

Students involved in this program expressed more interest in reading and writing than students in classes restricted to more traditional activities. They also performed better on tests of reading comprehension and oral and written literacy. Note that this approach not only responded to students' autonomy needs but also responded to their relatedness needs by allowing them to work together with classmates of their own choosing. A variation that might be used with any subject matter is to divide students into self-selected interest groups and allow them to do worthwhile content-related research projects.

RESPONDING TO STUDENTS' COMPETENCE NEEDS

People tend to enjoy and become absorbed in activities that are well matched to their current levels of knowledge and skill and thus provide optimal challenges that allow them to develop their competence (Elliot et al., 2000). This principle has several potential applications in classrooms.

First, *as a prerequisite, make sure that learning activities are in fact well matched to your students' levels of knowledge and skill.* If necessary, use the strategies presented in Chapters 3–5 to help students recognize and appreciate optimal challenges. Among activities that are optimally challenging, some are especially enjoyable or absorbing because they offer good opportunities for students to satisfy their competence needs. Examples include activities that (a) allow students to make active responses and get immediate feedback, (b) incorporate game-like features that most students find enjoyable, or (c) incorporate features that are associated with job satisfaction.

Emphasize Activities That Offer Opportunities to Make Active Responses and Get Immediate Feedback

Active responses. Students tend to prefer activities that allow them to respond actively—to interact with you or with one another, manipulate materials, or do something other than just listen or read. Routine recitation, boardwork, or seatwork activities provide only limited potential for active response. *Students should get frequent opportunities to go beyond simple question-answer formats in order to do projects, experiments, discussions, role play, simulations, computerized learning activities, educational games, or creative applications.*

Even within traditional lesson formats, you can create opportunities for more active involvement by going beyond factual questions to stimulate students to discuss or debate issues, offer opinions about cause-and-effect relationships, speculate about hypothetical situations, or think creatively about problems. Students need to master basic facts, concepts, and definitions, but they also need frequent opportunities to apply, analyze, synthesize, or evaluate what they have learned at the knowledge or comprehension level.

Also, *avoid overemphasis on convergent questions that admit to only a single correct answer.* In leading a discussion of a story or text chapter, for example, include questions that invite students to tell what they thought were the most interesting or important aspects, and why (Sansone & Morgan, 1992). Include frequent opportunities for students to state opinions, make predictions, suggest sources of action, formulate solutions to problems, or engage in other forms of divergent thinking.

Literacy should include dramatic readings and prose and poetry composition; mathematics should include realistic problem-solving and application opportunities; science should include experiments and other laboratory work; social studies should include debates, research projects, and simulation exercises; and art, music, and physical education should include opportunities to use developing skills in authentic application activities, not just to practice the skills in isolation. Such activities allow students to feel that school learning involves *doing* something.

Students prefer active over passive forms of learning. For example, 11- and 12-year-olds interviewed by Cooper and McIntyre (1994) associated effective teaching with methods that produced high levels of imaginative and practical involvement: storytelling by the teacher (which they found engaging even though it is a listening activity), drama and role-play, visual stimuli (photographs, drawings, diagrams, videos), whole-class and small-group discussion, and opportunities to collaborate in brainstorming, problem solving, or developing a group product.

Immediate feedback.   Activities that offer the greatest potential for enjoyment and flow experiences allow students to respond actively and get immediate feedback that they can use to guide subsequent responses. This feedback element is an important reason for the popularity of computer games and other pastimes featured in arcades (Malone & Lepper, 1987). Automatic feedback features are also built into many educational games and computerized learning systems.

You can provide such feedback yourself when leading a class or a small group through a lesson or when circulating to supervise progress on independent work. When you are less available for immediate response (such as when you are teaching a small group), you can still arrange for students working independently to get feedback by consulting answer keys; following instructions about how to check their work; consulting with an aide, adult volunteer, or appointed student helper; or discussing their work in pairs or small groups.

Although it is not always necessary for learning purposes, *immediate* feedback enhances the psychological impact of an activity. Most students are eager to receive and respond to immediate feedback when learning something for the first time, but less enthused about going back to try to relearn something that "we did already."

Incorporate Game-like Features into Learning Activities

Many learning and application activities can be structured to include features typically associated with games or recreational pastimes (Keller, 1983; Lepper & Cordova, 1992; Malone & Lepper, 1987). With a bit of imagination, ordinary assignments can be transformed into "test yourself" challenges, puzzles, or brain teasers. Some such activities involve clear goals but require students to solve problems, avoid traps, or overcome obstacles in order to reach the goals. For example, students might be asked to suggest possible solutions to a science or engineering problem or to find a shortcut for a tedious mathematical procedure. Other such activities challenge students to "find the problem" by identifying the goal itself and then developing a method for reaching it. Many "explore and discover" activities follow this model.

For example, McKenzie (1975) described three ways to introduce mystery to inquiry in social studies or science. First, as a way to lead students to discover a concept or generalization, provide them with examples of phenomena that seem to be unrelated. Then state that all of the cases are alike in some way and challenge them to discover the similarity. The resultant discovery will be a definition of a concept or a statement of a generalization. For example, pictures of pioneers on the frontier, the Wright brothers with their plane, African American students integrating a segregated school, and an astronaut might be presented along with the challenge, "All of these people are *pioneers*. Can you figure out what pioneers have in common?"

A variation on this method is to provide a set of clues, such as artifacts, divergent historical accounts of an event, or other data arranged to tell some story, then to ask students to reconstruct the event by acting as a detective (or an archaeologist or historian). A third technique is to present some situation that seems predictable and ask students what they think will happen. After they make predictions, demonstrate that something unexpected happens, then challenge the class to explain why. For example, introduce the concept of gravity by dropping pairs of objects together to illustrate that a smaller, lighter object such as a coin will reach the floor just as quickly as a larger, heavier object such as a baseball (contrary to most students' expectations).

Some game-like activities involve elements of suspense or hidden information that emerges as the activity is completed (puzzles that convey a message or provide the answer to a question once they are filled in). Others involve a degree of randomness or uncertainty about the outcome of performance on any given trial (knowledge games that cover a variety of topics at several difficulty levels and assign questions according to card draws or dice rolls—Trivial Pursuit is an example).

Covington (1992) described games and simulations that engage students in cooperative learning and higher-order thinking as they work to develop explanations for puzzling phenomena (e.g., how birds can migrate for thousands of miles and yet keep returning to the same place each year) or solutions to technical problems (e.g., how to use x-rays to destroy a cancerous tumor without harming the surrounding healthy tissue). When designed as opportunities to apply principles developed through instruction in school subjects, these game-like activities can have powerful motivational as well as instructional value.

Note that most of these game-like features involve presenting intellectual challenges to individuals working alone or groups working cooperatively. This illustrates that game-like features are much broader than games or competitions. *The game-like features described here are less distracting from learning objectives and more effective in promoting motivation to learn than competitive games that emphasize speed in supplying memorized facts rather than thoughtful integration or application of learning.*

Ideas from Research on Job Characteristics

Industrial psychologists have studied workplace conditions and job characteristics that affect workers' job satisfaction (Parker & Wall, 1998; Warr, 2007). Many of their findings overlap with what is said in this chapter about school tasks that support intrinsic motivation (autonomy, active responses that yield immediate feedback, collaboration with peers). However, three features of satisfying work have not yet received much attention in educational research: skill variety, task identity, and task significance (Hackman

& Oldham, 1980; Millette & Gagné, 2008). All three have implications for designing activities that respond to students' competence needs.

Skill variety.   Skill variety refers to the range of different skills needed to carry out an activity. *Workers tend to enjoy jobs that include a variety of tasks that provide opportunities to use a variety of skills*, but not jobs that involve constant repetition of the same task. *Students show the same preferences.*

Alleman and Brophy (1993–94) interviewed college students about learning activities they remembered from K–12 social studies. Responses were coded for what was said about the cognitive and affective outcomes of the activities. Desirable affective outcomes were coded when the students reported that an activity had produced interesting learning or enabled them to empathize with the people being studied. Negative assessments were coded when the students disparaged activities as pointless (e.g., learning about state birds) or as boring and repetitive (worksheets or assignments such as reading a chapter in the text and then answering questions about it).

The students frequently mentioned desirable affective outcomes, and never expressed negative assessments, when describing (a) thematic units (such as on pioneer life or Brazil) that included a variety of information and activities, (b) field trips, (c) discussion and debate activities, or (d) pageant or role-enactment activities. They expressed less enthusiastic, but still generally positive, reactions to simulation activities, research projects, construction projects, and lecture/presentation activities. In contrast, there were many complaints about boring, repetitive seatwork, especially if it had to be done individually and silently).

Task identity.   Task identity refers to the opportunity to do a complete job from beginning to end. *Workers tend to enjoy jobs that allow them to create a product that they can point to and identify with* more than jobs that do not yield such tangible evidence of the fruits of their labor. Students probably respond similarly to learning activities. That is, they are likely to prefer tasks that have meaning or integrity in their own right over tasks that are mere subparts of some larger entity, and are likely to experience a satisfying sense of accomplishment when they finish such tasks. Ideally, task completion will yield a finished product that students can use or display (a map, diagram, or other illustration; an essay or report; a scale model; or something other than just another ditto or workbook page).

Motivating students can be challenging because knowledge is decontextualized in school (Bruner, 1966; Lepper & Henderlong, 2002). Abstract principles and skills that have wide application are taught in circumstances far removed from those in which they will be used. Also, much school knowledge is modularized—broken into component parts taught separately. One result of this decontextualization and modularization is to remove much of the intrinsic motivation potential from school learning. You can recapture some of this potential by creating authentic activities that resemble the situated learning that occurs in out-of-school settings.

Scholars who have studied learning in home and job settings believe that it is a mistake to separate knowing from doing, or what is learned from how it is learned and used (Lave & Wenger, 1991; Rogoff, Turkanis, & Bartlett, 2001). They believe that learning is *situated*; that is, that knowledge is adapted to the settings, purposes, and tasks to which it is applied (and for which it was constructed in the first place). If we want students to learn and retain knowledge in a form that makes it usable for application, we need to make it possible for them to develop that knowledge in the natural setting, using methods and tasks suited to that setting. In this view, the ideal model for schooling is on-the-job training that occurs as experienced mentors work with novices or apprentices.

Obviously, there are limits to the degree to which in-school learning can be shifted to out-of-school settings. However, the notion of situated learning has implications for in-school instruction as well: *be conscious of potential applications when selecting and planning your teaching of curricular content, and emphasize those applications in developing the content with students.*

Also, as much as possible, allow students to learn through engagement in authentic tasks. *Authentic tasks* require using what is being learned for accomplishing the very sorts of life applications that justify the inclusion of this learning in the curriculum in the first place. If it is not possible to engage students in actual life applications, at least engage them in realistic simulations of these applications.

Theory and research on task identity as a job characteristic and on situated learning and authentic tasks in education lead to similar ideas about the kinds of learning activities that are intrinsically motivating. They underscore the value of engaging students in authentic life applications of the knowledge and skills they are learning in school, especially applications that yield some conclusion or product that students can appreciate as a significant accomplishment.

Task significance.   Task significance refers to the impact that the job has on other people, both immediately within the workplace and potentially in other contexts. It connects with educators' notions of task authenticity and with the principle of teaching school subjects with an eye toward applications to life outside of school. You can enhance your students' perceptions of the significance of learning activities by structuring them as opportunities to develop and apply big ideas. Also, occasionally incorporate activities of special significance such as service learning projects, student-led assessment conferences (in which students present their work portfolios to their families), or science or social studies projects that culminate in some service to the community or lobbying of local authorities to adopt some policy or take some action.

RESPONDING TO STUDENTS' RELATEDNESS NEEDS

You can go a long way toward meeting your students' relatedness needs by establishing your classroom as the kind of learning community described in chapter 2. Be a supportive teacher who cares about your students as persons and helps them succeed as learners (Furrer & Skinner, 2003). In addition, teach them to act as members of a learning community by listening carefully and responding thoughtfully during lessons and discussions and by supporting one another's learning when working in pairs or groups.

In this kind of collaborative climate, students will be able to please both you and their classmates (and thus meet their relatedness needs) simply by acting in accordance with learning community values. *A prevailing norm of "We're all in this together, learning and helping one another learn" creates alignment among the actions needed to satisfy needs for autonomy, competence, and relatedness.* Therefore, students can meet all of these needs simultaneously by asking and answering questions, working collaboratively on assignments, and engaging in other everyday learning activities. Such alignment does not exist in competitive or hostile climates, where students may be unable to meet their relatedness needs or able to meet them only at cost to their sense of autonomy or their self-concept.

Provide Frequent Opportunities for Students to Collaborate With Peers

In classrooms that do feature a positive interpersonal climate and norms of collaboration, students are likely to experience enhanced intrinsic motivation when they participate in learning activities that allow them to interact with their classmates. You can foster this by scheduling activities such as discussion, debate, role-play, or simulation. In addition, you can shift many practice and application activities from solitary seatwork to collaborations that allow students to work together in pairs or small groups to tutor one another, discuss issues, solve problems, or produce a report, display, or some other group product. Cooperative learning activities offer motivational benefits because they respond to students' relatedness needs, as well as potential learning benefits because they engage students in the social construction of knowledge.

Emphasize Purely Cooperative Learning Formats

The student team learning methods described in chapter 6 allow for cooperative learning among teammates, but they also involve competing against other teams and focusing on preparing for tests. Consequently, they are primarily extrinsic approaches to motivation. However, other approaches to paired or small-group learning are purely cooperative and thus likely to enhance students' intrinsic motivation. Three of the best known are Learning Together, Group Investigation, and Jigsaw.

Learning Together. Learning Together was developed by David and Roger Johnson (Johnson & Johnson, 1999; Johnson, Johnson, Holubec, & Roy, 1984). In this model, students work in four- or five-member groups to develop a single group product. *Learning Together incorporates four key features:*

1. *Positive interdependence.* Students are interdependent with other members of their group in achieving a successful group product. Positive interdependence can be structured through mutual goals (goal interdependence); division of labor (task interdependence); dividing materials, resources, or information among group members (resource interdependence); assigning students unique roles (role interdependence); or giving group rewards (reward interdependence).
2. *Face-to-face interaction among students.* Activities that call for significant interaction among group members are preferred over activities that can be accomplished by having group members work on their own.
3. *Individual accountability.* Mechanisms are needed to ensure that each group member has clear objectives for which he or she will be held accountable and receives any needed assessment, feedback, or instructional assistance.
4. *Instructing students in appropriate interpersonal or small-group skills.* Students cannot merely be placed together and told to cooperate. They need instruction in skills such as asking and answering questions, ensuring that everyone participates actively and is treated with respect, and assigning tasks and organizing cooperative efforts.

Group Investigation. Group Investigation was developed by Shlomo Sharan and his colleagues in Israel (Sharan & Sharan, 1976; Sharan et al., 1984). In this model, students form their own two- to six-member groups to work together using cooperative inquiry, group discussion, and planning and carrying out of projects. Each group chooses a topic from a unit studied by the whole class, breaks this topic into individual tasks, and carries out the activities needed to prepare a group report. Eventually, the group makes a presentation or display to communicate its findings to the class and is evaluated based on the quality of this report.

Jigsaw. Developed by Aronson, Blaney, Stephan, Sikes, and Snapp (1978), Jigsaw ensures active individual participation and group cooperation by arranging tasks so that each group member possesses unique information and has a special role to play. The group product cannot be completed unless each member does his or her part, just as a jigsaw puzzle cannot be completed unless each piece is included. For example, information needed to compose a biography might be broken into early life, first accomplishments, major setbacks, later life, and world events occurring during the person's lifetime. One member of each group would be given access to the relevant information and assigned responsibility for one of the five sections of the biography, and other group members would be assigned to other sections. Members of different groups who were working on the same section would meet together in "expert groups" to discuss their sections. Then they would return to their regular groups and take turns teaching their group mates about their sections. Because the only way that students can learn about sections other than their own is to listen carefully to their groupmates, they are motivated to support and show interest in one another's work. The students then prepare biographies or take quizzes on the material individually.

A variation entitled Jigsaw II was developed by Robert Slavin (1995). Here, the teacher does not need to provide each student with unique materials. Instead, all students begin by reading a common narrative and then each group member is given a separate topic on which to become an expert. This adaptation also can be used with the original Jigsaw. If it is adopted without also incorporating the team competition features of Jigsaw II (see chapter 6), it will simplify Jigsaw but still preserve its purely cooperative format.

Another way to differentiate roles within groups is to assign group members specific responsibilities for ensuring that the group functions effectively. For example, one member might monitor turn taking and participation, a second might record whatever needs to be written down, a third might identify points of agreement and disagreement, and a fourth might press for arguments and evidence to support stated opinions (Johnson & Johnson, 1999).

Small-group cooperative learning methods respond to students' relatedness needs. They promote friendships and prosocial interaction among students who differ in achievement, gender, race, ethnicity, and handicapping conditions, and have positive effects on outcomes such as self- esteem, academic self-confidence, liking for the class, liking and feeling liked by classmates, and dispositions toward empathy and social cooperation (Johnson & Johnson, 2009; Miller & Hertz-Lazarowitz, 1992; Slavin, 1995). They are especially motivating for struggling students, particularly when these students realize that their efforts are indispensable to the group's success (Weber & Hertel, 2007).

Certain qualifications on the use of cooperative learning methods should be noted. First, although most students prefer to collaborate with peers, some prefer to work alone. You may have good reasons for requiring such students to work with peers under some circumstances, but whenever you are using cooperative learning purely for intrinsic motivation reasons, you should allow students who want to work alone to do so. Second, group members may become distracted from learning goals if they begin to socialize, have difficulty negotiating roles, or find that some individuals are not fulfilling their responsibilities. Third, the intrinsic motivational benefits of cooperative formats do not guarantee accomplishment of your instructional goals. To ensure that cooperative approaches yield acceptable learning outcomes, make sure that the tasks you assign are suited to the cooperative learning format that you want your students to follow, prepare the students to collaborate effectively, and monitor group interactions and intervene if necessary (Gillies, 2003; Herrenkohl & Guerra, 1998; McCaslin & Good, 1996).

Pairs/partners.   Some cooperative learning formats call for pairs of students to work together as partners (Fuchs et al., 2000; King, 1999; Zajac & Hartup, 1997). Many language arts programs, for example, call for pairs of students to listen to each other read or spell and provide corrective feedback, or to read and respond to each other's written compositions. Also, many teachers assign pairs of students to act as study partners who correct and provide feedback concerning each other's mathematics assignments, to act as laboratory partners in carrying out science experiments, or to collaborate in "study buddy" relationships in working on homework assignments. Less formally, they may invite students to seek help from classmates (within certain guidelines, such as that helpers should not merely give answers but provide clues or explanations to enable helpees to move forward on their own and eventually accomplish the learning goal) (Antil, Jenkins, Wayne, & Vadasy, 1998; McManus & Gettinger, 1996).

Techniques have been developed to create interdependence between partners and encourage them to collaborate fruitfully. One is *scripted cooperation* (Dansereau, 1988; O'Donnell, 1996; O'Donnell & Dansereau, 1992). As applied to a text study assignment, scripted cooperation begins with breaking the text into sections. Both partners read the first section, then put the material away. One partner plays the role of "recaller" and states all of the information that he or she can remember. The other partner plays the role of "listener-detector" by listening carefully and attempting to detect errors or omissions in the recall. Both partners then share ideas about how to elaborate the information to make it more memorable (e.g., by developing analogies or generating images). When both partners can restate the gist of this section successfully, they move on to the next section but switch roles. They proceed in this manner, switching roles each time they start a new section, until they complete the material to be studied. Research indicates that pairs using the scripted cooperation method tend to learn more than students who study alone or pairs who are asked to study together but not instructed to use the techniques of alternation of roles, overt rehearsal, active listening, and collaborative elaboration on the content.

Slavin (1996) emphasized that group goals combined with individual accountability are usually needed to ensure that students help their partners or teammates to meet their individual goals. However, these features may not be needed when students form voluntary study groups (indicating that they already are motivated to help one another), when they are enacting cooperative learning models that call for them to carry out specific roles (thus ensuring that help is provided), or when the activity calls for higher-order thinking and negotiation of multiple opinions rather than following a clear path to resolution of a problem or controversy (in which case students will benefit from hearing one another thinking aloud).

SELF-DETERMINATION THEORY: LOOKING AHEAD

In its early stages, self-determination theory appeared to have limited potential for classroom application, because it was focused on intrinsic motivation. However, it has added the continuum of extrinsic regulation that ranges from external regulation through introjected regulation and identified regulation to integrated regulation. This recognizes that students often willingly pursue learning goals that they recognize as important, even though they may not find them intrinsically interesting or enjoyable. It also opens the way for investigations of ways that socializers might affect students' motivation, especially by helping them to appreciate the value of social regulations that apply to them (including expectations that they learn the school's curriculum).

In a related shift, Deci and Ryan have begun to emphasize that the key to understanding motivational dynamics is not an intrinsic vs. extrinsic motivation dichotomy, but the degree to which the person perceives rewards or other extrinsic features of the situation as informational versus controlling.

The Three Basic Needs

Self-determination theory still has its critics, however (Buunk & Nauta, 2000; Carver & Scheier, 2000). Some objections focus on identification of autonomy, competence, and relatedness as three basic needs. Critics have suggested that this list ought to be expanded to include such possibilities as self-preservation needs, safety needs, self-esteem needs, or self-actualization needs. Deci and Ryan (2000) have responded by clarifying that their theory focuses on psychological needs (so it assumes people's physical well-being while investigating factors affecting their psychological well-being), and that needs for self-esteem and self-actualization are implied in the need for competence (especially when it is considered in tandem with the needs for autonomy and relatedness). Also, given the logical circularity that previous need theories encountered when they began proliferating the numbers of needs included, they are hesitant to extend their list without compelling evidence of a need to do so.

Their hesitancy is understandable. So far, a great deal of research supports the notion that autonomy, competence, and relatedness are basic needs that must be satisfied to allow people to enjoy a sense of well-being and position them to engage in intrinsically motivated pursuits. Furthermore, these basic principles appear to apply across all cultures, including cultures that contrast in other aspects of motivation (Hagger, Chatzisarantis, Barkoukis, Wang, & Baranowski, 2005; Levesque, Zuehlke, Stanek, & Ryan, 2004; Vansteenkiste et al., 2005).

However, Sheldon, Elliot, Kim, and Kasser (2001) asked American and Korean college students to think about the most satisfying recent event in their lives and rate their feelings during this event, using descriptors reflecting satisfaction of 10 potential needs: self-esteem, relatedness, autonomy, competence, pleasure-stimulation, physical thriving, self-actualization-meaning, security, popularity-influence, and money-luxury. The ordering of those needs reflects the frequency with which they appeared in the

American responses. American students were especially likely to indicate that highly satisfying experiences were related to satisfaction of needs for self-esteem, relatedness, autonomy, or competence. The Korean responses were similar, except that relatedness needs replaced self-esteem needs at the top of the list (reflecting a difference between a collectivist and an individualist society—see chapter 11).

These data were supportive of Maslow's (1962) list of basic needs (although not his need hierarchy) and even more supportive of Deci and Ryan's identification of autonomy, competence, and relatedness as universal fundamental needs. However, they also suggested that self-esteem might be worth treating as a separate basic need, not just as an extension of the need for competence.

Additional support for the basic nature of Deci and Ryan's three primary needs can be seen in work done on people's sense of well-being. Reis, Sheldon, Gable, Roscoe, and Ryan (2000) asked college students to keep diaries for two weeks, reporting on their social activities and related moods and need satisfactions. Daily fluctuations in emotional well-being were closely related to the degree to which autonomy, competence, and relatedness needs were being satisfied. Also, Sheldon and Elliot (1998) asked college students about personal goals that they would seek to attain in the coming weeks (e.g., get more exercise, get at least a B in chemistry), then contacted them again later to find out their degree of effort expended and success attained in pursuing these goals. The results indicated that autonomous motivation (intrinsic or identified) predicted goal attainment but controlled motivation (externally regulated or introjected) did not. The students had focused on goals involving activities they personally viewed as interesting, important, or enjoyable, but were less invested in goals that they had listed primarily because someone (parents, instructors) or something else ("ought" feelings associated with potential shame, guilt, or anxiety) was compelling them to do so. Koestner, Lekes, Powers, and Chicoine (2002) found similar results in another study.

The Value of Choices

Several recent studies indicate the need to qualify claims about the value of providing choices (Katz & Assor, 2007; Patall, Cooper, & Robinson, 2008). First, although providing students with opportunities to choose a reading selection or other learning task can enhance their reported enjoyment of the task or their sense of confidence or control as they engage in it, these affective benefits usually are not accompanied by cognitive benefits—the students do not do better on learning measures than students who are not given the opportunity to choose (Flowerday & Schraw, 2003; Schraw, Flowerday, & Reisetter, 1998; Tafarodi, Milne, & Smith, 1999). More generally, although choice is related positively to affective aspects of engagement such as intrinsic motivation, feelings of satisfaction, and reduced anxiety, it has less of an influence, and often none at all, on cognitive aspects such as strategy use, recall of main ideas, or generating inferences (Schraw et al., 1998). Sometimes choice does not even affect intrinsic motivation, especially if the available choices are all similar or if none is especially appealing (d'Ailly, 2002; Flowerday, Schraw, & Stevens, 2004; Reeve, Nix, & Hamm, 2003).

A second qualification is that the choice set should feature options that allow students to engage in activities with autonomous (intrinsic or identified) motivation. Assor and colleagues (2002) found that students in Grades 3–8 in Israel could differentiate among three types of autonomy-enhancing teacher behaviors (fostering relevance, allowing criticism, and providing choice), as well as three types of autonomy-suppressing behaviors (suppressing criticism, intruding, and forcing unmeaningful acts). Of these teacher behaviors, the two that had the most important effects on students' feelings toward learning and cognitive engagement were fostering relevance and suppressing criticism. Offering choices of learning activities frequently was ineffective because the students did not perceive a connection between any of the choices and their personal goals and interests. The authors emphasized the importance of both making sure that the choices do in fact have value (i.e., are authentic activities) and helping students to perceive that value and thus appreciate the importance of the activities. As they put it in the title of their article, "Choice is good, but relevance is excellent" (p. 261).

A third qualification is that the number and variety of choices need to be calibrated to the students' current readiness to choose sensibly. Choice can be unappealing or even anxiety-producing if students are unsure about which alternatives are best for them (Koh, 2006) or believe that certain options threaten their need satisfaction (Katz & Assor, 2007). Schwartz (2000) has argued that opportunities for autonomy, self-determination, and choice can become excessive to the point that they are experienced as a kind of tyranny. This implies that an optimal number of choices is best in a given situation, rather than that "more is better."

Iyengar and Lepper (2000) supported this conclusion in three studies in which people were presented with an extensive array of choices (24 or 30) or a more limited array (6). In each case, the people presented with more choices expressed greater initial satisfaction than the people presented with a limited array, but follow-up data indicated better results for the limited-choice condition.

Two of the studies involved opportunities to sample jams or chocolates. In each case, people were more likely to purchase the foods if they were shown only six choices, and also more likely to express satisfaction with their choices later. The third study was done in a college classroom. Students were given the opportunity to write a two-page essay as an extra-credit assignment, selecting from either six or 30 potential essay topics. Students given six options were more likely to complete the assignment, and their essays were of higher quality. So, "too many" choices may be initially appealing but nevertheless undermine choosers' subsequent satisfaction and motivation. Other researchers have shown that a limited, optimal number of choices is preferable to either too few or too many (Shah & Wolford, 2007).

A fourth qualification is cultural. Iyengar and Lepper (1999) have shown that motivation (and performance) are optimized for people with independent selves (e.g., most Americans) when they are allowed to make personal choices, but optimized for people with interdependent selves (e.g., most East Asians) when the choices are made for them by valued in-group members. Bao and Lam (2008) reported similar results, but only for students who had close relationships with their mothers or teachers (who were choosing for them).

Other Issues

Carver and Scheier (2000) noted that many forms of intrinsically rewarding activity do not involve a competence dimension at all, and that people sometimes find activities intrinsically rewarding even though they are unskilled at them (e.g., people who are not good at particular sports but participate in them regularly because they enjoy doing so). Similarly, many intrinsically motivated activities are pursued when one is alone, so they do not involve a relatedness dimension, and some students do not especially value opportunities to interact with peers as they work on school assignments (Isaac, Sansone, & Smith, 1999; Sansone & Smith, 2002).

Some critics believe that needs for autonomy and for relatedness will inevitably clash in some situations. Deci and Ryan's response has been to clarify that motivation refers to subjective experience and that satisfying the need for autonomy involves experiencing perceptions of self-determination rather than necessarily acting independently of outside influences. This is an elegant solution at the theoretical level, but it moves their theory away from issues of greatest concern to policymakers and the general public (which focus on how to get students to study hard and ultimately do well on tests). Although it is important not to confuse motivation with performance, it also is important to take into account learning (not just motivation) in developing implications for teachers.

Students in a motivation class taught by the author have identified a related concern: the distinction between motivating and controlling students' behavior can constrict people's perceptions of the relevance or power of motivational principles. For example, people juggling multiple agendas will tend to give first priority to things that they must do because of extrinsic pressure reasons, and only secondary priority to things that they are intrinsically motivated to do but do not have to do. Several East Asian students, for example, have suggested that students from their countries were so controlled by extrinsic pressures (at least prior to taking the high-stakes tests that determined their future opportunities) that the term "motivation" would have limited applicability to attempts to explain or change their behavior. Even if they began to develop intrinsic motivation to pursue certain topics, they wouldn't have the time to do so.

There are many parallels between the intrinsic-extrinsic motivation literature and the goal theory literature. Intrinsic motivation theorists emphasize that extrinsic pressures preoccupy people with getting rewards with minimal effort, whereas goal theorists emphasize that performance pressures preoccupy people with preserving an image of competence. In both cases, resources that might have been devoted to maximizing the quality of learning or accomplishments are diverted to other goals. Also, intrinsic regulation (like mastery motivation) is associated with psychological well being in learning situations, whereas identified (extrinsic) regulation (like outcome goals or performance approach motivation) is associated with level of achievement (Burton, Lydon, D'Alessandro, & Koestner, 2006).

There also are many parallels between self-determination theory and goal theory, as Deci and Ryan (2000) have acknowledged and Standage, Duda, and Ntoumanis (2003) have demonstrated empirically. Although self-determination theory features value issues and emphasizes intrinsic motivation whereas goal theory features expectancy issues and emphasizes achievement motivation, the two theories yield similar descriptions of optimal classroom conditions (favoring intrinsic motivation and learning goals). Both theories get a great deal of mileage from manipulating a few key concepts, particularly when making predictions about and explaining relationships among motivational variables. Both are less impressive, however, when attention shifts to relationships between motivational variables and learning variables, especially when the focus is on school learning over the long haul rather than learning displayed during brief laboratory experiments.

SUMMARY

Recent theorizing has shifted from portraying intrinsic and extrinsic motivation as incompatible opposites. It is now recognized that relative autonomy increases as one moves from purely extrinsic motivational situations to purely intrinsic ones. Furthermore, the notion that extrinsic motivational strategies will necessarily erode intrinsic motivation has receded in favor of recognition that extrinsic strategies can be used in ways that complement intrinsic strategies. Even so, most motivational theorists argue that intrinsic strategies are preferable because they lead to higher quality task engagement and support the development of continuing intrinsic interest in the topic or activity.

Definitions of intrinsic motivation focus on the perception that one's actions are self-determined, so suggestions to teachers emphasize encouraging students to maintain or develop this perception. Self-determination theory emphasizes strategies that respond to students' needs for autonomy, competence, and relatedness.

You can respond to your students' autonomy needs by encouraging them to function as autonomous learners and allowing them frequent opportunities to make choices. Learning centers provide one way to build autonomy and choice opportunities into their everyday classroom experiences.

You can respond to your students' competence needs by making sure that learning activities are well matched to their current levels of knowledge and skill, by emphasizing activities that offer opportunities for them to make active responses and get immediate feedback, by incorporating game-like features into learning activities, and by emphasizing authentic activities and life applications that feature skill variety, task identity, task significance, and related characteristics that tend to make work enjoyable.

You can respond to your students' relatedness needs primarily by establishing your classroom as the kind of learning community described in chapter 2. In addition, you can provide frequent opportunities for your students to collaborate with one another, especially by using purely cooperative small-group learning formats (Learning Together, Group Investigation, or Jigsaw) or by allowing students to work together in pairs.

Like goal theory, self-determination theory has succeeded in synthesizing a great many findings from motivational research by manipulating a few key concepts. However, it is more applicable to the affective than the cognitive aspects of engagement in school activities, and more successful in predicting and explaining relationships among motivational variables than relationships between motivational variables and learning outcomes. For the latter purpose, its implications concerning encouraging identified regulation are more applicable than its implications concerning intrinsic motivation.

REFLECTION QUESTIONS

1. What is the difference between intrinsic motivation and motivation to learn?
2. Why do intrinsic motivation theorists emphasize that autonomy perceptions are subjective and independent of external pressures and constraints?
3. When operating out of identified regulation motivation, we do things because we view them as important. Yet Deci and Ryan view this as extrinsic rather than intrinsic motivation. Why?

4. How is it that certain experiences (e.g., felt obligations and associated potential for shame or guilt) are recognized as internal, yet construed as outside of our sense of self?

5. Why is there no necessary contradiction between our need for autonomy and our need for relatedness if a significant other (such as a teacher) wants us to do something that differs from what we would have chosen to do on our own?

6. Assess your current approach to teaching with respect to autonomy support. Can you see ways to become more autonomy supportive?

7. Given the qualifications on offering choices as a motivational technique, when and how will you present choice opportunities to your students?

8. Why is it that optimal autonomy support involves a gradual transfer-of-responsibility approach to granting autonomy (that is, maintaining an optimal level of structure and control) rather than eliminating structure and control entirely?

9. Left to their own devices, students often make bad choices. Therefore, should teachers restrict their options, scaffold their decision making, let them learn from natural consequences, or what?

10. In your own words, what is the appeal of activities that afford opportunities to make active responses and get immediate feedback? Can you identify ways to infuse more such activities into your teaching?

11. Similarly, what is it about skill variety, task identity, and task importance that adds appeal to learning activities? Can you identify ways to infuse more activities that offer these features into your teaching?

12. What are the key differences between the cooperative learning models described in this chapter and those described in chapter 6? Why does the author favor the purely cooperative models?

13. Cooperative learning has become very popular, for good reason, but it can be overused or used inappropriately. What are some situations when teacher-led instruction is more appropriate than learning independently in collaboration with peers? When an individual task structure is more appropriate than a cooperative task structure?

14. Parallels between self-determination theory and goal theory are identified near the end of the chapter. What are some of the differences between these two theories? Do any of these differences suggest contrasting implications for teaching?

REFERENCES

Adie, J., Duda, J., & Ntoumanis, N. (2008). Autonomy support, basic need satisfaction and the optimal functioning of adult male and female sport participants: A test of basic needs theory. *Motivation and Emotion, 32,* 189–199.

Alexander, P., Kulikowich, J., & Jetton, T. (1994). The role of subject-matter knowledge and interest in the processing of linear and nonlinear text. *Review of Educational Research, 64,* 201–252.

Alleman, J., & Brophy, J. (1993–94). Teaching that lasts: College students' reports of learning activities experienced in elementary school social studies. *Social Science Record, 30*(2), 36–48; *31*(1), 42–46.

Antil, L., Jenkins, J., Wayne, S., & Vadasy, P. (1998). Cooperative learning: Prevalence, conceptualizations, and the relation between research and practice. *American Educational Research Journal, 35,* 419–454.

Aronson, E., Blaney, N., Stephan, C., Sikes, J., & Snapp, M. (1978). *The Jigsaw classroom.* Beverly Hills, CA: Sage.

Assor, A., Kaplan, H., Kanat-Maymon, Y., & Roth, G. (2005). Directly controlling teacher behaviors as predictors of poor motivation and engagement in girls and boys: The role of anger and anxiety. *Learning and Instruction, 15,* 397–413.

Assor, A., Kaplan, H., & Roth, G. (2002). Choice is good, but relevance is excellent: Autonomy-enhancing and suppressing teacher behaviours predicting students' engagement in schoolwork. *British Journal of Educational Psychology, 72*, 261–278.

Bao, X., & Lam, S. (2008). Who makes the choice? Rethinking the role of autonomy and relatedness in Chinese children's motivation. *Child Development, 79*, 269–283.

Black, A., & Deci, E. (2000). The effects of instructors' autonomy support and students' autonomous motivation on learning organic chemistry: A self-determination theory perspective. *Science Education, 84*, 740–756.

Bozack, A., Vega, R., McCaslin, M., & Good, T. (2008). Teacher support of student autonomy in comprehensive school reform classrooms. *Teachers College Record, 110*, 2389–2407.

Bruner, J. (1966). *The culture of education*. Cambridge,MA: Harvard University Press.

Burton, K., Lydon, J., D'Alessandro, D., & Koestner, R. (2006). The differential effects of intrinsic and identified motivation on well-being and performance: Prospective, experimental, and implicit approaches to self-determination theory. *Journal of Personality and Social Psychology, 91*, 750–762.

Buunk, B., & Nauta, A. (2000). Why intraindividual needs are not enough: Human motivation is primarily social. *Psychological Inquiry, 11*, 279–283.

Carver, C., & Scheier, M. (2000). Autonomy and self-regulation. *Psychological Inquiry, 11*, 284–291.

Collier, G. (1994). *Social origins of mental ability*. New York: Wiley.

Condry, J., & Stokker, L. (1992). Overview of special issue on intrinsic motivation. *Motivation and Emotion, 16*, 157–164.

Conroy, D., & Coatsworth, J. D. (2007). Coaching behaviors associated with changes in fear of failure: Changes in self-talk and need satisfaction as potential mechanisms. *Journal of Personality, 75*, 383–419.

Conti, R. (2001). College goals: Do self-determined and carefully considered goals predict intrinsic motivation, academic performance, and adjustment during the first semester? *Social Psychology of Education, 4*, 189–211.

Cooper, P., & McIntyre, D. (1994). Patterns of interaction between teachers' and students' classroom thinking, and their implications for the provision of learning opportunities. *Teaching and Teacher Education, 10*, 633–646.

Covington, M. (1992). *Making the grade*. Cambridge, UK: Cambridge University Press.

Csikszentmihalyi, M. (1993). *The evolving self: A psychology for the third millennium*. New York: HarperCollins.

d'Ailly, H. (2002, April). *A distinctive cultural and gender difference in children's interest and effort in learning: The impact of choice and testing*. Paper presented at the annual meeting of the American Educational Research Association, New Orleans.

Dansereau, D. (1988). Cooperative learning strategies. In C. Weinstein, E. Goetz, & P. Alexander (Eds.), *Learning and study strategies: Issues in assessment, instruction, and evaluation* (pp. 103–120). San Diego, CA: Academic Press.

Deci, E., & Ryan, R. (1994). Promoting self-determined education. *Scandinavian Journal of Educational Research, 38*, 3–14.

Deci, E., & Ryan, R. (2000). The "what" and the "why" of goal pursuits: Human needs and the self-determination of behavior. *Psychological Inquiry, 11*, 227–268.

Deci, E., & Ryan, R. (2008). Facilitating optimal motivation and psychological well-being across life's domains. *Canadian Psychology, 49*, 14–23.

Deci, E., Schwartz, A., Sheinman, L., & Ryan, R. (1981). An instrument to assess adults' orientations toward control versus autonomy with children: Reflections on intrinsic motivation and perceived competence. *Journal of Educational Psychology, 73*, 642–650.

Eckblad, G. (1981). *Scheme theory: A conceptual framework for cognitive-motivational processes*. New York: Academic Press.

Edmunds, J., Ntoumanis, N., & Duda, J. (2007). Testing a self-determination theory-based teaching style intervention in the exercise domain. *European Journal of Social Psychology, 38*, 375–388.

Elliot, A., Faler, J., McGregor, H., Campbell, W., Sedikides, C., & Harackiewicz, J. (2000). Competence valuation as a strategic intrinsic motivation process. *Personality and Social Psychology Bulletin, 26*, 780–794.

Filak, V., & Sheldon, K. (2008). Teacher support, student motivation, student need-satisfaction and college teacher-course evaluations: Testing a sequential path model. *Educational Psychology, 28*, 711–724.

Flowerday, T., & Schraw, G. (2003). The effect of choice on cognitive and affective engagement. *Journal of Educational Research, 96*, 207–215

Flowerday, T., Schraw, G., & Stevens, J. (2004). The role of choice and interest in reader engagement. *Journal of Experimental Education, 72*, 93–114.

Fuchs, L., Fuchs, D., Kazden, S., Karns, K., Calhoon, M., Hamlett, C., & Hewlett, S. (2000). Effects of workgroup structure and size on student productivity during collaborative work on complex tasks. *Elementary School Journal, 100*, 183–212.

Furrer, C., & Skinner, E. (2003). Sense of relatedness as a factor in children's academic engagement and perfor-mance. *Journal of Educational Psychology, 95,* 148–162.

Garcia, T., & Pintrich, P. (1996). The effects of autonomy on motivation and performance in the college class-room. *Contemporary Educational Psychology, 21,* 477–486.

Gillies, R. (2003). The behaviors, interactions, and perceptions of junior high school students during small-group learning. *Journal of Educational Psychology, 95,* 137–147.

Grolnick, W., & Ryan, R. (1989). Parent styles associated with children's self-regulation and competence in school. *Journal of Educational Psychology, 81,* 143–154.

Guay, F., Boggiano, A., & Vallerand, R. (2001). Autonomy support, intrinsic motivation, and perceived compe-tence: Conceptual and empirical linkages. *Personality and Social Psychology Bulletin, 27,* 643–650.

Guay, F., Ratelle, C., & Chanal, J. (2008). Optimal learning in optimal contexts: The role of self-determination in education. *Canadian Psychology, 49,* 233–240.

Hackman, J. R., & Oldham, G. (1980). *Work redesign.* Reading, MA: Addison-Wesley.

Hagger, M., Chatzisarantis, N., Barkoukis, V., Wang, C. K. J., & Baranowski, J. (2005). Perceived autonomy support in physical education and leisure-time physical activity: A cross-cultural evaluation of the trans-contextual model. *Journal of Educational Psychology, 97,* 376–390.

Hardré, P., & Reeve, J. (2003). A motivational model of rural students' intentions to persist in, versus drop out, of high school. *Journal of Educational Psychology, 95,* 347–356.

Hayamizu, T. (1997). Between intrinsic and extrinsic motivation: Examination of reasons for academic study based on the theory of internalization. *Japanese Psychological Research, 39,* 98–108.

Heppner, W., Kernis, M., Nezlek, J., Foster, J., Lakey, C., & Goldman, B. (2008). Within-person relationships among daily self-esteem, need satisfaction, and authenticity. *Psychological Science, 19,* 1140–1145.

Herrenkohl, L. & Guerra, M. (1998). Participant structures, scientific discourse, and student engagement in fourth grade. *Cognition and Instruction, 16,* 431–473.

Hodgins, H., Koestner, R., & Duncan, N. (1996). On the compatibility of autonomy and relatedness. *Personality and Social Psychology Bulletin, 22,* 227–237.

Isaac, J., Sansone, C., & Smith, J. (1999). Other people as a source of interest in an activity. *Journal of Experimen-tal Social Psychology, 35,* 239–265.

Iyengar, S., & Lepper, M. (1999). Rethinking the value of choice: A cultural perspective on intrinsic motivation. *Journal of Personality and Social Psychology, 76,* 349–366.

Iyengar, S., & Lepper, M. (2000). When choice is demotivating: Can one desire too much of a good thing? *Journal of Personality and Social Psychology, 79,* 995–1006.

Jang, H. (2008). Supporting students' motivation, engagement, and learning during an uninteresting activity. *Journal of Educational Psychology, 100,* 798–811.

Johnson, D., & Johnson, R. (1999). *Learning together and alone: Cooperative, competitive, and individualistic learning* (5th ed.). Boston: Allyn & Bacon.

Johnson, D., & Johnson, R. (2009). An educational psychology success story: Social interdependence theory and cooperative learning. *Educational Researcher, 38,* 365–379.

Johnson, D., Johnson, R., Holubec, E., & Roy, P. (1984). *Circles of learning: Cooperation in the classroom.* Alex-andria, VA: Association for Supervision and Curriculum Development.

Katz, I., & Assor, A. (2007). When choice motivates and when it does not. *Educational Psychology Review, 19,* 429–442.

Keller, J. (1983). Motivational design of instruction. In C. Reigeluth (Ed.), *Instructional-design theories and models: An overview of their current status* (pp. 383–434). Hillsdale, NJ: Erlbaum.

King, A. (1999). Discourse patterns for mediating peer learning. In A. O'Donnell & A. King (Eds.), *Cognitive perspectives on peer learning* (pp. 87–115). Mahwah, NJ: Erlbaum.

Koestner, R. (2008). Reaching one's personal goals: A motivational perspective focused on autonomy. *Canadian Psychology, 49,* 60–67.

Koestner, R., Horberg, E., Gaudreau, P., Powers, T., Di Dio, P., Bryan, C., Jochum, R., & Salter, N. (2006). Bol-stering implementation plans for the long haul: The benefits of simultaneously boosting self-concordance or self-efficacy. *Personality and Social Psychology Bulletin, 32,* 1547–1558.

Koestner, R., Lekes, N., Powers, T., & Chicoine, E. (2002). Attaining personal goals: Self-concordance plus implementation intentions equals success. *Journal of Personality and Social Psychology, 83,* 231–244.

Krapp, A. (2005). Basic needs and the development of interest and intrinsic motivational orientations. *Learning and Instruction, 15,* 381–395.

Lave, J., & Wenger, E. (1991). *Situated learning: Legitimate peripheral participation.* Cambridge, UK: Cambridge University Press.

Lee, E. (2005). The relationship of motivation and flow experience to academic procrastination in university students. *Journal of Genetic Psychology, 166,* 5–14.

Legault, L., Green-Demers, I., & Pelletier, L. (2006). Why do high school students lack motivation in the classroom? Toward an understanding of academic amotivation and the role of social support. *Journal of Educational Psychology, 98,* 567–582.

Lepper, M., & Cordova, D. (1992). A desire to be taught: Instructional consequences of intrinsic motivation. *Motivation and Emotion, 16,* 187–208.

Lepper, M., & Henderlong, J. (2002). Turning "play" into "work" and "work" into "play." In C Sansone & J. Harackiewicz (Eds.), *Intrinsic and extrinsic motivation: the search for optimal motivation and performance* (pp. 257–307). San Diego, CA: Academic Press.

Levesque, C., Zuehlke, A. N., Stanek, L., & Ryan, R. (2004). Autonomy and competence in German and American university students: A comparative study based on self-determination theory. *Journal of Educational Psychology, 96,* 68–84.

Liu, W., Wang, C. K. J., Tan, O., Koh, C., & Ee, J. (2008). A self-determination approach to understanding students' motivation in project work. *Learning and Individual Differences, 19,* 139–145.

Losier, G., & Koestner, R. (1999). Intrinsic versus identified regulation in distinct political campaigns: The consequences of following politics for pleasure versus personal meaningfulness. *Personality and Social Psychology Bulletin, 25,* 287–298.

Malone, T., & Lepper, M. (1987). Making learning fun: A taxonomy of intrinsic motivation for learning. In R. Snow & M. Farr (Eds.), *Aptitude, learning, and instruction: III. Conative and affective process analysis* (pp. 223–253). Hillsdale, NJ: Erlbaum.

Maslow, A. (1962). *Toward a psychology of being.* Princeton, NJ: VanNostrand.

McCaslin, M., & Good, T. (1996). *Listening in classrooms.* New York: HarperCollins.

McKenzie, G. (1975). Some myths and methods on motivation social study. *The Social Studies, 66,* 24–28.

McManus, S., & Gettinger, M. (1996). Teacher and student evaluations of cooperative learning and observed interactive behaviors. *Journal of Educational Research, 90,* 13–22.

Miller, N., & Hertz-Lazarowitz, R. (Eds.). (1992). *Interaction in cooperative groups: The theoretical anatomy of group learning.* New York: Cambridge University Press.

Millette, V., & Gagné, M. (2008). Designing volunteers' tasks to maximize motivation, satisfaction and performance: The impact of job characteristics on volunteer engagement. *Motivation and Emotion, 32,* 11–22.

Miserandino, M. (1996). Children who do well in school: Individual differences in perceived competence and autonomy in above-average children. *Journal of Educational Psychology, 88,* 203–214.

Morrow, L. (1992). The impact of a literature-based program on literacy achievement, use of literature, and attitudes of children from minority backgrounds. *Reading Research Quarterly, 27,* 250–275.

Morrow, L. (1993). *Developing literacy in the early years: Helping children read and write.* Boston: Allyn & Bacon.

Noels, K., Clement, R., & Pelletier, L. (1999). Perceptions of teachers' communicative style and students' intrinsic and extrinsic motivation. *Modern Language Journal, 83,* 23–34.

Norwich, B. (1999). Pupils' reasons for learning and behaving and for not learning and behaving in English and maths lessons in a secondary school. *British Journal of Educational Psychology, 69,* 547–569.

Ntoumanis, N. (2005). A prospective study of participation in optional school physical education using a self-determination theory framework. *Journal of Educational Psychology, 97,* 444–453.

O'Donnell, A. (1996). Effects of explicit incentives on scripted and unscripted cooperation. *Journal of Educational Psychology, 88,* 74–86.

O'Donnell, A., & Dansereau, D. (1992). Scripted cooperation in student dyads: A method for analyzing and enhancing academic learning and performance. In N. Miller & R. Hertz-Lazarowitz (Eds.), *Interaction in cooperative groups: The theoretical anatomy of group learning* (pp. 121–140). New York: Cambridge University Press.

Ommundsen, Y., & Kvalo, S. (2007). Autonomy-mastery, supportive or performance focused? Different teacher behaviours and pupils' outcomes in physical education. *Scandinavian Journal of Educational Research, 51,* 385–413.

Otis, N., Grouzet, F., & Pelletier, L. (2005). Latent motivational change in an academic setting: A 3-year longitudinal study. *Journal of Educational Psychology, 97,* 170–183.

Parker, S., & Wall, T. (1998). *Job and work design.* London: Sage.

Patall, E., Cooper, H., & Robinson, J. (2008). The effects of choice on intrinsic motivation and related outcomes: A meta-analysis of research findings. *Psychological Bulletin, 134,* 270–300.

Pelletier, L., Fortier, M., Vallerand, R., & Briere, N. (2002). Associations among perceived autonomy support, focus of self-regulation, and persistence: A prospective study. *Motivation and Emotion, 25,* 279–306.

Pelletier, L., Fortier, M., Vallerand, R., Tuson, K., Briere, N., & Blais, M. (1995). Toward a new measure of intrinsic motivation, extrinsic motivation, and amotivation in sports: The Sport Motivation Scale (SMS). *Journal of Sport and Exercise Psychology, 17,* 33–53.

Ratelle, C., Guay, F., Vallerand, R., Larose, S., & Senècal, C. (2007). Autonomous, controlled, and amotivated types of academic motivation: A person-oriented analysis. *Journal of Educational Psychology, 99,* 734–746.

Reeve, J. (2009). Why teachers adopt a controlling motivational style toward students and how they can become more autonomy supportive. *Educational Psychologist, 44,* 159–175.

Reeve, J., & Jang, H. (2006). What teachers say and do to support students' autonomy during a learning activity. *Journal of Educational Psychology, 98,* 209–218.

Reeve, J., Jang, H., Carrell, D., Jeon, S., & Barch, J. (2004). Enhancing students' engagement by increasing teachers' autonomy support. *Motivation and Emotion, 28,* 147–169.

Reeve, J., Nix, G., & Hamm, D. (2003). Testing models of the experience of self-determination in intrinsic motivation and the conundrum of choice. *Journal of Educational Psychology, 95*(2), 375–392.

Reinboth, M., Duda, J., & Ntoumanis, N. (2004). Dimensions of coaching behavior, need satisfaction, and the psychological and physical welfare of young athletes. *Motivation and Emotion, 28,* 297–313.

Reis, H., Sheldon, K., Gable, S., Roscoe, J., & Ryan, R. (2000). Daily well-being: The role of autonomy, competence, and relatedness. *Personality and Social Psychology Bulletin, 26,* 419–435.

Renninger, K., Hidi, S., & Krapp, A. (Eds.). (1992). *The role of interest in learning and development.* Hillsdale, NJ: Erlbaum.

Reynolds, P. L., & Symons, S. (2001). Motivational variables and children's text search. *Journal of Educational Psychology, 93,* 14–22.

Rogoff, B., Turkanis, C., & Bartlett, L. (2001). *Learning together: Children and adults in a school community.* New York: Oxford University Press.

Ryan, R., & Connell, J. (1989). Perceived locus of causality and internalization: Examining reasons for acting in two domains. *Journal of Personality and Social Psychology, 57,* 749–761.

Ryan, R., Connell, J., & Grolnick, W. (1992). When achievement is not intrinsically motivated: A theory of internalization and self-regulation in school. In A. Boggiano & T. Pittman (Eds.), *Achievement and motivation: A social-developmental perspective* (pp. 167–188). Cambridge, UK: Cambridge University Press.

Ryan, R., & Deci, E. (2006). Self-regulation and the problem of human autonomy: Does psychology need choice, self-determination, and will? *Journal of Personality, 74,* 1557–1585.

Ryan, R., & Grolnick, W. (1986). Origins and pawns in the classroom: Self-report and projective assessments of individual differences in children's perceptions. *Journal of Personality and Social Psychology, 50,* 550–558.

Ryan, R., Huta, V., & Deci, E. (2008). Living well: A self-determination theory perspective on eudaimonia. *Journal of Happiness Studies, 9,* 139–170.

Ryan, R., & LaGuardia, J. (1999). Achievement motivation within a pressured society: Intrinsic and extrinsic motivations to learn and the politics of school reform. In T. Urdan (Ed.), *The role of context* (*Advances in motivation and achievement* series, Vol. 11, pp. 45–85). Stamford, CT: JAI Press.

Ryan, R., Rigby, C. S., & Przybylski, A. (2006). The motivational pull of video games: A self-determination theory approach. *Motivation and Emotion, 30,* 347–363.

Sansone, C., & Morgan, C. (1992). Intrinsic motivation and education: Competence in context. *Motivation and Emotion, 16,* 249–270.

Sansone, C., & Smith, J. (2002). Interest and self-regulation: The relation between having to and wanting to. In C. Sansone & J. Harackiewicz (Eds.), *Intrinsic and extrinsic motivation: The search for optimal motivation and performance* (pp. 341–372). San Diego, CA: Academic Press.

Schaffner, E., & Schiefele, U. (2007). The effect of experimental manipulation of student motivation on the situational representation of text. *Learning and Instruction, 17,* 755–772.

Schiefele, U. (1991). Interest, learning, and motivation. *Educational Psychologist, 26,* 299–323.

Schraw, G., Flowerday, T., & Reisetter, M. (1998). The role of choice in reader engagement. *Journal of Educational Psychology, 90,* 705–714.

Schwartz, B. (2000). Self-determination: The tyranny of freedom. *American Psychologist, 55,* 79–88.

Shah, A., & Wolford, G. (2007). Buying behavior as a function of parametric variation of number of choices. *Psychological Science, 18,* 369–370.

Sharan, S., Kussel, P., Hertz-Lazarowitz, R., Bejarano, Y., Raviv, S., & Sharan, Y. (1984). *Cooperative learning in the classroom: Research in desegregated schools.* Hillsdale, NJ: Erlbaum.

Sharan, S., & Sharan, Y. (1976). *Small-group teaching.* Englewood Cliffs, NJ: Educational Technology Publications.

Sheldon, K., & Elliot, A. (1998). Not all personal goals are personal: Comparing autonomous and controlled reasons for goals as predictors of effort and attainment. *Personality and Social Psychology Bulletin, 24,* 546–557.

Sheldon, K., Elliot, A., Kim, Y., & Kasser, T. (2001). What is satisfying about satisfying events? Testing 10 candidate psychological needs. *Journal of Personality and Social Psychology, 80,* 325–339.

Sheldon, K., & Filak, V. (2008). Manipulating autonomy, competence, and relatedness support in a game-learning context: New evidence that all three needs matter. *British Journal of Social Psychology, 47,* 267–283.

Sheldon, K., & Kasser, T. (1998). Pursuing personal goals: Skills enable progress but not all progress is beneficial. *Personality and Social Psychology Bulletin, 24,* 1319–1331.

Shih, S. (2008). The relation of self-determination and achievement goals to Taiwanese eighth graders' behavioral and emotional engagement in schoolwork. *Elementary School Journal, 108*, 313–334.

Skinner, E., Furrer, C., Marchand, G., & Kindermann, T. (2008). Engagement and disaffection in the classroom: Part of a larger motivational dynamic? *Journal of Educational Psychology, 100*, 765–781.

Slavin, R. (1995). *Cooperative learning: Theory, research, and practice* (2nd ed.). Boston: Allyn & Bacon.

Slavin, R. (1996). Research on cooperative learning and achievement: What we know, what we need to know. *Contemporary Educational Psychology, 21*, 43–69.

Soenens, B., & Vansteenskiste, M. (2005). Antecedents and outcomes of self-determination in three life domains: The role of parents' and teachers' autonomy support. *Journal of Youth and Adolescence, 34*, 589–604.

Standage, M., Duda, J., & Ntoumanis, N. (2003). A model of contextual motivation in physical education: Using constructs from self-determination and achievement goal theories to predict physical activity intentions. *Journal of Educational Psychology, 95*, 97–110.

Standage, M., Duda, J., & Ntoumanis, N. (2005). A test of self-determination theory in school physical education. *British Journal of Educational Psychology, 75*, 411–433.

Starnes, B., & Paris, C. (2000). Choosing to learn. *Phi Delta Kappan, 81*, 392–397.

Stefanou, C., Perencevich, K., Di Cintio, M., & Turner, J. (2004). Supporting autonomy in the classroom: Ways teachers encourage student decision making and ownership. *Educational Psychologist, 39*, 97–110.

Sweet, A., Guthrie, J., & Ng, M. (1998). Teacher perceptions and student reading motivation. *Journal of Educational Psychology, 90*, 210–223.

Tafarodi, R., Milne, A., & Smith, A. (1999). The confidence of choice: Evidence for an augmentation effect on self-perceived performance. *Personality and Social Psychology Bulletin, 25*, 1405–1416.

Taylor, I., & Ntoumanis, N. (2007). Teacher motivational strategies and student self-determination in physical education. *Journal of Educational Psychology, 99*, 747–760.

Tsai, Y., Kunter, M., Lüdtke, O., Trautwein, U., & Ryan, R. (2008). What makes lessons interesting? The role of situational and individual factors in three school subjects. *Journal of Educational Psychology, 100*, 460–472.

Valas, H., & Sovik, N. (1994). Variables affecting students' intrinsic motivation for school mathematics: Two empirical studies based on Deci and Ryan's theory on motivation. *Learning and Instruction, 3*, 281–298.

Vallerand, R., Fortier, M., & Guay, F. (1997). Self-determination and persistence in a real-life setting: Toward a motivational model of high school drop out. *Journal of Personality and Social Psychology, 72*, 1161–1176.

Vansteenkiste, M., Lens, W., & Deci, E. (2006). Intrinsic versus extrinsic goal contents in self-determination theory: Another look at the quality of academic motivation. *Educational Psychologist, 41*, 19–31.

Vansteenkiste, M., Simons, J., Lens, W., Sheldon, K., & Deci, E. (2004a). Motivating learning, performance, and persistence: The synergistic effects of intrinsic goal contents and autonomy supportive contexts. *Journal of Personality and Social Psychology, 87*, 246–260.

Vansteenkiste, M., Simons, J., Lens, W., Soenens, B., & Matos, L. (2005a). Examining the impact of extrinsic versus intrinsic goal framing and internally controlling versus autonomy-supportive communication style upon early adolescents' academic achievement. *Child Development, 76*, 483–501.

Vansteenkiste, M., Simons, J., Lens, W., Soenens, B., Matos, L., & Lacante, M. (2004b). Less is sometimes more: Goal content matters. *Journal of Educational Psychology, 96*, 755–764.

Vansteenkiste, M., Timmermans, T., Lens, W., Soenens, B., & Van den Broeck, A. (2008). Does extrinsic goal framing enhance extrinsic goal-oriented individuals' learning and performance? An experimental test of the match perspective versus self-determination theory. *Journal of Educational Psychology, 100*, 387–397.

Vansteenkiste, M., Zhou, M., Lens, W., & Soenens, B. (2005b). Experiences of autonomy and control among Chinese learners: Vitalizing or immobilizing? *Journal of Educational Psychology, 97*, 468–483.

Warr, P. (2007). *Work, happiness, and unhappiness*. Mahwah, NJ: Erlbaum.

Weber, B., & Hertel, G. (2007). Motivation gains of inferior group members: A meta-analytical review. *Journal of Personality and Social Psychology, 93*, 973–993.

Weinstein, R. (2002). *Reaching higher: The power of expectations in schooling*. Cambridge, MA: Harvard University Press.

White, R. (1959). Motivation reconsidered: The concept of competence. *Psychological Review, 66*, 297–333.

Wiley, C., Good, T., & McCaslin, M. (2008). Comprehensive school reform instructional practices throughout a school year: The role of subject matter, grade level, and time of year. *Teachers College Record, 110*, 2361–2388.

Wong, M. (2000). The relations among causality orientations, academic experience, academic performance, and academic commitment. *Personality and Social Psychology Bulletin, 26*, 315–326.

Worthy, J., Patterson, E., Salas, R., Prater, S., & Turner, M. (2002). "More than just reading": The human factor in reaching resistant readers. *Reading Research and Instruction, 41*, 177–202.

Yamauchi, H., & Tanaka, K. (1998). Relations of autonomy, self-referenced beliefs and self-regulated learning among Japanese children. *Psychological Reports, 82*, 803–816.

Zajac, R., & Hartup, W. (1997). Friends as coworkers: Research review. *Elementary School Journal, 98*(1), 3–13.

8

Other Ways to Support Students' Intrinsic Motivation

(handwritten marginal note: Online discussion)

Chapter 7 reviewed self-determination theory and presented ideas for supporting students' intrinsic motivation by meeting their needs for autonomy, competence, and relatedness. This chapter presents ideas about supporting students' intrinsic motivation that are derived from other sources, especially theory and research about interest and curiosity and teachers' suggestions based on their practical experience.

Research on student interest by Renninger and Hidi (2002) included a seventh-grader named Sam who had broad interests and did well in most subjects. When asked to describe the subjects he liked best, he wrote:

> I have several favorite subjects: reading, math, history, science, sports, woodshop, art, and music. What I like about reading is the fact that I can get a picture in my mind of a story without it being visual. I like math because I am pretty good at it and I like the challenge of tough math problems. I also like history because I like learning about what life was like in past years and we probably can learn some lessons from it. I like science because I like seeing how things work. I like sports because I like getting my energy out and I am pretty good at them. I like woodshop because I like building things. I like art because I like working with my hands and creating objects out of clay. I like music because I like playing all kinds of instruments and I like learning about the different kinds of music in the world. (p. 185)

THEORY AND RESEARCH ON INTEREST

Interest implies focused attention to a lesson, text passage, or learning activity that occurs because the learner values or has positive affective responses to its content or processes. Some authors treat interest as a form of intrinsic motivation, but others distinguish it by virtue of the fact that interest is focused on particular content or activities. *Interesting activities provide learners with forms of input or opportunities for response that they find rewarding and want to pursue* (Ainley, 2006; Schraw & Lehman, 2001; Silvia, 2008).

Possible sources of intrinsic interest in activities include the following:

- genetically based temperament or predispositions (e.g., high-arousal people are more likely to prefer active pursuits, whereas low-arousal people are more likely to prefer quieter ones);
- fun, enjoyment;
- relevance/utility to one's agendas;
- self-actualization potential (allows one to feel empowered, creative);
- meaningful, satisfying (allows one to experience new understandings, take satisfaction in achieving new insights or syntheses of knowledge);
- identification/self-projection (allows one to project oneself into a situation, such as by identifying with a central character in a story, simulation, or historical text);
- identification/assimilation to self (exposure to an activity makes one want to engage in it, to learn more about it, etc.).

Bergin (1999) reviewed the literature on factors that influence interest or related states such as attention, curiosity, or engagement. Factors that influence continuing interest include: a sense of belongingness in the task or situation because it reflects cultural values, personal identity, or social support; connection to one's emotions; opportunities to develop or demonstrate one's competence; relevance or utility to one's goals; or opportunity to extend one's knowledge in content domain. Situational factors that can draw attention and elicit at least temporary interest include: opportunities to engage in hands-on activity; recognition of discrepancy between what we think is true and what the situation implies; novelty; opportunities to share food or social interaction; author visibility in texts; opportunity to observe models who display competence or are rewarded for performing the behavior of interest; opportunity to play games or work on puzzles; themes relating to topics widely viewed as interesting (animal or human life, injury or death, sex, scandal, and so on); opportunities to enjoy fantasy elements embedded in certain activities; humor; and oral or written presentations organized within narrative formats.

Most authors distinguish between individual interest and situational interest. *Individual interest* (also known as *personal interest* or *topic interest*) refers to an enduring disposition to engage with particular content or activities whenever opportunities arise. *Situational interest* is triggered in the moment, emerging in response to something in the situation that catches our attention and motivates us to focus on it and explore it further. Situational interest may dissipate quickly (as when we investigate an unexpected sound and discover that it was just the wind blowing something over), or it can become the basis for more sustained investigation and learning (as when an encounter with an interesting anecdote about Albert Einstein motivates a reading of his biography, which, in turn, motivates a more sustained individual interest in nuclear physics).

Individual Interest

Research on relationships between interest and achievement provides some support for the strategy of capitalizing on students' existing motivation by *adapting the curriculum to students' individual interests.* One way is to offer activity choices that allow them to pursue those interests. Another way is to use stable individual interests (e.g., in sports) to provide contexts for mathematical problems, writing assignments, or other skill-development activities (Renninger & Hidi, 2002). When working in areas of individual interest, students display heightened attention, concentration, persistence, mastery orientation, positive affect, immediate comprehension of the material, and subsequent test performance (Ainley, Corrigan, & Richardson, 2005; Durik & Matarazzo, 2009; Durik, Vida, & Eccles, 2006; Guthrie et al., 2007; Harackiewicz, Durik, Barron, Linnenbrink-Garcia, & Tauer, 2008; Inoue, 2007; Katz, Assor, Kanat-Maymon, & Bereby-Meyer, 2006; Krapp, 2002; Renninger, 2009). Among dyslexic students, strong individual interests in certain topics often supply the motivation they need to persist in learning about those topics, and in process, develop more efficient reading skills than they would have otherwise (Fink, 1998).

Students usually have larger and better organized networks of prior knowledge in their areas of individual interest than in other content domains. This makes it easier for them to assimilate new information in their high-interest areas. However, such interest will not necessarily translate into attainment of curricular goals. For example, Sam, the seventh-grader quoted at the beginning of the chapter, said that he enjoyed reading because he enjoyed depicting the events of stories in his mind. This individual interest should serve him well during literacy activities that call for comprehending stories and relating personal reactions to them. However, it may not provide much motivation for activities that call for analyzing stories with respect to genre characteristics. Here, Sam is likely to need assistance in forming appropriate learning goals and maintaining attention to his learning strategies (Linnenbrink & Pintrich, 2000).

Situational Interest

Other motivational strategies call for *manipulating learning content or activities so as to stimulate situational interest.* Situational interest is more controllable by teachers than individual interest. Stimulating it promotes learning and often leads to development of individual interest (Schraw, Flowerday, & Lehman, 2001).

Hidi and Renninger (2006) proposed a four-phase model of interest development:

1. *Triggered Situational Intent.* Situational interest is triggered by features of a text, instructional condition, or learning environment.
2. *Maintained Situational Intent.* This situational interest is maintained through task meaningfulness, personal involvement, social support, or some other factor that sustains engagement in the activity.
3. *Emerging Individual Interest.* Individual interest begins to emerge as the learner begins to value opportunities to reengage in preferred activities and starts to generate questions or in other ways to regulate his or her own involvement in these activities.
4. *Well-Developed Individual Interest.* Nascent individual interests blossom into well-developed individual interests if the learner continues to find the domain or activity rewarding and progresses to deeper and more creative forms of engagement.

Interest does not necessarily progress through these four phases (in fact, well-developed individual interest in particular content domains is infrequent). In each phase, interest develops (if it does) through *triggering*: interactions or circumstances promote content-related uncertainty, surprise, novelty, complexity, or incongruity and lead to reorganization of the learner's thinking. In earlier phases, interest development might be triggered by group work in the classroom or a personally meaningful learning context. In later phases, triggers might include content-informed scaffolding (via teachers' questions or assignments) or curiosity questions generated by the learners themselves. Situational interest usually is primarily affective, but developing individual interest usually becomes increasingly cognitive (Renninger, 2009; Renninger, Bachrach, & Posey, 2008).

Texts. Much of the work on situational interest has focused on the reading of text, by identifying aspects of text associated with reader interest or ways that texts can be made more interesting to students. Manipulations of learning content have focused on three aspects of texts: coherence, vividness, and seductive details (Schraw & Lehman, 2001).

Coherence affects readers' ability to recognize the text's main ideas. Students not only learn more from easy-to-follow texts, but rate them as more interesting than less coherent tests.

Vividness refers to text segments that stand out because they are surprising, create suspense, or are otherwise engaging. Vivid text segments tend to be rated as more interesting and remembered better than less vivid segments.

Seductive details are unimportant to the text's main themes but highly interesting because they deal with controversial or sensational topics such as sex, death, or romantic intrigue. They are likely to be remembered—so much so that they interfere with memory for important text content (Harp & Mayer, 1998). Therefore, any details added to "spice up" a presentation should support, or at least not interfere with, attainment of the learning goals.

Besides coherence, vividness, and seductive details, other aspects of texts that stimulate interest include imagery, characters with whom readers can identify, emotionally charged or provocative content, content that is familiar but not too familiar, and relevance to the readers' personal goals (Schraw, 1997).

Interest is usually accompanied by emotional responses, which are usually but not always positive. Readers might be very interested in reading about sadistic torturers or the Holocaust, for example, even though the texts provoke responses of horror or disgust (Ainley, Corrigan, & Richardson, 2005).

Wade, Buxton, and Kelly (1999) asked college students to read expository texts and then tell what they found interesting. Interest was associated with information that was unexpected, important, new, or valued; connections that the readers made between the text and their prior knowledge; imagery and descriptive language; and connections made by the authors using comparisons and analogies. The major factor associated with low interest was low coherence or difficult vocabulary that made the text hard to follow. Once again, interest is more closely related to the overall value and coherence of a text than to isolated "grabbers" inserted into individual segments. There is no need to spice up texts with seductive details. Instead, present students with coherent renderings of new information that they value.

Activities. Independent of their potential interest in its content, learners might be interested in an activity's processes. If such interest is not already present, teachers may be able to stimulate it by encouraging students to expand their goals and task-engagement strategies so as to make the activity more interesting for them. For example, students might make the task of copying letters from a template more interesting by: competing against themselves or a friend, competing against time, trying to increase the artfulness of their tracings, varying their procedure, or sorting and categorizing different problems (Bergin, 1999; Hidi, 2002; Jang, 2008; Sansone & Thoman, 2006; Schraw & Lehman, 2001). These or other interest-enhancing task transformations might be encouraged so long as they support progress toward learning goals.

Chen, Darst, and Pangrazi (2001) examined the activity aspects of situational interest in physical education classes. They asked students to rate activities on the degree to which they: were new to them (novelty), were experienced as enjoyable (instant enjoyment), stimulated curiosity or interest in exploring the activity (exploration intention), required focused attention (attention demand), and were complex and difficult (challenge). Interest was associated primarily with instant enjoyment and secondarily with novelty and exploration intention. Attention demand was less clearly related and challenge was unrelated. Students are unlikely to perceive overly challenging activities as enjoyable or interesting.

Pfaffman (2003) asked high school students to think about their favorite class and rate the importance of reasons that might explain why they enjoyed it. Reasons related to learning (learning strategies and methods, reading about the subject, learning about dates, places, people, or things), creation (seeing the fruits of their labor, expressing themselves, creating something new or rare), or flow (overcoming new challenges, having clear goals and feedback, doing something as an end in itself) tended to be rated highly. Social (to be liked, to belong to a group, to share conversation) and extrinsic (to gain social stature, to win competitions, or to be better than others) reasons were rated much lower. In short, students' favorite classes were classes that they found intrinsically rewarding. Covington (1999) reported similar patterns in college students' reports about what aspects of their classes they most valued.

Askell-Williams and Lawson (2001) asked middle school students to identify the features of interesting lessons. Along with features related to meeting their needs for autonomy, competence, and relatedness, the students frequently mentioned hands-on activities, experiments, work that relates to the outside world, and activities that allow them to design or make things, use their imaginations or be creative, or do a variety of different things.

Technology.   Technology has long been recognized as a "catch" factor capable of eliciting students' situational interest in learning activities. Teachers' opportunities for taking advantage of technology's motivational properties have mushroomed in recent years, especially with the accumulation of websites offering content or activities that support learning. In all subjects, but especially in science and social studies, there has been a proliferation of technology-based instructional models, units, and lessons suitable for use in K–12 teaching, including many that explicitly that incorporate motivational principles. Most of them involve engaging students in inquiry or problem solving, often collaboratively and in ways that take advantage of Web 2.0 applications that enable students to create, edit, or comment on postings available at websites (e.g., a program that calls for students to research and then create their own wikis about historical topics). Research on these innovations indicates that they routinely increase student interest and engagement in the learning activities, and frequently lead to development of more sustained individual interest in and enhanced learning about the topic (Boll, Hammond, & Ferster, 2008; Brand, Collver, & Kasarda, 2008; Harmer & Kates, 2007; Heafner & Friedman, 2008; Ioannou, Brown, Hannifin, & Boyer, 2009; Mistler-Jackson & Songer, 2000; Oliver, 2008; Wang & Reeves, 2006).

ADAPTING ACTIVITIES TO STUDENTS' INTERESTS

To the extent that doing so will support your instructional goals, you can select reading assignments and design your classroom presentations to feature elements that enhance their interest value for students. For example, Hidi and Baird (1988) found that students' *interest was enhanced when the main ideas in an expository text were elaborated through insertions that featured the following motivational principles*: (a) *character identification* (information about people with whom the students could identify, such as those whose inventions or discoveries led to the knowledge under study); (b) *novelty* (content that was interesting because it was new or unusual); (c) *life theme* (applications or other connections to the students' lives outside of school); and (d) *activity level* (content that included reference to intense activities or strong emotions).

Means, Jonassen, and Dwyer (1997) increased students' interest in and learning from texts by addressing material that brought out connections between the text content and the students' lives. Students' perceptions of the relevance of text content can be increased

---

Box 8.1   Attempts to Make Texts More Interesting

For a time, it was believed that the interest potential and even the comprehensibility of textbooks could be improved by revising them into a zesty, magazine-style of writing. This approach focused on making the content more dramatic by adding vivid anecdotes and details focused more around people than events. It also involved writing more engaging prose that featured fewer passive sentences and abstract words; more memorable images and colorful picture words; strong, vivid verbs; and added colloquialisms and metaphors. Early experiments with these revised texts appeared promising.

However, findings accumulated over time indicated that magazine-style texts usually did not produce higher ratings of interest or enjoyment, and even when they did, they reduced students' learning of key ideas. The magazine-style writing reduced the coherence of text passages (making it harder for students to recognize and remember linkages among key ideas). Also, the inserted anecdotes and interesting details often proved to be more "seductive" than instructive (they focused attention on side issues at the expense of important content). Eventually, it became clear that the best combination of motivational and learning outcomes can be expected from texts that structure content into networks of connected information that cohere around important ideas (Britton, VanDusen, Gulgoz, & Glynn, 1989; Duffy et al., 1989; Garner, Alexander, Gillingham, Kulikowich, & Brown, 1991; Graves et al., 1991; McKeown & Beck, 1994; Wade, Alexander, Schraw, & Kulikowich, 1995).

These findings probably also apply to the content and organization of presentations made by teachers or conveyed through instructional media. The larger principle is that content representations or embellishments made for motivational purposes are likely to have desirable effects if they help students to recognize and remember key ideas, but not if they focus them on trivia. Similarly, motivational embellishments of learning activities should be designed to support students' accomplishment of your instructional goals and not be distracting "bells and whistles."

by asking them to adopt a particular perspective or to read with a particular purpose in mind (Narvaez, van den Broek, & Ruiz, 1999; Schraw & Dennison, 1994).

Whenever instructional goals can be accomplished using a variety of examples or activities, incorporate content that students find interesting or activities they find enjoyable. People, fads, or events that are currently prominent in the news or the youth culture can be worked into everyday lessons as applications of the concepts being learned. For example, a history teacher pointed out that the Ark of the Covenant mentioned in the ancient history text was the same ark featured in the movie *Raiders of the Lost Ark.* Similarly, a geography teacher sparked interest in studying the coordinates (latitude and longitude) by noting that the sunken remains of the *Titanic* can be located easily, even though they lie hundreds of miles out to sea, because the discoverers fixed the location precisely using the coordinates.

Another way to incorporate interests into activities is to *encourage students to ask questions and make comments about the topic.* Relevant questions and comments create "teachable moments." They indicate interest on the part of students who make them, and chances are good that other students will share this interest.

It also is helpful, from both instructional and motivational points of view, to plan lessons and assignments that *include divergent questions and opportunities for students to express opinions, make evaluations, or in other ways respond personally to the content.* For example, after reviewing information about the Christians and the lions, the gladiators, and other excesses of the Roman circuses, a history teacher asked his students how otherwise cultured people could take pleasure in such cruelty. This led to a productive discussion in which students developed insights about issues such as violence in sports and in contemporary society generally, and the difference between enjoyment of pleasures and indulgence in excesses. This same teacher, after describing life in Athens and Sparta, asked students which city they would rather live in and why. Again, this led to a lively discussion that included parallels to modern nations that focus on building military strength (at a cost in quality of civilian life) versus maintaining more balanced priorities.

ADAPTING TRADITIONAL LEARNING ACTIVITIES TO ENHANCE THEIR INTRINSIC MOTIVATION POTENTIAL

Conventional school learning activities can be altered or embellished to increase their intrinsic motivation potential. Adjustments might enhance four sources of intrinsic motivation: (a) challenge (adjust difficulty levels so that tasks are optimally challenging); (b) curiosity (include elements that will stimulate curiosity); (c) control (offer choices or in other ways encourage students to experience a sense of self-determination); and (d) fantasy (embellish activities in ways that encourage students to engage in them with a playful set, identification with fictional characters, or involvement in a world of fantasy; Malone & Lepper, 1987; Wang & Reeves, 2006). Challenge and control issues were discussed in chapter 7. Curiosity and embellishment strategies are discussed in the following sections.

Induce Curiosity or Suspense

When stimulating curiosity, do so in ways that foster development of continuing interest in the key ideas around which broad knowledge networks are structured. Otherwise, students may focus on seductive but trivial details or lose interest once their initial curiosity is satisfied (Friedlander, 1965; Loewenstein, 1994; Reio, 2008).

Covington and Teel (1996) suggested two strategies for stimulating curiosity: question asking, and discovering mysteries, puzzles, and oddities. *Question asking* can be used to stimulate curiosity about an upcoming topic ("As we begin our study of France, what questions do you have about that country?"), or to renew enthusiasm following its initial development ("What would you like to know about France that wasn't addressed in the textbook?"). *Discovering mysteries, puzzles, and oddities* involves asking students to bring up for discussion anything in their readings that seems incongruous or surprising.

Some teachers incorporate curiosity-stimulating techniques within frequently used *routines*. For example, a mathematics teacher began most classes with an intriguing problem which was written on the board but covered by a rolled down map. His students quickly learned to anticipate the moment when he would roll up the map and "allow" them to see the problem. When he did, he usually had their full attention. Another teacher concealed props within a large box that she placed on her desk on days when she was going to do some interesting demonstration. Again, all eyes were on her when she opened that box.

Karmos and Karmos (1983) described a mathematics teacher who often started lessons by saying "Last night, I went down to my basement and I found...." The first time, he told of finding a tree that doubled its number of branches each hour, and then used this "discovery" as the basis for posing interesting mathematics problems. Things "found in his basement" on other occasions included alligators and a diesel train. Whenever he said "Last night, I went down to my basement...," his students knew they could anticipate a preposterous claim followed by some interesting problems.

A topic or activity need not be new in order to generate curiosity. We often develop curiosity about certain aspects of familiar topics, especially when we experience doubt or confusion because we have become aware that our existing ideas appear to be contradictory or incomplete. This motivates us to want to acquire information that will allow us to resolve the gaps or discrepancies in our thinking (Abdi, 2005; Berlyne, 1960).

You can stimulate curiosity or suspense by posing questions or doing "set ups" that make students feel the need to resolve some ambiguity or obtain more information. To prepare students to read about Russia, for example, you could ask them if they know how many time zones there are in Russia or how the United States acquired Alaska. It is mind-boggling for most students to discover that one country encompasses 11 time zones or that the United States purchased Alaska from Russia.

Whether students find such facts interesting depends largely on the degree to which their teachers stimulate curiosity about them and provide contexts for thinking about their associations with prior knowledge or beliefs. This example further illustrates two important points made earlier: Interest resides in people rather than in topics or activities, and the motivation that develops in particular situations results from interactions among persons, tasks, and the larger social context.

You can stimulate your students' curiosity about a topic and encourage them to generate interest in it by (a) asking them to speculate or make predictions about what they will be learning; (b) raising questions that successful completion of the activity will enable them to answer; and (c) where relevant, showing them that their existing knowledge is not sufficient to enable them to accomplish some valued objective, is internally inconsistent, is inconsistent with new information, or is currently scattered but can be organized around certain general principles or powerful ideas (Malone & Lepper, 1987; Yell, Scheurman, & Reynolds, 2004).

Keller (1983) noted that one way to stimulate curiosity is to *put students into an active information-processing or problem-solving mode as you introduce learning activities*. You can do this by posing interesting questions or problems for students to address as they engage in the activity. For example, you might introduce the concept of condensation by calling students' attention to the water that begins to appear on the outside of a glass of ice water, and asking them to explain why. If necessary, prompt their thinking by suggesting seemingly plausible possibilities ("Is the water seeping through the glass?")

Reeve (1996) suggested five strategies for stimulating curiosity: suspense, guessing and feedback, playing to students' sense of knowing, controversy, and contradiction.

Suspense strategies focus attention on competing hypotheses or problems with uncertain conclusions. By inviting students to consider competing answers to questions such as what caused the Civil War or why the dinosaurs became extinct, you can create a sense of mental struggle within them. Students, especially those prone to say "just tell us the answer," can learn to experience the satisfactions of seeking answers to challenging intellectual questions.

The strategy of *guessing and feedback* involves introducing a topic by giving students a pretest or leading them through a prior knowledge activity that requires them to answer specific questions. The questions should be connected to key ideas and likely to be answered incorrectly (Which is the northernmost state: Colorado, Kansas, or Nebraska?). Knowledge that one has guessed incorrectly piques curiosity to learn more about the topic.

Playing to students' sense of knowing is a related strategy that applies when students already possess considerable prior knowledge. For example, by the time they reach junior high school, most students have had a great deal of exposure to U.S. maps and geography. If they have begun to respond with boredom or complacency, a question such as "Name the eight states that border the Great Lakes" might restimulate their interest, because most of them will be able to identify many but not all of these states.

Controversy strategies involve eliciting divergent opinions and then inviting students to resolve them through sustained discussion. In the process, students may recognize the need to consult reference materials or conduct other research to obtain information.

The *contradiction* strategy is used after students have assimilated a body of information and formed a conclusion. At this point, you introduce information that contradicts the conclusion, forces students to recognize that the issue is more complicated than they thought, and stimulates them to develop more complete understandings. For example, you might first establish that sodium and chloride are poisons, then point out that when combined as sodium chloride, they constitute basic table salt. Or, having established that humans "sit atop the evolutionary ladder," you might point out that there are more insects than any other species, and their combined weight exceeds that of all animals.

Embellish Learning Activities with Appealing Fantasy Elements

Research on embellishing learning activities with fantasy elements has been done by Mark Lepper and his colleagues (Lepper & Cordova, 1992; Lepper & Hodell, 1989). One study was done with a mathematics program on the Cartesian coordinates. In the unembellished version, students were asked to find a "hidden dot" lying beneath one of the intersections of an 11×11 Cartesian grid, with axes labeled from -5 to $+5$. Students were to find the dot by guessing its location. After each incorrect guess, they were provided with written and visual feedback (an arrow indicating the direction in which the hidden dot lay relative to the point guessed). When they eventually guessed correctly, they were given congratulatory feedback.

In the embellished version, students were invited to help a fantasy character hunt for hidden treasures buried on a desert island. When correct guesses were made, small icons representing a treasure (e.g., an ivory comb, a silver goblet, or a rusty hook) appeared on the screen, accompanied by sound effects.

In another study, students used a computerized graphics program to (a) draw lines connecting objects on the screen, (b) negotiate a series of mazes, and (c) construct geometric shapes. The unembellished versions simply called for constructing the lines or shapes. The embellished versions involved constructing the same lines or shapes within one of three fantasy contexts: a pirate in search of buried treasure, a detective hunting down criminals, or an astronaut seeking out new planets in space.

Cordova and Lepper (1996) and Iyengar and Lepper (1999) demonstrated the value of personalizing the fantasy elements of learning activities. They allowed elementary students to make choices concerning instructionally irrelevant and seemingly trivial aspects of the activities (e.g., naming the spaceship and including several friends as crew members). Yet, the students both learned more and showed greater interest in such activities when given the personalization options.

Another successful use of personalization was reported by deSousa and Oakhill (1996). They asked eight- and nine-year-old children to study text passages and attempt to detect problems such as prior knowledge violations, internal inconsistencies, and nonsense words. Some children were simply asked to edit the passage, but others were asked to pretend to be detectives while looking for the problems. The "detectives" found the task more interesting and were more successful in detecting the problems.

Schank and Cleary (1995) developed elaborately embellished computerized learning opportunities that incorporated simulation-based learning by doing, incidental learning, learning by reflection, case-based teaching, or learning by exploring. For example, a program for teaching languages leads students through scenarios that require them to use the language they are learning (e.g., arriving in the country by plane and going through customs, finding transportation, and checking in at a hotel). At each step, students interact with simulated people who appear in video clips and respond to what they say. When these communications are successful, the students move on to the next scenario. When communication breaks down, the program offers them options for getting help and then returning to the situation.

An incidental learning program teaches U.S. geography and map skills by allowing students to take simulated car trips. They begin with a map of the country, click on a state, then zoom in on a city. Students then can travel from city to city along the interstate highway system. When they reach a chosen destination, they can watch video clips that feature sports highlights, movies, music videos, amusement parks, or historical footage associated with the location. In the process, they familiarize themselves with U.S. states and cities and learn to plan travel using maps.

A case-based approach to teaching biological principles invites students to create their own animal by taking an existing animal and changing it in some way. They begin by selecting possibilities from lists of animals and potential changes, then explore the ramifications of the "created" animal by answering questions. If they select a fish that has wings, for example, the program might ask them to reflect on why the ability to fly would be useful to a fish, when this ability might be used, or what might be some limitations on its use. In the process, they view videos relating to these questions.

An elaborate simulation activity called Broadcast News allows groups of high school students to produce their own news shows on current events, working with real news sources from a day in the recent past. Students follow actual television news procedures and use video equipment to research, write, and edit stories; prioritize and sequence the stories for inclusion in the newscast; then put it all together under "live taping" conditions.

Research on embellishments of conventional learning activities has shown that students prefer the embellished versions and usually show improved learning outcomes. Furthermore, these effects are not restricted to children. Moreno and Mayer (2000) engaged college students in multimedia science lessons presented either in neutral, third-person language or in more personalized, first- and second-person language. The introduction to the neutral version read, "This program is about what type of plants survive in different planets. For each planet, a plant will be designed. The goal is to learn what type of roots, stem, and leaves allow plants to survive in each environment. Some hints are provided throughout the program." The parallel personalized version read, "You are about to start a journey where you will be visiting different planets. For each planet, you will need to design a plant. Your mission is to learn what type of roots, stem, and leaves will allow your plant to survive in each environment. I will be guiding you through by giving out some hints." Students given the personalized version learned the content more thoroughly and were able to apply it more successfully. The self-referential language of the personalized version encouraged students to elaborate the content, and its conversational format allowed them to learn with less cognitive effort.

Personalization effects have even been demonstrated with college students using quite simple techniques. In one study, students learned about plant survival mechanisms through a multimedia educational game in which an on-screen agent spoke to them in either a personalized or a non-personalized style. The content was the same; the only difference was that in the personalized style the agent used first- or second-person language rather than third-person language (Moreno & Mayer, 2004).

In a second study, the personalization treatment was even more minimal. Here, students learned from narrated animations explaining how the human respiratory system works. The 100-word narration was the same for both groups except that the personalized version used "your" in 12 places where the non-personalized version used "the" ("…During inhaling, the [your] diaphragm moves down creating more space for the [your] lungs, air enters through the [your] nose or mouth, moves down through the [your] throat and bronchial tubes to tiny air sacs in the [your] lungs…"; Mayer, Fennell, Farmer, & Campbell, 2004). Remarkably, students who experienced the personalized treatments showed higher achievement than students who experienced the non-personalized treatments in these studies.

Fantasy elements add interest value to activities because they allow students to identify with fantasy characters, feel emotional reactions, and vicariously experience situations that may not be open to them in real life. Fantasy environments can evoke mental images of physical or social situations that are not actually present and thus produce the cognitive advantages that accrue from linking the known to the unfamiliar. *Especially useful are fantasy elements that provide helpful metaphors for learning new skills* (the family metaphor for mathematical set concepts) *or real-world contexts within which the skills can be used* (simulating running a lemonade stand).

However, Lepper and Cordova (1992) cautioned that motivational embellishment strategies do not always have beneficial effects. *The best results can be expected when the embellishments draw attention to the key ideas or processes that the activity is designed to teach, and students must learn them in order to complete the activity successfully.* Where fantasy elements do not support learning in this fashion, they may function merely as "bells and whistles" that enhance the affective aspects of intrinsic motivation but do not engage the cognitive aspects that produce desired learning outcomes. Students may learn no more, or even less, than they would from conventional versions of the same activities (Sansone & Smith, 2000; Lepper & Henderlong, 2000).

Fantasy embellishments do not need to be as elaborate as the ones already described. Anand and Ross (1987) showed that both motivational and learning benefits resulted when problems on division of fractions were personalized by incorporating references to the students or to people or things with whom they identified (the teacher, their friends, or their favorite foods). You can introduce fantasy or imagination elements into your everyday instruction that will engage your students' emotions or allow them to experience events vicariously. In studying poems or stories, for example, you can encourage students to debate the authors' motives in writing the works or to learn about formative experiences in the authors' lives. In studying scientific or mathematical principles and methods, you can help students to appreciate the practical problems that needed to be solved or the personal motives of the discoverers that led to development of the knowledge or skills being taught.

Alternatively, you can set up *role-play or simulation activities* that allow students to identify with real or fictional characters or to deal with academic content in direct, personalized ways. Rather than just assign students to read history, for example, you can make it come alive by arranging for them to role play Columbus and his crew debating what to do after 30 days at sea (or at the secondary level, to role play the American, British, and Russian leaders meeting at Yalta). Simulations that engage students in social perspective taking (by requiring them to adopt the attitudes and beliefs of particular individuals or role representatives, yet understand and negotiate with others who represent contrasting attitudes and beliefs) appear to be notably motivating as well as educational (Gehlbach et al., 2008; Lay & Smarick, 2006; Pace, Bishel, Beck, Holquist, & Makowski, 1990).

To dramatize the importance of a secret ballot, you might have students act out an election scene in a totalitarian state where one must get a pencil from the election supervisors (i.e., officials of the ruling party) if one wishes to write in names instead of voting for the single slate of candidates. To demonstrate the efficiency of assembly lines, you might organize some of your students into an assembly line making sandwiches or collating information packets.

Elaborate simulations have been developed for social studies, particularly economics. For example, Kourilsky (1983) designed the Mini-Society program to teach 7- to 12-year-olds primarily about economics and secondarily about government, career, consumer, and value issues through participation in economic activities followed by debriefing of what was learned. The simulation is a market economy couched within a democratic society. Students create within their classroom a mini-society that includes a name, a flag, a currency system, civil servants, and some initial mechanisms through which citizens can earn money through good citizenship or accomplishments (as a way to introduce money into circulation). Then they set up and run businesses that offer goods or services in exchange for mini-society money. In the process, they collaborate with partners to plan and run businesses; vote on taxes, government services, and other policy issues; and engage in analysis and decision making on issues in economics and government.

A popular economics simulation for secondary students acquaints them with investing principles by inviting them to establish a simulated investment portfolio. They allocate a given sum to an initial set of investments of their own choosing, then "manage" the portfolio by making any desired changes and updating the associated bookkeeping. The simulated investments are tracked and discussed periodically so that students can understand what would have happened if they had been investing real money and try to determine why some investments worked out better than others.

Simulation activities are not confined to full-scale drama, role play, simulation games, and other "major productions." *More modest simulation exercises can be incorporated into everyday instruction.* You can invite students to briefly project themselves into fictional or nonfictional situations under study by asking them "If you were (the story's hero, the president of the United States, a homeless person, etc.), what would you think or feel when that happened? What actions might you take?" In teaching a mathematical procedure, you might ask students to identify everyday problems that the procedure might be used to solve. Material on totalitarian societies might be "brought home" by asking students to imagine and talk about what it would be like to seek housing in a country where the government owned all of the property or to get accurate information about world events in a country where the government controlled all of the media. Reports on states, nations, or cultures might be written as travel brochures or newspaper articles, with students asked to keep their chosen purpose and audience in mind when deciding what to include and how to present it. Such fantasy or simulation activities do not take much time or require special preparations, but they can stimulate students to relate to the content more personally and take greater interest in it.

INSTRUCTIONAL APPROACHES THAT REFLECT MULTIPLE PRINCIPLES WORKING IN COMBINATION

Several broad educational philosophies incorporate principles for connecting with students' existing intrinsic motivation or designing learning activities to be intrinsically motivating (progressive education, discovery learning, open education, Foxfire, whole language). These principles also are emphasized in models for incorporating motivational principles into curriculum and instruction. The TARGET program described in chapter 4 is one example. Two others are the motivated literacy approach to language arts instruction and the project-based learning approach to social studies and science instruction.

Motivated Literacy

Julianne Turner (1993, 1995) described the motivated literacy approach to beginning literacy instruction, defining it as an emphasis on open tasks over closed tasks. Teachers who emphasized *closed tasks* taught a literacy curriculum focused heavily on teacher-directed skills lessons followed by seatwork assignments. Students worked individually, attempting to provide correct answers to closed-ended questions. In contrast, teachers who favored a motivated literacy approach emphasized more open tasks. *Open tasks* included interactive-constructive tasks, in which students could manipulate materials to reach an outcome (such as in a game) or arrange words to reconstruct a nursery rhyme; partner reading, in which two students shared the oral reading of a story; composition, in which students wrote on self-selected topics; and tradebook reading, in which they read self-selected books.

Open tasks allow students to decide what information to use and how they want to use it to solve some larger problem. They feature characteristics associated with intrinsic motivation: challenge and self-improvement, autonomy, the pursuit of individual interests, and social collaboration. Emphasis on open tasks promoted greater engagement in literacy activities, as indicated by increased reading strategy use, persistence, and accomplishment of learning goals. Some examples of open tasks are as follows.

Several teachers reproduced texts from stories or nursery rhymes on oaktag board, cut the sentences into individual words, and then invited their students to reconstruct the sentences. This activity was challenging for even the best readers, yet still accessible to readers at lower levels. It required students to use strategies including designing a plan, rehearsing, decoding, monitoring for upper- and lowercase letters and punctuation, sequencing, and backtracking for comprehension. Frequently, they tried many arrangements, rereading each time to determine if they were satisfied with their construction.

Other teachers designed multiple activities that supported their instructional goals and then allowed students to select from them. One classroom featured a week-long celebration of *Clifford's Birthday Party* (Bridwell, 1988). Activity options included writing about the party described in the book, writing about a parallel party held in the classroom, writing party invitations, making a list of party supplies, drawing and labeling Clifford's gifts, and reading other Clifford books. In carrying out these activities, the students created products that showed care, planning, and originality and sparked task-oriented conversations. Turner attributed this in part to the students' opportunities to select activities that they found most interesting.

Several teachers allowed their students to work with selected partners to choose and sequence their learning activities. They helped each pair to think through their choices, make decisions about how to plan and monitor their work, evaluate their products, and note things to keep in mind for the future.

Some teachers connected with students' interests by allowing them to select books to read. This supported students' engagement during oral reading times and encouraged them to persist in reading difficult texts. Similarly, composition opportunities often allowed students to explore topics of importance to them. In one class, for example, all of the students wrote about butterflies, but their compositions ranged from discussions of the life cycle to pretend fantasies.

The students often worked in pairs or small groups, which allowed them to pique one another's curiosity, share interests, and model expertise that classmates could emulate. Open tasks are more conducive to student collaboration than closed tasks that allow for only one approach or answer.

Miller and Meece (1999), in a study of third graders, also found a preference for open and challenging tasks. Students reported feeling creative, experiencing positive emotions, and taking satisfaction in working hard at high-challenge tasks, but feeling bored and not engaged in productive thinking when working on low-challenge tasks.

Anderman (1993) described a motivating approach to writing instruction. In this study, third and fourth graders were asked to spend time each day writing in journals about any topic they wished to address. In weekly feedback sessions, they read their writings to the teacher and other students. Over time, they not only developed their writing abilities but acquired a continuing desire to engage in journal writing.

Project-Based Learning

Phyllis Blumenfeld and her colleagues (1991) described *project-based learning*, a comprehensive approach that incorporates several principles for capitalizing on students' intrinsic motivation. It calls for engaging students in *projects*: relatively long-term, problem-focused, and meaningful units of instruction that integrate concepts from a number of fields of study. Students pursue solutions to authentic problems by asking and refining questions, debating ideas, making predictions, designing plans or experiments, collecting and analyzing data, drawing conclusions, communicating their ideas and findings to others, asking new questions, and creating products.

There are two essential components to projects: they require a question or problem that organizes and drives activities, and the activities culminate in a final product that addresses the driving question. The final products represent the students' problem solutions, organized and presented in a form (e.g., a model, report, videotape, or computer program) that can be shared and critiqued. Feedback from others permits students to reflect on and extend their emergent knowledge and to revise their products if necessary. Project-based learning incorporates the following motivational features: Tasks are varied and include novel elements, problems are authentic and challenging, students exercise choice in deciding what to do and how to do it, they collaborate with peers in carrying out the work, and the work leads to closure via production of the final product.

These motivational features do not guarantee that students will acquire needed information, generate and test solutions, and evaluate their findings carefully. Teachers need to make sure that students possess whatever subject-matter knowledge and research skills are required to complete their projects successfully, learn key ideas and skills in the process of carrying them out, view the projects as authentic, and value the products they create.

Howard Gardner (1991) proposed a radical restructuring of K–12 schooling in which students would spend most of their time engaged in project-based learning. Projects can be developed for any subject, although they are especially well suited to science and social studies. Blumenfeld et al. (1991) suggested ways in which projects can be designed to maximize their motivational impact. Some of these involve using emerging technologies that enable students to work with computerized databases in conducting their research or to use computerized design, video technology, and other innovations in developing their products. Singer, Marx, Krajcik, and Chambers (2000) drew on experiences using project-based learning in middle schools to identify principles for designing projects and for scaffolding students' work to ensure that they engage in desired forms of collaborative inquiry. For examples of projects developed for the elementary grades, visit www.project-approach.com.

TEACHERS' EXPERIENCE-BASED MOTIVATIONAL STRATEGIES

When teachers are asked to describe the strategies they use to motivate their students, the experience-based strategies they report mostly resemble the intrinsic motivational strategies presented in this and the previous chapter. For example, all of the 36 teachers interviewed by Flowerday and Schraw (2000) endorsed offering choices. They believed that increased choice leads to increased interest, engagement, and learning, especially for students who do not show much motivation for school activities. They also felt that choice increases students' ownership of the activity and thus their motivation to learn. They suggested two strategies to use when students may choose unproductively if left on their own: (a) provide a menu of selections suited to the instructional goals but also likely to be attractive to students, and (b) scaffold students' choice-making by helping them take into account criteria such as whether they are likely to find the task engaging and be able to complete it successfully.

Nolen and Nicholls (1994) investigated teachers' beliefs about different motivational strategies. They found that the teachers favored encouraging cooperative learning, offering stimulating tasks, giving choices, and attributing thought and interest ("I've noticed how much you enjoy problems that make you think.") over praising, publicizing superior performance, or using extrinsic rewards.

Hootstein (1995) interviewed eighth-grade teachers about the strategies they used to motivate students to learn U.S. history. The 10 most frequently mentioned strategies were: having students role-play characters in historical simulations (mentioned by 83% of the teachers), projects that result in the creation of products (60%), playing games to review material for tests (44%), relating history to current events or to students' lives (44%), historical novels (44%), thought-provoking questions (33%), guest speakers from the community (33%), historical videos and films (28%), cooperative learning activities (28%), and small-scale hands-on experiences (28%).

Hootstein (1995) also showed the eighth graders the strategies mentioned by their teachers and asked which would most motivate them to want to learn U.S. history. Role playing historical characters was mentioned most often, followed by group discussions and teacher attempts to make the subject interesting, to relate it to current events or their own interests, or to inject humor through jokes, stories, or anecdotes. Here is additional evidence that students do not necessarily need technology, games, or various "bells and whistles" to enjoy learning, and even enjoy relatively passive forms of learning if their teacher makes the material interesting to them.

Zahorik (1996) asked teachers to write papers on (a) what makes for a good learning experience, (b) a very interesting activity they had used, (c) how they created interest, and (d) subject-matter facts and concepts they had found to be interesting to students. The teachers' papers once again emphasized intrinsic motivational strategies, although in ways that underscored their limitations as well as their strengths.

Strategies for generating interest in learning were concentrated in eight categories. All of the teachers mentioned *hands-on activities*. Examples included manipulatives such as pattern blocks in mathematics; playing games of all kinds; simulations, role play, and drama; projects such as growing seedlings in science or making television commercials in Spanish; and solving problems or puzzles such as determining the sugar content of chewing gum.

Personalized content was mentioned by 65% of the teachers. These responses took three forms: tying content to students' prior knowledge, experiences, or interests (beginning a unit on weather by having students discuss their experiences with tornados); allowing students to generate the content to be studied, often through teacher-student planning; and selecting from the required curriculum that content which is likely to interest students (appealing novels; rules for how married names are composed in Spanish).

Also mentioned by 65% of the teachers were *student trust techniques* that show respect for students' intelligence, integrity, and pride. They permit students to share their ideas and experiences through dialogue, reporting, debating, and displaying work; to make decisions for themselves and use their creativity; or to develop ownership of classroom events through involvement in planning units and choosing activities.

Group tasks were mentioned by 55% of the teachers. These were activities that students carried out cooperatively in small groups, such as a science demonstration on water evaporation and condensation.

The remaining categories included using a *variety of materials* (29%), *teacher enthusiasm* (28%), *practical activities that have utility outside of school or produce a useful product* (17%), and using a *variety of activities* (11%). In speaking of variety, the teachers especially mentioned materials, resources, or activities that were atypical in some way, such as field trips, guest speakers, artifacts, or animals. Examples of teacher enthusiasm included being humorous and emphasizing fun, describing personal experiences to students, participating in tasks as an equal group member, showing excitement, and communicating a sense of purpose, direction, or organization. One teacher dressed up as a story character. Another told students about her recent trip to Spain. Practical activities included artwork that could be used as gifts, producing a book for others to read, learning how to read a menu, planning a trip to a national park, and discussing contraception.

Among activities that they avoided for motivational reasons, teachers mentioned *sedentary activities* (explaining, giving directions, reviewing, testing, reading textbooks, doing workbooks, taking notes); *unsuitable tasks* (too difficult or extensive, or too easy or redundant); *artificial tasks* that have no perceived utility outside of school; *student distrust* (unilateral teacher actions in areas where student choice could have been provided); and *teacher insipidity* (the teacher displaying lack of enthusiasm, caring, fun, or involvement).

The teachers had disappointingly little to say about putting students into contact with inherently interesting content. They focused more on topics than ideas, and usually called for adding interesting elements rather than helping students to develop appreciation for the content base itself. They reported that their students were interested in the following categories of topics: *human* (anything that has to do with people or culture, such as the skeleton, food, family, diseases, pets, weapons, holidays, sex, death, violence, or money); *now* (topics of current importance in the students' lives, such as television, drugs, fashion, music, gangs, shopping malls, and slang); *nature* (topics relating to the physical and biological world, such as dinosaurs, giraffes, the sea, ecology, wolves, and weather); and *functional* (practical or useful topics, such as safety, consumerism, map reading, the stock market, or computers).

When the teachers did mention content, many of their responses referred to very limited ideas or specific facts (such as that Van Gogh cut off his own ear). However, some, especially secondary teachers, did mention more broadly applicable ideas (no country exists that does not need another country for something; plants and animals exist in symbiotic relationships; the passive voice is used in Spanish to shift blame away from persons).

Zahorik expressed concern that *hands-on activities often were treated more as ends than as means*. At least a third seemed unlikely to lead to important learning. For example, a fifth-grade social studies unit on the 1950s included activities calling for singing Elvis Presley songs, impersonating Elvis, writing essays speculating on whether

Elvis was still alive, and critiquing Elvis's movies. *Hands-on* activities will not produce important learning unless they include *minds-on* features that engage students in thinking about powerful ideas (Duckworth, Easley, Hawkins, & Henriques, 1990; Flick, 1993; Loucks-Horsley et al., 1990; Roth, 1992).

The key to the minds-on aspects of learning activities is getting students in touch with the powerful ideas that anchor content structures, reflect major instructional goals, and provide the basis for authentic applications. To support significant learning, intrinsic motivation needs to include the cognitive/learning aspects associated with motivation to learn, not just the affective/fun aspects associated with interest or enjoyment.

Middleton (1995) studied the motivational beliefs of teachers and students in middle-school mathematics classes. He found that both groups emphasized both expectancy and value issues when discussing motivation, although high-achieving students emphasized value (they wanted activities to be interesting) and low-achieving students emphasized control (they wanted activities that they could handle without difficulty).

Teachers' beliefs about what makes mathematics intrinsically motivating affected their students' motivational ideas. For example, one teacher believed that involving his students in applications to real-life problems was the key. His students were especially likely to report that application activities were more fun than other mathematics activities. Another teacher believed that her students were most motivated when they found the work easy, and in fact this is what her students reported. These findings show how you can shape your students' motivational orientations, not just react to them.

This same point was emphasized by Mitchell (1993), who followed up on an idea originally suggested by John Dewey in *distinguishing between catching and holding students' interest*. Mitchell's research in secondary mathematics classrooms suggested that motivational techniques such as presenting students with brain teasers or puzzles, allowing them to work on computers, or allowing them to work in groups were effective in *catching* initial interest in mathematical learning activities but not in *holding* that interest in ways that led to significant learning. The latter outcome was associated with *content emphases that featured meaningfulness* (students could appreciate the content's applications to life outside of school) and *instructional methods that allowed involvement* (students spent most of their time engaged in active learning and application activities, not just watching and listening). Subsequent studies at the college level also found that "hold" factors were better predictors of continuing interest in the subject than "catch" factors (Harackiewicz, Barron, Tauer, Carter, & Elliot, 2000; Harackiewicz et al., 2008), although "catch" factors appeared necessary to engage learners with low initial interest (Durik & Harackiewicz, 2007).

CONCLUSION

Schooling should be as enjoyable as it can be for both teachers and students. Therefore, whenever your instructional objectives can be met through a variety of activities, emphasize activities that students find rewarding and avoid ones that they find boring or aversive. However, bear in mind *two important limitations on what you can accomplish through intrinsic motivational strategies*.

First, your opportunities to use these strategies are limited. You have to teach the whole curriculum, not just the parts that appeal to students. Even when activities are enjoyable to students, learning still requires concentration and effort.

Second, although intrinsic motivational strategies should increase students' enjoyment of classroom activities, they do not directly stimulate intentions to accomplish the activities' learning goals. Therefore, even when you are able to use intrinsic motivational strategies, you will need to supplement them with strategies for stimulating students' motivation to learn (see chapter 9). Otherwise, students may enjoy your activities but fail to derive the intended knowledge or skills from them.

The motives, goals, and strategies that your students develop in response to learning activities will depend both on the activities themselves and on how you present and scaffold them. In this regard, note that *our colloquial language for discussing intrinsic motivation is misleading.* We commonly describe certain topics or tasks as "intrinsically interesting" and speak of engaging in activities "for their own sake." Such language implies that motivation resides in activities rather than in people. In reality, *people generate intrinsic motivation; it is not somehow built into topics or tasks.* When we are intrinsically motivated, we do something not for *its* sake but for *our* sake—because doing so provides us with enjoyable stimulation or satisfaction.

Students who are motivated solely by grades or other extrinsic rewards will do what they must to prepare for your tests, but then forget most of what they learned. It is better when students find academic activities intrinsically rewarding. Even then, however, they may not learn what you would like them to learn if the basis for their intrinsic motivation is primarily affective (they enjoy the activity) rather than cognitive (they find it interesting, meaningful, or worthwhile to learn what the activity is designed to teach). Consequently, it will be important for you to *motivate students to learn*—to seek to gain the intended learning and to set goals and use cognitive strategies that will enable them to do so.

SUMMARY

This chapter complements chapter 7 by considering strategies for supporting students' intrinsic motivation that go beyond those involved in meeting students' needs for autonomy, competence, and relatedness. Many of these strategies are rooted in theory and research on interest, which implies a cognitive and affective relationship between a student and particular content domains or learning activities. You can tap the motivational potential of students' stable individual interests by incorporating them into the curriculum and by offering activity choices that allow students to pursue their interests while at the same time accomplishing curricular goals. In addition, you can stimulate situational interest in a topic or activity by arousing curiosity, posing questions, creating suspense, or taking other actions likely to make the content more interesting or the activities more enjoyable for students.

Other approaches involve adapting activities to students' interests or embellishing them to enhance their intrinsic motivation potential. Conventional activities can be cast within a fantasy format that allows students to take the roles of fantasy characters in carrying out goal-oriented tasks. Many computerized games and learning programs take this approach. Less elaborately, you can incorporate drama, simulation, role play, and other fantasy elements in ways that make everyday activities more personalized and emotionally engaging for students.

Broad educational philosophies have been built around the principle of engaging students in learning activities designed to be intrinsically motivating. Recently, more focused models for incorporating motivational principles into curriculum and instruction have been developed, including the TARGET program described in chapter 4 and the motivated literacy and project-based learning models described in this chapter.

Research indicates that teachers emphasize intrinsic motivational strategies, but sometimes implement them in ways that do not engage students with powerful ideas. Hands-on activities do not guarantee minds-on learning.

To make school as enjoyable as it can be for your students, emphasize activities that they find rewarding and avoid ones that they find boring or aversive, but do so in ways that address the entire curriculum and ensure that your students accomplish your instructional goals. Even intrinsically motivated students may not do so if their motivation is primarily active/fun oriented rather than cognitive/learning oriented. Consequently, even when you are able to use intrinsic motivational strategies, you also will need to use the motivation-to-learn strategies described in chapter 9.

REFLECTION QUESTIONS

1. In considering literature selections for potential use in lessons or assignments, how could you distinguish selections that are interesting but also supportive of your curricular goals from selections that are long on seductive details but short on curricular value?
2. Why is it that individual interest in a topic will not necessarily translate into attainment of curricular goals?
3. Consider the process aspects of your curriculum (basic literacy and mathematics skills, oral presentation and discussion skills, inquiry, problem solving, decision making). Can you identify ways to develop these skills within contexts that your students will find interesting or enjoyable?
4. How can you encourage students to ask questions and make comments about lesson topics?
5. Do you view motivational embellishments as cost-effective interventions? If so, when and how would you use them? If not, why not?
6. How might you stimulate curiosity and suspense more frequently in your teaching? Might some of these strategies be incorporated as recurring routines?
7. What does it mean to put students into an active information-processing or problem-solving mode as you introduce learning activities? How can you do this?
8. Can you identify places where role-play, simulation, drama, or historical recreation might be used productively in learning activities?
9. How does practitioner wisdom compare to motivational theories as a source for useful ideas about motivating students to learn, especially with respect to the distinction between catching and holding interest?
10. Why is it important to note that when we are intrinsically motivated, we study or do something not for its sake but for our sake?

REFERENCES

Abdi, S. W. (2005). *Motivating elementary & middle school students with selected physical science activities.* Boston: Pearson.

Ainley, M. (2006). Connecting with learning: Motivation, affect, and cognition in interest processes. *Educational Psychology Review, 18*, 391–405.

Ainley, M., Corrigan, M., & Richardson, N. (2005). Students, tasks, and emotions: Identifying the contribution of emotions to students' reading of popular culture and popular science texts. *Learning and Instruction, 15*, 433–447.

Anand, P., & Ross, S. (1987). A computer-based strategy for personalizing verbal problems in teaching mathematics. *Educational Communication and Technology Journal, 35*, 151–162.

Anderman, E. (1993). *The zone of proximal development as a context for motivation.* Educational Resource Information Center (ERIC) Document No. Ed 374 631.

Askell-Williams, H., & Lawson, M. (2001). Mapping students' perceptions of interesting class lessons. *Social Psychology of Education, 5*, 127–147.

Bergin, D. (1999). Influences on classroom interest. *Educational Psychologist, 34*, 87–98.

Berlyne, D. (1960). *Conflict, arousal, and curiosity.* New York: McGraw-Hill.

Blumenfeld, P., Soloway, E., Marx, R., Krajcik, J., Guzdial, M., & Palincsar, A. (1991). Motivating project-based learning: Sustaining the doing, supporting the learning. *Educational Psychologist, 26*, 369–398.

Boll, G., Hammond, T., & Ferster, B. (2008). Developing Web 2.0 tools for support of historical inquiry in social studies. *Computers in the Schools, 25*, 275–287.

Brand, B., Collver, M., & Kasarda, M. (2008). Motivating students with robotics. *Science Teacher, 75*(4), 44–49.

Bridwell, N. (1988). *Clifford's birthday party.* New York: Scholastic.

Britton, B., VanDusen, L., Gulgoz, S., & Glynn, S. (1989). Instructional texts rewritten by five expert teams: Revision and retention improvement. *Journal of Educational Psychology, 81*, 226–239.

Chen, A., Darst, P., & Pangrazi, R. (2001). An examination of situational interest and its sources. *British Journal of Educational Psychology, 71*, 383–400.

Cordova, D., & Lepper, M. (1996). Intrinsic motivation and the process of learning: Beneficial effects of contextualization, personalization, and choice. *Journal of Educational Psychology, 88*, 715–730.

Covington, M. (1999). Caring about learning: The nature and nurturing of subject-matter appreciation. *Educational Psychologist, 34*, 127–136.

Covington, M., & Teel, K. (1996). *Overcoming student failure: Changing motives and incentives for learning.* Washington, DC: American Psychological Association.

deSousa, I., & Oakhill, J. (1996). Do levels of interest have an effect on children's comprehension-monitoring performance? *British Journal of Educational Psychology, 66*, 471–482.

Duckworth, E., Easley, J., Hawkins, D., & Henriques, A. (1990). *Science education: A minds-on approach for the elementary years.* Hillsdale, NJ: Erlbaum.

Duffy, T., Higgins, L., Mehlenbacher, B.,Cochran, C., Wallis, D., Hill, C., et al. (1989). Models for the design of instructional text. *Reading Research Quarterly, 24*, 434–456.

Durik, A., & Harackiewicz, J. (2007). Different strokes for different folks: How individual interest moderates the effects of situational factors on task interest. *Journal of Educational Psychology, 99*, 597–610.

Durik, A., & Matarazzo, K. (2009). Revved up or turned off? How domain knowledge changes the relationship between perceived task complexity and task interest. *Learning and Individual Differences, 19*, 155–159.

Durik, A., Vida, M., & Eccles, J. (2006). Task values and ability beliefs as predictors of high school literacy choices: A developmental analysis. *Journal of Educational Psychology, 98*, 382–393.

Fink, R. (1998). Literacy development in successful men and women with dyslexia. *Annals of Dyslexia, 48*, 311–342.

Flick, L. (1993). The meanings of hands-on science. *Journal of Science Teacher Education, 4*, 1–8.

Flowerday, T., & Schraw, G. (2000). Teacher beliefs about instructional choice: A phenomenological study. *Journal of Educational Psychology, 92*, 634–645.

Friedlander, B. (1965). A psychologist's second thoughts on concepts, curiosity, and discovery in teaching and learning. *Harvard Educational Review, 35*, 18–38.

Gardner, H. (1991). *The unschooled mind: How children think and how schools should teach.* New York: Basic Books.

Garner, R., Alexander, P., Gillingham, M., Kulikowich, J., & Brown, R. (1991). Interest and learning from text. *American Educational Research Journal, 28*, 643–659.

Gehlbach, A., Brown, S., Ioannou, A., Boyer, M., Hudson, N., Niv-Solomon, A., et al. (2008). Increasing interest in social studies: Social perspective taking and self-efficacy in stimulating simulations. *Contemporary Educational Psychology, 33*, 894–914.

Graves, M., Prenn, M., Earle, J., Thompson, M., Johnson, V., & Slater, W. (1991). Improving instructional text: Some lessons learned. *Reading Research Quarterly, 26*, 111–121.

Guthrie, J., Hoa, A. L., Wigfield, A., Tonks, S., Humenick, N., & Littles, E. (2007). Reading motivation and reading comprehension growth in the later elementary years. *Contemporary Educational Psychology, 32*, 282–313.

Harackiewicz, J., Barron, K., Tauer, J., Carter, S., & Elliot, A. (2000). Short-term and long-term consequences of achievement goals in college: Predicting continued interest and performance over time. *Journal of Educational Psychology, 92*, 316–330.

Harackiewicz, J., Durik, A., Barron, K., Linnenbrink-Garcia, L., & Tauer, J. (2008). The role of achievement goals in the development of interest: Reciprocal relations between achievement goals, interest, and performance. *Journal of Educational Psychology, 100*, 105–122.

Harmer, A., & Kates, W. (2007). Designing for learner engagement in middle school science: Technology, inquiry, & the hierarchies of engagement. *Computers in the Schools, 24*, 105–124.

Harp, S., & Mayer, R. (1998). How seductive details do their damage: A theory of cognitive interest in science learning. *Journal of Educational Psychology, 90*, 414–434.

Heafner, T., & Friedman, A. (2008). Wikis and constructivism in secondary social studies: Fostering a deep understanding. *Computers in the Schools, 25*, 288–302.

Hidi, S. (2002). An interest researcher's perspective: The effects of extrinsic and intrinsic factors on motivation. In C. Sansone & J. Harackiewicz (Eds.), *Intrinsic and extrinsic motivation: The search for optimal motivation and performance* (pp. 309–339). San Diego, CA: Academic Press.

Hidi, S., & Baird, W. (1988). Strategies for increasing text-based interest and students' recall of expository texts. *Reading Research Quarterly, 23*, 465–483.

Hidi, S., & Renninger, K. A. (2006). The four-phase model of interest development. *Educational Psychologist, 41*, 111–127.

Hootstein, H. (1995). Motivational strategies of middle school social studies teachers. *Social Education, 59*, 23–26.

Inoue, N. (2007). Why face a challenge?: The reason behind intrinsically motivated students' spontaneous choice of challenging tasks. *Learning and Individual Differences, 17*, 251–259.

Ioannou, A., Brown, S., Hannifin, R., & Boyer, M. (2009). Can multimedia make kids care about social studies? The GlobalEd problem-based learning simulation. *Computers in the Schools, 26*, 63–81.

Iyengar, S., & Lepper, M. (1999). Rethinking the role of choice: A cultural perspective on intrinsic motivation. *Journal of Personality and Social Psychology, 76*, 349–366.

Jang, H. (2008). Supporting students' motivation, engagement, and learning during an uninteresting activity. *Journal of Educational Psychology, 100*, 798–811.

Karmos, J., & Karmos, A. (1983). A closer look at classroom boredom. *Action in Teacher Education, 5*, 49–55.

Katz, I., Assor, A., Kanat-Maymon, Y., & Bereby-Meyer, Y. (2006). Interest as a motivational resource: Feedback and gender matter, but interest makes the difference. *Social Psychology of Education, 9*, 27–42.

Keller, J. (1983). Motivational design of instruction. In C. Reigeluth (Ed.), *Instructional-design theories and models: An overview of their current status* (pp. 383–434). Hillsdale, NJ: Erlbaum.

Kourilsky, M. (1983). *Mini-Society: Experiencing real-world economics in the elementary school classroom.* Menlo Park, CA: Addison-Wesley.

Krapp, A. (2002). An educational-psychological theory of interest and its relation to SDT. In E. Deci & R. Ryan (Eds.), *Handbook of self-determination research* (pp. 405–427). Rochester, NY: University of Rochester Press.

Lay, J., & Smarick, K. (2006). Simulating a senate office: The impact on student knowledge and attitudes. *Journal of Political Science Education, 2*, 131–146.

Lepper, M., & Cordova, D. (1992). A desire to be taught: Instructional consequences of intrinsic motivation. *Motivation and Emotion, 16*, 187–208.

Lepper, M., & Henderlong, J. (2000). Turning "play" into "work" and "work" into "play": Twenty-five years of research on intrinsic versus extrinsic motivation. In C. Sansone & J. Harackiewicz (Eds.), *Intrinsic and extrinsic motivation: The search for optimal motivation and performance* (pp. 257–307). San Diego, CA: Academic Press.

Lepper, M., & Hodell, M. (1989). *Intrinsic motivation in the classroom. In C. Ames & R. Ames (Eds.), Research on motivation in education. Volume 3: Goals and cognitions* (pp. 73–105). San Diego, CA: Academic Press.

Linnenbrink, E., & Pintrich, P. (2000). Multiple pathways to learning and achievement: The role of goal orientation in fostering adaptive motivation, affect, and cognition. In C. Sansone & J. Harackiewicz (Eds.), *Intrinsic and extrinsic motivation: The search for optimal motivation and performance* (pp. 196–230). San Diego, CA: Academic Press.

Loucks-Horsley, S., Capitan, R., Carlson, M., Kuerbis, P., Clark, R., Melle, G., et al. (1990). *Elementary school science for the '90s.* Alexandria, VA: Association for Supervision and Curriculum Development.

Loewenstein, G. (1994). The psychology of curiosity: A review and reinterpretation. *Psychological Bulletin, 116*, 75–98.

Malone, T., & Lepper, M. (1987). Making learning fun: A taxonomy of intrinsic motivation for learning. In R. Snow & M. Farr (Eds.), *Aptitude, learning, and instruction: III. Conative and affective process analysis* (pp. 223–253). Hillsdale, NJ: Erlbaum.

Mayer, R., Fennell, S., Farmer, L., & Campbell, J. (2004). A personalization effect in multimedia learning: Students learn better when words are in conversational style rather than formal style. *Journal of Educational Psychology, 96,* 389–395.

McKeown, M., & Beck, I. (1994). Making sense of accounts of history: Why young students don't and how they might. In G. Leinhardt, I. Beck, & C. Stainton (Eds.), *Teaching and learning in history* (pp. 1–26). Hillsdale, NJ: Erlbaum.

Means, T., Jonassen, D., & Dwyer, F. (1997). Enhancing relevance: Embedded ARCS strategies vs. purpose. *Educational Technology Research and Development, 45,* 5–17.

Middleton, J. (1995). A study of intrinsic motivation in the mathematics classroom: A personal constructs approach. *Journal for Research in Mathematics Education, 26,* 254–279.

Miller, S., & Meece, J. (1999). Third graders' motivational preferences for reading and writing tasks. *Elementary School Journal, 100,* 19–35.

Mistler-Jackson, M., & Songer, N. (2000). Student motivation and internet technology: Are students empowered to learn science? *Journal of Research in Science Teaching, 37,* 459–479.

Mitchell, M. (1993). Situational interest: Its multifaceted structure in the secondary school mathematics classroom. *Journal of Educational Psychology, 85,* 424–436.

Moreno, R., & Mayer, R. (2000). Engaging students in active learning: The case for personalized multimedia messages. *Journal of Educational Psychology, 92,* 724–733.

Moreno, R., & Mayer, R. (2004). Personalized messages that promote science learning in virtual environments. *Journal of Educational Psychology, 96,* 165–173.

Narvaez, D., van den Broek, P., & Ruiz, A. (1999). The influence of reading purpose on inference generation and comprehension in reading. *Journal of Educational Psychology, 91,* 488–496.

Nolen, S., & Nicholls, J. (1994). A place to begin (again) in research on student motivation: Teachers' beliefs. *Teaching and Teacher Education, 10,* 57–69.

Oliver, R. (2008). Engaging first year students using a Web-supported inquiry-based learning setting. *Higher Education, 55,* 285–301.

Pace, D., Bishel, B., Beck, R., Holquist, P., & Makowski, G. (1990). Structure and spontaneity: Pedagogical tensions in the construction of a simulation of the Cuban missile crisis. *History Teacher, 24* (1), 53–65.

Pfaffman, J. (2003, April). *What makes hobbies motivating and their relationship to education.* Paper presented at the annual meeting of the American Educational Research Association, Chicago.

Reeve, J. (1996). *Motivating others: Nurturing inner motivational resources.* Boston: Allyn & Bacon.

Reio, Jr., T. (2008). Curiosity and primary source materials: Making history come alive. In D. McInerney & A. Liem (Eds.), *Teaching and learning: International best practice* (pp. 169–190). Greenwich, CT: Information Age.

Renninger, K. A. (2009). Interest and identity development in instruction: An inductive model. *Educational Psychologist, 44,* 105–118.

Renninger, K. A., Bachrach, J., & Posey, S. (2008). Learner interest and achievement motivation. In M. Maehr, S. Karabenick, & T. Urdan (Eds.), *Social psychological perspectives (Advances in motivation and achievement* series, Vol. 15, pp. 461–491). Bingley, UK: Emerald.

Renninger, K. A., & Hidi, S. (2002). Student interest and achievement: Developmental issues raised by a case study. In A. Wigfield & J. Eccles (Eds.), *Development of achievement motivation* (pp 173–195). San Diego, CA: Academic Press.

Roth, K. (1992). Science education: It's not enough to "do" or "relate." In M. Pearsall (Ed.), *Scope, sequence, and coordination of secondary school science: Relevant research* (Vol. 2, pp. 151–164). Washington, DC: National Science Teachers Association.

Sansone, C., & Smith, J. (2000). Interest and self-regulation: The relation between having to and wanting to. In C. Sansone & J. Harackiewicz (Eds.), *Intrinsic and extrinsic motivation: The search for optimal motivation and performance* (pp. 341–372). San Diego, CA: Academic Press.

Sansone, C., & Thoman, D. (2006). Maintaining activity engagement: Individual differences in the processes of self-regulating motivation. *Journal of Personality, 74,* 1697–1720.

Schank, R., & Cleary, C. (1995). *Engines for education.* Hillsdale, NJ: Erlbaum.

Schraw, G. (1997). Situational interest in literary text. *Contemporary Educational Psychology, 22,* 436–456.

Schraw, G., & Dennison, R. (1994). The effect of reader purpose on interest and recall. *Journal of Reading Behavior, 26,* 1–18.

Schraw, G., Flowerday, T., & Lehman, S. (2001). Increasing situational interest in the classroom. *Educational Psychology Review, 13,* 211–224.

Schraw, G., & Lehman, S. (2001). Situational interest: A review of the literature and directions for future research. *Educational Psychology Review, 13,* 23–52.

Silvia, P. (2008). Interest–the curious emotion. *Current Directions in Psychological Science, 17,* 57–60.

Singer, J., Marx, R., Krajcik, J., & Chambers, J. (2000). Constructing extended inquiry projects: Curriculum materials for science education reform. *Educational Psychologist, 35,* 165–178.

Turner, J. (1993). A motivational perspective on literacy instruction. In D. Leu & C. Kinzer (Eds.), *Examining central issues in literacy research, theory, and practice: Forty-second Yearbook of the National Reading Conference* (pp. 153–161). Chicago: National Reading Conference, Inc.

Turner, J. (1995). The influence of classroom contexts on young children's motivation for literacy. *Reading Research Quarterly, 30,* 410–441.

Wade, S., Alexander, P., Schraw, G., & Kulikowich, J. (1995). The perils of criticism: Response to Goetz and Sadowski. *Reading Research Quarterly, 30,* 512–515.

Wade, S., Buxton, W., & Kelly, M. (1999). Using think-alouds to examine reader-text interest. *Reading Research Quarterly, 34,* 195–216.

Wang, S., & Reeves, T. (2006). The effects of a Web-based learning environment on student motivation in a high school earth science course. *Education Technology Research and Development, 54,* 597–621.

Yell, M., Scheurman, G., & Reynolds, K. (2004). The anticipation guide: Motivating students to find out about history. *Social Education, 68,* 361–363.

Zahorik, J. (1996). Elementary and secondary teachers' reports of how they make learning interesting. *Elementary School Journal, 96,* 551–564.

9

Stimulating Students' Motivation to Learn

In short, intrinsic motivation cannot constitute a sufficient and stable motivational basis for schooling in general or a predesigned curriculum in particular. It will ... encourage an orientation toward activity based on immediate satisfaction rather than on values. Contrary to claims made by some psychologists, intrinsically motivated students will not be consistently motivated. Certain aspects of the curriculum will interest them, while others will not; at times they will study, and at times they will not. Thus, students who rely exclusively on intrinsic motivation are likely to neglect a large part of their schoolwork.

Most students, however, do not do this. The average student in a good school tends to do the work ... even when a subject does not arouse high intrinsic motivation and even when rewards and punishments are not salient. What, then, is the source of such students' hard work?... the students share the belief of the curriculum designers that the program is desirable and valuable. (Nisan, 1992, pp. 129–130)

MOTIVATION TO LEARN

I share the view expressed by Mordecai Nisan, which is why I place more emphasis on motivation to learn than on intrinsic motivation. By *motivation to learn*, I mean a student's tendency to find learning activities meaningful and worthwhile and to try to get the intended benefits from them. In contrast to intrinsic motivation, which is primarily an affective response to an activity, motivation to learn is primarily a cognitive response involving attempts to make sense of the activity, understand the knowledge it develops, and master the skills that it promotes. *Interest leading to play or casual exploration is not the same as motivated and focused learning.* If students construe a situation as play, they usually will not activate relevant learning schemas to systematically extract the gist of the experience and "organize and file" it for later application.

Unfortunately, value concepts tend to be defined in ways that limit their applicability to learning situations. Definitions of valuing typically focus on utility value (e.g., engaging in an activity to acquire a skill or certification that is needed to advance one's career goals). They seldom emphasize experiences such as the satisfaction of achieving new insights, aesthetic appreciation of the content or skill, or awareness of its role in improving the quality of our lives. Meanwhile, definitions of interest and intrinsic motivation tend to focus on their affective aspects (e.g., fun, pleasure, or enjoyment), without paying much attention to their cognitive aspects (e.g., absorption, satisfaction, self-realization).

School learning is mostly cognitive—abstract concepts and verbally coded information. To make good progress, students need to develop and use *generative learning strategies* (Weinstein & Mayer, 1986). That is, they need to process information actively, relate it to their existing knowledge, make sure they understand it, and so on. Therefore, motivating students to learn includes not only stimulating them to see the value of what they are learning, but also providing them with guidance about how to go about learning it.

Students can be motivated to learn from an activity even if they do not find its content interesting or its processes enjoyable. They may not get to choose the activity, but they can choose to make the most of the learning opportunities it affords (see Box 9.1). *In essence, motivation to learn is adoption of learning goals and related strategies; it is not linked directly to either extrinsic motivation or intrinsic motivation.*

RELATED MOTIVATIONAL CONCEPTS

Motivation to learn overlaps considerably with the "learning" or "mastery" orientations described by goal theorists. It is a broader concept, however, meant to apply not only to achievement situations that involve specific goals but also to other situations in or out of school that offer the potential for learning.

Motivation to learn also overlaps with the learning orientation described by Marshall (1994). Classes with a *learning orientation* emphasized the purposes of the learning and the strategies required to figure things out. Teachers framed lessons and assignments in terms of what students would learn from them and emphasized the importance of constructing understandings over supplying "right answers" and completing worksheets. In contrast, in classes that featured a *work orientation*, students viewed assignments as tasks to be completed. They frequently did not understand the purposes of activities, and they engaged in them using surface-level information processing and retention strategies. Their teachers made frequent references to "work" and the need to get "work" finished. Their curricula emphasized answer sheets and workbooks, whereas the learning-oriented teachers offered many more open-ended and authentic tasks.

Penny Oldfather has described *the continuing impulse to learn* as an ongoing engagement with learning characterized by intense involvement, curiosity, and a search for understanding that goes well beyond situational interest in a topic or activity. Developing it requires creating classroom cultures in which students connect who they are to what they do in school (Oldfather & West, 1999).

Other authors have put forth similar trait-like concepts of motivation to learn. Flum and Kaplan (2006) described exploratory orientation as active seeking and processing of information to create self-relevant meaning, particularly as it relates to one's personal identity and future agendas. Renninger, Sansone, and Smith (2004) described love of learning, defined to include valuing of learning content or activities, mastery orientation, and well developed individual interests. Nisan has written about the importance of cultivating the sense of the desirable (Nisan, 1992) or sense of the worthy (Nisan & Shalif, 2006) with respect to learning goals, so that students will value what they are learning.

Box 9.1   Motivation to Learn as a Felt Obligation

Intrinsic motivation and motivation to learn often go together and operate in a mutually supportive fashion. However, each can occur independently of the other. Lee and Brophy (1996) described students with contrasting motivational patterns that illustrated the combinations that occur. Students were observed in sixth-grade science classes and described in terms of their motivation to learn science.

Students who were intrinsically motivated to learn science displayed both intrinsic interest in the subject and motivation to learn it. Jason was inquisitive, curious, and active in his attempts to construct scientific knowledge. He expanded lesson content to relate it to his prior knowledge or personal experience. He paid close attention to lessons and pointed out mistakes, ambiguities, or places where further elaboration was needed in the curriculum unit or the teacher's explanations. Sometimes he posed challenging questions or engaged in debates until he convinced the teacher of his ideas or was convinced by the teacher's explanations. He contributed to class discussions by proposing alternative or novel ideas and demonstrated leadership in small-group work. When he had extra time he helped other students, checked and elaborated his answers in the activity book, or pursued his curiosity and interest in the subject. He also reported science experiences outside of class, such as growing sugar crystals on a paper clip at home after seeing the activity demonstrated on a televised science program.

Other students demonstrated the goal of understanding science, but did not show the intrinsic motivation or self-initiation seen in students like Jason. Sara's cognitive engagement was confined to the lesson content and activity requirements assigned by the teacher. She recognized conceptual conflicts and tried to modify misconceptions into scientific conceptions. When she didn't understand something said in class, she would say so and ask for clarification. She volunteered during lessons and did her assignments conscientiously. She was clearly motivated to learn science with understanding and willing to invest the time, effort, and strategies needed to do so. However, she and other students who shared her pattern did not demonstrate intrinsic interest in science or enjoyment in carrying out scientific activities. Instead, they seemed to be motivated by a duty-bound sense of obligation.

Neil displayed the inconsistency that results when a student's pattern includes intrinsic motivation but not motivation to learn. He displayed keen interest and initiative in some situations but was inattentive and uninvolved in others. In interviews, he described the former activities as fun (e.g., experiments on water evaporation and condensation), but said that he didn't enjoy the latter activities (e.g., writing in the activity book). Thus, the quality of Neil's engagement depended on his interest (intrinsic motivation). He did not display any consistent motivation to learn science independently of his interest in particular topics or activities.

Finally, some students were unmotivated to learn science. Kim was often inattentive to lessons and prone to use strategies designed to minimize her effort in completing work. She rarely volunteered in class and, when called on as a nonvolunteer, she made feeble responses or said "I don't know." In small-group activities, her interactions were social rather than academic. She readily accepted other students' ideas and copied their answers instead of trying to make sense of what was being taught. She also left some questions unanswered. She and other task avoidant students (as well as one task resistant student) displayed both a lack of intrinsic motivation and a lack of motivation to learn science.

Thorkildsen, Nolen, and Fournier (1994) interviewed 7- to 12-year-old students about the fairness of selected practices that teachers might use to motivate their students to learn. One group favored practices that would help students to find the material more interesting, challenging, and intrinsically meaningful, and thus promote the desire to understand new ideas. Their responses suggested a combination of intrinsic motivation and motivation to learn. A second group favored practices that encouraged students to work diligently to get a good education. These students appeared to possess a dutiful commitment to education and thus motivation to learn, but not intrinsic motivation. Finally, a third group favored extrinsic incentive systems that would reward students for their efforts or accomplishments. These students did not possess either intrinsic motivation or motivation to learn, although they did express a willingness to work in exchange for extrinsic rewards.

Other investigators speak of student involvement, which refers to "minds-on" immersion in learning activities, featuring deep concentration, growth in understanding, and commitment to persist until valued goals have been accomplished (Reed & Schallert, 1993). Classrooms that supported high involvement featured inquiry and discussion of problem-solving strategies rather than recitation and rote learning methods. The teachers challenged their students to engage in deep thinking and take intellectual risks, but also provided them with whatever scaffolding and encouragement they needed to learn with understanding (Turner et al., 1998).

Authors writing about curiosity or interest sometimes describe subtypes that resemble motivation to learn. Kintsch (1980) distinguished between emotional interest and cognitive interest in a text. *Emotional interest* refers to the arousal of feelings in response to text features that initially catch attention, whereas *cognitive interest* is a more intellectual response to the text's content. Cognitive interest can be stimulated by encouraging students to define learning goals for themselves, pursue their individual interests in meaningful ways, and experience self-determination as they do so (Alexander, 1997).

Authors also have begun to draw contrasts between the traditionally emphasized affective forms of intrinsic motivation that apply mostly to recreational activities, and cognitive forms that apply better to learning activities. Reiss (2004) suggested that intrinsic motivation theorists have erred in assuming that people engage in intrinsically motivated behavior simply because it is enjoyable. He pointed out that people often engage willingly in activities that are not fun or pleasurable in the usual sense of the words, and that may involve strenuous work or even exposure to anxieties or dangers (e.g., mountain climbing). He also suggested that people ordinarily engage in learning activities not for pleasure but for satisfaction of one or more of 16 basic desires (including curiosity, or the desire for knowledge).

Waterman (2005) has distinguished between two forms of enjoyment that may be derived from activities: hedonic and eudaimonic. *Hedonic* pleasures can be experienced through simple participation, without engaging in effortful or goal-oriented action sequences. Examples include dining at a restaurant, watching television, or window shopping at a mall. _Eudaimonic_ pleasures result from sustained goal-oriented efforts, especially during activities that challenge us to realize our potentials. Examples include rock climbing, composing music, acting on stage, and writing computer code.

Two common forms of eudaimonic pleasure are flow and personal expressiveness. _Flow_ experiences occur when we become completely absorbed in activities. They are associated with a balance between challenge and skill. Feelings of _personal expressiveness_ are associated with opportunities to experience self-realization (especially during identity-related activities that allow us to express our daimon, or true self). Both forms of eudaimonic pleasures tend to be more focused and associated with peak experiences than interest, which is a more general but less intense form of motivation (Schwartz & Waterman, 2006; Waterman, 2005). Some activities only offer the potential for hedonic pleasures, but others, including worthwhile learning activities, offer the potential for both hedonic and eudaimonic pleasures.

These cognitive forms of motivation deserve theoretical and research attention, because relative to hedonic forms, they relate more closely to motivation to learn in school, and more generally, to the richness and rewards of people's subjective experiences. People who report more curiosity, desire for knowledge, and eudaimonic forms of motivation to learn also score higher on measures of general life satisfaction and sense of well being (Kashdan & Steger, 2007; Ryan, Huta, & Deci, 2006; Steger, Kashdan, & Oishi, 2008; Waterman, Schwartz, & Conti, 2008).

BRINGING STUDENTS TO THE LESSON

Blumenfeld, Puro, and Mergendoller (1992) developed a concept of student motivation to learn that combines motivation and cognitive engagement. In fifth- and sixth-grade science classes in which students reported lower motivation to learn, teachers focused on recitation, quizzes, and grades. In classes in which students reported higher motivation to learn, teachers stressed big ideas, highlighted the value of science by showing how it connects to everyday events, and expressed their enthusiasm by relating their personal scientific experiences. They made conceptual material more concrete and interesting by providing examples and connecting the material to their students' experiences or to current events. They also assigned more varied tasks and encouraged students to cooperate in small groups.

Four factors characterized the classes in which students reported greater motivation to learn:

1. _Opportunities to learn._ The teachers (a) focused lessons around mid-level concepts that were substantive but not overwhelming to students; (b) made the main ideas evident in presentations, demonstrations, discussions, and assignments; (c) developed concepts by presenting concrete illustrations of scientific principles and relating unfamiliar information to students' personal knowledge; (d) made explicit connections between new information and things that students had learned previously, and pointed out relationships among new ideas by stressing similarities and differences; (e) elaborated extensively on textbook readings rather than allowing the book to "carry the lesson"; (f) guided students' thinking when posing high-level questions; and (g) asked students to summarize, make comparisons between

related concepts, and apply the information they were learning. These methods provided students with frequent opportunities to learn, and where necessary, helped them to do so.

2. *Press*. The teachers pressed for thinking through their expectations for lesson participation, their questions to students, and their follow-up to students' responses. They (a) required students to explain and justify their answers; (b) prompted, reframed the question, or broke it into smaller parts when students were unsure, and probed students when their understanding was unclear; (c) monitored for comprehension rather than procedural correctness; (d) encouraged responses from all students through techniques such as asking them to vote or to debate the merits of different ideas (rather than allowing a small subgroup to dominate the lessons); and (e) supplemented the "short answer" assignments in the workbooks by adding questions that required explanations of results or alternative representations such as diagrams or charts. They required their students to actively think about what they were hearing or reading, instead of just passively monitoring it or trying to memorize it.

3. *Support*. The teachers supported students' attempts to understand through modeling and scaffolding. They (a) modeled thinking, suggested strategies, and worked with students to solve problems when the students had difficulty (instead of just providing answers); (b) reduced the procedural complexity of manipulative tasks by demonstrating procedures, highlighting problems, providing examples, or allowing for planning time; and (c) encouraged collaborative efforts by requiring all students to make contributions to the group. Thus, besides exerting a consistent press, these teachers gave their students whatever help they needed to enable them to meet their thinking and learning demands.

4. *Evaluation*. These teachers' evaluation and accountability systems emphasized understanding and learning rather than work completion or right answers. They used mistakes as ways to help students check their thinking, and they explicitly encouraged students to take risks. Finally, they allowed students who had done poorly to redo assignments or retake quizzes.

All four of these factors needed to be present and working together. One teacher's students reported high motivation but low cognitive engagement. He typically began lessons by trying to pique students' interest using humor, dramatic visual aids, connections to students' experiences, or his own enthusiasm. However, he did not follow up by using teaching techniques that encourage high cognitive engagement. He relied heavily on presenting information, then asking questions that required only repetition or simple paraphrasing of the reading. He did not ask his students to make and justify predictions, to relate points under discussion to prior knowledge, or to summarize or extend their learning. He sometimes inserted comments or questions designed to sustain students' interest, but he did not provide them with opportunities to synthesize or apply what they were learning.

In summarizing their findings, Blumenfeld and colleagues (1992) stated that *teachers need to do two things in order to motivate their students to learn*: *bring the lesson to the students* by providing opportunities for them to learn and stimulating them to see value in the learning, and *bring the students to the lesson* by requiring them to think about and use the material and supporting their efforts to do so. The teacher just described did a good job of enhancing interest in his lessons, but he did not consistently "bring the students to the lesson" by requiring them to think about the material and supporting their learning efforts.

Middleton and Midgley (2002) provided additional support for bringing students to the lesson in a study of middle school math classes. Students had higher self-efficacy perceptions, engaged in more self-regulated learning, and were more willing to seek help in classes they perceived as high in press for understanding. Productive press for understanding challenges students to think deeply about the content, rather than merely demanding good performance on assignments and tests.

PAVING THE WAY FOR MOTIVATION TO LEARN: SOCIALIZING

Appreciation for Learning Activities

Students do not need to enjoy school activities to be motivated to learn from them, but they do need to perceive the activities as meaningful and worthwhile. To develop these perceptions in your students, you will need to (a) make sure that your curriculum content and learning activities actually are meaningful and worthwhile, and (b) develop this content and scaffold your students' engagement in learning activities in ways that enable them to see and appreciate their value.

To ground these efforts, *focus your curriculum on content that is at least potentially relevant to students and applicable to their lives outside of school.* People assume that the curriculum reflects consensus beliefs about what is important for young people to learn—that it empowers them with knowledge, skills, and dispositions that enable them to function effectively in modern society. However, current curricula have been described as mile-wide but inch-deep, trivial pursuit, or parade of facts—not structured around powerful ideas. Furthermore, even when a content strand does have significant potential value, it may be taught in a way that is too abstract or otherwise ineffective to enable students to appreciate it. With respect to its potential for student appreciation, curricular content might be classified within one of five categories:

1. Content that has value that students already recognize and appreciate.
2. Content that has value that is recognized by curriculum makers and teachers and could be taught in ways that lead students to appreciate its value.
3. Content that has value that is recognized by curriculum makers and teachers, but the potential for appreciating it lies beyond the students' current capacities.
4. Content that has potential value and could be appreciated by students (at least at certain grade levels), but curriculum makers and teachers currently cannot articulate this value clearly enough to enable them to represent it effectively in instructional materials or scaffold students' appreciation of it during teaching.
5. Content that lacks significant value (and therefore does not belong in the curriculum).

I believe that much of what is in current school curricula lacks sufficient justification. We often hear that learning is its own reward, but this saying assumes that there is good reason for the learning. I submit that there is no good reason for students to learn a lot of the specialized vocabulary, unnecessary detail, and sheer trivia that is included in most school curricula, nor for engaging in activities such as alphabetizing the state capitals. We need to prune this kind of pointless content from the curriculum.

I also believe that much of the school curriculum fits into the fourth category: it does have potential value, but we have lost sight of the reasons for including it. We need to rediscover and articulate the life-application bases for retaining this content and teach it accordingly.

If your instructional planning is guided by appropriate purposes and goals phrased in terms of student outcomes, your curriculum should feature content that students can appreciate as worthwhile and activities that they can appreciate as authentic. This will help them to learn with awareness of each activity's purposes and goals.

Curricula developed in this goal-oriented fashion will consist of coherent *networks of connected content structured around powerful ideas*. These powerful ideas will be developed in sufficient depth to promote deep understanding of their meanings and connections, appreciation of their significance, and exploration of their applications to life outside of school. As much as possible, this learning will occur through engagement in *authentic activities* that require using what is being learned for accomplishing the very sorts of life applications that justify inclusion of this content in the curriculum in the first place.

Assuming that your curriculum content and learning activities are meaningful and worthwhile, how can you help your students to appreciate their value? *Consider the following examples*:

1. Two seemingly similar classmates have the same exposure to the same learning opportunities (hearing or reading a selection from a story book or history text; watching a video that dramatizes a story or depicts a historical event). As a result, one of the students gets "turned on" to that literary genre or historical era, but the other does not. Why?

2. A teacher wants to teach *King Lear* (or the U.S. Constitution, or photosynthesis) in ways that motivate students to appreciate Shakespeare (or civics, or biology), value it, and seek to learn more about it on their own.

What motivational concepts or principles might help us to explain Example 1 or formulate good advice to the teacher in Example 2? First, two features of the learning situation need to be in place to set the stage for motivated learning: (a) a motivationally optimal match with the learner's current characteristics, and (b) content and activities that are perceived as relevant to the learner's personal identity or agendas.

Optimal Matching (The Motivational Zone of Proximal Development)

Models of cognitive development and learning typically include an optimal match principle: The best learning activities are optimally challenging, being neither too easy nor too difficult for the learner. Sociocultural models extend this idea to include the role of the teacher in optimizing the match, because mediation (via modeling, coaching, and scaffolding) can transform an activity that is too difficult for self-guided learning into an activity that lies within the zone of proximal development for mentor-guided learning (Tharp & Gallimore, 1988).

Similar principles apply in the motivational sphere. *The motivational optimal match principle* postulates that the features of a learning activity must match the learner's prior knowledge and experiences in such a way as to stimulate interest in pursuing the learning. *A match exists when the activity is familiar enough to be recognizable as a learning opportunity, and attractive enough to interest the learner in pursuing it.* A mismatch would occur if the activity were overly familiar to the point that the learner had become satiated with it (at least temporarily), if it were so unfamiliar that the learner could not understand or appreciate its potential value, or if the learner's prior experiences with it had been unrewarding.

The optimal match principle also implies a motivational analog of the "zone of proximal development" concept: mentors can help learners begin to see the value in learning opportunities that they have not yet come to appreciate (and might never come to appreciate) on their own. Motivationally effective teachers make school learning experiences meaningful for students not only in the cognitive sense (enabling them to learn the content with understanding) but also in the motivational sense (enabling them to appreciate its value, particularly its potential applications in their lives outside of school).

The learning of reading, writing, swimming, or other basic skills has obvious utility to almost everyone. However, as John Dewey and others have pointed out, most school content originated as practical knowledge derived through situational problem solving, but, as it got systematized within what became the disciplines, it got formulated more abstractly and separated from its situated origins (Hansen, 2006). Consequently, for much of what we teach in school, especially the more abstract content and higher order processes, the reasons for learning it are not obvious. Students may not appreciate the value of this content unless their learning is scaffolded in ways that help them to do so.

In summary, a learning situation is optimal from a motivational standpoint when it features curricular content and learning activities that are well matched to the learner's current characteristics because they are either (a) already familiar to the learners and valued as learning opportunities worth pursuing or (b) less familiar or valued, but nevertheless *within the learners' motivational zones of proximal development, so they can begin to value them if the teacher mediates their learning experiences effectively* (see Table 9.1).

Identification/Self-Relevance Perceptions

Different learners will respond differently to the same learning opportunity. To explain these individual differences in interests and appreciations, *we need concepts that describe the "task attraction" or "rewarding experience" elements of the optimal match. At minimum, learners must perceive some relevance of the learning opportunity to their personal agendas.* Better yet, they should respond in a more personal or intense fashion—in effect, saying to themselves, "I am that," "I want to do that," "This is for me," etc.

The concept of *identification* is useful here. People can identify not only with a person or model, but also with an interest area or genre of knowledge or skill (hereafter called a learning domain; Barron, 2006; Renninger, 2009). They even can identify with academics in general, to the extent that they feel that they belong in their academic environment and value academic achievement (Walker, Greene, & Mansell, 2006). Lawrence Kohlberg (1966) featured the concept in his gender-role identification theory: As toddlers and young children become aware that they are either boys or girls, they become motivated to explore and identify with anything (e.g., types of clothing, toys, skills, or recreation activities) that is linked to their own gender. That is, boys tend to develop preferences for and motivation to pursue "male" interests, and girls "female" interests (Martin & Ruble, 2004).

TABLE 9.1
Theoretical Schematic: Intersections of the Cognitive and Motivational Readiness Dimensions, Including the Zones of Proximal Development

	Above the Motivational ZPD[a]	Within the Motivational ZPD[b]	Below the Motivational ZPD[c]
Above the cognitive ZPD (not yet able to learn)	Potential learning goal is beyond the learners' current cognitive and motivational capacities, even with mediation.	Mediation could help learners appreciate the value of the potential learning goal, but could not overcome current limitations in their cognitive capacities.	Learners already appreciate the value of the domain, but attainment of the potential learning goal is beyond their current cognitive capacities, even with mediation.
Within the cognitive ZPD (able to learn with mediation)	Mediation could help learners attain the potential learning goal, but could not overcome current limitations in their capacities for coming to appreciate the learning domain.	The learning goal lies within both the cognitive and the motivational ZPDs, so effective mediation should produce learning and appreciation.	Learners already appreciate the value of the domain and could attain the potential learning goal with effective mediation.
Below the cognitive ZPD (has learned already)	Learners already have attained the learning goal via rote processes, but they are not yet ready to appreciate the value of this learning domain, even with mediation.	Learners already have attained the learning goal via rote processes, and they could learn to appreciate the value of the learning domain with effective mediation.	Learners have already attained the learning goal as meaningful learning within a context of appreciation for the value of the learning domain.

Note: ZPD = zone of proximal development
[a]Not yet able to appreciate. [b]Can learn to appreciate with mediation. [c]Appreciates already.

Also useful are various *self-concepts*, including ideal selves or possible selves (Markus & Nurius, 1986). For example, reading about and identifying with fictional characters or historical figures they find inspirational is one way for students to explore possible future selves (Alvermann & Heron, 2001; Daisey & Josè-Kampfner, 2002; Richardson & Eccles, 2007). As children develop, their self-concepts become articulated and spawn self-relevance perceptions that may apply to any aspect of life. To the extent that *self-relevance perceptions* become attached to particular learning domains or activities, they begin to guide learners' decision making regarding the potential value of learning opportunities (see Box 9.2).

In summary, if a learning opportunity is located within the learners' motivational zone of proximal development, it is *possible* for them to come to appreciate the value of the learning. Such appreciation is much more *likely* to develop if they perceive the learning as relevant to their personal agendas. If self-relevance is not already obvious to them, their teacher will need to mediate their learning so as to encourage the desired self-relevance perceptions to develop (Hannover, 1998; Van Etten, Pressley, McInerney, & Liem, 2008).

Box 9.2   Identity and Self-Concepts

In everyday usage, the term *self* refers to the direct feeling that people have of privileged access to their own thoughts, feelings, and sensations. In contrast, the term *self-concept* refers to the totality of inferences that we make about ourselves. The latter term is misleading because we do not possess a single, unified self-concept so much as a loosely connected set of ideas, inferences, and illusions about ourselves (Baumeister, 1997). In addition to ideas about who and what we are, we possess ideas about who and what we might become (possible selves), what we would like to be or become ideally (ideal selves), and what we think we ought to be or become (ought selves). Dejected emotions (sadness, disappointment) arise when we note discrepancies between our perceived self and our ideal self, and agitated emotions (e.g., anxiety, guilt) arise when we see discrepancies between our perceived self and our ought self (Higgins, 1987).

Self-esteem refers to the value that we place on ourselves. It is the evaluative component of self-concept. Besides producing the negative emotions just described, awareness of discrepancies between our perceived self and our ideal or ought self threatens self-esteem. Typically this leads to redoubled efforts at coping (e.g., studying harder), or where this is not feasible or effective, resorting to defense mechanisms (e.g., self-handicapping; Zirkel, 2000). In the school setting, these aspects of self-concept are closely associated with success or failure in achievement situations, and thus with the expectancy aspects of motivation. Research indicates that interventions leading to improved achievement are also likely to lead to improved self-esteem, but interventions focused on boosting self-esteem are unlikely to lead to improved achievement (Baumeister, Campbell, Krueger, & Vohs, 2003).

The value aspects of motivation are associated more with the descriptive aspects of self-concept, especially our ideas about our traits, dispositions, values, interests, preferences, and so on. We gravitate toward learning opportunities that we view as supportive of our perceived, ideal, or ought selves; we are indifferent toward learning opportunities that we view as irrelevant to us; and we seek to avoid learning opportunities that we view as likely to make us become something that we do not wish to become (Eccles, 2009; Hagger & Chatzisarantis, 2006; McCaslin, 2009).

This is especially the case with the inner core of self-concepts that constitute our *identity*. People living in contemporary western societies tend to focus on identifying and exploring their unique individualities—"finding themselves" and establishing coherent identities. Interestingly, this was not always the case and still is not the case in many other societies. More traditional and collective societies place relatively little importance on unique individual qualities. Instead, they emphasize the functions that people fulfill according to their place in society, and people's identities are closely bound up with their social rank, family ties, and occupations (Baumeister, 1997).

In contemporary western societies, people do not feel bound by these traditional ascribed roles and identities. Instead, they focus on creating their own identities, and in the process, adopting relatively coherent and usually strongly held views on who they are, what they believe and value, and the implications of this for their everyday actions (including their responses to potential learning activities). Motivating students to invest in learning opportunities implies helping them to see these opportunities as congruent with their perceived actual or ideal selves, or if necessary, with their perceived ought selves.

TEACHERS OFTEN NEED TO SCAFFOLD STUDENTS' APPRECIATION OF THEIR LEARNING, BY HELPING THEM TO BUILD MOTIVATED LEARNING SCHEMAS

Creating motivationally optimal learning situations requires attention to both curriculum and instruction. *A goal-oriented curriculum is crucial, because unless there are good reasons for learning something and authentic activities to use as vehicles for developing this learning, there is no basis for appreciating the learning. Instruction is crucial as well, because optimally mediated learning experiences raise students' consciousness of the purposes and goals of each activity and help them to build schemas that will enable them to learn with understanding, appreciation, and life application* (and thus to derive the motivational benefits as well as the knowledge and skill benefits that the learning activities are designed to develop). Relationships between learning goals, zones of proximal development, curricular choices, and teacher mediation of students' learning experiences are illustrated in Table 9.2.

Much of what we teach in school, especially in the humanities and social sciences, is primarily cognitive rather than perceptual or sensorimotor, and often is relatively abstract and complex. Consequently, so are the aesthetic and other forms of satisfaction that may be experienced in learning this content, as well as the processes involved in applying it to life outside of school. Students are not likely to experience the satisfactions and acquire the application potentials that school learning opportunities offer unless we do a better job of building these outcomes into our instructional goals. This is why, instead of just talking about teaching school subjects for understanding, I prefer to talk about teaching them for understanding, appreciation, and life application.

I include the term *appreciation* as a reminder that *students should not merely understand what they are learning but value it because they see good reasons for learning it.* These reasons include not only practical applications but ways that the learning might enrich students' repertoires of insights and recognitions or otherwise enhance the quality of their inner lives. I include the term *life application* as a reminder that *students should experience authentic activities that will enable them to apply what they are learning to their lives outside of school.* Many so-called "application exercises" do not qualify as authentic activities because they are too artificial. Even so-called "authentic activities" often are far removed from everyday life and have application potential only for specialists in the disciplines. Most students' life applications of school subjects involve

TABLE 9.2

Theoretical Schematic: Planning Curriculum and Instruction for Cognitively and Motivationally Optimal Learning

---

Goals: Identify domain knowledge, skill, attitude, value, and dispositional outcomes most worth developing.

ZPD filters: Identify potential learning goals that lie within the learners' cognitive ZPDs and are either below or within their motivational ZPDs.

Curricular choices: Within ZPD guidelines, choose content that optimally blends all three curricular sources (society's needs, learners' current capacities, and knowledge that has enduring value) and focus on authentic activities that provide a basis for learning for understanding, appreciation, and life application.

Mediation: Model, coach, and scaffold in ways that help learners both to acquire meaningful understanding and to value this learning as self-relevant and applicable to life outside of school.

Note: ZPD = zone of proximal development.

acting as consumers/appliers of discipline-based knowledge, not as disciplinary practitioners engaged in producing such knowledge.

The notion of learning with understanding, appreciation, and attention to life applications implies much more than mere interest in a topic, and it includes cognitive strategies and metacognitive control components along with affective components. It requires activating a network of related schemas—cluster of insights, skills, values, and dispositions that enable students to understand what it means to engage in school activities with the intention of accomplishing their learning goals and with awareness of the strategies they use in attempting to do so. The total network cannot be taught directly, although some of its cognitive and skills components can. In addition, its value and dispositional components can be developed through modeling and communication of attitudes, beliefs, values, expectations, and dispositions relating to motivation to learn.

Like other schemas, motivated learning schemas differ on dimensions such as generic vs. situation-specific or sketchy and uncertain vs. well developed, elaborated, and coordinated. The schemas that are most instantly accessible for information processing and problem solving tend to be domain- and situation-specific. They enable experts who know their way around a domain to immediately begin exploring new exposures to it by activating well-developed and integrated schemas. In contrast, novices must grope for clues as to what the domain is all about, what cues are significant, and how to proceed (see Figures 9.1 and 9.2).

These principles apply as much to the motivational aspects of learning as to the information processing aspects. Students who are ignorant (or misled) about a learning domain (e.g., studying dramatic plays) cannot generate much appreciation for the domain because they are unable to see its potential. Lacking concepts (e.g., foreshadowing, Achilles Heel) and strategies (e.g., analyzing plot developments and making predictions based on them, noting clues to characters' personal strengths and flaws) to guide their information processing, they are not yet able to experience many of the insights and satisfactions that studying dramatic plays offers. Even those who appreciate the play as a story may not find much personal relevance in it unless they have learned, for example, to identify with dramatic characters and think about how they (the students) might act in parallel situations.

The point here is that *learners may need teacher scaffolding to develop schema networks that include motivational as well as cognitive components before they can engage in certain learning activities with appreciation (not just learning) goals and can experience some of the satisfactions or other benefits that they afford.* Students do not need much motivational scaffolding to induce motivated learning of primarily physical sports and recreation activities. Relatively brief observation of models playing kickball, ping pong, pinball, or simple computer games may be enough to convey a basic sense of the nature of the activity, how to engage in it, and what kinds of rewards or satisfactions to expect. However, extensive scaffolding may be required to build students' readiness to appreciate typical school content and learning activities, especially as the curriculum moves away from basic skills. For advanced content in the humanities and social studies, motivated learning may not become possible for most students unless their teachers provide sufficient scaffolding to enable them to begin to appreciate the kinds of value afforded by the domain and explore it in ways that enable them to experience its satisfactions.

The potential for valuing school learning lies in the affordances it offers to students. The most notable of these affordances are a) the insights and understandings afforded by the big ideas that anchor content networks, and b) the information-processing, problem-

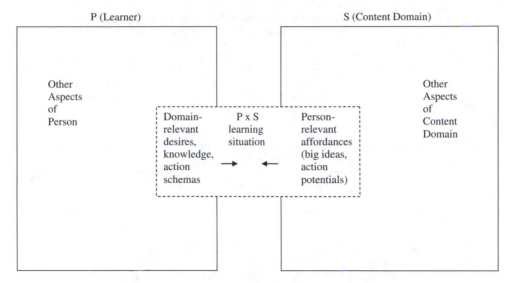

As persons learn about the affordances of action arenas (including school content domains), they develop schemas for exploiting them (or at least, the ones they value). Productive learning experiences occur when persons activate domain-relevant schemas (motive/goal/strategy networks) for exploiting the domain's learning-relevant affordances (big ideas, authentic activities). Sometimes this involves nothing more than using well-developed schemas to exploit familiar affordances and produce routine learning experiences, but at other times it involves generating and perfecting new schemas for exploiting newly discovered affordances. In these cases, the results include increases not only in domain-relevant knowledge networks and action schemas, but also in appreciation of the domain's affordances.

FIGURE 9.1 Person × situation model of motivated learning.

solving, and decision-making opportunities afforded by activities designed to develop and apply these big ideas.

Powerful ideas expand and enrich the quality of students' subjective lives, providing them with lenses through which to construe their observations and experiences, schemas into which they can assimilate novel elements, connections that they can make and draw inferences from, potential for recognizing and appreciating the aesthetic qualities of the objects or events that they encounter, and so on. These ideas and associated intellectual skills also empower them with tools for processing information, solving problems, and making decisions efficiently. These kinds of educational outcomes are applicable to a broad range of situations experienced throughout life, in contrast to the more specific outcomes usually associated with the terms attainment value and utility value.

If a curriculum strand has significant value for students, it will be because its content network is structured around big ideas that provide a basis for authentic applications to life outside of school. This implies the need to structure curricula around big ideas and authentic activities, because these two curricular components afford learning activities that students are most likely to value (for their enrichment satisfactions and empowerment benefits).

Note that this argument is not just another call for making curriculum and instruction more relevant to students. It does include recognition of the motivational value of connecting with students' current interests and agendas, but it does not begin with the

A. At a given point in his or her development, a learner's knowledge about a domain's affordances and how to exploit them can be depicted as follows:

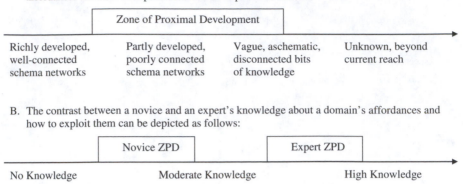

B. The contrast between a novice and an expert's knowledge about a domain's affordances and how to exploit them can be depicted as follows:

Knowledge may be propositional (what), procedural (how), or conditional (when, where, why). These three types may be developed unevenly, especially in school curricula. Bases for appreciation of value lie in conditional knowledge of when, where, and why to use the procedural knowledge to apply the propositional knowledge, especially in the service of self-relevant agendas.

C. Experts bring more domain-relevant schemas to learning situations involving the domain, and they are aware of many more of the domain's potentially achievable affordances:

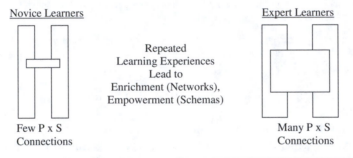

FIGURE 9.2 Development of domain expertise within and across learners.

students. Instead, it begins with curricular aims, purposes, and goals. It calls for articulating the knowledge, skills, values, dispositions, and appreciations that are intended as outcomes of particular content strands, then asking how these strands might be represented and how students' learning of them might be scaffolded in ways that encourage realization of the intended outcomes. Fundamentally, it focuses on crafting curriculum and instruction to scaffold students' development toward those outcomes, not limiting curriculum and instruction to cater to students' current interests and agendas. Furthermore, it emphasizes that intended outcomes include changes in the motivational aspects of learning (i.e., inducing students not just to acquire the desired knowledge and skills but to appreciate their value).

Teaching for appreciation is very different from "making learning fun" and similar hedonic prescriptions. It clarifies and scaffolds attainment of aims and purposes, emphasizing outcomes of enrichment or empowerment (not hedonic pleasure). It involves doing something minds-on with the content (processing, reacting, applying, etc.), but this need not involve hands-on activities. Making sure that students experience the intended benefits or satisfactions is the key.

Doing so can be challenging, however, because many of the benefits and satisfactions afforded by school learning are not well represented by popular ideas about motivation. When we talk about motivation, we typically refer to fun, pleasure, enjoyment, or excitement. However, the potentially motivating experiences that occur during acquisition and use of school content usually do not involve physical thrills, basic emotional reactions, or immersion in multi-sensory overload. Instead, they are primarily cognitive (achieving insights, making connections, etc.). They can come to be very compelling and highly valued, but they are best described using terms such as enrichment or empowerment, not pleasure or fun. Table 9.3 lists some of the major benefits and satisfactions derivable from acquiring and using school content, along with affordances of school content domains that are more versus less likely to enable learners to experience these benefits and satisfactions.

In summary, to explain the mediated acquisition of new valuing of or interest in domain-specific activities, we need a concept of scaffolded appreciation. This concept assumes that motivated functioning in a domain is schema-driven. When novices can observe what is involved in carrying out the activity and can "see the point to it" immediately, mere exposure may be sufficient to stimulate rapid development of needed schemas. For less transparent activities, however, especially *in cognitive domains like those taught in school, a mentor needs to scaffold novices' exposures so as to provide a "take" or entry point that will allow them to experience activities in the domain as meaningful and satisfying.* Both in selecting activities in which to engage learners and in scaffolding their subsequent engagement, the mentor's work should be guided by motivational goals as well as learning goals.

These ideas might seem novel at first, but they are just motivational applications of well-established principles of sociocultural learning, especially as it relates to the development of schemas and domain expertise (Alexander, 2003; Kaplan & Maehr, 2007; Nolen & Ward, 2008). Young people acquire most of their self-referenced attitudes, beliefs, expectations, and dispositions to action through exposure to socializing influences. Parents, teachers, peers, social institutions, and the media convey expectations not only about how people (in general and in various categories such as male/female, child/ teenager/adult, etc.) should act, but also about how they should think and feel. This includes attitudes and beliefs about the nature of learning in particular content domains—whom these learning experiences are meant for, whether they are enjoyable or worth pursuing, and if so, what one will get out of them.

Depending on the extent and nature of their prior experiences, particular learners (e.g., high school students) might have contrasting ideas about a potential learning experience (e.g., upcoming study of *King Lear*). Some might hold counterproductive attitudes and beliefs (Shakespeare is boring, difficult, and "not for me"). Others might have productive attitudes and beliefs (Shakespeare is well worth study for his gripping plots, rich characterizations, and deep insights into the human condition, and *King Lear* is considered one of his masterpieces). Still others might have no strongly formed attitudes and only vague beliefs (Shakespeare is supposed to be a great playwright, but he wrote a long time ago, so I wonder if I will like the play). The latter students will develop clearer attitudes and beliefs through their experiences during the unit, including both the input they receive from their teacher and classmates and their own emergent responses as they read and discuss the play.

TABLE 9.3
Potential Affordances, Benefits, and Satisfactions of School Content Domains

A. Potential Benefits and Satisfactions of School Learning
Enrichment of knowledge networks
Empowerment via new or more developed schemas
Absorption in content or activity
Aesthetic appreciations
Applications to life, personal agendas
Articulating tacit knowledge
Becoming more discriminating about one's desires
Clearing up misconceptions
Enriched perceptions, analyses, experiences
Forming hypotheses, opinions
Making meaning, connections
New insights, A-ha experiences
Personalization of content, applications
Recognition of connections to prior knowledge, life applications
Self-realization, flow

B. Affordances of School Content Domains

More Enabling of Appreciation of Value	*Less Enabling of Appreciation of Value*
Apply, Analyze, Evaluate, Synthesize/Create	Know, Remember
Connected Network of Knowledge	Isolated Bits of Information
Authentic Application	Part-skills Practice
Process Actively, Construct Meaning	Passive Intake
Learn Big Ideas	Enjoy Seductive Details
Restructure Knowledge Network, Apply in Sustained Activity	Satisfy Isolated Curiosity
Transformative Ideas	Inert Knowledge
Hold Factors (sustain engagement) Meaningful/ Life Applicable Involvement/Active Learning	Catch Factors (elicit initial engagement but do not sustain it)
Topic/Personal Interest Self-Relevance	Situational Interest
Valued Proximal Goal	No Goal, Non-valued Goal, or Remote Goal
Identified Regulation, Intrinsic Motivation (to Learn)	Extrinsic Motivation, Introjected Regulation
Intrinsic Value, Identity-related Forms of Attainment or Utility Value	No Recognized Value, Extrinsic Forms of Attainment or Utility Value
Eudaimonic (Flow, Self-Expression)	Hedonic (Fun, Enjoyment)

Modeling, Coaching, and Scaffolding Motivated Learning

Many theories could be brought to bear in identifying methods to help students to appreciate what they are learning and to develop motivated learning schemas. However, given that I have depicted these appreciations and schemas as acquired through sociocultural learning and talked about nurturing them within the motivational zone of proximal development, I will stick with sociocultural terms and speak of *the teacher as a mentor mediating the motivated learning of student novices through modeling, coaching, and scaffolding.* These terms usually are defined in ways that focus on the cognitive aspects of teaching and learning, but their definitions are easily extended to address the motivational aspects.

Modeling.   Teachers and other mentors can nurture motivation to learn by socializing as they instruct. One powerful socializing mechanism is modeling, particularly cognitive modeling that includes overt verbalization of the thinking that guides one's behavior when engaged in an activity. Appreciation-oriented modeling of engagement in a learning activity (e.g., reading *King Lear*) would communicate not just the strategies used to accomplish tasks (e.g., answering questions about the plot, characterization, etc.), but also the thoughts and feelings involved in savoring the experience and enjoying the aesthetic satisfactions it offers (e.g., making connections between characterization and plot elements depicted in the play and parallel elements in our own lives, putting ourselves in the place of Lear and thinking about how we might handle the dilemmas he faced, etc.). For example, a teacher described by Blank and White (1999) introduced *Hamlet* by posing the following question to his class: "Imagine you've been away from home for several years. When you come back, you find that your father has died and your mother, a few weeks after your father's death, has married your father's brother. Then you start uncovering clues that lead you to think that your uncle may have been responsible for your father's death. What do you think you would do under the circumstances?"

Other forms of socialization (besides modeling) are also helpful, notably direct instruction about motivated learning and comments designed to induce positive attitudes, beliefs, and expectations about the learning domain. However, these methods merely *tell* students that worthwhile experiences await them if they pursue the domain. Cognitive modeling *shows* them what these experiences look and feel like. *Good cognitive modeling should convey* not only the strategies needed to meet the demands of the task, but also *the aesthetic experiences, personal satisfactions, celebrations of new insights, pleasures taken in familiar recognitions, and other manifestations of what it looks and feels like to engage in motivated learning with appreciation of its affordances and enjoyment of its benefits and satisfactions.* As students acquire the needed schemas, they too can begin to anticipate, enhance, and savor the benefits and satisfactions that can be derived from exploiting a learning domain's affordances (Bryant & Veroff, 2007; Gresalfi, Martin, Hand, & Greeno, 2009).

Coaching. Preparatory instruction, hints, and cues given to guide students' task responses, as well as feedback given following their responses, communicate information about what to do or avoid doing. However, such coaching can also convey enthusiasm for the activity, help students to experience the satisfactions that it offers, and stimulate appreciation of the nature and progress of their learning. *Appreciation-oriented coaching* helps students to take satisfactions in, develop connections among, or draw implications from their insights as they learn (e.g., by cueing them to think about key aspects of the personalities or motives of the characters in the play, complimenting them on the insights they have developed about these characters, or inviting them to speculate about what these insights portend about the outcome of the drama or tell us about Shakespeare's view of the human condition).

Scaffolding. Mentors also scaffold novices' development of expertise in a domain, gradually transferring responsibility for guiding learning to the novices as their expertise develops. Scaffolding can include developing learners' capacities for valuing and deriving satisfactions from the domain (gradually transferring responsibility for managing these motivational aspects of engagement to the learners as they acquire the capacities for doing so).

Appreciation-oriented scaffolding would begin with (a) *selecting* appropriate learning activities in the first place, then following through by (b) *framing* them in ways that inform students about the activities' purposes and about what students can expect to get out of them, (c) providing *coaching* that includes making statements or asking questions that draw students' attention to benefits or satisfactions of the learning experience (i.e., helping the students to appreciate the activity's affordances), and (d) providing *feedback* that stimulates students to appreciate their developing expertise. *Appreciation-oriented feedback* provides not just knowledge of results but also commentary on noteworthy qualitative features of the learners' responses or accomplishments, especially features that suggest developing interests or talents that might be pursued further. Where appropriate, the initial feedback might be followed up with questions to learners about why they chose the general approach they chose or how they might improve or elaborate on what they have accomplished so far.

These forms of scaffolding *communicate in subtle ways the notion that the learner not only is doing something worthwhile, but is doing it in ways that represent seriousness of purpose, growth in knowledge or craftsmanship, and aesthetic qualities that reflect his or her individuality.* Table 9.4 illustrates how appreciation-oriented modeling, coaching, and feedback provided in the process of scaffolding students' learning experiences can address the motivational as well as the cognitive aspects of learning.

Dewey and Transformative Experiences

The writings of John Dewey (1938, 1958) have inspired recent theory and research on ways in which teachers can mediate students' encounters with powerful ideas so as to foster transformative experiences. Transformative experiences occur when we learn something that enables us to see some aspect of the world in a new way, such that we find new meaning in it and value the experience. For example, if an encounter with Monet's

TABLE 9.4
Theoretical Schematic: Scaffolding Both the Cognitive and the Motivational Aspects of Optimal Learning

Cognitive Aspects	Motivational Aspects
Modeling	
Convey key ideas and model strategies for learning these ideas and using them to accomplish authentic applications.	Convey reasons why this is worth learning, when and why we use it, and how it looks and feels when we do (verbalize self-monitoring and appreciation of growth in one's own knowledge, artistry, craftsmanship, etc.)
Coaching	
Cue attention to key foci at each step in the learning process; use questions or reminders to help learners negotiate the process and overcome temporary confusion or misdirected efforts.	Provide goal reminders and cues to next steps in the process in ways that develop learners' appreciation for the learning domain and for their own development of domain-specific knowledge and skill.
Feedback	
Provide timely feedback about correctness of response; explain reasons for errors and how to avoid or correct them; build capacity for self-monitoring and evaluation.	Provide feedback that calls learners' attention to developments in their knowledge or skill, ability to anticipate and prevent problems, or make corrections smoothly; signs of artistry or craftsmanship in their work; or unique "signature" elements indicative of their personal style of operating in this domain.

paintings becomes a transformative experience, the person may acquire a richer perception of the world—taking more notice of light, shadows, and colors, and, in general, seeing the world through Monet's eyes. Neo-Deweyan motivational theorists have noted that encounters with powerful ideas also have this potential, and have developed ways to design transformational learning experiences (Girod, 2000; Pugh & Girod, 2007; Girod & Wong, 2002; Girod, Rau, & Schepige, 2003; Wong et al., 2001).

Pugh (2002) applied these ideas to teaching science in high school. Modeling and scaffolding were prominent features of his approach. He began a zoology unit on adaptation and evolution by inviting students to talk about their favorite animals. He then shared some personal experiences with wild animals and showed home video footage of encounters with a moose and a grizzly bear. Next, he expressed his fascination with animals and said that one purpose of the upcoming unit would be to learn to appreciate animals better, explaining that ... *every animal ... is designed to survive and thrive in a particular environment. And when you learn how to see animals in terms of how they're adapted to their environment, every animal becomes an amazing creation* (p. 1108).

To awaken students' anticipation about how the concept of adaptation could enable them to see animals in exciting, new ways, he foreshadowed by telling them that they would learn to see the polar bear as a walking greenhouse and the common cat as a marvel of nature. He added that every animal has a historical record hidden within it, and evolution is the lens that allows us to read that record.

Pugh frequently modeled his thinking as he noted examples of adaptation in everyday observations of animals, as well as generated adaptation-related questions (e.g., seeing a flock of Canadian geese and wondering whether their combination of a black head with a white neck has an adaptive purpose). He also scaffolded students' initial attempts to see and discuss animals in terms of adaptations, by using their shoes as a metaphor for the relationship between form, function, and environment, and then guiding the students as they examined photos or videos of animals to identify aspects of their appearance or physical features that suggest adaptation (such as features that might make them more successful predators or make it harder for predators to see or catch them). He also encouraged students to notice and record signs of adaptation that they encountered outside of class. Analyses indicated that, compared to a parallel class taught using a case approach, the transformative experiences class learned the key ideas (adaptation and evolution) more thoroughly. They also more frequently discussed them, noticed applications outside of class, and reported related transformative experiences. The students found these key concepts to be both interesting and valuable.

One of your implicit goals as a teacher should be to make all of the big ideas you teach become transformative for your students. If flow is the ultimate manifestation of intrinsically motivated application of skills, transformative experiences are the ultimate manifestations of intrinsically motivated application of ideas.

SOCIALIZING MOTIVATION TO LEARN AS A GENERAL DISPOSITION

Each person has a unique motivational system, developed in response to experiences and to socialization from significant others in his or her life. Teachers are important "significant others." Rather than just accommodate classroom activities to students' existing motivational systems, teachers can *shape* those systems through socialization designed to develop students' motivation to learn. You can both socialize your students' motivation to learn as a general disposition and stimulate its emergence in particular teaching situations by bringing it to the forefront relative to other motives that may be operating at the time.

There are three general strategies for establishing a favorable context in which to socialize students' motivation to learn. These strategies involve helping students come to understand that classrooms are primarily places for learning, and that acquiring the knowledge and skills taught there enhances the quality of their lives (not just their grades).

Model Your Own Motivation to Learn

Model interest in learning throughout all of your interactions with students. This will encourage them to value learning as a self-actualizing activity that produces personal satisfaction and enriches their lives. Besides teaching what is in the textbooks, call attention to school learning applications in everyday living, in the local environment, or in current events. *Share your thinking* about such applications—show your students how educated people use concepts learned in school to understand and respond to everyday experiences in their lives and to news about events occurring elsewhere.

Without being preachy about it, relate personal experiences illustrating how you use literacy knowledge to communicate or express yourself effectively in important life situations, how you use mathematical or scientific knowledge to solve everyday household-engineering or repair problems, or how you use social studies knowledge to help you appreciate things that you see in your travels or to understand the significance of events in the news. *Through such modeling, help your students come to see how it is both stimulating and satisfying to understand (or even just to think, wonder, or make predictions about) what is happening in the world around us.*

Much of your modeling will occur during everyday instruction. It may be subtle or indirect, but, if it is displayed consistently, it will have cumulative effects on your students' attitudes and beliefs. *One important place to model curiosity and interest in learning is when responding to students' questions.* Questions usually indicate that students are interested in the topic and actively thinking about it rather than just listening passively. Consequently, be prepared to respond in ways that show that you value such questions. First, acknowledge or praise the question itself: "That's a good question, Latonya. It does seem strange that the people of Boston would throw the tea into the water, doesn't it?" Then, answer the question or refer it to the class: "How about it, class? Why would they throw the tea into the water instead of taking it home with them?"

You also can model curiosity in responding to questions for which you do not have ready answers: "I never thought about that before. Why didn't they take the tea home? They must have decided not to steal it but to throw it into the water instead. How come?" At this point, you could continue to think aloud in this vein or else invite suggestions from the class. If no one is prepared to answer the question, suggest some strategy to address it. You might promise to get the answer for the student, or better yet, invite the student to go to the library or the internet to find the answer and then report back to the class.

Other occasions for modeling curiosity and interest in learning arise when you convey information about your life outside of school. If you read a book, magazine article, or newspaper item of interest, mention it so that students can read it for themselves if they wish (better yet, make the item available for loan). Also, announce television programs, museum exhibits, or other special events of educational or cultural value.

You also can model curiosity and interest in learning through comments made in passing during class. Without belaboring the point, you can communicate that you regularly read the newspaper ("I read in the paper that…"), watch the news ("Last night on the news they showed…"), and participate in various educational and cultural pursuits. Your students should be aware that you think carefully about and participate in elections, keep abreast of current events, and otherwise show evidence of an active, inquiring mind.

For example, a junior high school teacher used modeling in connection with an assignment involving reading about current events. He began by noting that he read the editorial page regularly, sometimes agreeing and sometimes disagreeing, but always finding the ideas thought provoking. He went on to discuss a forthcoming summit meeting, noting that he was initially pessimistic about it but had become more optimistic as he became better informed by reading the paper and watching news programs. This led to discussion of the positions of the United States and other countries on issues addressed at the meeting. The teacher went on to note that, although he was sharing his own position on the issues discussed that day, he usually withheld his positions on issues discussed in class to encourage students to think for themselves and avoid inhibiting any who might disagree with him. He probably increased his students' interest in newspaper articles and television programs about current events, as well as giving them a model to follow in responding to those news sources in active, thoughtful ways.

Communicate Desirable Expectations and Attributions

In your everyday teaching, routinely project attitudes, beliefs, expectations, and attributions (statements about the reasons for your students' behavior) implying that students share your enthusiasm for learning. To the extent that you *treat students as if they already are eager learners*, they will be likely to become eager learners. Let them know that they are expected to be curious, to want to learn with understanding, and to want to apply what they are learning to their everyday lives (Marshall, 1987).

Minimally, this means avoiding suggestions that students will dislike academic activities or work on them only to get good grades. More directly, it means treating students as active, motivated learners who care about their learning and are trying to learn with understanding (Blumenfeld & Meece, 1988).

For example, an elementary teacher communicated positive expectations by announcing that she intended to make her students into "social scientists." She referred to this idea frequently in comments such as, "Since you are social scientists, you will recognize that the description of this area as a tropical rain forest has implications about what kinds of crops will grow there," or "Thinking as social scientists, what conclusions might we draw from this information?" Besides cueing her students to use disciplinary conventions for handling evidence and drawing conclusions, such comments encouraged them to identify with the social science disciplines and to connect what they were learning with their lives outside of school.

As another example, consider this teacher's treatment of division with remainders:

Teacher: We started out with 18 links and divided them into groups of 3, so how many groups are we going to get?

Anthony: Six.

Teacher: Six groups. You're right. We could say 6 groups of 3 make 18, right? OK, this time let's say I'm going to take away one. How many would I have then? [Several students say 17.] Seventeen. I want someone to come up and put these 17 links into groups of two. How many groups do you end up with?

Brenda: Eight groups plus one left over.

Teacher: Can't you put it in with one of the others? [Brenda shakes her head.] No. So we counted 8 groups of 2, but what else have we got?

Brenda: One left over.

Teacher: One left over. OK, in math, what do we call a leftover?

Lyle: A remainder.

Teacher: Right. So this problem is a little more interesting—we have a remainder.

In the process of teaching about division with remainders, this teacher is also socializing attitudes about mathematics. She presents the concept of remainders in a positive way that encourages students to view division with interest and confidence. Another teacher might have introduced this new level of complexity with a sense of futility or irritation ("You don't know what to do now, do you?" "This problem has a remainder, so it's more difficult"). If made consistently, such comments would lead students to view division as complicated and frustrating.

Minimize Performance Anxiety

Motivation to learn is likely to develop most fully when students are goal oriented but relaxed enough to be able to concentrate on the activity without worrying about whether they can meet performance expectations. You can encourage this by making clear distinctions between instructional activities designed to promote learning and tests designed to evaluate performance. Most classroom activities should be structured as learning experiences rather than as performance assessments.

To the extent that learning activities include testlike events (recitation questions, practice exercises), portray these as opportunities for your students to work with and apply what they are learning rather than as opportunities for you to test their mastery. If you want your students to engage in academic activities with motivation to learn (which implies a willingness to take intellectual risks and make mistakes), you will need to protect them from anxiety or premature concern about performance adequacy.

Eventually you will have to evaluate their performance and assign grades. Until that point, however, emphasize learning rather than performance, and encourage students to respond to evaluations in terms of "Let's assess our progress and learn from our mistakes," rather than "Let's see who knows it and who doesn't." If necessary, add statements such as "We're here to learn, and you can't do that without making mistakes," and caution students against laughing at the mistakes made by classmates.

STIMULATING STUDENTS' MOTIVATION TO LEARN IN SPECIFIC LEARNING SITUATIONS

Using the three general strategies just described will encourage your students to develop motivation to learn as a general disposition. You then can supplement these general strategies by using the following specific strategies during the learning situations that you create each day. These strategies are designed to stimulate students' motivation to learn what an activity is designed to teach. They are grouped within three categories: strategies for shaping students' expectations about the learning, strategies for inducing motivation to learn, and strategies for scaffolding students' learning efforts.

STRATEGIES FOR SHAPING STUDENTS' EXPECTATIONS ABOUT THE LEARNING

Students are more likely to be motivated to learn if they expect the learning to be interesting or important. You can foster these expectations by being enthusiastic when introducing learning activities and by shifting into an intense communication style when explaining things that are especially important.

Be Enthusiastic (Regularly)

Students take cues from their teachers about how to respond to school activities. If you present a topic or assignment with enthusiasm, suggesting that it is interesting, important, or worthwhile, your students are likely to adopt this same attitude (Bettencourt, Gillett, Gall, & Hull, 1983; Kunter et al., 2008; Long & Hoy, 2006; Patrick, Turner, Meyer, & Midgley, 2003; Turner et al., 2002).

Projecting enthusiasm does not mean pep talks or phony theatrics. Instead, it means identifying good reasons for viewing a topic as interesting, meaningful, or important and then communicating these reasons to your students when teaching about the topic. You can use dramatics or forceful salesmanship if you are comfortable with these techniques, but if not, low-key but sincere statements of the value that you place on a topic will be just as effective (Cabello & Terrell, 1994). Even a brief comment showing that a topic is food for thought or illustrating how it is interesting, unique, or different from previously studied topics may be sufficient. *The primary objective of projecting enthusiasm is to induce students to value the topic or activity, not to amuse, entertain, or excite them.*

A history teacher generated a great deal of interest by enthusiastically explaining to his students that during the Middle Ages, the Mediterranean Sea was the center of the world. Its seaports were major trade centers and places like England were outposts of civilization, but this changed with discovery of the New World and the emergence of new centers of trade and culture. His presentation included references to maps, reminders about the primary modes of transportation at the time, and characterizations of the attitudes of the people and their knowledge about other countries and trade possibilities.

Another teacher brought ancient Israel alive by enthusiastically telling his students about David as the slayer of Goliath and ancestor of Jesus, Abraham leading his people to the Promised Land, Solomon as a wise man and builder of the temple, and Moses as the man who presented the Ten Commandments and led the people out of the wilderness. This lesson included locating Jerusalem, Israel, and the Sinai Peninsula on a map and speculating about whether the temple might be rebuilt in modern Jerusalem (noting that a major Moslem temple is located next to the spot occupied by Solomon's temple). In each of these examples, the teacher was able to parlay personal interest and detailed knowledge about a topic into an effective presentation that sparked interest and elicited many questions and comments.

The potential power of teacher enthusiasm is captured in the following quotation explaining why certain teachers find a permanent place in their students' memories:

> What intrigues students most about these teachers is their enthusiasm for subjects that seemed boring and purposeless in other teachers' classes. Memorable teachers challenge students to expect more than just recognition or a paycheck from the work they choose. Why is Mr. Phillips so fired up about differential equations? How could Ms. Patrelli get so excited about the Crusades? Sometimes it is an encounter with just such a teacher that inspires students to reconsider the intrinsic rewards of exploring a domain of knowledge. (Csikzentmihalyi, Rathunde, & Whalen, 1993, pp. 184–185)

Be Intense (Selectively)

Learn to use timing, nonverbal expressions and gestures, cueing, and other verbal techniques to project a level of intensity that tells students that material is especially important and deserves close attention. You might begin an intense presentation with a direct statement of the importance of the message ("I'm going to show you how to invert fractions—now pay close attention and make sure that you understand when and why to do it, and how to do it"). Then present the message itself, using techniques that convey intensity and cue attention: a slow-paced, step-by-step presentation during which you emphasize key words, use unusual voice modulations or exaggerated gestures that focus attention on key terms or procedural steps, and scan the group following each step to look for signs of understanding or confusion (and to allow anyone with a question to ask it immediately). In addition to your words, everything about your tone and manner should communicate to students that what is being said is important and that they should give it full attention and ask questions about anything they do not understand.

You cannot be intense all the time, and even if you could, your students would adjust to it, so it would lose its effectiveness. Therefore, *reserve intensity for times in which you want to communicate "This is especially important; pay close attention."* Likely occasions include introduction of important new terms or definitions, especially those that might be confusing to students; demonstration of procedures (preparing paint in an art class, serving a volleyball, or handling scientific equipment); modeling of problem-solving techniques, especially when giving instructions for assignments; and any instruction that is intended to eliminate misconceptions (and thus requires making students aware that although they think they already understand, their "knowledge" may be incorrect). Exaggerated intensity is less appropriate for more routine situations, although whenever you are covering new or complex material, it is wise to slow the pace and be alert for signs of confusion or student desire to ask a question.

STRATEGIES FOR INDUCING MOTIVATION TO LEARN

Regardless of extrinsic incentives, intrinsic interest, or whatever other motivational influences may be operating, you will need to motivate your students to learn what your lessons and activities are designed to teach. This requires introducing and carrying out learning activities in ways that keep both you and the students *goal oriented—*

developing knowledge and skills in ways that support understanding, appreciation, and life application.

Awareness of curricular goals should guide both your teaching and your students' learning. Be mindful of the primary learning outcomes that each activity is designed to develop and how these fit within the curriculum as a whole. This will enable you to make good decisions about what content to emphasize, how to frame it so students can appreciate its value, and how to develop it so they can apply it in and out of school.

Similarly, *clarity about learning goals will help your students to focus on key ideas and applications and thus to learn with a sense of purpose.* To the extent that students are aware of learning goals, they will be more likely to monitor their progress, seek help if they need it, and persist until they have learned what they are supposed to learn. Also, to the extent that your presentations are clear and easy to follow, your students will be more likely to find the content meaningful and worthwhile (Mottet et al., 2008; Seidel, Rimmele, & Prenzel, 2005).

This assumes that your lessons and activities are focused on major instructional goals and phrased in terms of desired student outcomes. You will need to implement the principles outlined in chapter 2 concerning goal-oriented planning, adapting instructional materials in the light of your major goals, structuring content around powerful ideas developed in depth, and emphasizing authentic activities and assignments. Within the context created by this approach, you can use the following strategies to induce motivation to learn in particular situations.

Induce Dissonance or Cognitive Conflict

If a topic is familiar, students may think they already know all about it and thus may listen to presentations or read texts with little attention or thought. You can counter this tendency by pointing out unexpected, incongruous, or paradoxical aspects of the content; by calling attention to unusual or exotic elements; by noting exceptions to general rules; or by challenging students to solve the "mystery" that underlies a paradox. One teacher implemented several of these principles when he introduced a unit on the Middle Ages by telling students that they would learn about "our ancestors" who chose to remain illiterate and persecuted people who did not share their religion. Later, he contrasted the Moslem advances in mathematics, science, and the construction of libraries with the illiteracy of most Christian kings and lords. This stimulated his mostly Christian students to develop empathy with and appreciation for the culture of the Moslems of the Middle Ages, instead of viewing them only as faceless enemies of Christian crusaders.

A teacher used dissonance to stimulate curiosity about the Persian empire by noting that Darius was popular with the people he conquered and asking students to anticipate reasons why this was so. Another introduced the Trojan War by telling students that they would read about "how just one horse enabled the Greeks to win a major battle against the Trojans." Another introduced a video on the fall of the Roman Empire by saying, "Some say that the factors that led to the decay of the Roman Empire are currently at work in the United States—as you watch the video, see if you notice parallels."

United States history is full of opportunities to create dissonance, especially in students whose prior exposures have been confined to overly sanitized versions. Topics such as the Trail of Tears, the Japanese internment during World War II, or CIA involvement in undermining foreign governments can be startling eye openers, especially if approached not just as past history but as grist for discussions about whether such things might still happen today or what their implications might be for government policy.

The school curriculum includes a great many "strange but true" phenomena, especially in mathematics and science. By calling attention to these, you can get your students to begin asking themselves "How can that be?" Otherwise, they may treat the material as just more information to be absorbed without even noticing that it seems to contradict their previous learning.

Conceptual change teaching. Sometimes students' prior learning includes misconceptions about important concepts. For example, science units on plants typically emphasize their roles as food producers via the photosynthesis process. Students enter knowing little about photosynthesis but a great deal about food for people. They know that food is something that you eat, that it is taken in from the outside environment, and that there are many different kinds of food. This knowledge produces distorted understandings in students who assume that food for plants is similar to food for people, because plants' only source of food is that which they manufacture themselves (they transform light energy from the sun into chemical potential energy stored in food by combining the light energy with carbon dioxide, water, and minerals). Neither soil nor fertilizers (even if called "plant food") are taken in as food or consumed for energy.

To understand this, students must restructure their thinking about the nature of food, focusing on its scientific definition as potential energy for metabolism rather than on reasoning by analogy from their prior experiences with food for humans. Posner Strike, Hewson, and Gertzog (1982) suggested that four conditions must be satisfied if students are to be induced to change their understandings: (a) dissatisfaction with existing concepts must be induced and the new concepts must (b) be intelligible to the students, (c) be initially plausible, and (d) appear fruitful. These ideas underlie what has become known as *conceptual change teaching* (Echevarria, 2003).

Anderson and Roth (1989) used conceptual change teaching to help middle school students understand plants' food production. They began by asking students to define food—and food for plants—and to respond to a problem. This provided information about the students' initial conceptions and made the students more aware of them. Next, they gave students explanations about different ways of defining food, including its scientific definition. Then they posed questions that allowed students to appreciate how this new definition of food could explain everyday phenomena (Is water food? Juice? Vitamin pills? Can people live on vitamin pills alone? Why or why not?). They also asked students to write their ideas about how plants get food, to write about what kind of food plants use, and to diagram how food moves inside a plant.

As they developed information about plants and food production, they frequently referred back to these early exercises, drawing contrasts between scientific explanations and students' prior knowledge. The students engaged in experimental observations of plants, discussion of similarities and differences between plants and animals, comparisons of materials taken into plants with materials made by plants during photosynthesis, and comparisons between energy-containing and non-energy-containing materials that people consume. These activities encouraged students to make connections between their own ideas and scientific concepts, as well as to use their newly structured conceptions to make predictions and develop more satisfying explanations of everyday phenomena.

Kathleen Roth (1996, 2002) extended the conceptual change teaching model to history teaching, and noted that it can be used with any subject. The key steps include:

1. establish a question or problem in a way that engages students' interest and then elicit students' ideas about it (students will see that their peers have many ideas different from their own);
2. engage students in exploring phenomena related to the question or problem (preferably through hands-on experiences that will challenge their preconceptions), allowing them opportunities to think through their ideas, gather new evidence, and consider whether their initial ideas still make sense;
3. once students realize the need for new ideas, present scientific explanations and encourage students to compare these with their previous ideas and determine whether they make sense in light of the evidence;
4. provide students with opportunities to apply the scientific concepts to explain real-world situations, and
5. engage students in reflecting on how their ideas have changed and exploring connections between the newly learned scientific ideas and other ideas.

Alexander, Fives, Buehl, & Mulhern (2002) incorporated aspects of conceptual change teaching into a "teaching as persuasion" model for middle school science. The instruction involved conventional content concerning Galileo's study of planetary movements leading to the conclusion that the earth revolves around the sun instead of vice versa. However, the lesson was framed as an investigation to address a motivating question ("Should scientific evidence be kept from the public if it will cause confusion or unrest?"), and content was developed with emphasis on Galileo's struggles to promote his scientific discoveries in the face of ridicule and banishment. A role-play activity asked students to assume the position of a designated character in the dispute (Galileo, Ptolemy, Copernicus, Pope Urban VIII, or Cardinal Bellermine). The students also wrote reactions to several readings, and, as a culminating activity, re-evaluated their original responses to the motivating question. Persuasion classes showed deeper comprehension and greater interest than classes taught more conventionally.

Make Abstract Content More Personal, Concrete, or Familiar

Definitions, principles, and other abstractions may have little meaning for students unless made more concrete. One way to accomplish this is to relate experiences or anecdotes illustrating how the content applies to the lives of individuals that your students are interested in or likely to identify with.

For example, a junior high teacher personalized his instruction about slavery in ancient times by reading aloud a brief selection about Spartacus. When covering the crusades, he emphasized the Children's Crusade, noting that the children involved were "your age and younger" and that most died before the crusade ended in failure. He also made poignant connections to contemporary Iran, where religion-based zeal led preadolescents to volunteer to go to war. Another teacher brought the medieval guilds alive for her students by describing them in detail and soliciting the students' reactions to the fact that if they had lived during the Middle Ages and wanted to become a journeyman, they would have had to leave their homes as children and spend seven years apprenticed to a master craftsman.

Make abstractions concrete by conducting demonstrations or by showing objects, pictures, or videos. In studying a country, for example, teach about its people and culture in addition to its physical features and products. Show students what the country looks like and help them to imagine what it would be like to live there. Perhaps include children's literature sources that offer stories set in the country or follow members of a representative family through a typical day or week in their lives.

Help your students to relate new or strange content to their existing knowledge by using examples or analogies that refer to familiar concepts, objects, or events. For example, I have seen teachers make the following connections:

- the Nile River flooding and its effects on Egyptian customs compared to the spring flooding in Michigan rivers and its effects on local customs;
- the Washington Monument as a modern example of an obelisk;
- three times the size of modern domed football stadiums as the size of the largest Roman coliseums;
- identification of students in the class (or failing that, famous personalities) descended from the ancient peoples or the geographical areas being studied;
- linking of students' family names to the guilds (Smith, Tanner, Miller, Baker);
- similarities in climate and potential for flower raising and dairy farming as reasons why the Dutch were drawn to the Holland, Michigan, area;
- similarities between customs associated with the Roman Saturn Festival and customs associated with modern Christmas festivities; and
- explaining how the medieval social and political systems worked by describing the local area as part of the outlying lands surrounding a manor based in Lansing, which, in turn, would be under the protection of and would pay taxes to "the king of Detroit."

View your texts as outlines to be elaborated on, not as the entire curriculum. For example, one text that I studied explained Russia's exit from World War I by saying only that "the revolution came and a new government was established." This does not enable students to understand and visualize events surrounding the Russian revolution. To do so, you would need to elaborate on the text by explaining why and how the communists and others organized political and eventual military resistance to the Czar's regime, killed or expelled the Czar's family and key officials, and established a new government. Such elaboration on the text creates a meaningful story that students can explain in their own words because they can relate it to their prior knowledge and visualize the events to which it refers. Now they can actively process the content instead of just trying to memorize it.

The preceding example also illustrates another technique for making content more concrete and personal for students: *Dramatize by telling stories or at least representing the content within narrative formats.* In contrast to analytic or impersonal explanatory formats, narrative formats contain the key features of stories: a focus on central figures pursuing some goal, a plot that involves conflict or some barriers to accomplishment of the goal, a resolution that involves success or failure, and the implications of this for subsequent events. Egan (1990) has written about the power of narratives for capturing students' imaginations. He suggested that 8- 15-year-olds are highly responsive to the narrative format, and especially to dramatic stories featuring inspiring hero figures struggling to accomplish great feats or to right the wrongs of the world. This narrative approach can be applied not only in language arts and history, but in mathematics and science as well (in stories about struggles to solve mathematical problems, unlock scientific mysteries, or develop important inventions).

You may need to adapt your curriculum to make sure that it features gender equity and suitable connections to the ethnic and cultural backgrounds of your students. Certain students may feel excluded and lose interest if they come to believe that a school subject is about "them" rather than "us" (Alton-Lee, Nuthall, & Patrick, 1993; Epstein, 2009). Consequently, your treatment of history should include sufficient attention to social history, women's roles, and the lives of everyday people along with political and military events, and explore multiple perspectives on their meanings and implications. Similarly, your material on literature, biography, the arts and sciences, or society and culture should include sufficient attention to contributions by women and members of minority groups, especially groups represented in your class.

Research assignments connected with this content should include opportunities for students to choose biographical subjects, literature selections, or historical events on which to focus. In this way, those who wish to do so can pursue their interests in content with which they identify in part because of its relevance to gender or cultural identity issues that are important to them.

Induce Task Interest or Appreciation

You can induce appreciation for a topic or activity by explaining why students should value it. If it has connections with something they already recognize as interesting or important, note these connections. If the knowledge or skills to be taught have applications to everyday living, point out these applications, especially those that will allow students to solve problems or accomplish goals that are important to them. Also, mention any new or challenging aspects of activities that students can anticipate.

Sometimes, instead of just telling students why the content they are about to learn is valuable, you can arrange for them to discover this for themselves by engaging them with a question or problem that requires the content for its solution. This approach is most applicable with mathematical or scientific principles and procedures. Most of these principles were developed as by-products of attempts to understand some important phenomenon or solve some practical problem, and since then, other important applications have accumulated. You can make use of these applications when introducing and developing the content.

Arts and humanities knowledge usually lacks direct practical applications, but it has value as grist for developing insights into the human condition and advances in personal identity and self-actualization. *Stories,* for example, whether fictional or historical, usually can be framed with reference to enduring dilemmas or common problems with which your students can identify. Such stories have value not just as entertainment or cultural literacy knowledge but as case studies and food for thought about the trade-offs involved in alternative ways of responding to situations that provoke fear, rage, jealousy, conflicting loyalties, moral dilemmas, or other powerful emotions. In exposing your students to such stories, encourage them to put themselves in the place of the hero or another key character and to think about how they might have handled the depicted situations. In considering works of art, help your students not only to appreciate the artist's interpretation of the theme but also to develop their own interpretation and think about how they might express it artistically.

Information about people in the past or in other cultures can be rendered more meaningful to students by helping them to appreciate how these people's experiences contrast with their own geographical and cultural experiences. For example, a junior high teacher motivated students to read about the ancient Greek legal system by noting that it was similar to ours in many ways but it called for 501 jurors. He also motivated his students to study the map of Greece by explaining that even though no place in Greece is more than 40 miles from the sea, its jagged contours give it far more coastline than most larger countries.

Sivan and Roehler (1986) studied introductions to activities conducted during small-group reading instruction. They found that when teachers introduced activities with emphasis on the value of the activities themselves or of the knowledge or skills that the activities would develop, students engaged in the activities with an enhanced sense of their usefulness and with greater metacognitive awareness of their learning strategies and progress. Sansone, Weir, Harpster, and Morgan (1992) and Reeve, Jang, Hardre, and Omura (2002) reported similar benefits to informing students about the value of text content.

Keller (1987) recommended six strategies for enhancing students' perceptions of the relevance or value of curricular content: connecting the content with students' existing past experiences, skills, and interests; emphasizing the present worth of the content (how students can use it in their lives right now); emphasizing the future usefulness of the content; linking the content to specific student needs; allowing students autonomy and choice in determining how to accomplish goals; and using modeling by personally demonstrating the value of the content or recruiting former students to testify to its value.

Frymier and Shulman (1995) identified 12 strategies for helping students appreciate the relevance or value of their learning, and asked students to rate how frequently their teachers used them:

- uses examples to make the content relevant to me;
- provides explanations that make the content relevant to me;
- uses exercises or explanations that demonstrate the importance of the content;
- explicitly states how the material relates to my career goals or my life in general;
- links content to other areas of content;
- asks me to apply content to my own interests;
- gives assignments that involve applying the content to my career interests;
- helps me to understand the importance of the content;
- uses own experiences to introduce or demonstrate a concept;
- uses student experiences to demonstrate or introduce a concept;
- uses discussion to help me understand the relevance of the topic;
- uses current events to apply a topic.

Students reported greater motivation when their teachers used more of these strategies (Frymier, 2002).

Frymier also reported a few instances in which relevance manipulations did not produce significant results, prompting her to observe that students differ in their needs, interests, and personal agendas, so that some may not be persuaded by their teacher's attempt to highlight a learning activity's relevance or importance. I would add that learning activities also differ in their potential affordances and applications, so that some ought to be perceived as relevant and important by most students (if framed properly by their teachers), but others do not have significant relevance or serve important purposes (Legault, Green-Demers, & Pelletier, 2006).

Newton (2000) noted that helping students appreciate content often involves embedding the content within a wider context, thus restoring some of the threads that were removed from a larger web when the content was isolated for study. This might be done by asking questions that relate to its relevance, eliciting prior knowledge about it, or setting the scene in ways that highlight the human needs that the content can satisfy. For example, a unit on genetics might be introduced through discussion of beliefs about inheritance before Mendel, how Mendel's discoveries changed our understanding of genetic mechanisms, and how this knowledge eventually led to plant hybridization, cloning, the human genome project, and other contemporary applications of genetic knowledge.

Induce Students to Generate Their Own Motivation to Learn

You can induce your students to generate their own motivation to learn by asking them to think about topics or activities in relation to their own interests or preconceptions. For example, ask them to identify questions they would like to get answered or to note things that they find surprising as they read. *These techniques help students to understand that motivation to learn must come from within themselves—that it is a property of the learner rather than the activity.*

Ortiz (1983) emphasized to students that their motivational responses to a text— whether interest or boredom—are generated by them and not inherent in the text itself. To illustrate, she engaged students in activities such as thinking of ways to make reading a page from the phone book interesting, reading a text and then sharing reasons why they did or did not find it interesting, and analyzing what was going through their minds at times when they did or did not find a text interesting. These exercises helped students to realize that they need to generate interest themselves and to acquire a repertoire of strategies for doing so.

One popular way to induce students to generate their own motivation to learn is the K-W-L technique (Ogle, 1986). K-W-L promotes learning by helping students to retrieve relevant background knowledge and learn with awareness of purpose and accomplishment. It unfolds through several steps. First, as they are about to begin study of a topic, students write down what they already <u>K</u>now (or think they know) about the topic and what they <u>W</u>ant to learn about it. Alternatively, this step can be done as a teacher-led group activity, in which students' responses are listed publicly.

The next steps occur during study of the topic. Here, you address any misconceptions that emerged in your students' "K" responses and provide answers (or arrange for the students themselves to get answers) to the questions raised in their "W" responses.

Finally, as a culmination of their study of the topic, students write what they <u>L</u>earned about it. At this time, they also revisit their earlier "K" and "W" responses. They may see a need to change some of these earlier statements, if part of what they thought they knew was incorrect.

Spires and Donley (1998) noted that *giving students permission to bring their personal knowledge encourages them to establish the relevance of content to their own interests and purposes.* They recommended teaching students to take note of their personal reactions, things that the content reminds them of, or connections to other knowledge or experience. Students using this strategy showed better comprehension of and improved attitudes toward text materials they studied.

STRATEGIES FOR SCAFFOLDING STUDENTS' LEARNING EFFORTS

Scaffolding strategies are needed to complement motivational strategies because, as Blumenfeld and colleagues (1992) noted, *motivating students to learn requires not only bringing the lesson to them but bringing them to the lesson.* You are off to a good start if you present students with worthwhile learning activities and introduce them in ways that help students to appreciate their value. You need to follow this up, however, *by asking questions or assigning tasks that will require students to think critically and creatively about the content; apply it in activities calling for inquiry, problem solving, or decision making; and get feedback. In the process, you can supplement and scaffold your students' efforts* by providing them with learning goals and advance organizers, modeling task-related thinking and problem solving, and helping them to learn with metacognitive awareness and control of their own learning strategies.

State Learning Goals and Provide Advance Organizers

Learners retain more when their learning is goal-directed and structured around key concepts, so introduce activities by stating their goals and by providing advance organizers that characterize what will be learned in general terms. These techniques *call students' attention to the benefits that they should derive from engaging in the activity and help them establish a learning set to use in guiding their responses to it* (Lane, Newman, & Bull, 1988; Marshall, 1987). As used here, the term *learning goal* is meant to have a broader meaning than *behavioral objective* or *instructional objective.* The learning goals likely to contribute to students' motivation to learn are broader and phrased in terms of the added capacities (knowledge, insights, coping strategies) that students will acquire, preferably with reference to their applications in life outside of school.

When introducing a lesson or activity, it seems natural to make sure that students understand what they will be doing and why. However, few teachers do so systematically (Urdan, 2001).

For example, Newby (1991) observed 30 first-year elementary teachers over a four-month period, developing thick-description records of classroom discourse and activities. These data were later analyzed for four motivational strategies: focusing attention, emphasizing relevance, building confidence, or imposing rewards and punishments. The teachers averaged 10.4 strategies per hour. However, 58% of these were reward or punishment strategies, and most of the rest (27%) were attention-focusing strategies. Only 7.1% involved building students' confidence, and only 7.5% were relevance strategies that involved explaining the value of the learning or why it was being taught. Thus, these teachers mentioned the purpose or value of learning less than once per hour.

Anderson, Brubaker, Alleman-Brooks, and Duffy (1985) found that first-grade teachers' presentations of assignments typically included procedural directions, but seldom called attention to the purposes and meanings of the work. Only 5% described the purpose of the assignment, and only 1.5% included explicit descriptions of the cognitive strategies to use. The work was mostly low-level and repetitive, the directions seldom included statements about what would be learned or how it related to other learning, and the teachers' monitoring focused on work completion rather than levels of understanding.

The result was summarized in what one student said to himself as he finished a worksheet: "I don't know what it means, but I did it." Many students (especially low achievers) did not understand how to do their assignments. Rather than ask their teachers or get help in other ways, they often were content to respond randomly or rely on response sets (such as alternating true-false answers or picking one from a list of new words to fill the blank in a sentence without reading the sentence itself). Low achievers tended to be more concerned about finishing assignments than understanding the content they were supposed to be learning. High achievers completed most assignments successfully and showed less concern about finishing on time, but even they showed little understanding of the assignments' content-related purposes.

These findings are not unique. Rohrkemper and Bershon (1984) interviewed elementary students about what was on their minds when they worked on assignments. They found that of 49 students, 2 were concerned only about getting finished, 45 were concerned about getting the answers correct, but only 2 mentioned trying to understand what was being taught.

If we want students to be aware of the goals of learning activities and appreciate their potential for promoting personal growth and enhancing quality of life, we will need to draw the students' attention to these goals and potentials. Teachers do not do this nearly as much as they should. For example, Green (2002) interviewed two teachers about their motivational strategies and observed them in their classrooms. Each teacher mentioned both expectancy aspects (e.g., help students become comfortable and confident as learners) and value aspects (e.g., elicit their interest and help them understand the importance of learning activities) in describing her ideas about motivation. Yet, each made reference to usefulness or importance only three times during approximately 15 hours of teaching. Their motivational attempts were focused on expectancy issues. Most came during comments to individual students after activities had begun, rather than in comments to the whole class when introducing the activities.

One of my own studies yielded similar findings (see Box 9.3). Unfortunately, it appears that most teachers, even those who are effective in other respects, do not introduce learning activities in ways that are likely to stimulate their students' motivation to learn.

Plan Questions and Activities to Help Students Develop and Apply Powerful Ideas

Once you have clarified the purposes and goals of an activity and provided any needed introduction to its content base, ask questions and engage students in activities designed to help them develop their understanding by processing and applying the content. Emphasize questions and activities that will stimulate students to reflect on what they are learning and engage in thoughtful discussion of its meanings and implications. You may occasionally need to use drill activities to reinforce learning that must be memorized, as well as recitation activities to check and correct understanding of basic knowledge that must be in place to anchor subsequent learning activities. However, most of your questions should be asked not just to monitor comprehension but to stimulate students to think about the content, connect it to their prior knowledge, articulate their understandings of it, and begin to explore its applications (Turner et al., 2002; Turner, Meyer, Midgley, & Patrick, 2003).

Types of questions. Questioning ordinarily should not take the form of rapidly paced drills or attempts to elicit miscellaneous facts. Instead, *use questions as means for engaging students with the content. Stimulate them to process that content actively and*

Box 9.3   Teachers' Task Introductions

Brophy, Rohrkemper, Rashid, and Goldberger (1983) observed reading and mathematics instruction in intermediate-grade classrooms to test predictions about relationships between the expectations that teachers established when introducing tasks to their students and the apparent levels of engagement displayed by the students once the tasks were begun. As expected, low levels of student engagement were observed on tasks that the teachers had introduced by communicating negative expectations (that the tasks would be boring or that the students would not enjoy them). However, task introductions in which teachers communicated positive expectations were not associated with the highest levels of student engagement. Instead, student engagement was highest when the teachers launched directly into tasks without making introductory statements about them.

Later analyses of these data by Brophy and Kher (1986) suggested that these teachers' positive task introductions did not have much impact on their students' motivation to learn because (1) they did not occur often enough; (2) when they did occur, they usually were too short or sketchy to do much good; and (3) whatever good they might have done was probably negated by other statements likely to undermine their students' motivation to learn. Only about a third of the teachers' task introductions included comments judged likely to have positive effects on student motivation, and most of these were brief predictions that the students would enjoy the task or would do well on it. In about 100 hours of classroom observation, only 9 task introductions were noted that included substantive information about motivation to learn:

- These are not elementary, high school, or college words; these are living-level words. You'll use them every day in life. If you plan to be a writer or enjoy reading, you'll need these words.
- Remember, the essential thing is to do them correctly, not to be the first to finish.
- I think you will like this book. Someone picked it out for me, and it's really good.
- This is a really strange story. It's written in the first person, so that the person talking is the one who wrote the story about his experience. It has some pretty interesting words in it. They are on the board.
- The stories in this book are more interesting than the ones in the earlier level books. They are more challenging because the stories and vocabulary are more difficult. Reading improves with practice, just like basketball. If you never shoot baskets except when you are in the game, you are not going to be very good. Same with reading. You can't do without it.
- Answer the comprehension questions with complete sentences. All these stories are very interesting. You'll enjoy them.
- You girls should like this story because it is a feminist story. You boys will enjoy yours too. Your story is especially interesting. I want you to be sure to read it. It's a mystery, and you'll enjoy it.
- Percent is very important. Banks use it for interest loans, and so on. So it is important that you pay attention.

- You're going to need to know fractions for math next year. You will need fractions in the world to come.

Notice how minimal and essentially barren most of these remarks are. They do not go into enough detail to be very meaningful or memorable for most students, and many have a perfunctory quality suggesting that the teacher was going through the motions without much enthusiasm or conviction. Also, most of the teachers' remarks to students concerned procedural demands and evaluations of work quality or progress rather than description of the task itself or what the students might get out of it. No teacher was ever observed to suggest that a task had self-actualization value (i.e., that students could develop knowledge or skills that would bring them pleasure or personal satisfaction). Middleton (1995) reported the same finding for middle school mathematics classes.

Furthermore, any desirable effects that the teachers' occasional positive task introductions may have had were probably undercut by remarks such as the following:

- Today's lesson is nothing new if you've been here.
- If you get done by 10 o'clock, you can go outside.
- Your scores will tell me whether we need to stay with multiplication for another week. If you are talking, I will deduct 10 points from your scores.
- This penmanship assignment means that sometimes in life you just can't do what you want to do. The next time you have to do something you don't want to do, just think "Well, that's part of life."
- Get your nose in the book, otherwise I'll give you a writing assignment.
- You don't expect me to give you baby work every day, do you?
- You've been working real hard today, so let's stop early.
- You'll have to work real quietly, otherwise you'll have to do more assignments.
- My talkers are going to get a third page to do during lunch.
- We don't have a huge amount to do, but it will be time-consuming.
- This test is to see who the really smart ones are.

It is important to note that the teachers observed in this study were all experienced and if anything better than average as a group. Yet, they seldom took advantage of opportunities to stimulate their students' motivation to learn in the process of introducing academic activities; when they did, their positive task introductions were too short and sketchy to be very effective; and they frequently violated important motivational principles by bribing or threatening students to create extrinsic work pressures, portraying tasks as boring or pointless, or even treating them as if they were punishments in themselves. To avoid displaying such patterns yourself, it will be important for you to monitor your teaching consistently enough to allow you to notice and initiate corrective actions if you begin to drift into counterproductive habits (see Good & Brophy, 2008, concerning developing awareness of your classroom teaching).

"make it their own" by rephrasing it into their own words and considering its meanings and implications. The idea is to build an integrated network of knowledge structured around powerful ideas, not to stimulate rote memorizing of miscellaneous information.

For each subtopic to be developed, ask questions in sequences designed to help students construct connected understandings. Use different question sequences to accommodate different instructional goals. To develop an unfamiliar topic, for example, you might begin with questions designed to stimulate interest in the topic or help students connect it to their prior experiences, then move to questions designed to elicit key ideas, then move to questions calling for reflection on or application of these ideas. If students already have prior knowledge about a topic, you might wish to place them into an application mode immediately, such as by posing a problem, eliciting alternative solution suggestions and rationales, and then engaging the class in a reflective discussion of these ideas.

It is not possible to develop complete scripts for question sequences and proceed through them rigidly, because students' responses are only partially predictable in advance. It would not be wise to attempt this in any case, because you will want to adapt lesson plans to developing situations and take advantage of "teachable moments" that students create by asking questions or making comments that are worth pursuing. Nevertheless, *an important part of goal-oriented teaching is the planning of purposeful sequences of questions designed to help students construct key understandings.* Such planned question sequences are much more likely to yield thoughtful classroom discourse than the inefficient patterns of questioning that occur when teachers have not thought through their purposes for developing a particular topic.

Questioning technique.   Good questioning technique can enhance the power of your questions to stimulate student thinking. First, *address most of your questions to the entire class rather than to a single student.* This will encourage all students to think about the question, not just the designated individual. Second, *before calling on anyone to respond, allow sufficient wait time to enable students to process and formulate responses.* You may need to emphasize to students that you are more interested in thoughtfulness and quality than speed of response, as well as to discourage overly eager students from blurting out answers. Finally, *distribute response opportunities widely rather than allow a few students to answer most of your questions.* Students learn more if they are actively involved in discussions than if they sit passively without participating, and distributing response opportunities helps keep all students attentive and accountable.

Using questions that call for content-based thinking and problem solving, initiate patterns of discourse that evolve into *exchanges of views*, in which students respond to one another as well as to you, and respond to statements as well as to questions. Dillon (1988, 1990) has shown that *teachers' statements can be just as effective as their questions for producing lengthy and insightful responses during discussions.* Questions may even impede discussions, if they are perceived as attempts to test students rather than to solicit their ideas. Instead of continuing to ask questions, you sometimes can sustain discussions nicely by simply remaining silent; asking students to respond to what their classmates have said; probing for elaboration ("Tell us more about that" or "Perhaps you could give some examples"); asking indirect questions ("I wonder what makes you think that"); summarizing or restating what a student has said; or simply making some declarative statement that adds to the discussion and invites further comment from students.

When collecting responses to a problem-solving or decision-making question, record the responses (list them on the board, a chart, or an overhead screen), but *do not evaluate them immediately*. Continue collecting and recording as long as anyone has new suggestions to contribute, then invite students to develop arguments for or against selected alternatives. Such discussions should be conducted within learning community norms as described in chapter 2. That is, students should understand that the purpose of reflective discussion is to work collaboratively to deepen their understandings. They will need to listen carefully, respond thoughtfully, and participate assertively but respectfully. Both in advancing their own ideas and in responding to those of classmates, they should build a case based on relevant evidence and arguments and avoid divisive or other inappropriate comments.

Thoughtful discourse.   Newmann (1990) described classroom discourse patterns that develop *thoughtfulness*: persistent desire that claims be supported by reasons (and that the reasons themselves be scrutinized), tendency to be reflective by taking time to think through problems rather than acting impulsively or automatically accepting the views of others, curiosity to explore new questions, and flexibility to entertain alternative and original solutions to problems. Based on observations in high school social studies classes, Newmann identified six key indicators of thoughtfulness:

1. Classroom discourse focuses on sustained examination of a few topics rather than superficial coverage of many.
2. The discourse is characterized by substantive coherence and continuity.
3. Students are given sufficient time to think before being required to answer questions.
4. The teacher presses students to clarify or justify their assertions, rather than accepting and reinforcing them indiscriminately.
5. The teacher models the characteristics of a thoughtful person (showing interest in students' ideas and suggestions for solving problems, modeling problem-solving processes rather than just giving answers, and acknowledging the difficulties involved in gaining clear understandings of problematic topics)
6. Students generate original and unconventional ideas in the course of the interaction.

Classes that displayed these characteristics were demanding, so students viewed them as more difficult and challenging than their other classes. However, they also described them as more engaging and interesting. Here again is evidence that the key to motivation to learn is minds-on engagement with powerful ideas.

Newmann (1992) later developed a theory of student engagement that took into account the authenticity of learning activities along with thoughtfulness during classroom discourse. A subsequent survey indicated that students who reported experiencing more authentic work also reported higher engagement. This relationship held up across social class, race/ethnicity, and grade levels (Marks, 2000).

Minds-on learning.   MacIver, Young, and Washburn (2002) reviewed reform literature in major school subjects and found convergence on active, meaning-oriented teaching as optimal. In a study of what makes science classes engaging and worthwhile, they asked middle school students to report on the frequencies with which their classes offered: (a) minds-on learning opportunities (generate a hypothesis to explain why something happened, offer an opinion on a scientific issue, generate questions or topics for the class to investigate, explain answers to partners or teammates and make sure that they understand the material, discuss careers in science, write in a personal science journal); (b) hands-on opportunities to design, carry out, and interpret experiments (do experiments, write about the results, explain the results, interpret data, design an experiment); and (c) going beyond the textbook (read articles on science, do a report, discuss a science news event). There were somewhat positive relationships for hands-on opportunities, and much stronger relationships for minds-on opportunities and going beyond the textbook, with students' reports of valuing their science classes and perceiving their teachers as caring about their feelings and learning progress. Once again, note that the minds-on aspects of these classes, not the hands-on aspects, were associated most closely with students' motivation to learn.

Other studies suggest similar implications. Whether their methodologies involved classroom observation of teachers who differed in motivational effectiveness or interviews with students about instructional practices they found motivating or demotivating, the findings consistently point to *thoughtful discourse about big ideas* and *authentic activities with life applications* as promoting student engagement in learning, and to disconnected recitation and fill-in-the-blank seatwork as discouraging such engagement (Certo, Cauley, Moxley, & Chafin, 2008; Raphael, Pressley, & Mohan, 2008).

Model Task-Related Thinking and Problem Solving

The information-processing and problem-solving strategies needed for thinking about particular content or responding to particular tasks may be unknown to many of your students unless you make them overt and observable by modeling them. Your modeling should show the thinking that goes into selecting the general approach to use, deciding on what options to take at choice points that arise during the process, checking on progress as one goes along, and making certain that one is on the right track. It also should include recovery from false starts and from use of inappropriate strategies, so your students can see how to develop a successful strategy even after getting off to a bad start (Schunk & Hanson, 1985).

This kind of *cognitive modeling is powerful not just as an instructional device but as a way to show students what it means to approach a task with motivation to learn*. That is, it allows you to model the attitudes, beliefs, and strategies that are associated with such motivation (patience, confidence, persistence in seeking solutions through information processing and rational decision making, benefiting from the information supplied by mistakes rather than giving up in frustration, concentrating on the task and how to respond to it rather than focusing on the self and worrying about one's limitations).

Induce Metacognitive Awareness and Control of Learning Strategies

When motivated to learn, students process information actively by concentrating their attention, making sure they understand, integrating new information with existing knowledge, and storing this information in a form that will allow them to remember it and use it later. Students are most likely to do these things effectively if they do them with *metacognitive awareness*—conscious selection of appropriate strategies, monitoring of their effectiveness, noting and correcting their mistakes, and shifting to new strategies if necessary.

You can help your students remain aware of their goals and strategy decisions by structuring and scaffolding their engagement in learning activities. To the extent needed, this might include pre-activity instructions that emphasize its purposes and goals, questions or cues offered during the activity to help keep students aware of the processes they are using in responding to it, and post-activity debriefing that focuses on appreciating what has been accomplished (Brophy & Alleman, 1991; Jones & Idol, 1990; Rosenshine & Guenther, 1992).

A complete activity might include the following stages:

1. *Introduction* (communicate the goals of the activity and cue relevant prior knowledge and response strategies)
2. *Initial scaffolding* (explain and demonstrate procedures if necessary, then ask questions to develop key ideas and make sure that students understand what to do before releasing them to work on their own)
3. *Independent work* (release students to work individually or with peers, but monitor their progress and intervene when necessary)
4. *Debriefing/reflection/assessment* (revisit the activity's primary goals and assess the degree to which they have been accomplished)

This sequence operationalizes the point that *effective activities require not just physical actions or time on task but cognitive engagement with important ideas.* Inductive or discovery learning activities will unfold through different stages, but even these activities require an optimal type and amount of structuring and scaffolding to maximize their impact.

1. *Introduction.* Students will need to understand the intended purposes of the activity and what these imply about how they should respond to it. *Good introductions to activities fulfill at least four functions*: (a) stimulating students' interest in or recognition of the value of the activity; (b) communicating its purposes and goals; (d) cueing relevant prior knowledge and response strategies; and (d) establishing a learning set by helping students to understand what they will be doing, what they will have accomplished when they are finished, and how these accomplishments will be communicated or evaluated. Information about purposes and goals should emphasize cognitive and affective engagement with powerful ideas, not just instructional objectives in the narrower sense. Cueing of prior knowledge might include comparison or contrast with previous activities, asking students to use their knowledge to make predictions about the upcoming activity, explaining where the activity fits within a sequence or bigger picture, or helping students make connections between its content and their personal knowledge or experiences. To guide students' thinking during a presentation, video, or film, you might distribute a partial outline for them to fill in or a series of questions to answer as the lesson unfolds.
2. *Initial scaffolding.* Before releasing students to work mostly on their own, provide whatever explicit explanation and modeling they need in order to understand what to do, how to do it, and why it is important. To the extent that the activity calls

for skills that need to be taught rather than merely cued, your scaffolding should include explicit explanation and modeling of strategic use of these skills.

3. *Independent work.* Once students have been released to work individually or collaboratively, monitor their efforts and provide any additional scaffolding or responsive elaboration on the instructions that may be needed to structure or simplify the task, clear up confusion or misconceptions, or help students to diagnose and develop repair strategies when they have made mistakes or used inappropriate strategies. These interventions should not involve doing tasks for students or simplifying them to the point that they no longer engage the students in the cognitive processes needed to accomplish the activity's goals. Instead, scaffold within the students' zones of proximal development in ways that allow them to handle as much of the task as they can at the moment but also to progress toward fully independent and successful performance.

    Students will need *feedback*—not only information about correctness of responses but also diagnosis of the reasons for errors and explanation of how their performance might be improved. To the extent possible, provide such feedback immediately as you circulate to monitor students' progress.

4. *Debriefing/reflection/assessment.* Bring activities to closure in ways that link them back to their intended goals and purposes. Provide students with opportunities to assess their learning and to correct and learn from their mistakes. Ordinarily, you should include a post-activity debriefing or reflection that reemphasizes purposes and goals, reflects on how (and how well) they have been accomplished, and reminds students about where the activity fits within the larger unit or curriculum strand.

SELF-REGULATED LEARNING

Rohrkemper and Corno (1988) suggested that the highest form of cognitive engagement that students can use to learn in classrooms is *self-regulated learning*—active learning in which they assume responsibility for motivating themselves to learn with understanding. Self-regulated learning should be the ultimate goal of your motivational efforts.

You can set the stage for development of self-regulated learning by using teaching strategies that foster intrinsic motivation and motivation to learn. Within this context, you then can promote self-regulated learning more directly by (a) clarifying goals, modeling strategies, and otherwise working to ensure that students' learning is meaningful and strategic; and (b) withdrawing these learning supports when they are no longer needed and providing opportunities for students to work with increasing autonomy on tasks that challenge them to integrate and apply what they are learning.

Teaching learning skills and strategies empowers students by helping them to truly understand what they are learning (which should improve their attitudes toward it) and to generalize and apply it to tasks of their own choosing. Students' need for instruction in strategy use recedes as their expertise develops. At first they may need interventions designed to increase their awareness and deliberate use of learning strategies, but this kind of assistance can be faded as they begin to acquire the skills of expert learners (e.g., abilities to diagnose the reasons for learning problems and to focus immediately on the most likely solutions, to develop short cuts through longer processes, and to use certain strategies automatically without having to make conscious decisions to do so).

CONCLUSION

The motivational strategies developed throughout this book are potentially quite powerful, especially if used systematically and in complementary ways. This entails establishing your classroom as a learning community as described in chapter 2, then infusing motivational elements into your unit, weekly, and daily planning. Units should be structured around powerful ideas and include a variety of learning activities and formats. Individual activities should be appropriately challenging and scaffolded so as to address the expectancy aspects of students' motivation, and the combination of the activity itself, its content base, and the way that you introduce and scaffold it should address the value aspects of your students' motivation in multiple ways.

The idea here is to create what Ford (1992) called *motivational insurance* when designing activities and social contexts for your classroom. The most motivating activities and experiences in life afford opportunities for simultaneous pursuit and attainment of many different goals. From a motivational standpoint, the most desirable classroom activities make it possible for students to accomplish the teacher's instructional goals while at the same time accomplishing many of their own personal and social goals. This provides motivational insurance against the possibility that no relevant goal will be activated.

SUMMARY

Various conceptions of motivation to learn, including my own, emphasize its cognitive elements—the information processing, sensemaking, and advances in comprehension or mastery that occur when students are seeking to gain the intended learning benefits from a classroom activity. The term connotes minds-on cognitive engagement with powerful ideas. Motivation to learn in this sense is not guaranteed by interest in a topic or even hands-on involvement in an activity. It requires opportunities to learn through exposure to curriculum content and learning activities, teacher pressure and support for such learning, and follow-through in the form of evaluation and accountability systems that lead to additional learning opportunities if necessary.

As a significant person in your students' lives, you can socialize their motivation. Pave the way for motivation to learn by making sure that your curriculum content and learning activities are meaningful and worthwhile, then developing the content and scaffolding your students' engagement in the activities in ways that enable them to see and appreciate their value. Work in the zone of proximal development (motivationally as well as cognitively), help students to see curriculum content as self-relevant and identify with it, and scaffold their appreciation of their learning by using modeling, coaching, and feedback to build motivated learning schemas.

Three general strategies for socializing enduring dispositions to value learning and thus to approach learning situations thoughtfully and purposefully are modeling motivation to learn in your own everyday teaching, communicating related expectations and attributions about your students by treating them as if they already are eager learners, and avoiding practices that create anxiety and distract students from learning goals to performance goals. These strategies may be viewed as elaborations on the notion of establishing your classroom as a learning community (as described in chapter 2).

Within the context established by these general strategies, you can use more specific techniques to stimulate your students' motivation to learn in the specific learning situations that you create each day. These include strategies for shaping students' expectations about the learning, for inducing motivation to learn, and for scaffolding their learning efforts.

Two strategies for shaping students' expectations about the learning are being enthusiastic (regularly) and being intense (selectively). You should routinely project enthusiasm for lessons and activities. You may be dramatic or entertaining in the process, but the point is to induce students to value the topic or activity. At times when you are communicating something particularly important, project a level of intensity that alerts students to the need to pay especially close attention.

Strategies for inducing motivation to learn are designed to help your students focus on learning goals and become cognitively engaged with the key ideas that lessons and activities are designed to develop. These include inducing dissonance or cognitive conflict when introducing the lesson or activity; making abstract content more personal, concrete, or familiar to students by linking it to their experience; inducing task interest or appreciation; and inducing students to generate their own motivation to learn.

Strategies for scaffolding students' learning efforts are needed to help students understand the purpose and nature of an activity and then support their efforts to accomplish its goals (to the extent that such support is needed). Scaffolding strategies include stating learning goals and providing advance organizers when introducing the activity, modeling task-related thinking and problem solving whenever these are not already familiar to students, and inducing metacognitive awareness and control of learning strategies.

The motivational picture is never complete without inclusion of these strategies for motivating students to learn. Even in learning situations in which students are confident that they can achieve success with reasonable effort, are aware of opportunities to earn rewards, and are motivated to engage in the activity because they are interested in the topic or enjoy the processes involved, they will not necessarily be motivated to learn unless you also stimulate and scaffold their learning efforts using some of the strategies presented in this chapter.

REFLECTION QUESTIONS

1. Why does the author emphasize motivation to learn over intrinsic motivation?
2. Why can't the value and dispositional aspects of motivation to learn be taught directly?
3. What does it mean to bring the lesson to the students and bring the students to the lesson?
4. What does it mean to say that teachers should scaffold students' engagement in learning activities to achieve an optimal match within the motivational zone of proximal development?
5. Is your identity simply some synthesis of the culturally defined roles you play, or is it something more than that? If so, what?
6. What are some possible selves that might influence students' motivation in classrooms? How might you shape or respond to them in ways that support the students' motivation to learn?
7. What is the best way to address students' self-esteem problems?
8. Representatives of academic disciplines sometimes define authentic activities as activities that call for students to do what disciplinary practitioners do, using the

discourse genres and inquiry tools that they use. Why does the author prefer a definition that emphasizes life applications?

9. What does it mean to say that the reach of learners' vision concerning the affordances embedded in potential learning opportunities limits their perceived options? How can teachers enrich this vision by scaffolding appreciation?

10. What does modeling convey about the functional value of behavior besides whether it results in success or failure?

11. Why might otherwise sensible and effective teachers act like those described in Box 9.3?

12. How might teachers cast themselves as enablers who provide self-actualizing opportunities and help students learn to exploit them?

13. Have you had transformative experiences through encounters with powerful ideas? How can you develop big ideas so as to pave the way for transformative experiences in your students?

14. The author suggests calling attention to unexpected, incongruous, exotic, or paradoxical aspects of content to create dissonance. However, this can be done poorly or carried too far. Identify some better and worse ways of creating dissonance with respect to three topics that you teach.

15. How might principles of conceptual change teaching apply to your curriculum?

16. Think of a few topics in your curriculum that currently do not engage your students. Can you think of ways to make this material more concrete and personally meaningful to the students using personal anecdotes, demonstrations, visuals, examples, analogies, stories, or cultural connections? Plan to incorporate these features the next time you teach the topics.

17. How might you challenge students to generate their own motivation to learn say, poetry?

18. Research suggests that you probably will not consistently introduce lessons and activities effectively unless you include attention to expectancy and value issues as part of a developed planning routine. What other considerations should go into your planning routine?

19. For at least one lesson that you teach or are likely to teach, write out an introduction that is likely to motivate your students to learn and a sequence of questions that is likely to produce thoughtful discourse structured around powerful ideas.

20. What does it mean to make the strange familiar or the familiar strange?

21. Write out some examples of motivational feedback that you might give to your students, especially when they are working on important but unexciting tasks.

22. Should teachers be encouraged to make learning fun for their students, or what?

23. An intrinsic motivational theorist might ask, "Instead of engaging in all of these manipulations to get students to engage in tasks that they are not much interested in, wouldn't it be simpler and better all around to change the tasks?" Is this good advice? Always, sometimes, or never?

REFERENCES

Alexander, P. (1997). Knowledge-seeking and self-schema: A case for the motivational dimensions of exposition. *Educational Psychologist, 32,* 80–94.

Alexander, P. (2003). The development of expertise: The journey from acclamation to proficiency. *Educational Researcher, 32*(8), 10–14.

Alexander, P., Fives, H., Buehl, M., & Mulhern, J. (2002). Teaching as persuasion. *Teaching and Teacher Education, 18,* 795–813.

Alton-Lee, A., Nuthall, G., & Patrick, J. (1993). Reframing classroom research: A lesson from the private world of children. *Harvard Educational Review, 63,* 50–84.

Alvermann, D., & Heron, A. (2001). Literacy identity work: Playing to learn with popular media. *Journal of Adolescent and Adult Literacy, 45,* 118–122.

Anderson, C., & Roth, K. (1989). Teaching for meaningful and self-regulated learning of science. In J. Brophy (Ed.), *Advances in research on teaching* (Vol. 1, pp. 265–309). Greenwich, CT: JAI.

Anderson, L., Brubaker, N., Alleman-Brooks, J., & Duffy, G. (1985). A qualitative study of seatwork in first-grade classrooms. *Elementary School Journal, 86,* 123–140.

Barron, B. (2006). Interest and self-sustained learning as catalysts of development: A learning ecology perspective. *Human Development, 49,* 193–224.

Baumeister, R. (1997). Identity, self-concept, and self-esteem: The self lost and found. In R. Hogan, J. Johnson, & S. Briggs (Eds.), *Handbook of personality psychology* (pp. 681–710). San Diego, CA: Academic Press.

Baumeister, R., Campbell, J., Krueger, J., & Vohs, K. (2003). Does high self-esteem cause better performance, interpersonal success, happiness, or healthier lifestyles? *Psychological Science in the Public Interest, 4,* 1–44.

Bettencourt, E., Gillett, M., Gall, M., & Hull, R. (1983). Effects of teacher enthusiasm training on student on-task behavior and achievement. *American Educational Research Journal, 20,* 435–450.

Blank, M., & White, S. (1999). Activating the zone of proximal development in the school: Obstacles and solutions. In P. Lloyd & C. Fernyhough (Eds.), *Lev Vygotsky: Critical assessments* (pp. 331–350). London: Routledge.

Blumenfeld, P., & Meece, J. (1988). Task factors, teacher behavior, and students' involvement and use of learning strategies in science. *Elementary School Journal, 88,* 235–250.

Blumenfeld, P., Puro, P., & Mergendoller, J. (1992). Translating motivation into thoughtfulness. In H. Marshall (Ed.), *Redefining student learning: Roots of educational change* (pp. 207–239). Norwood, NJ: Ablex.

Brophy, J., & Alleman, J. (1991). Activities as instructional tools: A framework for analysis and evaluation. *Educational Researcher, 20*(4), 9–23.

Brophy, J., & Kher, N. (1986). Teacher socialization as a mechanism for developing student motivation to learn. In R. Feldman (Ed.), *Social psychology applied to education* (pp. 257–288). New York: Cambridge University Press.

Brophy, J., Rohkemper, M., Rashid, H., & Goldberger, M. (1983). Relationships between teachers' presentations of classroom tasks and students' engagement in those tasks. *Journal of Educational Psychology, 75,* 544–552.

Bryant, F., & Veroff, J. (2007). *Savoring: A new model of positive experience.* Mahwah, NJ: Erlbaum.

Cabello, B., & Terrell, R. (1994). Making students feel like family: How teachers create warm and caring classroom climates. *Journal of Classroom Interaction, 29,* 17–23.

Certo, J., Cauley, K., Moxley, K., & Chafin, C. (2008). An argument for authenticity: Adolescents' perspectives on standards-based reform. *High School Journal, 91,* 26–39.

Csikzentmihalyi, M., Rathunde, K., & Whalen, S. (1993). *Talented teenagers: The roots of success and failure.* New York: Cambridge University Press.

Daisey, P., & Josè-Kampfner, C. (2002). The power of story to expand possible selves for Latina middle school students. *Journal of Adolescent and Adult Literacy, 45,* 578–587.

Dewey, J. (1938). *Experience and education.* New York: Collier.

Dewey, J. (1958). *Art as experience.* New York: Capricorn. (original work published in 1934)

Dillon, J. (Ed.). (1988). *Questioning and teaching: A manual of practice.* London: Croom Helm.

Dillon, J. (Ed.). (1990). *The practice of questioning.* New York: Routledge.

Eccles, J. (2009). Who am I and what am I going to do with my life? Personal and collective identities as motivators of action. *Educational Psychologist, 44,* 78–89.

Echevarria, M. (2003). Anomalies as a catalyst for middle school students' knowledge construction and scientific reasoning during science inquiry. *Journal of Educational Psychology, 95,* 357–374.

Egan, K. (1990). *Romantic understanding: The development of rationality and imagination, ages 8–15.* New York: Routledge.

Epstein, T. (2009). *Interpreting national history: Race, identity, and pedagogy in classrooms and communities.* New York: Routledge.

Flum, H., & Kaplan, A. (2006). Exploratory orientation as an educational goal. *Educational Psychologist, 41,* 99–110.

Ford, M. (1992). *Motivating humans: Goals, emotions, and personal agency beliefs.* Newbury Park, CA: Sage.

Frymier, A. (2002). Making content relevant to students. In J. Chesebro & J. McCroskey (Eds.), *Communication for teachers* (pp. 83–92). Boston: Allyn & Bacon.

Frymier, A., & Shulman, G. (1995). "What's in it for me?": Increasing content relevance to enhance students' motivation. *Communication Education, 44,* 40–50.

Girod, M. (2000). Rocks as windows into the past. *Science and Children, 56,* 72–75.

Girod, M., Rau, C., & Schepige, A. (2003). Appreciating the beauty of science ideas: Teaching for aesthetic understanding. *Science Education, 87,* 574–587.

Girod, M., & Wong, D. (2002). An aesthetic (Deweyan) perspective on science learning: Case studies of three fourth graders. *Elementary School Journal, 102,* 199–224.

Good, T., & Brophy, J. (2008). *Looking in classrooms* (10th ed.). Boston: Allyn & Bacon.

Gresalfi, M., Martin, T., Hand, V., & Greeno, J. (2009). Constructing competence: An analysis of student participation in the activity systems of mathematics classrooms. *Educational Studies in Mathematics, 70,* 49–70.

Green, S. (2002). Using an expectancy-value approach to examine teachers' motivational strategies. *Teaching and Teacher Education, 18,* 989–1005.

Hagger, M., & Chatzisarantis, L. (2006). Self-identity and the theory of planned behaviour: Between-and within-participants analyses. *British Journal of Social Psychology, 45,* 731–357.

Hannover, B. (1998). The development of self-concept and interests. In L. Hoffman, A. Krapp, A., Renninger, K. A., & Baumert, J. (Eds.), *Interest and learning: Proceedings of the Seeon Conference on Interest and Gender* (pp. 105–125). Kiel, Germany: Institute for Science and Education at the University of Kiel.

Hansen, D. (2006). Dewey's book of the moral self. In D. Hansen (Ed.), *John Dewey and our educational prospect: A critical engagement with Dewey's Democracy and Education* (pp. 165–188). Albany: State University of New York Press.

Higgins, E. T. (1987). Self-discrepancy: A theory relating self and affect. *Psychological Review, 94,* 319–340.

Jones, B., & Idol, L. (Eds.). (1990). *Dimensions of thinking and cognitive instruction.* Hillsdale, NJ: Erlbaum.

Kaplan, A., & Maehr, M. (2007). The contributions and prospects of goal orientation theory. *Educational Psychology Review, 19,* 141–184.

Kashdan, T., & Steger, M. (2007). Curiosity and pathways to well-being and meaning in life: Traits, states, and everyday behaviors. *Motivation and Emotion, 31,* 159–173.

Keller, J. (1987). Strategies for stimulating the motivation to learn. *Performance and Instruction, 26*(8), 1–7.

Kintsch, W. (1980). Learning from text, levels of comprehension, or: Why anyone would read a story anyway. *Poetics, 9,* 87–89.

Kohlberg, L. (1966). A cognitive-developmental analysis of children's sex-role concepts and attitudes. In E. Maccoby (Ed.), *The development of sex differences* (pp. 82–172). Stanford, CA: Stanford University Press.

Kunter, M., Tsai, Y., Klusmann, U., Brunner, M., Krauss, S., & Baumert, J. (2008). Students' and mathematics teachers' perceptions of teacher enthusiasm and instruction. *Learning and Instruction, 18,* 468–482.

Lane, D., Newman, D., & Bull, K. (1988). The relationship of student interest and advance organizer effectiveness. *Contemporary Educational Psychology, 13,* 15–25.

Lee, O., & Brophy, J. (1996). Motivational patterns observed in sixth- grade science classrooms. *Journal of Research in Science Teaching, 33,* 303–318.

Legault, L., Green-Demers, I., & Pelletier, L. (2006). Why do high school students lack motivation in the classroom? Toward an understanding of academic amotivation and the role of social support. *Journal of Educational Psychology, 98,* 567–582.

Long, J., & Hoy, A. (2006). Interested instructors: A composite portrait of individual differences and effectiveness. *Teaching and Teacher Education, 22,* 303–314.

MacIver, D., Young, E., & Washburn, B. (2002). Instructional practices and motivation during middle school (with special attention to science). In A. Wigfield & J. Eccles (Eds.), *Development of achievement motivation* (pp. 333–351). San Diego, CA: Academic Press.

Marks, H. (2000). Student engagement in instructional activity: Patterns in the elementary, middle, and high school years. *American Educational Research Journal, 37,* 153–184.

Markus, H., & Nurius, P. (1986). Possible selves. *American Psychologist, 41,* 954–969.

Marshall, H. (1987). Motivational strategies of three fifth-grade teachers. *Elementary School Journal, 88,* 135–150.

Marshall, H. (1994). Children's understanding of academic tasks: Work, play, or learning. *Journal of Research in Childhood Education, 9,* 35–46.

Martin, C., & Ruble, D. (2004). Children's search for gender cues: Cognitive perspectives on gender development. *Current Directions in Psychological Science, 13,* 67–70.

McCaslin, M. (2009). Co-regulation of student motivation and emergent identity. *Educational Psychologist, 44,* 137–146.

Middleton, J. (1995). A study of intrinsic motivation in the mathematics classroom: A personal constructs approach. *Journal for Research in Mathematics Education, 26,* 254–279.

Middleton, M., & Midgley, C. (2002). Beyond motivation: Middle school students' perceptions of press for understanding in math. *Contemporary Educational Psychology, 27,* 373–391.

Mottet, T., Garza, R., Beebe, S., Houser, M., Jurrells, S., & Furler, L. (2008). Instructional communication predictors of ninth-grade students' affective learning in math and science. *Communication Education, 57,* 333–355.

Newby, T. (1991). Classroom motivation: Strategies of first-year teachers. *Journal of Educational Psychology, 83,* 195–200.

Newmann, F. (1990). Qualities of thoughtful social studies classes: An empirical profile. *Journal of Curriculum Studies, 22,* 253–275.

Newmann, F. (Ed.). (1992). *Student engagement and achievement in American secondary schools.* New York: Teachers College Press.

Newton, D. (2000). *Teaching for understanding: What it is and how to do it.* London: Routledge/Falmer.

Nisan, M. (1992). Beyond intrinsic motivation: Cultivating a "sense of the desirable." In F. Oser, A. Dick, & J. Patry (Eds.), *Effective and responsible teaching: The new synthesis* (pp. 126–138). San Francisco: Jossey-Bass.

Nisan, M., & Shalif, Y. (2006). The sense of the worthy as a motivation for studying: The case of the Yeshiva. *Interchange, 37,* 363–394.

Nolen, S., & Ward, C. (2008). Sociocultural and situative approaches to studying motivation. In M. Maehr, S. Karabenick, & T. Urdan (Eds.), *Social psychological perspectives (Advances in motivation and achievement series, Vol. 15* (pp. 425–460). Bingley, UK: Emerald.

Ogle, D. (1986). K-W-L: A teaching model that develops active reading of expository text. *Reading Teacher, 39,* 564–570.

Oldfather, P., & West, J. (1999). *Learning through children's eyes: Social constructivism and the desire to learn.* Washington, DC: American Psychological Association.

Ortiz, R. (1983). Generating interest in reading. *Journal of Reading, 27,* 113–119.

Patrick, H., Turner, J., Meyer, D., & Midgley, C. (2003). How teachers establish psychological environments during the first days of school: Associations with avoidance in mathematics. *Teachers College Record, 105,* 1521–1558.

Posner, G., Strike, K., Hewson, K., & Gertzog, W. (1982). Accommodation of a scientific conception: Toward a theory of conceptual change. *Science Education, 66,* 211–228.

Pugh, K. (2002). Teaching for transformative experiences in science: An investigation of the effectiveness of two instructional elements. *Teachers College Record, 104,* 1101–1137.

Pugh, K., & Girod, M. (2007). Science, art and experience: Constructing a science pedagogy from Dewey's aesthetics. *Journal of Science Teacher Education, 18,* 9–27.

Raphael, L., Pressley, M., & Mohan, L. (2008). Engaging instruction in middle school classrooms: An observational study of nine teachers. *Elementary School Journal, 109,* 61–81.

Reed, J., & Schallert, D. (1993). The nature of involvement in academic discourse tasks. *Journal of Educational Psychology, 85,* 253–266.

Reeve, J., Jang, H., Hardre, P., & Omura, M. (2002). Providing a rationale in an autonomy-supportive way to motivate others during an uninteresting activity. *Motivation and Emotion, 26,* 183–207.

Reiss, S. (2004). Multifaceted nature of intrinsic motivation: The theory of 16 basic desires. *Review of General Psychology, 8,* 179–193.

Renninger, K. A. (2009). Interest and identity development in instruction: An inductive model. *Educational Psychologist, 44,* 105–118.

Renninger, K. A., Sansone, C., & Smith, J. (2004). Love of learning. In C. Peterson & M. Seligman (Eds.), *Character strengths and virtues: A handbook and classification* (pp. 161–179). New York: Oxford University Press.

Richardson, P., & Eccles, J. (2007). Rewards of reading: Toward the development of possible selves and identities. *International Journal of Educational Research, 46,* 341–356.

Rohrkemper, M., & Bershon, B. (1984). Elementary school students' reports of the causes and effects of problem difficulty in mathematics. *Elementary School Journal, 85,* 127–147.

Rohrkemper, M., & Corno, L. (1988). Success and failure on classroom tasks: Adaptive learning and classroom teaching. *Elementary School Journal, 88,* 297–312.

Rosenshine, B., & Guenther, J. (1992). Using scaffolds for teaching higher level cognitive strategies. In J. Keefe & H. Walberg (Eds.), *Teaching for thinking* (pp. 35–47). Reston, VA: National Association of Secondary School Principals.

Roth, K. (1996). Making learners and concepts central: A conceptual change approach to learner-centered fifth-grade American history planning and teaching. In J. Brophy (Ed.), *Advances in research on teaching* (Vol. 6, *Teaching and learning history,* pp. 115–182). Greenwich, CT: JAI.

Roth, K. (2002). Talking to understand science. In J. Brophy (Ed.), *Social constructivist teaching: Affordances and constraints* (pp. 197–262). New York: Elsevier Science.

Ryan, R., Huta, V., & Deci, E. (2006). Living well: A self-determination theory perspective on eudaimonia. *Journal of Happiness Studies, 9,* 139–170.

Sansone, C., Weir, C., Harpster, L., & Morgan, C. (1992). Once a boring task always a boring task? Interest as a self-regulatory mechanism. *Journal of Personality and Social Psychology, 63,* 379–390.

Schunk, D., & Hanson, A. (1985). Peer models: Influence on children's self-efficacy and achievement. *Journal of Educational Psychology, 77*, 313–322.

Schwartz, S., & Waterman, A. (2006). Changing interests: A longitudinal study of intrinsic motivation for personally salient activities. *Journal of Research in Personality, 40*, 1119–1136.

Seidel, T., Rimmele, R., & Prenzel, M. (2005). Clarity and coherence of lesson goals as a scaffold for student learning. *Learning and Instruction, 15*, 539–556.

Sivan, E., & Roehler, L. (1986). Motivational statements in explicit teacher explanations and their relationship to students' metacognition in reading. *National Reading Conference Yearbook, 35*, 178–184.

Spires, H., & Donley, J. (1998). Prior knowledge activation: Inducing engagement with informational texts. *Journal of Educational Psychology, 90*, 249–260.

Steger, M., Kashdan, T., & Oishi, S. (2008). Being good by doing good: Daily eudaimonic activity and well-being. *Journal of Research in Personality, 42*, 22–42.

Tharp, R., & Gallimore, R. (1988). *Rousing minds to life: Teaching, learning, and school in social context.* Cambridge, UK: Cambridge University Press.

Thorkildsen, T., Nolen, S., & Fournier, J. (1994). What is fair? Children's critiques of practices that influence motivation. *Journal of Educational Psychology, 86*, 475–486.

Turner, J., Meyer, D., Cox, K., Logan, C., Di Cintio, M., & Thomas, C. (1998). Creating contexts for involvement in mathematics. *Journal of Educational Psychology, 90*, 730–745.

Turner, J., Midgley, C., Meyer, D., Gheen, M., Anderman, E., Kang, Y., & Patrick, H. (2002). The classroom environment and students' reports of avoidance strategies in mathematics: A multimethod study. *Journal of Educational Psychology, 94*, 88–106.

Turner, J., Meyer, D., Midgley, C., & Patrick, H. (2003). Teacher discourse and sixth-graders' reported affect and achievement behaviors in two high mastery/high performance mathematics classrooms. *Elementary School Journal, 103*, 357–382.

Urdan, T. (2001). Contextual influences on motivation and performance: An examination of achievement goal structures. In F. Salili, C. Y. Chiu, & Y. Y. Hong (Eds.), *Student motivation: The culture and context of learning* (pp. 171–201). New York: Plenum.

Van Etten, S., Pressley, M., McInerney, D., & Liem, A. (2008). College seniors' theory of their academic motivation. *Journal of Educational Psychology, 100*, 812–828.

Walker, C., Greene, B., & Mansell, R. (2006). Identification with academics, intrinsic/extrinsic motivation, and self-efficacy as predictors of cognitive engagement. *Learning and Individual Differences, 16*, 1–12.

Waterman, A. (2005). When effort is enjoyed: Two studies of intrinsic motivation for personally salient activities. *Motivation and Emotion, 29*, 165–188.

Waterman, A., Schwartz, S., & Conti, R. (2008). The implications of two conceptions of happiness (hedonic enjoyment and eudaimonia) for the understanding of intrinsic motivation. *Journal of Happiness Studies, 9*, 41–79.

Weinstein, C., & Mayer, R. (1986). The teaching of learning strategies. In M. Wittrock (Ed.), *Handbook of research on teaching* (3rd ed., pp. 315–327). New York: Macmillan.

Wong, E., Pugh, K., & The Dewey Ideas Group at Michigan State University. (2001). Learning science: A Deweyan perspective. *Journal of Research in Science Teaching, 38*, 317–336.

Zirkel, S. (2000). Social intelligence: The development and maintenance of purposive behavior. In R. Bar-On & J. Parker (Eds.), *The handbook of emotional intelligence: Theory, development, assessment, and application at home, school, and in the workplace* (pp. 3–27). San Francisco: Jossey-Bass.

10

Socializing Uninterested or Alienated Students

Apathy, not discouragement, is the ultimate motivational problem facing teachers. Students who display learned helplessness, failure syndrome, or related performance concerns frequently lose their focus on learning and require special motivational treatment (see chapter 5). However, they usually value learning and would like to be able to complete learning activities successfully.

In contrast, *apathetic students* are uninterested in or even alienated from school learning: They don't find it meaningful or worthwhile, don't want to engage in it, don't value it even when they know that they can achieve success with reasonable effort, and may even resist it if they fear that it will lead to unwanted responsibilities or make them into someone that they do not want to become (Goodnow, 1996). You will need to make sustained efforts to resocialize such students' attitudes and beliefs: show them what it means to engage in school activities with motivation to learn, nurture their desire to do so, and follow up with appropriate structuring and scaffolding of their learning efforts.

Students who have not developed motivation-to-learn schemas view school activities as imposed demands rather than learning opportunities, so they engage in them (if at all) only enough to stay out of trouble. They give little consideration to learning goals, let alone to appreciating the value of the learning or taking pride in their accomplishments.

There is little theory-based research on strategies for dealing with uninterested or alienated students. However, it is possible to suggest several sets of principles based on what is known about the socialization of value-based motivation in homes, schools, and work settings (Baumrind, 1991; Damon, 1995; Epstein, 1989; Grusec & Goodnow, 1994).

CONSIDER CONTRACTING AND INCENTIVE SYSTEMS

Students who find no value in school activities are candidates for *contracting* (offering incentives in exchange for specified accomplishments). Incentives are especially useful with students who know what they are supposed to do and are capable of doing it if they put their minds to it, but currently are not conscientious or motivated enough to do so *consistently* (i.e., apathetic or alienated students whose motivational problems primarily involve value issues rather than expectancy issues).

Contracting provides built-in opportunities for teacher–student collaboration in negotiating expectations and rewards. If perfect performance is currently an unreasonable expectation, negotiations might yield specifications calling for rewarding a level of improvement that the student views as reasonable and the teacher is willing to accept (at least for now). Contracting also provides opportunities to offer students choices of rewards, thus ensuring that the intended reward is experienced as such.

In *contingency contracting*, you confer with the student about possible alternatives and then jointly draw up a contract that specifies what the student will be expected to do in order to earn contingent rewards. The contract can be purely oral, although it helps to formalize it by having the student write down its details. Solicit the student's input about the extent and nature of required accomplishments (challenging but doable with reasonable effort) and desired rewards. If appropriate, specify several levels of potential accomplishment linked to differential levels of reward, so the student could earn a lesser reward even if he does not qualify for his most preferred reward.

Contracting can be subsumed within an "earned points" version of a *token economy system*, in which students earn point credits by fulfilling contracts. The credits then can be spent on rewards selected from a menu. The biggest rewards cost the most points and thus require the most sustained levels of effort and accomplishment.

Most motivation theorists urge caution in using such incentive systems because they can undermine students' intrinsic motivation to engage in the rewarded activities. Where such intrinsic motivation is lacking, however, there is nothing to undermine. Thus, at least in areas where apathetic students clearly have no intrinsic motivation, you have nothing to lose by using extrinsic incentives.

However, the qualifications and guidelines on how to use rewards (see chapter 6) still apply, especially if you want to move apathetic students away from dependence on these incentives and toward self-regulated motivation to learn. Therefore, avoid offering incentives in ways that reinforce these students' tendencies to view lessons and assignments as unwelcome impositions that must be endured for extrinsic reasons. Instead, *use contracting approaches that include collaborative goal setting, and take advantage of the opportunities provided by the goal-setting negotiations to help the students begin to appreciate the value of what they are learning.*

Emphasize authentic activities, phrase goal statements in terms of learning accomplishments rather than tasks completed, and use qualitative criteria for assessing progress. Revisit these goals and assessment criteria during post-activity debriefings, and elicit summaries and critiques of accomplishments from the students themselves. If the activity has yielded some noteworthy product, offer to display it or suggest that the student share it with classmates or family members.

The point here is not merely to deflect attention from extrinsic rewards, but to *provide the students with concepts and language that they can use to appreciate and take pride in their accomplishments.* Students can't appreciate what they don't see or understand. They need concepts and language to help them articulate learning goals, assess progress, and think about end products in terms of understandings, skills, or accomplishments (not merely task completion or compliance with minimal requirements).

Richly descriptive language is especially important for practice activities in subjects such as grammar, computation, or penmanship. To begin with, students should be aware that such practice is important because the ultimate goals—writing and problem solving in life situations—cannot be accomplished efficiently until key subskills are mastered to levels of smooth, accurate performance, so they can be applied "effortlessly" when needed. Analogies to the importance of skill practice in preparing for athletic or musical performance might be useful here.

In addition, provide concepts and language to describe the immediate outcomes of learning efforts. It is more meaningful and motivating to think about "understanding why slavery flourished in the south but not in the north" rather than "studying history," to "learn to divide when there is both a decimal point and a remainder" rather than to "do your math problems," or to "learn to adjust your writing position so that you stay on the line and maintain the same slant as you move across the page" rather than to "practice your penmanship." Use richly descriptive goal characterizations like these when introducing such activities. As students begin to work on them, phrase your feedback with reference to these goals. In assessing their completed work, refer to specific, qualitative aspects of their performance instead of confining yourself to grades or general evaluative comments.

It *may* be helpful to explain to apathetic students why learning can be empowering and self-actualizing. However, it almost certainly *will* be helpful to arrange conditions that allow them to experience these outcomes directly. Therefore, whether or not you use incentive systems, be sure to negotiate goals and provide feedback in language that they can use to plan and assess their learning. *By engaging these students in the processes of setting goals and reflecting on their work, you lead them through first-hand experiences in what it means to engage in academic activities with motivation to learn.*

As these processes become more familiar, the students can begin to engage in them more naturally without feeling pressed to respond to unfamiliar demands. This will leave more of their cognitive resources free to think about the purposes, meanings, and potential applications of what they are learning. Eventually they should begin to do this spontaneously and thus start to generate and build on their own motivation to learn (Thorkildsen, 1988; Vallacher & Wegner, 1987).

DEVELOP AND WORK WITHIN A CLOSE RELATIONSHIP WITH THE STUDENT

Chapter 2 emphasizes that you can become your own most valuable motivational tool by building close relationships with students and establishing yourself as a supportive and helpful resource person. *It is important to do this with all students, but especially with uninterested or alienated students who don't find much value in school learning.* These students are already moving in undesirable directions, so they need to be turned around. You will need to exert counterpressures against whatever forces have led them to become apathetic or resistant learners. If failure syndrome problems are also present, you will have to work on these too, using the techniques described in chapter 5. Sometimes students dismiss a content area or type of learning activity as boring or useless because they fear failure and want to establish an excuse for not trying hard.

Whether or not they are compounded by failure syndrome problems, well-established apathy or resistance problems will not be cleared up quickly with a brief talk or a single key experience. *You will need to work for and accept gradual progress, and to stay patient and supportive even if you encounter skepticism or resistance.* Be prepared for such reactions, at least from students whose apathy has "hardened" into a well-articulated belief system. After all, why should these students take seriously your attempts to portray school learning as worthwhile if their own prior experiences tell them otherwise?

To establish a potential for succeeding with apathetic students, show them that you care about them personally as individuals and are concerned about their present and future best interests. *Help them to see that their prior experiences have been limited or distorted*—that despite the grading system, the basic reason for engaging in learning activities is to acquire the empowerment and self-actualization potential that these activities are designed to develop (see Box 10.1). A great deal of modeling, socialization, and reflective discussion of learning experiences will be required to accomplish this agenda. For these efforts to have much effect, your relationships with these students will have to be such that they value your opinions and want to please you.

Box 10.1 Self-Actualization Motives for School Learning

Furst and Steele (1986) interviewed older adults who had enrolled (not necessarily for credit) in courses at universities, asking them why they had done so. Their responses are interesting because most of them focused on self-actualization rather than extrinsic reasons.

1. *Keeping up/becoming involved.* To keep up with what is going on in the world; reexamine my perspectives on contemporary issues; become better able to cope with the challenges of daily living; become more effective as a citizen; improve my ability to participate in community work; participate in group activity; or share a common interest with my spouse or friend.
2. *Fulfillment.* To develop an unfulfilled talent; supplement a narrow previous education; pursue earlier interests that I could not get around to before; or complete some previously unfinished learning.
3. *Stimulation and self-maintenance.* To get relief from boredom; get a change from the routine of home or work; maintain or enhance my self-respect; keep my mind active and alert by making intellectual demands on it; or feel a sense of achievement.
4. *Practical achievement.* To acquire knowledge of a particular subject; learn a specific skill; feel a sense of achievement; prepare myself for retirement living; or satisfy a desire to develop new interests.
5. *Self-understanding/personal adjustment.* To gain insight into personal problems; get help with a crisis in my personal life; or reexamine myself and my role in life.
6. *Formal attainment and recognition.* To earn a degree, diploma, or certificate; or increase others' respect for me.
7. *Qualifying for privileges.* To qualify for privileges such as use of library or swimming pool, or to participate in group activities.
8. *Prerequisite knowledge.* To acquire knowledge to help with other educational courses or to gain insight into human relations.
9. *Intellectual stimulation and enjoyment.* To learn just for the joy of learning or to satisfy an inquiring mind.

Most of these reasons for learning appear just as applicable to K–12 students as to older learners. You can cultivate their development in your students by frequently making reference to them and by asking questions that lead students to discover them.

In getting to know apathetic students, take note of the situations in which they do or do not accomplish learning goals, and adjust accordingly. Also, get them talking about their school experiences in ways that help you to capitalize on their existing motivation. Ask them about content areas and types of activities or learning formats that they find conducive to learning, and about ways that other learning experiences might be made more worthwhile. Simply providing such students with opportunities for input is likely to improve your relationships with them and their attitudes toward learning. Also, their responses may include specific suggestions that lead to improved performance.

DISCOVER AND BUILD ON EXISTING INTERESTS

Another reason for developing good relationships with apathetic students is to learn about their values and interests. Some of these might provide starting points for nurturing their motivation to learn. For example, *almost any substantive interest can become the basis for developing literacy skills*. Students might read books or magazines about sports and entertainment personalities, automobile customizing, computer games, or other topics popular in the youth culture, then write reports summarizing and reflecting on what they read. This may be less desirable than having them read and write about science or social studies topics, but at least it provides opportunities for applying literacy skills and perhaps developing some important dispositions (reading for key ideas, reflecting on and communicating about them). You might consider suggesting that these students subscribe to favorite magazines, or give them subscriptions as gifts or as rewards for fulfilling achievement contracts. Other possibilities include arranging for students to follow up on recent experiences by reading about topics featured in field trips or popular movies or television shows, as well as encouraging students to recommend books to one another and discuss things they have read (Williams, 1996).

Certain apathetic students will possess social motivation that you can use to substitute in part for their lack of motivation to learn. They might learn little or nothing if left to work individually but accomplish some important learning goals if paired with classmates who are more oriented toward learning. You might make frequent use of partner learning formats with these students in the short run, while developing their capacities for self-regulated learning. You might also arrange for them to spend time with older students or alumni who value learning and could share life experiences that would help them to see that they should too (Tjas, Nelsen, & Taylor, 1997).

HELP STUDENTS TO DEVELOP AND SUSTAIN MORE POSITIVE ATTITUDES TOWARD SCHOOL WORK

To develop stable individual interests in apathetic students and use these as bases for motivating their learning, you need to go beyond inducing curiosity or situational interest. In addition, *help these students to see that it is in their own best interests to learn what you are trying to teach them*.

Mordecai Nisan (1992) made a similar point in stating that schooling does not aim to provide satisfaction of what is *desired* by students, but instead to cultivate in them what the culture construes as *desirable*. Ultimately, schooling is based on values rooted in images of a state of human perfection that is worth aspiring to attain. Apathetic students need help in understanding that they owe it to themselves to take advantage of the opportunities that schooling offers to develop self-actualized personal identities, as well as the knowledge, skills, values, and dispositions that they will need to function effectively in society.

When phrased in such language, the sense of the desirable sounds are very abstract. However, Nisan's research showed that first-, fourth-, and seventh-graders already possessed intuitive versions of this value. When asked to express opinions about a scenario that involved a child who did not attend school, large majorities at all three grade levels viewed failure to attend school as undesirable, even when the child was depicted as living in a country in which school attendance was not required and not common. Most supported laws requiring school attendance, based on concern about children's long-term well-being. They viewed schooling as necessary for proper development.

At some level, students understand that it is in their own best interests not only to attend school but to strive to accomplish learning goals. Apathetic students have suppressed this realization, so you will have to help them rediscover it and confront its implications through sympathetic yet persistent comments and questions. Emphasize that securing their long-run best interests requires progress in all aspects of the curriculum, not just the ones they enjoy.

Just as intrinsic motivation resides in persons, not activities, the same is true of negative reactions to school. Emphasize this when working with students who view learning activities as aversive. If these activities are well suited to their current learning needs, the students' aversive experiences are caused by their own negative attitudes and expectations, not by anything inherent to the activities themselves. Other students find these activities meaningful, worthwhile, and even enjoyable; they will too if they learn to engage in them with a more positive mindset.

Green-Demers, Pelletier, Stewart, and Gushue (1998) found that learners could sustain their motivation to work carefully on necessary but boring practice tasks by taking steps to make the tasks more interesting or to remind themselves of their importance. Productive motivation-boosting strategies included: challenge enhancement (challenging themselves by trying to perform the tasks more quickly, efficiently, or perfectly), introduction of variety (juggling the order of subtasks or trying out new ways of approaching them), and generating self-relevant rationales (reminding themselves why the tasks were important and would support progress toward larger goals).

Csikzentmihalyi (1993) has noted that *people can learn to experience flow even in routine activities if they seek out challenges and relish stretching their limits.* For example, they might "complexify" an otherwise boring activity by trying to do it artistically, seeking to increase their efficiency, or setting goals that convert the activity into something more challenging and interesting. In school, students can develop strategies for managing their affective responses to learning activities, and use these strategies to avoid becoming distracted by boredom, frustration, or other negative emotions. You can assist by helping your students make efficient use of the coping strategies they have developed on their own, as well as by teaching them new ones.

Oldfather (1992) interviewed fifth- and sixth-graders about their strategies for getting started and staying focused on boring tasks. Several emphasized accepting the idea that there was a significant purpose behind everything they were asked to do. For example, Suki found her science project boring but believed that "I have to think of it as important, because if you thought it wasn't important, you wouldn't do anything about it." Phil identified two factors that helped him overcome resistance to a task: observing peers enjoying the task and gaining a sense of competence (recognizing that he could "figure it out" if he applied himself, and thus expand his repertoire of knowledge and skills).

McCaslin and Good (1996) spoke of *scaffolding students' motivation by asking them questions such as the following*:

Do you like the unit we have been studying? How come? (Why not?)
What about _____ interests (bores) you?
Do you think that when you like something or find it interesting it is easier to learn? Is it easier to remember?
Are there ways that you can try to make work more interesting or fun for you?
What are some of the things you do?
Does that seem to help you learn?
Why do you suppose that is?
Have you ever tried _____? (p. 20)

Besides calling students' attention to useful strategies, such scaffolding encourages honest communication because it "legitimizes" the students' view that engagement in learning activities is sometimes boring or aversive. It doesn't endorse this view, but it acknowledges that the students believe it and makes it OK to talk about it.

Making Work More Enjoyable or Satisfying

Many suggestions have been made to adults who would like to derive more satisfaction from their jobs. You can adapt these suggestions as ways to help apathetic students learn to take more satisfaction from their school work.

Waitley and Witt (1985) emphasized that work fulfillment resides at least as much in the worker's attitude as in the work itself. They told of three construction workers who were asked to talk about their jobs. The first mostly complained about negative aspects (demanding boss, frustrations caused by bad weather or poor materials). The second emphasized the steps involved in carrying out discrete tasks (mixing mortar, positioning a brick properly, troweling and scraping). The third worker, who derived the most satisfaction from the job, explained that he was building a cathedral!

Waitley and Witt (1985) identified several techniques used by workers to make their jobs more rewarding and enjoyable:

- Focus more on what you expect to accomplish than on the difficulties you expect to encounter
- Develop plans and goal sequences to guide your work but also get feedback and be prepared to revise plans when necessary
- Emphasize perseverance and flexibility over attempts to be perfect from the beginning
- Make routine work more interesting by treating it as a game, trying to surpass self-imposed quotas, do individual portions perfectly, or discover how you can add personal creativity to it
- Learn to enjoy the challenge of solving problems and to take satisfaction in a job well done
- Congregate with people who share similar attitudes and expectations, while avoiding people who lack goals or who are more into complaining than coping.

Cameron and Elusorr (1986) also offered suggestions for making work more interesting. Most are based on psychological principles but some are based on Zen philosophy, especially the notion of present focus.

Present focus. If you stay absorbed in what you are doing, you won't be watching the clock. Therefore, when you show up for a task, really show up: Be there, pay close attention to what you are doing, focus on it, and do it fully. If you catch your mind wandering, notice where it went and why. Make a note of any business that needs to be attended to later, but then refocus on the task at hand.

Rituals. Starter rituals help you to get into present focus. For example, a "clearing ritual" in which you set up your equipment or clear your desk and arrange your papers might be a useful transition from other activities into getting ready to study or work.

Ride the waves. Don't let situations that are imperfect or do not work out well gnaw at you. Care about what you do, do your best, analyze and try to deal with problems, but don't give up or do less than your best merely because you know that things are not going to be perfect.

A personalized approach. Bring creativity to the job. If you must deal with certain recurring difficulties, stop looking at them as handicaps and begin to view them as opportunities or challenges. If things are going so smoothly that you get bored, return to present focus by striving to meet personally set goals or varying your routines.

Make a game of it. Turn work into play by creating a game that you can play while doing the job. A medical technician might occasionally take time out to view slides as if she were an art critic, a bartender might become a connoisseur of cliches that he hears from boring customers, a grocery bagger might try to pack items so that they come out level at the fill line, and a waitress might learn the habits of regulars and make bets with herself on their orders.

See your work as an art form. Any action can be performed with a sense of aesthetics, so seek ways to do your work gracefully or to produce an end product that is visually or otherwise pleasing in addition to functional.

See your work as a teacher. Discover what there is to learn about it. Analyze when you are bored and when you are not, to get ideas about how to minimize boredom. Also, learn more about the work itself (possibilities for using equipment, ways to do the job more efficiently, shortcuts to use and cues for recognizing when they are relevant).

Find a rhythm to your work. Finding natural rhythms or cycles in work can help make it more enjoyable and reduce the sense that "it never lets up." If possible, take time away from some continuous task so as to vary it with another task and give yourself a chance to relax from that particular form of effort.

Unwind. When pressure gets to you, let your mind slip into something more comfortable. Alternate periods of intense concentration with brief periods of relaxation. If you can't walk around or take a break, sit back, close your eyes, and meditate briefly. Sharing jokes and finding humor on the job help too.

Seek excellence. Learn to seek excellence in doing your work and taking satisfaction from doing so. Use the following techniques: *just the details* (Pay attention to each detail of the job and do it carefully. This combines present focus with the notion of taking pride in each separate small piece of the job as part of what is involved in completing the job as a whole successfully) and *your life depends on it* (Do the work as if your life depended on doing it well. Think of it as something that you are going to dedicate to people you care about or are going to sign with your name when you finish).

Students develop some of these techniques on their own, although often only the less adaptive ones (see Box 10.2). You might teach them some of the more adaptive techniques, which should help them to derive satisfaction in the process of carrying out assignments and to sustain the self-regulation needed to see the work through to completion. Techniques for making work more enjoyable should go a long way toward reducing apathy and resistance. However, they apply more to routine tasks calling for expert performance than to tasks designed as learning experiences for novices. Consequently, *even if you do all of the things already suggested in this chapter, you will still need to socialize apathetic students' motivation to learn.*

SOCIALIZE APATHETIC STUDENTS' MOTIVATION TO LEARN

Values and attitudes ordinarily are acquired primarily through exposure to respected *models* who exhibit them, rather than through more typical instruction. However, they also can be socialized through *persuasive communication* (if students accept the message) and developed through *participation in powerful learning experiences* that foster them. You can socialize motivation to learn indirectly through modeling, persuasion, and scaffolding of students' learning experiences, but you cannot transmit it directly through instruction because it includes elements of emotional involvement and personal commitment that can come only from the students themselves (Gagne', Briggs, & Wager, 1988).

Socializing motivation to learn is difficult with apathetic students who have not had much exposure to experiences that help them understand what it means to engage in learning activities with the intention of gaining the benefits they were designed to develop. The task is even more challenging with alienated students who have come to view schooling as aversive, because it requires changing existing attitudes and values in addition to building new ones.

You cannot force students to change their attitudes and values, not even with sanctions such as punishments or failing grades. You may be able to force them to do at least a minimum amount of work by requiring them to complete assignments during recess periods, after school, or in in-school detention programs. However, getting work out of students is not the same as motivating them to learn. *Therefore, it is better to minimize your reliance on coercive methods and instead build and work within more productive teacher-student relationships.*

Apathetic students need consistent application of the strategies described in chapter 9, supplemented by more individualized treatment tailored to their personal characteristics and needs. *Attempts to develop their motivation to learn need to be relentless, yet subtle.* You won't get far if the students perceive you as nagging them, manipulating them, or attempting to force your will on them. Instead, *help them to see you as enabling or empowering them* by opening doors to self-actualization and teaching them to exploit unrecognized potentials.

> ### Box 10.2   Students' Coping Strategies
>
> Students develop strategies for coping with situations in which they find school-work aversive or discouraging. McCaslin (1990) interviewed sixth graders about how they handled the "hard stuff" in mathematics. The following excerpts are from interviews with best friends. Both girls persistently tried to solve math problems, but the first did so mostly to get finished so that she could interact with her friends. She made strategic use of fantasies connected with this social goal as a way to help her get through the rough spots:
>
>> A lot of times I get sick of things so I just want to stop. And I do… I always, whenever I'm working and I just get sick of working, I just stop because I can't stand it anymore. I think of things that I like to do. Like in school, I'm going to play with my friends, I think of all the things that are fun that we do, and stuff. But I have to get this done and right before I can go to do that. (pp. 42–43)
>
> In contrast, her friend focused on learning with understanding (not just getting correct answers), but was less successful in avoiding the frustration and worry that accompanied failure to solve difficult problems easily. Lacking her friend's ability to use fantasy strategically, she had to distract herself by engaging in alternative activities.
>
>> Well, I think I'm going to get them all wrong. And I kind of feel like I have to get up and walk around and think about it. I feel like I have to stop and work on something else for a little bit. I might get up and work on spelling for a minute 'cause that's pretty easy and I don't have to think about it, 'cause spelling I just know the answers and they're right there. I can't think about the math and what I'm going to do…(It's time for a break) when I get pretty frustrated, I think to myself "You can't do this," and I start tearing, I start biting my pencil. Then I know I have to get up and do something else. I just get so frustrated with it I can't think.… I start to fiddle with my hands, go like that. I know I have to do something else. 'Cause I really get mad. I don't take a real long (break) time, maybe just 10 minutes. Then I come back to work again. Just to get it out of my mind for a minute. (p. 43)
>
> Students differ dramatically in the strategies they employ for setting goals, addressing task demands, and seeking to make "repairs" when their initial efforts do not succeed. You can help apathetic or discouraged students learn to cope with situational pressures by teaching them strategies for doing so. However, emphasize strategies that help students to see value and take satisfaction in the work over strategies that merely provide temporary relief from what they continue to view as an aversive situation.

Apathetic students need the same curiosity-, interest-, and reflection-stimulating experiences that other students do, but they need to encounter them more frequently and carry them out in more personal, intense, and sustained ways. They especially need to be stimulated to reflect on and communicate about their learning. Therefore, *keep focusing them on the self-actualizing potential of learning experiences* by asking them questions about the content or by making assignments that require them to think about and appreciate new insights, to form and explain opinions, to develop explanations, or to make connections or applications. Scaffold their engagement in learning activities and their post- activity reflections to make sure that they experience empowering or self-actualizing outcomes. Your goal is to *induce them to identify with these experiences*—to connect learning experiences with their self-concepts and to begin to develop images of their ideal selves that cast them as open-minded, active learners (see Box 10.3).

To the extent that apathetic students are open to considering it and capable of understanding it, consider trying a "hard sell" approach to socializing their motivation to learn. Perhaps begin by informing them that they have missed the boat on some important opportunities for self-actualization, and that you want to give them a second chance.

Ask them questions to initiate discussions about why schools and libraries exist, why people go to museums or watch educational programs, why they read newspapers and magazines, and why they travel and seek other opportunities to broaden their lives.

Box 10.3   Develop Students' Self-Schemas as Motivated Learners

Markus and Nurius (1986) have developed the concept of possible selves—cognitive representations of oneself in the future. Possible selves represent the selves that a person could become, would like to become, or is afraid of becoming. To the extent that people have developed clear notions of possible selves, they can mobilize their energies toward becoming their ideal selves and avoiding movement in the direction of possible selves that they do not want to develop.

Overall movement toward ideal possible selves is supported by the development of *self-schemas* in particular domains of functioning. Cross and Markus (1994) showed that competent functioning in a domain requires both domain-specific ability and a self-schema for this ability. Optimal progress in mathematics, for example, requires both steady development of needed mathematical knowledge and recognition that one possesses this knowledge and can use it to solve problems.

Self-schemas represent one's domain-specific abilities and one's experiences in the domain. *Schematic* students possess well-developed self-schemas in a domain. They can use these self-schemas to make quick and confident judgments, to adapt flexibly to different information-processing goals, and to accurately retrieve information relevant to the domain. They are sensitive to schema-relevant information and pay close attention to it. As a result, they are attuned to schema-relevant situations and ready to exercise schema-relevant abilities when needed. They value these self-schemas, assigning them critical personal importance.

In contrast, students who are *aschematic* in that same domain have not developed well-articulated and valued self-schemas. They may possess as much domain-specific ability as schematic students and may even display equivalent competence when pressured or motivated to do so. However, they are not as likely as schematic students to seek out opportunities to activate their domain-specific competencies, recognize these opportunities when they arise, or exploit them as fully or persistently.

These ideas about possible selves and self-schemas apply well to the ideas presented in this book about the development of motivation to learn as a general disposition. Learning situations (in or out of school) constitute one important domain of functioning in life. People who develop well-articulated self-schemas relating to this domain will tend to recognize and value learning situations and to engage in them with motivation to learn. More generally, their possible selves will include ideals featuring an open, active mind and a tendency to be reflective about their experience. They will also recognize passive or closed-minded individuals as possible selves to be avoided.

In contrast, the kinds of apathetic students discussed in this chapter are aschematic in the domain of motivation to learn. The experiences and socialization influences that have shaped their development have not led them to understand what it means to engage in learning activities with motivation to learn, to value doing so as part of becoming a fully self-actualized person, or to develop aspirations for higher education and the kinds of occupations that require it.

This may also be true of some of your more academically motivated students, especially if they come from lower socioeconomic or minority backgrounds. Any aspirations to higher education that these aschematic students may have are more likely to be nonfunctional, wishful thinking or fantasies rather than informed decisions accompanied by implementation plans for goal pursuit (Day, Borkowski, Deitmeyer, Howsepian, & Saenz, 1992; Dunkel, 2000; Kendzierski & Whitaker, 1997; Oettingen & Mayer, 2002; Yowell, 2002). You will need to help these aschematic students by providing them with opportunities for needed experiences, scaffolding their engagement in the experiences, and inducing them to reflect on what they have accomplished and its implications for their self-schemas and future possible selves.

Oyserman, Bybee, and Terry (2006) developed a possible-selves intervention for low-income and minority eighth graders. It was designed to help them develop more schematic possible selves as successful students who cared about school and were willing and able to meet its demands through persistent efforts and self-regulated learning. Compared to control students, program participants showed improved motivation and conduct, better attendance, and better grades and standardized test scores.

Also, model and provide examples of ways that people with active minds can bring the world to themselves by using their own resources, without depending on other people or media to bring things to them. Draw on examples from your own life to illustrate motivation to learn and the self-talk that accompanies it, while *articulating values such as the following*:

Get worthwhile payoffs from your investments of time and effort. Whenever you engage in some activity (and especially when your engagement is required), do so in ways that produce useful outcomes and do not leave you feeling that you have wasted time and effort. If you are going to study, learn. Get the most out of the experience by focusing on the meanings and potential applications of key ideas.

Take satisfaction in gaining understanding. Learn to take pleasure in acquiring information and to experience satisfaction in coming to understand how things work. Take time to appreciate the minor epiphanies represented by "aha" reactions, "so that's how it works" insights, or "I never knew that—I'll bet that's why ____" connections.

Enjoy the stimulation of novel or surprising input. New input stimulates the cognitive juices, especially when it extends knowledge of things that we are already interested in or when it violates our expectations, contrasts with what we are familiar with, or in some other way surprises us or makes us aware that our knowledge is incomplete. It is fascinating to learn about lifestyles or actions that we have never considered or thought possible.

Enjoy vicarious experiences. Especially in reading fiction, but also in keeping up with current events or reading in the social sciences, there are opportunities to identify with focal characters or project ourselves into the situations being depicted. This allows us to vicariously experience what happens to the people in these situations, and to think about how we would respond in their place.

Appreciate expansion of self-knowledge. Whenever we learn about particular people or about the human condition in general, we learn more about ourselves. This includes similarities and contrasts with other people as well as information about the motives and intentions that underlie behavior, about different ways of handling life situations, and so on.

Take pride in becoming a well-informed person and citizen. Expanding our knowledge and using our cognitive abilities are important parts of what it means to be a fully functioning person. These activities provides bases for us to take satisfaction in feeling that we are aware of what is going on in the world, that we can follow news and current events knowledgeably, that we are informed voters, and that we have developed well-articulated opinions on policy issues or matters that come up in social discussion.

Along with providing such modeling and expectations yourself, *expose your apathetic students to peers or people with whom they identify who model active minds at work.* For example, in an intervention study designed to encourage 7- to 11-year-old students to become more intrinsically motivated learners, Hennessey, Amabile, and Martinage (1989) had the students watch videotapes that included the following dialogue:

Adult: Tommy, of all the things your teacher gives you to do in school, think about the one thing you like to do best and tell me about it.

Tommy: Well, I like social studies the best. I like learning about how other people live in different parts of the world. It's also fun because you get to do lots of projects and reports. I like doing projects because you can learn a lot about something on your own. I work hard on my projects and when I come up with good ideas, I feel good. When you are working on something that you thought of, and that's interesting to you, it's more fun to do.

Adult: So, one of the reasons you like social studies so much is because you get to learn about things on your own. And it makes you feel good when you do things for yourself; it makes it more interesting. That's great! (p. 216).

As part of socializing motivation to learn in apathetic students, expose them to selected videotapes from television talk shows (or at least make reference to certain common types of participants on these shows) in order to draw contrasts between active and passive or closed minds. Draw distinctions between the content and style of communication displayed by interesting, well-informed, and obviously reflective guests and the guests who defeat their own best interests by impulsively blurting out ill-considered ideas, loudly repeating counterproductive arguments, undermining their own credibility, and causing other guests and onlookers to respond to them with derision or irritation. Point out that these people did not have to become the way they are—most of them are not stupid but are passive, unreflective, willfully ignorant, or defensively aggressive rather than open to new information or ideas. They never learned to ask what things mean, why they are important, or what their implications might be for personal or social decision making.

Where it may be productive to do so, you might go on to point out that despite the diversity and richness of the self-actualization opportunities that the modern world presents, some people maintain very restricted mental lives. They think only about work, daily needs, and popular culture. They are not desirable as spouses, parents, friends, or coworkers because they have nothing to say, prattle on about trivia, or aggressively spout uninformed opinions rather than engage in mutually satisfying conversations. They got this way by passing through school without taking advantage of the opportunities it offers, rationalizing by finding everything to be "boring" or "stupid."

The point of all this to emphasize with apathetic students is that schooling is not intended just to teach them basic skills and prepare them for jobs; in addition, it is intended to help them realize their human potential more fully in all aspects of their lives. To put it bluntly, schooling is intended to help them become the kinds of people that others admire rather than the kinds that are mostly ignored because they just pass their time like cows chewing cud or are mostly looked down upon because they act like the people who embarrass themselves on scandal-oriented talk shows.

TEACH SKILLS FOR SELF-REGULATED LEARNING AND STUDYING

Many students, but especially apathetic or alienated students, will need instruction in cognitive and metacognitive skills for learning and studying effectively. You can teach them to become more aware of their goals during task engagement, to monitor their selection of strategies to use in pursuing those goals, to note the effects of these strategies and adjust them if necessary, and to control their affective responses to these unfolding events (Bruning & Horn, 2000; Hartman, 2001; Pintrich, 2000; Zimmerman & Schunk, 2001). For example, Pressley and Beard El-Dinary (1993) reviewed evidence supporting the value of teaching students how to manage six aspects of self-regulated learning:

Actively preparing to learn. Teach students to prepare to learn actively by mobilizing their resources and approaching tasks in thoughtful ways: getting ready to concentrate, previewing tasks by noting their nature and objectives, and in the case of complex tasks, developing plans before trying to respond to them.

Committing material to memory. If material must be memorized, teach students techniques for doing so efficiently. Such techniques include active rehearsal; repeating, copying, or underlining key words; making notes; or using imagery or other mnemonic strategies.

Encoding or elaborating on the information presented. Ordinarily you will not want students to memorize information but instead to retain its gist and be able to apply it later. Teach them strategies for identifying and retaining main ideas: paraphrasing and summarizing information to put it into their own words, relating it to what they already know, and assessing their understanding by asking themselves questions.

Organizing and structuring the content. Students also need to learn to structure extensive content by dividing it into sequences or clusters. Teach them to note the main ideas of paragraphs, outline the material, and notice and use the structuring devices built into it. Also, teach them strategies for effective note-taking (Devine, 1987; Kiewra et al., 1991).

Monitoring comprehension. In giving instructions for assignments, remind students to remain aware of the learning goals, the strategies they use to pursue those goals, and the corrective efforts they undertake if the strategies have not been effective. Also, teach them strategies for coping with confusion or mistakes: backing up and rereading, looking up definitions, identifying places in the text where the confusing point is discussed, searching the recent progression of topics for information that has been missed or misunderstood, retracing steps to see whether the strategy has been applied correctly, and generating possible alternative strategies.

Maintaining appropriate affect. Finally, model and instruct your students in ways of approaching academic activities with desirable affect (relaxed but alert and prepared to concentrate, ready to enjoy or at least take satisfaction in engaging in the task). Also, teach them ways to avoid undesirable affect (anger, anxiety, etc.). Such instruction should include taking satisfaction in accomplishments and using coping skills to respond to frustration or failure (reassuring self-talk, refocusing of attention on the task at hand, and use of the comprehension-monitoring strategies listed at the end of the previous paragraph).

A literacy program developed by a team of university researchers and elementary school teachers illustrates application of many of the strategies suggested here for scaffolding students' learning efforts (see Box 10.4). Butler (1998) similarly reported positive findings from a program for teaching strategies in the context of writing instruction. Generally, strategy teaching that is embedded in the regular curriculum (and thus is learned in the context of application) is more likely to be effective than more generic strategy instruction, including instruction that occurs in pull-out programs for struggling students (Hattie, Biggs, & Purdie, 1996).

TEACH VOLITIONAL CONTROL STRATEGIES

In many learning situations, some students possess goal clarity, motivation to learn, and the strategies needed to do so, but fail to follow through because they become distracted, fatigued, or preoccupied with competing goals. In recognition of this, some motivational theorists distinguish between motivation and volition (Corno, 2001; Kuhl & Beckmann, 1985).

Motivation refers to the adoption of goals and the development of goal-related plans. *Volition* refers to actions taken to follow through on those plans and make sure that they are implemented. Such actions include concentrating on the task at hand, buckling down to get to work, resisting distractions, and persisting in the face of difficulties.

You may need to teach at least some of your students volitional control strategies such as the following:

- *metacognitive control* (thinking of initial steps to take in order to get started right away; going back over work to check it and making revisions before turning it in);

Box 10.4   Concept-Oriented Reading Instruction

Concept-Oriented Reading Instruction (CORI) is an approach to teaching reading, writing, and science that incorporates principles for motivating students and scaffolding their use of learning strategies (Guthrie, McRae, & Klauda, 2007; Guthrie, Wigfield, & Perencevich, 2004). It incorporates four general phases:

1. *Observe and personalize.* The first step was to provide opportunities to observe concrete objects and events (a tree, flower, cricket, caterpillar, or bird nest, for example). Following such observations, students brainstormed to identify questions to explore with additional observations, data collection, reading, writing, and discussion.
2. *Search and retrieve.* Through teacher modeling and scaffolded practice, students learned how to conduct research by clarifying the questions, collecting and organizing observations and resource materials, extracting relevant information, and recording it in a form that supported later use.
3. *Comprehend and integrate.* Students also were taught strategies for processing the source materials they used: noting and summarizing main topics and critical details, drawing comparisons, relating illustrations to texts, evaluating texts, and taking into account the author's point of view. They also learned strategies for elaborating on texts by looking up additional information, combining material from separate sources, and recoding notes and reflections.
4. *Communicate to others.* Finally, students learned to synthesize and communicate information to others through forms that included a written report, a class-authored book, dioramas, charts, and informational stories.

Students in the CORI program showed concurrent developments in their intrinsic motivation for reading and the quality of their literacy engagement. They became more involved, curious, and social in their literacy activities, read about a broader range of topics, and displayed developments in strategies such as searching for information in multiple texts, representing ideas through drawing and writing, and transferring conceptual knowledge to new situations. The authors concluded that classroom contexts that support development of intrinsic motivation and literacy engagement are (a) observational, encouraging students to initiate learning by generating their own questions from real-world observations; (b) conceptual, focusing on substantive topics rather than reading skills; (c) self-directing, supporting student autonomy and choice of topics, books, and collaborating peers; (d) metacognitive, with explicit teaching of reading strategies, problem solving, and composing; (e) collaborative, emphasizing social construction of meaning within communities of learners; (f) expressive, creating opportunities for self-expression through writing, debating, and group interaction; and (g) coherent, emphasizing connections between classroom activities and tasks across the day, week, and month.

- *motivation control* (reminding oneself to concentrate and focus on task goals; generating ways to carry out the task that will make it more enjoyable, challenging, or reassuring; imagining completing the task successfully and enjoying the satisfaction of doing so);

- *emotion control* (reassuring oneself when bothered by fear of failure or doubts about one's ability; activating strategies that one has learned for coping when confused or frustrated);
- *controlling the task situation* (developing and revising a step-by-step plan for getting complex tasks accomplished; moving away from noise and distractions; gathering all needed materials before beginning the work); and
- *controlling others in the task setting* (asking for help from teacher or classmates; asking others to stop bothering or interrupting).

With highly distractible students, you may need to provide study carrels or other distraction-reduced work environments in addition to teaching them strategies for maintaining their engagement in learning activities.

When working with apathetic or alienated students, supplement work on motivational issues (goal commitment) with work on volitional issues (specific plans for when, where, and how the commitment will be carried out). Ostensible goal commitments are much more likely to be carried through to fruition if accompanied by specific implementation intentions (Armor & Taylor, 2003; Fishbach & Trope, 2008; Gollwitzer, Parks-Stamm, Jaudas, & Sheeran, 2008; Koestner, Lekes, Powers, & Chicoine, 2002).

Students with expectancy-related problems will need attention to aspects of volition that involve managing frustration and negative emotions and maintaining productive task engagement (Randi & Corno, 2000; Turner, Husman, & Schallert, 2002; Wolters, 2003). In contrast, *apathetic and alienated students are likely to need work on aspects of volition that involve formulating clear and firm implementation intentions.* Help these students learn to follow through on goal commitments by planning: when and where they will do the work (estimating and budgeting for the necessary time); how they will protect this time from other interests and commitments; when and how they will assemble any needed materials; and if necessary, how they will divide the work into a series of subtasks (with associated time schedules).

Students who have particular trouble getting started and following through on assignments can learn to benefit from the "strategic automaticity" or "proceduralization" of implementation intentions. Encourage them to establish standard routines for working in particular places at particular times: develop a "start-up ritual" (e.g., clearing the workspace of all but needed materials, arranged in ready-for-use alignments); turn off the television, the phone, or other potential distractions; do assignments for different subjects in the same order each time. Standardized procedures and work habits reduce students' needs to make specific implementation plans and help them to begin work more quickly and stick with it more consistently.

CONCLUSION

Apathetic students do not value what schooling has to offer and thus are indifferent or resistant to it. You can use threats and sanctions to compel them to perform to some minimum standard, but if you want to "get through" to them and resocialize their values, you will have to do it by modeling, communicating attitudes, expectations, and attributions, and arranging for them to engage in experiences that foster the development of motivation to learn.

Assuming appropriate curriculum and instruction, there are many good reasons for taking advantage of what school has to offer. Unfortunately, the reasons typically emphasized to apathetic students tend to focus on "tickets" to advancement in society (you need knowledge, skills, diplomas, etc., to get good jobs). These are valid reasons and should be emphasized to some degree, but they focus on extrinsically imposed requirements rather than learning. Also, they are easy for apathetic students to dismiss because they can always point to people who dropped out of school but nevertheless achieved at least material success in our society.

Consequently, your best chances of "getting through" to apathetic students lie in helping them to appreciate the empowerment and self-actualization outcomes that result from consistently engaging in school learning activities with motivation to learn. These ideas may be abstract, but even elementary students have at least intuitive understanding of their meaning and recognition of their validity. Students can recognize the differences between people who are admired because they are thoughtful, well-informed, and open-minded and people who are ignored because they are passive or are rejected because they are boorish.

The key is to help unmotivated and resistant students see that these personal qualities are rooted in values and dispositions toward learning. This realization should encourage them to develop values and dispositions relating to motivation to learn, not only to help ensure their success in school but also to help them become fully functioning in all aspects of their lives.

SUMMARY

This chapter suggested strategies for working with apathetic students who are uninterested in or alienated from school learning. Many of these students also display expectancy-related motivational problems and therefore also require treatment using the strategies described in chapter 5. Whether or not expectancy-related problems are present, apathetic students need modeling, socialization, and engagement in experiences that develop their motivation to learn.

Apathetic students require the same strategies for addressing the value-related aspects of motivation that were recommended for use with the class as a whole—the strategies described in chapters 6–8 and especially in chapter 9. However, these strategies will need to be applied more insistently and in more personalized ways in an attempt to "get through" to these students.

Contracting and incentive systems are widely recommended for use with apathetic students, in part because there is less need to fear undermining intrinsic motivation. These strategies can be helpful, but if they are to function as motivation builders rather than mere performance incentives, they will need to be implemented in ways that focus students' attention on learning goals and on the empowerment and self-actualization satisfactions that may be derived from attaining them.

It is important to develop and work within close relationships with apathetic students. For one thing, you will need to display patience and determination in pushing for steady progress despite setbacks or resistance, and this is difficult to do if you don't have a good relationship with the student. Also, your modeling and socialization efforts will be more successful if the student likes you and wants to please you.

In an effort to make schooling more intrinsically rewarding for apathetic students, discover and build on their existing interests, especially topical interests that might provide a basis for assignments or social interests that might sustain their learning efforts. Also, make sure that these students understand the purpose and value of learning activities and assignments. At some level, most of them realize that school activities are designed with their own best interests in mind, but many of them will not appreciate the relevance or potential application value of a particular activity unless it is pointed out to them.

To help apathetic students develop and sustain more positive attitudes toward school work, teach them strategies for making work more enjoyable or satisfying and for sustaining their efforts through volitional control. If they experience learning activities as aversive even though these activities are well suited to their current abilities and needs, help them to understand that they are causing their own problems—that their negative experiences flow from their own negative attitudes rather than from anything inherent in the work.

Finally, make determined efforts to socialize apathetic students' motivation to learn. With many of these students, you will need to work not only to induce them to *value* motivation to learn, but also to *understand* what this concept means and what it feels like as it is experienced in the process of engaging in learning activities. In this regard, explanations are likely to be helpful; exposure to and discussion of modeled examples (positive and negative) will be even more helpful; but most helpful will be opportunities to engage in activities that promote motivation to learn, scaffolded in ways that develop their appreciation of learning as empowering and self-actualizing. This may need to include teaching the students how to establish better metacognitive and volitional control of their learning efforts.

REFLECTION QUESTIONS

1. Why does the author claim that apathy is an even more serious motivational problem than discouragement?
2. Might you consider using contracting and incentive systems with certain students? Which ones? How would the systems work and how would you present them to the students?
3. Why do students often need to be taught (or at least, guided to discover) what it means to engage in learning activities with motivation to learn?
4. How can you provide students with concepts and language that they can use to appreciate and take pride in their accomplishments?
5. Think of an apathetic or alienated student you know (or if necessary, imagine one), and develop a plan for helping this student appreciate the value of schooling.
6. Why is it that many techniques for helping apathetic students become more active learners involve complexifying simple tasks, not just simplifying complex ones?
7. How can goal setting help make tasks meaningful and worthwhile for students who currently do not see value in them?
8. Why is it important to note that goals can be qualitative, not just quantitative (e.g., revise a poem until you are satisfied that it conveys the images that you want to convey)?
9. How might you engage apathetic or alienated students in problem-solving discussions that might help them begin to view school activities more positively and begin to take satisfaction from them?

10. If you should decide that certain apathetic or alienated students need a hard-sell approach, how could you implement it in ways that would not damage your relationship with the students?

11. If you suspected that part of the problem with some apathetic or alienated students was that they had never learned to study effectively, how could you teach them learning and volitional control strategies that would make them more self-regulated learners?

REFERENCES

Armor, D., & Taylor, S. (2003). The effects of mindset on behavior: Self-regulation in deliberative and implemental frames of mind. *Personality and Social Psychology Bulletin, 29,* 86–95.

Baumrind, D. (1991). Effective parenting during the early adolescent transition. In P. Cowan & M. Hetherington (Eds.), *Family transitions* (pp. 111–164). Hillsdale, NJ: Erlbaum.

Bruning, R., & Horn, C. (2000). Developing motivation to write. *Educational Psychologist, 35,* 25–37.

Butler, D. (1998). The strategic content learning approach to promoting self-regulated learning: A report of three studies. *Journal of Educational Psychology, 90,* 682–697.

Cameron, C., & Elusorr, S. (1986). *Thank God it's Monday: Making your work fulfilling and finding fulfilling work.* Los Angeles: Jeremy P. Tarcher, Inc.

Corno, L. (2001). Volitional aspects of self-regulated learning. In B. Zimmerman & D. Schunk (Eds.), *Self-regulated learning and academic achievement: Theoretical perspectives* (2nd ed., pp. 191–225). Mahwah, NJ: Erlbaum.

Cross, S., & Markus, H. (1994). Self-schemas, possible selves, and competent performance. *Journal of Educational Psychology, 86,* 423–438.

Csikzentmihalyi, M. (1993). *The evolving self: A psychology for the third millennium.* New York: HarperCollins.

Damon, W. (1995). *Greater expectations: Overcoming the culture of indulgence in America's homes and schools.* New York: The Free Press.

Day, J., Borkowski, J., Deitmeyer, D., Howsepian, B., & Saenz, D. (1992). Possible selves and academic achievement. In L. Winegar & J. Valsiner (Eds.), *Children's development within social context (Vol. 2: Research and methodology)* (pp. 181–201). Hillsdale, NJ: Erlbaum.

Devine, T. (1987). *Teaching study skills: A guide for teachers* (2nd ed.). Boston: Allyn & Bacon.

Dunkel, C. (2000). Possible selves as a mechanism for identity exploration. *Journal of Adolescence, 23,* 519–529.

Epstein, J. (1989). Family structures and student motivation: A developmental perspective. In C. Ames & R. Ames (Eds.), *Research on motivation in education* (Vol. 3, pp. 259–295). San Diego, CA: Academic Press.

Fishbach, A., & Trope, Y. (2008). Implicit and explicit counteractive self-control. In J. Shah & W. Gardner (Eds.), *Handbook of Motivation Science* (pp. 281–341). New York: Guilford.

Furst, E., & Steele, B. (1986). Motivational orientations of older adults in university courses described by factor and cluster analyses. *Journal of Experimental Education, 54,* 193–201.

Gagné, R., Briggs, L., & Wager, W. (1988). *Principles of instructional design* (3rd ed.). New York: Holt, Rinehart & Winston.

Gollwitzer, P., Parks-Stamm, E., Jaudas, A., & Sheeran, P. (2008). Flexible tenacity in goal pursuit. In J. Shah & W. Garner (Eds.), *Handbook of motivation science* (pp. 325–341). New York: Guilford.

Goodnow, J. (1996). Acceptable ignorance, negotiable disagreement: Alternative views of learning. In D. Olson & N. Torrance (Eds.), *The handbook of education and human development: New models of learning, teaching and schooling* (pp. 345–367). Cambridge, MA: Blackwell.

Green-Demers, I., Pelletier, L., Stewart, D., & Gushue, N. (1998). Coping with the less interesting aspects of training: Toward a model of interest and motivation enhancement in individual sports. *Basic and Applied Social Psychology, 20,* 251–261.

Grusec, J., & Goodnow, J. (1994). Impact of parental discipline methods on the child's internalization of values: A reconceptualization of current points of view. *Developmental Psychology, 30,* 4–19.

Guthrie, J., McRae, A., & Klauda, S. (2007). Contributions of Concept-Oriented Reading Instruction to knowledge about interventions for motivations in reading. *Educational Psychologist, 42,* 237–250.

Guthrie, J., Wigfield, A., & Perencevich, K. (2004). *Motivating reading comprehension: Concept-oriented reading instruction.* Mahwah, NJ: Erlbaum.

Hartman, H. (Ed.). (2001). *Metacognition in learning and instruction: Theory, research and practice.* Boston: Kluwer.

Hattie, J., Biggs, J., & Purdie, N. (1996). Effects of learning skills interventions on student learning: A meta-analysis. *Review of Educational Research, 66,* 99–136.

Hennessey, B., Amabile, T., & Martinage, M. (1989). Immunizing children against the negative effects of reward. *Contemporary Educational Psychology, 14,* 212–227.

Kiewra, K., Dubois, N., Christian, D., McShane, A., Meyerhoffer, M., & Roskelley, D. (1991). Note-taking functions and techniques. *Journal of Educational Psychology, 83,* 240–245.

Koestner, R., Lekes, N., Powers, T., & Chicoine, E. (2002). Attaining personal goals: Self-concordance plus implementation intentions equals success. *Journal of Personality and Social Psychology, 83,* 231–244.

Kuhl, J., & Beckmann, J. (Eds.). (1985). *Action control: From cognition to behavior.* New York: Springer-Verlag.

Markus, H., & Nurius, P. (1986). Possible selves. *American Psychologist, 41,* 954–969.

McCaslin, M. (1990). Motivated literacy. In J. Zutell & S. McCormick (Eds.), *Literacy theory and research: Analyses for multiple paradigms* (39th yearbook, pp. 35–50). Rochester, NY: National Reading Conference, Inc.

McCaslin, M., & Good, T. (1996). *Listening in classrooms.* New York: HarperCollins.

Nisan, M. (1992). Beyond intrinsic motivation: Cultivating a "sense of the desirable." In F. Oser, A. Dick, & J. Patry (Eds.), *Effective and responsible teaching: The new synthesis* (pp. 126–138). San Francisco: Jossey- Bass.

Oettingen, G., & Mayer, D. (2002). The motivating function of thinking about the future: Expectations vs. fantasies. *Journal of Personality and Social Psychology, 83,* 1198–1212.

Oldfather, P. (1992, April). *My body feels completely wrong: Students' experiences when lacking motivation for academic tasks.* Paper presented at the annual meeting of the American Educational Research Association, San Francisco.

Oyserman, D., Bybee, D., & Terry, K. (2006). Possible selves and academic outcomes: How and when possible selves impel action. *Journal of Personal and Social Psychology, 91,* 188–204.

Pintrich, P. (2000). The role of goal orientation in self-regulated learning. In M. Boekaerts, P. Pintrich, & M. Zeidner (Eds.), *Handbook of self-regulation* (pp. 451–502). San Diego, CA: Academic Press.

Pressley, M., & Beard El-Dinary, P. (Guest Eds.). (1993). Special issue on strategies instruction. *Elementary School Journal, 94,* 105–284.

Randi, J., & Corno, L. (2000). Teacher innovations in self-regulated learning. In M. Boekaerts, P. Pintrich, & M. Zeidner (Eds.), *Handbook of self-regulation* (pp. 651–685). San Diego, CA: Academic Press.

Thorkildsen, T. (1988). Theories of education among academically able adolescents. *Contemporary Educational Psychology, 13,* 323–330.

Tjas, K., Nelsen, E., & Taylor, M. (1997). Successful alumni as role models for high school youth. *High School Journal, 80,* 103–110.

Turner, J., Husman, J., & Schallert, D. (2002). The importance of students' goals in their emotional experience of academic failure: Investigating the precursors and consequences of shame. *Educational Psychologist, 37,* 79–89.

Vallacher, R., & Wegner, D. (1987). What do people think they're doing? Action identification and human behavior. *Psychological Review, 94,* 3–15.

Waitley, D., & Witt, R. (1985). *The joy of working.* New York: Dodd, Mead.

Williams, W. (1996). *The reluctant reader: How to get and keep kids reading.* New York: Warner Books.

Wolters, C. (2003). Regulation of motivation: Evaluating an underemphasized aspect of self-regulated learning. *Educational Psychologist, 38,* 189–205.

Yowell, C. (2002). Dreams of the future: The pursuit of education and career possible selves among ninth grade Latino youth. *Applied Developmental Science, 6*(2), 62–72.

Zimmerman, B., & Schunk, D. (Eds.). (2001). *Self-regulated learning and academic achievement: Theoretical perspectives* (2nd ed.). Mahwah, NJ: Erlbaum.

11

Adapting to Differences in Students' Motivational Patterns

And there is the poignant story of Sandy and math baseball. It appears that Sandy's fears about mathematics began in the third grade when her teacher's favorite mathematics game was a variant on the spelling bee called math baseball. Two captains were appointed from the class, and they chose teams for the game. The teams lined up on either side of the room, lead-off batters closest to the blackboard. The teacher "pitched" a problem and the lead-off batters ran to the blackboard and solved it as fast as they could. The one who came to the correct solution in the shortest time scored a run.

Sandy wasn't a fast runner, so she was usually at a disadvantage before she even started the calculation. And although she was very accurate in doing arithmetic calculations, Sandy was slower than a lot of the other children. So she could never score a run for her team. Even though other pupils didn't say anything to her, Sandy knew she was a liability to her friends, and she grew to dread these episodes of public problem solving. Sandy never recovered her initial enjoyment of mathematics. She couldn't take comfort in the fact that she got the right answers and did well on tests, because in the most important area—respect among friends—she didn't feel successful at all. (Brush, 1980, p. 14)

Sandy's story illustrates two points that are noted later in this chapter: Compared to boys, girls are less likely to be motivated by involvement in competitions and more likely to question their abilities in mathematics. Such differences complicate your motivational efforts: Some strategies work well with boys but not girls, or vice versa. Similar complications can arise when students differ in developmental levels, cognitive or learning styles, or cultural backgrounds.

The "math baseball" game violates several important motivational principles, so it is not surprising that it had negative effects on Sandy and probably other students as well. If you avoid such ill-considered "motivational" strategies, you are unlikely to have significant negative effects on students. However, the strategies you do use may have uneven positive effects because of individual and group differences in students' motivational patterns. To the extent that such differences exist, they may lead you to use different motivational strategies with different students.

THEORETICAL POSITIONS ON GROUP AND INDIVIDUAL DIFFERENCES

Learners are individuals and must be treated as such if we expect to optimize their motivation and learning. As an abstract proposition, this statement is compelling. However, we immediately encounter complexities when we seek to apply it to particular students. Over time, a great many claims have been made that teachers need to accommodate this or that dimension of difference among students, but few of these claims have been backed by research establishing that (a) differences on the dimension are important enough to justify the effort it would take for teachers to assess students and provide differentiated curriculum and instruction to different subgroups; (b) the suggestions made about differentiating instruction are feasible under normal classroom conditions; and (c) if provided, such differentiated treatment would serve the long-run best interests of the students.

For the most part, the motivational strategies suggested in this book are based on psychological principles believed to apply to people in general, regardless of age, gender, social class, race, cultural background, or personal characteristics. Many motivational theorists would expect these strategies to affect all students similarly rather than to produce contrasting reactions in different subgroups. Certain principles might be more relevant to certain situations (e.g., introducing an activity vs. providing feedback to students' responses), but the principles would apply to all students.

Other motivational theorists would maintain that efforts to implement motivational principles need to be tailored not only to situations but to students. They might agree that you can use the same basic set of motivational strategies with all students but argue the need to use some strategies more frequently or intensively with students who belong to certain subgroups or have developed certain personal characteristics.

Still other motivational theorists would argue that you face a more complex situation—that different students need different motivational strategies because any given strategy is likely to increase motivation in some students but decrease it in others. For example, anxious and dependent students respond well to praise and encouragement but not to challenge or criticism, whereas confident and independent students show the opposite pattern. Some students prefer material rewards, others prefer symbolic rewards, and still others prefer special privilege or teacher rewards.

Eden (1975) developed a model that incorporated this idea. His model assumes that, for a given person in a given situation, certain motives are relevant but others are not. Therefore, the effect of tying task engagement to a motive will depend on the relevance of that motive to the person at the time. If task engagement produces a relevant motivational consequence, there is likely to be an (probably substantial) increase in motivation to perform the task. However, if task engagement produces some irrelevant motivational outcome, there is likely to be a (probably small but real) decrease in motivation to perform the task. Eden presented some evidence in support of this model (although not from classrooms).

Intrinsic motivational theorists might interpret Eden's work as further evidence of the need to provide students with choices of what assignments to do and when and how to do them. Extrinsic motivational theorists might interpret it as further evidence that teachers should not rely on a few incentives but instead offer students a variety of rewards from which to choose, so that all of them will be able to work toward incentives that they find appealing.

These implications are valid as far as they go, but they don't take into account the limited applicability of intrinsic and extrinsic motivational approaches in classrooms or the need to move beyond catering to students' existing motivational systems in order to develop new ones, especially motivation to learn.

A PERSPECTIVE ON ACCOMMODATING STUDENTS' PREFERENCES

I have already noted that *accommodating students' existing motivational systems does nothing to move them in directions that you would like to see them move*. In addition, there are two other reasons for proceeding cautiously when adapting motivational strategies to student differences. First, *accommodating students' preferences is not the same as meeting their needs*. Allowing students to choose their own learning methods or arranging to teach them as they prefer to be taught may *reduce* their achievement, even if it improves their attitudes (Clark, 1982; Dorsel, 1975; Flowerday & Schraw, 2003; Hannafin & Sullivan, 1996; Schofield, 1981; Trout & Crawley, 1985).

Second, *accommodating students' existing personal characteristics is likely to reinforce those characteristics, including ones that you would prefer to change*. For example, it is tempting to respond reciprocally to passive or alienated students by minimizing your interactions with them—calling on them only when they raise their hands and avoiding them during work times unless they indicate a need for help. This might maximize both your comfort and theirs, but it would not be in their best interests.

Even where it may be desirable to treat different students differently, your opportunities to do so will be limited unless you teach in a setting with a very low student/teacher ratio. If you teach a typical class of 20 or more students, you will have to focus most of your instruction on the class as a whole and work at the margins to adapt to individual differences.

With respect to students' motivation, the most important individual differences lie in the degree to which they: value what schooling has to offer, believe that they can meet its demands if they invest reasonable effort, and emphasize learning goals instead of less desirable goals. These aspects of students' motivation have been the focus of the first 10 chapters of the book.

The remainder of this chapter will focus on other dimensions that may provide a basis for differentiating your treatment of different individuals or subgroups. As you read this and any other advice about differentiating your motivational strategies, however, *keep in mind that your primary responsibility is to induce your students to move in desirable directions, not just to cater to their current preferences and interests*.

In considering suggestions made to teachers for differentiating curriculum and instruction, I begin with one of the better researched variables: the cognitive style dimension of psychological differentiation.

DIFFERENCES IN PSYCHOLOGICAL DIFFERENTIATION

Cognitive style refers to the ways that people process information and use strategies to respond to tasks. For example, people differ in their tendencies to attend to global features versus fine details, to classify into a few large categories versus many smaller ones, or to make quick, impulsive decisions versus employing a slower, more painstaking approach to problem solving. Cognitive styles are called styles rather than abilities because they refer to *how* people process information and solve problems, not *how well*.

A cognitive-style dimension that has implications for motivation is *psychological differentiation*, also known as *field dependence versus field independence* or as *global versus analytic perceptual style* (Saracho, 1997; Witkin, Moore, Goodenough, & Cox, 1977). People who are low in psychological differentiation (*field dependent*) have difficulty differentiating stimuli from the contexts in which they are embedded, so their perceptions are easily affected by manipulations of the surrounding context. In contrast, people who are high in psychological differentiation (*field independent*) perceive more analytically. They can separate stimuli from context, so their perceptions are less affected when changes in context are introduced.

These differences apply to social perceptions as well as perceptions of the physical world. Consequently, field-dependent people's opinions are strongly affected by those of other people, whereas field-independent people are more likely to resist social pressures and make up their minds on the basis of their own perceptions. In ambiguous social situations, field-dependent people are more attentive to and make more use of prevailing social frames of reference, monitor the faces of others for cues as to what they are thinking, attend more to verbal messages with social content, and get physically closer to and interact more with others. As a result, they tend to be liked by other people and perceived as warm, tactful, considerate, socially outgoing, and affectionate. In contrast, field-independent people have a more abstract, theoretical, analytical, and impersonal orientation. This makes them more able to resist external pressures toward conformity, but also more likely to be perceived as cold, distant, or insensitive.

In classrooms, field-dependent students prefer to learn in groups and to interact frequently with teachers, whereas field-independent students prefer more independent and individualized learning opportunities. They also tend to prefer and do better in mathematics and science, whereas field-dependent students tend to prefer and do better in the humanities and social sciences (Billington, Baron-Cohen, & Wheelwright, 2007).

Most students do not consistently reflect these extremes of psychological differentiation, but they may tend more toward one cognitive style than the other. To the extent that they do, they are likely to be happier in school if they spend most of their time focusing on content and learning within formats matched to their preferences. However, it is not clear that such differentiated treatment would serve their long-run best interests. Extremely field independent students have social adjustment problems, and extremely field dependent students are conforming to the point that they seem to lack minds of their own. These extreme students might be better off in the long run if they could learn to appreciate and function more frequently in their nonpreferred orientation.

Therefore, learn to recognize and respect both orientations and to build on students' strengths but also work on their areas of weakness. You might structure field-dependent students' learning experiences enough to enable them to cope effectively, provide frequent encouragement and praise, be supportive when noting their mistakes, and allow them to learn in collaboration with peers most of the time. Field-independent students do not need as much personal support and encouragement, although they will require explicit feedback. With these students, it may be more important for you to respect their needs for privacy and distance, to avoid penalizing them unreasonably for low social participation, and to allow them frequent opportunities to operate autonomously.

LEARNING STYLES AND MULTIPLE INTELLIGENCES

Much attention has been focused on the notion of learning styles, especially by people who offer workshops or sell materials purported to help teachers assess their students' learning styles and follow up with differentiated curriculum and instruction. Learning style inventories address questions such as the following: Are the students "verbal learners" who prefer to listen to information, or "visual learners" who prefer to read it or see it displayed graphically? Do they prefer to learn alone or with others? Do they prefer to study for frequent short periods or fewer longer periods? Do they like to study in silence; with soothing musical or "white noise" backgrounds; or in potentially distracting environments (amid people who are conversing or near a playing radio or television)?

For example, McCarthy (1980, 1990) identified four learning styles by locating students on two dimensions: perceiving (concrete sensing/feeling vs. more abstract thinking) and processing (active doing vs. reflective watching). Combinations of high and low scores on these dimensions produce four learning styles:

1. *Imaginative learners* perceive information concretely and process it reflectively. They listen, share, and seek to integrate school experience with self experience.
2. *Analytic learners* perceive information abstractly and process it reflectively. They appreciate both details and ideas, tend to think sequentially, and value ideas more than people.
3. *Commonsense learners* perceive information abstractly and process it actively. They tend to be pragmatic learners who value concrete problem solving and like to "tinker" and experiment to learn by discovery.
4. *Dynamic learners* perceive information concretely and process it actively. They tend to integrate experience and application, are enthusiastic about new learning, ready to engage in trial-and-error learning, and adept at risk taking.

McCarthy designed the 4MAT system, a model for designing units of study that accommodate the four learning styles as well as the supposed hemispheric (left- vs. right-brain) preferences of students. Intended to be applicable to any content area or grade level, it calls for an eight-step cycle of instruction and learning activities relating to the unit topic. Each of the four learning styles is represented by two steps in the cycle, one designed to facilitate right-brain learning and the other to facilitate left-brain learning. If the teacher follows the full cycle, each individual student's learning style will be addressed during at least one-fourth of the instructional time. During other parts of the cycle the learner will be "stretched," learning other ways to solve problems. McCarthy reported positive results from an intervention done with elementary students.

Wilkerson and White (1988) tested the 4MAT system against a more conventional science unit on machines taught to third graders. The 4MAT version unfolded as follows:

Step 1: Students visualize machines experienced in everyday life, then draw pictures of their mental images (right mode lesson for imaginative learners).
Step 2: Students work in small groups to discuss how the machines they have drawn make work easier (left mode lesson for imaginative learners).
Step 3: Students view a filmstrip depicting six simple machines, then draw pictures of them. Also, teacher holds up objects (e.g., fishing reel, scissors) and students

Unit of study

point to the same types of machines as the objects (right mode lesson for analytic learners).

Step 4: Using the overhead projector, teacher explains characteristics of each of the six machines. Then, students use a flannel board to match new words from the unit with their definitions (left mode lesson for analytic learners).

Step 5: Teacher reads students a book about machines. Then, students complete three worksheets reviewing concepts taught in Steps 4 and 5 (left mode lesson for commonsense learners).

Step 6: Wooden models of simple machines, examples of compound machines, and task cards are placed at work stations. Small groups examine the machines and discuss potential responses to questions written on the task cards (right mode lesson for commonsense learners).

Step 7: Each student is given 11 word cards. Teacher asks questions about machines and students answer by holding up one of their word cards. Then, each student is given a piece of transparency film and asked to draw a compound machine that would make work easier (left mode lesson for dynamic learners).

Step 8: The pieces of transparency film are used to make a film strip that is shown to the class. As their drawings come up, individual students explain how the machines they drew would work (right mode lesson for dynamic learners).

While the 4MAT group was working through this cycle, the conventional group read from the textbook, provided oral and written responses to questions based on this material, and engaged in activities that included making a lever, conducting an experiment on inclined planes, completing a crossword puzzle that reviewed the six simple machines, making a bar graph showing the numbers of machines found in their homes, and watching a commercial filmstrip about machines. Assessment data indicated that the 4MAT approach produced modest but favorable effects on students' attitudes and achievement.

McCarthy and the 4MAT system are unusual within the learning styles literature, for three reasons. First, intervention studies were done with elementary students and encompassed a significant portion of the curriculum and instruction they experienced. Most learning style studies have been done at the high school and (especially) the college level, and interventions have been restricted to variations in study or test environments.

Second, McCarthy noted the need to help students "stretch" to function in learning modes they use infrequently. Unfortunately, most learning style advocates only emphasize catering to students' existing preferences.

Finally, reports of research on the 4MAT system have been published in respected research journals. Unfortunately, most of the sources cited by advocates of learning styles are either position pieces unsupported by research or dissertations and other unpublished studies (Carbo, 1997; Dunn & Dunn, 1992; Dunn, Gorman, Griggs, Olson, & Beasley, 1995).

Lack of Research Support for Claimed Effects

The credibility of learning styles enthusiasts is questionable because: (a) they tend to make outlandish claims for the effectiveness of the measurement inventories and instructional models they sell; (b) most of the studies purporting to support learning style approaches are too flawed to survive the peer review standards of research journals; and (c) most of these studies have been conducted by people with vested interests in positive results who gave instructions designed to maximize the treatment groups' enthusiasm and positive expectations (Cassidy, 2004; Coffield, Moseley, Hall, & Ecclestone, 2004; Kavale & LeFever, 2007; Klein, 2003; Stahl, 1999; Willingham, 2005).

Stellwagen (2001) contrasted the enthusiasm for learning styles among many school administrators and teachers with the skepticism or rejection typically expressed by researchers. He found that professional journals (e.g., *Educational Leadership, NASSP Bulletin*) typically waxed enthusiastic about learning styles and related fads such as brain-based learning, but research journals consistently published reports questioning the value of both the instruments purporting to measure learning styles and the educational programs based on them. He noted that even the 4MAT approach showed only mixed results in 18 dissertation studies (no new studies of the effects of the 4MAT system have appeared in major journals for 20 years now).

Stellwagen (2001) contrasted the claims of Rita Dunn about her learning style inventory with the conclusions drawn by independent investigators (e.g., no evidence for educational benefits, not recommended as a diagnostic tool, "has no redeeming value"). He also expressed concern that learning style categories were being misapplied in ways that led to stereotyping and potentially prejudicial treatment of students.

Similarly, Stahl (1999) critiqued Marie Carbo's claims for her so-called reading style inventory and noted that most of the "research" claims of Carbo and the Dunns are citations to dissertations by their own students. He went on to suggest that learning styles have enduring popularity, despite a paucity of supporting evidence, for the same reason that fortune telling does: They produce statements that are specific enough to sound predictive but ambiguous enough to apply to many different situations.

Like other reviewers who pay close attention to the research literature, I do not see much validity in the claims made by those who urge teachers to assess their students with learning style inventories and follow up with differentiated curriculum and instruction. First, the research bases supporting these urgings are thin to nonexistent. Second, a single teacher working with 20 or more students does not have time to plan and implement much individualized instruction. With respect to student motivation, much more is to be gained by focusing on students' learning goals, values, and expectancies than on the variables emphasized in cognitive or learning style inventories.

Brain-Based Education and Multiple Intelligences

Similar comments apply to schemes for differentiating instruction according to student profiles developed using supposed measures of brain hemisphere preferences or multiple intelligences. Scientific examinations of claims about supposedly brain-based education routinely conclude that knowledge about brain functioning has not progressed to a level that would support recommendations about curriculum and instruction, so claims that educational programs are based on brain research simply have no validity (Bergen & Coscia, 2002; Bruer, 1999; Jensen, 2000).

Similarly, although Howard Gardner has updated his multiple intelligences model (Gardner, 1999) and also published a book about educational assessments and interventions based on it (Gardner, 1993), scientific reviewers routinely conclude that there are conceptual problems with his theory (particularly, misapplication of the term "intelligences"), psychometric problems with his measuring instruments (validity not yet demonstrated), a lack of clarity and specificity about what multiple intelligences theory implies about educational practice, and a lack of systematic research on (let alone clear support for) educational programs supposedly based on this theory (Klein, 2003; Visser, Ashton, & Vernon, 2006; Waterhouse, 2006).

Krechevsky and Seidel (2001) suggested that multiple intelligences theory implies the need to individualize students' education as much as possible, teach subjects in more than one way, use project-based learning, and infuse the arts throughout the curriculum. However, they cautioned that the theory should not be taken as a mandate to teach every topic in seven or eight ways. For example, asking students to sing songs about operations learned in a unit on fractions, or playing classical music in the background during the lessons, are not meaningful uses of music to support mathematics learning. They also cautioned against labeling or stereotyping students and against overemphasizing celebration of students' strengths without paying sufficient attention to their weaknesses.

CONCLUSIONS REGARDING LEARNING STYLES AND MULTIPLE INTELLIGENCES

Individual difference concepts such as cognitive styles, multiple intelligences, or learning styles can be useful to teachers if adopted only loosely and used primarily as reminders of the value of including a variety of learning activities and formats in the curriculum. However, scientific validity and practical feasibility problems arise if such concepts are emphasized to the extent of seeking to develop individual curricular prescriptions for each student.

It is worthwhile to learn about your students' preferences and to accommodate them by providing opportunities for autonomy and choice whenever doing so will support progress toward learning goals. Sometimes such accommodation is not feasible or advisable, however. For example, to attain certain learning goals, students must engage in processes they might prefer to avoid (presentations to the class, debates, cooperative work on a group project). Or, you might have to limit certain students' opportunities to pursue favorite topics or learn in their preferred mode, because if they spent too much time indulging these preferences they would fail to develop knowledge or skills needed in school or in life generally. You can accommodate such preferences much of the time, however, and doing so will increase your students' opportunities to experience intrinsic motivation (see Box 11.1).

CHANGES WITH AGE IN STUDENTS' MOTIVATIONAL PATTERNS

Different grade levels present somewhat different motivational challenges because of age-related changes in students' motivational patterns. *Most students begin schooling enthusiastically, but then show progressive deterioration on measures of school-related attitudes, curiosity, and intrinsic motivation* (Corpus, McClintic-Gilbert, & Hayenga, 2009; Gottfried, Fleming, & Gottfried, 2001; Harter, 1999; Linnenbrink-Garcia & Fredricks, 2008; Wigfield & Eccles, 2002).

Most students in the early grades show positive (actually, unrealistically high) self-concepts and success expectations. These persist until about age seven, when they begin to show more consistent relationships with test scores and other more objective measures.

> ### Box 11.1   Preferences Identified as Elements of Learning Styles
>
> One problem with the notion of learning styles and its potential application in classrooms is the seemingly limitless variety of learner preferences and other potential bases for differentiating instruction. Listed below are just some of the dimensions identified in the learning styles literature:
>
> - Type of lighting (natural, incandescent, fluorescent)
> - Brightness of lighting
> - Sound (quiet; various types of music, radio or TV; ambient noise in social settings)
> - Room temperature and humidity
> - Seating accommodations (desks, straightbacked chairs, easy chairs, pillows on floor, etc.)
> - Body position while studying (standing, sitting, reclining)
> - Need for imposed structure versus desire to do things in one's own way
> - Preferring to learn alone, with a partner, in a small group, as part of a team, or with an adult or expert tutor
> - Preferring an adult or expert tutor to act in an authoritative versus a collegial manner
> - Preference for routine and predictability versus variety and unpredictability
> - Preference for certain learning modalities over others (visual, auditory, tactile, kinesthetic)
> - Variations in alertness levels and readiness to study connected to time of day
> - Preferring to sit still versus move around while learning
> - Global versus analytic information processing style
> - Right- versus left-brain information processing style
> - Impulsive versus reflective style of processing information or making decisions
> - Preference for sustained study periods versus shorter periods interspersed with frequent breaks
> - Opportunity to eat, drink, or chew on something while studying
> - Working on one thing at a time until it is finished versus enjoying working on several things simultaneously and leaving many things unfinished
> - Conforming versus resistant to authority
> - Preferring to be taught directly versus to discover for self
> - Preferring to develop a close relationship with the teacher versus to maintain a distance
> - Relying on intuition and insight versus inductive or deductive reasoning
> - Getting started right away versus requiring warm-up
> - Evaluation mode preferences (short answer tests, essay tests, portfolios, projects)
> - Preferring individual versus cooperative versus competitive task structures
> - Oriented toward extrinsic rewards versus intrinsic satisfactions

(continued)

Box 11.1   Continued

- Confident, exploratory, willing to learn from mistakes versus anxious, teacher-dependent, perfectionistic
- Focusing on the big picture versus the details
- Preferring deductive, rule-example sequence versus inductive, example-rule sequence
- Preferring focus on people using narrative approaches versus focus on things using analytic approaches
- Preferring whole versus part learning of complex skills (observing demonstrations of the complete sequence and then attempting to duplicate it versus taking one step at a time)
- Preferring receptive learning by watching and listening versus active learning by doing
- Emphasizing rote memorizing versus generative learning strategies

For most of these variables (and many others that could have been listed), there is little or no classroom-based research to support claims that matching instruction to student preferences will produce significant improvements in learning outcomes. Even if there were an abundance of such evidence, however, few teachers would have the time and resources needed to assess students on these so-called learning style variables, develop individual prescriptions, and proceed accordingly. However, you can accommodate many of these preferences by avoiding unnecessarily rigid behavioral requirements and by providing students with opportunities to exercise autonomy and make choices in self-regulating their learning. Within limits, for example, rules regulating behavior when working on assignments might allow students to move around the room, collaborate with peers, or leave their desk to work somewhere else. Choice options might include variations not only in topics but in the kinds of information processing required (visual versus auditory input or output, focus on the big picture versus attention to detail, etc.). In general, unless you become aware of good reasons not to, you probably should accommodate students' requests or demonstrated preferences for opportunities to engage in certain kinds of learning or styles of working.

As students become better at interpreting the feedback they receive, and as they begin to compare themselves with peers, their self-assessments become more accurate (Stipek & MacIver, 1989). To the extent that they begin to experience failure and understand its implications, they become susceptible to learned helplessness and other failure syndrome problems. However, even students who doubt their abilities usually do not begin to give up consistently until they are about 10 years old (Nicholls & Miller, 1984).

Younger students attend primarily to their own accomplishments rather than those of classmates, so they tend to feel competent and successful if they complete a task or show improvement in their work. They tend to attribute success more to effort than ability, and to believe that they can increase their levels of ability by investing the effort needed to do so. As they develop, however, they begin to see effort and ability as inversely related. By the time they reach seventh grade, most are well aware that the need to expend considerable effort on a task implies limitations in domain-related abilities (Linnenbrink-Garcia & Fredricks, 2008).

Young children's inflated perceptions of their own competence and lack of sophistication in making social comparisons and interpreting feedback provide certain advantages to primary-grade teachers. Their students are less susceptible to learned helplessness problems, because failure does not faze them the way it fazes older students who are more aware of its potential implications (Miller, 1985). Also, younger students are less likely to feel embarrassed or to infer that their teacher believes that they lack ability if they are praised for effort (Barker & Graham, 1987; Lord, Umezaki, & Darley, 1990).

These findings imply that primary-grade teachers can afford to be more spontaneous in scaffolding their students' learning, giving them feedback, and praising both their efforts and their accomplishments. Even so, teachers in these grades should follow the praising guidelines given in chapter 6. They also should provide primarily informative rather than evaluative feedback and focus their students' attention on appreciating their accomplishments to date and building on them in the future, not on comparisons with classmates. If feedback emphasizes social comparisons or normative evaluations, even kindergarten students will experience failure and begin to lower their self-evaluations of ability (Butler, 1990; Licht, 1992; Stipek & Daniels, 1988).

Transitional Grades

Within the general trend of steady decreases in intrinsic motivation and self-perceptions of ability, there is a tendency for noteworthy drops to occur when students shift from elementary to middle or junior high schools, or from middle or junior high schools to high schools. Negative effects on motivation are especially likely following the first shift, because it entails movement from a more supportive to a less supportive learning environment. Compared to elementary classrooms, middle school and junior high classrooms confront students with greater emphasis on teacher control and discipline; fewer opportunities to engage in decision making, choice, or self-management; less personal and positive teacher-student relationships; more frequent use of practices such as whole-class teaching, ability grouping, and public evaluation of work; and more stringent standards for grading. The enhanced salience of performance feedback and social comparison, within the context of a new reference group, causes many students to reevaluate their academic abilities (Anderman & Maehr, 1994; Eccles & Roeser, 2009; Otis, Grouzet, & Pelletier, 2005; Wigfield & Eccles, 2002).

New levels of schooling need not be so stressful or destructive to students' motivation. When middle and junior high schools provide more personalized and supportive environments suited to their students' psychological needs, the students do not demonstrate the same declines in motivation seen in traditional schools (Corpus, McClintic-Gilbert, & Hayenga, 2009; Eccles & Roeser, 2009; Meece, Herman, & McCombs, 2003; Skinner, Furrer, Marchand, & Kindermann, 2008).

School-level changes such as creating "schools within schools" and smaller learning environments, block scheduling and flexible use of time, and assigning an adult advisor to each student can help ease transitions to higher levels of schooling. Even more importantly, teachers can establish their classrooms as learning communities. Teachers at higher school levels who work with students just entering from lower levels should go out of their way to welcome these students, make them feel comfortable, and scaffold their learning efforts in ways that help them to feel confident. They also should provide their students with frequent autonomy and choice opportunities, because they value these opportunities more than younger students do and because they are better equipped to handle them.

Developments in Children's Interests

Connecting with students' interests is one way to stimulate intrinsic motivation and perhaps motivation to learn. Jersild and Tasch (1949) conducted a massive survey of the interests of students in Grades 1–12, and numerous smaller studies have also been conducted (Hurlock, 1964). These studies indicated that interests become differentiated with age, so that younger students have more interests in common than older students. At all ages, however, students tend to be more interested in stories and other content dealing with people than in content dealing with impersonal topics, and to prefer learning experiences that involve active doing over those that are confined to watching and listening.

Students' responses to questions about their interests are heavily influenced by their prior experiences. Consequently, these responses say more about the students' past exposure to interest-generating experiences than about their probable responses to potential future experiences. Even so, certain documented trends are worth noting.

Primary-grade students' interests center on themselves and their personal and family experiences. In school, they tend to prefer language arts, mathematics, and art over science, social studies, and local or world news. For reading, they tend to enjoy stories about other children and familiar experiences; tales of fantasy, fun, and humor; and narratives featuring acts of kindness or bravery.

Neitzel, Alexander, and Johnson (2008) gathered information about the interests that pre-kindergarten children displayed at home and later observed these children as kindergartners. They found that children's interests (e.g., in topics such as trains, ocean life, or weather; construction toys; rule-bound games; storybooks; arts and creative activities; or dramatic play) were associated with the kinds of contributions they made to class discussions and the kinds of books and learning activities they preferred to pursue when given opportunities to make choices.

Students in the intermediate grades tend to be more interested in realistic stories —tales of adventure, sportsmanship, or the work of inventors. They also develop interests in nature study, and more generally, in science and social studies topics. They tend to become interested in subjects in which they are successful, but not subjects that are difficult for them. Whereas younger students talk mostly about their own play and recreation or their family and home activities, students in the middle grades talk more about family vacations and other trips away from the local setting, books they have been reading, and television, movies, and other entertainment and youth culture activities.

These trends continue as students progress through secondary schools, but their interests broaden to include topics from history and the social sciences and current events in the news, including events occurring in other parts of the world. High school students also develop interests in self-improvement, self-understanding, and vocations (Massey, Gebhardt, & Garnefski, 2008). The emergence of these interests reflects progression from a focus on competence (What are my areas of strength and weakness?) to a focus on identity (What kind of person do I want to become, in terms of personal values, lifestyle, occupation, etc.?).

You can generate opportunities to connect with interests by administering and following up on interest inventories and by allowing for choices of topics for reading assignments and learning projects. Also, familiarize yourself with literature selections and computerized learning programs that are especially appealing to students at your grade level. Consult with other teachers and librarians for suggestions in these areas, and visit literacy websites that list children's books popular at different ages.

Developments in Students' Preferences Regarding Curriculum and Instruction

Many younger students find it difficult to sustain attention to lengthy activities, especially information presentations. Consequently, it is wise to emphasize hands-on learning activities in the early grades, to keep presentations and discussions relatively short, and to intersperse them with activities that call for more active forms of learning.

Older students can sustain attention to longer presentations and discussions, and they often enjoy doing so. However, they become increasingly impatient with presentations that mostly require them to commit transmitted information to memory. Instead, they want more interactive discussion of curricular topics, including discussion of their controversial aspects (Nicholls, Nelson, & Gleaves, 1995).

GENDER DIFFERENCES

As children develop, they are exposed to *gender role socialization* suggesting that certain family and social roles, occupations, personal attributes, and ways of dressing and behaving are primarily feminine, while others are primarily masculine. Gender role socialization is modeled by the individuals they encounter in their personal lives and in the media, expressed directly in the messages they receive from their parents and peers (and sometimes their teachers; Li, 1999; Tenenbaum & Leaper, 2003; Tiedemann, 2000), and reinforced through communication of expectations concerning such things as the toys and games they will want to play with, the books they will enjoy reading, or the things that they will want to do in school or in their free time (DeLoache, Simcock, & Macari, 2007; Johnson, Alexander, Spencer, Leibham, & Neitzel, 2004; Martin, Ruble, & Szkrybalo, 2002).

The more restrictive aspects of traditional gender roles have loosened over the last century. Even so, many activities are still associated primarily with one gender or the other. To the extent that an activity is gender typed, teachers and students may anticipate gender differences in interest and enjoyment in the activity, and perhaps also in success expectancies and performance attributions (Diekman & Eagly, 2008).

Attitudes and Beliefs About School Subjects

Boys tend to value and enjoy mathematics and science more than language arts, but girls show the opposite pattern. These differences extend to preferences within subject areas, as well. In reading, for example, boys are more oriented to non-fiction texts, while girls tend to prefer fiction. Within fiction, boys tend to prefer action, adventure, and sports themes, whereas girls tend to prefer plots focusing on romance or personal relationships (Dreher, 2003; Millard, 1997; Wigfield & Eccles, 2002). Some researchers view these differences merely as carryovers from traditional socialization designed to prepare boys primarily to be breadwinners but girls primarily to be wives and mothers. They anticipate further reductions in gender differences in response to continued reductions in gender role specialization in the home and workplace.

Others urge teachers to try to reduce gender differences in response to school subjects, especially if the differences encompass not only value perceptions but also beliefs about ability and related attributional inferences. Concern is greatest with respect to science and especially mathematics, because many girls believe themselves to possess less domain-specific ability than boys, or tend to attribute their successes to luck or other external factors but to attribute their failures to lack of ability (Bornholt, Goodnow, & Cooney, 1994; Eccles et al., 1989; Guimond & Roussel, 2001; Hoffmann, 2002; Nosek, Banaji, & Greenwald, 2002; Stipek & Gralinski, 1991).

Boys are more likely to credit their successes to high ability but attribute their failures to bad luck, lack of interest, low effort, or other causes that do not imply a lack of ability (Blatchford, 1992; Eccles, 1987; Miller, 1986). These differences make girls more vulnerable to learned helplessness and other failure syndrome problems, especially in subjects like mathematics or science where the girls might suspect limitations in their domain-specific abilities.

Starting around fifth grade and continuing thereafter, girls' ability beliefs and expectancies for future success in mathematics and science tend to drop below those of boys, even though their grades in these subjects are as good or better than boys' grades. Girls also are more likely to opt out of mathematics and science classes when they begin to get the opportunity to do so, thus cutting themselves off from future career opportunities that require academic preparation in these subjects. These patterns develop as much among brighter girls as among other girls, although the underrepresentation of higher achieving women in mathematics and science-related careers is due mostly to value-related preferences rather than doubts about their abilities (Ceci, Williams, & Barnett, 2009). Also, students in general and girls in particular sometimes develop negative attitudes towards mathematics and science for reasons that have little to do with gender roles (e.g., those subjects are tightly rule bound and have little room for personal creativity or expressiveness; Hannover & Kessels, 2004).

Boys generally place less value on engaging in academic activities than girls do, so the quality of their engagement is more variable. They are more likely than girls to adopt work-avoidant goals or display task resistance. When they adopt learning or performance goals, however, they are likely to focus on achieving mastery or competitive success. In contrast, girls are more likely to focus on putting forth their best efforts and pleasing their teachers (Berndt & Miller, 1990; Blatchford, 1992; Boggiano, Main, & Katz, 1991; Harter, 1975; Pomerantz, Altermatt, & Saxon, 2002; Ratelle, Guay, Vallerand, Larose, & Senécal 2007). These differences show up often enough to be cause for concern because they further contribute to girls' vulnerability to learned helplessness (because girls more consistently put forth their best efforts and therefore tend to attribute failures to lack of ability, whereas boys more consistently credit their successes to high ability but explain away their failures).

Interactions with Teachers

Boys are more active and salient in classrooms than girls. They have more of almost every kind of interaction that occurs between students and teachers. The differences are greatest for interactions that boys initiate themselves by calling out answers or by misbehaving and drawing some form of teacher intervention, but teachers also initiate interactions more frequently with boys, especially to give them procedural instructions, check their progress on assignments, or generally monitor and control their activities (Brophy, 1985; Garrahy, 2001; Harter, 1999).

Researchers also have identified differences in the ways teachers interact with boys versus girls. In particular, words of encouragement or feedback directed to boys tend to focus exclusively on their achievement striving and accomplishments, but some of what is said to girls in parallel situations focuses instead on neatness, following directions, speaking clearly, or showing good manners. Teachers sometimes pay more attention to, ask more thought-provoking questions of, or provide more extensive feedback to boys in mathematics or science classes but to girls in language arts classes. When groups of students work on computers or carry out scientific experiments, boys are more likely to take active roles but girls are more likely to act as recorders or just observers.

These trends are observed in varying degrees in almost all classrooms, regardless of whether the teachers are male or female. Thus, they are rooted in the gender role expectations that most people acquire through socialization into our culture. Many reflect gender differences in styles of participation in social conversation that carry over into classrooms: men speak more often and frequently interrupt women; listeners pay more attention to male speakers, even when female speakers use similar styles and make similar points; women participate less actively in conversations but do more gazing and passive listening; and women often transform declarative statements into more tentative statements that reduce their ability to influence others ("We could solve this problem using the Pythagorean Theorem, couldn't we?") (Brookfield & Preskill, 1999; Sadker & Sadker, 1994).

Recommendations

Clear-cut teacher favoritism of one gender over the other is rare. Gender differences in teacher–student interaction patterns tend to be relatively small in quantity and subtle in quality. Most reflect gender differences in student behavior that impact on teachers, rather than consistent teacher tendencies to treat boys and girls differently in parallel situations. Even so, it is wise to remain conscious of gender issues, not only to avoid inappropriate gender discrimination, but also to take advantage of opportunities to free your students from counterproductive restrictions built into traditional gender role concepts (Hoffmann, 2002).

Help your boys to take full advantage of reading and writing opportunities, and, in particular, to appreciate poetry and other forms of literature that they might view as feminine. Information about books popular with boys can be found at www.guysread. com. Similarly, help your girls to value and develop their full potential in mathematics and science (for ideas and resources, see http://girlstech.douglass.rutgers.edu).

In developing content, use examples and problem contexts that will interest girls as well as boys. Stimulate their interest in and willingness to take courses in these subjects and help them to realize that they can be successful if they apply reasonable effort. Both value- and expectancy-related issues in motivation relating to mathematics and science can be overcome, by emphasizing the roles of social discourse and personal creativity in these subjects (Kessels, Rau, & Hannover, 2006) and providing modeling and socialization to develop domain and career self-efficacy (Luzzo, Hasper, Albert, Bibby, & Martinelli, Jr., 1999).

Also, where necessary, encourage girls to become more active in the classroom. Make systematic efforts to observe and get to know each girl as an individual (especially girls who achieve satisfactorily and appear to be well adjusted but rarely initiate contact with you or assert themselves in the classroom). Encourage these girls to speak their minds, call on them to participate if they do not volunteer, assign them to leadership roles for group projects, and take other actions to encourage them to become more assertive. Broaden their perspectives by helping them to realize that the full spectrum of career opportunities is open to them and by using learning experiences such as stories involving females in leadership positions or discussions or assignments focusing on the work of female scientists.

Most teachers have been doing these things in recent years, and along with changes in curriculum materials and pervasive messages about gender equality in the culture generally, they have had a significant effect. Gender gaps in mathematics and science achievement are disappearing rapidly (Martinot & Désert, 2007). In fact, gender-related concerns about student motivation and achievement have begun to shift to boys, because recent trends indicate that fewer boys are earning good grades in school, graduating from high school, or attending college (Head, 1999).

DIFFERENCES IN FAMILY AND CULTURAL BACKGROUNDS WITHIN AMERICAN SOCIETY

Students from lower social class backgrounds or from racial or ethnic minority groups may experience difficulties at school to the extent that the values, language, behavioral expectations, and other aspects of the school culture contrast with what these students have been exposed to in their families and local subcultures. However, these difficulties can be minimized by teachers who are knowledgeable about and respectful of their students' home cultures and who work with the assets that the students bring to school with them rather than focus on deficiencies or problems (Anderman & Anderman, 1999).

Theory and research on these issues have developed in ways that reflect these distinctions. Early studies focused on group comparisons and yielded conclusions suggesting, for example, that lower-class students preferred material rewards whereas middle-class students preferred intrinsic rewards, that Hispanic students were oriented toward cooperative learning, that Native American students responded negatively to public praise, and that African American students had lower success expectations and less favorable attribution patterns than other students.

Subsequent research indicated that these and other sweeping statements about group differences were either incorrect or exaggerated, and that in any case, general sociological categories such as social class, race, ethnicity, or minority group membership were not nearly as useful as knowledge about individual students' family backgrounds and home cultures for understanding and suggesting ways to improve their adjustment to schooling. When researchers focused on specific families, and especially on the frequency and nature of the interactions that children had with their parents, they discovered many dimensions of family life and home culture that affect the degree to which children are comfortable at school, prepared to meet its challenges successfully, and confident in their ability to do so (Baker, Scher, & Mackler, 1997; Ginsburg & Bronstein, 1993; Grolnick & Ryan, 1989; Massey, Gebhardt, & Garnefski, 2008).

Many of these family factors that affect students' motivation at school are included in Joyce Epstein's (1989) TARGET model that led to Carole Ames's TARGET intervention model described in chapter 4. Epstein referred to the TARGET variables as family structures. The six structures and some of their influences on student motivation are as follows.

Task structure.   The task structure includes all activities conducted at home that may be related to school learning (household chores, play and hobby activities, school assignments done as homework, learning opportunities designed by the parents). Some families do much more than others to prepare their children for school and support their schooling experiences. They interact with their children frequently in cognitively stimulating ways, provide them with instruction and learning opportunities suited to their developmental levels (reading to them, teaching them to tell time and tie shoe laces, or teaching them the letters of the alphabet or how to write their names during the preschool years, and discussing their school work with them in later years), expose them to educational games and media at home, take them to museums and zoos, and encourage their talents and interests. Interaction around these activities builds important knowledge and skills and also has positive effects on children's developing curiosity, interest, attitudes toward school, acceptance of challenge, and tendency to engage in activities with learning goals rather than less desirable goals.

Authority structure.   The authority structure concerns the types and frequencies of children's responsibilities, self-directed activities, and opportunities to participate in family decision making. Families support their children's development of desirable motivational patterns by using authoritative childrearing methods that include age-appropriate sharing of authority, negotiation of rules and expectations, and opportunities for children to make their own decisions. These home experiences develop desirable motivational patterns on variables such as locus of control, personal responsibility, efficacy perceptions, tendency to seek success and not fear failure, and orientation toward self-regulated learning (but with readiness to interact effectively with teachers and participate in discussions and projects with other students). Families that rely on authoritarian or laissez-faire childrearing methods develop less desirable motivational patterns in their children.

Reward structure.   The reward structure refers to the degree to which parents pay attention to and reward their children's efforts and accomplishments. Parents support their children's school motivation by emphasizing encouragement and reward over threat and punishment, and by focusing their encouragement and rewards on school-related accomplishments (not just accomplishments in sports or other areas). It also helps if parents recognize improvement as well as excellence, cooperative as well as competitive behavior, and intrinsic satisfactions as well as extrinsic rewards.

Grouping structure.   Students' readiness to get along and collaborate with peers is affected by the degree to which their families encourage them to display nurturing behavior (in caring for younger siblings or elderly family members), monitor their interactions with peers and teach them to negotiate plans and resolve disagreements productively, model tolerance and appreciation of diversity, and help them to balance responsibilities to peers with responsibilities to parents, teachers, and others in their lives.

Evaluation structure.   The evaluation structure concerns the standards set for learning and behavior, the procedures used for monitoring and evaluating attainment of those standards, and the methods used to provide feedback about accomplishments and needed improvements. Supportive parental activities within this structure include emphasizing private and informative feedback over public and evaluative judgments, being flexible in adjusting standards to accommodate developments in children's abilities, and discussing the reasons for and implications of these developments in ways that help children to appreciate their accomplishments and set appropriate goals in the future.

Time structure.   The time structure concerns the schedules that families set for their children's activities and assignments. Especially when children have busy schedules (music lessons, sports, homework, chores, etc.), it is important for them to learn to develop realistic plans and manage their time effectively. Parents need to see that their children have sufficient time to do all they are expected to do, but also to see that these things are, in fact, accomplished and that a high priority is placed on school-related tasks if time is tight.

When parents fail to do these things that help prepare children for school and support their progress as students, it is usually because they do not realize their importance or know how to do them. Most parents care about their children's success at school and will respond positively to information sharing and requests from teachers. Furthermore, one of the distinctive features of the teachers and schools that are most effective with students at risk for school failure is that they reach out to these students' families, get to know them, keep them informed of what is going on at school, and involve them in decision making.

Stereotype Threat

Claude Steele (1997) has shown that members of stereotyped groups may perform below their capacities on tasks that their group is expected to do poorly on, especially if they are reminded of their group membership. For example, in the United State there are stereotyped expectations that African American students will perform poorly on tests of intelligence or academic achievement (Brown, 1998). Even subtle reminders of this expectation can cause African American students to become concerned about confirming this stereotype when they take tests, and this concern can distract the students from the tests and reduce their coping capacities in the same ways that efficacy concerns and fear of failure can (Schmader, Johns, & Forbes, 2008). Steele and Aronson (1995) demonstrated these dynamics in studies indicating that African American students showed variable levels of test performance, depending on how the test was presented. They did not do as well when the test was described as diagnostic of intellectual ability or when they were asked to identify their race immediately before taking it.

Steele (1997) noted that African American students' repeated experiences with stereotype threat, especially if they find themselves confirming the stereotype, can erode their motivation and ultimately lead to academic disidentification. Other scholars also have noted problems of academic disidentification among African American students, especially males (Major, Spencer, Schmader, Wolfe, & Crocker, 1998; Ogbu, 2002; Osborne, 1997; Voelkl, 1997) and some also have reported similar patterns for Latino students (Cordeiro & Carspecken, 1993; Griffin, 2002; Hudley & Graham, 2001).

Although demonstrated originally with African American students, stereotype threat phenomena can occur with respect to members of any group who might be expected to perform poorly in a particular domain, especially if they are reminded of their membership in the group when they are about to perform. So far, this has been demonstrated for Latino students (Hollis-Sawyer & Sawyer, 2008), for women on tests of mathematics ability (O'Brien & Crandall, 2003; Shih, Pittinski, & Ambady, 1999; Spencer, Steele, & Quinn, 1999), for men on an affective processing task (Leyens, Désert, Croizet, & Darcis, 2000), for European American students relative to Asian American students on a mathematics test (Aronson, Lustina, Keough, Brown, & Steele, 1999), for White athletes relative to Black athletes on an ostensible test of natural athletic ability (Stone, Lynch, Sjomeling, & Darley, 1999), and for students from lower socioeconomic status backgrounds relative to students from higher socioeconomic status backgrounds (Harrison, Stevens, Monty, & Coakley, 2006). For a review, see Steele, Spencer, and Aronson (2002).

The process can also work in reverse. Members of groups who are expected to excel in a domain can receive a stereotype "lift" or "boost" if they are reminded of their group membership as they are about to take a test in the domain. The size of the effect depends on the degree to which the person is aware of the stereotype and believes that it is valid (Chatard, Selimbegović, Konan, & Mugny, 2008; Walton & Cohen, 2003).

Both stereotype threat and stereotype boost effects were demonstrated in a simple but ingenious experiment done by Ambady, Shih, Kim, and Pittinsky (2001) with Asian American girls in grades K–8. Prior to taking a mathematics test, some of these girls were subtly reminded of their Asian heritage, while others were subtly reminded of their female gender. Analyses indicated that both at grades K–2 and at grades 6–8, the "Asians" outperformed the "females." In grades 3–5, however, when children go through a developmental stage that features gender chauvinism (believing that their own sex is superior to the other), the "females" outperformed the "Asians." A follow-up study with Asian American boys produced parallel findings indicating that stereotype lift effects were primarily associated with reminders of their Asian heritage, except at grades 3–5, when they were primarily associated with reminders of their male gender. Parallel results also were reported by Yopyk and Prentice (2005), who found that student athletes who had been primed to think about their identities as students did better on a math test than other student-athletes who had been primed to think about their identities as athletes.

Cohen, Steele, and Ross (1999) have suggested that wise teachers will create optimistic relationships with at-risk students, focusing not on academic problems and failures but on encouraging these students to feel a sense of belonging in the classroom and helping them to reach realistic achievement goals. They stressed that in interacting with these students, and especially when giving feedback on their work, teachers should combine articulation of high standards with expression of confidence that the students can meet these standards if they apply themselves. Other authors typically emphasize combining a warm and welcoming orientation toward these students and their families with persistent and determined efforts to help them achieve their potentials. These suggestions are supported by research indicating that potential victims of stereotype threat can be helped to perform more successfully by priming feelings of confidence, recognition that individuals do not necessarily reflect group norms and that ability can be improved incrementally, and that difficulties can be surmounted with effort and practice, as well as by exposing them to successful role models from their own group (Cohen & Garcia, 2008; Dweck & Grant, 2008; Marx & Roman, 2002; McIntyre, Paulson, & Lord, 2003; Schmader, Forbes, Zhang, & Mendes, 2009; Smith & Hung, 2008).

Motivating Minority and At-Risk Students

It is important to establish collaborative relationships with all of your students' parents, but especially with the parents of students who are struggling, apathetic, or resistant to you or your curriculum. The parents may have had similar problems in school them-selves, may feel guilty about their child's problems, or may be inhibited or suspicious at first in dealing with you (if they view teachers primarily as authority figures capable of getting their child into trouble). However, they are likely to be grateful and become more responsive if they see that you care about their child and want to work with them to pursue the child's best interests, not merely to give them bad news and then expect them to "do something."

The same is true of their child. Minority students and others whose family back-grounds place them at risk for school failure do especially well with teachers who share warm, personal interactions with them but also hold high expectations for their aca-demic progress, require them to perform up to their capabilities, and see that they progress as far and as fast as they are able. These teachers break through social-class differences, cultural differences, language differences, and other potential barriers to communication in order to form close relationships with at-risk students, but they use these relationships to maximize the students' learning progress, not merely to provide friendship or sympathy to them (Baker, 1998; Delpit, 1992; Hayes, Ryan, & Zseller, 1994; Kleinfeld, 1975; Siddle-Walker, 1992; Tucker et al., 2002).

At-risk students also do especially well in classrooms that offer warm, inviting social environments (Elias & Haynes, 2008; Lewis & Kim, 2008). Therefore, help your students to value diversity, learn from one another, and appreciate different languages and tradi-tions. Treat the cultures that they bring to school as assets that provide students with foundations of background knowledge to support their learning efforts and provide you with opportunities to enrich the curriculum for everyone. Think in terms of helping minority students to become fully bicultural rather than in terms of replacing one cul-ture with another. If you are unfamiliar with a culture that is represented in your class-room, educate yourself by reading about it, talking with community leaders, visiting homes, and most importantly, talking with students to learn about their past history and future aspirations.

For example, Moll (1992) interviewed the families of students enrolled in a bilingual education class to identify resources available in the community that might be capital-ized upon at the school, which was located in a primarily Spanish-speaking minority community. He identified the following *funds of knowledge* possessed by members of these households: ranching and farming (horsemanship, animal husbandry, soil and irrigation systems, crop planting, hunting, tracking, dressing game); mining (timbering, minerals, blasting, equipment operation and maintenance); economics (business, mar-ket values, appraising, renting and selling, loans, labor laws, building codes, consumer knowledge, accounting, sales); household management (budgets, child care, cooking, appliance repairs); material and scientific knowledge (construction, carpentry, roof-ing, masonry, painting, design and architecture); repairs (airplane, automobile, trac-tor, house maintenance); contemporary medicine (drugs, first-aid procedures, anatomy, midwifery); folk medicine (herbal knowledge, folk cures); and religion (catechism, bap-tisms, bible studies, moral knowledge and ethics).

Moll and Gonzalez (1997) noted that teachers could usefully integrate these funds of knowledge into classrooms through such activities as having students do research on community issues, understanding the architectural principles used in building commu-nity houses, or developing awareness of how the community functioned socially. They also emphasized the value of integrating parents intellectually into the life of the school. Similarly, Leacock (1969) noted that opportunities for connecting the curriculum to the students' home backgrounds are often missed because instruction stays too close to what is in the textbooks. As an example, she noted "community helpers" lessons in elementary social studies classes. Usually some students in a class have parents who are police officers, fire fighters, postal workers, and other service workers studied in these units, but few teachers think to invite these parents to come to the classroom and talk about their jobs.

If necessary, modify your curricula to infuse a multicultural perspective and feature the cultures represented by your students. Modifications might include a somewhat different selection of content (especially in history and literature) as well as treatment of many more topics as issues open to multiple perspectives rather than as bodies of factual information that admit to only a single interpretation. In covering cultures and customs, emphasize instructional materials that focus on universal human experiences and parallels between comparable cultural practices over materials that encourage chauvinism by promoting stereotypes focusing on exotic practices. Expose students to literature or multimedia content sources that feature models who come from minority groups represented in your classroom and portray these models in ways that encourage all students to identify with them. In addition, expose your students to actual, living models by arranging for classroom speakers, field trips, or current events discussions that will raise minority students' consciousness of roles and accomplishments to which they might aspire.

Knapp (1995) analyzed ways in which teachers working in ethnically heterogeneous classrooms responded to the cultural diversity of their students. Some did not respond constructively because they held negative stereotypes of certain ethnic or socioeconomic groups. They treated students from these groups in ways that limited their learning opportunities.

In contrast, constructive teachers held more positive expectations of their students and possessed a basic knowledge of their cultures. The most effective ones explicitly communicated to students that their cultural backgrounds were not problems to be overcome but rather strengths to be acknowledged and drawn upon in schooling. For example, here is Knapp's description of a bilingual teacher of a class composed of Hispanic, African American, and White students:

> Mr. Callio holds high expectations for his students and demands strict accountability for the work assigned to them. He recognizes that his students do not arrive at school with all the skills he would like them to have and plans his instruction accordingly. At the same time, his approach builds in a respect for the strengths and backgrounds of the students in his class. For example, Mr. Callio's classroom is alive with pictures from different parts of the world, showing the different ethnic, racial, and cultural groups represented in his students. One display reads "Yo soy Latin y orgulloso" ("I am Latin and proud of it") in big letters surrounded by pictures of pyramids, indigenous Mesoamericans, and other Latino faces. Another reads "I am African American and proud" and displays pictures of African people, places, and artifacts. Mr. Callio argues that it is imperative to provide positive self-images and role models if a teacher expects students to be driven to succeed. Mr. Callio uses his Spanish extensively in the classroom—and not simply to help those students with limited English proficiency. Rather, he argues that Spanish is an important language to know and encourages his monolingual English speakers to try to learn it. One of the top students in the class,

an African-American male, regularly tries to piece together Spanish sentences. (Knapp, 1995, p. 39)

COUNTERACTING PEER PRESSURES

A positive approach that honors diversity and focuses on helping all students to achieve their potentials should carry you a long way in motivating your students to learn. This includes most students considered to be at risk for school failure because of their social class, racial, or ethnic backgrounds. These students usually want to be successful at school and often have integrated academic achievement into their ethnic or racial identities (Carter, 2008; Lewis & Kim, 2008; Darling, Molina, Sanders, Lee, & Zhao, 2008; Nasir, McLaughlin, & Jones, 2009). However, you may encounter resistance from alienated students who have come to view putting forth consistent effort in school as "selling out," "sucking up to teachers," or "acting White" (Taylor & Graham, 2007). You will need to take actions designed to turn these students around, and, in the meantime, to minimize their negative influences on classmates.

The most effective way to turn around resistant students is to put them in contact with respected models with whom they identify and ask the models to help these students see that their attitudes undermine their own best interests. Ideal models might be teenagers and young adults who formerly attended your school and can relate true stories that illustrate how life paths begin to diverge when students their age decide either to take advantage of or to reject what schooling has to offer them.

In addition, try to resocialize resistant students' attitudes, whatever your (and their) social class and ethnic backgrounds may be. Toward this end, I recommend three strategies. First, do not scoff at the students' ideas (about "acting White," etc.) or dismiss them out of hand. Accept them as genuinely held beliefs, although beliefs that you do not share. If you try to undermine these beliefs using persuasion methods, make sure that everything about your tone and manner and all of your arguments communicate your concern about their best interests. If they view your behavior as an attempt to manipulate them for your own purposes, your persuasion attempts will backfire. In the case of minority group students, even if they concede your good intentions, they may believe that you essentially are pressuring them to give up their cultural heritage in exchange for economic opportunities in the larger society (Secada & Lightfoot, 1993).

Second, draw these students out by using "active listening," reflection, and related counseling techniques. In private conversations, ask them to elaborate on their views and listen carefully. Occasionally, paraphrase or reflect to show that you have understood what the student is saying ("So, your friends taunt you when you contribute good ideas to class discussion or get good grades on tests. How does that make you feel?"). If you continue in this vein, the student may begin to see for himself that he doesn't really believe what peers are telling him, that the peers are pursuing their own questionable agendas rather than acting as true friends concerned about his best interests, that they are pressuring him to subvert his own values, and that he needs to find ways to resist this peer pressure without significant cost to his social relationships (or perhaps to cultivate friendships with more compatible peers).

Third, with students who begin to develop such insights, you might use the "inoculation" techniques that have been developed for helping people to cope with stressful situations. For example, techniques for helping timid children to become more assertive include role playing or discussing vignettes in which someone ignores or mistreats them, then analyzing how the situation might be handled effectively or how the role-played response might have been improved. Similar techniques can be used to help socially pressured students plan ahead for and practice possible responses to situations in which peers taunt them for displaying motivation to learn at school.

Along with your own efforts, improvements in the school's culture and in school-community relations will be needed to turn around the most hostile and resistant students, especially if they belong to a local subculture that distrusts schooling as an institution. You cannot simply wait for these improvements to occur, however, because you must work with your students each day, dealing with them and the school milieu as they are at the moment. You may not be able to eliminate resistant students' negative attitudes toward the school as a whole, but at least you can get them to view you as an exception and begin to "go along with the program" in your classroom. Whatever the apparent odds against you, you will maximize your chances to succeed with these students if you follow the suggestions made in this book, especially those calling for making yourself and your classroom attractive to students, modeling motivation to learn, communicating positive expectations and attributions, and connecting with students' home cultures.

CONTRASTS BETWEEN NATIONS AND WORLD REGIONS

Ideas about motivation developed within the United States and other Western cultures are based on theory and research developed primarily in these nations and published primarily in English. We tend to think of these ideas as "the" psychology of motivation—reflective of a common human condition and thus equally applicable everywhere. Indeed, this assumption is often supported by evidence, indicating for example that people from different countries around the world show similar patterns of basic needs (Ryan & Deci, 2006; Sheldon, Elliot, Kim, & Kasser, 2001; Vansteenkiste, Lens, Soenens, & Luyckx, 2006; Yamaguchi et al., 2007) or attribution of school performances to causes (Little & Lopez, 1997). However, comparative research also has identified interesting contrasts between nations and world regions.

For example, Hufton, Elliott, and Illushin (2002) found that Russian adolescents were more likely to attribute high achievement to ability than to effort, yet reported spending more time on schoolwork and in other respects investing more effort than American and British adolescents. Furthermore, they maintained task engagement even though their teachers were short on praise and long on correction, and they maintained a mastery orientation even though their activities involved following a prescribed curriculum and seldom featured opportunities for autonomy or choice making. This pattern reflected a pervasive Russian cultural value on becoming an educated person. Russian children are socialized from their earliest years to value education and become strongly motivated to acquire it. Teachers are seen as necessary guides and supporters (not imposers) in pursuing these goals, and classmates are seen as collaborators (not competitors). Consequently, teacher correction is construed as help and valued as such. Education is defined by the school curriculum, so students feel little need for choice of learning task or autonomy in working. Given this socialization, there is less need for Russian teachers to work on the value aspects of motivation, compared to British and American teachers.

Perhaps the most pervasive cultural differences are between people from Western nations (e.g., the United States and western Europe) and people from East Asia (e.g., China, Korea, and Japan). The former countries are individualistic and tend to produce people whose self-concepts emphasize uniqueness and independence from others, whereas the latter nations are collectivistic and tend to produce people whose self-concepts are interdependent (Heine & Buchtel, 2009; Kitayama, Duffy, & Uchida, 2007; Morling & Kitayama, 2008).

Western psychological thinking tends to assume that a key facet of development is movement toward an increasingly differentiated and individuated self-concept. Most of our motivational concepts make or imply reference to the self, whether they refer to expectancy aspects (self-efficacy perceptions, internal locus of control, self-worth protection, etc.), value aspects (self-relevance perceptions, identification, personal interests, etc.), intrinsic aspects (choices perceived as autonomous are seen as emanating from oneself), or extrinsic aspects (feeling external pressure to perform, such that our behavior is not self-determined). *In contrast, East Asian people are socialized to think more in terms of their families and other relationships than their individual identities, being part of an interdependent social network, and pursuing agendas more as a member of a group than as an individual.* They usually do not develop acute consciousness of a unique self or need to differentiate themselves from others. They tend to be oriented toward harmonizing themselves with others rather than toward achieving self-actualization by accomplishing a personal agenda.

In attributing behavior to causes, East Asians tend to make fewer references to personal dispositions but more references to situational factors. This enables them to be more tolerant of contradictions and more able to adjust themselves to conflicting situational demands than Westerners, who are more concerned about self-consistency (Heine, 2007; Spencer-Rodgers, Boucher, Mori, Wang, & Peng, 2009). Some scholars have claimed that East Asians are more likely than Westerners to emphasize effort rather than ability in explaining achievement, and have suggested that this attributional pattern is advantageous to the motivation of East Asian students and helps explain their superior performance on international achievement tests (Stevenson & Stigler, 1992). However, other scholars have questioned these claims and put forth evidence to refute them (Bempechat & Drago-Severson, 1999; Pomerantz, Ng, & Wang, 2008) or have pointed out that the "model minority" stereotype (Li & Wang, 2008) and a pervasive emphasis on effort over ability place struggling East Asian students in a difficult bind—even though they work harder than their peers, they still earn relatively low grades, leading to additional anxiety and stress because parents and teachers interpret their poor performance as reflecting inadequate effort (Grant & Dweck, 2001; Hong, 2001).

Other findings have indicated that East Asians have less need to maintain a sense of self-consistency and less need for positive self-regard, so they tend to be less self-aggrandizing and more self-critical when talking about themselves (Heine & Hamamura, 2007). East Asians also tend to be more comfortable subordinating their personal agendas to those of their families or groups. For example, interdependent goal pursuit (pursuing goals to please parents and friends) increases the perceived benefit of goal attainment for East Asian students but not American students (Oishi & Diener, 2001) and people with interdependent selves are more likely than people with independent selves to be intrinsically motivated when choices are made for them by trusted significant others than when they make the choices themselves (Bao & Lam, 2008; Iyengar & Lepper, 2002; Pöhlmann, Carranza, Hannover, & Iyengar, 2007). These cultural differences have been attributed to differences in philosophical and religious beliefs about the human condition (Heine, 2007), as well as to differences in societal expectations that lead parents to socialize their children toward socially valued and adaptive behavior patterns (Kitayama & Imada, 2008; Morling & Kitayama, 2008; Yamagishi, Hashimoto, & Schug, 2008).

Finally, Americans tend to focus on self-enhancement, so they seek to "stick out," adopting primarily approach motivation and attending primarily to opportunities. In contrast, East Asians tend to focus more on "fitting in," and to be more concerned about loss of face (social devaluation for failing to live up to expectations), so they are relatively more attentive to potential dangers and likely to adopt avoidance motivation focused on preventing mistakes (Heine, 2007; Zusho, Pintrich, & Cortina, 2005).

Gaskins (1999) summarized *the Zen Buddhist perspective* on human psychology and motivation. He noted that Buddhism treats self-concept as both a delusion (what we recognize as a self or permanent essence is actually an ever-changing configuration of energies or processes that is meaningful only within particular contexts) and a barrier to the achievement of contentment (which involves emptying ourselves of filters that we create between ourselves and aspects of our experience, thus freeing ourselves to experience the moment "just as it is," and to appreciate our interfusion with all things). These notions seem contradictory to Western notions at first, but in many respects they lead to similar principles concerning motivation in education. For example, descriptions of flow or of adopting a learning orientation (in which the person is immersed in the task and not thinking about the self) seem quite similar to Buddhist notions of what it means to be "in the moment." Similarly, although concerns about failure might lead Western students to fear personal embarrassment but East Asian students to fear bringing shame to their families or groups, it would seem that principles drawn from efficacy theory, attribution theory, goal theory, and related notions should apply equally well in both situations.

Comparisons of Eastern and Western thinking about motivation have not yet yielded clear implications for practice. However, even if it ultimately turns out that most of the principles developed in Western research prove to have universal applicability (or require only minor tweaking to adapt them to Eastern contexts), it will be useful to know which aspects of our theorizing appear to be universal and which appear to be culturally bound. As anthropologists like to remind us, we learn more about the human condition and our own places within it by "making the familiar strange" and "making the strange familiar."

CONCLUSION

You may have noticed that even though this chapter deals with individual and group differences, it frequently reemphasizes strategies presented in previous chapters and recommends individualizing along the margins of a general motivational approach to the class as a whole rather than using very different methods with different students. There are three reasons for this. First, psychological theory and research, both on motivation in particular and on the human condition in general, indicates that humans are much more similar than different. A particular motive might be less relevant for some people than for others, but to the extent that the motive is applicable in a given situation, research-based principles relating to the motive should apply to everyone.

Second, empirical research bears out these theoretical expectations. Discouraged students may need more attention to the expectancy-related aspects of motivation whereas apathetic students may need more attention to the value- related aspects, boys may need more encouragement in language arts and girls more encouragement in mathematics and science, members of minority groups may have a greater need for exposure to models with whom they can identify, and so on. However, these distinctions lie in the details of implementation of motivational principles, not in the principles themselves. What has been said in this book about the desirability of learning goals relative to performance or work avoidant goals, about the value of inducing students to attribute their successes to the combination of sufficient ability and reasonable effort but to attribute their failures to insufficient effort or strategy knowledge, about helping students to see that schooling is designed to empower them to pursue their own best interests and achieve self-actualization goals, and so on, are principles that you can apply with all of your students, whoever they may be.

Finally, much of my own research has focused on the dynamics of teacher- student interactions, particularly as they are affected by teachers' and students' attitudes, beliefs, and expectations. This work has sensitized me to the problems of rigid expectations, labeling effects, and stereotyping that often result when teachers think of their classes as collections of subgroups (Blacks vs. Whites, boys vs. girls, high achievers vs. low achievers, cooperative students vs. troublemakers, etc.) or think of individual students in terms of stereotyped labels (gifted, learning disabled, hyperactive, low functioning, emotionally disturbed, etc.). Up to a point, descriptive categories and labels are necessary and help us to understand students and plan to meet their needs. However, if we lose sight of students' individuality and begin to think about them primarily in terms of category labels, we may begin to notice only those things about them that fit our stereotypes and start to interact with them in ways that cause our expectations to function as self-fulfilling prophecies.

Thus, there is danger in pigeonholing students and thinking about motivation in terms of the contrasting needs of different subgroups or student types. I believe that you will be a more successful motivator if you learn general principles and strategies and use these to establish your classroom as a learning community, then supplement by providing individual students with whatever special emphases or motivational extras they may need.

SUMMARY

Motivational theorists differ in the relative emphasis they place on general principles assumed to apply universally versus specialized principles intended for use with particular subgroups or student types. Most such theorists, including myself, emphasize principles that are believed to apply universally but may have more relevance in certain situations or with certain students than others. However, some theorists have called for using different strategies with different students.

Some schemes for differentiating motivational strategies amount to nothing more than accommodating students' content or activity preferences. There are at least three reasons for proceeding with caution in adopting such strategies: accommodating students' existing preferences does nothing to develop their motivation to learn or in other ways to move them in directions you would like to see them move; accommodating their preferences is not the same as meeting their needs; and accommodating their preferences may have the effect of reinforcing personal characteristics that ought to be changed. Consequently, any plans for individualizing motivational strategies should be designed to meet the students' needs and long-run best interests, not just to accommodate their current preferences. In addition to these theoretical concerns, there is also the important practical constraint of feasibility: Teachers working with 20 or more students need to focus their curriculum and instruction on the class as a whole. They do not have the time or resources to plan a unique program for each individual student.

Within this perspective, the chapter considers claims and suggestions made to teachers for differentiating curriculum and instruction so as to optimize students' motivation. One of the better researched bases for planning contrasting approaches is the cognitive style dimension of psychological differentiation. Field dependent students are people-oriented in their content interests and prefer to learn in close collaboration with others. Field independent students have more theoretical and analytic interests and prefer to learn more autonomously and individually. You might want to accommodate these preferences most of the time, although students who represent the extremes of this dimension need to learn to function effectively in situations that call for their non-preferred cognitive style.

Much of what you hear about individualizing your approaches to motivation will be based on the notion of learning styles. Often these ideas will be presented by people who are eager to sell you learning style inventories and other assessment devices or manuals outlining their learning style models. They are likely to imply that implementing these models will quickly produce remarkable improvements in students' motivation and achievement. In fact, the research base supporting these models is thin to nonexistent (depending on the model) and characterized by questionable scientific procedures and interpretations of findings. You probably should accommodate students' preferences when doing so will not interfere with accomplishment of learning goals. However, there is little reason to believe that it will be worth your while to purchase assessment instruments and seek to implement elaborate models of differentiated instruction based on these learning style notions. The same is true of models based on supposed multiple intelligences or brain hemisphere preferences.

Developmental differences in children's cognitive abilities and motivational needs and interests make certain strategies more or less relevant at particular grade levels. Young children's inattention to social comparisons and limited understanding of the implications of failure feedback make them less likely than older students to emphasize performance goals over learning goals or to develop learned helplessness problems. Such problems can develop even in these students, however, if teachers fail to follow the guidelines in chapters 2–5. Teachers at higher levels of schooling who deal with transitional students coming in from lower levels should go out of their way to make sure that these students adjust smoothly to the new school and do not suffer dramatic drops in their self-perceptions of ability.

Motivational problems relating to rigid gender roles are less serious than they used to be. Nevertheless, many activities are still gender typed, and this may inhibit some students' interest in them. All students need help in overcoming the rigidities of traditional gender roles and learning to develop their potentials in areas that they associate with the opposite gender. In addition, some students (especially girls with respect to mathematics or science) need to be helped to realize that claims of large gender differences in ability in different subject areas are incorrect, and that they have the ability to succeed if they apply reasonable effort in subjects traditionally associated with the opposite gender.

Early research on student social class, race, and ethnicity produced sweeping generalizations which have come to be recognized as incorrect, exaggerated, or misinterpreted. Subsequent research has shifted attention from these general sociological labels to investigation of individual students' family and cultural experiences as factors influencing the students' readiness for and successful functioning in school. Also, investigations of minority groups have shifted from identifying supposed deficits to developing understanding of the prior experiences and cultural backgrounds that children bring to school and how these may be used as strengths to build on.

Students may be anxious or conflicted at school if the expectations and culture they encounter there contrast with what the students experience in the rest of their lives. Teachers who are successful with minority-group and other at-risk students develop good personal relationships with these students and their families and embrace their languages and cultures. However, they also work to maximize the students' academic progress, not merely to provide them with friendship or sympathy. You are most likely to help each of your students to get maximal empowerment and self-actualization benefits from being in your class if you think in terms of using the same basic motivational principles to pursue the same basic learning goals with all of them, rather than in terms of using different principles to pursue different goals with different subgroups or individuals.

Interesting cultural differences in motivational patterns have been noted, especially relating to contrasts between individualist cultures that develop independent selves and collectivist cultures that develop interdependent selves. As with contrasts between subgroups of Americans, these differences are relative rather than absolute, so they may require minor adaptations of basic principles that apply to everyone, but not wholesale differential treatment of students from different cultures. All students need an emphasis on motivation to learn within a learning community as described in chapter 2.

REFLECTION QUESTIONS

1. The author has described several contrasting positions on the importance of group and individual differences and their possible implications for accommodating curriculum and instruction. Write out your own position on these issues and discuss it with colleagues.

2. Do you recognize yourself as being either primarily field dependent or primarily field independent (rather than more mixed)? If so, how will you adjust your natural teaching tendencies in order to be more effective with students whose psychological differentiation pattern contrasts with your own?

3. Given the history of mixed and frequently negative research findings, what explains the persistent popularity of ideas about adapting teaching to students' supposed cognitive styles, learning styles, brain hemisphere preferences, or multiple intelligences? Are there productive ways to use some of these concepts to improve instructional planning? What negative effects might they have if used inappropriately?

4. How might it be helpful and/or harmful to tell teachers that certain of their students are visual learners but others are verbal learners? What if these characterizations are also passed along to the students?

5. What do you make of the loss of intrinsic motivation as children progress through school?

6. Do you think that particular motivational techniques ought to be either emphasized or minimized with younger students? With older students?

7. Suppose that you were to teach two sections of the same class. The sections would be comparable in every other respect but one would include only male students and the other only female students. What, if anything, would you do differently in planning your general approach to instruction, your curriculum, and your learning activities for the two sections? List any differences you would include and discuss your lists with colleagues.

8. Repeat the previous exercise, this time pretending that all sections contain both male and female students but one consists exclusively of European American students, another of African American students, and a third of Latino students. Again, list and discuss what, if anything, you would do differently in these sections. What do your lists imply about your position on accommodating group differences?

9. Why do adolescent girls' self-efficacy perceptions as mathematics and science learners drop, even though they continue to earn better grades than boys? What can you do about this?

10. Along with a majority of American-born children, your class includes three students whose families emigrated from Mexico and two whose families emigrated from Vietnam. What, if anything, will you need to do differently with these five immigrant students than you do with the rest of your class?

11. What should you do if confronted with outright resistance to your curriculum and teaching efforts?

12. If you were asked to adapt this book to be used as a text in China or Japan, would you change any of its basic principles? If so, which ones, and why?

REFERENCES

Ambady, N., Shih, M., Kim, A., & Pittinsky, T. (2001). Stereotype susceptibility in children: Effects of identity activation on quantitative performance. *Psychological Science, 12,* 385–390.

Anderman, E., & Maehr, M. (1994). Motivation and schooling in the middle grades. *Review of Educational Research, 64,* 207–309.

Anderman, L., &. Anderman, E. (1999). Social influences on school adjustment: Families, peers, neighborhoods, and culture [Special issue]. *Educational Psychologist, 34,* 1–70.

Aronson, J., Lustina, M., Keough, K., Brown, J., & Steele, C. (1999). When White men can't do math: Necessary and sufficient factors in stereotype threat. *Journal of Experimental Social Psychology, 35,* 29–46.

Baker, J. (1998). The social context of school satisfaction among urban, low-income, African-American students. *School Psychology Quarterly, 13,* 25–44.

Baker, L., Scher, D., & Mackler, K. (1997). Home and family influences on motivations for reading. *Educational Psychologist, 32,* 69–82.

Bao, X., & Lam, S. (2008). Who makes the choice? Rethinking the role of autonomy and relatedness in Chinese children's motivation. *Child Development, 79,* 269–283.

Barker, G., & Graham, S. (1987). Developmental study of praise and blame as attributional cues. *Journal of Educational Psychology, 79,* 62–66.

Bempechat, J., & Drago-Severson, E. (1999). Cross-national differences in academic achievement: Beyond etic conceptions of children's understandings. *Review of Educational Research, 69,* 287–314.

Bergen, D., & Coscia, J. (2002). *Brain research and childhood education.* Olney, MD: Association for Childhood Education International.

Berndt, T., & Miller, K. (1990). Expectancies, values, and achievement in junior high school. *Journal of Educational Psychology, 82,* 319–326.

Billington, J., Baron-Cohen, S., & Wheelwright, S. (2007). Cognitive style predicts entry into physical sciences and humanities: Questionnaire and performance tests of empathy and systemizing. *Learning and Individual Differences, 17,* 260–268.

Blatchford, P. (1992). Academic self-assessment at 7 and 11 years: Its accuracy and association with ethnic group and sex. *British Journal of Educational Psychology, 62,* 35–44.

Boggiano, A., Main, D., & Katz, P. (1991). Mastery motivation in boys and girls: The role of intrinsic versus extrinsic motivation. *Sex Roles, 25,* 511–520.

Bornholt, L., Goodnow, J., & Cooney, G. (1994). Influences of gender stereotypes on adolescents' perceptions of their own achievement. *American Educational Research Journal, 31,* 675–692.

Brookfield, S., & Preskill, S. (1999). *Discussion as a way of teaching: Tools and techniques for democratic classrooms.* San Francisco: Jossey-Bass.

Brophy, J. (1985). Interactions of male and female students with male and female teachers. In L. Wilkinson & C. Marrett (Eds.), *Gender influences in classroom interaction* (pp. 115–142). Orlando, FL: Academic Press.

Brown, L. (1998). Ethnic stigma as a contextual experience: A possible selves perspective. *Personality and Social Psychology Bulletin, 24,* 163–172.

Bruer, J. (1999). In search of … brain-based education. *Phi Delta Kappan, 80,* 649–657.

Brush, L. (1980). *Encouraging girls in mathematics: The problem and the solution.* Cambridge, MA: Abt.

Butler, R. (1990). The effects of mastery and competitive conditions on self-assessment at different ages. *Child Development, 61,* 201–210.

Carbo, M. (1997). *What every principal should know about teaching reading: How to raise test scores and nurture a love of reading.* Syosset, NY: National Reading Styles Institute.

Carter, D. (2008). Achievement as resistance: The development of a critical race achievement ideology among Black achievers. *Harvard Educational Review, 78,* 466–497.

Cassidy, S. (2004). Learning styles: An overview of theories, models, and measures. *Educational Psychology, 24,* 419–441.

Ceci, S., Williams, W., & Barnett, S. (2009). Women's underrepresentation in science: Sociocultural and biological considerations. *Psychological Bulletin, 135,* 218–261.

Chatard, A., Selimbegović, L., Konan, B., & Mugny, G. (2008). Performance boosts in the classroom: Stereotype endorsement and prejudice moderate stereotype lift. *Journal of Experimental Social Psychology, 44,* 1421–1424.

Clark, R. (1982). Antagonism between achievement and enjoyment in ATI studies. *Educational Psychologist, 17,* 92–101.

Coffield, F., Moseley, D., Hall, E., & Ecclestone, K. (2004). *Should we be using learning styles? What research has to say to practice.* London: Learning and Skills Research Centre.

Cohen, G., & Garcia, J. (2008). Identity, belonging, and achievement: A model, interventions, implications. *Current Directions in Psychological Science, 17,* 365–369.

Cohen, G., Steele, C., & Ross, L. (1999). The mentor's dilemma: Providing critical feedback across the racial divide. *Personality and Social Psychology Bulletin, 25,* 1302–1318.

Cordeiro, P., & Carspecken, P. (1993). How a minority of the minority succeed: A case study of 20 Hispanic achievers. *Qualitative Studies in Education, 6,* 277–290.

Corpus, J., McClintic-Gilbert, M., & Hayenga, A. (2009). Within-year changes in children's intrinsic and extrinsic motivational orientations: Contextual predictors and academic outcomes. *Contemporary Educational Psychology, 34,* 154–166.

Darling, E., Molina, K., Sanders, M., Lee, F., & Zhao, Y. (2008). Belonging and achieving: The role of identity integration. In M. Maehr, S. Karabenick, & T. Urdan (Eds.), *Social psychological perspectives (Advances in motivation and achievement* series (Vol. 15, pp. 241–273). Bingley, UK: Emerald.

DeLoache, J., Simcock, G., & Macari, S. (2007). Planes, trains, automobiles –and tea sets: Extremely intense interests in very young children. *Developmental Psychology, 43,* 1579–1586.

Delpit, L. (1992). Acquisition of literate discourse: Bowing before the master? *Theory Into Practice, 31,* 296–302.

Diekman, A., & Eagly, A. (2008). Of men, women, and motivation: A role congruity account. In J. Shah & W. Gardner (Eds.), *Handbook of motivation science* (pp. 434–447). New York: Guilford.

Dorsel, T. (1975). Preference-success assumption in education. *Journal of Educational Psychology, 67,* 514–520.

Dreher, M. (2003). Motivating struggling readers by tapping the potential of information books. *Reading and Writing Quarterly: Overcoming Learning Difficulties, 19,* 25–38.

Dunn, R., & Dunn, K. (1992). *Teaching elementary students through their individual learning styles.* Boston: Allyn & Bacon.

Dunn, R., Gorman, B., Griggs, S., Olson, J., & Beasley, M. (1995). A meta-analytic validation of the Dunn and Dunn model of learning-style preferences. *Journal of Educational Research, 88,* 353–362.

Dweck, C., & Grant, H. (2008). Self-theories, goals, and meaning. In J. Shah & W. Gardner (Eds.), *Handbook of motivation science* (pp. 405–416). New York: Guilford.

Eccles, J. (1987). Gender roles and women's achievement related decisions. *Psychology of Women Quarterly*, *11*, 135–172.

Eccles, J., & Roeser, R. (2009). Schools, academic motivation, and stage-environment fit. In R. Lerner & L. Steinberg (Eds.), *Handbook of Adolescent Psychology* (3rd ed., Vol. 1, pp. 404–434). New York: Wiley.

Eccles, J., Wigfield, A., Flanagan, C., Miller, C., Reuman, D., & Yee, D. (1989). Self-concepts, domain values, and self-esteem: Relations and changes at early adolescence. *Journal of Personality and Social Psychology*, *57*, 283– 310.

Eden, D. (1975). Intrinsic and extrinsic rewards and motives: Replication and extension with Kibbutz workers. *Journal of Applied Social Psychology*, *5*, 348–361.

Elias, M., & Haynes, N. (2008). Social competence, social support, and academic achievement in minority, low-income, urban elementary children. *School Psychology Quarterly*, *23*, 474–495.

Epstein, J. (1989). Family structures and student motivation: A developmental perspective. In C. Ames & R. Ames (Eds.), *Research on motivation in education. Vol. 3: Goals and cognitions* (pp. 259–295). San Diego, CA: Academic Press.

Flowerday, T., & Schraw, G. (2003). Effect of choice on cognitive and affective engagement. *Journal of Educational Research*, *96*, 207–215.

Gardner, H. (1993). *Multiple intelligences: The theory in practice*. New York: Basic Books.

Gardner, H. (1999). *Intelligence reframed: Multiple intelligences in the 21st century*. New York: Basic Books.

Garrahy, D. (2001). Three third-grade teachers' gender-related beliefs and behavior. *Elementary School Journal*, *102*, 81–94.

Gaskins, R. (1999). "Adding legs to a snake": A reanalysis of motivation and the pursuit of happiness from a Zen Buddhist perspective. *Journal of Educational Psychology*, *91*, 204–215.

Ginsburg, G., & Bronstein, P. (1993). Family factors related to children's intrinsic/extrinsic motivational orientation and academic performance. *Child Development*, *64*, 1461–1474.

Gottfried, A.E., Fleming, J., & Gottfried, A.W. (2001). Continuity of academic intrinsic motivation from childhood through late adolescence: A longitudinal study. *Journal of Educational Psychology*, *93*, 3–13.

Grant, H., & Dweck, C. (2001). Cross-cultural response to failure: Considering outcome attributions with different goals. In F. Salili, C. Chiu, & Y. Hong (Eds.), *Student motivation: The culture and context of learning* (pp. 203–219). New York: Kluwer/Plenum.

Griffin, B. (2002). Academic disidentification, race, and high school dropouts. *High School Journal*, *85*(4), 71–81.

Grolnick, W., & Ryan, R. (1989). Parent styles associated with children's self-regulation and competence in school. *Journal of Educational Psychology*, *81*, 143–154.

Guimond, S., & Roussel, L. (2001). Bragging about one's school grades: Gender stereotyping and students' perceptions of their abilities in science, mathematics, and language. *Social Psychology of Education*, *4*, 275–293.

Hannafin, R., & Sullivan, H. (1996). Preferences and learner control over amount of instruction. *Journal of Educational Psychology*, *88*, 162–173.

Hannover, B., & Kessels, U. (2004). Self-to-prototype matching as a strategy for making academic choices. Why high school students do not like math and science. *Learning and Instruction*, *14*, 51–67.

Harrison, L., Stevens, C., Monty, A., & Coakley, C. (2006). The consequences of stereotype threat on the academic performance of White and non-White lower income college students. *Social Psychology of Education*, *9*, 341–357.

Harter, S. (1975). Developmental differences in the manifestation of mastery motivation on problem-solving tasks. *Child Development*, *46*, 370–378.

Harter, S. (1999). *The construction of the self: A developmental perspective*. New York: Guilford.

Hayes, C., Ryan, A., & Zseller, E. (1994). The middle school child's perceptions of caring teachers. *American Journal of Education*, *103*, 1–19.

Head, J. (1999). *Understanding the boys: Issues of behaviour and achievement*. London: Falmer.

Heine, S. (2007). Culture and motivation: What motivates people to act in the ways that they do? In S. Kitamaya & D. Cohen (Eds.), *Handbook of Cultural Psychology* (pp. 714–733). New York: Guilford.

Heine, S., & Buchtel, E. (2009). Personality: The universal and the culturally specific. *Annual Review of Psychology*, *60*, 369–394.

Heine, S., & Hamamura, T. (2007). In search of East Asian self-enhancement. *Personality and Social Psychology Review*, *11*, 4–27.

Hoffmann, L. (2002). Promoting girls' interest and achievement in physics classes for beginners. *Learning and Instruction*, *12*, 447–465.

Hollis-Sawyer, L., & Sawyer, T. (2008). Potential stereotype threat and face validity effects on cognitive-based test performance in the classroom. *Educational Psychology*, *28*, 291–304.

Hong, Y. (2001). Chinese students' and teachers' inferences of effort and ability. In F. Salili, C. Chiu, & Y. Hong (Eds.), *Student motivation: The culture and context of learning* (pp. 105–120). New York: Kluwer/Plenum.

Hudley, C., & Graham, S. (2001). Stereotypes of achievement striving among early adolescents. *Social Psychology of Education, 5,* 201–224.

Hufton, N., Elliott, J., & Illushin, L. (2002). Achievement motivation across cultures: Some puzzles and their implications for future research. *New Directions for Child and Adolescent Development, 96,* 65–85.

Hurlock, E. (1964). *Child development* (4th ed.). New York: McGraw-Hill.

Iyengar, S., & Lepper, M. (2002). Choice and its consequences: On the costs and benefits of self-determination. In A. Tesser, D. Stapel, & J. Wood (Eds.), *Self and motivation: Emerging psychological perspectives* (pp. 71–96). Washington, DC: American Psychological Association.

Jensen, E. (2000). Brain-based learning: A reality check. *Educational Leadership, 57*(7), 76–80.

Jersild, A., & Tasch, R. (1949). *Children's interests and what they suggest for education.* New York: Bureau of Publications, Teachers College, Columbia University.

Johnson, K., Alexander, J., Spencer, S., Leibham, M., & Neitzel, C. (2004). Factors associated with the early emergence of intense interests within conceptual domains. *Cognitive Development, 19,* 325–343.

Kavale, K., & LeFever, G. (2007). Dunn and Dunn model of learning-style preferences: Critique of Lovelace meta-analysis. *Journal of Educational Research, 101,* 94–97.

Kessels, U., Rau, M., & Hannover, B. (2006). What goes well with physics? Measuring and altering the image of science. *British Journal of Educational Psychology, 76,* 761–780.

Kitayama, S., Duffy, S., & Uchida, Y. (2007). Self as cultural mode of being. In S. Kitayama & D. Cohen (Eds.), *Handbook of cultural psychology* (pp. 136–174). New York: Guilford.

Kitayama, S., & Imada, T. (2008). Defending cultural self: A dual-process analysis of cognitive dissonance. In M. Maehr, S. Karabenick, & T. Urdan (Eds.), *Social psychological perspectives (Advances in motivation and achievement* series (Vol. 15, pp. 171–207). Bingley, UK: Emerald.

Klein, P. (2003). Rethinking the multiplicity of cognitive resources and curricular representations: Alternatives to "learning styles" and "multiple intelligences." *Journal of Curriculum Studies, 35,* 45–81.

Kleinfeld, J. (1975). Effective teachers of Indian and Eskimo students. *School Review, 83,* 301–344.

Knapp, M. (1995). *Teaching for meaning in high-poverty classrooms.* New York: Teachers College Press.

Krechevsky, M., & Seidel, S. (2001). Minds at work: Applying multiple intelligences in the classroom. In J. Collins & D. Cook (Eds.), *Understanding learning: Influences and outcomes* (pp. 44–59). London: Paul Chapman.

Leacock, E. (1969). *Teaching and learning in city schools.* New York: Basic Books.

Lewis, J., & Kim, E. (2008). A desire to learn: African American children's positive attitudes toward learning within school cultures of low expectations. *Teachers College Record, 110,* 1304–1329.

Leyens, J., Desert, M., Croizet, J., & Darcis, C. (2000). Stereotype threat: Are lower status and history of stigmatization preconditions of stereotype threat? *Personality and Social Psychology Bulletin, 26,* 1189–1199.

Li, G., & Wang, L. (Eds.). Model minority myths revisited: An interdisciplinary approach to demystifying Asian-American educational experiences. Charlotte, NC: Information Age.

Li, Q. (1999). Teachers' beliefs and gender differences in mathematics: A review. *Educational Research, 41,* 63–76.

Licht, B. (1992). The achievement-related perceptions of children with learning problems: A developmental analysis. In D. Schunk & J. Meece (Eds.), *Student perceptions in the classroom* (pp. 247–264). Hillsdale, NJ: Erlbaum.

Linnenbrink-Garcia, L., & Fredricks, J. (2008). Developmental perspectives on achievement motivation: Personal and contextual influences. In J. Shah & W. Gardner (Eds.), *Handbook of motivation science* (pp. 448–464). New York: Guilford.

Little, T., & Lopez, D. (1997). Regularities in the development of children's causality beliefs about school performance across six sociocultural contexts. *Developmental Psychology, 33,* 165–175.

Lord, C., Umezaki, K., & Darley, J. (1990). Developmental differences in decoding the meanings of the appraisal actions of teachers. *Child Development, 61,* 191–200.

Luzzo, D., Hasper, P., Albert, K., Bibby, M., & Martinelli, Jr. E. (1999). Effects of self-efficacy-enhancing interventions on the math/science self-efficacy and career interests, goals, and actions of career undecided college students. *Journal of Counseling Psychology, 46,* 233–243.

Major, B., Spencer, S., Schmader, T., Wolfe, C., & Crocker, J. (1998). Coping with negative stereotypes about intellectual performance: The role of psychological disengagement. *Personality and Social Psychology Bulletin, 24,* 34–50.

Martin, C., Ruble, D., & Szkrybalo, J. (2002). Cognitive theories of early gender development. *Psychological Bulletin, 128,* 903–933.

Martinot, D., & Désert, M. (2007). Awareness of a gender stereotype, personal beliefs and self-perceptions regarding math ability: When boys do not surpass girls. *Social Psychology of Education, 10,* 455–471.

Marx, D., & Roman, J. (2002). Female role models: Protecting women's math test performance. *Personality and Social Psychology Bulletin, 28,* 1183–1193.

Massey, E., Gebhardt, W., & Garnefski, N. (2008). Adolescent goal content and pursuit: A review of the literature from the past 16 years. *Developmental Review, 28*, 421–460.

McCarthy, B. (1980). *The 4MAT system*. Oakbrook, IL: Excel.

McCarthy, B. (1990). Using the 4MAT system to bring learning styles to school. *Educational Leadership, 48*, 31–37.

McIntyre, R., Paulson, R., & Lord, C. (2003). Alleviating women's mathematics stereotype threat through salience of group achievements. *Journal of Experimental Social Psychology, 39*, 83–90.

Meece, J., Herman, B., & McCombs, B. (2003). Relations of learner-centered teaching practices to adolescents' achievement goals. *International Journal of Educational Research, 39*, 457–475.

Millard, E. (1997). Differently literate: Boys, girls and the schooling of literacy. London: Falmer.

Miller, A. (1985). A developmental study of the cognitive basis of performance impairment after failure. *Journal of Personality and Social Psychology, 49*, 529–538.

Miller, A. (1986). Performance impairment after failure: Mechanism and sex differences. *Journal of Educational Psychology, 78*, 486–491.

Moll, L. (1992). Bilingual classroom studies and community analysis. *Educational Researcher, 21*, 20–24.

Moll, L., & Gonzalez, N. (1997). Teachers as social scientists: Learning about culture from household research. In P. Hall (Ed.), *Race, ethnicity, and multiculturalism: Policy and practice* (pp. 89–114). New York: Garland.

Morling, B., & Kitayama, S. (2008). Culture and motivation. In J. Shah & W. Gardner (Eds.), *Handbook of motivation science* (pp. 417–433). New York: Guilford.

Nasir, N., McLaughlin, M., & Jones, A. (2009). What does it mean to be African American? Constructions of race and academic identity in an urban public school. *American Educational Research Journal, 46*, 73–114.

Neitzel, C., Alexander, J., & Johnson, K. (2008). Children's early interest-based activities in the home and subsequent information contributions and pursuits in kindergarten. *Journal of Educational Psychology, 100*, 782–797.

Nicholls, J., & Miller, A. (1984). Development and its discontents: The differentiation of the concept of ability. In J. Nicholls (Ed.), *The development of achievement motivation* (pp. 185–218). Greenwich, CT: JAI.

Nicholls, J., Nelson, J., & Gleaves, K. (1995). Learning "facts" versus learning that most questions have many answers: Student evaluations of contrasting curriculum. *Journal of Educational Psychology, 87*, 253–260.

Nosek, B., Banaji, M., & Greenwald, A. (2002). Math = male, me = female, therefore math [not equal to] me. *Journal of Personality and Social Psychology, 83*, 44–59.

O'Brien, L., & Crandall, C. (2003). Stereotype threat and arousal: Effects on women's math performance. *Personality and Social Psychology Bulletin, 29*, 782–789.

Ogbu, J. (2002). *Black American students in an affluent suburb: A study of academic disengagement*. Mahwah, NJ: Erlbaum.

Oishi, S., & Diener, E. (2001). Goals, culture, and subjective well-being. *Personality and Social Psychology Bulletin, 27*, 1674–1682.

Osborne, J. (1997). Race and academic disidentification. *Journal of Educational Psychology, 89*, 728–735.

Otis, N., Grouzet, F., & Pelletier, L. (2005). Latent motivational change in an academic setting: A 3-year longitudinal study. *Journal of Educational Psychology, 97*, 170–183.

Pöhlmann, C., Carranza, E., Hannover, B., & Iyengar, S. (2007). Repercussions of self-construal for self-relevant and other-relevant choice. *Social Cognition, 25*, 284–305.

Pomerantz, E., Altermatt, E., & Saxon, J. (2002). Making the grade but feeling distressed: Gender differences in academic performance and internal distress. *Journal of Educational Psychology, 94*, 396–404.

Pomerantz, E., Ng, F., & Wang, Q. (2008). Culture, parenting, and motivation: The case of East Asia and the United States. In M. Maehr, S. Karabenick, & T. Urdan (Eds.), *Social psychological perspectives (Advances in motivation and achievement series* (Vol. 15, pp. 209–240). Bingley, UK: Emerald.

Ratelle, C., Guay, F., Vallerand, R., Larose, S., & Senécal, C. (2007). Autonomous, controlled, and amotivated types of academic motivation: A person-oriented analysis. *Journal of Educational Psychology, 99*, 734–746.

Ryan, R., & Deci, E. (2006). Self-regulation and the problem of human autonomy: Does psychology need choice, self-determination, and will? *Journal of Personality, 74*, 1557–1585.

Sadker, M., & Sadker, D. (1994). *Failing at fairness: How America's schools cheat girls*. New York: Scribner.

Saracho, O. (1997). Teachers' and students' cognitive styles in early childhood education. Westport, CT: Bergin & Garvey.

Schmader, T., Forbes, C., Zhang, S., & Mendes, W. (2009). A metacognitive perspective on the cognitive deficits experienced in intellectually threatening environments. *Personality and Social Psychology Bulletin, 35*, 584–596.

Schmader, T., Johns, M., & Forbes, C. (2008). An integrated process model of stereotype threat effects on performance. *Psychological Review, 115*, 336–356.

Schofield, H. (1981). Teacher effects on cognitive and affective pupil outcomes in elementary school mathematics. *Journal of Educational Psychology, 73*, 462–471.

Secada, W., & Lightfoot, T. (1993). Symbols and the political context of bilingual education in the United States. In M. Arias & U. Casanova (Eds.), *Bilingual education: Politics, practice, and research* (pp. 36–64). Chicago: University of Chicago Press.

Sheldon, K., Elliot, A., Kim, Y., & Kasser, T. (2001). What is satisfying about satisfying events? Testing 10 candidate psychological needs. *Journal of Personality and Social Psychology, 80,* 325–339.

Shih, M., Pittinski, T., & Ambady, N. (1999). Shifts in women's quantitative performance in response to implicit sociocultural identification. *Psychological Science, 10,* 80–90.

Siddle-Walker, E. (1992). Falling asleep and failure among African- American students: Rethinking assumptions about process teaching. *Theory Into Practice, 31,* 321–327.

Skinner, E., Furrer, C., Marchand, G., & Kindermann, T. (2008). Engagement and disaffection in the classroom: Part of a larger motivational dynamic? *Journal of Educational Psychology, 100,* 765–781.

Smith, C., & Hung, L. (2008). Stereotype threat: Effects on education. *Social Psychology of Education, 11,* 243–257.

Spencer, S., Steele, C., & Quinn, D. (1999). Under suspicion of inability: Stereotype threat and women's math performance. *Journal of Experimental Social Psychology, 35,* 4–28.

Spencer-Rodgers, J., Boucher, H., Mori, S., Wang, L., & Peng, K. (2009). The dialectical self-concept: Contradiction, change, and holism in East Asian cultures. *Personality and Social Psychology Bulletin, 35,* 29–44.

Stahl, S. (1999). Different strokes for different folks? A critique of learning styles. *American Educator, 23*(3), 27–31.

Steele, C. (1997). A threat in the air: How stereotypes shape intellectual identity and performance. *American Psychologist, 52,* 613–629.

Steele, C., & Aronson, J. (1995). Stereotype threat and the intellectual test performance of African Americans. *Journal of Personality and Social Psychology, 69,* 797–811.

Steele, C., Spencer, S., & Aronson, J. (2002). Contending with group image: The psychology of stereotype and social identity threat. In M. Zanna (Ed.), *Advances in experimental social psychology* (Vol. 34, pp. 379–440). San Diego, CA: Academic Press.

Stellwagen, J. (2001). A challenge to the learning style advocates. *Clearinghouse, 74,* 265–268.

Stevenson, H., & Stigler, J. (1992). *The learning gap.* New York: Summit

Stipek, D., & Daniels, D. (1988). Declining perceptions of competence: A consequence of changes in the child or in the educational environment? *Journal of Educational Psychology, 80,* 352–356.

Stipek, D., & Gralinski, J. (1991). Gender differences in children's achievement-related beliefs and emotional responses to success and failure in mathematics. *Journal of Educational Psychology, 83 ,* 361–371.

Stipek, D., & MacIver, D. (1989). Developmental change in children's assessment of intellectual competence. *Child Development, 60,* 521–538.

Stone, J., Lynch, C., Sjomeling, M., & Darley, J. (1999). Stereotype threat effects on Black and White athletic performance. *Journal of Personality and Social Psychology, 77,* 1213–1227.

Taylor, A., & Graham, S. (2007). An examination of the relationship between achievement values and perceptions of barriers among low-SES African American and Latino students. *Journal of Educational Psychology, 99,* 52–64.

Tenenbaum, H., & Leaper, C. (2003). Parent-child conversations about science: The socialization of gender inequities? *Developmental Psychology, 39,* 34–47.

Tiedemann, J. (2000). Parents' gender stereotypes and teachers' beliefs as predictors of children's concept of their mathematical ability in elementary school. *Journal of Educational Psychology, 92,* 144–151.

Trout, J., & Crawley, F. (1985). The effects of matching instructional strategy with selected student characteristics on ninth-grade physical science students' attitudes and achievement. *Journal of Research in Science Teaching, 22,* 407–419.

Tucker, C., Zayco, R., Herman, K., Reinke, W., Trujillo, M., Carraway, K., Wallack, C., & Ivery, P. (2002). Teacher and child variables as predictors of academic engagement among low-income African American children. *Psychology in the Schools, 39,* 477–488.

Vansteenkiste, M., Lens, W., Soenens, B., & Luyckx, K. (2006). Autonomy and relatedness among Chinese sojourners and applicants: Conflictual or independent predictors of well-being and adjustment? *Motivation and Emotion, 30,* 273–282.

Visser, B., Ashton, M., & Vernon, P. (2006). Beyond *g*: Putting multiple intelligences theory to the test. *Intelligence, 34,* 487–502.

Voelkl, K. (1997). Identification with school. *American Journal of Education, 105,* 294–318.

Walton, G., & Cohen, G. (2003). Stereotype lift. *Journal of Experimental Social Psychology, 39,* 456–467.

Waterhouse, L. (2006). Multiple intelligences, the Mozart effect, and emotional intelligence: A critical review. *Educational Psychologist, 41,* 207–225.

Wigfield, A., & Eccles, J. (2002). The development of competence beliefs, expectancies for success, and achievement values from childhood through adolescence. In A. Wigfield & J. Eccles (Eds.), *Development of achievement motivation* (pp. 91–121). San Diego: Academic Press.

Wilkerson, R., & White, K. (1988). Effects of the 4MAT system of instruction on students' achievement, retention, and attitudes. *Elementary School Journal, 88,* 357–368.

Willingham, D. (2005, Summer). Do visual, auditory, and kinesthetic learners need visual, auditory, and kinesthetic instruction? *American Educator, 29*(2), 31–35, 44.

Witkin, H., Moore, C., Goodenough, D., & Cox, P. (1977). Field-dependent and field-independent cognitive styles and their educational implications. *Review of Educational Research, 47,* 1–64.

Yamagishi, T., Hashimoto, H., & Schug, J. (2008). Preferences versus strategies as explanations for culture-specific behavior. *Psychological Science, 19,* 579–584.

Yamaguchi, S., Greenwald, A., Banaji, M., Murakami, F., Chen, D., Shiomura, K., et al. (2007). Apparent universality of positive implicit self-esteem. *Psychological Science, 18,* 498–500.

Yopyk, D., & Prentice, D. (2005). Am I an athlete or a student? Identity salience and stereotype threat in student-athletes. *Basic and Applied Social Psychology, 27,* 329–336.

Zusho, A., Pintrich, P., & Cortina, K. (2005). Motives, goals, and adaptive patterns of performance in Asian-American and Anglo-American students. *Learning and Individual Differences, 15,* 141–158.

12

Looking Back and Ahead: Integrating Motivational Goals into Your Planning and Teaching

If you have read through the rest of the book before turning to this chapter, you may be feeling that motivation is much more complicated than you thought. You also may be daunted at the prospect of trying to integrate so many principles into your teaching. This is understandable. After all, in the very first chapter I described factors built into schooling that limit your motivational options (the high student/teacher ratios, the public nature of much teacher–student interaction, the need to work through the curriculum and assign grades instead of just acting as a mentor and resource person).

Then, in subsequent chapters, I developed a lengthy list of motivational principles for you to keep in mind, frequently attaching qualifications on when or how they should be used: If used as incentives, rewards should be delivered in ways that communicate verification of accomplishment rather than exercise of authority; praise should be communicated mostly in private; feedback should emphasize advances in knowledge or skill rather than normative comparisons; value-oriented strategies should focus on developing motivation to learn, not just connecting with existing intrinsic motivation; and so on. Many principles require not just using a strategy but doing so in just the right way (delivering the right kinds of praise in the right situations, attributing successes to one set of causes but failures to another). In addition, you may need to make adjustments in response to developments in students (continuing to provide just the right levels of challenge as students gain confidence, doing less structuring and scaffolding but giving them more responsibility for self-regulation as they develop expertise).

Clearly, motivation is complicated. Therefore, it is important for you to face up to this fact and learn to address the complexities involved. You won't be a very effective motivator if you overrely on a few techniques or rules of thumb.

However, certain factors make these complexities more manageable than they might be otherwise. For one thing, you can become your own most powerful motivational tool by establishing productive relationships with students. This alone will carry you a long way and minimize the likelihood that any mishandling of particular situations will have lasting demotivating effects. Also, motivational principles complement principles of good curriculum and instruction, so the complete set of principles can be learned and implemented as an internally consistent and pedagogically powerful package (see Box 12.1). Another simplifier is that efforts to incorporate motivational elements into your teaching can focus on establishing your classroom as a learning community and planning curriculum and instruction for the class as a whole. You will need to supplement this with adaptations or motivational extras designed to meet special needs, but you will not have to develop unique motivational prescriptions for each student in your class.

Finally, it is worth repeating that this book has synthesized the motivational literature specifically for teachers. Although it may not seem like it at this point, its content has been streamlined and focused in two important ways. First, I have culled from a much larger scholarly literature the material that I think you ought to know to help you to motivate your students. A great many topics and details were omitted because they lack teaching implications. Second, I have organized the content around principles that you might use in your classroom, rather than just presenting general coverage of the motivational literature and leaving it to you to try to figure out whether and how it might apply to your teaching.

Even so, I recognize that this content is lengthy and complex. Other scholars interested in motivation in education also have recognized these complexities and developed organizing schemes to simplify the content for teachers and help them with their planning. I will summarize three of these before proceeding to my own scheme.

THE TARGET CATEGORIES

The TARGET categories (task, authority, reward, grouping, evaluation, and time) identify six structures that teachers can work through to motivate their students to engage in learning activities. One way for you to systematically incorporate motivational principles into your planning is to check your curricular and instructional plans against the TARGET model guidelines summarized in Table 4.2.

KELLER'S MODEL

John Keller (1983) synthesized many motivational principles within four dimensions: interest, relevance, expectancy, and outcomes.

1. *Interest*: the extent to which curiosity is aroused and sustained over time. Keller suggested five strategies for stimulating and maintaining interest: (a) use novel, incongruous, conflictual, or paradoxical events, or arouse attention through an abrupt change in the status quo; (b) use anecdotes and other devices to inject a personal, emotional element into otherwise purely intellectual or procedural material; (c) give students opportunities to learn more about things they already know about and are interested in, but also give them moderate doses of the unfamiliar; (d) use analogies to make the strange familiar and the familiar strange; (e) guide students into a process of question generation and inquiry.
2. *Relevance*: perception that the instruction is related to personal needs or goals. Motivation increases when students perceive that a learning activity will satisfy

Box 12.1   Motivational Saturation

Pressley et al. (2003) illustrated the complementary nature of the strategies empha-sized in this book. They developed detailed descriptions of the curricular, instruc-tional, motivational, and classroom management practices of elementary teachers who were remarkably successful motivators who kept their students productively engaged in worthwhile academic activities all day long.

Close investigation revealed that these teachers did not rely on just a few key techniques but instead saturated their classrooms with motivation. They were exceptionally positive people, both about their students and about their own potential for making an important difference in the students' lives. They cared deeply about their students and expressed that care as determination to ensure that all of them would learn. Following is a partial list of the motivational elements observed in their classrooms: learning their students' names immediately and using them frequently; listening carefully and responding compassionately when students expressed thoughts, needs, or concerns; emphasizing that the classroom was a community where respect and good manners were expected; introducing the curriculum with enthusiasm, projecting high but realistic expectations and expressing confidence that the students would be able to meet them; providing a lot of generic praise and encouragement to the class as a whole but also a lot of spe-cific informative praise to individuals; modeling expected procedures and making sure that students understood them, emphasizing self-regulation in behavior and learning; flooding the classroom with reading materials, many linked to current instructional units; displaying and celebrating student accomplishments, such as final drafts of stories written by students; emphasizing individual trajectories and improvement in giving feedback to students; encouraging cooperative learning; presenting content in ways likely to make it interesting to students; making certain that what they taught was worth learning and that their students appreciated its value; making connections between new learning and what students already knew; giving tasks that were optimally challenging and helping students to appreciate the progress they had made over time; emphasizing effort as the key to progress; being available to students when they were working on assignments to provide help if needed; making sure that students understood big ideas and reviewing them fre-quently; encouraging students to communicate personal reactions to readings or other class activities; using a variety of instructional strategies and activities and offering choices when feasible; teaching students strategies for learning and solv-ing problems; involving the students' families; and avoiding demotivating prac-tices such as personal aloofness, nagging criticism, boring work, poorly planned activities, and so on.

A final noteworthy characteristic of these most impressive teachers was that they were always looking to improve (unlike several less impressive teachers, who confidently viewed themselves as outstanding when they clearly were not). Cur-ricular differences were especially important: Many of the other teachers were generally positive and supportive in their interactions with students, but were less successful as motivators and instructors because they taught mile-wide but inch-deep curricula featuring mostly reading, memorizing, and filling in blanks on assignment sheets. For more on this study, see Bogner, Raphael, and Pressley (2002) and Dolezal (2003). A later study documented similar patterns of motivational saturation in the classrooms of outstanding teachers at the middle school level (Raphael, Pressley, & Mohan, 2008).

basic motives such as needs for achievement, power, or affiliation. Strategies for increasing personal relevance call for providing opportunities to achieve under conditions of moderate risk; making instruction responsive to the power motive by providing opportunities for choice, responsibility, and interpersonal influence; and satisfying the need for affiliation by establishing trust and providing opportunities for no-risk, cooperative interaction.

3. *Expectancy:* perceived likelihood of achieving success through personal control. Keller suggested four strategies for increasing success expectancies: provide consistent success experiences (on meaningful tasks), be clear about requirements for success, use techniques that offer personal control, and provide attributional feedback relating success to personal effort and ability.

4. *Outcomes:* the satisfaction of goal accomplishment and its effects on motivation for engaging in similar activities in the future. Keller suggested emphasizing the rewards that come naturally from successful completion of the activity rather than using artificial extrinsic rewards, as well as emphasizing praise and informative feedback over threats, surveillance, or external performance evaluations.

As with the TARGET model, you can use Keller's model as a checklist against which to evaluate your instructional plans.

WLODKOWSKI'S MODEL

Raymond Wlodkowski (1984) suggested a time continuum model for building motivational strategies into instructional planning. It identifies three critical periods in a learning sequence in which particular motivational strategies will have the most impact: attitude and needs strategies at the beginning of the activity, stimulation and affect strategies during the activity, and competence and reinforcement strategies when ending the activity.

Attitude strategies address the question "What can I do to establish positive student attitudes toward the learning situation, as well as to establish the expectation that students will be able to meet its demands successfully?" They include sharing something of value with students (task-related anecdotes, humor, or personal experiences), listening to them with empathy, treating them with warmth and acceptance, modeling enthusiasm for the subject, communicating positive expectations and encouragement, and helping students to set realistic goals.

Needs strategies address the question "How can I best meet the needs of the students?" They include making sure that students are physically comfortable and free from fear or anxiety, establishing a collaborative learning environment and being encouraging rather than critical in responding to students, structuring learning experiences and arranging for creation of products that support students' sense of identity and self-esteem, and including divergent thinking and exploration elements that appeal to students' needs for self-actualization.

Stimulation strategies address the question "What about this learning activity will continuously stimulate students' attention and sustain their engagement in the activity?" This includes using voice, body language, props, and other communication skills; relating material to students' interests; using humor, examples, analogies, or stories to personalize the content; asking questions, especially questions that call for higher order thinking; and using spontaneity, unpredictability, or dissonance induction to periodically restimulate students' alertness and thoughtfulness.

Affective strategies address the question "How can I make the affective experience and emotional climate for this activity positive for students?" They include maintaining a positive group atmosphere, presenting content and asking questions that will engage students' emotions, and connecting the learning with things that are important in their lives outside of school.

Competence strategies address the question "How will this learning activity increase or affirm students' feelings of competence?" They involve first making sure that students appreciate their progress by providing informative feedback and facilitating successful task completion, then encouraging students to take credit for these accomplishments by attributing them to sufficient ability plus reasonable effort.

Reinforcement strategies address the question "What reinforcement will this learning activity provide for students?" They include calling students' attention to positive natural consequences of successful task completion, as well as providing them with praise or rewards (in ways consistent with the guidelines given in chapter 6).

Wlodkowski's three-stage time continuum is worth keeping in mind as a way to make sure that you address motivational issues when planning how you will introduce an activity, what will occur as the activity unfolds, and how you will bring it to closure.

INCORPORATING PRINCIPLES PRESENTED IN THIS BOOK

To help you take into account all of the principles presented in this book, I have provided the list of motivational strategies presented in Box 12.2 and the following set of questions to consider when planning curriculum and instruction. You may want to simplify, elaborate, or otherwise adapt these tools to your personal needs.

If you are a new teacher or a teacher who is planning a new course from scratch, you can incorporate motivational strategies by building them directly into the planning process. If you are already working with adopted curriculum guidelines and instructional materials, you can incorporate the strategies by adjusting existing plans as needed. One way to do so is to use Box 12.2 as a menu of potential strategies from which to choose or a checklist against which to assess your instructional plans. Another way is to ask yourself the following sets of questions to stimulate your thinking as you develop your plans.

Questions to Consider for All Activities

The following questions should be considered in planning for any learning activity. First, what are its *goals*? Why will your students be learning this content or skill? When and

---

Box 12.2   Summary of Motivational Principles and Strategies

A. General Principles

1. Focus on developing motivation to learn as your primary goal
2. Think in terms of shaping students' motivational development, not just connecting with their current motivational systems
3. Make yourself and your classroom attractive to students
4. Use authoritative management and socialization strategies
5. Establish your classroom as a learning community whose members engage in learning activities collaboratively
6. Emphasize learning goals and criterion-referenced attainment goals, but not peer comparisons or performance-avoidance goals
7. Teach things that are worth learning, in ways that help students to appreciate their value
8. Teach for understanding, appreciation, and application of the learning
9. Attend to both the expectancy- and the value-related aspects of students' motivation
10. Show students that you care about their progress and are available to help them succeed

B. Strategies for Supporting Students' Confidence as Learners

1. Program for success (continuous progress achieved with reasonable effort)
2. Help students to set goals, evaluate their progress, and recognize effort-outcome linkages
3. Emphasize informative feedback rather than grades or student comparisons
4. Provide extra support to struggling low achievers
5. Resocialize students with failure syndrome problems
6. Help self-worth protective students shift emphasis from performance goals to learning goals
7. Resocialize the attitudes of underachievers and encourage their commitment to appropriately challenging goals

C. Strategies for Motivating Through Extrinsic Incentives

1. Praise and reward students for making progress toward performance/improvement standards
2. Deliver praise and rewards in ways that encourage students to appreciate their learning
3. Call attention to the instrumental value of the learning
4. Perhaps use competition occasionally but depersonalize it, equalize opportunities for success, and focus attention on learning goals

D. Strategies for Connecting with Students' Intrinsic Motivation

1. Respond to students' autonomy needs by encouraging them to function as autonomous learners and allowing them to make choices

(continued)

Box 12.2   Continued

2. Respond to students' competence needs by emphasizing activities that offer opportunities to make active responses and get immediate feedback, incorporating game-like features into learning activities, and assigning tasks that feature skill variety, task identity, and task significance
3. Respond to students' relatedness needs by providing them with frequent opportunities to collaborate with peers, especially within purely cooperative learning formats
4. Adapt learning activities to students' interests
5. Embellish traditional learning activities with simulation or fantasy elements
6. Combine hands-on activities with minds-on learning

E. Strategies for Stimulating Students' Motivation to Learn

1. Socialize motivation to learn as a general disposition by modeling your own motivation to learn, communicating desirable expectations and attributions, and minimizing students' performance anxiety
2. Shape students' expectations about learning by being enthusiastic (regularly) and by being intense (when material is especially important and requires close attention)
3. Stimulate situational motivation to learn by inducing curiosity or suspense; inducing dissonance or cognitive conflict; making abstract content more personal, concrete, or familiar; inducing task interest or appreciation; or inducing students to generate their own motivation to learn
4. Scaffold students' learning efforts by stating learning goals and providing advance organizers, planning questions and activities to help students develop and apply powerful ideas, modeling task related thinking and problem solving, inducing metacognitive awareness and control of learning strategies, teaching skills for self-regulated learning and studying, and teaching volitional control strategies
5. Resocialize the attitudes and behavior of apathetic students by developing and working in close relationships with them, using contracting and incentive systems, discovering and building on their existing interests, helping them to develop and sustain more positive attitudes towards schoolwork, and socializing their motivation to learn

F. Adaptations to the Needs of Individual Students

1. Where feasible, accommodate students' preferences based on differences in cognitive or learning styles, age-related abilities and needs, age- and gender-related interests, or family and cultural backgrounds that may be associated with social class, race, or ethnicity
2. In making any such accommodations, however, emphasize the students' long-run best interests over their current preferences (if these conflict)

> ### G. Your Development as a Motivator
>
> 1. Work on your own self-efficacy perceptions, performance attributions, etc. with respect to your development of knowledge and skills in the domain of student motivation
> 2. Work on metacognitive monitoring and self-regulation of your emotional reactions and of the strategy adjustments that you make in working to motivate difficult students (stay goal-focused and resist temptations to give into frustration or provocation)
> 3. Finally, reflect regularly to identify ways to improve your motivational "batting average"

how might they use it after they learn it? Answers to these questions suggest information that should be conveyed when introducing the activity.

Before getting into the activity itself, is there a way to characterize it using general terms that indicate its nature and provide students with organizing concepts? If so, frame it using such advance organizers.

What elements of the activity could you focus on to create interest, identify practical applications, or induce curiosity, suspense, or dissonance? Does the activity include interesting information or build skills that students are eager to develop? Does it contain unusual or surprising information? Can the content be related to events in the news or in students' lives? Are there aspects that they are likely to find surprising or difficult to believe? Are there ways to stimulate curiosity or create suspense by posing interesting questions?

Questions to Consider for Listening and Reading Activities

You might consider the following questions when planning activities that require students to follow an oral presentation, watch a visual presentation, or learn by reading. First, what aspects of the content are interesting, noteworthy, or important, and why? Identify reasons for enthusiasm about the topic, and communicate these to students.

Can you relate personal experiences or display artifacts related to the content? Do you know anecdotes about the experiences of others or about how the knowledge was discovered? Will the lesson contain sufficient variety in the cognitive levels of information communicated and the types of responses demanded? If there will be too much uninterrupted lecture or reading, how might you break it up by asking questions, initiating discussion, or allowing time for students to take notes or do a brief assignment?

How should students respond to the presentation or text? Take notes or summarize key ideas? Keep particular issues or questions in mind as they listen or read? Outline the material or respond to a study guide? Identify organizational structures embedded in the material? If you want them to do something more specific than just pay attention, then tell them what to do, and if necessary, help by supplying questions, outlines, study guides, or information about how the material is organized.

Is there some key point that students might easily miss if not forewarned? Are there abstractions that will not be meaningful without additional explanation or concrete examples? Are there concepts that may be troublesome because they are subtle or difficult, because they are not well explained in the text, or because they conflict with the students' experiences? If so, you may want to call attention to these trouble spots to prepare students for viewing or reading.

Questions to Consider for Activities That Require Active Response

You might consider the following questions when planning activities that require students to do something more than just listen or read (e.g., answer questions, prepare a report, or work on a project). Is the activity presented as an opportunity to apply knowledge or develop skills rather than as a test (unless it is a test)? When and how might students be encouraged to ask questions or seek help?

Does the activity demand new or complex responses that ought to be modeled? If so, what steps should be modeled at what level of detail? Will you need to model important hypothesis-testing strategies (considering alternatives at a choice point and then selecting the correct one after reasoning or brief experimentation) or troubleshooting or repair strategies (responding to confusion or errors with diagnosis of the problem or generation of alternative strategies)?

When, how, and from whom will students get feedback? What should they do if they do not understand a question or are not sure about how to get started? What should they do when they think they are finished? How might they be encouraged to check their work, generate and respond to their own questions about it, or engage in follow-up discourse with peers?

The suggestions given here are not intended to be implemented as a set of rigid procedures. Instead, they are meant to be brought to life in the same way that you bring the curriculum to life: by bringing your personality and past experiences to the teaching role and implementing instructional units in ways that combine professional creativity with applied science. You may have to consciously prepare and practice using certain strategies at first, but eventually they will become second nature to you and get implemented in ways marked by your own personal touches.

MAINTAINING YOUR OWN MOTIVATION AS A TEACHER

This book has focused on applications of motivational principles to students' engagement in learning activities. However, these principles also apply to teachers' engagement in teaching activities. Keeping this in mind may help you to analyze and deal with any difficulties you may encounter in seeking to motivate your students to learn.

For example, students are likely to use more desirable learning strategies when they engage with learning goals rather than performance goals and when they are primarily seeking to understand what they are learning rather than responding to extrinsic pressures. The same is true of you as you engage in your teaching responsibilities.

Ideally, your planning and teaching would reflect your beliefs about the nature of your students' needs and about what constitutes a good professional effort to meet them. You would feel well prepared to meet those needs and would confidently set about doing so by establishing realistic goals, employing suitable strategies, monitoring their effectiveness, adjusting accordingly, and then taking satisfaction in seeing the goals accomplished. While engaged in these activities you would be in a flow-like state, focusing on the goals and processes involved rather than evaluating yourself in terms of success or failure. Subsequently you might engage in attributional thinking, by enjoying your successes (which you would attribute to the combination of sufficient ability and reasonable effort) and analyzing any failures with an eye toward developing plans for overcoming them. You would attribute these failures to reliance on incorrect information or inappropriate strategies, or perhaps to failure to persist long enough or put forth sufficient effort, but not to inherent limitations on your potential as a motivator or your students' potential for becoming motivated to learn.

Unfortunately, this ideal is difficult to attain routinely and impossible to sustain continuously. For one thing, you won't be operating under ideal conditions of intrinsic motivation. You will have limited opportunity to decide what goals to establish and how to pursue them. You will be expected to comply with state and district curriculum standards and guidelines, your time schedule may be regimented, your instructional resources will be limited and may include textbooks or other materials that you would not have selected on your own, and your students may be tested using standardized instruments that you may view as inappropriate. Your attempts to deemphasize extrinsic incentives or competitions may be resisted by students, parents, or administrators.

These and other externally imposed constraints and pressures can get you down. Experiments have shown that when two groups of teachers are asked to teach the same content or skills to comparable classes of students, the group instructed simply to help their students understand the content or master the skills tends to teach more efficiently and elicit better student achievement than the group instructed to prepare students to pass an achievement test. The former teachers place more emphasis on conceptual learning, are more responsive to their students' questions, and are generally more relaxed and supportive. The latter teachers are more controlling, pressuring their students to master what the test is going to cover but doing so in counterproductive ways (Engel & Randall, 2009; Flink, Boggiano, Main, Barrett, and Katz, 1992). Similarly ironic relationships have been documented in interviews with practicing teachers (Pelletier, Levesque, & Legault, 2002). In general, the attachment of high-stakes consequences to most states' curricular guidelines and assessment programs has had negative effects on teachers' motivation and instruction (Certo, Cauley, Moxley, & Chafin, 2008; Ciani, Summers, & Easter, 2008).

To prevent such external pressures from having similar effects on you, you will need to develop sufficient confidence in your efficacy as a teaching professional to enable you to exercise some autonomy in setting goals for your students. The importance of this was shown in studies conducted by Fred Newmann (1992) on thoughtfulness in high school social studies classes. In classrooms high in thoughtfulness, interaction focused on sustained examination of a few topics rather than superficial coverage of many; the discourse displayed substantive coherence and continuity; students were given sufficient time to think before being required to answer questions; the teachers pressed the students to clarify or justify their assertions; the teachers modeled the characteristics of a thoughtful person; and the students generated many original and unconventional ideas. In contrast, other classrooms featured lecture, recitation, and seatwork. If the teachers did attempt to emphasize discussion, they did not foster much thoughtfulness because they skipped from topic to topic or accepted students' contributions uncritically.

Interviews indicated that teachers whose classrooms were high in thoughtfulness emphasized long-range and far-reaching dispositional goals in addition to more immediate knowledge and skill objectives. Furthermore, although they felt pressure to cover more content, they experienced this pressure primarily as external and resisted it by emphasizing depth of topic development. The other teachers experienced it primarily as internal pressure and succumbed to it by emphasizing breadth of coverage.

In the current climate of achievement standards backed by high-stakes testing programs, there is increased pressure on teachers to elicit high test scores. Many respond by narrowing the curriculum and teaching to the test. This demotivates students and has counterproductive effects on their learning. Several studies (reviewed in Good & Brophy, 2008) have shown that an emphasis on teaching for understanding not only leads to better achievement of higher-order outcomes but also produces comparable or better achievement of the lower-order outcomes that are usually emphasized on standardized tests. Therefore, take courage. *If you find yourself confronted by counterproductive emphases on high-stakes testing programs, don't allow these pressures to dislodge you from teaching your subjects for understanding and thus enjoying the learning and motivational benefits that this emphasis brings.* Also, make sure that your students see you as allied with them in preparing to handle the tests successfully, not as allied with the tests as part of an oppressive system that is set up to embarrass them.

Typically, you will be trying to pursue several agendas simultaneously. Consequently, you often will have to accept partial solutions to motivational problems or suspend your motivational goals temporarily while you deal with time constraints or classroom management problems. You will need to develop concepts and language for describing types and levels of motivational success in these situations, so you can recognize and take satisfaction in your accomplishments and learn to set realistic goals, assess progress, and reinforce yourself accordingly.

You also may need to work on your efficacy perceptions and failure attributions. That is, *as you acquire motivational skills, you should recognize that you are doing so and appreciate these developments within an incremental view of your motivational ability.* Positive perceptions of your motivational efficacy will help you to develop confidence and persistence in supporting your students' self-regulated learning, whereas low self-efficacy perceptions may leave you with a tendency to give up easily when you encounter difficulties, a controlling orientation toward students, and the belief that extrinsic rewards are necessary to motivate them (Brady & Wolfson, 2008; Scharlach, 2008; Thompson, Warren, & Carter, 2004; Woolfolk, Rosoff, & Hoy, 1990).

In working with difficult students, you will need to support positive self-efficacy perceptions with productive management of your strategies and emotions. Just as students learning mathematics have to learn to cope with difficult problems by staying task-focused and avoiding attributional thinking or emotional reactions that lead to frustration and learned helplessness, so do teachers who encounter motivational problems such as failure syndrome, apathy, or resistance. You may be tempted to give up attempts to solve these problems by attributing failures to uncontrollable causes (your own limitations as a motivator or undesirable student motivation patterns that are too well-established to be changed). Many teachers develop these helplessness-inducing attributions and end up shifting from persistent motivational attempts to tacit bargains in which they lower their standards in exchange for classroom cooperation (Sedlak, Wheeler, Pullin, & Cusick, 1986). To continue to work productively with difficult students, you need to *commit yourself to pursuing challenging but reachable motivational goals, stay positive and task-focused when you encounter setbacks, and sustain the belief that you will begin to succeed more consistently as you discover and perfect the right strategies.* Novice teachers who are faced with challenges to their teaching efficacy can overcome them if they assess their strengths and weaknesses honestly, develop plans for improvement, seek feedback and help from colleagues, and make incremental progress (Gregoire, 2003; Milner, 2002; Rosenfeld & Rosenfeld, 2008; Ross & Bruce, 2007). They are likely to do so if they are passionate about teaching, especially if they value it for primarily intrinsic reasons (Carbonneau, Vallerand, Fernet, & Guay, 2008; Day, 2004; Roth, Assor, Kanat-Maymon, & Kaplan, 2007), and if they adopt mastery rather than performance orientations when they set their own teaching goals (Butler & Shibaz, 2008; Hoffmann, Huff, Patterson, & Nietfeld, 2009).

In this regard, you may find it helpful to consider a parallel between your own situation and that facing major league baseball players when they take their turn at bat. Although highly skilled, these hitters are more likely to make an out than to hit safely. Even the best of them succeed only about 3 times in 10 opportunities (i.e., bat .300), and success is even less likely if they are facing a tough pitcher. Yet, they come to the plate intending to get a hit and reasonably confident that they will succeed in doing so if they maintain concentration on their goals and strategies. You are in a parallel situation as a teacher. It is unrealistic to expect to bat 1.000 (i.e., succeed with every student in every situation). However, if you stay positive and maintain focus, you may raise your motivational "batting average" from say .400 to .800 in favorable situations, or from say .200 to .500 in more difficult situations.

Management of emotional reactions is even more important for teachers seeking to motivate students than for students seeking to learn. Even though they can be frustrating, learning problems are impersonal—they just sit there, as it were, waiting for students to solve them. Unmotivated students, however, are human beings involved in personal relationships with their teachers. They can and often do frustrate the teachers by failing to respond positively to motivational strategies and by expressing hostility or rejection, challenging the teachers' authority, or in other ways creating additional problems. This can lead to vicious cycles of negative action and reaction that culminate in mutual avoidance or hostility (Birch & Ladd, 1998; Brophy & Evertson, 1981; Georgiou, Christou, Stavrinides, & Panaoura, 2002).

When faced with consistent sullenness or resistance from certain students, teachers' natural tendencies are to attribute the students' behavior to internal, stable, and controllable causes; to perceive their provocations as intentional and become angry in response; and to treat the students in an authoritarian or punitive fashion. Such reactions are understandable, but they are not appropriate for teachers who have professional obligations toward their students, including students who are "undeserving." Acting on these natural response tendencies leads to counterproductive expectations and behavior, resulting in deterioration of teacher-student relationships and escalation of the behavior problems.

Thus, it will be important for you to recognize what is happening when these vicious cycles occur, to inhibit your natural but counterproductive reactions, and to replace them with more professional responses. In the process, you will need to "be the adult" by staying positive, focusing on goals, and pursuing strategies designed to resocialize the students' attitudes and behavior (Jennings & Greenberg, 2009; Sutton, Mudrey-Camino, & Knight, 2009).

For more information about the behavioral causes and emotional dynamics that underlie such problems, see Brophy and Evertson (1981). For more information about types of problem students and strategies for working with them, see Brophy (1996). Finally, for information about ways to monitor and get feedback about your interactions with students and to work together with fellow teachers to improve your effectiveness, see Good and Brophy (2008).

SUMMARY AND CONCLUSION

Given the many principles presented in this book and the qualifications attached to most of them, it is safe to say that motivation is a large and complicated topic. However, you can get off to a very good start by making yourself and your classroom attractive to students and establishing the kind of learning community described in chapter 2. Also, you will find that the motivational principles presented here complement the curricular and instructional principles involved in teaching for understanding, so you can learn the larger set of principles as an integrated approach to teaching.

Many of the principles outlined in this book are included within the categories of the TARGET model, the Keller model, or the Wlodkowski model. All of the major principles are summarized in Box 12.2. To systematically build these motivational principles into your instructional planning, you can use these sources as checklists against which to assess your instructional plans. An alternative method is to answer the sets of questions included in the chapter (one set for all activities, a second for listening and reading activities, and a third for activities that require active response).

The book concludes with a section on maintaining your own motivation as a teacher. It points out that you need to develop confident efficacy perceptions, set challenging but reachable goals, adopt an incremental view of your developing motivational skills, attribute successes and failures accordingly, manage your emotions, self-regulate your selection and adjustment of strategies, and so on, in order to sustain optimal motivation to fulfill your potential in the domain of motivating students to learn. In short, you need to develop the same kinds of motivational characteristics in this domain as you want your students to develop in academic knowledge and skill domains.

In the process, you will need to learn to feel autonomously self-regulated and derive intrinsic satisfaction from your work despite curriculum mandates, testing programs, and other extrinsic constraints and pressures. In this regard, bear in mind the point made in chapter 7 that the perception of autonomy is determined by the subjective experience of the person, not by the presence or absence of extrinsic pressures.

Prepare yourself to deal with students who are sullen or hostile in their personal reactions to you. Read books or take courses in managing classrooms and dealing with problem students, so as to inoculate yourself against the natural but counterproductive tendency to slip into vicious cycles of negativity with them. If you stay professional, positive, and goal-oriented with these students, and especially if you communicate that you care about them despite their provocative behavior, you will gradually turn them around.

Finally, if you haven't done so already, go back and take a look at your answers to the questions posed in chapter 1. To what extent are they congruent with the theory and research on motivation in education? Are there any clear discrepancies? If so, develop a plan for resolving the issues that underlie them.

REFLECTION QUESTIONS

1. What are the relative advantages of the TARGET system, the Keller system, the Wlodkowski system, and my system (Table 12.2) as tools for incorporating motivational considerations into instructional planning?
2. From a motivational standpoint, what are the pros and cons of state standards, curriculum guides, and testing programs?
3. Why would teachers with low perceptions of their own teaching efficacy be more prone to criticize students than other teachers?
4. Do lack of confidence in your potential to become an excellent teacher, entity views of students' ability or motivational characteristics, or other expectancy-related problems stand as obstacles to your professional development? If so, what can you do to address these problems effectively?
5. How can you monitor your motivational batting average and make adjustments where necessary?
6. If you teach under difficult circumstances, what steps can you take to ensure that you continue to pursue challenging but realistic goals, take satisfactions in achieving them, stay positive, and avoid burnout?

REFERENCES

Birch, S., & Ladd, G. (1998). Children's interpersonal behaviors and the teacher-child relationship. *Developmental Psychology, 34*, 934–946.

Bogner, K., Raphael, L., & Pressley, M. (2002). How grade-1 teachers motivate literate activity by their students. *Scientific Studies of Reading, 6*, 135–165.

Brady, K., & Woolfson, L. (2008). What teacher factors influence their attributions for children's difficulties in learning? *British Journal of Educational Psychology, 78*, 527–544.

Brophy, J. (1996). *Teaching problem students*. New York: Guilford.

Brophy, J., & Evertson, C. (1981). *Student characteristics and teaching*. New York: Longman.

Butler, R., & Shibaz, L. (2008). Achievement goals for teaching as predictors of students' perceptions of instructional practices and students' help-seeking and cheating. *Learning and Instruction, 18*, 453–467.

Carbonneau, N., Vallerand, R., Fernet, C., & Guay, F. (2008). The role of passion for teaching in intrapersonal and interpersonal outcomes. *Journal of Educational Psychology, 100*, 977–987.

Certo, J., Cauley, K., Moxley, K., & Chafin, C. (2008). An argument for authenticity: Adolescents' perspectives on standards-based reform. *High School Journal, 91*, 26–39

Ciani, K., Summers, J., & Easter, M. (2008). A "top-down" analysis of high school teacher motivation. *Contemporary Educational Psychology, 33*, 533–560.

Day, C. (2004). *A passion for teaching*. London: Routledge Falmer.

Dolezal, S., Mohan Welsh, L., Pressley, M., & Vincent, M. (2003). How nine third-grade teachers motivate student academic engagement. *Elementary School Journal, 103*, 239–267.

Engel, S., & Randall, K. (2009). How teachers respond to children's inquiry. *American Educational Research Journal, 46*, 183–202.

Flink, C., Boggiano, A., Main, D., Barrett, M., & Katz, P. (1992). Children's achievement-related behaviors: The role of extrinsic and intrinsic motivational orientations. In A. Boggiano & T. Pittman (Eds.), *Achievement and motivation: A social-developmental perspective* (pp. 189–214). Cambridge, UK: Cambridge University Press.

Georgiou, S., Christou, C., Stavrinides, P., & Panaoura, G. (2002). Teacher attributions of student failure and teacher behavior toward the failing student. *Psychology in the Schools, 39*, 583–595.

Good, T., & Brophy, J. (2008). *Looking in classrooms* (10th ed.). Boston: Allyn & Bacon.

Gregoire, M. (2003). Is it a challenge or a threat? A dual process model of teachers' cognition and appraisal processes during conceptual change. *Educational Psychology Review, 15*, 147–179.

Hoffmann, K., Huff, J., Patterson, A., & Nietfeld, J. (2009). Elementary teachers' use and perception of rewards in the classroom. *Teaching and Teacher Education, 25*, 843–849.

Jennings, P., & Greenberg, M. (2009). The prosocial classroom: Teacher social and emotional competence in relation to student and classroom outcomes. *Review of Educational Research, 79,* 491–525.

Keller, J. (1983). Motivational design of instruction. In C. Reigeluth (Ed.), *Instructional-design theories and models: An overview of their current status* (pp. 383–434). Hillsdale, NJ: Erlbaum.

Milner, H. R. (2002). A case study of an experienced English teacher's self-efficacy and persistence through "crisis" situations: Theoretical and practical considerations. *High School Journal, 86,* 28–35.

Newmann, F. (1992). *Student engagement and achievement in American secondary schools.* New York: Teachers College Press.

Pelletier, L., Levesque, C., & Legault, L. (2002). Pressure from above and pressure from below as determinants of teachers' motivation and teaching behaviors. *Journal of Educational Psychology, 94,* 186–196.

Pressley, M., Dolezal, S., Raphael, L., Mohan, L., Roehrig, A., & Bogner, K. (2003). *Motivating primary grade students.* New York: Guilford.

Raphael, L., Pressley, M., & Mohan, L. (2008). Engaging instruction in middle school classrooms: An observational study of nine teachers. *Elementary School Journal, 109,* 61–81.

Rosenfeld, M., & Rosenfeld, S. (2008). Developing effective teacher beliefs about learners: The role of sensitizing teachers to individual learning differences. *Educational Psychology, 28,* 245–272.

Ross, J., & Bruce, C. (2007). Teacher self-assessment: A mechanism for facilitating professional growth. *Teaching and Teacher Education, 23,* 146–159.

Roth, G., Assor, A., Kanat-Maymon, Y., & Kaplan, H. (2007). Autonomous motivation for teaching: How self-determined teaching may lead to self-determined learning. *Journal of Educational Psychology, 99,* 761–774.

Scharlach, T. (2008). These kids just aren't motivated to read: The influence of preservice teachers' beliefs on their expectations, instruction, and evaluation of struggling readers. *Literacy Research and Instruction, 47,* 158–173.

Sedlak, M., Wheeler, C., Pullin, D., & Cusick, P. (1986). *Selling students short: Classroom bargains and academic reform in the American high school.* New York: Teachers College Press.

Sutton, R., Mudrey-Camino, R., & Knight, C. (2009). Teachers' emotion regulation and classroom management. *Theory Into Practice, 48,* 130–137.

Thompson, G., Warren, S., & Carter, L. (2004). It's not my fault: Predicting high school teachers who blame parents and students for students' low achievement. *High School Journal, 87,* 5–14.

Wlodkowski, R. (1984). *Motivation and teaching: A practical guide.* Washington, DC: National Education Association.

Woolfolk, A., Rosoff, B., & Hoy, W. (1990). Teachers' sense of efficacy and their beliefs about managing students. *Teaching and Teacher Education, 6,* 137–148.

Author Index

Subject Index